Y0-BZY-411

ROY W. GOODY

Mission College, Santa Clara, California

THE INTELLIGENT MICROCOMPUTER

Second Edition

SCIENCE RESEARCH ASSOCIATES, INC.

Chicago, Henley-on-Thames, Sydney, Toronto

An IBM Company

Acquisition Editor	Michael Carrigg
Project Editor	Byron Riggan
Compositor	Graphic Typesetting Service
Illustrator	John Foster
Cover Designer	Harry Voight
Text Designer	Judith Olson

Cover Photo courtesy of Hewlett-Packard Company

Appendixes I–VI (pp. 413–429) reproduced by permission of Intel Corporation

Library of Congress Cataloging-in-Publication Data

Goody, Roy W.
    The intelligent microcomputer.

    Includes index.
    1. Microcomputers.   I. Title.
QA76.5.G627   1986   004.1'6   85-14371
ISBN 0-574-21615-4

Copyright © Science Research Associates, Inc. 1982, 1986. All rights reserved. No part of this publication may be reproduced, stored in a retrieval system, or transmitted in any form or by any means, electronic, mechanical, photocopying, recording, or otherwise, without the prior written permission of Science Research Associates, Inc.

Printed in the United States of America

10   9   8   7   6   5   4   3   2

To George and June Goody

preface

If learning about the complex field of microcomputers can be compared to scaling a high peak, then this book is written as a staircase. It is designed to provide the beginning- to intermediate-level technician or electronics-technology (ET) engineering student a gradual, step-by-step, upward learning path, eliminating the sharp rises and gaps that often impede progress. The Contents lists the steps in the staircase and divides the material into 27 easily scaled chapters. Depending on the pace of presentation, these chapters might be divided appropriately into two sections for a two-semester or two-quarter series of courses.

Emphasizing the major aspects of hardware design (configuring), program development, interfacing, and applications, the material in this book is based on the *inventor's approach*. That is, on successful completion of the material, you will be able to design and troubleshoot a simple microprocessor-based system starting completely from scratch. The scope and depth are sufficient for both the technician, who must test and troubleshoot the system, and the engineer, who must design and develop the system.

Little or no previous knowledge of computers is required. Prerequisites are a basic background in ac/dc and semiconductor electronics, experience in the use of the hexadecimal number system, and a working knowledge of digital circuits and gates. No review of basic digital concepts and number systems is included; it is assumed that you have completed a course in basic digital concepts before undertaking microcomputer studies.

This book is based on the popular Intel family of microprocessors (the 8080, 8085, 8048, 8086, and 80286 to name the most prominent). However, the bulk of the presentation will center on the popular 8-bit 8080/8085, microprocessors which represent the ideal level of complexity for those just entering the field. The study of these real devices and real systems, whose characteristics can be reproduced in the laboratory, is deemed to be the most effective way to focus the mind on this complex subject. The basic principles gained from a study of the Intel product family can, of course, be easily applied to any comparable microprocessor on the market. (*The Versatile Microcomputer* is a Motorola 6800-based version of this text.)

To those who are familiar with the first edition, this second edition has been updated to reflect the latest technology, and it has been expanded in both scope and depth. To give several examples, there are sections on CAD/CAE, operating systems, integrated RAMs, layered networks, structured programming, and in-circuit emulation (ICE). The number of worked-out examples and sample programs has been greatly expanded, and there is a new chapter covering the 80186 and 80286 microprocessors.

A major addition is the inclusion in Chapters 14 through 21 of a number of *machine assembly updates,* providing information to keep pace with the increasing availability of machine assemblers. Although all machine assembly was done on an Intel Series II Development System to demonstrate the tools and methods used within industry, the machine assembly process is very similar to those presently available for the more popular personal computers (such as the IBM PC and Apple II).

To enhance the software development skills of the student, the Questions and Problems sections at the end of each chapter suggest nearly 60 programs (in addition to those presented in the text) that can be written and tested. The solutions to all suggested programs are given in the *Instructor's Guide*. All programs listed in this text and in the *Instructor's Guide* can be run without modification on the Intel SDK-85 single-board computer (with only minor modifications required to run on any 8080/8085-based single-board computer).

To summarize, the *content* of this book is grounded in fundamentals: design, troubleshooting, and interfacing in a balanced hardware/software environment. The *theme* of this book, however, is quite different, for it keeps an eye on the future, and in the future one subject will dominate the field of computers: *artificial intelligence*.

Therefore, to further increase enthusiasm and to make the material more readable, this book takes full advantage of the notion of the computer as an intelligent machine (an android). Indeed, if you set out to build a functioning intelligent machine, what major steps would you follow? First you would fashion the anatomy of the system (assemble the hardware). Next you would study its basic bodily processes and metabolism (basic processing action). You would then

v

bring it to life (initiate processor action), send it off to school to be taught (programmed) many useful skills, and finally train it to live successfully in the real world (interfacing and applications). These are also the steps in the staircase along which this book is organized.

Also within the theme of artificial intelligence (AI), the text makes occasional reference to the evolutionary parallel between human and computer. The author has chosen this parallel as a natural way to introduce a number of computer concepts. No attempt is made to convince you that a machine will someday be the equal of a human being. The subjects of artificial intelligence and natural selection are used primarily as vehicles to motivate your interest and perhaps to make the material more exciting and fascinating. On the other hand, the similarities between computers and people should in no way be construed as mere fantasy; moreover, it is predicted that after completing this book you will come to regard your home computer a little more like your family pet (a living creature) and a little less like your family car (a simple tool).

Roy W. Goody

contents

THE INTELLIGENT MICROCOMPUTER
Second Edition

chapter 1

The Microcomputer: An Overview

The microcomputer has flourished because—like its animal-kingdom counterpart—it found a fertile niche in the electronic environment and survived by being the fittest of the species.

In this chapter we will look at the historical development of the microcomputer and examine its fundamental nature. As you will see, we can learn a great deal about the computer by studying ourselves.

THE MICROCOMPUTER REVOLUTION

By the turn of this century the first industrial revolution, which began in England around 1720, was well under way, and machine power was replacing muscle power at an ever-increasing pace. Since the early 1970s a second and far more profound industrial revolution has gathered strength. This time, however, machine power will enhance and replace not the muscle power of the human species but the *brain* power.

The machine we are talking about is, of course, the computer. But computers are not all that new. Why then has the microprocessor—essentially a computer on a chip—ushered in the second industrial revolution?

Strangely enough, the answer to this question can be found on the Salisbury Plain in southwest England—the site of Stonehenge. This curious arrangement of 30-ton stones, each hewn from a distant quarry and transported hundreds of miles, is actually an ancient neolithic computer, constructed 500 years after the Egyptian pyramids to predict eclipses and other celestial events. Clearly, if today's computers were of Stonehenge design—requiring 30-ton components and hundreds of years to design and construct, fashioned from hard-to-get materials, dedicated to a single purpose, slow, inaccurate, and very limited in power—the second industrial revolution would not be taking place. But today's microprocessor-based computers are just the opposite. They are inexpensive, ultrasmall, lightweight, multipurpose, highly accurate, breathtakingly fast, and incredibly powerful—and the second industrial revolution is under way.

MICROPROCESSORS AND EXISTING SYSTEMS

To be more specific, microcomputers are successfully filling a wide gap in the electronic-design spectrum between ordinary arrays of gates and registers (called *combinational* or *random logic*) and minicomputers. Toward one end of the gap, microcomputers are replacing hardware with software, and toward the other end, they are replacing numerous discrete computer components with a handful of very large scale integrated (VLSI) chips, each containing 50,000 or more transistors on a single chip of silicon. Any combinational-logic circuit of 30 or more gates is a prime candidate to be replaced by a microprocessor, and any computer system of today—including mainframe computers—may soon be replaced by a handful of VLSI blocks.

MICROPROCESSOR DESIGN

Microprocessors are unique in the world of electronic design because successful designers and users must have a balanced knowledge of hardware, programming, and interfacing. No longer do we have the luxury of specializing either in hardware design or pure programming. Sometimes a design problem is best solved with extensive programming, using only the simplest of external hardware. At other times a careful combination of VLSI blocks will provide the best overall solution. Once this balanced approach is accepted, the rewards will be faster, more powerful, and less costly system designs.

MICROPROCESSORS AND MICROCOMPUTERS DEFINED

In a single sentence, a *microcomputer* is a system containing a *microprocessor*. A *microprocessor* is a VLSI programmable logic device on a single silicon chip, less than $\frac{1}{4}$ inch on a side, usually containing all necessary computer com-

1

ponents except memory and input/output (I/O) ports. A *microcomputer* is an entire computer system, including a microprocessor, external memory, and I/O devices. Occasionally, the entire computer system is integrated on a single chip (the 8048 family), although means are usually provided for adding extra memory and I/O ports.

Compared to mini- and mainframe computers, a microcomputer is usually smaller and less expensive, and often does not include the wide variety of expensive peripherals, such as cathode-ray tube (CRT) or disk memory. Microcomputers normally require less memory, are slower, and often are dedicated to a specific task, whereas mini- and mainframe computers are usually very high speed, general-purpose systems. However, the realm of the microcomputer overlaps into the area now dominated by the minicomputer, and soon will push into the area occupied by mainframe systems. Clearly it is difficult to define a system that is constantly changing; and, compared to human beings, computers are changing and adapting at an explosive pace!

MICROCOMPUTER APPLICATIONS

Even more important than the replacement of existing circuits and systems are the thousands of applications lying within the design gap between combinational-logic arrays and minicomputers—applications only the microprocessor can bring to life. The applications are so vast that the microprocessor revolution has already spawned an electronic age, in which an army of willing servants watches over us from morning to night. We wake up to a microprocessor-controlled alarm clock, read a newspaper that was edited and printed by a microcomputer-based word processor, and watch the morning news on television as a microprocessor fine-tunes the picture. We leave our homes guarded by a microprocessor "watchman," drive to work as a microprocessor instantly adjusts the car's timing and fuel/air mixture for optimum performance, and converse over a microprocessor-controlled CB radio. Our commute is speeded up by micro-processor-based traffic-control systems, our on-the-job productivity is increased by computerized inventory systems, and our workrooms are environmentally controlled by a microprocessor. We shop at a store where an intelligent (microprocessor-controlled) cash register inputs data to a central computer system that automatically inventories and orders merchandise. We go out for dinner and have our meal ordered and cooked under microprocessor control, and our drinks dispensed with a microcomputerized mixing machine. Then we go to bed and dream.

When we wake up it will be the future and our alarm will talk to us in perfect English. Our home computer will accurately forecast the weather and diagnose our ailments. We will realize how much we have come to rely on our computer

for its *judgment* as well as its knowledge, and it will be hard to tell whether we are still dreaming.

A BRIEF HISTORY

Like most inventions, the microprocessor resulted from the gradual blend of many scientific trends. Those most important to the development of the microprocessor were the mathematical, electronic, and computer trends. As shown in Figure 1.1, several important milestones finally led to today's advanced microprocessor.

- *The early days:* The first calculations were done on the human hand. From this simple beginning the familiar decimal, binary, and hexadecimal number systems eventually evolved. The first mechanical device to make use of number systems was the *abacus,* a calculating device that dates back before the birth of Christ and is still used today.

- *1642—Calculating machine:* Blaise Pascal invented the first "desk calculator." It was strictly a mechanical device, using systems of gears to add and subtract. Since the precision machining of parts was still many years away, the idea slowly died. (But Pascal's name did not die away, for a popular high-level computer language is named after him.)

- *1801—Automatic loom:* Joseph Jacquard's idea revolutionized the weaving industry and was destined to resurface many years later in the computer industry. It was an automatic loom that used punched cards (IBM cards!) to control the pattern.

- *1833—"Analytical engine":* Charles Babbage, more than any other computer pioneer, deserves the title "father of modern digital computers." His "analytical engine," developed to calculate and print mathematical tables, incorporated many of the principles of modern digital computers. Babbage was the first to envision the stored-program concept, in which all numbers *and* instructions were read before calculations began. In other words, once programmed, the machine worked without human intervention. Unfortunately, for a number of practical reasons that plague all inventions ahead of their time, it was never developed beyond the prototype stage.

- *1854—Boolean algebra:* Can formal logic be described mathematically? George Boole discovered that it could, and he developed a symbolic form of logic called *Boolean algebra,* a subject familiar to every student of digital electronics. The door to computer design was now wide open.

- *1890—Electric tabulating machine:* Herman Hollerith developed the first true data-processing machine. Using

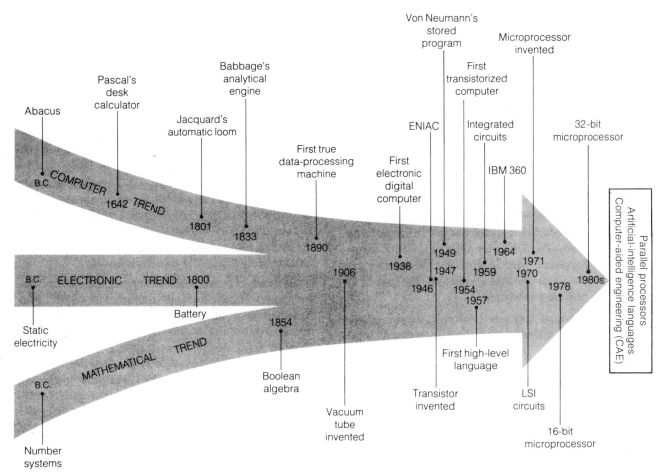

Figure 1.1 Technological trends and milestones in microprocessor development.

his machine, the task of tabulating the 1890 census was reduced from 20 to 3 years.

- *1906—Vacuum tube:* The electronic pathway began in earnest with the application of the triode vacuum tube, invented by Lee De Forest in 1906. Mathematical manipulations could now be done electronically rather than mechanically, with a quantum jump from seconds to milliseconds in processing speed.

- *1938—Electronic digital computer:* John V. Atanasoff formulated the basic ideas for computer memory and associated logic, and built the first electronic digital computer. Based on vacuum tubes, it paved the way for all work to follow.

- *1946—Large-scale electronic digital computer:* Prompted by the wartime need to calculate ballistic tables to produce trajectories for artillery and bombing, the U.S. Army funded the Electronic Numerical Integrator and Calculator (ENIAC) project. Completed in 1946, ENIAC was the first large-scale electronic digital calculating machine.

By today's standards it was a monster. Composed of 18,000 vacuum tubes, it weighed in at 30 tons, occupied 1,500 square feet, and consumed 130,000 watts of power. However, it could multiply two numbers in about 3 milliseconds, a thousand times faster than ever before—and without the use of a single moving part. It was turned off for the last time in 1955.

- *1949—Stored-program computer:* Although ENIAC could perform individual mathematical operations at high speed, it had to wait for each instruction to be entered by its human operators. Intent on removing this human factor, John von Neumann picked up on the stored-program concept first conceived by Babbage and proposed placing computer instructions as well as data in the computer's memory. Whenever a sequence of instructions was to be performed, the computer could read in each instruction from memory without waiting for human intervention. Storing the program inside the computer along with the data allows today's computers to operate at high speed (and distinguishes a computer from a calculator).

With the stored-program concept, the last major hurdle to modern computer design was crossed, and in May of 1949 the first digital computer based on the stored-program concept went into operation. Named the Electronic Delay Storage Automatic Calculator (EDSAC), it set the stage for all computers to follow.

- *1954—Transistorized computer:* Although based on electronics, ENIAC and EDSAC were still of "Stonehenge" design—far too big, bulky, and power consuming to command widespread attention. In 1947, however, a breakthrough was made that can only be described in fairy-tale terms, for like Alice in Wonderland, the solid-state research it set in motion was destined to shrink the size of computers a thousandfold and more. Invented by John Bardeen, W. H. Brattain, and W. B. Shockley at Bell Laboratories in 1947, the transistor was the seed from which the second industrial revolution sprouted.

  The first product of this seed sprouted in 1954 with the introduction of the TRAnsistor DIgital Computer (TRADIC). By 1960 hundreds of transistorized computers were in operation, processing data faster and at lower cost than ever before. The days of the vacuum tube were numbered.

- *1957—High-level language:* Primarily because of their awesome size, the early vacuum-tube computers quickly acquired a public image of "giant brains," fearsome machines to be viewed with apprehension and mistrust. This image was largely undeserved, of course, for these early computers were very crude, and in one area in particular—languages—they were downright primitive. The only language these early machines understood was machine language—the language of ones and zeros—a language that made programming a cumbersome, error-prone, and difficult endeavor.

  The first major breakthrough in language development was made by an IBM research team headed by John Backus. Primarily interested in developing a language to solve mathematical calculations, the team devised a way of writing a program using mathematical notation instead of machine language. Using common typewriter symbols to write and enter the program, the computer would then translate (compile) the sequence of symbols into the required machine-language instructions.

  Introduced in 1957, the language was called *FORTRAN* (for FORmula TRANslation) and is still in widespread use today. By 1960 numerous high-level languages were in use, including COBOL (COmmon Business-Oriented Language), which gave the business community many of the same advantages that FORTRAN gave the scientific community.

- *1959—Integrated circuit:* By applying the principles of photolithography to flat surfaces of silicon, and by developing the method of solid-state diffusion for introducing the impurities that create p and n regions, engineers found they could construct entire circuits, consisting of many transistors, on a single chip of silicon. This was the basis of the integrated circuit, a technology that was to show the same explosive growth in sophistication as took place in the human brain during the end of the last ice age.

- *1964—Integrated-circuit computer:* On April 7, 1964, IBM introduced the standard mainframe computer, the System/360 (called 360 because the system was said to encompass the full range of scientific and business applications). Using highly reliable, mass-produced, integrated circuits, it could perform in 1 second nearly a half million computations at a cost of less than 10 cents. The System/360 also introduced a number of new input/output and auxiliary storage devices.

- *1970—Large-scale integrated (LSI) circuit:* From the early 1960s to the early 1970s, the maximum complexity of integrated circuits doubled approximately every 18 months. By 1970 more than 15,000 transistors could be etched onto a single chip of silicon, an achievement that made the handheld calculator feasible.

- *1971 to present—era of the microprocessor:* In 1971 the computer, electronic, and mathematical trends came together in a unique way, and the microprocessor emerged on the scene—initially with little fanfare. In less than 15 years, though, it went from a simple 4-bit LSI device developed for calculators (the Intel 4004), to the iAPX386, a 32-bit SLSI (super large scale integrated) enhanced microprocessor family that forms the heart of a system resembling a mainframe computer.

- *Sometime in the future—first true intelligent machine:* In the field of microprocessors, the future blends with the past so quickly that no historical survey would be complete without a word about what lies ahead. Most far-reaching of all is a fourth scientific trend that is now merging with the ongoing development of the microprocessor. This fourth trend, known as *artificial intelligence,* will combine with the new parallel array processors to produce the true intelligent machine. Unlike the human brain, which must depend on the relatively slow process of biological change, the intelligent machine made of silicon is under no such restrictions. We can only wonder where the new technology will lead us. Soon a true learning machine will emerge, *one able to modify its program based on learning experience.* What would be the result if we taught two such learning machines to play chess, and what if they were pitted against each other, playing games at the speed of light for a month or a year? At the end of the time, what would we find? Perhaps a new way of thinking, or a new philosophy, or a new mathematics—or perhaps something we would not be able to understand at all!

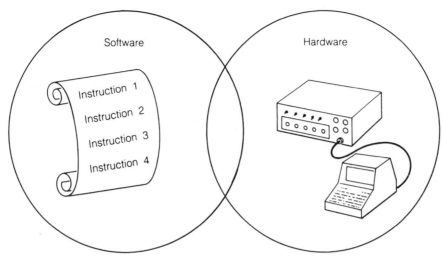

Figure 1.2 A computerized solution to a problem—both software and hardware required.

THE FUNDAMENTAL PRINCIPLES OF COMPUTER ACTION

The apparent similarity between people and computers presents us with an exciting possibility: If computers and humans do things in a similar way, then to develop the more basic concepts of computer action perhaps we can begin by studying ourselves.

What separates us and other members of the animal kingdom from the world of inanimate objects? The answer is very straightforward: we perform tasks; we do things.

To use an everyday example, consider a major-league outfielder catching a baseball. Even the most cursory analysis of this simple task reveals that it is composed of individual steps, taken in sequential order:

Track ball
Run under ball
Raise glove
Catch ball

Each step in the sequence commands a specific operation. In computer terminology, each command is called an *instruction*. To complete the task of catching a baseball, then, we simply go through the instructions in order. *A computer performs a task in precisely the same way.* Therefore, by studying our own actions, we already have uncovered perhaps the most fundamental of all computer concepts. Seven of these concepts are described below.

1. *A computer performs a task by processing a sequential list of instructions.*

Of course, it is important for us to write the list of instructions in the proper order. If any of the steps is incorrectly listed, the task probably could not be completed.

2. *To carry out a task by way of computer action, we require both the list of instructions (the software) and the physical circuitry (the hardware).*

To catch a baseball, we require two major items: the list of instructions and the collection of physical components (player, baseball, and glove). When applied to computers, the sequential list of instructions is known as *software;* the physical computer circuitry and peripheral components are known as *hardware* (see Figure 1.2).

3. *Each instruction given to a computer generally consists of a verb portion (the operation code) and an object portion (the operand).*

As listed below, each instruction written for a person is also made up of two parts—a verb or action portion and a noun or object portion:

Verb	*Object*
track	ball
run under	ball
raise	glove
catch	ball

4. *As each instruction is carried out (executed), the operation code (verb) directs the activities of the operand (object).*

As each instruction of our baseball routine is processed, the verb or action portion directs the activities of the object portion, and the instruction is carried out—or *executed*. Since this is true of all instructions carried out by people, it is also true of all instructions carried out by computers.

5. *Programming a computer means entering the proper sequence of instructions into its memory.*

During training, a baseball player quickly commits to memory the sequence of instructions for catching a baseball. In other words, the player has *learned* the sequence of steps. In computer terminology, learning is known as *programming,* and it consists of storing the sequence of instructions in memory. As previously noted, the concept of a stored program—that is, placing the instructions in memory before they are needed—was one of the great historical advances made in computer technology.

6. *A computer consists of five basic hardware blocks: input, output, memory, arithmetic/logic unit (ALU), and control unit.* (CPU)

We know that the system software—or program—can be broken down into a sequence of instructions. Can the system hardware, for both human being and computer, also be broken down into a number of individual blocks? For people we find that it can, and catching a baseball puts five major parts of anatomy (hardware) into play:

- The *eye* (input port) tracks the flight of the ball.
- The *voice* (output port) calls for the ball.
- The *memory* holds the sequence of instructions.
- The *computation and logic area of the brain* (arithmetic/logic unit, or ALU) computes the ball's trajectory.

- The *central nervous system* (control unit) times and sequences the overall process.

As shown in Figure 1.3, these five basic hardware elements are also common to every computer.

The control unit and the ALU are often combined in a single unit known as the *central processing unit*—or simply CPU (the CPU is often a single microprocessor chip, such as the 8080/8085).

7. *The basic processing cycle of a computer system consists of input of data, manipulation of data, and output or display of result.*

Human beings generally interact with their environment in a three-step process: we take in information, manipulate it mentally, and output the result. The overall processing cycle of a computer follows the same pattern: input, process, and output.

BEYOND THE FUNDAMENTAL CONCEPTS

When described in their most basic terms—as we have done in this chapter—the actions that human beings take to catch a baseball or perform other common tasks do not seem complex. It appears we use our marvelous mental machines with little regard for the intricate operations involved. Unfortu-

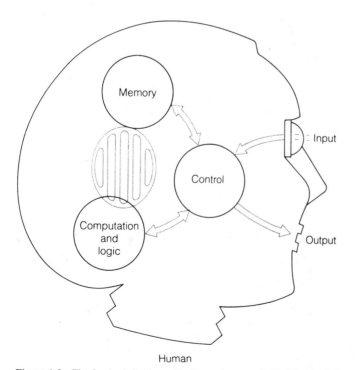

Human

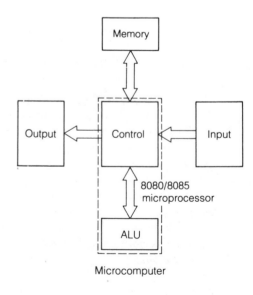

Microcomputer

Figure 1.3 The five basic hardware blocks are the same for both human being and computer.

nately, we cannot take computers so lightly, for to design and troubleshoot computer systems we must understand precisely how every component functions and interacts, and how every signal and waveform carries forward the processing cycle. The tasks before us are clear:

- The five blocks of the computer system must be opened up and the inner workings revealed.

- The processing action itself must be studied in detail.

- The computer's vocabulary (all the instructions it can follow) must be learned, and all instructions must be converted to a form the computer will understand (English will not do). In addition, the computer must be taught (programmed) to perform simple tasks.

- All the factors allowing a computer to operate efficiently in a real-world environment must be covered.

- More advanced, later-generation computer systems must be introduced.

Each of these tasks corresponds closely to Parts I, II, III, IV, and V of this book.

QUESTIONS AND PROBLEMS

1. List some ways in which you think people and computers are alike, and list ways in which they are not.
2. What is the difference between a microprocessor and a microcomputer?
3. What does VLSI stand for?
4. When a combinational-logic array is replaced by a microprocessor, why can the chip count usually be reduced?
5. What significant computer development do we owe to Charles Babbage? *STORED-PROGRAM CONCEPT*
6. List some of the microprocessor/microcomputer applications you have recently encountered.
7. Name several characteristics of a *high-level* language.
8. What is the major difference between a computer and a calculator? *IS programmable*
9. Name the first and most fundamental of all computer concepts.
10. What is each step in a program called?
11. Why is it important to list the steps in a program in proper sequence?
12. What is the difference between *hardware* and *software*?
13. In technical terms, what do the (a) "verb" and (b) "object" of each instruction correspond to?
14. Programming a computer corresponds to what process in human beings?
15. What are the five major hardware blocks of a computer? To what human anatomical feature does each correspond, and what is the basic function of each?
16. How is a recipe like a computer program?
17. If *sequential* (or serial) processing refers to executing instructions one-at-a-time *in sequence*, to what do you think *parallel* (array) processing refers?
18. What present-day technological innovation comes the closest to "computers designing other computers"? (Hint: What does *CAE* stand for?)

do problems before Wednesday's class

unknown Computer aided Engineering

part 1

Hardware:
The Anatomy of a Computer

Armed with a knowledge of the most fundamental principles of computer action, we will now construct an intelligent machine from scratch.

In Part I, we will assemble, one at a time, the five hardware blocks that constitute the *anatomy* of the computer. The computer's anatomy is often called its *architecture*—the total collection of circuits, registers, and interconnecting lines that make up the physical system. When we have added all five components—and have completed Part I—the system will be ready to assume the characteristics of a true intelligent machine.

chapter 2

The Bus System

"Beauty of style and harmony and grace and good rhythm depend on simplicity." (Plato, *The Republic,* 4th century B.C.) This remarkable insight by Plato might be called the *designer's creed*. If our computer system is going to perform with style and harmony, it must be simple.

Unfortunately, the potential for complexity is enormous. A single CPU, for example, may be called on to communicate with hundreds of peripheral circuits. Imagine the overall complexity of such a system if we had to provide a *unique* path between the CPU and every peripheral. Indeed, the number of pins required on the CPU would alone make such an approach prohibitive. Before microcomputers could evolve, this data roadblock had to be cleared away.

THE BUS CONCEPT

As with so many contemporary problems, the solution had already been demonstrated—it merely had to be applied to computers. Simply look at the neighborhood you live in. Your community may be a small one, with just five homes, but providing a *unique* roadway between each home results in a system of great complexity (see Figure 2.1*a*). As demonstrated by Figure 2.1*b*, the solution is well known: interconnect the five homes with a single intersection.

An <u>intersection</u> is a *common* area fed by all pathways, and its use results in a simpler system. To avoid conflicts, of course, we have to take great care that vehicles traveling

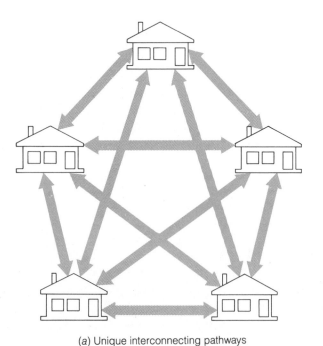

(*a*) Unique interconnecting pathways
that result in complex system

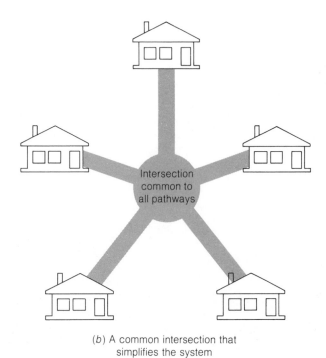

(*b*) A common intersection that
simplifies the system

Figure 2.1   The bus concept.

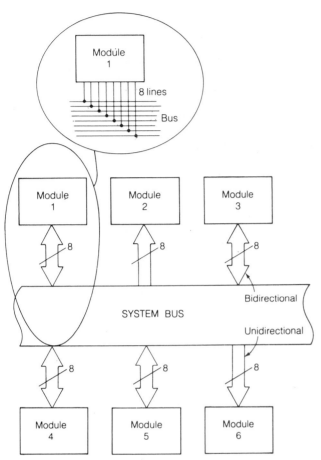

Figure 2.2 A bus-organized system.

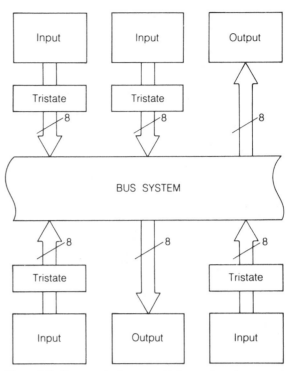

Figure 2.3 Bus-organized system with inputs tristated.

on separate pathways do not attempt to use the intersection at the same time. In other words, they must take turns using the common medium, a process known as *time multiplexing*.

Microcomputers have adopted this hardware-saving configuration. The single transmission medium, known as a *bus*, consists of an array of *common* conductors into which all circuit elements tap. The bus concept allows for a very simple arrangement of components (see Figure 2.2).

Of course, all peripheral modules feeding the common bus system will have to share its use through the process of time multiplexing. First, one peripheral circuit transmits its data with full and exclusive use of the transmitting medium; then, in the next time slot, another peripheral circuit has full use of the common bus system. *Clearly, only one circuit module at a time can transmit data onto the common bus.*

BUS-SYSTEM CATEGORIES

Because it greatly simplifies the overall system, all 8-bit microcomputers use the bus concept. Furthermore, all microcomputers break down the bus system into four bus-

strip categories. Each bus-strip category in turn consists of a number of "parallel" conductors:

- *Data bus*—The data bus consists of eight bidirectional conductors and carries data and instructions back and forth between the various circuit locations. The eight parallel data lines, carrying eight bits of information simultaneously, make the 8080/8085 microprocessor a parallel processor. These 8-bit words are known as *bytes*.

- *Address bus*—The address bus consists of 16 lines and is used to locate data within memory or I/O ports. Since 65,536 different binary numbers can be specified with 16 bits ($2^{16} = 65,536$), the address bus can locate, or point out, one particular byte of data among 65,536 possible locations (65,536 = 64K, where 1K = 1,024).

- *Control bus*—The control bus carries the various timing signals used to regulate and sequence the transfer of data and to carry out various processes. The number of lines is arbitrary because the control bus is a catchall bus— that is, it contains signals that do not fit into the other bus-strip categories.

- *Power bus*—The power bus for most microcomputers consists of two lines: + 5 volts and ground. Occasionally, for older microprocessors and components, additional lines are needed. For instance, the 8080 microprocessor requires − 5 and + 12-volt supplies in addition to the standard + 5 volts. Component manufacturers

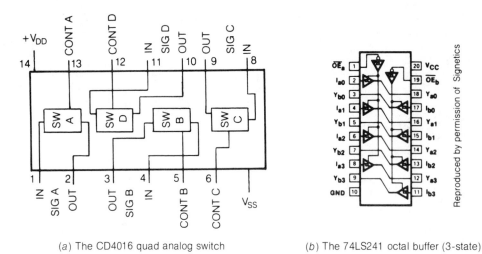

(a) The CD4016 quad analog switch

(b) The 74LS241 octal buffer (3-state)

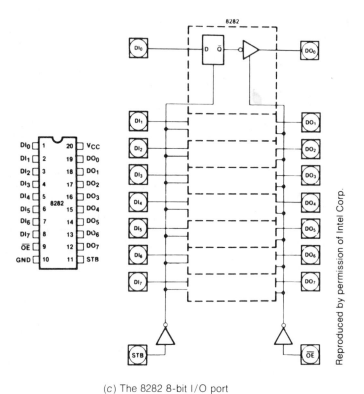

(c) The 8282 8-bit I/O port

Figure 2.4 Three typical tristate circuits.

clearly intend to produce circuits which run on a single + 5-volt supply and which are fully TTL compatible. (To simplify future diagrams, the power bus usually will be deleted.)

TRISTATE CIRCUITS

The bus concept and time multiplexing go hand in hand. When one roadway is transmitting vehicles into an intersection, all others must be isolated. Traffic signals provide the

necessary isolation by giving the green light to only one roadway at a time.

In electronics, the tristate circuit acts as the traffic signal, controlling the flow of data onto the data bus. It must have a transmitting state (green light) and an isolation state (red light). When in the transmitting state, either a logic 1 or a logic 0 can pass through to the data bus. When in the isolation state, the output floats and enters a high-impedance (Z) condition. Since three states are possible, we call the circuit a *tristate circuit*. The three states are:

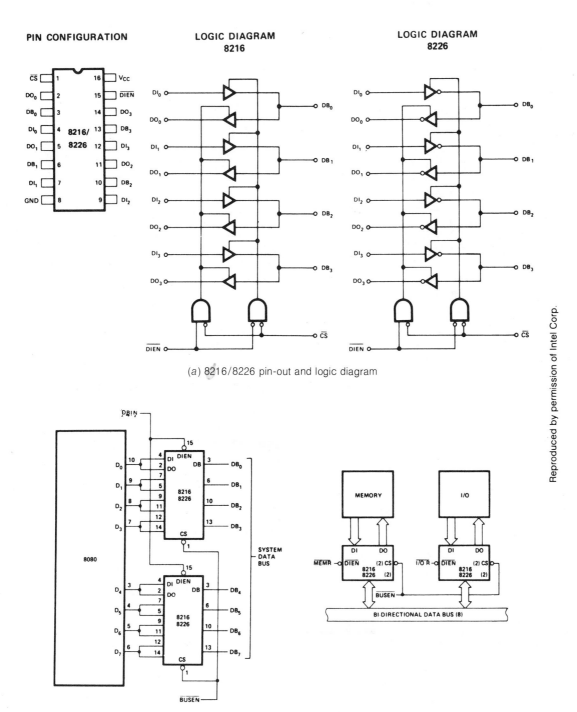

(a) 8216/8226 pin-out and logic diagram

(b) Bus-system buffering using the 8216/8226 bidirectional bus driver

Figure 2.5 The 8216/8226 4-bit, bidirectional bus driver.

Reproduced by permission of Intel Corp.

0	transmitting state (logic 0)
1	transmitting state (logic 1)
high Z	isolation state

A high-impedance state accomplishes the necessary isolation since it does not prevent the single actively transmit-ting circuit from driving the data-bus lines high or low, as required. Devices receiving information from the data bus, on the other hand, need not be tristated, for conflicts of information between receiving circuits are not possible (once you leave an intersection, there is no need for further traffic control). However, the output circuits should present to the bus a reasonably high input impedance to avoid overloading the bus lines.

When tristate circuits are added to all input devices, notice how simple a bus-organized system becomes (Figure 2.3). The beauty of the bus system lies in the ease with which new circuits or modules can be added into the computer system. Simply tie the address, data, control, and power lines directly into the system bus.

EXAMPLES OF TRISTATE CIRCUITS

To implement a time-multiplexed bus system, a whole family of tristate circuits has evolved. We will look at three examples:

- The CD4016 quad bilateral switch shown in Figure 2.4*a* is a set of four analog switches that can be used for tristate functions. The circuit operation is very simple. When any given control line is high, the circuit is transmitting information, and the output state equals the input state. When the control line goes low, the circuit assumes the high-impedance state and does not prevent another circuit from transmitting onto the bus. The inherent high input impedance and low power drain of this chip simplify the job of the designer.

- The 74LS241 octal buffer (tristate) is similar to the CD4016. However, the 74LS241 integrates eight buffers within a single chip and, as a member of the TTL family, has different I/O characteristics (see Figure 2.4*b*).

- The 8282 8-bit latch (a simplified version of the popular 8212) is a member of the newer family of tristate circuits and can be configured for either input or output operation (see Figure 2.4*c*). Eight tristate buffers are included within each chip, making the 8282 specifically designed for use with 8-bit microprocessors. For added flexibility, a D latch is paired with each tristate buffer. Output enable (OE) controls the tristate buffers, and strobe (STB) clocks data through the D latches. We will be using the 8282 shortly when the first two hardware blocks are added to our intelligent-machine system.

BUFFERING THE BUS LINES

For a small, single-board system, the current drive capability of the 8080/8085 (a single TTL load) is adequate. For large multiboard systems, however, MOS and CMOS microprocessors and circuits often lack the required power to drive the system bus, and a *buffer* or *driver* must be interfaced between the CPU and system bus. If memory and I/O ports are MOS or CMOS devices, they too may require buffering.

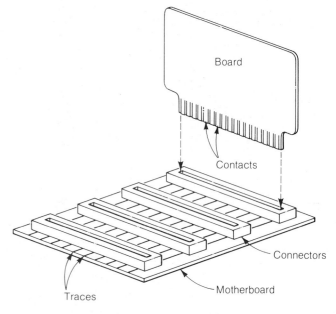

Figure 2.6 The motherboard concept.

Buffer/drivers fall into one of three categories:

1. *Transmitters,* which buffer the signals sent to the bus
2. *Receivers,* which buffer the signals sent from the bus
3. *Transceivers,* which perform both of the above processes

The 8216/8226 4-bit, parallel, bidirectional bus driver (Figure 2.5*a*) is a typical buffer, offering high output-drive capability and tristate outputs. Figure 2.5*b* shows the 8216/8226 used as a transceiver to buffer the bidirectional data bus.

COMMON BUS STANDARDS

Standardization eliminates redundancy and improves efficiency. The English language, for example, is a standard form of communication, used by a great number of diverse peoples. For the same reasons, a number of widely adopted bus standards presently are found in the microcomputer world (with several others under development). We will examine a few of the more popular bus standards.

S-100 Bus

Like so many standards, the S-100 bus was not originally designed to be a standard. It was developed by MITS, Inc., in 1975 for their 8080-based Altair computer. Others soon adopted the S-100 format, and it quickly became an industry standard.

The S-100 bus is a collection of 100 data, address, con-

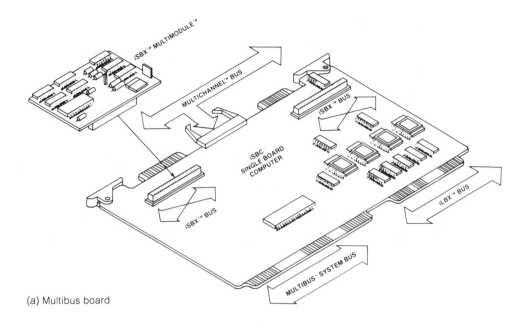

(a) Multibus board

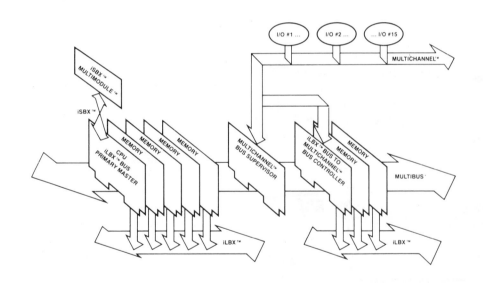

(b) System architecture

Figure 2.7   The Multibus system.
Reproduced by permission of Intel Corporation.

trol, and power signals. Its major appeal was the adoption of the "motherboard" concept (Figure 2.6). A motherboard is a printed-circuit board holding 100 parallel foil strips, with several 100-pin edge connectors soldered to the foil. Circuit boards (10 by 5.5 inches) are added to the system by merely plugging them into the edge connectors at right angles. Consequently, a flood of S-100 compatible modules—memory boards, I/O boards, and others—soon became available.

However, the original S-100 bus—developed in an era when 16-bit processors, multiprocessing, and megabyte memories were unheard of—was unable to keep up with new developments. To maintain the popular S-100 concept, yet meet the needs of modern systems, the IEEE-696 standard was developed. Among its improved features are a 24-bit address bus (16 megabytes), 16-bit data bus, 11 interrupt inputs, and provisions for multiprocessing. This new general-purpose interface system should ensure compatibility with present and future S-100 computer systems.

Multibus

Like the new S-100 standard, Intel Corporation's Multibus standard—also appropriate for both 8-bit and 16-bit devices—is specifically designed to accept a wide variety of system modules. Unlike the S-100 standard, however, the Multibus system is actually four buses in one. The reason, as always, is the need to provide for increasingly complex solutions. A single bus structure was simply too "one dimensional" (*all* interconnections between modules were by way of the single system bus).

The diagram of Figure 2.7 reveals the four-bus Multibus structure. A variety of 6.75- by 12-inch CPU, memory, and I/O boards can be quickly assembled by plugging them into a Multibus card cage. Let's briefly review the rational behind each of the four buses:

- The *Multibus system bus* is the main bus structure. All system modules are interconnected via a rigid backplane motherboard that holds edge connectors to accept each Multibus module. Its 86 lines include 24 address lines (16 Mbytes), 16 data lines (bidirectional), 8 multilevel interrupt lines, an extensive control array, and a number of redundant power and ground lines.
- The *iLBX bus* provides an additional 16 Mbytes of *local* memory (memory allocated only to those boards interconnected via the iLBX bus). By eliminating the need to access memory only over a single common bus, parallel (simultaneous) operation is possible and performance is greatly enhanced.
- To allow for custom variations, the Multibus package includes the *iSBX Multimodule* bus. As shown in Figure 2.7a, several small iSBX Multimodule cards can be added to each main board to provide added capability without the need for additional Multibus boards.
- The *Multichannel bus* was created to allow data exchanges between modules via *direct memory access* (DMA). Direct memory access, fully explained in Chapter 18, is an ultra-high speed technique of transferring blocks of data between peripherals without the intervention of the CPU.

The Multibus system bus supports two basic types of modules: *master* and *slave*. The master controls the bus, transmitting address and command signals; the slave merely receives signals. A Multibus system may have a number of bus masters. Since only one bus master can control the bus at one time, bus arbitration logic is included with the Multibus scheme. To allow for speed variations between master and slave, an asynchronous *(handshaking)* scheme is used for data transfers. For example, when the master initiates a read operation ("Give me some data"), it must wait for an *acknowledge* signal from the slave ("Here it is") indicating the data is now available on the bus. (*Handshaking* is a topic of Chapter 18.)

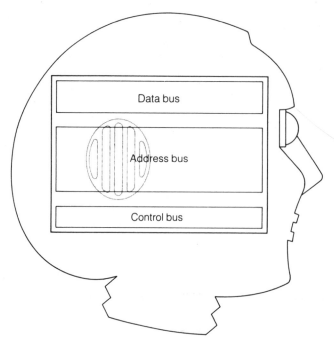

Figure 2.8   Thinking-machine design under way.

The Intel-developed Multibus (officially designated IEEE-796) has gained widespread acceptance in the microcomputer industry.

Multibus II

For applications involving the new complex, high-speed 32-bit systems that are coming onto the market, we can select the more advanced *Multibus II*.

As expected, Multibus II expands on the multiple-bus structure of Multibus I. The clock speed was increased, support for 32-bit processors was added, the size of local memory (via the private iLBX II bus) was increased to 64 Mbytes, the number of possible bus masters was expanded, and a special serial bus (iSSB) was added. To improve reliability, the Multibus II has adopted the Eurocard mechanical standard for its backplane connections. In addition, Multibus II offers a more generalized system design that supports practically any microprocessor.

INTELLIGENT-MACHINE DESIGN

With an appreciation of the advantages of a bus-organized system, we can now begin the design of our intelligent machine.

Adding a bus system to simplify the overall computer architecture, our system is on its way (Figure 2.8). So far it is a system that Plato would have approved of; it is a system that will lead to inherent simplicity.

QUESTIONS AND PROBLEMS

1. How does the bus concept simplify the overall hardware configuration of a computer?
2. What is another term for *time multiplexing?*
3. How many circuit modules are allowed to transmit data *onto* the bus at the same time? Why? *1 to avoid conflicts*
4. What are the four bus-strip categories of a microcomputer bus system, and what general function is provided by each?
5. What does the term *floating* mean?
6. What are the three states of a tristate circuit?
7. What function is performed by the $\overline{\text{OE}}$ (output enable) line of the 8282 8-bit I/O port?
8. What is a *motherboard?* In general, why can boards be plugged into the motherboard at any position (what distinguishes one board from another)?
9. Why is it sometimes necessary to buffer the bus lines?
10. What does *bidirectional* mean?
11. What is a transceiver?
12. *Theoretically*, how many modules can simultaneously *receive* information from the common bus?
13. Name several advantages of a multibus structure over a single *bus* structure.
14. What is *local* or *private* memory?

3. So as not to interfere w/flow of other data

5. isolation state, — entering high impedance condition.

12. any, all, infinite because receiving devices are not tristated.
Yet if only 1 can be transmitted at a time, then only one can be received.

chapter 3

Input and Output Ports

At the very beginnings of brain development, when the Earth belonged to tiny multicellular organisms, the first nervous systems were simple sensory receptors designed to sense the heat, light, and chemical makeup of their ocean environment and to respond by simple reflex action.

In this chapter we will follow the pattern of nature and make the first circuits added to our intelligent machine its "eyes," "ears," and "voice"—simple *input ports* and simple *output ports*. (More complex I/O circuits and techniques will be introduced in future chapters.)

THE INPUT PORT

An input port is a conduit for channeling information from the outside world to the internal data bus. As we learned in the previous chapter, however, all information transmitted onto the data bus must be tristated; otherwise data from two sources would collide on the data bus, and the information would be garbled.

The 8282 8-bit I/O port has built-in tristate buffers and will satisfy all the requirements for input-port operation (see Figure 3.1). When we examine the internal circuitry of the

8282, we find all eight tristate buffers controlled by the active-low output-enable (OE) line. When OE is pulled low, the data present at the eight input lines pass through the port and appear on the eight output lines. When the OE control line is inactive (high), the output lines are driven to their high-impedance state. Since simple input ports generally do not require latches, the eight D latches are made transparent to the incoming data by placing a high on the strobe line. (The D latches are level active, passing the input to the output when STB is high, and latching the data on the high-to-low transition.)

Adding two 8282s to our system, our thinking machine is now endowed with sensory inputs (see Figure 3.2). When the computer wishes to "read," it pulls port 1's OE line low. Information flows from the outside world to the data bus. When this OE line is high and the output buffers are in their high-impedance state, port 2 can take its turn at transmitting

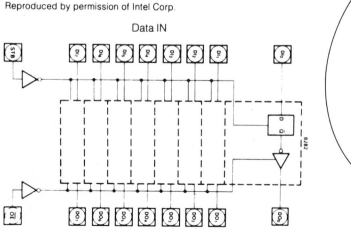

Reproduced by permission of Intel Corp.

Figure 3.1 The 8282 8-bit I/O port with three-state outputs.

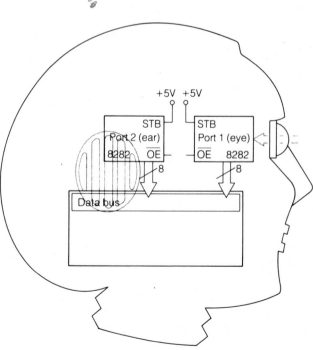

Figure 3.2 Sensory input ports added to intelligent machine.

data onto the data bus. By taking turns, all input ports can share the common data bus.

Our developing system can now read and listen at various times—by time multiplexing. But how does it choose what it wants to do—if it wants to read rather than listen? How does it single out the one correct input port from all the others in the system? And once it has found the right input port, how does it know precisely *when* to activate the port?

A careful look at the process of *data transfer* will help provide the answers. After all, reading and listening are nothing more than data-transfer operations.

Data Transfer

Suppose you plan to travel by air between San Francisco and New York. When you purchase your plane ticket, you must be able to answer two important questions:

1. *Where* am I and *where* am I going?
2. *When* will I leave?

In short, traveling from one location to another is a *where/ when* operation. First you specify your source and destination, and then you pinpoint the exact time of your trip.

Data-transfer operations within a computer system are also where/when operations:

1. *Where:* With the help of signals on the address bus, both the source and the destination of the data transfer are determined.
2. *When:* Control-bus signals then open the gates of the selected source and destination, allowing the data to flow between source and destination.

These considerations lead to the standard waveforms for data transfer (Figure 3.3). The waveforms constitute a where/ when data-transfer operation and must occur whenever

information is transferred from one computer location to another.

Note that the *when* part of the operation occurs *within* the time of the *where* part. This all-important address/control phasing ensures that the address will have time to stabilize before data flows and will remain stable throughout the entire transfer process. (Imagine the confusion if data were allowed to flow before the changing address bus settled down to point to a single memory or port location.) Also shown are the two major 8080/8085 specifications for address/control phasing (both t_{AC} and t_{CA} are typically over 100 nsec).

By convention the crisscrossing lines of the address waveforms simply indicate a change from one address to the next. That is, whenever an address changes, typically some of the address bits will go high, some will go low, and some will remain unchanged. The dotted lines of the data waveforms indicate a floating or indeterminate state. Also note the typically active-low control signals.

8282/Bus Interfacing

To summarize our progress to date, we have our 8282 8-bit input-port chip with its $\overline{OE}$ line to allow the flow of information through the chip when pulled active low. We also know that any transfer of data must follow a where/when process using signals from the address and control bus. Are we now ready to complete the design and tie in the 8282 to the system bus, adding any necessary interfacing circuitry?

One problem is that the interface circuitry depends on the microprocessor we ultimately choose to run the system. For example, as shown below, the 8080 and 8085 specify control information in slightly different ways:

8080 control bus		8085 control bus	
_____	I/O R	_____	$\overline{RD}$
_____	I/O W	_____	$\overline{WR}$
_____	MEM R	_____	$IO/\overline{M}$
_____	MEM W		

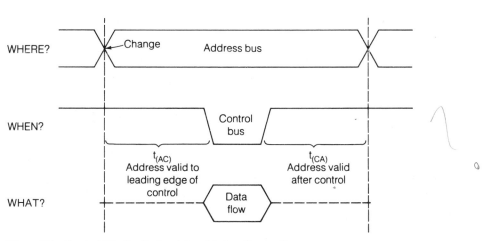

Figure 3.3 Standard (idealized) where/when data transfer waveforms.

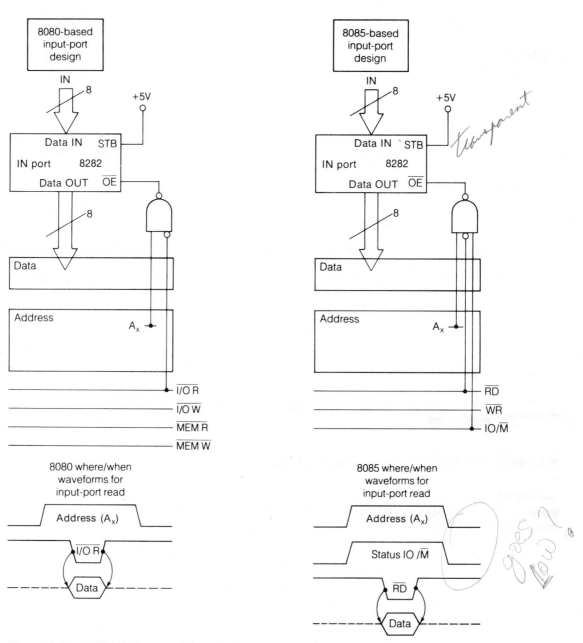

Figure 3.4   Final 8080/8085 input-port design and address/control waveforms (Address line Ax is arbitrary).

The question is: how will these control-bus lines behave during an input-port data transfer? Since we are familiar with basic Boolean notation (and simple abbreviations for memory, input/output, and read/write), the answer is seen at a glance:

- For 8080-based systems, $\overline{\text{I/O R}}$ (Input/Output Read) will go active low and all other control lines will remain high.
- For $\overline{8085}$-based systems, $\overline{\text{RD}}$ (read) will go active low and $\overline{\text{WR}}$ (write) will remain high. IO/$\overline{\text{M}}$ (Input-Output/Memory) will go high to specify the port-address space rather than the memory-address space. Although tech-

nically known as a *status* line, think of the IO/$\overline{\text{M}}$ line as part of the address, since it helps to pinpoint a specific location by separating the port space from the memory space. Since there is no room on the address bus, however, it is placed on the control bus.

The Final Input-Port Design

Blending all the information, we arrive at the final input-port design for both 8080- and 8085-based systems (Figure 3.4).

To read in information through the input port to the data bus, simply sequence the address/control lines according to the where/when waveforms. In both cases a single address line, attached directly to one of the 16 available lines, is all we require to address the input port. As we will see in chapter 5, this is a reasonable assumption for small systems. (The arrows on the input waveforms indicate a cause/effect relationship—the control bus *causes* data to flow.)

Interfacing Additional Input Ports

Interfacing additional 8282-based input ports to the bus system is quite simple since there is only one difference in interfacing circuitry between the various input ports: *the address signal for each is attached to a different line on the address bus*. With each input port receiving a unique address, the computer will easily be able to distinguish between them.

General Input-Port Design

Although our input-port design was developed around a specific chip—the 8282—the basic principles must hold for all input ports:

- All input ports must include tristate buffers in order to implement the requirements of time multiplexing.

- All input-port operations must be controlled by a where/when operation.

- And all input ports must include the interfacing circuitry required to correctly enable the tristate buffers when fed the proper address and control signals.

The Input-Port in Action

Adding two input ports (8085-based) to our intelligent machine, it now possesses the ability to "see" and "hear" (Figure 3.5). As a final test of our input-port design, hold up a data word to the machine's "eyes" and follow through the where/when sequence as it reads the word to the internal data bus:

1. The where process begins with the address of input port 1 (eye) appearing on the address bus. Simultaneously, the IO/$\overline{\text{M}}$ line goes high.

2. After the address and IO/$\overline{\text{M}}$ lines have been given time to fully stabilize, the read control line ($\overline{\text{RD}}$) goes active low, completely enabling NAND gate 1 and driving the OE line active low.

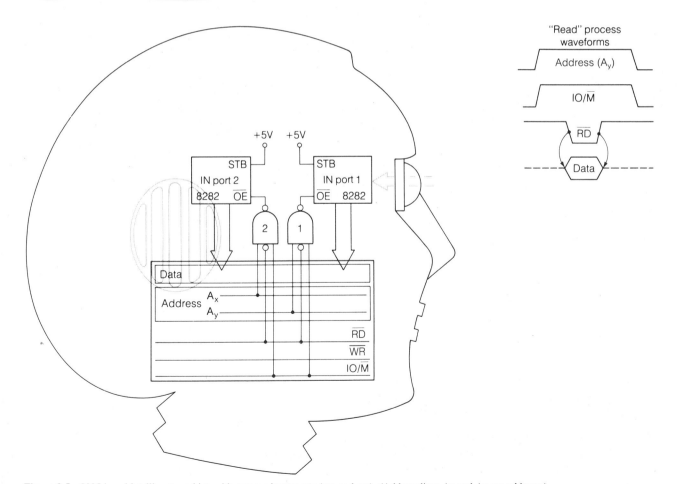

Figure 3.5   8085-based intelligent machine with sensory input ports (eye and ear). (Address lines Ax and Ay are arbitrary.)

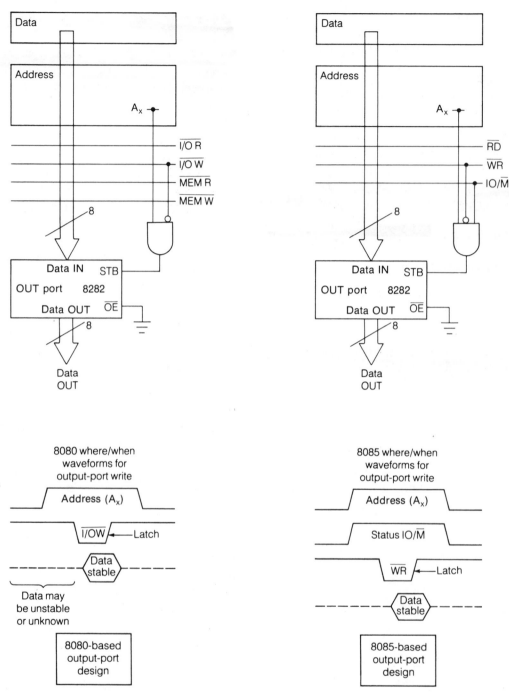

Figure 3.6 Final 8080/8085 output-port design and data-transfer waveforms.

3. The data word flows from the outside world, through the selected 8282 input port, and onto the data bus.

4. The read control line goes high, shutting off the flow of data.

5. To make sure the tristate buffers are fully disabled before the address is changed, an additional address-hold period is provided after the read control line goes inactive.

THE OUTPUT PORT

Our computer system is now endowed with simple input ports and has the means to sense its environment. That, however, is not enough. It must also be able to respond to the information it has taken in. In other words, it must be given a voice—an *output port*.

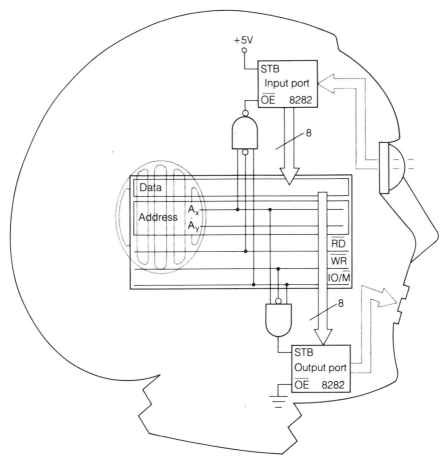

Figure 3.7   8085-based intelligent machine with input port (eye) and output port (voice).

Comparison of Input and Output Ports

Since both reading and speaking involve a simple transfer of data, the structure of both input and output ports will be similar. For example, the output port will also use the 8282 chip.

An output port, however, differs from an input port in two ways. First, an output port does not need tristate buffers. Remember, when information is *received* from the data bus, rather than being *transmitted* onto it, there can be no conflict of data. Therefore the tristate buffers are permanently enabled by grounding the $\overline{OE}$ line.

The second significant difference between an input port and an output port is the presence of latches to catch and hold the outported information. Latches are especially important when the computer is speaking to people, for we need time to take in the information. In addition, clocked latches provide a means of passing to the outside world only the data-bus information of interest. (If we ask the computer to add two numbers, we are usually interested in only the final answer, not the intermediate information appearing on the data bus.)

These two differences between input and output ports also will require a slight change in the interfacing circuitry between 8282 and bus system.

The Complete Output-Port Design

The final output-port design is shown in Figure 3.6. By driving the strobe line (STB) with the combined bus signals, we can properly clock the output data into the latches. (Again, remember, we permanently enabled the tristate buffers by tying the output-enable line low.)

To transfer data from the data bus to the output-port latches, simply sequence the proper address/control bus lines according to the where/when data-transfer format. (Note the differences between the output and input waveforms: the write rather than the read control line goes active low, and the information on the data bus must be stable before the write control lines go high.)

INTELLIGENT-MACHINE UPDATE

As shown in Figure 3.7, our computer system now has (at least physically) an "eye" and a "voice"—an *input port* and an *output port*. But it cannot see and it cannot speak—at least on its own—for that requires additional circuitry to control and time the input and output processes. This additional circuitry will be added in a future chapter. First, however, we must endow our intelligent machine with a memory.

QUESTIONS AND PROBLEMS

1. What is the purpose of an input port? Of an output port?
2. Why must an input port be tristated?
3. Output enable ($\overline{OE}$) controls what internal circuits within the 8282? Strobe (STB) controls what internal circuits?
4. What two steps are involved in all data-transfer processes?
5. What is the function of the address bus in a data-transfer operation? Of the control bus?
6. What is the difference between the 8080 and 8085 control buses?
7. Go through the precise steps required in an 8080-based system to both input and output data. Do the same procedure for an 8085-based system.
8. How are ports (input or output) added to a computer system?
9. Name three general principles that must hold for all input ports.
10. Why is the control line active for a shorter period of time than the address lines?
11. Why is *read* a particularly appropriate term for the input-port operation? Why is *write* a reasonable term to use for the output-port operation?
12. How can the terms *address, status,* and *control* all apply to the IO/$\overline{M}$ signal?
13. Why can both an input port and an output port be tied to the same address line (as shown in Figure 3.7)?
14. How can we tell at a glance that IO/$\overline{M}$ will be high for port operations and low for memory operations?
15. Redesign the system of Figure 3.7, using 8212s rather than 8282s.
16. Why is it more important for the address to be stable before activation of the write control line than the read control line?
17. Although latches are not essential for input-port operation, under what conditions might they be used?
18. Redraw the idealized input-port read waveforms of Figure 3.4, showing the effects of propagation delay (delay between control-line switching and data flow). By researching the specifications of the input-port circuitry, determine an expected value of the propagation delay.
19. Referring to Figure 3.6, why is it important for the data to be stable when the write control line goes high?
20. Redesign the system shown in Figure 3.7 using a single 8205 (3205) 3-in/8-out decoder instead of the AND/NAND gates.

chapter 4

Introduction to
Memory/Memory Hierarchy

There exists in this world a memory of remarkable properties. Its retention ability is so vast that 1,000 bits of information can be absorbed every second for more than one hundred years and still not overflow its capacity. It accepts information of various word lengths—sometimes up to thousands of bits per word. It functions reliably for many decades, weighs no more than 3 pounds, is very compact, and is so structured that the failure of one small part does not prevent the overall system from functioning.

Such a memory, of course, is our own!

Even though we cannot hope to equal the power and complexity of the human mind soon, we will find once again that the computer's memory needs and our own memory needs are closely related.

MEMORY HIERARCHY

Our own memory is hierarchical. Short-term memory (memory at the tip of our tongues) resides in electrical activity. If the idea to be remembered is important enough and persists long enough, however, the electrical activity is thought to give rise to protein synthesis, a more permanent form of memory.

Computer memory systems are also hierarchical and consist of up to three major levels:

- Primary, or main
- Secondary, or auxiliary
- Backup

All microcomputer systems contain primary memory, but the need for secondary and backup systems depends on the specific application. As always, the goal is to optimize performance and cost.

Primary Memory

Primary memory is closely matched to the CPU and is available for instant communication. To qualify for primary status, therefore, the memory must be fast—fast enough to keep up with today's state-of-the-art microprocessors. As we will see in the following chapter, primary memory's high speed results from its parallel, random-access organization. Most small-scale, dedicated microcomputer systems (those designed for a specific task) contain only primary memory. For larger systems in which additional storage capacity is required, however, primary memory becomes a financial burden and we must look elsewhere.

Secondary Memory

By a change in technology and an increase in capacity, secondary memory stores information at a *lower cost per bit*. To achieve these features, secondary memory adds aspects of *sequential* access (to access a given location, the system must pass through all intermediate locations). Using part random-access and part sequential-access organization, secondary memory operates at moderate speed.

Secondary memory (also called *storage*) serves as a readily accessible data library. Since data and programs of immediate use are always stored in primary memory, blocks of data are transferred back and forth as required between primary and secondary memory.

Backup Memory

In a perfect world in which equipment failures and operator errors are unknown, the need for backup memory would be greatly reduced. In the real world, however, systems crash and mistakes are made. Despite the very high data-reliability specifications of today's secondary systems, many computer operators will not be satisfied until their data are resting securely on a nonvolatile backup shelf. A common mode of operation is for the database in primary or secondary memory to be moved to backup at regular intervals.

In addition, many computer applications generate continuous blocks of new data that must be periodically stored away, giving rise to the need for a high-capacity, low-cost, long-term, permanent storage medium (archival storage). Since speed is not a critical factor with such a backup system, further relaxing the access time has allowed the devel-

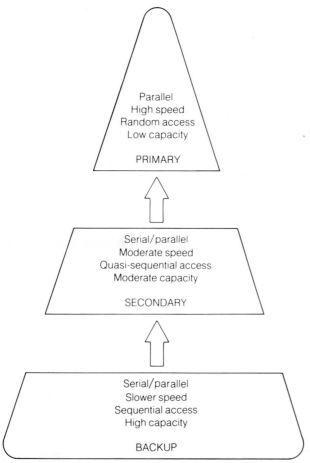

Figure 4.1 Primary/secondary/backup memory hierarchy.

opment of high-capacity, low-cost backup storage systems. Figure 4.1 diagrams the memory hierarchy of a microcomputer system.

THE MICROCOMPUTER MEMORY SPECTRUM

At each hierarchical level, the microcomputer designer is faced with a wide choice:

Primary	Secondary	Backup
Static	Floppy disk	Floppy disk
Dynamic	Winchester disk	Magnetic tape
Magnetic core	Bubble	Video tape
	Optical	Optical

Each of these memory types will be discussed in detail in the following two chapters, so only a few general comments will be made here. (Note that several types of memory can serve both secondary and backup functions.)

Three important factors entering into the selection of a memory type are access time (speed), capacity, and cost.

Figure 4.2 shows the tradeoffs involved in these three factors for the various categories of memory.

For 8080/8085-based systems, primary memory is generally limited to 64K—a tiny memory space all but swallowed up by the 200K to 1 Gbyte (1000 Mbytes) capacity of secondary and backup storage systems. Remember, however, that the price you pay for large storage capacity is speed. Primary memory is the only hierarchical level the CPU can "converse with" at its own natural high rate of speed.

All memory systems, of course, are application dependent. A microcomputer controller assigned the task of regulating the fuel/air mixture of an automobile under varying load conditions will use only primary memory. (Controllers are the subject of Chapter 20.)

On the other hand, a word processor may require copious amounts of storage space to file away the many pages of material produced each day. At regular intervals, selected material may be copied onto the backup device.

Only when the application is known is it possible to recommend a particular memory ensemble.

VIRTUAL MEMORY

Memory management, even for large systems, would be a simple process if all memory were of the high-speed primary variety. Of necessity, however, much of the data and programs must be stored in the lower-cost, high-capacity secondary systems. Since the computer usually works directly on primary memory only, it is obvious that some fancy data exchanges between primary and secondary memory will have to take place.

The problem was solved in the late 1950s with a concept called *virtual memory*. The programmer writes programs as if the entire memory space were primary memory. When the virtual-memory management system finds a requested address unavailable in primary memory (referred to as a *page fault*), it automatically initiates a swap procedure and exchanges a block of primary memory with a block of secondary memory (a process known as *folding* or *overlaying*).

To work successfully, virtual memory takes full advantage of the tendency for program activity to *cluster* around small portions of memory. As activity gradually shifts to other memory regions, these areas of secondary storage are automatically accessed and brought into main memory. If program action is not well clustered, the numerous accesses to secondary memory severely limit performance, and result in a condition known as *thrashing.*

Through the use of cache memory, even primary memory itself can be enhanced using virtual-memory concepts. *Cache memory* is a small block of ultrahigh-speed primary memory interposed between the CPU and the basic main (primary) memory. By taking advantage of program clustering and

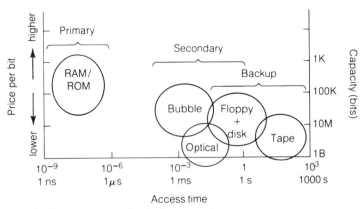

Figure 4.2   Primary/secondary/backup comparison.

applying the same overlaying techniques that we did with secondary memory, the processor "sees" a main memory system of near cache speed.

Virtual memory is an example of a mainframe concept gradually working its way into the micro world. Some newer 16-bit and 32-bit microprocessors, such as the Intel 80286 and Motorola 68010, have included provisions for virtual-memory management. (The 80286 is overviewed in Chapter 26.)

THE MEMORY MAP

Books are a convenient way of storing information. One advantage is that information can be categorized according to page and chapter. Given the page on which it is contained, information can be located quickly. These techniques can be carried over to any memory system.

Consider the entire 64K of 8080/8085-based primary memory space to be a book. Further, imagine the book to have 256 pages. Each page contains 256 words, and each word is made up of 8 letters. If we apply this convention to 8-bit microcomputers and say that a byte of data is word 17H on page 20H, we have an instant feeling for the data location among the full 64K of memory space. (Using the Intel convention, hexadecimal numbers are followed by an H.)

To make the analogy more graphic, the 256 pages are often shown on a chart called a *memory map* (Figure 4.3). The pages can be designated by decimal numbers, but more commonly are given in hexadecimal form. A memory map is therefore a linear arrangement of memory pages. Quite often the pages are grouped together in sizes (chapters, perhaps) to match the memory chips used with the system.

The concept of pages is particularly well suited to 16-bit addresses. As diagrammed below, the pages and words are split evenly between the two highest-order hex digits and the two lowest-order hex digits:

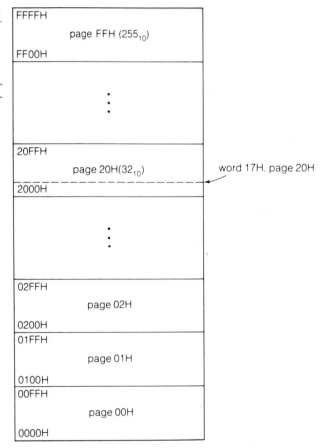

Figure 4.3   Memory map for 64K system.

$$A_{15}\ A_{14}\ A_{13}\ A_{12}\ A_{11}\ A_{10}\ A_9\ A_8 \qquad A_7\ A_6\ A_5\ A_4\ A_3\ A_2\ A_1\ A_0$$
$$\ \ 0\ \ \ 0\ \ \ 1\ \ \ 0\ \ \ 0\ \ \ 0\ \ \ 0\ \ 0 \qquad \ \ 0\ \ \ 0\ \ \ 0\ \ \ 1\ \ \ 0\ \ \ 1\ \ \ 1\ \ 1$$

page 20H   word 17H

The memory-map convention can easily be carried over to large-scale memory systems. For example, the 20-bit address of the 8088/86 16-bit microprocessor (chapter 25), contains 4K *pages* (1 Mbyte), designated by the three highest-order hexadecimal digits:

$$A_{19} \ldots A_8 \qquad A_7 \ldots A_0$$
$$000000100000 \qquad 00010111$$

$$\underbrace{} \qquad \underbrace{}$$

page 020H   word 17H

INTELLIGENT-MACHINE UPDATE

Nature long ago realized that one type of memory was insufficient to enable its more intelligent forms of life to survive and prosper in a complex world. We now know that the same holds true for our intelligent machine, and with the following two chapters we will make sure that an inadequate memory system will not hold it back from evolving into a higher form of intelligence.

QUESTIONS AND PROBLEMS

1. What are the three levels in the memory hierarchy of a microcomputer?
2. What one characteristic, more than any other, distinguishes primary (main) memory?
3. List the three hierarchical levels of memory in terms of (a) speed and (b) capacity.
4. What is *archival storage?*
5. The data and programs that the computer is currently working on are most likely contained in what hierarchical level of memory?
6. How does virtual memory make the programmer's job easier?
7. Define each of the following as it relates to virtual memory:
   - Page Fault
   - Folding or Overlaying
   - Clustering
   - Thrashing
8. Draw a memory map for a 64K system consisting of 4K memory modules. How many pages are contained within each module?
9. Write the hexadecimal address of page 102 word 17 (both in base 10).
10. What is the difference between *random* and *sequential* memory organization?
11. What is *cache memory?*
12. Name one type of memory that can serve as either secondary or backup memory.
13. What is the difference between a gigabyte (Gbyte) and a billion?
14. What is the difference between 10 and 10H?

chapter 5

Primary Memory

Evidence suggests that our minds store large amounts of information in the form of holograms or vast interconnecting neuronal patterns. Since the same neuron assemblies are involved in the storage of many different ideas (only the interconnecting patterns differ), many thoughts require approximately the same period of time to retrieve. This *random-access* technique was chosen by nature to speed up the process of recall.

The same random-access techniques (every storage location accessed in the same period of time), coupled with parallel architecture (all 8 bits are moved about and processed simultaneously as a unit), have produced memory systems fast enough to keep pace with the central processing unit. These are called *primary memory systems*.

Four types of primary memory, all found in microcomputer systems, will be covered in this chapter:

- Static RAM √
- Dynamic RAM √
- Magnetic-core RAM √
- ROM √

RAM VS ROM

To survive, we require two distinct types of memory. First, we require at birth a permanent memory to regulate the automatic processes of breathing and heartbeat. Second, we need memory space to receive new information that comes to us through our life experiences. Otherwise, we could never learn anything new—such as how to multiply or how to ride a bicycle.

These same two categories of memory are found in computer systems and are known as *RAM* and *ROM*. Unfortunately, the strict definitions of RAM and ROM do not always match conventional usage. The definitions that follow appear to be the most universally accepted:

- *RAM (Random-Access Memory):* a parallel memory unit composed of integrated-circuit memory chips that are truly random access in nature, have both read and write

capability, and are usually volatile (stored information is lost when the power is removed).
- *ROM (Read-Only Memory):* a memory array composed of integrated-circuit memory chips that are truly random access in nature, possess only the read capability, and are nonvolatile (stored information is protected when the power is removed).

Clearly, based on the above definitions, RAM and ROM usually refer to *primary* memory components. No universally accepted definitions of RAM and ROM exist, however, and the final determination must be based on the context in which they are used.

STATIC RAM

Perhaps the most popular form of primary memory for small systems, and the one we will give the greatest coverage, is *static* RAM (memory requiring only dc power supplies). Following the conventional description of RAM, it is a parallel, read/write, random-access, volatile memory, available in standard dual-in-line, integrated-circuit packages (DIP).

One way to approach the study of static RAM is to follow the lead of nature again. Nature designs living systems by natural selection, beginning with the simple and gradually building to the more complex. Our study of static RAM will follow the same approach. Always keep in mind that the internal RAM circuits developed here will show only the essential features and may not necessarily be the precise circuitry used in an actual static-RAM device.

The Basic RAM Memory Cell

From a "primeval ocean" of simple electronic components emerged the basic static-RAM memory cell shown in Figure 5.1. Already it possesses several human characteristics: it can remember, recall, and learn a single bit of information. In memory terminology, these properties are known as *store, read,* and *write*.

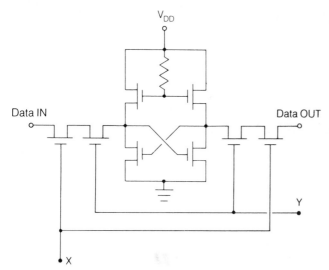

Figure 5.1   The basic MOS static-RAM cell.

the memory cell, both X *and* Y lines must be high. If either X *or* Y is low, the information is blocked. The upper two transistors are active loads, and are substituted for resistors because they require less physical (silicon) space. (However, a new polysilicon technology, promising high resistance in IC dimensions, may reverse the trend.)

Adding bus-interface circuitry, we arrive at the system of Figure 5.2. The data-out line ultimately will transmit information onto the data bus and is therefore time-multiplexed with a tristate buffer. The tristate buffer in the data-in line isolates the memory cell, except during the time information is written into the cell. The data-in and data-out lines join together and form a single line to the data bus.

The design is simple and efficient. A flip-flop stores the logic 1 or logic 0 by way of positive-feedback latching action. To extract (read) the logic state of the cell, simple sense the drain voltage of either transistor. To set (write) a logic value into the cell, simply gain control over either gate. The AND gate barriers, spliced into both the data-in and date-out lines, provide a means for addressing the cell. To select (address)

A Multicelled 4 × 1 Static RAM

With the power of addressability, our one-celled memory unit can now evolve into a multicelled system—one capable of remembering many bits of information. We will begin our design with a four-celled memory system that can store, read, and write four separate unique bits of information. Such a system is known as a *4 × 1 static RAM*. The first number specifies the number of individually addressable memory locations, and the second number specifies the number of bits stored in each addressable location. Therefore, a 4 × 1

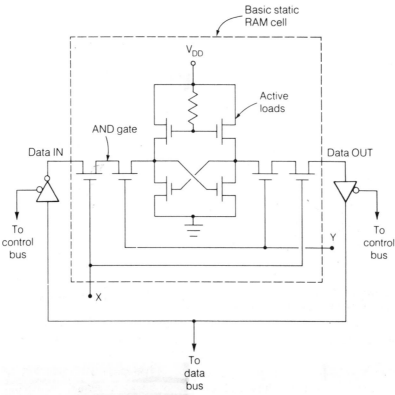

Fiure 5.2   Static-RAM cell with bus-interface circuitry added.

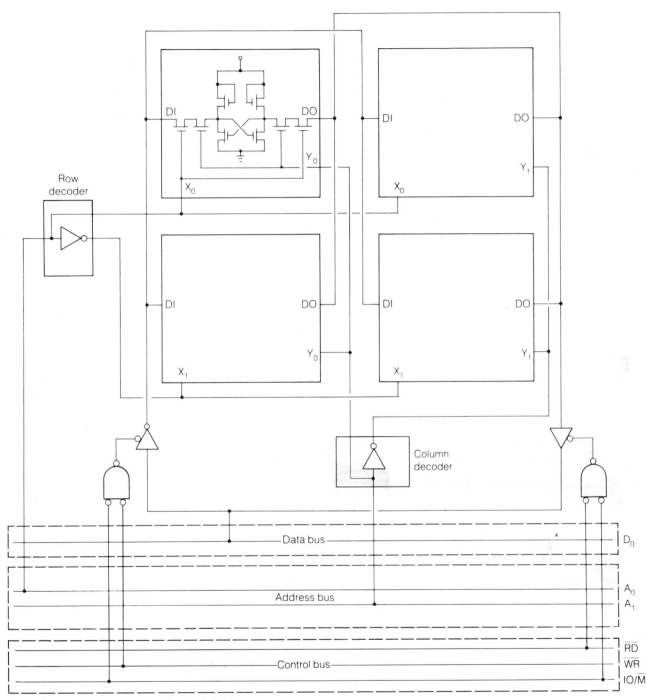

Figure 5.3 4 × 1 static RAM interfaced with 8085 bus.

static RAM has four addressable memory locations, each storing one bit of information. (Of course, such a small RAM system would find little acceptance on the open market, but it does illustrate the principles involved.)

A complete 4 × 1 static RAM—tied into an 8085-based bus system—is shown in Figure 5.3. To simplify the diagram, three of the memory cells are shown purely in block form.

The 4 × 1 static-RAM system is involved in two activities:

- Memory *write into* the selected (addressed) cell
- Memory *read from* the selected (addressed) cell

Since both activities are merely data-transfer operations, we can immediately write the where/when data-transfer waveforms required to carry out each process (Figure 5.4).

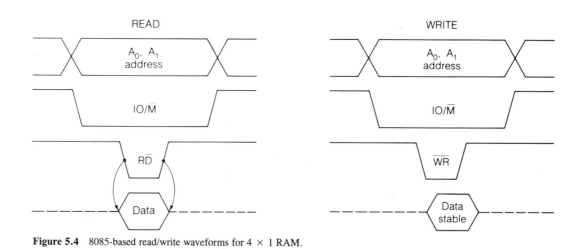

Figure 5.4 8085-based read/write waveforms for 4 × 1 RAM.

To see how the memory system works, let us go through the read process, using the simple two-step where/when sequence (refer to Figures 5.3 and 5.4).

- *Step 1—Address the memory cell:* The address of the selected memory cell (00, 01, 10, or 11) is placed on the address bus. Address bit A_0 goes to the row decoder and address bit A_1 goes to the column decoder. It is the function of the decoders (simple 1-in/2-out inverters in this case) to select one particular row and one particular column out of all the rows and columns that interlace the array of memory cells, a process known as *coincident-selection addressing*. Clearly, only the memory cell where the selected row and column cross is fully enabled (remember that both X *and* Y must be high in order to enable the cell). Note how the IO/$\overline{M}$ line completes the addressing by selecting the memory space rather than the I/O space.

- *Step 2—Pull the read ($\overline{RD}$) control line low:* When $\overline{RD}$ is cycled low (after the address has fully stabilized), the data bit stored in the addressed memory cell passes through the tristate buffers and onto the data bus.

An analysis of the memory write process for our 4 × 1 RAM is left as an exercise.

A 4 × 4 Static RAM

So far our simple 4 × 1 RAM system can remember only two-valued data: is it hot or cold, night or day, high or low? To remember the actual temperature, or time, or elevation, we must increase the bit size of our memory words. Four bits per word, for example, would give us 16 value levels to choose from.

To expand our 4 × 1 RAM into a 4 × 4 RAM is simple. All we need to do is clone four identical 4 × 1 systems and arrange them side by side in planes, as shown in Figure 5.5.

Each memory operation will now involve a half byte (a nibble). The two address lines are simply extended to include the three additional 4 × 1 planes, and an address appearing on the address bus will enable four like cells, one in each plane. Although the address lines are common to all four planes, the four independent data lines are not, and as shown each plane feeds a unique data-bus line. When a read or write control line is activated, information will flow four bits at a time onto or from the four-line data bus.

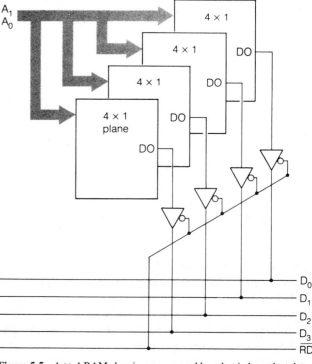

Figure 5.5 4 × 4 RAM showing common address but independent data lines.

Bit vs Word Organization

A 4 × 4 RAM contains sixteen memory cells. When the cells are organized as a 16 × 1 RAM it is called a *bit-organized* memory, and when organized as a 4 × 4 RAM it is called a *word-organized* memory. Figure 5.6 compares the bit-organized with the word-organized memory for our small-scale, 16-cell system. As we will see later in this chapter, speed, application, and type of memory are three important factors influencing the choice between bit and word organization.

The 2114A 1024 × 4 Static RAM

Continuing with our evolutionary process, we next extend the size of each plane from 4 bits to 1,024 bits, and create a 1,024 × 4 static RAM, the size of the 2114A—a popular, commercially available product (Figure 5.7a). The memory array, row and column decoders, and input/output tristate buffers are apparent.

Figure 5.7b details the read/write waveforms for the 2114A. Basically, they are standard where/when data-transfer waveforms, showing the effects of propagation delay. To read, $\overline{CS}$ is pulled low and $\overline{WE}$ remains high; to write, both $\overline{CS}$ and $\overline{WE}$ are pulled low. A detailed account of the many specifications can be found in the *Intel Memory Components Handbook*.

Larger RAM Systems

By expanding the number of memory planes and the number of storage locations within each plane, it appears we could continue this process of RAM evolution indefinitely. In fact, this evolutionary expansion is going on continuously, and 256K × 8—and even larger—RAMs will soon be commonplace.

The memory-addressing capabilities of the microprocessor chip are expanding even faster, however. Just when we satisfy the 64K × 8 needs of the 8080/8085 family, we must look toward the 80286 with its 16-megabyte addressing capability. The conclusion is inescapable: *to build very large prime-memory arrays, we will have to combine existing RAM chips*.

Memory Arrays

The 2114A will serve as an example of how to form large memory arrays by combining individual static chips. First of all, to satisfy the need for an 8-bit memory system, two 1K × 4 RAM chips are placed in tandem to produce a 1K × 8 RAM module (Figure 5.8). With the address lines tied in common, an address sent to the memory module will point to the same 4-bit word location within each chip. One chip then handles the low-order four bits of data while the other handles the high-order four bits. (As bytewide mem-

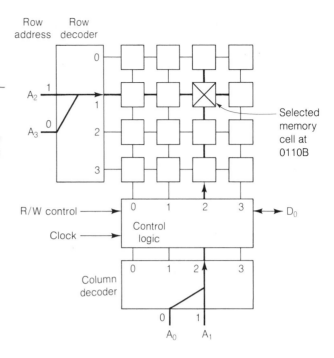

(a) Bit-organized 16 × 1 memory array

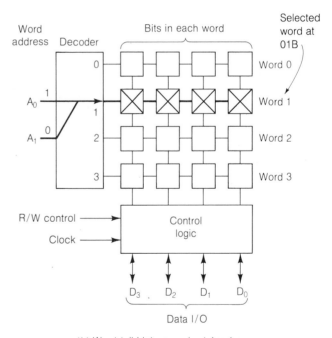

(b) Word (nibble) -organized 4 × 4 memory array

Figure 5.6 Bit vs word organized memory.

ories become more available, this tandem arrangement will be unnecessary.) Our task is to combine these 1K × 8 RAM modules to form large arrays—perhaps as large as 64K × 8.

A question naturally arises whenever a memory system contains more than one memory module. For example, if

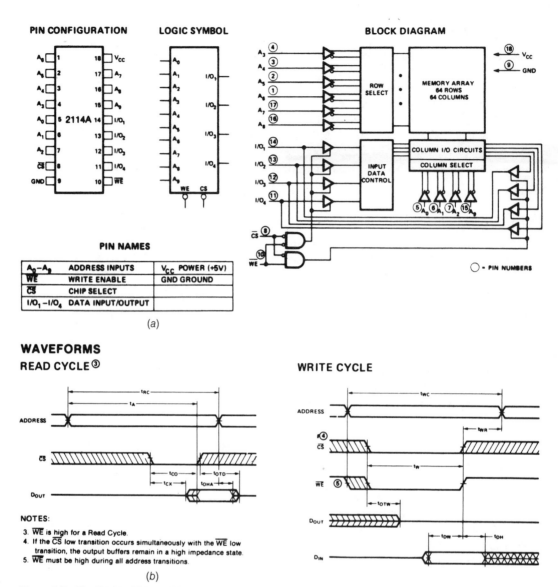

Figure 5.7 The 2114A 1024 × 4-bit static RAM: *a)* Pin-out and block diagram. *b)* Read/write waveforms. *Reproduced by permission of Intel Corporation.*

all RAM modules consist of two 2114As in tandem, then all modules must be fed the identical address lines A_0 through A_9 ($2^{10} = 1,024$) in order to single out the correct memory location from the 1,024 possible locations. But the memory location we wish to access lies within a *particular* RAM module. How can the computer single out this one particular 1K × 8 RAM module from all the others in the system?

The problem is not at all unique to electronics. Most large cities, for example, contain a street named Broadway. How does the post office select the correct Broadway from among the hundreds available? By adding town information to the street address, of course. In like manner the 16-line address bus can be divided into two sections (Figure 5.9):

• The *high-level* address lines A_{10} through A_{15}, which can be termed *town* addressing lines, are used to single out

one particular 1K × 8 memory module from all the others in the system.

• The *low-level* address lines A_0 through A_9, which can be termed *street* addressing lines, are used to single out the correct one of 1,024 memory locations within the selected "town" module.

The exact dividing line between *high-level* and *low-level* address lines depends on the size of the memory modules used.

At the chip stage, high-level addressing is handled by the Chip-Select (CS) input to the 2114A. All memory chips contain one or more CS input pins (sometimes they are called *Chip Enable*, or CE), and their purpose is to enable the entire chip. Referring back to Figure 5.7a, locate the two AND gates fed by the $\overline{CS}$ and $\overline{WE}$ input lines. In a sense, the two

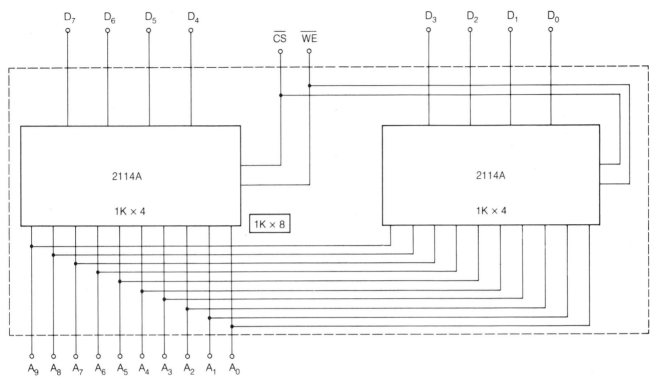

Figure 5.8 A 1K × 4 RAM module formed by combining two 1K × 4 2114A chips.

AND gates are "guarding the gates" to the memory array. Unless $\overline{CS}$ is active low, the entire chip is tristated and no data information can pass through the tristate buffers.

Linear vs Decoded High-Level Addressing

For our 2114A-based RAM system, so far we know the following: the chip-select inputs to each 1K × 8 RAM module will be attached to high-level address lines A_{10} through A_{15}. The next question is: exactly how will the tie-in be made? The simplest method, if we anticipate no more than six 1K × 8 modules in our system, is to assign each memory module its own unique high-level address line. This hardware-saving technique is called *linear addressing;* with six high-level address lines available, it can support up to six 1K × 8 RAM modules to form a 6K × 8 system.

If additional memory is required, the high-level address lines can be decoded, allowing up to 64 1K × 8 memory modules, for a grand total of 64K (65,536) memory locations (more than enough for most medium-scale applications). Figure 5.10 compares the linear and decoded addressing schemes for a memory system consisting of two 1K × 8 RAM modules.

Very Large Memory Arrays

A full 64K × 8 RAM system, the largest an 8080/8085-based system can directly address, can be called a *very large memory array*. To provide high-level addressing for the required 64 1K × 8 RAM modules, we must fully decode the high-level address lines, making use of all address combinations. The following decoder chips are readily available:

74155	2-in/4-out	
8205	3-in/8-out	
74154	4-in/16-out	

Figure 5.9 High-level/low-level addressing for 1K × 8 modules.

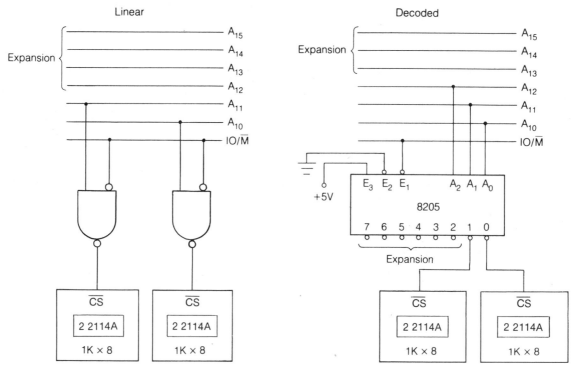

Figure 5.10 Comparison of linear and decoded addressing (8085 system).

Unfortunately, the list does not include a 6-in/64-out decoder, precisely what we need to select one out of 64 RAM modules (the chip would have an unconventionally large number of pins). Perhaps we can arrange an array of decoders—say the popular 8205s—and simulate our unavailable 1-of-64 decoder. We can, and the technique is closely related to the U.S. Postal Service's zip code.

Looking over the solution (Figure 5.11), we note how it takes on a three-tiered pyramid structure. Let's see how a data "letter" winds its way through the decoder array to a single address.

First, we split the 16-bit address into the high-level "town" and low-level "street" portions. The six "town" binary address bits (A_{15}–A_{10}) are analogous to the postal service's zip code, for they will route the data to the correct memory module from among the 64 possible choices. The 10 "street" binary address bits (A_9–A_0) will then complete the job and route the data to the correct 1-of-1024 locations within the selected "town" module.

The three highest-order address bits (A_{15}, A_{14}, and A_{13}) go to the top of the 8205 pyramid and are analogous to the leftmost numbers of the zip code. These three binary numbers select one of the eight 8205s in the second tier, and subdivide the entire 64K memory space into 1-of-8 8K subspaces. (In like manner the leftmost digit in the zip code subdivides the entire United States into ten subregions.)

The next three address lines (A_{12}, A_{11}, and A_{10}) are analogous to the lowest numbers of the zip code and activate

one of the eight outputs of the enabled 8205, which in turn selects one of the 64 1K RAM modules. Note how the zip-code technique homes in on the correct module ("town") by successive subdivisions of the total address space. Low-level ("street") address lines A_0 through A_9 then finish the job by addressing the correct single-word location within the selected RAM module.

To avoid the two-tiered array of decoders, with their built-in complexity and propagation delay, we might select larger memory chips. For example, using the popular 16K × 1 RAM chips to form 16K × 8 modules, our full 64K system requires only four modules and takes on the simpler arrangement of Figure 5.12. (Note that only address lines A_{14} and A_{15} are high level.)

On those rare occasions when 64K of prime memory would be insufficient (for an 8-bit system), we can employ *bank-switching* tactics and obtain additional high-level address lines from our output ports. Figure 5.13a shows how to expand our 64K system to 128K (two 64K banks) by outporting the additional address line A_{16}. The price we pay for bank switching is increased software complexity and slower speed. (The system must always be aware of which 64K bank it is presently accessing and therefore is no longer totally random access.)

Another popular technique of expanding primary memory beyond the normal 64K limits is known as *mapping RAM*, and is illustrated in Figure 5.13b. First, the microprocessor initializes the 8 × 8 mapping RAM by sending 8 bytes of

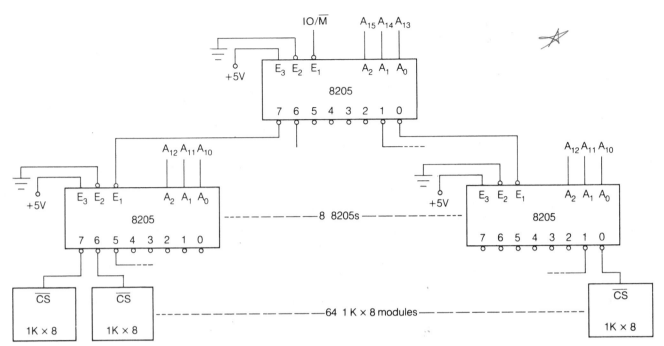

Figure 5.11   Fully decoded 64K RAM system using 1K × 8 modules (only high-level address lines shown).

address information via the data bus. When generating an address during a memory access, the upper 3 address bits (A_{13}, A_{14}, and A_{15}) are sent to the mapping RAM. The 8 output lines are then merged with address lines A_0 through A_{12} to form a 21-line address (2 megabytes). Since any data from 00 to FFH can be written to the mapping RAM, both megabytes are accessible.

We have now completed our RAM evolution, from a simple one-celled memory unit to a jellyfishlike large memory array of 2M locations. Since most primary memory systems lie between these two extremes, it is the responsibility of the design engineer to produce the most efficient RAM system for the application at hand. Clearly, the job of the designer will be simplified as the newer high-density (multimegabit) chips become available.

Foldback Memory

Foldback memory is an unavoidable trait of linear addressing. To see how memory is folded back, imagine a single 2114A 1K × 8 RAM module linearly addressed by tying its active-high chip select to address line A_{15} (Figure 5.14). If you were asked to list the four pages of memory occupied by this RAM module, perhaps you would respond 80H, 81H, 82H, and 83H. And you would be right—those four pages of memory extend from 8000H through 83FFH.

But when you move on to the next word past location 83FFH—to the first word of page 84H—address line A_{15} is still high, so the first location in the RAM module is again addressed. In other words, page 84H is an exact copy of page 80H, page 85H an exact copy of 81H, page 86H an exact copy of 82H, page 87H an exact copy of 83H; the entire last half of the memory book, pages 80H through FFH, are all exact copies spaced four pages apart. The reason is that address line A_{15} is high for all those pages, and therefore the 1K × 8 RAM module is always selected.

It follows that no other RAM modules may be placed at these "folded-back" pages; therefore, in a sense, the folded-back pages are wasted (unavailable). For small systems, however, you can afford to waste memory space, and since linear addressing saves hardware (decoders), it is often the preferable technique. (To avoid folding back memory locations, the high-level address lines must be fully decoded.)

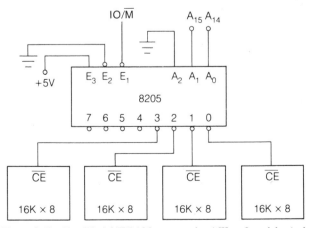

Figure 5.12   Simplified 64K RAM system using 16K × 8 modules (only high-level address lines shown).

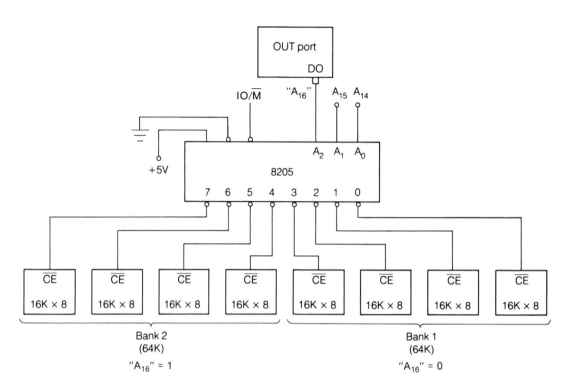

(a) Using bank switching to double the primary memory to 128K × 8

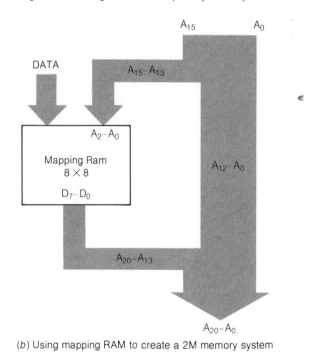

(b) Using mapping RAM to create a 2M memory system

Figure 5.13 Memory expansion techniques.

One way to identify foldback locations is to start from address 0000H and count up in binary. What is the first range of addresses that will access all the locations of the chip (8000H through 83FFH in Figure 5.14)? Continue counting up in binary, identifying all other address blocks that also will access the chip. These are the foldback locations.

Figure 5.15 illustrates how the SDK-85 single-board computer (shown in photo) addresses its 256 × 8 RAM block contained within the 8155 chip. (The 8155 includes I/O ports and timer in addition to its 1 page of RAM.) It is left as an exercise to determine the addressing technique as well as page and foldback locations.

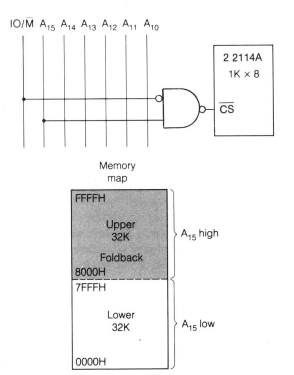

Figure 5.14 Linear addressing scheme resulting in four-page foldback over entire upper 32K of memory space.

RAM Performance

Cost, reliability, availability, size (density), and speed are the five factors most important to the acceptance of a RAM chip on the marketplace—and progress is occurring on all fronts. It is in speed, however, that the real horse race is taking place. As microprocessors become faster and faster, RAM cannot afford to be the weak link in the speed chain (16-bit processors—as explained in Chapter 25—use a technique called *prefetching* to reduce the need for superfast RAM).

The following three terms describing speed are most commonly seen (of these three, *access time* is the most widely used):

- *Access time (t_A):* The time span from the start of the read cycle (address applied) to the time when valid data are available at the output pins.

- *Read-cycle time (t_{RC}):* Total time span required for a read operation, from beginning to end.

- *Write-cycle time (t_{WC}):* Total time span required for a write operation, from beginning to end.

Referring back to Figure 5.7*b*, the 2114A 1K × 4 static RAM has an access time (t_A) of approximately 200 nanoseconds and a write-cycle time (t_{WC}) and read-cycle time (t_{RC}) of approximately 250 nanoseconds.

What is interesting about the performance specifications of the 2114A, a popular "workhorse" RAM, is that it is quite slow by state-of-the-art standards. HMOS II, CHMOS, and Hi-CMOS are all technologies taking dead aim at an access time of 15 nsec, clearly encroaching into areas once the sole property of bipolar. For example, the 2115H high speed static RAM—based on Intel's advanced HMOS II technology—provides 1024 × 1-bit organization with an access time as low as 25 nsec. (The very highest speed RAMs are usually offered in bit-wide format.) Using ECL technology, access times below 10 nsec are inevitable, and Gallium Arsenide (GaAs) technology, with a fivefold improvement in electron mobility, promises to surpass the 1 nsec barrier.

Still faster times are promised with the still-experimental *Josephson-junction* semiconductors. An OR gate fashioned with this superconducting technology could have a switching speed of 10 picoseconds! (A picosecond is to 1 second as 1 second is to 32,000 years.)

The ultimate technology for speed, if you include those still on the drawing board, is based on *light*. These all-optical speed-of-light devices, capable of operating at 5 gigabits per second, are based on a resonance/threshold effect. To provide the AND function, for example, two light beams are combined. Only when both light inputs are present will the input exceed a threshold and enter a resonator circuit to be amplified.

When matching a RAM chip to a computer, however, access time is not the only consideration. Inherent in the interface between RAM and CPU is propagation delay composed of logic delay, capacitive-loading delay, and transit-time delay. Logic delay is the time it takes a signal to pass through the various decoders and buffers standing between CPU and RAM. Capacitive-loading delay is a function of the distributed capacitance throughout the system. Transit time is the time required to traverse the printed-circuit traces. As RAM access times fall, these once insignificant delay factors become of major importance.

Another factor related to RAM performance is power drain, and here CMOS—often called the ideal technology—is the recognized leader. No technology can match its automatic power-down feature and ultra-low standby power drain. CMOS 16K static RAM chips have been tested with a standby power draw of a mere 1 microwatt! For battery-powered operation, CMOS is the logical choice. Add to this CMOS's ability to function over a wider power-supply range, its vastly improved speed, its high noise rejection, and its immunity from ionizing alpha-particle radiation, and it is easy to see why CMOS technology is poised to become the reigning technology of the computer industry.

DYNAMIC RAM

Compared to static RAM (SRAM), dynamic RAM (DRAM) seems to take a step backward, for the logic state is retained in the oldest electronic storage device known: the capacitor.

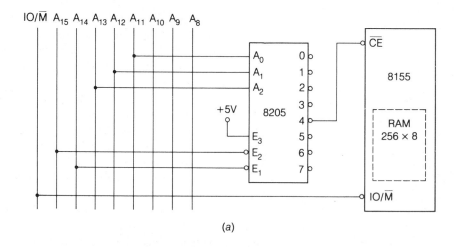

(a)

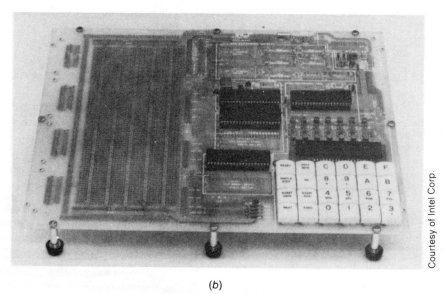

(b)

Figure 5.15 SDK-85 addressing: *a)* High-level addressing scheme. *b)* SDK-85 single-board computer.

But the key to the success of dynamic RAM is simplicity (Plato's creed), and it clearly shows up in Figure 5.16 when a dynamic-RAM cell is compared side by side to a static-RAM cell (C_s, the storage capacitor, is actually the 10^{-15} farad built-in drain to substrate capacitance).

One immediate benefit of simplicity is density, since many more memory cells can be etched on a single silicon chip (which is why ultrahigh-density memory chips—such as the $1M \times 1$—are generally DRAMs). When the density goes up, the cost per cell is greatly reduced. Dynamic RAM is fast, with access times as low as 50 ns, and it offers a low-power quiescent state (10 mW standby and 150 mW active are typical). In addition, dynamic RAMs now available require only a single $+5$-volt power supply, rather than the usual three voltages. These are the major reasons why dynamic RAM generally outsells static RAM by a wide margin.

Nevertheless, for memory systems of approximately 16K bytes or less, static RAM is not only preferred, but cheaper—

and for good reason. The problem with storing information by capacitors is that they leak. In fact, they leak so badly that, unless precautions are taken, all the information will drain away in just a couple of milliseconds. (Static RAM, remember, uses positive-feedback latching action to store information and in no way is subject to loss of data through capacitive leakage.)

We cannot prevent the storage capacitors from discharging, but we can periodically renew their state—a process called *refreshing*. Turning first to the simplified diagram of Figure 5.17*a*, let's see how reading, writing, and refreshing (the three "Rs" of dynamic RAM) are accomplished on a small-scale 4×1 DRAM.

First of all, in order to reduce the number of address pins required, our simplified 4×1 DRAM *time-multiplexes* its two address lines over the same pins. The first address (A0) is called the *row* address, and the second (A1) is called the *column* address. As shown in Figure 5.17*b*, the row address

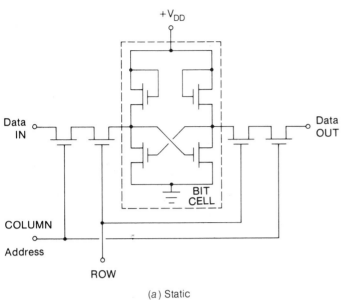

+V_DD

Data IN

Data OUT

BIT CELL

COLUMN

Address

ROW

(a) Static

Data IN/OUT

COLUMN ADDRESS

ROW ADDRESS

BIT CELL

+V

(b) Dynamic

Figure 5.16 Comparison of RAM cells.

is latched internal to the DRAM by the falling edge of $\overline{RAS}$ (Row Address Strobe) and the column address is latched by the falling edge of $\overline{CAS}$ (Column Address Strobe). The address inputs normally are supplied by a DRAM controller, which oversees the operation of the DRAM system.

The real problem with designing and operating DRAMs is the need to maintain refreshing while allowing read and write operations. An elegant solution was found by keying $\overline{RAS}$ and $\overline{CAS}$ to specific operations:

- Whenever $\overline{RAS}$ is activated, *the entire addressed row* is automatically refreshed (each column has its own refresh amplifier).

- Whenever $\overline{CAS}$ is activated, the I/O buffers are enabled (read if $\overline{WE}$ is high; write if $\overline{WE}$ is low).

Therefore, whenever a memory cell is accessed (either read or write), *the entire addressed row is automatically refreshed during the $\overline{RAS}$ portion of the cycle.* However, because we certainly cannot count on every row being addressed at least every 2 msec during normal operation, the DRAM controller activates the *refresh only* ($\overline{RAS}$-only) cycle whenever necessary (see Figure 5.17c).

Refreshing can take place in the burst mode (all cells refreshed during a single time period by cycling through all row addresses) or by cycle stealing (refreshing done in small intervals between normal memory operations). Cycle stealing normally is preferred, since it allows refreshing to take place without tying up the memory for long periods of time. A major function of the DRAM controller is to *arbitrate* between the need for refreshing and the read/write requests from the CPU. Since refreshing cannot be put off, the DRAM

controller must occasionally suspend a read or write operation by pulling the CPU's READY line low (the READY signal is fully explained in Chapter 9).

When we expand our simple two-row/two-column DRAM array to four blocks of 128 rows by 128 columns, we create the 2164A 64K × 1 dynamic RAM, a popular state-of-the-art chip marketed by Intel Corp. Looking inside the 2164A (Figure 5.18a) we see the memory arrays, the address latch, the row and column decoders, and the I/O buffers. As with our simple 4 × 1 DRAM, the $\overline{RAS}$ and $\overline{CAS}$ signals of Figure 5.18b demultiplex the row and column addresses. Note that $\overline{WE}$ goes low during a write operation. For refresh-only operations, Figure 5.18c shows that only the $\overline{RAS}$ signal is activated. In order to simplify a 2164A DRAM system, the 8203 dynamic RAM controller provides all the signals necessary to control up to 64 DRAM devices, including addressing, refreshing, and arbitration. In systems where reliability is critical, the 8206 *error detection and correction unit* (see Chapter 6) can be included in the DRAM system.

Dynamic RAM has also been caught up in the CMOS revolution, as Intel Corp. recently introduced the 51C64 and 51C65 64K × 1 CMOS dynamic RAMs. As expected, their most attractive features are related to power. Operating power dissipation is under 200 mW, and in a special standby mode the current drain drops to 100 microamps and the refresh period is extended to 64 msec.

All refreshing schemes, however, will soon be a thing of the past as the new *integrated* RAMs become readily available. Combining the best features of the static RAM (SRAM) and dynamic RAM (DRAM), the integrated RAM (iRAM) is an entire dynamic RAM system integrated onto a single chip. Because all DRAM control logic—including the memory array, refresh logic, arbitration, and control logic—is

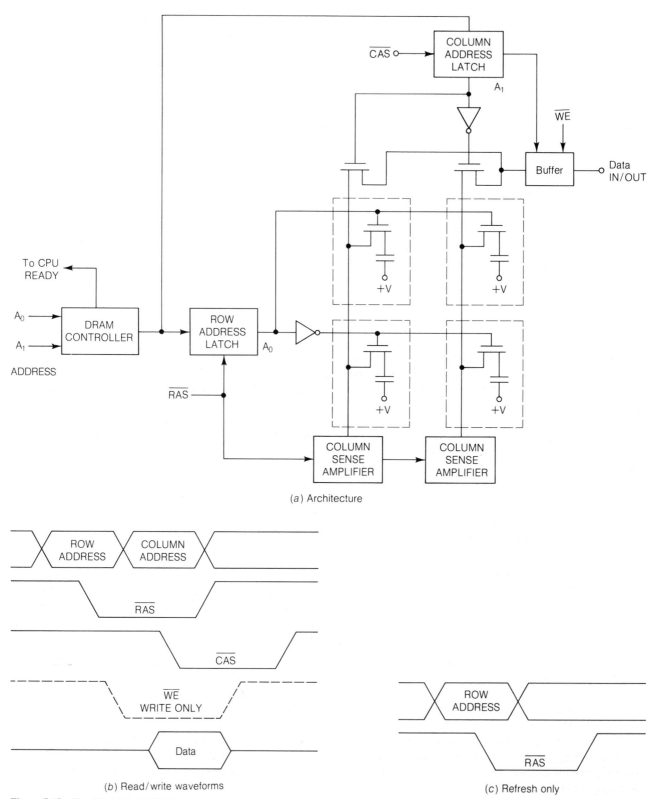

(a) Architecture

(b) Read/write waveforms

(c) Refresh only

Figure 5.17   Simplified 4 × 1 DRAM system.

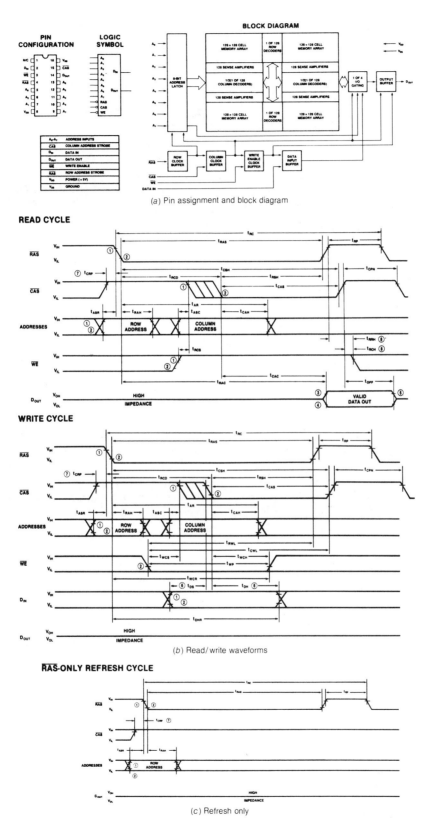

Figure 5.18   The 2164A 64K × 1 dynamic RAM.
Reproduced by permission of Intel Corporation.

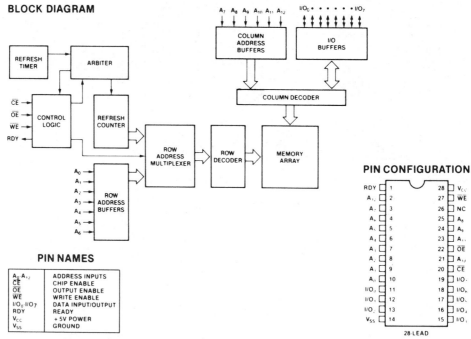

PIN NAMES

A_0-A_{12}	ADDRESS INPUTS
$\overline{CE}$	CHIP ENABLE
$\overline{OE}$	OUTPUT ENABLE
$\overline{WE}$	WRITE ENABLE
I/O_0-I/O_7	DATA INPUT/OUTPUT
RDY	READY
V_{CC}	+ 5V POWER
V_{SS}	GROUND

Figure 5.19 The Intel 2186A 8K × 8 iRAM.
Reproduced by permission of Intel Corporation.

internal, the iRAM is self-refreshing and appears to the user as if it is nearly static. (The older *pseudo-* or *quasistatic* RAM integrates all DRAM functions except the arbiter—the most critical of all.)

The Intel 2186A of Figure 5.19 is an 8K × 8-bit iRAM featuring a 250 nsec access time, single + 5V operation, byte-wide architecture, a standardized format, and low active and standby current drains. To the circuit designer, the only major difference between the iRAM and a fully static RAM is the presence of the RDY output, used to notify the CPU (via the READY input) that a read or write operation must wait for the completion of a refresh operation.

ONE-LINE VS TWO-LINE CONTROL

Both the 2114A SRAM and 2186A iRAM follow standard pin-out formats. Yet, when we isolate the control lines and compare them side by side (Figure 5.20), we note a major difference. The 2114A uses a *one-line* control scheme, while the newer 2186A adopts the more effective *two-line* control scheme.

The problem with one-line control is *bus contention*: when two devices simultaneously drive the same bus lines. During the time the address switches from one 2114A module to the other, there may be a brief time when both will be addressed, and therefore both will be sending information to the data bus at the same time. If one chip attempts to pull a given bit line high, while another attempts to pull the same line low, a shorted condition arises, and the resulting voltage

and current spikes on the power supply can trigger a whole host of problems—including false triggering, race conditions, invalid data, and reflections.

One solution to the problem is to qualify the chip select lines with the $\overline{RD}$ and $\overline{WR}$ lines (Figure 5.21a). When switching from one address to the next, new data will not appear on the data bus lines until the address has fully stabilized and the previous device has been switched off the bus. Although the bus contention problem has been solved, we have added external components and have increased the propagation delay time.

Two-line control, used by the 2186A iRAM, is a more effective solution to the problem of bus contention. Referring to Figure 5.21b, the additional output enable ($\overline{OE}$) line qualifies the read process without the use of any additional external hardware. As we will see later in this chapter, two-

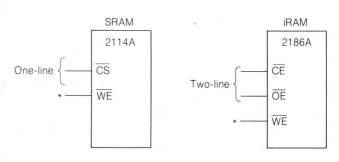

*$\overline{WE}$ is always present to
qualify the write process

Figure 5.20 One-line vs two-line control.

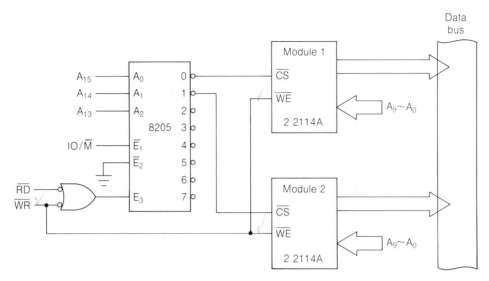

(a) Qualifying $\overline{CS}$ with $\overline{RD}$ or $\overline{WR}$ eliminates bus contention but increases complexity and propagation delay

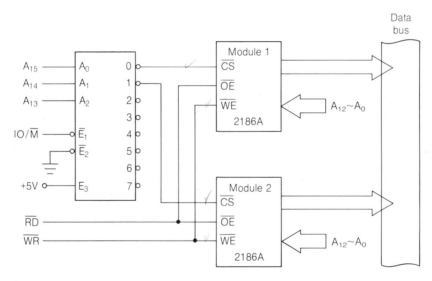

(b) Two-line control eliminates bus contention automatically

Figure 5.21   Eliminating bus contention.

line control is part of the JEDEC (Joint Electron Device Engineering Council) *byte-wide universal memory* standard.

MAGNETIC-CORE RAM

It is surprising, considering the rapid advance of memory technology, to find magnetic-core memory still available—surprising since this type of RAM was among the very first developed. However, it has a combination of characteristics found nowhere else: nonvolatility coupled with 1-μsec access times. Magnetic-core memory also is rugged and highly resistant to temperature and radiation.

Data storage takes place in tiny ferromagnetic doughnuts (toroids) called *magnetic cores*. When the magnetic domains are lined up in one direction (and latched in place by self-reinforcing action), a logic 1 is stored; when latched in the opposite direction, a logic 0. If sufficient current is sent through the center of the core, it will flip from one state to the next (obeying the well-known hysteresis curve).

Addressing

A core is addressed by threading wires through the array in the manner of cross streets (see Figure 5.22*a*). Each wire carries only half the amount of current required to rotate the

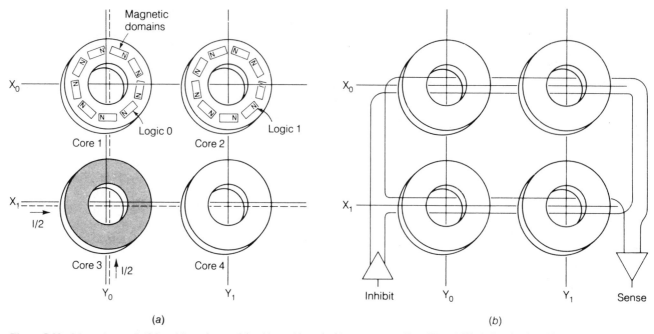

Figure 5.22 Magnetic-core RAM: *a)* Magnetic core 3 is addressed by coincident current on lines X1 and Y0. *b)* Read/write/addressing technique.

magnetic domains. To address memory core 3, for example, wires X_1 and Y_0 are activated. Only at the intersection of X_1 and Y_0 is there sufficient current to rotate the magnetic domains from one state to another (this is known as *coincident current selection*). Combined XY current in one direction produces the logic 1 state; combined XY current in the reverse direction causes the domains to flip, resulting in the reverse logic state.

Reading and Writing

The read and write processes rely on a single sense wire and a single inhibit wire threaded through the entire array (Figure 5.22*b*), as if forming a string of beads. The memory-read and memory-write processes are unusual because each involves a full read/write sequence. To read out the contents of a memory location, we first force the selected core to the logic 0 state by sending current through the proper XY cross wires in the logic 0 direction. If the core was initially in the logic 1 state, a change occurred in the magnetic flux and, following Faraday's law (voltage is proportional to rate of change of magnetic flux), the sense wire received a voltage pulse indicating a logic 1 was indeed stored in the cell. However, the process of accessing the memory cell was destructive— we destroyed the logic 1 initially stored in the cell. We therefore reverse the current in the selected XY wires and write the logic 1 back into the cell, thereby restoring the cell to its original logic state.

If the core was initially in the logic 0 state, however, no change occurred in the magnetic flux and the sense wire received no voltage pulse (indicating a logic 0 was stored in

the cell). This time, when the XY current is reversed, we activate the inhibit wire and prevent the writing of a logic 1 into the cell, thereby preserving the original logic 0 condition.

The memory-write process also consists of a read/write sequence, but it is much simpler. First, the selected cell is forced to the zero state. The XY current is reversed and logic 1 current sent through the selected cell. If a logic 1 is to be written into the cell, the inhibit wire is not activated. If a logic 0 is to be written, the inhibit wire is activated. Although magnetic-core memory is still being used, its high cost and low density make it unsuitable for most applications.

READ-ONLY MEMORY

Read-only memory (ROM), the second major category of primary memory, is associated with *instincts*—behavioral actions developed over thousands of years and passed along from one generation to the next. Instincts represent those programs that we simply cannot afford to forget or to have altered in any way, and ROM holds those programs the *computer* cannot afford to "forget" or to have altered in any way.

Because microcomputers are often dedicated to a specific purpose, they have a strong need for ROM. To use an everyday example, the typical camera now on the market is a "smart" camera. It can automatically determine the correct lens settings (and even the correct focus) to give the best picture in any given environment. As expected, it is controlled by a microcomputer—a miniature brain doing the work for us. In a sense, the camera knows what to do instinctively, and the program that makes this possible certainly cannot be lost when the camera is stored on the shelf. So the camera must have a permanent memory.

ROM Properties

In general, *ROM is a nonvolatile memory array whose contents, once programmed, cannot be altered by the microprocessor using the memory.* Although this general definition of ROM has been stretched somewhat by the emergence of the EE-PROM (to be covered shortly), all members of the ROM family are integrated-circuit, high-speed, random-access, parallel devices—properties well suited to the requirements of a "smart" camera.

Programs stored in ROM have hardware-like properties because they are permanent and based on internal physical connections. But, since they are programs, they also must have properties of software. Since programs stored in ROM have properties of both hardware and software, a new term was coined: *firmware*. Firmware refers to software instructions permanently contained in a ROM.

ROM Categories

The two major categories of read-only memory are ROM and PROM. ROM is custom-programmed read-only memory, meaning the programming is done at the factory during the manufacturing process. (Here the term *ROM* is more restrictive and refers only to the specific category of read-only memory that is custom-programmed at the factory.)

PROM (programmable read-only memory) must be programmed by the customer after the manufacturing process is complete (in the field).

Which read-only memory should we choose for our product—ROM or PROM? It depends on where we are in the manufacturing process. Suppose our product is the "smart" camera mentioned earlier. There are two major stages of manufacturing: development and production. We will consider them in reverse order.

The prototype model works as expected, and the software has been fully debugged. Development complete, you are ready to go into production, expecting to produce at least 100,000 camera units a year. Now—which memory category should you choose? Which one goes hand in hand with production? The answer is ROM.

Factory-Programmed ROM

ROM is the best choice for the production phase for a very important reason: less cost per unit. The process of manufacturing and ordering a ROM will tell us why.

Since a ROM is programmed at the factory, we must supply a program listing when placing our order. Acceptable formats include floppy disk, magnetic tape, a master ROM or PROM from which to copy, or computer punched cards. The 68364, shown in Figure 5.23, is a popular 8K × 8 factory-programmed ROM (it is common for ROMs to be available in bytewide format).

When the order arrives at the factory, a batch of 8K × 8 silicon chips, in which all but the very last manufacturing step has been completed, is taken off the shelf. The only missing step is to connect (or leave floating) the gate of each transistor according to the program ordered by the customer. This is accomplished in the final manufacturing step when a mask is prepared from the customer's order sheet and used

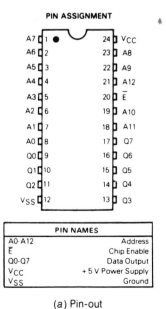

(*a*) Pin-out

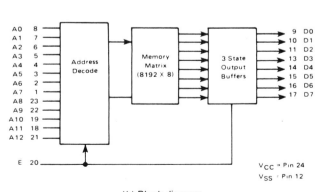

(*b*) Block diagram

Figure 5.23   The 68364 factory-programmed ROM.

to selectively etch away a layer of aluminum, leaving the correct interconnecting pattern (see Figure 5.24). For this reason, factory-programmed ROM is also called *mask-programmable ROM*.

Note how simple the entire structure is: one transistor per cell keeps the cost down and the density high. Leaving only the last manufacturing step undone until the customer's order arrives reduces the turnaround time. There is no question that ROMs are best for large-volume orders when the software has been fully tested.

Large-density MOS ROMs (16K and up) are available that access in less that 80 ns, and super-density 1 Mbit and larger ROMs will soon be commonplace.

Now let us back up to the development stage, when the entire manufacturing process is in a state of constant flux, and changes and improvements in both hardware and software occur quite often. Clearly, ROM would be inappropriate, for its cost is low only when large orders are placed, and the turnaround time, although short by manufacturing standards, is too long by development standards.

PROM

For development work, the logical choice is PROM, or programmable read-only memory. The crucial difference is that the programming of the chip is not tied to the manufacturing process. It can be done by the customer, often with relatively simple equipment. The only problem in the use of PROMs is the large variety available:

- EPROM
- Bipolar PROM
- CMOS PROM
- EE-PROM

This really is no problem at all, however, for until the recent development of the EE-PROM (to be covered shortly), one type on the PROM menu has all but captured the market. It is the first one on the list, EPROM, which stands for erasable programmable read-only memory.

EPROM   EPROMs are nearly the ultimate in convenience. They can be programmed and erased by the customer over and over again, more than a hundred times, as the software undergoes development. No wonder the EPROM has become such a vital tool in the development phase of microcomputer products.

Structurally, each EPROM memory cell is similar to that of a ROM with one major exception: an additional floating gate is placed in the insulating material separating the select gate and the drain/source connection (see Figure 5.25). As with the ROM, the select gate is activated when the cell is addressed.

In order to turn on the memory-cell transistor, both the select gate *and* the floating gate must be charged. If the floating gate is devoid of charges, the cell cannot turn on, even when the select gate is activated. Therefore, the presence of charges on the floating gate is equivalent to one logic state (usually a zero), and the absence of charge stores the alternate logic state (usually a one). It follows that an EPROM cell is programmed by either forcing charges on the floating gate or leaving it uncharged, according to the requirements of the program.

To place a charge on the floating gate and program the cell with a logic 0, a high voltage is placed on the select gate, sufficient to force electrons across the insulating barrier by avalanche breakdown (as shown in Figure 5.26a). The process can best be explained by referring to the classic potential-well diagrams of Figure 5.26b.

The amount of energy required to overcome the insulating energy barrier, called E_p, is supplied by the programmer in the form of a dc voltage. After each electron is forced over this energy hump, it is attracted to the floating gate and falls into the deep potential well, where it becomes trapped. So deep is this potential-well trap that some EPROM manufacturers claim memory-retention capabilities superior to even an elephant's, with the charge remaining on the floating gate for more than a hundred years.

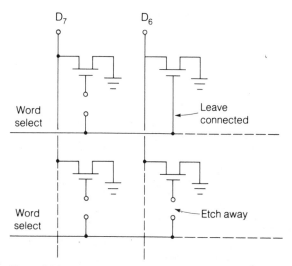

Figure 5.24   A portion of a factory-programmed MOS ROM.

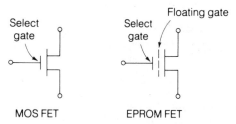

Figure 5.25   To form an EPROM memory cell, an extra floating gate is added to the basic MOS cell.

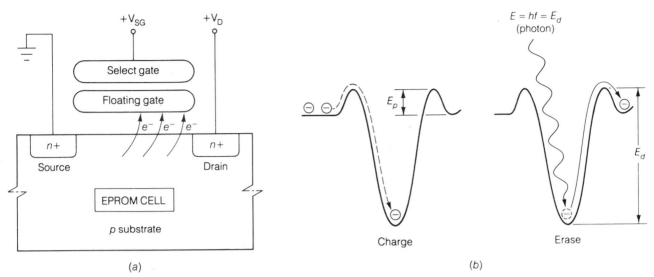

Figure 5.26 Programming the EPROM: *a)* Programming configuration. *b)* Potential-well diagrams.

To erase the memory cell, the stored changes must be pulled out of the potential well—and that takes energy, an amount equal to E_d. This energy is supplied by ultraviolet photons of the proper frequency (energy). It is light, then— ultraviolet light—that erases EPROMs. The process is simple, quick, and clean.

2764 EPROM The 2764 8K × 8 EPROM is a widely used state-of-the-art device, featuring a 200 ns access time, two-line control to eliminate bus contention, a standby power-down mode, and a single 5 volt supply (see Figure 5.27). To speed up the programming time, it uses Intel's special *intelligent programming algorithm,* which ensures that no more than the minimum necessary number of programming pulses is applied to each cell. The result is a five-fold reduction in the conventional 50 msec per byte programming time. We will follow the role of the 2764 as it might be used to develop a "smart" camera program. Remember, we are in the development phase and have just written an improved program we wish to try out.

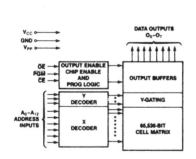

Figure 1. Block Diagram

Figure 2. Pin Configurations

PIN NAMES

A_0-A_{12}	ADDRESSES
$\overline{CE}$	CHIP ENABLE
$\overline{OE}$	OUTPUT ENABLE
O_0-O_7	OUTPUTS
$\overline{PGM}$	PROGRAM
N.C.	NO CONNECT

MODE SELECTION

MODE	$\overline{CE}$ (20)	$\overline{OE}$ (22)	$\overline{PGM}$ (27)	A_9 (24)	V_{PP} (1)	V_{CC} (28)	Outputs (11-13, 15-19)
Read	V_{IL}	V_{IL}	V_{IH}	X	V_{CC}	V_{CC}	D_{OUT}
Output Disable	V_{IL}	V_{IH}	V_{IH}	X	V_{CC}	V_{CC}	High Z
Standby	V_{IH}	X	X	X	V_{CC}	V_{CC}	High Z
Program	V_{IL}	V_{IH}	V_{IL}	X	V_{PP}	V_{CC}	D_{IN}
Verify	V_{IL}	V_{IL}	V_{IH}	X	V_{PP}	V_{CC}	D_{OUT}
Program Inhibit	V_{IH}	X	X	X	V_{PP}	V_{CC}	High Z
intelligent Identifier	V_{IL}	V_{IL}	V_{IH}	V_H	V_{CC}	V_{CC}	Code
intelligent Programming	V_{IL}	V_{IH}	V_{IL}	X	V_{PP}	V_{CC}	D_{IN}

1. X can be V_{IH} or V_{IL}
2. V_H = 12.0V ± 0.5V

*HMOS is a patented process of Intel Corporation.

Figure 5.27 The 2764 8K × 8 EPROM.
Reproduced by permission of Intel Corporation.

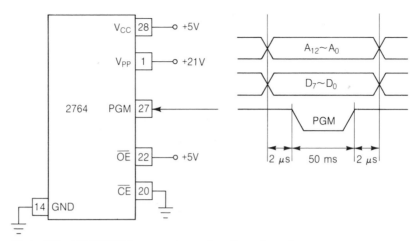

Figure 5.28   2764 EPROM programming configuration and waveforms.

First, erase the old program by exposing the quartz see-through window to ultraviolet light of the proper wavelength. Inexpensive EPROM erasers are on the market and readily available. Even sunlight and fluorescent light will erase EPROMs if they are exposed long enough (weeks for sunlight as opposed to years for fluorescent light), so it is advisable to cover the window if the EPROM contains valid information.

Referring to Figure 5.28, we program the EPROM with our newly developed camera routine by first placing the dc voltages at the pins shown. Then pulse the address, data, and program pins following the timing requirements provided by the manufacturer (also shown in Figure 5.28). With the 2764, you can program any location at any time, either individually, sequentially, or at random. To program EPROMs the user can choose from a wide variety of options, from development system attachments, to IBM PC add-ons, to portable field programmers (Figure 5.29).

Once programming is complete, tie in the 2764 to the system bus following the rules developed earlier in this chapter (see Figure 5.30). As shown, we have adopted linear addressing techniques and have tied chip enable to high-level address line A_{15}, placing our 8K of EPROM at pages 80H through 9FH and folded back over the upper 32K of memory space. (For large-scale EPROM systems, decoding techniques would be adopted.)

EPROM access times   By virtue of their design, EPROMs are inherently the slowest of all MOS technologies, typically about 350 to 450 nsec. To satisfy the needs of today's super-fast processors, however, EPROMs are now available with access times of 200 nsec. As with all memory categories,

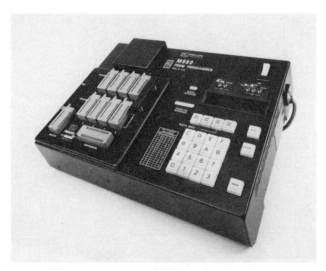

Figure 5.29   The M980 portable PROM programmer.
Courtesy ProLog Corporation.

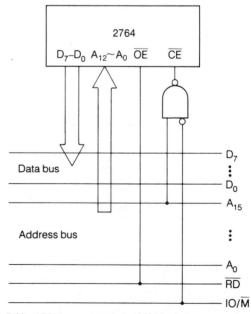

Figure 5.30   2764 bus-system tie-in (8085 bus).

there is every reason to believe that the advance of solid-state technology will sweep the EPROM into the sub-100-nsec range and beyond, even with devices as large as 256K.

ROMs vs EPROMS   As the price differential between ROMs and EPROMs narrows (today, EPROMs cost no more than twice as much as ROMs), and as the higher-density 256K (32K $\times$ 8) EPROMs fall in price, the more flexible EPROM will be used even in the production phase. One obvious advantage of EPROMs over ROMs is that last-minute software changes can be incorporated into the product shortly before shipment.

Bipolar PROM   At the present time, bipolar technology is the answer for sheer speed, with access times approaching 20 nsec. High speed must be important enough, however, to compensate for several disadvantages. First of all, bipolar PROMs are lower-density devices and hence more expensive. In addition, the program cannot be erased and the PROM reused. If you make a mistake in programming, you buy a new PROM. Bipolar PROMs also would not be suitable for battery operation because of their high current draw.

Bipolar PROMs work on the fusible-link principle and are very easy to program (see Figure 5.31). To program a logic 1, the fuse is left intact. To program a logic 0, the metal fuse is blown away by a high-current external programming pulse.

Many cell designs and fuse materials are presently in use. To overcome the drawbacks of low density, stacked-fuse bipolar technology using a polysilicon fuse looks the most promising. Stacked-fuse technology should be capable of producing a 64K, 25-nsec, bipolar PROM.

CMOS PROM   Where low-power operation is a must, the CMOS PROM is the answer. A typical 256 $\times$ 4 field-programmable CMOS PROM dissipates just 25 mW during low-power operation and 500 μW during low-power standby. CMOS PROMs are ideal for portable, battery-operated products where low-current draw is a must (as in our intelligent camera).

EE-PROM   Electrically Erasable PROMs (EE-PROMs or E^{2}PROMs) are the sleepers of the PROM family. When they fully awaken, they will do so with a flourish, eventually surpassing the EPROM in popularity.

The advantages of erasing PROMs electrically rather than by ultraviolet light are many: programs can be altered remotely (by phone), the expensive quartz window can be eliminated, individual locations can be erased, and computer systems will be able to adjust their own "permanent" programs without removing the chip from its system environment (thereby taking a major evolutionary step ahead of the animal kingdom). The technical and manufacturing problems are many, and some rather exotic technology is going into the effort.

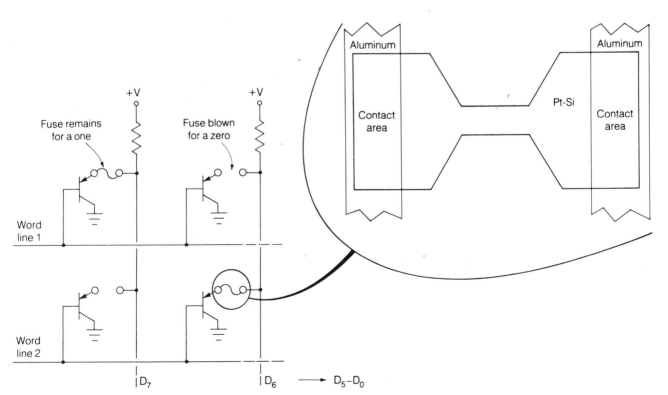

Figure 5.31   Programmed fusible-link PROM.

For example, the floating gates are both erased and programmed by electron tunneling (quantum-mechanical penetration of an energy barrier).

Intel's 2816A is a 2K × 8 EE-PROM featuring a 250-nsec access time, two-line control, and a 9-msec erase/write time. As shown in Figure 5.32a, it is pin compatible with the 2716, allowing easy system upgrade from EPROM to EE-PROM. Of special importance to the designer is the 2816A's 5-volt-only operation; the external 21 volt programming pulse required for earlier devices (the 2816) is now generated by on-chip circuitry. Of special importance to the user is the ability to write/erase any byte location at any time and in any order—over 10,000 times, with a data retention of over 10 years. As expected, the write/erase waveforms for the 2816A (Figure 5.32b) are similar to those of the 2764 EPROM.

An interesting offshoot of the 2816A is the "system friendly" 2817A EE-PROM. To show what a little intelligence can do, consider the process of writing or erasing individual bytes during normal computer operation. Referring to Figure 5.32b, you can see that the problem is to hold the write (WE) line active low for 9 ms during each write/erase operation. The 2817A skirts this requirement by including on-chip latches and timers. To write to a location, we use the same timing and waveforms *as if we were writing to a conventional static RAM*. Upon receiving the write pulse, the 2817A intelligent EE-PROM goes into a "turtle" mode, floating all data lines and pulling RDY/BUSY (pin 1) low. While off-line (in its shell), it performs the 9 msec write process internally. After the write/erase operation is completed, it notifies the CPU by driving BUSY high—and another write/erase operation can commence.

NONVOLATILE STATIC RAMS (NVRAMS)

The 2816 EE-PROM, with its fast read but slow write times, is the precursor of a major goal of memory research: the

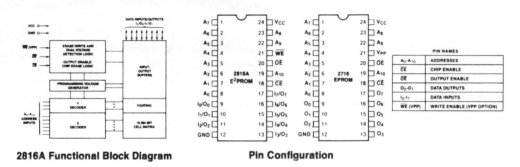

(a) 2816A block and pin diagrams showing pin compatibility with the 2716 EPROM

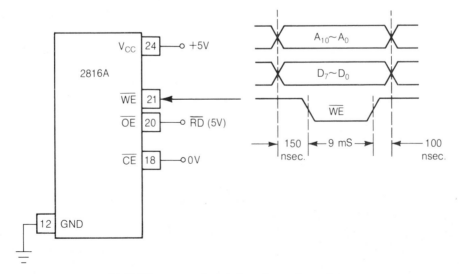

(b) 2816A programming configuration and waveforms

Figure 5.32 The 2816A E²PROM.
Reproduced by permission of Intel Corporation.

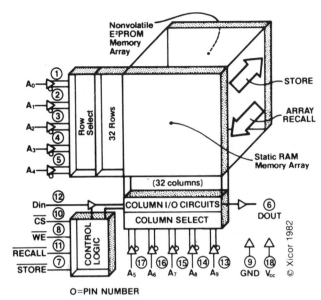

O=PIN NUMBER

Figure 5.33 EE-PROM (E²PROM) and static RAM combined to produce a non-volatile static RAM.

ory). By sending simple 5-volt signals to the X2201, data can be transferred back and forth between RAM and EE-PROM.

With a RAM-to-backup time of 2 ms, the X2201 will flourish in an environment where power failure is possible, where remote coding is required, and in general, wherever the convenience of a nonvolatile RAM is an important factor. For smaller NVRAM requirements, the designer can choose the X2804A 512 × 8 byte-wide NVRAM.

An even more direct nonvolatile solution is offered by Mostek's 16K MK48202 *Zeropower RAM*. Lithium cells are piggybacked on a conventional CMOS static RAM. When power goes down, the chip automatically switches to its built-in battery backup—and, if necessary, will retain the data for a decade!

nonvolatile static RAM. On drawing boards today are non-volatile static RAMs (fast EE-PROMs) offering write and erase times below 100 ns and billions of cycles of endurance (number of write/erase cycles possible before chip becomes unusable). Until such a technology comes of age, we will see many compromise nonvolatile solutions appearing on the market.

By adopting the "best of both worlds" philosophy, for example, the Xicor X2201 merges EE-PROM technology with static-RAM technology to provide a nonvolatile, 5-volt 1K × 1 static RAM (NVRAM). As diagrammed in Figure 5.33, a conventional 250 ns static RAM is overlaid bit for bit with a nonvolatile EE-PROM (called the *shadow mem-*

BYTEWIDE PIN-OUT STANDARDS

As we move from development to production, we generally replace EPROMs with less-expensive ROMs. As higher-density chips become available, we may replace 2K × 8 chips with 8K × 8 chips. Also, as newer technologies mature, we may eventually replace EPROMs with EE-PROMs. To make such memory-system upgrading quick and efficient, the Joint Electron Device Engineering Council (JEDEC) has approved standard 24-pin and 28-pin DIP sites for bytewide memories from 16K (2K × 8) to 256K (32K × 8) bits. All devices belonging to this compatible pin-out family can be used interchangeably in the same socket, including EPROMs, ROMs, EE-PROMs, bytewide static and dynamic RAMs, and iRAMs.

The 24/28-pin JEDEC standard is based on the Intel 2764 8K × 8 EPROM. As an example of the convenience of the standard, Figure 5.34 shows a possible density-upgrade path

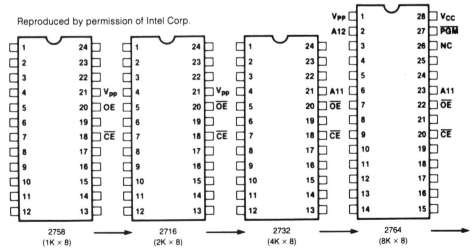

Figure 5.34 The JEDEC standard showing EPROM density upgrading.

for EPROMs. Anticipating the need for this density upgrading, the manufacturer can fit all memory boards with JEDEC-approved 28-pin sites. The lower-capacity 24-pin 2716 (2K × 8) would initially be inserted into each 28-pin site, leaving the upper four pins unoccupied. As the need for larger-density devices arises, they are substituted with direct replacement. (When passing from the 2716 to the 2732, a jumper must be included to accommodate the V_{pp}/A_{11} changeover.)

Although not all manufacturers have adopted the JEDEC standard, it is clearly desirable to have a standard pin-out format for all bytewide memories. However, when changing over to higher-density memory devices, the decoding scheme must allow for easy page-boundary adjustments. For example, when we convert from the 32K 2732 to the 64K 2764,

all page boundaries have to be doubled. To provide the decoding flexibility, a PROM is used as the decoding device. In practice, the PROM is programmed with a special decoding map, and a DIP switch feeds selected address inputs. A mode-selection table relates switch positions to device density. When a newer, higher-density device becomes available, the older devices are removed and the newer devices placed into the JEDEC 28-pin sites. To adjust the page boundaries, the DIP-switch input is set to a new value.

A RAM/ROM SYSTEM

A real microprocessor-based product—such as a "smart" camera—will contain a blend of both RAM and ROM. The

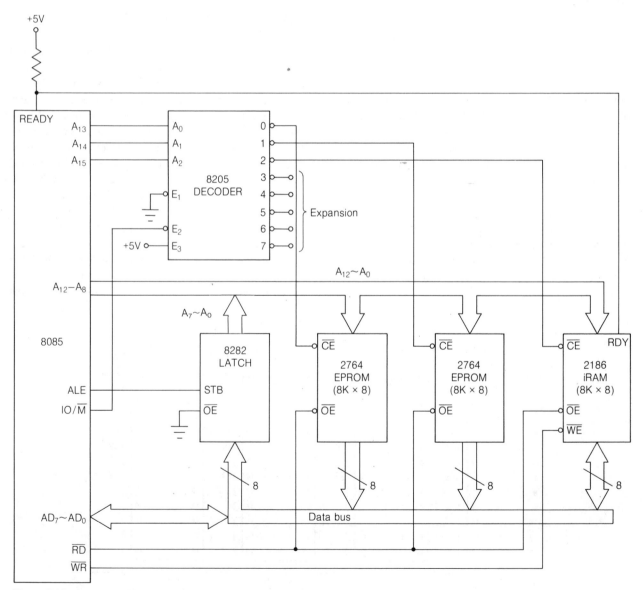

Figure 5.35 A typical 8085-based RAM/PROM memory system.

main purpose of ROM will be to hold the permanent stored program that runs the exposure process. ROM will also hold lookup tables and other constants (such as the value of pi) that do not change and must always be available. RAM (usually smaller in size) will be used as a scratchpad memory, storing temporary, intermediate calculations during mathematical operations or other processes.

Figure 5.35 depicts a typical 8085-based RAM/ROM system. Since studies have shown that the iRAM is cost effective in systems of from 8K to 64K, we have chosen the 2186 8K × 8 iRAM for our random access needs. Using all 8K × 8 byte wide chips, we have achieved 24K of byte-wide RAM/ROM memory with a simple, straightforward design. Since all chips are based on the JEDEC universal site standard, system upgrade and modification are a simple process.

LOGIC ARRAYS

Logic arrays represent the third phase of logic design. Although logic arrays are not classified strictly as memory devices, they are included here because they have several similarities with primary memory.

The first phase of logic design was the use of the conventional 54/74/74C family of TTL/CMOS-logic chips, with their quad OR and AND gates and hex inverters. This design approach was relatively expensive and consumed large amounts of PC board space.

The second phase, starting in the early 1970s, was the development of the microprocessor, in which logic operations were performed sequentially under the direction of software. Here, one VLSI chip (the microprocessor) replaced many discrete-logic chips. The microprocessor, along with its companion memory and peripheral chips, represents the *generalist* approach to electronic design. That is, based on a relatively small number of off-the-shelf parts, each with clearly defined behavior and performance characteristics, the designer could achieve a wide range of *specific* product goals.

This third phase (logic array) represents the *dedicated* approach, in which VLSI circuits are designed from the ground up to meet a specific application. In the past, high costs and a lack of IC designers have kept these *application-specific ICs* from making any significant inroads into the microprocessor-dominated marketplace. With advances in process technology and computer-aided-design (CAD), all that will soon change. *In the very near future, single-station CAD systems will routinely take the application-specific IC design process all the way from initial conception to final mask generation.* As the design environment improves, more and more manufacturers will turn to application-specific ICs to maintain their competitive edge.

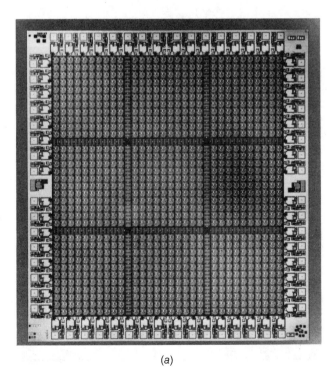

(a)

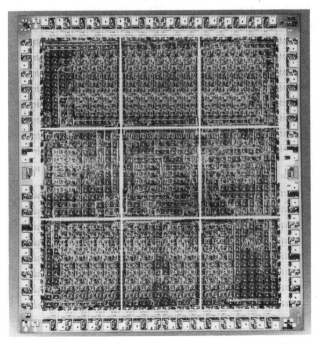

(b)

Figure 5.36 The 2,000 gate array: *a)* Uncommitted. *b)* Personalized. *Courtesy Interdesign.*

Categories of Logic Array

Once the decision has been made to go with application-specific ICs, the next step is to select the proper option from among the three available categories:

- Gate arrays (including the PAL and PLA)
- Standard cells
- Full custom

To help us decide which approach is best for our application, let's take a brief look at each area.

Gate arrays   Gate arrays encompass a large variety of approaches. The most basic and general form of the gate array (also called a *master slice*) is an array of uncommitted transistor cells. Moving up to a less basic format, Figure 5.36*a* reveals the layout of a typical medium-scale CMOS gate array. It is composed of 1,000 *matrix cells,* with each matrix cell containing a number of uncommitted components, including resistors, diodes, and transistors. When connected in their basic form, each matrix provides 2 two-input NOR gates, yielding a grand total of 2,000 gates. Around the outside of the matrix cell array are a number of *peripheral cells,* providing I/O interfacing to a wide variety of devices. When several matrix cells are combined, we create a number of standard circuit elements, such as flip-flops, counters, and schmitt triggers. Most of these commonly-used functions are available as *standard layout macros* (the manufacturer of the gate array provides a library of these standard interconnections). When these various standard functions are in turn interconnected, we create a "personalized" gate array (Figure 5.36*b*), filling a wide variety of applications—such as digital voltmeters, sound synthesizers, motor speed controls, and digital thermometers.

At a still higher level of complexity, the gate array provides a wide variety of basic cell elements. For example, the CMOS gate array shown in Figure 5.37 is designed specifically to accommodate both linear and digital functions on a single chip. The various analog/digital functions include MOS capacitors, zener diodes, analog switches, dedicated flip-flops, and fixed resistors. Using this rich combination of basic circuit elements, the designer can create such analog/digital systems as the RC oscillator, phase-locked loop, switched-capacitor filter, and A/D converter.

When designing with gate arrays, there are a number of options available. For small-scale operations, the customer is provided a design kit, such as that shown in Figure 5.38. Using adhesive overlays, the circuit is layed out on an enlarged sheet of the gate array. When the layout sheet arrives at the factory, a photographic master is taken and used to etch the correct interconnect pattern. As CAD/CAM (computer-aided design/computer-aided manufacturing) systems lower in cost, all steps from initial layout to final photographic mask, will

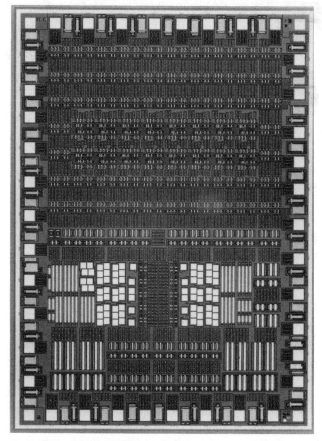

Figure 5.37   The analog/digital gate array. *Courtesy Interdesign.*

Courtesy of Interdesign, Inc.

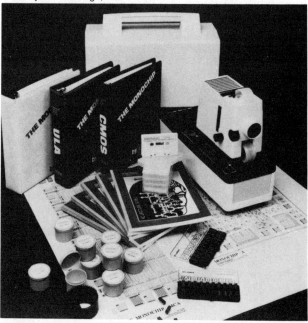

Figure 5.38   Gate-array design is simplified by kits supplying all required materials.

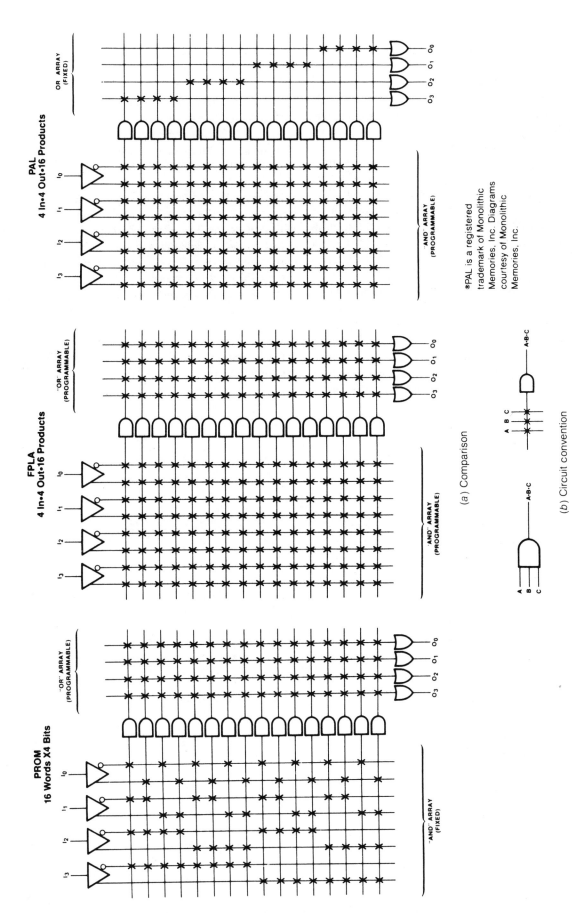

(a) Comparison

(b) Circuit convention

®PAL is a registered
trademark of Monolithic
Memories, Inc. Diagrams
courtesy of Monolithic
Memories, Inc.

Figure 5.39 PROMS, FPLAs, and PALs.

be fully computerized. Even prototype breadboarding and testing will be done by computer simulation. (CAD/CAM systems are discussed in Chapter 22.)

Besides CMOS technology, TTL, I²L, MOS, and ECL gate arrays are available, with ECL used primarily in high-speed mainframe computers. (Using ECL arrays, gate delays below .5 nsec have been achieved.)

The *PAL (programmable array logic)* and *FPLA (fuse-programmable logic array)* are special forms of basic gate arrays. Since the distinctions between the PAL and FPLA are quite subtle, Figure 5.39 compares them both with the more familiar PROM. All three arrays implement the familiar sum-of-products logic that is used to express any Boolean transfer function.

- The PROM consists of a fixed AND array whose outputs feed a programmable OR array. It is low cost and easy to program.

- The *FPLA* (also called *field-programmable logic array*) offers the designer a programmable AND array, feeding a fully programmable OR array. Full programmability of all interconnections allows the ultimate in flexibility.

However, this increased generality makes PLAs relatively expensive.

- The PAL consists of a programmable AND array feeding a fixed OR array. PALs occupy the middle ground between PROMs and PLAs—they are more flexible than PROMs but less expensive than PLAs. With propagation delays approaching 10 nsec, PALs can replace up to 90 percent of the entire 54/74 S and LS series logic.

Standard cells   Standard cell design is the hardware counterpart to modular software design. Unlike gate arrays, in which all but the last mask layer is predefined, a standard cell does not predefine any mask layers. Instead, a fully customized set of masks is created from "building blocks" (cells). Each cell—represented by a set of masks in a cell library—is a full-custom "standard" circuit, ranging from simple gates to UARTs (universal asynchronous receiver/transmitters), DACs (digital-to-analog converters), ALUs, etc. Supported by CAD techniques, the mask sets for each cell are combined (interconnected) to create a custom mask for the full circuit.

A special category of the standard cell is one containing

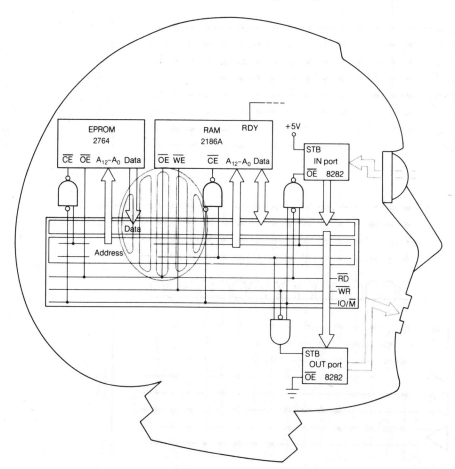

Figure 5.40   Intelligent machine with I/O ports, RAM, and PROM (eyes, voice, memory, and instincts).

a *core microprocessor,* such as Intel's 8085. Standard cells that include core microprocessors can offer great reductions in circuit board size and cost, while using standard and well-known circuit elements.

Full custom   A *full custom circuit* is one that is designed from the ground up to meet a specific application. There is no previously designed hardware (as with the gate array's transistor array) and no previously designed circuit elements (as with the standard cell's library of mask sets). In other words, with full custom design, no off-the-shelf hardware or software designs are used; the final circuit is a completely unique solution to a specific design goal.

Logic Arrays vs Microprocessors

To the designer, the various forms of logic arrays—in competition with microprocessors—may seem quite confusing. Which approach is best? As usual, it depends on all the factors that go into bringing a product to market. For artificial intelligence applications, the flexibility of software programmed logic (the microprocessor) is ideal. If low cost and fast turnaround are more important than high circuit density, the designer can look to the gate array. For moderate volume, semicustom systems, composed of standard digital and analog subcircuits, the standard cell approach may be most attractive. The full-custom approach—which maximizes use of the silicon area, and produces the highest performance circuits—may be best when the high front-end cost is overcome by high production volume. For prototyping (very fast turnaround) and low-volume applications, however, the low-cost, field-programmable PAL or FPLA may be the best choice. Clearly only a thorough investigation and comparison of all options will yield the most suitable approach.

INTELLIGENT-MACHINE UPDATE

When primary memory—RAM and PROM—is added to our intelligent machine (Figure 5.40), it takes yet another step toward its human creators. It can remember, recall, and learn—and with the addition of permanent memory (ROM), it is endowed with instincts. Still, for all its impressive memory capabilities, it is only an inanimate object, incapable of actions on its own. Clearly, the biggest step (bringing the computer "to life") has yet to be taken.

QUESTIONS AND PROBLEMS

1. List the major features normally found in a primary memory system.

2. List the major features normally associated with (a) a RAM and (b) a ROM system.

3. A static-RAM cell uses what process to store information?

4. What is the difference between *static* and *dynamic* RAM?

5. How is an individual static-RAM memory cell addressed?

6. For an 8080-based system, draw the where/when waveforms for both the memory-read and memory-write processes. Do the same for an 8085-based system.

7. With regard to a 2K $\times$ 8 RAM, what do the numbers 2K and 8 mean?

8. What is the purpose of a high-level address line?

9. What is the dividing line between high-level and low-level address lines for a system composed exclusively of 4K $\times$ 8 modules?

10. What is coincident address selection? What part do decoders play in the addressing process?

11. What is the difference between *linear* and *decoded* addressing?

12. Using linear addressing, place a 2K $\times$ 8 RAM module at page 40 (hex).

13. Design a memory system in which two 1K $\times$ 8 RAM modules occupy pages 80H to 87H consecutively.

14. Figure 5.15 depicts the 256 $\times$ 8 RAM system of the 8085-based SDK-85 single-board microcomputer. What addressing technique is used? By tracing through the high-level address lines, at what page is the memory located? To what locations is it folded back?

15. Draw the where/when diagram for the memory-read process and show what is meant by *access time.*

16. What is *bus contention?*

17. What is the difference between one-line and two-line control? What is the advantage of two-line control?

18. List the steps required for a memory-write process to the 2114A RAM (see Figure 5.7*b*).

19. For large-scale systems, why is dynamic RAM preferred over static RAM?

20. What is *refreshing?*

21. How does the iRAM arbitrate between read/write requests and internal refreshing?

22. How does a *refresh-only* cycle differ from a *read/write* cycle?

23. How is addressing done in magnetic-core memory?

24. What is the difference between PROM and (factory-programmed) ROM? Which one is used during the development stage of a new product?

25. How is information stored in an EPROM?

26. Why is it not possible to reprogram bipolar PROM?

27. What is the difference between an EPROM and EE-PROM?

28. What is *electron tunneling* and how is it related to the EE-PROM?

29. For a battery-powered system, what memory technology is preferred?

30. What is a *master slice?* How are the interconnections normally made?

31. What is the difference between a *gate array* and a *standard cell?*

32. Draw a memory map of the RAM/PROM system of Figure 5.35. Why is there no foldback?

33. A single 1K × 8 RAM module is linearly addressed by tying CE to line A_{14}. Draw the memory map, showing all addressed and foldback locations.

34. Show how a magnitude comparator (such as the 7485) might be used to provide "user-selectable" decoding for a memory module.

35. Redesign the system of Figure 5.40 using a single 8205 decoder instead of the AND/NAND gates.

36. Referring to Figure 5.10, what percentage of the 64K memory map is occupied by each 2K × 8 system (linear and decoded)?

chapter 6

Secondary and Backup Memory

Secondary and backup memory act as vast data warehouses. Their function is much like that of an ordinary library. A library is an information storehouse consisting of thousands of books. However, a person can actively read only a single book at a time. When one book is finished, it is placed back on the shelf and another is retrieved. Writers may even add to the information storehouse from time to time. For convenience and protection, all the information contained in the library (as well as books and newspapers no longer in circulation) is available on microfilm.

A microcomputer's memory is also an information library organized along similar lines. Primary memory corresponds to the single book that one is actively reading. Secondary memory is analogous to the thousands of readily available books stored on the shelves, and backup memory serves the same purpose as archives of securely stored rolls of microfilm.

By switching from random to sequential organization, secondary- and backup-memory systems have sacrificed speed to produce nonvolatile data libraries of high capacity and low cost. Although such systems cannot approach the mega-megaword capacity of the human mind, the secondary and backup systems coming into the market give all the capacity and power a microcomputer system is likely to require.

In this chapter we will cover the following types of secondary and backup memory (those memory types straddling both lists are commonly used for both secondary and backup functions):

Secondary	*Backup*
Winchester Disk	Magnetic tape
Bubble	Cartridge and Cassette tape
Charge-coupled device	Video tape
Wafer-scale technology	Winchester (removable)
	Floppy disk
	Optical

THIN-FILM MAGNETIC TECHNOLOGY

With the exception of bubble and optical memory, all secondary- and backup-memory systems store information in a similar manner. The storage medium is a thin layer of iron oxide. Suspended within this magnetic slurry are billions of tiny magnetic, needlelike particles a thousand times thinner than human hair. Each iron atom in the particle exhibits its own earthlike magnetic field. The iron atoms tend to align themselves along the axis of the elongated particle, turning each particle into a tiny bar magnet.

During manufacture of the memory element, the iron-oxide liquid is spread thinly on the surface of a disk or tape support material in the presence of an external magnetic field. When the iron-oxide slurry has dried, all magnetic particles will be aligned in the same north-south direction. Since the magnetic field strength in the critical region just above the magnetic film is the sum of all magnetic particles beneath, this mutual alignment assures the strongest possible field strength. (To reduce noise, some magnetic systems use a random alignment of magnetic particles.)

The whole system is useful as a memory device because of two distinct magnetic configurations. As seen in Figure 6.1, the iron atoms can align and latch themselves in one of two states. (Remember, only the magnetic state of the iron atom turns, not the magnetic particles themselves.) Digital information is stored by a linear pattern of these two states of magnetic alignment.

Once the pattern has been established, the hysteresis properties of the magnetic material guarantee that the pattern will remain locked in place for long periods of time.

Reading and Writing

Reading information from the magnetic medium takes place by passing the linear patterns of magnetic alignment under a magnetic head (see Figure 6.2). A coil of wire on the magnetic head senses the changing magnetic pattern by the principle of induction (a voltage pulse appears whenever the magnetic alignment *changes*). The resulting voltage waveform is decoded by logic circuitry to recreate the serial pattern of ones and zeros originally stored on the magnetic medium.

The same magnetic head (known as the *read/write head*) can be used in the write mode. Sufficient current is forced

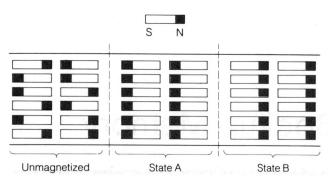

Unmagnetized   State A   State B

Figure 6.1 Digital two-state storage in a magnetic medium.

through the loops of wire to create a magnetic field. The direction of the magnetic field can be switched by changing the direction of the current flow. This switching magnetic field lays down the required pattern of magnetization as the magnetic medium passes beneath.

Recording Modes

It seems logical that magnetic alignment in one direction would store the logic 1 state, and magnetic alignment in the opposite direction would correspond to the logic 0 state. However, magnetic induction produces a voltage only when a *change* in magnetism is encountered. Following this constraint, a logic 1 is represented as a magnetic reversal, and a logic 0 as no reversal. This simple *non-return-to-zero current* (NRZI) mode appeared in the early 1950s with the introduction of the first magnetic tape storage units. Unfortunately, the NRZI mode was not *self-clocking* and required an extremely stable time base in order to maintain bit synchronization.

The solution was to integrate clock information in with data information. It turns out that if a flux transition occurs at least once every three bit cells, synchronization can be maintained with phase-locked loop techniques—and the system is self-clocking (a phase-locked loop, remember, exhibits a memory via its external RC network).

Historically, the first *self-clocking* data-encoding scheme was called *frequency modulation (FM)*. As shown in Figure 6.3*a*, the presence of a logic pulse (magnetic flux reversal) in the center of the bit cell stores a logic 1, and the absence stores the logic 0. A clock phase reversal at the boundary of every cell provides the steady repetitive signal required for phase lock. The technique is called frequency modulation because a sequence of all zeros has frequency *f,* and a sequence of all ones has a frequency of 2*f.* The problem with this "single-density" technique is inefficiency; one-half of the available 8-microsecond space (based on typical floppy disk speed) is used up by clock bits.

By using so-called "double-density" techniques, twice the information can be packed into the same space. Modified frequency modulation (MFM)—the simplest and most pop-

ular double-density technique—is demonstrated in Figure 6.3*b*. Clock bits are written into the data stream only if data bits have not been written into both the preceding and present bit cells. Because a bit cell never contains both a clock and a data bit, each cell can be made half as large (4 microseconds). Because a clock or a data bit (phase reversal) occurs at least once every third bit cell, and because the clock and data bits are harmonically related, the phase-lock condition is easy to achieve.

Since each clock pulse, present or not, still requires space (a clock window) on the recording medium, we can increase density further by totally eliminating the clock pulses. However, suppose we have a long string of zeros; how will we maintain synchronization? The answer is *group-coded recording* (GCR). By means of GCR (Figure 6.3*c*), each byte of data to be written to the disk is divided into two nibbles. Each nibble is translated into 5-bit codes *including at least one flux reversal to maintain synchronization*. Upon reading from the disk, the process is reversed. GCR encoded data uses approximately 65 percent of the space required for double-density recording (2.6 microseconds).

Formatting

In any storage medium, identification of the data, synchronization between memory and CPU, and detection of errors are just as important as the information itself. Therefore, data stored on a magnetic medium usually are cradled in a complex format that allows for identification, synchronization, buffering, and error detection. Figure 6.4 shows a typical format in which the data have been divided into a number of sectors. Each sector is identical in form and contains the following fields: marks, gaps, addresses, error-detection bytes, and data.

The gaps act as buffer zones between information-containing areas and allow time for such actions as head movement, switching between read and write modes, and compensation for slight differences between read and write speeds of the magnetic medium. The marks (often consisting of a series of ones) signal the start of address and data fields and provide synchronization between the data medium and the internal electronics. The address field gives the address of each sector and allows the system to verify the address of each data field. Space is provided in both the address and data fields to check for errors.

Error Detection

The error checks in both the address and data fields can be simple parity checks in which an extra parity bit is added to each data word so the total number of ones is even (for even parity) or odd (for odd parity). Periodic checking of the parity will reveal if a data bit has been inadvertently switched.

A more efficient method, which uses less overall space, is called the *checksum* method. All the data bytes in a data

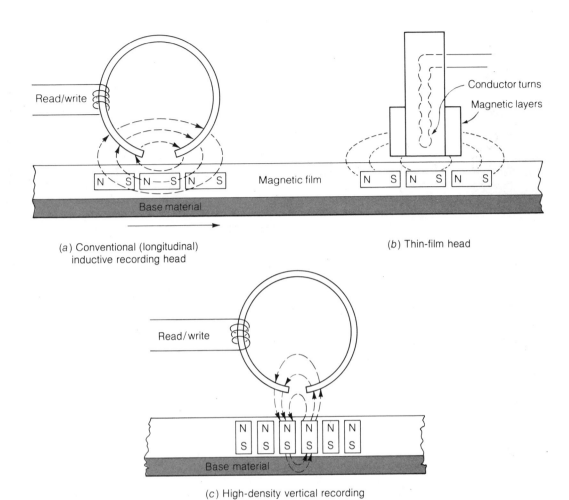

(a) Conventional (longitudinal) inductive recording head

(b) Thin-film head

(c) High-density vertical recording

Figure 6.2 Sensing (reading) and setting (writing) the magnetic domains.

field are added and any carries beyond two bytes are ignored. At any time, the data bytes can be added again and the new checksum compared with the original. If the sums agree, the data was probably transmitted without error.

Nearly the ultimate in error-checking sophistication is known as *cyclic redundancy checking* (CRC). This method is particularly well suited to the detection of multiple bit errors that occur in bursts—a common problem in data communication.

The CRC method is based on basic mathematical theory. First of all, we must understand how a block of digital data can be written as a polynomial. Arbitrarily choosing the data word 10011, we see how a polynomial is formed from the data word by using the data bits as coefficients for each term:

$$
\begin{array}{llccccc}
 & 1 & 0 & 0 & 1 & 1 \\
\text{Step 1:} & a_4x^4 & + a_3x^3 & + a_2x^2 & + a_1x & + a_0 \\
\text{Step 2:} & 1x^4 & + 0x^3 & + 0x^2 & + 1x & + 1 \\
\text{Step 3:} & x^4 & & & + x & + 1
\end{array}
$$

Therefore, $10011 = x^4 + x + 1$.

When this data polynomial (Dx) is divided by a generator polynomial (Gx), a remainder (Rx) is formed:

$$\frac{D(x)}{G(x)} = Q(x) + \frac{R(x)}{G(x)} \qquad \text{where } R(x) = \text{CRCC}$$

The remainder, which is shorter than the original polynomial, will be a unique number for each data block. The remainder is known as a *cyclic-redundancy-check character* (CRCC). Rewriting the equation, we see how errors are revealed:

$$\frac{D(x) - R(x)}{G(x)} = Q(x) + 0$$

That is, if the remainder is subtracted from the data polynomial and the result divided by the generator polynomial, the division takes place an even number of times and *no remainder will be generated*. This fact forms the basis of the CRC method.

As shown by Figure 6.5, three steps are involved in the CRC process:

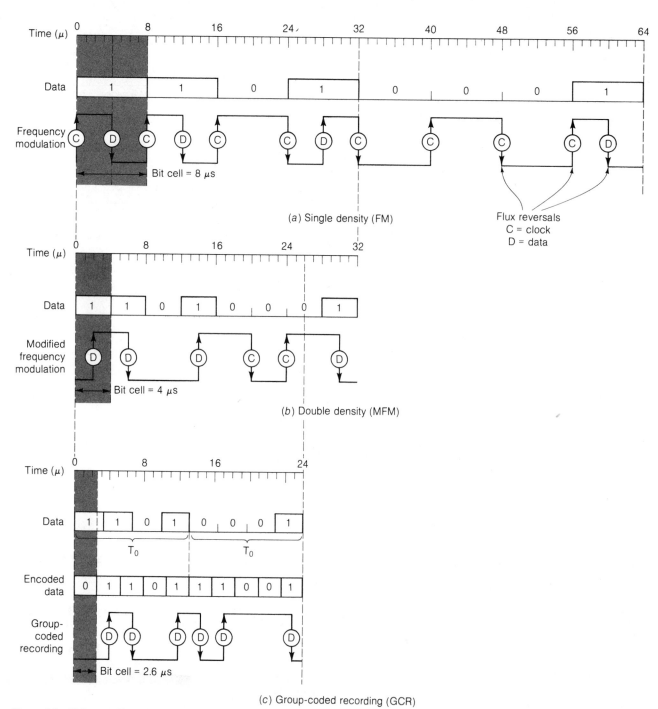

Figure 6.3 Major encoding techniques.

- *Step 1—Generation of the CRCC*. The data polynomial is divided by the generator polynomial to produce the CRCC (remainder polynomial).

- *Step 2—Transmission*. The CRCC is included with the data and transmitted.

- *Step 3—Error checking*. The CRCC remainder polynomial is subtracted from the data polynomial, and the result

is divided by the same generator polynomial. If the remainder is zero, the message was transmitted without error. If a remainder appears, it tells us the data stream picked up an error.

A popular generator polynomial is:

$$G(x) = x^{16} + x^{15} + x^5 + 1$$

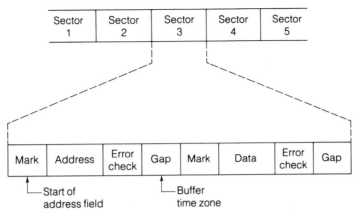

Figure 6.4   Formatting serial data.

The higher the order of the generator polynomial, the greater the probability of detecting an error, but the more difficult the implementation.

Error-Checking-and-Correcting (ECC) Codes

The spread of microcomputer systems to critical real-time operations—such as banking and process control—demands that errors be automatically detected *and* corrected. The CRCC method, highly effective in detecting errors, is not so effective in correcting them.

For intermittent errors, most often occurring in semiconductor memories, the *Hamming code* is the most common error-correcting code. By interspersing parity bits with data bits, an incorrect bit can be located and automatically toggled to the correct value. Figure 6.6 details the process for a 4-bit word. Let's follow the action and see how the number 9 (1001), which picked up an error in bit position 3 and incorrectly became a BH, is automatically corrected back to a 9.

The process begins with parity-bit generation. As shown in Figure 6.6*a*, three parity bits are generated from exclu-

sive-OR combinations of the 4 data bits and added to the data word at selected locations. During data storage in semiconductor memory, the data/parity word picked up an error in position 6 (perhaps due to an alpha particle). When the data word is read, the position of the error is obtained by exclusive-OR combinations of the data and parity bits. Once the error location is pinpointed, it is toggled to the correct value by a final exclusive-OR process (see Figure 6.6*b*).

Although error-correcting codes, such as the Hamming code, are bit wasteful and require complex on-board circuitry, memory boards with built-in ECC circuits can be 300 times more reliable than conventional memory boards.

SECONDARY MEMORY SYSTEMS

Floppy Disks

Convenience is the reason floppy-disk technology is such a popular form of auxiliary and backup storage for microcomputers. It is convenient to store music on records, and it is convenient to store binary data on floppy disks—a storage medium remarkably close in structure to an ordinary 45-rpm

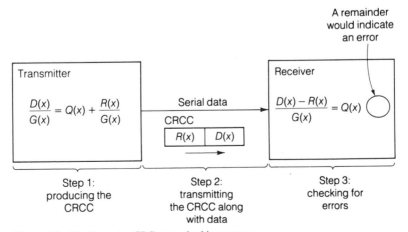

Figure 6.5   The three-step CRC error-checking process.

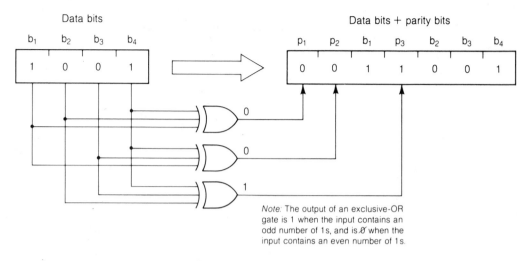

Note: The output of an exclusive-OR gate is 1 when the input contains an odd number of 1s, and is 0 when the input contains an even number of 1s.

(a) Parity bit generation for number 9

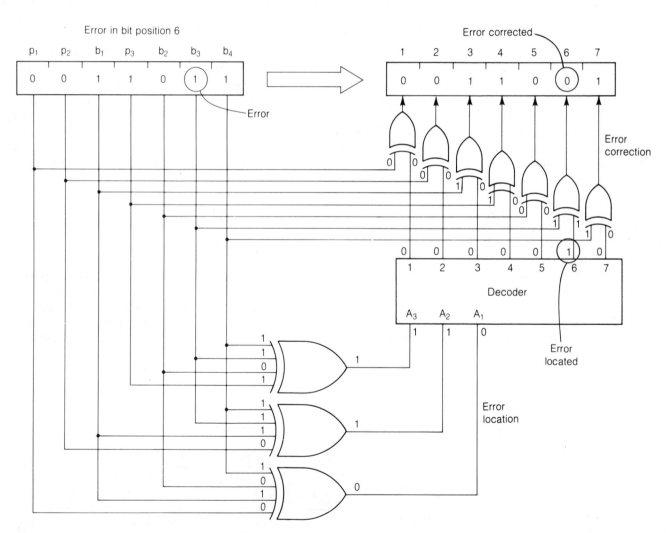

(b) Error correction first locates error bit position, then toggles error bit to correct value

Figure 6.6 Hamming error correction.

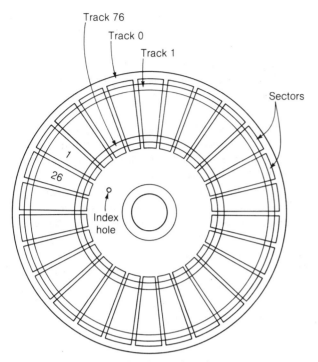

Figure 6.7 Diskette organized into tracks and sectors.

record. Flexibility of the recording medium (called a *diskette*) is achieved by the use of a thin section of Mylar as the base material on which the iron oxide is coated. Data are organized on the diskette in concentric tracks, each divided into a number of sectors (similar to a dart board). The standard 8-inch diskette illustrated in Figure 6.7 has 77 tracks and 26 sectors per track.

As shown in Figure 6.8, the diskette is contained within an envelope and is simply plugged into the record/play unit. During read or write activity, the diskette rotates within the low-friction plastic case at approximately 360 rpm. The radially shaped access slot allows the read/write head to move to the proper track and scan the surface of the disk. The large center hole allows the disk to be spun, and the small index hole is used to locate the first sector.

Figure 6.9 shows how the read/write head is positioned quickly and accurately within the access slot by the use of a stepper motor. Each circular step is translated into one track-to-track distance by a steel band wound over the motor's pulley.

Addressing A floppy disk is a semi-random-access device. To go from one track/sector location to another, it is not necessary to pass through all intermediate locations.

When an address is sent to the floppy disk system, the read/write head is positioned over the correct track. The system then locates the first sector by waiting for the index hole to pass between the light-source/photodetector combination. By counting sectors from that time, the drive circuitry can determine which sector is passing under the read/write head. To verify that the correct sector has been reached, each track can be formatted to contain the complete track/sector address. Because the IBM 3740 floppy-disk format is in such widespread use, it is presented in Figure 6.10. It includes the expected marks, gaps, addresses, error detection, and data fields.

A newly purchased disk usually is unformatted (blank). Most microcomputers (e.g., Apple II, IBM PC) provide a

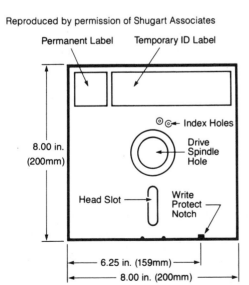

Figure 6.8 Floppy-disk envelope (left) plugged into record/play unit (right).

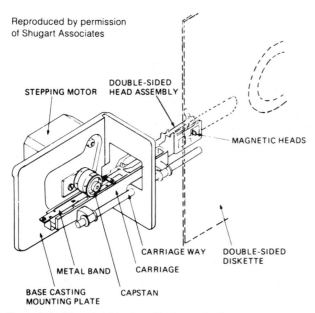

Reproduced by permission
of Shugart Associates

Figure 6.9   Linear-band head-positioning mechanism.

simple means for formatting blank disks. While running
under the *Disk Operating System* (DOS) program, simply
type a command such as:

>FORMAT A: (Carriage Return)

The FORMAT *utility* (program contained in DOS) carries
out the format operation on the disk stored in drive A, and
a track format similar to that of Figure 6.10 is written onto
the floppy disk (of course the data fields are left blank).
When track and sector identification is prerecorded by the
manufacturer, the diskette is called *preformatted*.

Soft-sectored vs hard-sectored format   The soft-sectored
format just covered relies on a single index hole and software
formatting to locate and verify data sectors. Hard sectoring
includes up to 32 sector holes (in addition to the index hole)
evenly spaced about the diskette to locate up to 32 corresponding sectors. Because the need for address bytes has
been largely eliminated, six additional sectors can be added
to each track. (Since addresses cannot be verified, the price
you pay for these six additional sectors is reduced reliability.)

Capacity   Using 73 tracks (four tracks normally contain
no data), with 26 sectors per track and 128 bytes of data per
sector, a quick calculation will show that the typical diskette
can store some 250,000 bytes of information. Double-density disks, which make use of the MFM encoding technique
of Figure 6.3*b,* can double this figure. And by using double-
sided, double-density diskettes (which require a special double-sided head assembly), we approach the magic 1-mega-
byte figure. Continued increases in bit density and improvements in head-positioning systems should soon provide the
10-megabyte, 8-inch floppy.

Speed and reliability   On the average it requires approximately one-fifth of a second to position the read/write head
over the correct sector (this is known as a *seek operation*).
Such a relatively long time is misleading, however, because
information is usually stored in large sequential blocks. Once
the correct starting sector has been located, data can be read
from the diskette at the rate of approximately 500 kbits/sec.

The term most commonly used to specify overall speed
is *average access time,* the average amount of time required
to access data from the beginning of a read operation to the
end. For floppy disks, average access times of 80 to 150 ms
are typical (a million times slower than primary memory).

Reliability of magnetic-based systems is determined by
the average number of bits that can be read from the system
before one bit is found to be in error. A typical reliability
value lies between 1 error per 10^8 and 1 error per 10^{10} bits
read. Since physical contact is made between diskette and
read/write head, the magnetic medium is subject to wear.
Therefore, another important reliability specification is mean
time between failure (MTBF)—typically 9,000 hours under
normal usage.

Disk controller and operating system   A floppy-disk controller is the interface electronics between the floppy-disk
system and the CPU. It must perform a wide variety of tasks:

- Read and write operations
- Parallel-to-serial and serial-to-parallel conversions
- Seek operations and other control commands
- Address verification
- CRC error detection
- Overall synchronization between CPU and floppy

These various functions are divided between hardware
(disk-controller board) and software (Disk Operating System). The primary function of the DOS is to manage the
transfer of data between primary and secondary memory.

As explained in greater depth in Chapter 22, modern Disk
Operating Systems—which are usually stored on floppy disk—
go beyond simple disk I/O operations, and allow the operator to perform a variety of operations on *files* (a named
program stored on a floppy disk).

The Minifloppy

The Minifloppy, a less-expensive, scaled-down version of
the full-size floppy disk storage system, has all but captured
the microcomputer market. The disk size is reduced from 8
to $5\frac{1}{4}$ inches, the number of tracks from 77 to 40, and the
number of sectors from 26 to 10, with a comparable reduction in total storage capacity (typically $\frac{1}{2}$ Mbyte using formatted double-sided, double-density). Especially popular are
the space-saving half-height minifloppy drives (Figure 6.11),

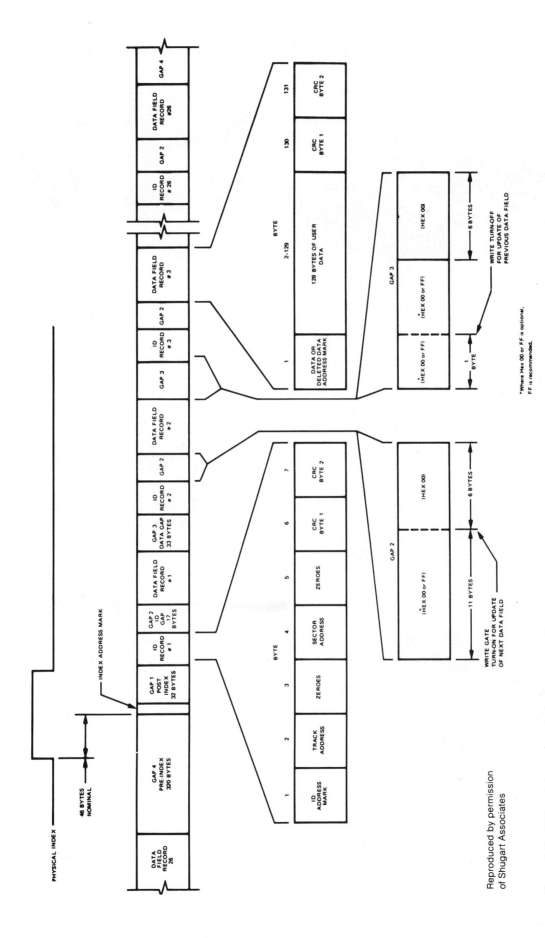

Reproduced by permission
of Shugart Associates

Figure 6.10 IBM track format.

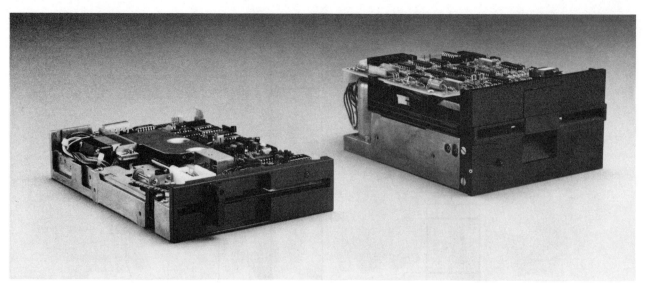

Figure 6.11   Half-height and full-height minifloppies.
Courtesy Shugart Corporation.

allowing two disk drives to fit into the same space normally reserved for a single drive.

As floppy disk technology matures, expect a dual-sided minifloppy diskette to hold more than 5 Mbytes of data—at no increase in price.

The Microfloppy

The newly emerging 3- to 4-inch *microfloppy* is further reducing the size of personal computers and is spearheading a number of significant departures from conventional design.

For example, the Shugart 350 illustrated in Figure 6.12 is a $3\frac{1}{2}$ inch double-sided microfloppy disk drive offering 1

Mbyte of capacity and using the new *hard-shell cartridge media* (the disk enclosed in a rigid plastic case with a head-slot shield that automatically recedes when the disk is inserted).

The microfloppy is smaller, sturdier, and easier to handle than the $5\frac{1}{4}$- and 8-inch floppy disks; it should make steady inroads into the conventional disk markets. Since the Microfloppy Industry Committee (MIC) has given its blessing to the $3\frac{1}{2}$ inch system shown in Figure 6.12, this intermediate size should gain favored market acceptance and emerge as the de facto standard.

RAM Disk

A basic tenet of memory hierarchy is that memory price is directly related to its speed. That is why a large program is broken into parts when stored on floppy disk; each piece loaded into main (primary) memory prior to its processing turn, and after execution that portion of primary memory used by the program section is freed for other purposes. Using *virtual memory* techniques, the computer automatically folds programs and data between primary and secondary memory.

However, with the dramatic drop in primary memory prices (approaching that of a floppy system), the *ramdisk* has emerged. A ramdisk is a circuit board of RAM chips that the computer treats as a disk drive. To use a ramdisk, simply transfer the information from floppy to ramdisk, and tell the computer (through special software) to access the ramdisk rather than the floppy disk. When finished, copy the ramdisk back to the floppy to save any updates. The primary advantage of a ramdisk is a 50-fold improvement in speed over the floppy.

Figure 6.12   The Shugart 1 M-byte microfloppy.
Courtesy Shugart Corporation.

Figure 6.13 A 70-megabyte, 8-inch Winchester showing aerodynamic head and head-positioning assembly. *Courtesy PRIAM Corporation.*

Winchester Disks

Disk memories strongly resemble floppy-disk systems (Figure 6.13). The major difference is that the iron-oxide recording medium is coated onto a rigid aluminum base rather than flexible Mylar. In general, disk systems represent a general upgrading in precision, performance, and price (although the cost per bit usually is lower than for a floppy system).

Like the floppy system, information is stored serially in concentric tracks (typically, 1,000 per surface) on the magnetic-film medium. The disk is spun at high speeds (3,600 rpm), and a precision stepper motor positions the read/write head over the proper track. Sophisticated controller circuitry accepts the commands from the CPU and directs and activates the read/write head.

Winchester technology, introduced by IBM in 1973, is a package of refinements to this basic disk system. It is now spreading throughout the microcomputer industry as fast as its namesake, the Winchester rifle, spread through the early West. (In its conceptual stage, the Winchester disk was a dual-drive, 30-megabyte system. Although no longer in use, this "30-30" arrangement accounts for the code name "Winchester.")

Included in the Winchester technology package are:

- A lightweight, aerodynamic read/write head that floats on an air cushion a mere half micrometer above the surface of the spinning disk.

- Sealed disk environment.
- Filtered internal atmosphere.
- Very thin magnetic-oxide coating.
- Very high reliability (1 bit in 10^{11}).
- High track and bit densities (over 1,000 tracks/in and over 10,000 bits/in are projected).
- Read/write head rests on lubricated disk surface when not in operation, thereby eliminating head "crashes" (catastrophic collision of head and disk).

A key feature of Winchester technology is the small gap between the read/write head and rotating disk. The smaller the gap, the greater the data density. When you realize that a fingerprint would deposit a "mountain" of oil some five times higher than the half-micrometer flying height of the read/write head, you begin to realize why the head/disk assembly operates in a hermetically sealed, filtered environment.

Disk sizes range from the recently available 3.5 and 3.9 inches (100 mm), to the floppy-compatible $5\frac{1}{4}$ and 8 inches, to the large-scale 14-inch unit, covering the capacity spectrum from 5 to 600 megabytes and more. The $5\frac{1}{4}$-inch half-height micro-Winchester (Figure 6.14) should prove popular with the microcomputer set. It is the same size as the half-height Minifloppy, yet can store a respectable 6–15 megabytes of unformatted data.

With an average access time approaching 25 ms and transfer rates exceeding 5 megabits per second (Mb/s), the Winchester far outstrips the floppy in performance.

Even the major drawback of the conventional Winchester when compared with the floppy (the permanently sealed Winchester disk cannot be removed and therefore offers no I/O capability) is overcome by the *removable* hard-disk cartridge. The removable Winchester disk offers all the advantages of the floppy, but with vastly increased storage capacity, access speed, reliability, and convenience of use.

Although removable hard disks are available in all four popular sizes (3.9, $5\frac{1}{4}$, 8 and 14 inches), only the more inexpensive 3.9-inch hard-disk cartridge is in a position to compete with the floppy disk. Only time will tell if the removable hard disk will relegate the floppy to the same fate as the nearly obsolete punched card and cassette tape.

The popularity of the Winchester guarantees that a steady stream of improvements and modifications will appear on the market. Two recent innovations—*thin-film heads* and *servo positioners* (which locate tracks by reading location information preset on the disk)—have already produced a half-height $5\frac{1}{4}$ Winchester with a storage capacity of over 100 Mbytes and an average access time of under 30 ms.

Bubble Memory

Although several companies have dropped out of the bubble-memory race, it still remains the rising star of secondary

Figure 6.14 The Seagate 12 M-byte half-height micro-Winchester. *Courtesy Seagate Associates.*

storage. Its major advantages over all other forms of secondary storage are its compact size and complete absence of mechanical moving parts. Like other secondary storage devices, it is nonvolatile.

Magnetic bubbles are tiny cylindrical regions of magnetic domains, aligned in opposite polarity to the magnetic domain about them. When viewed under polarized light, they resemble liquid bubbles. They are created by applying a strong magnetic field perpendicular to a thin sheet of magnetic material. Most of the magnetic dipoles will line up with the external magnetic field, but some will not. As the external field grows in strength, the opposing regions will shrink to less than one-millionth of a meter in diameter and become true magnetic bubbles. (If the external magnetic field is increased further, the bubbles will eventually disappear.) The presence of a bubble stores a logic 1, and the absence stores a logic 0. An external permanent magnet supplies the static field required to retain the data when power is removed.

Like liquid bubbles, magnetic bubbles can be made to propagate through their medium. To provide the moving force, various magnetic-alloy patterns (often called *chevrons* because of their shape) are placed on top of the film layer (Figure 6.15*a*). Rotating magnetic fields, produced by external orthogonal (right-angle) current-carrying coils, move the bubbles from chevron to chevron in shift-register fashion.

When in active storage, bubbles are synchronously circulated about in many small storage loops, like the rapidly moving teeth of a chain saw. As illustrated by Figure 6.15*b*, input and output tracks interconnect all the loops and provide a mainline pathway for the input and output of data. (Using many minor loops, rather than a single large storage loop, allows the addressed bubbles to circulate for a shorter average distance before they are read out, thereby greatly improving access times.)

The write process takes place when bubbles are injected into the input track and routed to the proper storage loop. (A bubble generator produces bubbles by replicating an existing bubble within the generator.) Reading takes place as the bubbles released to the output track pass beneath a special pattern of linked chevrons that detect a bubble by changing magnetoresistive properties.

The rotating storage loops give bubble memory its sequential characteristics and relatively slow access time (compared to primary memory) of approximately 5 to 40 ms. Once a block of data is in position, however, it streams out at the rate of over 400 kilobits per second (kb/s). And when several units are operated in parallel, transfer rates of over 100 Mb/s are possible. (In general, bubbles have faster access times than disks, but slower transfer rates.)

Nonvolatility, high storage capacity, fast access, compact size, and ruggedness are the properties that will guarantee bubble memory a place in the marketplace. Perhaps the first task assigned to bubble memory will be to reduce equipment size. Single devices storing 5 to 10 megabytes, in a medium no larger than the size of a postage stamp, should soon be commonplace. Although the interfacing problems have been challenging, single-board bubble-memory systems are now available that include all interfacing electronics.

Intel's i7114 4-Mbit bubble memory chip represents the present state-of-the-art. When combined with the companion 7224 *bubble memory controller* (BMC), interfacing to a host 8080/8085 CPU is as simple as with any *programmable peripheral chip* (the subject of Chapter 19). The host processor operates the bubble memory system by reading from, or writing to, specific registers within the BMC.

When four megabits of bubble memory are combined with error checking and correction (ECC) circuits and placed on an IBM PC-compatible board (Figure 6.16), we create the PC bubble disk, a secondary system that offers a high-speed, reliable alternative to the mini-Winchester.

Although working bubble memory systems are a reality, their sheer complexity and sophistication represents a hinderance when it competes with other forms of secondary memory. However, if past history is any guide, constant improvements in both design and production techniques will be made. It remains to be seen if the price/performance ratio of bubble memory will significantly displace the market position of floppy and Winchester disk systems.

Wafer-Scale Technology

Another contender for the title of "secondary memory champion" (presently held by the Winchester) is *wafer-scale tech-*

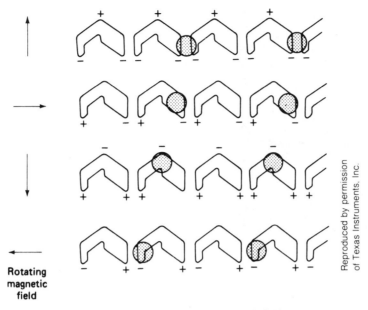

Reproduced by permission of Texas Instruments, Inc.

Rotating magnetic field

(a) Bubble propagated by rotating magnetic field

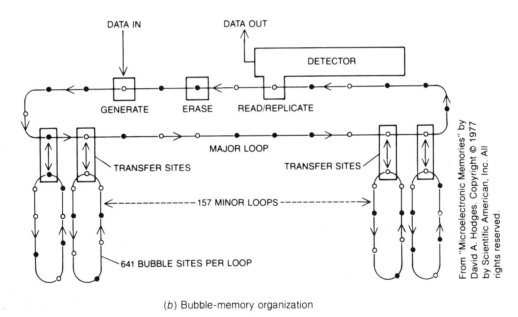

From "Microelectronic Memories" by David A. Hodges. Copyright © 1977 by Scientific American, Inc. All rights reserved.

(b) Bubble-memory organization

Figure 6.15 Bubble memory.

nology. Although it has suffered several recent setbacks, progress is being made.

A *wafer* is a large slab of silicon—some four inches in diameter and 6 to 12 mils thick—that can hold half a megabyte of serial memory. To the contest for market supremacy, it brings blinding speed coupled with low power requirements. It offers an estimated access time of 10 microseconds and a power consumption of 1 W—1,000 times faster and 1/10 the power of its mechanical rival.

For a circuit the size of the wafer-scale, yield (number of good chips) has been a major problem. Therefore, a key

element in the success of the wafer-scale will be the patented technique in which bad elements in a serial array are automatically bypassed.

With a potential cost per bit far below that of the Winchester, wafer-scale technology is a promising newcomer to the secondary memory field.

Charge-Coupled-Devices (CCD)

In basic terms, a CCD memory is a large-capacity, very fast, serial-shift register. Because data bits are stored and

Figure 6.16 The PC Bubble Disk
Curtesy Helix Laboratories.

From "Microelectronic Circuit Elements" by James D. Meindl. Copyright © 1977 by Scientific American, Inc. All rights reserved.

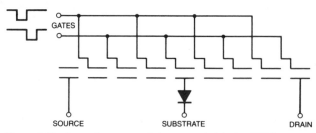

Figure 6.17 Internal structure of charge-coupled device (CCD).

a long string of gates placed between. By applying carefully phased pulses to alternate gates, charge packets injected at the source can be passed bucket-brigade fashion from transistor to transistor. A typical CCD memory array may have 4,096 storage cells with bits circulating at 5 million cycles per second.

Charge-coupled-device memories arrived on the scene with a great deal of fanfare, but have failed to live up to expectations. Charge-coupled technology, however, will "live on" because of its applications in imaging and filtering, where a repeating linear pattern of data is required.

BACKUP STORAGE DEVICES

The word *backup* implies protection, and indeed backup devices are often used to save data in the event of catastrophic failure. However, backup memory is more than a simple protection system. Since the spread of Winchester devices, with their typically nonremovable disks, the responsibility for program interchange and updates, exchange of databases, and archival storage has passed on to the backup system. To provide these services, backup memory systems must have the capacity for storing large amounts of information at low cost.

In addition to those secondary systems that also can provide backup functions (floppy and removable Winchester), backup memory for microcomputers includes:

- Half-inch magnetic tape
- Quarter-inch magnetic cartridge
- Cassette tape
- Video tape
- Optical

Although optical memory presently is used primarily for backup, recent advances in technology will soon find optical devices providing secondary functions as well.

Magnetic Tape

For proven reliability and low cost, magnetic-tape memory systems have few equals. They have provided reliable data

transferred in serial format, CCD memory is conceptually similar to bubble memory. The major difference lies in the method of bit storage and transfer.

Figure 6.17 shows the basic structure of a CCD. The source and drain of an MOS transistor are pulled apart and

storage for many years and have established an impressive track record of success.

The major advantage of magnetic-tape backup systems is their ability to store large amounts of information at low cost per bit. The major disadvantage is their slow access speed. Using sequential address exclusively, the tape is obliged to pass through all intermediate locations in order to arrive at the desired destination.

Present-day tape systems usually provide 2, 4, or 9 tracks (with future generation tape drives having up to 18 tracks), allowing information to be stored in parallel or serial (9 and 18 tracks allow room for parity bits). Data transfer to and from the tape system also can be either parallel or serial, depending on the interface.

Magnetic-tape drives come in either the conventional *start-stop* version or the newer *streaming-tape* option—the "talk of the town" in magnetic tape technology. Like Winchester technology, streaming-tape technology includes a package of features specifically designed to match well with today's high-speed computer systems. As the name implies, streaming-tape drives are designed to operate at full speed, with the need for frequent starts and stops largely overcome. Reading and writing is designed to take place "on the fly." By reducing the number of starts and stops, transfer rates above 150 kbytes/s are standard. Developed specifically for backup applications, streaming-tape technology has lowered the cost and improved the efficiency of both half-inch and quarter-inch tape systems.

Streaming operation depends on a double-buffering technique (Figure 6.18), which follows the classic producer/consumer problem. In the diagram, the Winchester disk is the producer, sending data to the ring of memory buffers, and the tape is the consumer, receiving information from the buffers. During data-transfer operations, the producer (disk) fills the first-in/first-out buffers from one end, while the tape (consumer) empties the buffers from the other. When data are to be written back into the Winchester from the tape, the roles of producer and consumer are reversed. The operation can be likened to filling a bucket in spurts, but allowing the water to flow out a hole in the bottom in a steady *stream* (of course, the bucket cannot be allowed either to overflow or to empty).

A disadvantage of streaming-tape drives is that the data on the tape cannot be directly accessed by the CPU. Start/stop tape drives, which store data in typically 4-kilobyte individually addressable blocks, overcome this drawback, but at much greater cost. Required to stop and start between each block of data, a high-torque motor is required to accelerate the tape to read/write speed in the required intergap distance.

Half-Inch Magnetic Tape

For very high-capacity backup storage at minimum cost, the half-inch streaming-tape systems have few equals (Figure 6.19). Nearly 100 Mbytes of data can be stored on a single reel of magnetic tape costing less than $10; 150-Mbyte storage on a single 7-inch reel is a realistic prediction. A complete half-inch system is no larger than the Winchester device it must back up, and great strides have been made in easing the once painful task of interfacing the tape drive to the computer system. Most half-inch systems are IBM compatible and are formatted accordingly. With a transfer rate of over 1 Mb/s, the half-inch streaming-tape system is effective backup for secondary systems of more than 30 or 40 Mbytes. With error rates of 10^{10} or better, the user can expect only a single error in 200 $10\frac{1}{2}$-inch reels of tape. With fully automatic loading, reels of tape can be interchanged quickly and easily, offering excellent I/O capability.

Quarter-Inch Cartridge Tape

When it comes to ease of handling and loading, quarter-inch cartridge-tape systems are unsurpassed. Operated as easily as a stereo or video-tape system, few memory devices so closely resemble a common consumer item (Figure 6.20). The tape is environmentally protected, compact, easily stored and transported, and can be used with no special training. Its 2- to 75-Mbyte capacity range is well matched to the Winchester disk and other midsized secondary systems, and

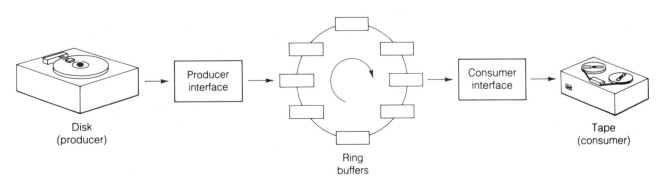

Figure 6.18 Double-buffering technique, which maintains data "streaming" to "consumer" at a steady rate.

Figure 6.19 Cipher half-inch streaming tape drive. *Courtesy Cipher Data Products.*

its transfer rate is approaching a healthy 1 Mb/s (allowing a typical Winchester to be backed up in minutes). It offers a reliability approaching that of the Winchester (10^{10} bits), and is available in conventional start/stop action or the new high-speed streaming action.

The Floppytape Cartridge

For those whose needs fall between secondary and backup—between the floppy and the tape drive—the industry offers the innovative *Floppytape Cartridge* (Figure 6.21). Designed to emulate the industry-standard $5\frac{1}{4}$-inch floppy disk system, the Floppytape offers a hefty 32 megabytes of capacity with a transfer rate of 500 kbits/sec. Of course, its use would be restricted to those applications that do not require the high speed, semirandom access nature of floppy disks.

Disk-Drive Controllers

To ease the task of interfacing any array of secondary/backup systems with the CPU, the *universal disk-drive controller* is the answer. The SA1400 disk-drive controller from Shugart Corporation (Figure 6.22) is a typical system, performing control functions and data transfers between CPU and a mixture of up to four Winchester, floppy, and quarter-inch cartridge drives.

As intelligent peripheral devices flourish, the need for a more sophisticated interface grows. The goal is universal mutual compatibility between all peripheral devices, allowing full intermixing of disk drives, tapes, printers, and all other popular intelligent peripherals—regardless of manufacturer and without modification to system software or hardware.

Although such as ideal situation probably will never materialize (too many opposing viewpoints), when the dust settles any proposed ANSI (American National Standards

Figure 6.20 Quarter-inch cartridge-tape system. *Courtesy Data Electronics.*

Institute) standard will most certainly resemble one of the following:

- Shugart Associates System Interface (SASI)
- Small Computer System Interface (SCSI)
- Intelligent Standard Interface (ISI)
- Intelligent Peripheral Interface (IPI)

Audio-Cassette Recording

Audio-cassette recording has prospered because it excels in one vital area: cost. To attain storage at ultralow cost, nearly

Figure 6.21 The floppytape cartridge tape drive. *Courtesy Cipher Data Products.*

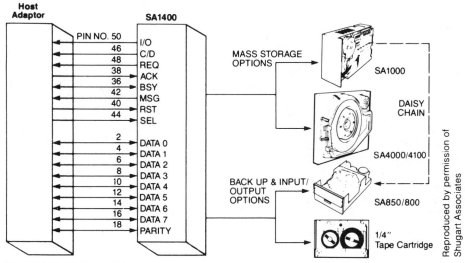

Figure 6.22 Universal disk-drive controller.

all other factors had to be sacrificed. Although a cassette can store up to 1 Mbyte of data, the data-transfer rate is only 150 bytes/s and the average access time can be several minutes. The tape is subject to wear from high frictional contact with the head, and the reliability is low (1 bit in 10^8). Furthermore, the operator must perform manually many of the control operations done automatically by other systems.

As with all magnetic-based systems, the digital information must be encoded into a form the recording medium can accept. Because low-cost recorders are plagued by limited frequency response (300 to 3000 Hz) and poor tape-speed control, any encoding scheme would have to account for these limitations. The most popular encoding technique used with cassette tapes is the hobbyist-oriented *Kansas City standard* (formulated by a committee that met in Kansas City in November 1975). Using frequency-shift-keying (FSK) techniques, the system converts each logic 1 bit to 8 cycles of 2400 Hz and each logic 0 bit to 4 cycles of 1200 Hz. Therefore, as shown in Figure 6.23, a Kansas City storage

system consists of three components. The *modulator* converts the digital stream of highs and lows (ones and zeros) to 2400 and 1200 Hz tones—which are recorded by the cassette deck. When the data are to be read back from the tape decks, the tones are converted back into high and low voltages *(demodulated)*.

Video-Cassette Recording

Accompanying the growing popularity of commercial videotape recorders (VTRs) are techniques for storing digital data on video cassettes. An inexpensive system is shown in Figure 6.24. Called the *Corvus mirror,* it interfaces between the Winchester disk and VTR and converts digital signals to video signals, suitable for recording directly onto a commercially available video recorder. It has a capacity of 100 million bytes and, using CRC techniques, an estimated non-recoverable error rate of one error per 15,000 hours. Data transfers at approximately 1.1 Mbauds, allowing the con-

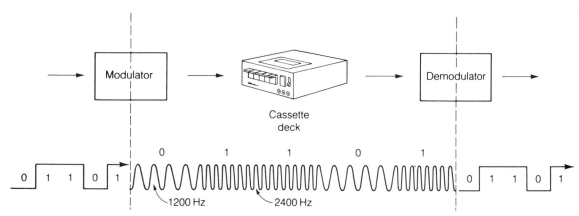

Figure 6.23 Kansas City Standard cassette storage.

Figure 6.24 The Corvus mirror, a low-cost, large-capacity, videotape backup for Winchester disk systems.

Figure 6.25 A one gigabyte (Gbyte) read-only optical storage system compared to an 8-inch floppy. *Courtesy Shugart Corporation.*

tents of an entire 10-Mbyte hard disk to be dumped to the VTR in 10 minutes.

Optical Storage

Since low cost per bit, high storage capacity, and I/O capability are the prime attributes of backup memory, optical storage systems should soon be prominent features on the secondary and backup storage "landscape."

The simplest optical (beam-addressed) memory device employs a laser beam to burn holes (1 micrometer in diameter) in the coating of a disk. A hole burned may be equivalent to a logic 1, and a hole not burned may be equivalent to a logic 0. During readout, another laser beam (of lower power) is positioned over the proper track of the disk, and it determines the logic value by reflected laser light—that is, if a hole is present, the light is transmitted; if not, the light is reflected.

Shugart Corporation's *Optimem 1000* optical disk drive (Figure 6.25) uses such laser technology to store 1,000 megabytes (1 Gbyte) of read-only information on a 12-inch disk. Its attractive cost-per-bit price tag and its ability to store large amounts of data at high density make the optical disk ideal for archival storage.

The problem with these early optical disk systems is that they are a read-only technology; the data, once written, cannot be changed. However, advances in magneto-optic materials will eventually produce the *erasable* optical disk. The basic theory is simple enough: Using a focused laser beam, heat a tiny portion of a magnetic alloy to its Curie temperature (the point at which the Ferromagnetic properties of the material disappear and it becomes most susceptible to magnetic change). A weak external field can then reverse the direction of the magnetic domains. When the laser beam is removed and the material cools, the domains are locked in place. Reading takes place when a polarized beam of laser light is bounced off the medium, and the logic state is determined by the degree of rotation of the plane of polarization.

Another read/write optical technology, which totally eliminates the magnetic medium, relys on reversible color changes. Using a special silver-zinc alloy, a laser beam changes its crystalline structure and hence its color (reflective) properties. Simplicity, higher access speed, and lower error rates will be the major benefits of this all-optical storage technology.

With the optical disk able to store a gigabyte of data on one side of a platter 30 cm in diameter, access data in under 100 ms, and transfer data at 500 kbytes/s, the Winchester disk is clearly an endangered species of secondary memory.

Secondary/Backup Hybrid Systems

When we combine the precision and capacity of the Winchester disk with the convenience and low cost of the cartridge backup, we create the fixed-disk/removable-cartridge memory system. It provides both secondary and backup capabilities in a single package.

A typical system may employ both fixed and removable Winchester disks in the same system. The removable cartridge is inserted above the fixed disks and engages with the drive-motor spindle and head-actuator assembly. When looking at this option, the user must weigh the relatively higher cost of the cartridges (compared to floppy and tape) against the precision, speed, and convenience of Winchester technology.

Another option (dubbed the "Flinchester" storage system) combines an 8-inch Winchester with a double-sided floppy-disk system. Also available in the area of hybrid secondary/backup systems is an 8-inch Winchester disk drive with an integrated cartridge-tape backup (Figure 6.26). We can expect the number of hybrid offerings to greatly increase in the years ahead.

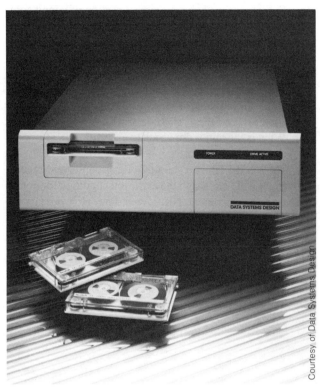

Figure 6.26 Hybrid Winchester/tape storage system.

SELECTING THE RIGHT SECONDARY/ BACKUP COMBINATION

Although the concept of backup is hardly a new idea, the spread of Winchester storage—the little giant of the secondary world—has reopened the entire question: What secondary/backup combination will best fit my needs? It is not an easy question to answer. The following list includes just a few of the considerations leading to the correct secondary/ backup choice:

- Do I need backup at all when using Winchester technology with its spectacular 1×10^{11} data-reliability specification?

- Must my entire database be backed up each day? Would it be efficient for me to back up an 80-Mbyte Winchester with a 1-Mbyte floppy, or should I choose the higher-capacity streaming-tape drives?

- Do I need I/O capability?

- How much access time do I need? For transitional (frequent) backup, the lower access times of the floppy are attractive. For daily backup, the lower-cost magnetic- or video-tape approach may be best.

- Who is going to use my system? Should I go for the convenience and ease of the quarter-inch cartridge?

- Can I easily integrate a backup device into my existing system? From the standpoint of file management and interfacing, the floppy is practically a twin of the Winchester. Is there a disk-drive controller to meet my needs?

- Are tape systems better for archival storage?

- Will I be transporting data (through the mail, for example)? If so, cartridge and floppy are excellent transportable mediums.

- Will the new removable hard-disk systems solve all my secondary/backup problems?

- How much can I afford to spend?

- How available are the various options?

- Should I opt for the newer video or optical backup techniques, even though they are not yet in widespread use?

Clearly, those shopping for the right secondary/backup combination should carefully consider their overall needs and not be persuaded solely on the basis of one or two outstanding features of each system.

INTELLIGENT-MACHINE UPDATE

With access to secondary and backup memory systems, our intelligent machine now has a vast data library at its disposal. No longer is it restricted to a small primary memory book of 256 pages. Now, with Winchester storage and archival backup, it has quick and easy access to the entire collected works of its software library. Endowed with ports to the outside world, and with a memory system of great speed, capacity, and flexibility, it is now ready for the final step— its passage into the second industrial revolution, the era of the true intelligent machine.

QUESTIONS AND PROBLEMS

1. Is secondary-memory access *random* or *sequential?* Are the data stored in a *parallel* or *serial* manner?

2. How is digital information stored in a thin-film magnetic system?

3. As the read/write head scans over a magnetic pattern, exactly when are voltage pulses produced?

4. Using modified frequency modulation, show how the hexadecimal word C2 is stored in a magnetic pattern.

5. In a formatted storage medium, what is the purpose of each of the following: marks, gaps, addresses, and error-detection bytes?

6. Which rotates faster, a floppy disk or a Winchester disk?

7. Which stores information at a greater density, a floppy disk or a Winchester disk?

8. What is the difference between a soft-sectored and a hard-sectored format?

9. Why is the access time of secondary memory slower than that of primary memory?

10. Name three functions of a floppy-disk controller.

11. When in operation, what is the major difference between floppy and Winchester heads?

12. What is a micro-Winchester?

13. What is a magnetic bubble?

14. How are magnetic bubbles propagated through a medium?

15. Why do memory systems often contain backup memory?

16. What is streaming-tape technology?

17. Of the three types of memory—primary, secondary, and backup—which stores information at the lowest cost per bit?

18. Name two advantages (a) of floppy-disk backup over tape backup; (b) of tape backup over floppy backup.

19. Generate a data polynomial for the data word 1101101.

20. Sometimes we can remember a section of a long composition only by going back to the beginning and leading up to the desired section. Does this mean our memories also exhibit (besides random-access properties) properties of serial or sequential access—similar to secondary-memory systems? Discuss.

21. Why does *vertical recording* increase storage density? (See Figure 6.2c.)

22. What is the major drawback to early all-optical storage systems?

23. How is the latest technology for group-coded recording (GCR) similar to the earliest technology for nonreturn-to-zero current (NRZI) recording? How does group-coded recording (GCR) eliminate the clock pulses, yet still maintain synchronization?

24. What happens to a magnetic material at its Curie temperature?

chapter 7

The Central Processing Unit: Introduction to Processing Action

For all its input/output and memory powers, our intelligent machine is only a puppet, with the outside world pulling on its bus-system strings—for as yet it can do nothing on its own. In this chapter all that will change, for we will add the final architectural block, the computer's *central processing unit* (CPU)—its central nervous system—the device that will control, sequence, and coordinate all activities. In our system, the central processing unit is the 8080/8085 microprocessor, consisting of the control unit (CU) and the arithmetic/logic unit (ALU) integrated within its 40-pin package (see Figure 7.1).

Since the CPU is by far the most complex module we will add to the system, this chapter will introduce only the most basic aspects of CPU architecture and processing action, leaving the many refinements to be added throughout the remainder of the book.

Based on an analogy using understandable, easy-to-read material, this brief chapter is designed to bring computer action alive and to pave the way into the complex world of computer architecture and processing action that lies ahead.

A COMPUTER ANALOGY

"All perception of truth is the detection of an analogy" (Thoreau, 1851). To truly understand a complex subject is to see an analogy within it. In this chapter we will bring out an everyday analogy that lies embedded in computer architecture and processing action. The analogy will provide a framework on which to build a complete, functioning microcomputer system.

To analogize a computer is to find something that is like a computer—something familiar to all of us, and something that can be described in familiar terms. And here it is: *an army base is like a computer.* The analogy is not at all far-fetched when you realize that the fundamental principle of computer action—a computer works by processing a sequential list of instructions—is also true of an army base. To perform any task on an army base is to process a sequential list of instructions. A typical process that takes place many times each day, and certainly involves a sequential list of instruc-

tions, is the task of transporting supplies from one location to another:

> Load supplies
> Add fuel
> Move truck

Load, add, and *move,* all verbs belonging to the 8080/8085 instruction set, will be studied in detail in Part III when the emphasis shifts to software.

The task before us is to build an army base from scratch—from the ground up—and to examine carefully its architecture, for it should look a great deal like the architecture of a microcomputer. We then will go through the process of transporting the supplies, watching carefully the steps that take place, for they should closely resemble basic processing action.

Ten Bright Ideas

The commanding officer assigned the responsibility of designing and operating the army base gets a series of ten bright ideas. After these ten bright ideas are implemented, the base will be constructed, and it will carry out the task at hand. As an added bonus, it will run itself with the greatest of efficiency, for therein will be distilled the essence of 150 years of computer technology.

Bright idea #1 Delegate authority.

The commanding officer cannot personally issue all the commands required to run an army base—that is obvious. So, to perform the task of transporting the supplies, he summons to the base three sergeants, each a specialist at issuing one particular command. Each sergeant, therefore, represents one *instruction:*

> Sergeant 1—Load supplies
> Sergeant 2—Add fuel
> Sergeant 3—Move truck

These three sergeants, not the commanding officer, will ultimately issue the three sequential commands for carrying

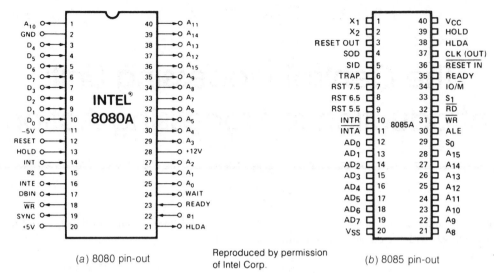

(a) 8080 pin-out

Reproduced by permission of Intel Corp.

(b) 8085 pin-out

Figure 7.1 8080/8085 comparison.

out the task. The three sergeants will live in a special housing area. Within a computer system this special housing area is the *stored program* in ROM (or RAM).

As noted in Chapter 1, each instruction consists of two parts. The verb part (load, add, move) we call the *operation code,* and the object part (supplies, fuel, truck) we call the *operand*.

Bright idea #2 House the sergeants in the same sequential order in which they will be giving their instructions.

If the sergeants live next to each other, in the same order in which they issue their commands, the sequencing process is greatly simplified.

Bright idea #3 Assign each housing unit a sequential house number.

Each sergeant can now be identified not by *who* he is, but by *where* he is (his address). That is, the commanding officer need no longer remember the contents of each house—only the addresses.

By assigning an address to each memory location, computers also can identify instructions by "pointing to them" with an address. (The results of the first three bright ideas are summarized in Figure 7.2.)

Bright idea #4 To sequence through the task, start at the lowest-numbered house address and count upward.

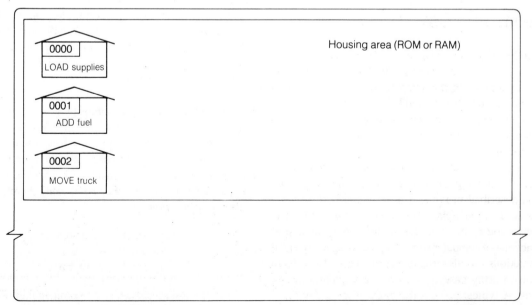

Figure 7.2 Army-base/computer analogy.

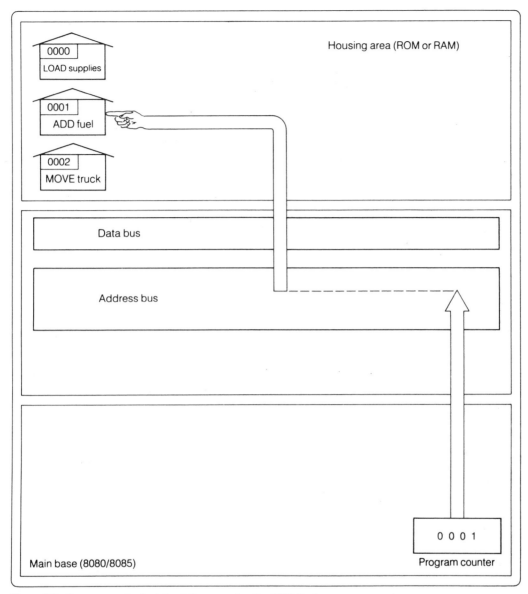

Figure 7.3 Program counter "pointing to" program location 0001 (hex).

This bright idea leads to a genuine revelation, for _we can process through a list of instructions by simply counting!_ And what are we counting? _Addresses_—an increasing sequence of housing unit addresses. It follows that the central authority for the entire army base—the headquarters of the whole operation—is a counter, not very different from the odometer in your car.

In a computer, this central authority, called the _program counter_ (PC), is a 16-bit counter inside the 8080/8085 microprocessor chip (Figure 7.3). The program counter holds the memory address of the instruction currently being processed. (Technically speaking, as we will see in future chapters, the present memory address in the program counter is latched into an internal bus-interfacing register early in each instruction-fetch operation, thereby freeing the pro-

gram counter to look ahead to the next instruction byte to be fetched.)

Think of the program counter as an incrementing _memory pointer,_ tying into the address bus and locating each instruction in sequential order. Note the common pathways (buses) interconnecting all sections of the base.

Bright idea #5 Separate the object of each instruction from the verb and place them into succeeding memory locations.

This action greatly increases efficiency since one sergeant can now direct the activities of many different objects. And, in computers, one operation code can direct the activities of many different operands.

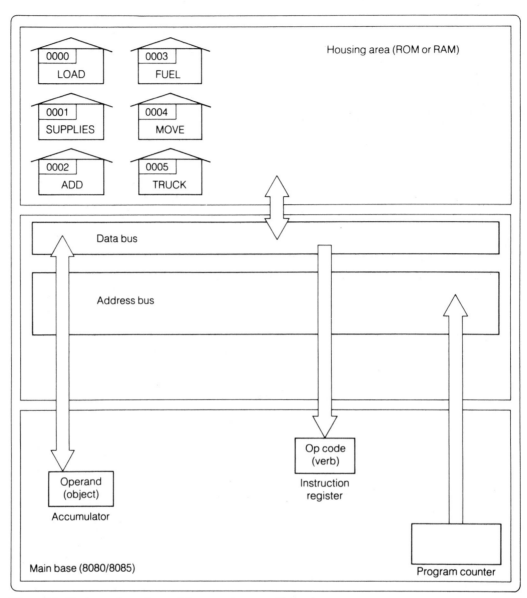

Figure 7.4 The instruction register and the accumulator are added to the system.

Bright idea # 6 To carry out an instruction, both the sergeant who issues the command and the object to be processed are brought into the main base. (The housing area is used only for storage.)

In computer language, bringing the operation code and the operand into the microprocessor chip is called a *fetch* operation. Of course, each fetch operation is a data transfer and must obey the *WHERE/WHEN* data-transfer process.

When fetched into the 8080/8085, the op code is sent to a new register, the special purpose *instruction register* that only holds op codes (see Figure 7.4). The operand goes to yet another new register, the *accumulator*—a register that only holds data and is one of the busiest registers within the microprocessor chip.

Bright idea #7 Place an instruction decoder next to the instruction register.

We already know how necessary it is to decipher the commands of an army sergeant. It is just as important to decipher (decode) each operation code fetched to the instruction register. Since each operation code is an 8-bit word, the instruction decoder will be a 1-of-256 decoder.

Bright idea #8 Add timing and control operations to the base to sequence the fetch and execution of each instruction.

Imagine the timing and control block to be a room full of telephone operators who can communicate instantly with every part of the base. To communicate with external components outside the main base (microprocessor chip), they

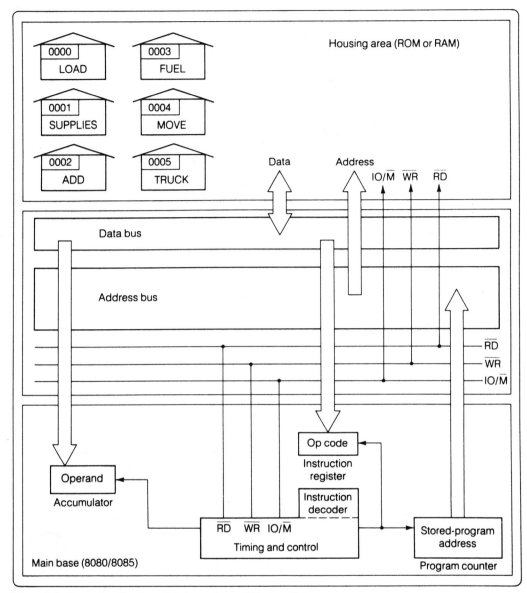

Figure 7.5   Instruction decoder and timing and control blocks added.

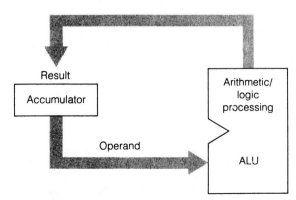

Figure 7.6   Accumulator/ALU processing loop.

send data, address, and control signals to the system bus (Figure 7.5).

Bright idea #9   Include a set of microprograms within the 8080/8085 main base to carry out the detailed processing of each instruction.

Remember the prime rule of computer action: *a computer works by processing a sequential list of instructions*. It follows that the processing of *each instruction* also requires a sequential list of *subinstructions*. These subinstructions, known as *microprograms* (or *microcode*), are permanently stored within the microprocessor chip in a special on-chip array of ROM known as *control storage*. (The sequential list of main instructions pulled from external memory is often

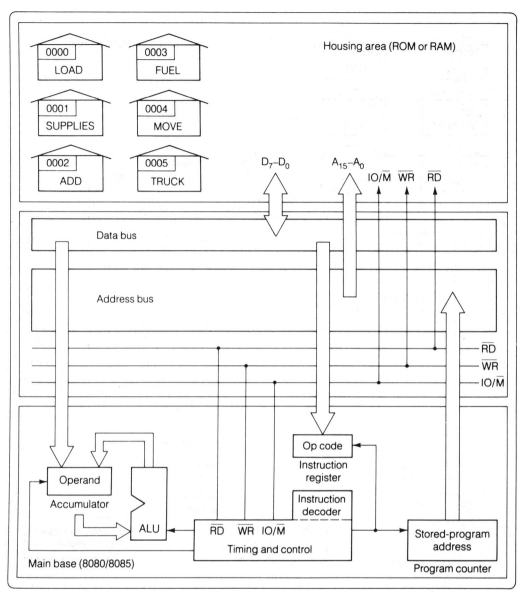

Figure 7.7 Final system, ready to carry out task.

called the *macroprogram.*) As soon as a main instruction is fetched, decoded, and identified, it triggers the sequential processing of the proper microprogram. (A built-in set of microprograms is really nothing new. Purchase a kitten at the pet shop and you will get a whole set of built-in microprograms—only they are called *instincts.*)

Bright idea #10 Create a place where instruction execution takes place. ALU!

Within the army base, this is where the sergeant's command is carried out (the verb acts on the object). Within the 8080/8085 microprocessor, this block is known as the *arithmetic/logic unit,* or simply ALU. During instruction exe-

cution, the operand moves from the accumulator to the ALU, where it is acted on by the operation code. As diagrammed in Figure 7.6, the result of the ALU action goes back to the accumulator—revealing why this register is called an accumulator: it accumulates the results of processing many instructions.

The Final System

All ten bright ideas have now been implemented, and Figure 7.7 shows the final system. Like all great innovations, the hardware design is ingenious, yet profoundly simple.

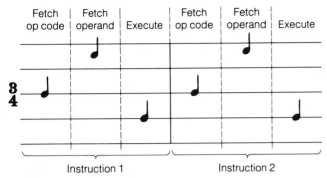

Figure 7.8 Ballad of computer processing—fetch op code, fetch operand, execute.

PROCESSING ACTION

Architecture in place, the commanding officer now initiates the task of transporting the supplies. The first step (shown completed in Figure 7.7) is to program the system (place the instructions—or sergeants—in their ROM locations in the proper order). This step is just about the only work the commanding officer must do. But he has to do it right. Almost any mistake in programming will abort the entire process (which lies at the base of the well-known computer adage "garbage in/garbage out").

The commanding officer next sets the program counter to point to the starting location of the program. A where/when data-transfer operation is initiated by timing and control, and the operation code "load" is fetched to the instruction register and decoded. Under direction of the "load" microprogram, the program counter is incremented to point to the next memory location. The object "supplies" is fetched to the accumulator by way of another where/when data-transfer process.

When both op code and operand have been fetched, the microprogram commands the execution phase, sending the object "supplies" to the ALU "loading room." There the supplies are loaded onto the truck, and the result returned to the accumulator.

The execution of the second instruction begins with the PC increment and op-code fetch of the second instruction. There really is no need to review the last two instructions, however, for they are processed in precisely the same way as the first.

In fact, the whole computing process has a definite recurring beat to it, an almost musical rhythm: fetch op code, fetch operand, execute—over and over again (see Figure 7.8).

Of course, there are variations on musical beats, and there are also variations on the basic processing action presented in this chapter. But an analogy can go only so far. An army base is not a computer; it is just similar to a computer. Still, if you have a feeling for basic processing action and generally understand the flow of data between the major registers, you are ready to proceed.

It should not surprise you to find in future chapters that the 8080/8085 contains more internal registers than we have seen so far and that the basic processing action introduced in this chapter can be modified in a number of ways.

INTELLIGENT-MACHINE UPDATE

If we interpret life as the ability to intelligently respond to the environment without outside control, then in this chapter we have identified the architecture and processes of computer life. If the basic processes of computer life are so simple, it remains to be seen how computers (as well as people) can perform such complex tasks.

QUESTIONS AND PROBLEMS

1. What kind of information does the program counter hold?
2. When a computer carries out a task by counting, what exactly is it counting?
3. What information is held in the instruction register?
4. After an operation code has been fetched, what is the very next process that takes place?
5. What is a *micro*program and how does it differ from a *macro*program? How is a microprogram like an instinct?
6. What kind of information does the accumulator hold?
7. How do the accumulator and ALU interact during instruction processing?
8. What exactly takes place when a computer is programmed?

part II

Basic Processing Action:
The Metabolism of a Computer

While we go about our daily business—working, playing, living—we are scarcely aware of the underlying metabolic activities that continuously go on inside our bodies. We breathe, pump blood, and digest food with little attention to the complex processes involved, for they are governed by the ancient, primordial parts of our mind. A doctor, on the other hand, must care about our metabolic processes, for they mirror our health and well-being.

A computer also has a metabolism—underlying currents of activity, cyclic in nature, that permit the computer to perform its operations. Interested only in results, the computer operator is scarcely aware they exist. To the troubleshooter, though, these underlying cycles and rhythms are the computer's vital signs, revealing the cause of a malfunction in the system. To the designer, they are the fundamental beat with which all parts of the system must synchronize.

The two chapters of Part II, then, cover fundamental processing action, beginning with an introduction to programming. By studying the processing action of a real program, the computer's cycles and waveforms will also be real—with results that can be reproduced in the laboratory.

chapter 8

Introduction to Programming and Program Processing

What does it mean to be alive? What is that mysterious essence separating animate from inanimate objects? For human beings, this question is ageless. For a computer, it can be answered exactly: a computer is "living" when it is processing a sequential list of instructions.

In this chapter we will write a program in the computer's own binary language; we will teach the computer a task by placing a program into its memory; and we will run the program, following through the processing action step by step. Quite simply, in this chapter we will bring the computer to life!

WRITING A PROGRAM

The first step in writing a program is to select a task—something you want the computer to do. Since this will be our very first program, the task should be a simple one. One way to assure simplicity is to select a task that can be learned by a lower-order member of the animal kingdom—such as a mynah bird. A mynah has the often embarrassing ability to repeat—or mimic—the sounds it hears. Because the routine is so simple, the mimic process will be the first task we will teach our computer. When we place a hexadecimal word before its "eyes," it will mimic the word.

The Instruction Set

First, to write a mimic program—indeed, to write anything—we need a vocabulary, a list of instructions that the computer can understand. This list of instructions is known as its *instruction set.* The basic instruction sets for both the 8080 and the 8085 are nearly identical, consisting of the same 72 types of instructions. However, the 8085 instruction set includes two additional instruction types, for a total of 74. The 8080/8085 instruction set summary appears in Figure 8.1, while a complete instruction set description (reprinted from the *MCS80/85 User's Manual*) is given in Appendix I.

To write a mimic program we must select the proper instructions from this list of 72 (74) and then place them into the correct sequential order.

The Flowchart

Since a complex program can easily consist of thousands of instructions, we will borrow a practice from the field of writing to help us organize our thoughts. Most novelists summarize or outline the flow of their story before filling in the final details. In computer programming, such an outline is known as a *flowchart;* it is a sequential arrangement of blocks—each block representing a portion of the total program.

Although dozens of block categories are used, those shown in Figure 8.2 are the most common ones. The type of operation determines the shape of the block element.

Even though the flowchart is a widely used programming aid, many programmers—particularly those using a structured, high-level language (explained in Chapter 22)—prefer other techniques. However, flowcharts are a useful tool for the beginning machine-language programmer and will be used extensively in this text.

The flowchart for the simple mimic process is easy to develop, since only an input followed by an output operation is involved. As shown in Figure 8.3, the main body of the flowchart therefore involves only parallelograms—the flowchart symbol for I/O operations.

As we can see, the programmer is free to write inside each block any information that will make the program flow easier to understand. The plain everyday language of Figure 8.3a is perfectly acceptable. If you prefer, however, you might choose more technical terms (Figure 8.3b).

WRITING THE SIMPLE MIMIC PROGRAM

The task before us is to select the proper sequence of instructions for carrying out the requirements of each flowchart block. For convenience, as shown in Figure 8.1, the 72 (74) types of instructions have been arranged into five major groups:

1. Data-transfer group
2. Arithmetic group

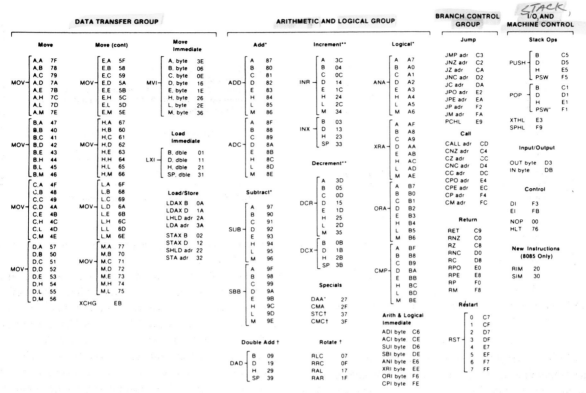

Figure 8.1 The 8080/8085 instruction set. *Reproduced by permission of Intel Corporation.*

3. Logic group
4. Branch group
5. Stack, I/O, machine-control group

Most of the instructions making up each of the five groups will be studied in detail in Part III when the emphasis shifts to software. For now, our task is to simply locate the single instruction required to carry out each block in the mimic program flowchart.

Block 1—The Start Block

Can you now carry out the requirements of block 1—the start block—by locating the correct instruction within the correct grouping? The answer is: no instruction at all is required to initiate (start) processor action. Simply free the READY and HOLD pins to the 8080/8085 and activity will

begin. To ensure that processor action will begin in a predictable manner, a RESET pulse is also sent to the CPU at start-up (the READY, HOLD, and RESET requests are described in Chapter 9).

Block 2—The Input Block

The second block does require an instruction. Let us make use of all available clues to locate the right instruction type among the 72 (74) choices. Since "listen" is an input operation and "ears" are input ports, perhaps you correctly selected the *IN-port* instruction from group 5. Let us take a close look at the IN-port instruction, as outlined in the 8080/8085 user's manual (see Figure 8.4).

Starting at the upper left, the IN-port designation is called a *mnemonic* and is a shorthand notation of what the instruction type accomplishes. Just to the right of the mnemonic is

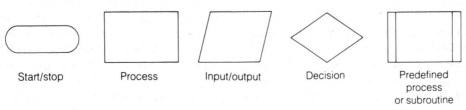

Start/stop   Process   Input/output   Decision   Predefined process or subroutine

Figure 8.2 Basic flowchart symbols.

Reproduced by permission of Intel Corp.

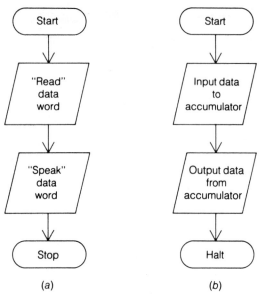

Figure 8.3   Mimic-process flowchart: *a)* ordinary language. *b)* more technical terms.

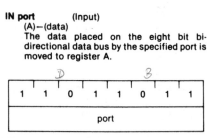

Figure 8.4   The IN-port instruction summary.

its full meaning (input). The most useful feature of mnemonics is that they are based on plain English and precisely follow the "verb/object" makeup of each instruction. The "verb" portion—the operation code—usually is easy to follow. "IN," for example, clearly defines a data-transfer operation, commanding the input of data to the accumulator. But what is the operand, *port?* The answer, once again, is found in the English language. Below the first instruction from our army-base analogy (load supplies), we will write the same command, but in a slightly different form:

Verb	*Object*
1. load	supplies
2. load	contents of warehouse 2040

Should warehouse 2040 contain the supplies, then both instructions produce the same result. In other words, the instruction does not have to tell *what* the data is—it can specify *where* it is. Therefore, as listed in the following summary, all instructions can be divided into two distinct categories:

- Category 1: The instruction contains the data (load *supplies*).
- Category 2: The instruction contains the address of the data (load *contents of warehouse 2040*).

Clearly, the word *port* falls into category 2, for it specifies a *location* where the data can be found.

More specifically, *port* represents an address—the address of a particular input port. This address must be supplied in binary form by the programmer. Since the port address is an 8-bit word, up to 256 input ports can be uniquely

addressed—more than enough for most small- to medium-scale applications.

To process this new type of instruction, another register—the WZ register pair—is included within the 8080/8085 microprocessor, as shown in Figure 8.5. (The WZ register pair is also known as the Memory Address Register—or MAR.) Unlike other register pairs to be introduced, the WZ register pair is inaccessible to the user (it is invisible).

Because the second category of instructions (those specifying the operand as an address) are more complex than the first category, an extra intermediate step is required during the processing action.

1st category	*2nd category*
1. fetch op code	1a. fetch op code
	1b. fetch operand to WZ
2. transfer data	2. transfer data

In the case of the IN-port instruction, this middle step is used to fetch the port address to the WZ register pair for temporary storage. This stored address is then used in the final step to select the proper input port for an input of data. Generally speaking, the WZ register pair (MAR) is used to address data during the execution phase; the program counter addresses instruction bytes during the instruction fetch phase.

As a final point of interest, when the port address (an 8-bit number) is fetched to the WZ register pair (a 16-bit register pair), it is copied into both the W and Z registers. When the WZ register contents are released onto the address bus during the input operation, the 8-bit port address will appear identically on both the upper and lower halves of the address bus. Although this is redundant, it is useful. All port-addressing lines can be divided between the upper and lower half of the address bus, thereby reducing address-bus loading.

Looking further into the instruction summary (Figure 8.4), we see that each instruction type is supplied with a plain English statement, spelling out exactly what the instruction will accomplish. For the IN-port instruction, it is: "The data placed on the 8-bit bidirectional data bus by the specified port is moved to register A."

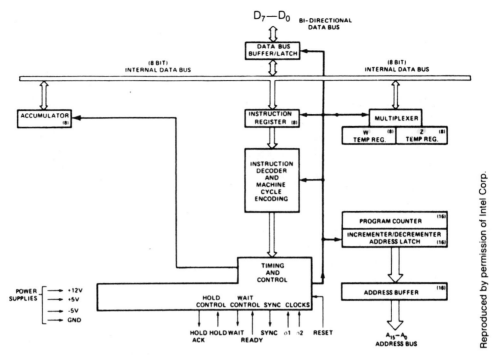

Figure 8.5   8080/8085 partial internal block diagram.

The symbolism below the IN-port mnemonic diagrams the instruction's purpose. The term on the right is the source and the term on the left is the destination. The data move in the direction of the arrow from source to destination. The parentheses are generally equivalent to the phrase "contents of." Therefore, this shorthand designation means: the *contents of* the specified port are moved to or become the *contents of* the accumulator.

The final part of the instruction summary is the actual binary instruction itself—the true language of the computer. The IN-port instruction is a two-byte instruction, with the first byte carrying the operation code ("verb"). This combination of ones and zeros is recognized by the computer as an input command. The second byte is the operand's address. It is the programmer's responsibility to fill in the second byte with the exact binary (or hex) address of the selected input port. *This binary address will, in turn, depend on how the port is tied into the address bus.*

Let's be specific and hardwire our input port at location 40H (the "H" indicates that 40 is a hexadecimal number). This means when 4040H appears on the address bus, the input port must be enabled (remember, 40H is repeated on both the high-order and low-order lines). As when addressing a memory chip, we can use either linear or decoded addressing techniques (or a combination of the two). Illustrating both techniques, Figure 8.6 shows how our input port is configured for address 40H operation. Using linear addressing we can uniquely specify (address) up to 8 input ports, while fully decoding the address lines allows us to

uniquely specify up to the maximum 256 input ports. (Note how address lines A_0 through A_7 are equivalent to lines A_8 through A_{15}.)

Placing 40H in the second byte of the IN-port instruction, the binary code for carrying out block 2 is now complete and can be placed beside the flowchart block (Figure 8.7). The binary and hexadecimal formats, of course, are for the computer. For the benefit of people, let us also keep the mnemonic notation.

Block 3—The OUT-Port Block

The third block basically commands the reverse operation. Its similarity to the second block will considerably simplify our job. If we agree that "to speak" is to output data, then clearly the instruction type below the IN-port instruction in the 8080/8085 user's manual will carry out the requirements of block 3 (see Figure 8.8a).

As with the IN-port instruction, it is the responsibility of the programmer to substitute the binary address of the output port for the word *port*. If we assume our output port is hardwired at address 20H, the output instruction takes on the form of Figure 8.8b.

Block 4—The Stop Block

Stop is really a command to the computer and is not part of the actual mimic process. The machine control group seems like a good place to look for a stop command.

Reproduced by permission of Intel Corp.

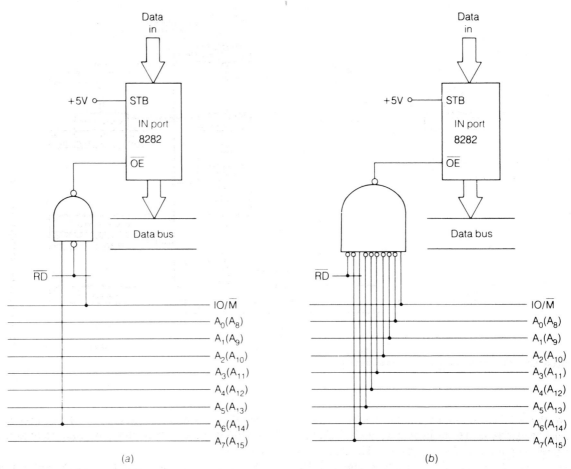

Figure 8.6 Addressing techniques for port 40H location (8085 bus): *a)* Linear. *b)* Decoded.

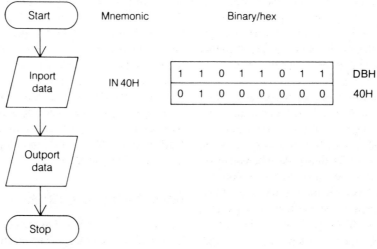

Figure 8.7 Block 2 completed.

Figure 8.8 Generating the block 3 instruction: *a)* The OUT-port instruction summary. *b)* OUT-port instruction for port 20H operation.

We quickly locate the *halt* instruction (Figure 8.9), which basically stops processor action. Unlike most instructions, the halt instruction does not require an operand. The same is true in English—the command "halt" usually stands alone.

The Complete Mimic Program

Adding the OUT-port and HLT instructions beside the proper flowchart blocks, our mimic program is complete (Figure 8.10).

In future chapters we will learn a number of shorthand techniques for writing programs and for translating them from English to binary (mnemonics to machine language).

TEACHING THE MIMIC TASK

The next step is to "teach" our computer to perform the mimic task. This is the easiest and quickest step of all, for we simply deposit the program into the computer's memory. Programming, as we know, is teaching. Programming is also learning; it just depends on your point of view. As we will see in later chapters, the "deposit" process usually is carried out by a special *monitor* program burned into ROM. To conform to the available RAM space of the SDK-85 single-

HLT   (Halt)

The processor is stopped. The registers and flags are unaffected. A second ALE is generated during the execution of HLT to strobe out the Halt cycle status information.

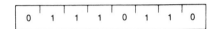

Figure 8.9 The halt instruction.

board computer, we will place the mimic program at page 20H.

Recall from our historical summary in Chapter 1 that the idea of programming, of placing the instructions as well as the data into memory—the *stored-program* concept—was one of the great forward leaps in computer technology, envisioned nearly 150 years ago by Babbage. When instructions are stored in the same form as data in the same memory, it is known as a Von Neumann or Princeton-class computer.

PERFORMING THE MIMIC TASK

Our computer has been taught the mimic process (programmed), and we are now ready to cross the threshold

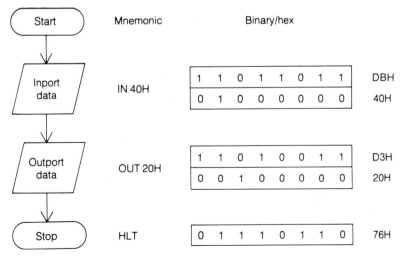

Figure 8.10 The complete mimic program.

between "living" and "nonliving" systems. When we place a data word before the computer's "eyes" and initiate processor action, it will "speak" the word. Not long ago such a process, performed by a mere machine, would have been regarded as sheer magic. (As science fiction author Arthur C. Clarke said, "Any sufficiently advanced technology is indistinguishable from magic.")

The Mimic Process

If life is fleeting for human beings, it is especially so for a computer, for the entire mimic process requires only 8 microseconds or so from start to finish. Let us see exactly what happens during those crucial 8 microseconds by taking an X-ray look inside our intelligent machine (Figure 8.11) and following the processing action step by step. (Remember, not all of the 8080/8085's internal structure is presented here—just those parts necessary to carry out the mimic task.)

Place an arbitrarily chosen data word—such as 77H—before the computer's "eyes," initiate processor action, and the following sequential operations will take place (continued reference to Figure 8.11 should be helpful):

- Step 1: The starting address of the program (2000H) is

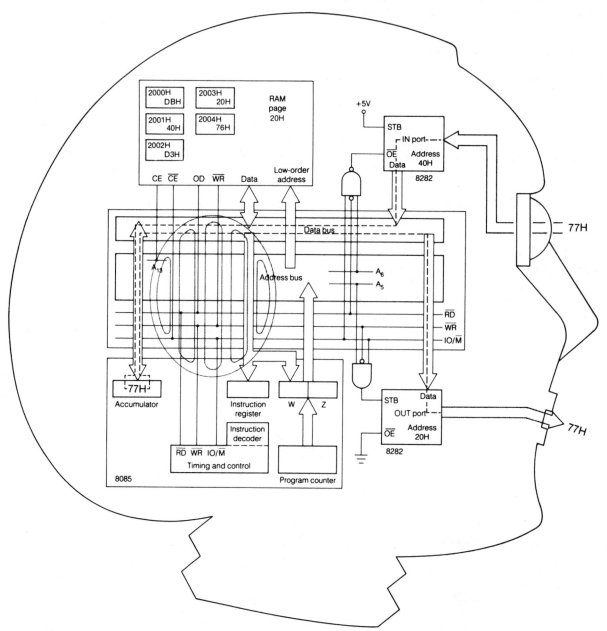

Figure 8.11 A mimic machine.

placed into the program counter (this is accomplished by the *monitor* program).

- Step 2: The program counter points to the first memory location in the program, and a where/when operation fetches the IN-port operation code (DBH) to the instruction register.

- Step 3: The IN-port op code is decoded and the proper microprogram selected.

- Step 4: The IN-port microprogram directs the program counter to increment to 2001H and another where/when data transfer fetches the port address (40H) to the WZ register pair via the data bus. The 8-bit port address is copied into both the W and Z registers. (The IN- and OUT-port instructions are the only category 2 instructions in the entire instruction set using an 8-bit address, and the only ones in which the WZ registers and high-level/low-level address lines are redundant.)

- Step 5: The third and final where/when data-transfer operation begins with the port address (4040H) in the WZ register pair pointing to the "eyes" of the computer, followed by the data word 77H IN-ported from the outside world to the accumulator.

- Step 6: The first instruction complete, timing and control increments the program counter to 2002H and fetches the OUT-port op code (D3H) to the instruction register.

- Step 7: Under direction of the decoded microprogram, the program counter is incremented to 2003H, and the address of the output port (20H) is fetched to the WZ register pair.

- Step 8: The port address in the WZ register pair (2020H) points to the "voice" of the computer, and the data in the accumulator (77H) are transferred to the addressed output port and latched in place.

- Step 9: The second instruction complete, the operation code for halt (76H) is fetched to the instruction register, decoded, and computer operation is stopped.

To exit the halt state and repeat the mimic process, we reset the microprocessor, which clears the program counter. (The process of initializing the program counter to 2000H must unavoidably remain vague at this time.)

SDK-85 Operation

For those who wish to test the MIMIC program of Figure 8.10 on the SDK-85 single-board computer (using existing ports 21H and 22H), modifications must be made to the beginning and ending of the program as shown in Figure 8.12 (see Appendix II for a complete explanation).

A PROBLEM WITH SYNTAX

Many times the meaning of a commonly used word conflicts with its historical definition, and an ambiguity arises. The word *operand* is a case in point. Historically, *operand* meant *the data operated upon by the op code*. However, with the advent of assembly-language programming (formally introduced in Chapter 13), *operand* has come to mean *the operand field of the instruction mnemonic*. The problem, as revealed by the IN-port instruction, is that the operand field of an instruction can be an address. For example, in the instruction IN 40H, what is the *operand?* Is it "40H," the input port's address, or is it the data to be input from the input port? Unfortunately, the answer is, it could be either; it depends on how the writer interprets the word *operand*. As is so often the case, the exact meaning of a word will depend on the context in which it is used.

However, we should be consistent, and we should be up-to-date. Since at the present time all programming (beyond the initial learning stage) is at least written at the assembly-language level (using mnemonics), we will adopt the more modern convention and define *operand* as *the operand field of the instruction mnemonic*. For example, in the instruction IN 40H, "40H" is the *operand*, while the information transferred from (or inported from) address 40H will be referred to as the *data* or the *value*.

INTELLIGENT-MACHINE UPDATE

In performing the mimic process, our computer has announced its existence to the world. In the remaining chapters it will develop beyond this infant state by expanding both its anatomy (hardware) and its vocabulary (software). As we will see, our intelligent machine has just begun to grow.

Address	Mnemonic		Hexadecimal
2000H	MVI	A,0EH	3EH,0EH
2002H	OUT	20H	D3H,20H
2004H	IN	21H	DBH,21H
2006H	OUT	22H	D3H,22H
2008H	RST	1	CFH

Figure 8.12   Modifying the MIMIC program for SDK-85 operation.

QUESTIONS AND PROBLEMS

1. What technique is used to give an overview of the program before the specific instructions are selected?
2. List the five major flowchart blocks and state the general process to which each corresponds.
3. List the five groups of 8080/8085 instructions.
4. Write the IN-port instruction (filling in the second byte) for each of the examples shown below:

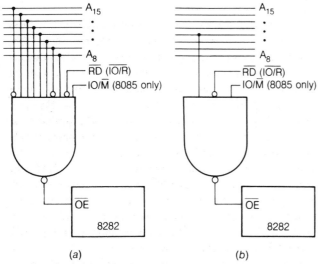

(a)   (b)

5. What is the purpose of the *mnemonic* form of each instruction?

6. When the second byte of the IN-port instruction is fetched, into what register is it placed?
7. Why does the IN-port instruction require three data transfers?
8. What aspect of computer operation corresponds to "teaching" or "learning"?
9. Why is our system restricted to 256 input and 256 output ports?
10. Could an input port and an output port use the same address? Explain.
11. Based on the linear addressing configuration of Figure 8.6a, how many input ports could be placed in the system?
12. List the steps involved in processing the OUT-port instruction.
13. Complete the following: When a port address is fetched, it goes to the _____ register pair via the _____ bus. When it is later used as a pointer, it leaves the _____ register pair via the _____ bus.
14. When wiring an input port for address 40H operation using linear addressing, why is address line A_6 equivalent to line A_{14}?
15. Referring to Figure 8.11, how does the linear tie-in to address line A_5 result in address 20H output-port operation?
16. If the instruction OUT 44H outports 0AH from the accumulator, what is the *operand* and what is the *data?*
17. Define the term *mnemonic* (consult a dictionary).

chapter 9

Timing and Multiplexing

Would a vague and general idea of human anatomy and bodily processes be enough to allow a doctor to diagnose and treat ailments? Would a vague and general idea of computer architecture and processing action be enough to allow a technician or engineer to diagnose and treat computer malfunctions?

The answer to both questions is no—a doctor and a technician must have a detailed knowledge of the systems they are working on. If we have any hope at all of doing design and troubleshooting work, we must increase our knowledge of 8080/8085 processing action.

There are two vital areas in which we are particularly deficient. One area can be called the computer's "metabolism"—its natural rhythms and timing cycles. The second area relates to interfacing, the microprocessor's link to the system bus. A careful look at the 8080 microprocessor (Figure 9.1a) reveals that the four control signals (I/OR, I/OW, MEM/R, and MEM/W) are not directly represented by any of the 40 pins. And on the 8085 (Figure 9.1b), what exactly is going on with pins 12 through 19? Are they used for

addresses or are they used for data? Or could they possibly be used for both?

Timing cycles and 8080/8085 bus interfacing, therefore, are the two major topics of this chapter.

THE SYSTEM CLOCK

A computer must have a "heartbeat," a precise clock pulse for generating all the necessary timing and sequencing signals required to run the entire system. A basic crystal-controlled oscillator will provide the necessary pulses. Beyond this, however, the 8080 and 8085 systems differ.

8080 Clock System

The 8080-system timing circuits have been placed in a separate 16-pin chip called the 8224 clock generator and driver. The 8224 timer chip has been assigned three major functions:

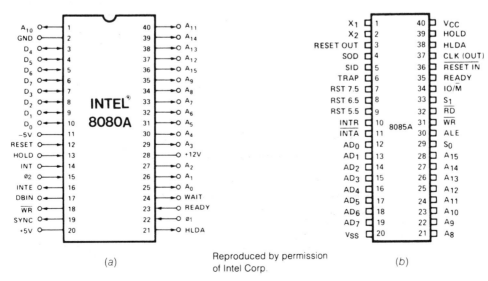

Reproduced by permission of Intel Corp.

Figure 9.1 8080 vs 8085: *a)* 8080 pin-out. *b)* 8085 pin-out.

- To provide the basic phase 1 and phase 2 timing signals required by the 8080 microprocessor
- To synchronize the RESET and $\overline{\text{WAIT}}$ requests
- To synchronize and provide the $\overline{\text{STSTB}}$ (status strobe) signal

(A full understanding of these signals should come with the completion of this chapter.)

A block diagram of the 8224 appears in Figure 9.2. Referring to the diagram, the phase 1 and phase 2 output signals are produced by the standard oscillator/counter/decoder combination. The phase 1 and phase 2 output waveforms, shown in idealized form below the block diagram, operate at $\frac{1}{9}$ the crystal frequency, which can vary between 3 and 20 MHz. A crystal frequency of 18.432 MHz is often recommended since it is easily divided down to the commonly used communication baud rates.

Also shown on the block diagram is the technique for synchronizing the sync, $\overline{\text{RESIN}}$, and RDYIN inputs to pro-

duce the $\overline{\text{STSTB}}$, RESET, and READY outputs, respectively. Other signals emanating from the 8224 include a direct buffered output from the crystal-controlled clock and a phase 2 TTL-compatible signal for external timing. Pin 13, labeled TANK, is provided for trimming overtone crystals.

8085 Clock System

In an 8085-based system, the 8224 clock functions have all been fully integrated within the 8085 microprocessor chip. The only external timing component required is the crystal. As illustrated in Figure 9.3, the crystal frequency passes through a toggle flip-flop to produce the phase 1 and phase 2 clock signals at half the crystal frequency. The phase 1 signal is made available on pin 37. The selected crystal frequency is often 6.144 MHz, for the same communications-related reason that 18.432 MHz is important to 8080-based systems. (The 8085 can also be driven at its X_1 and X_2 inputs by an LC- or RC-tuned circuit.)

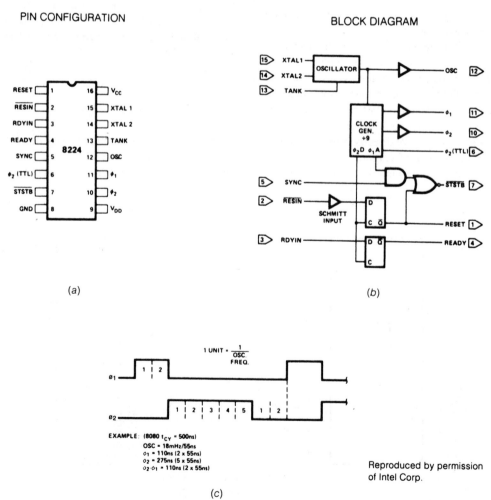

PIN CONFIGURATION

BLOCK DIAGRAM

(a)

(b)

(c)

Reproduced by permission of Intel Corp.

Figure 9.2   The 8224 timer: *a)* Pin-out. *b)* Internal block diagram. *c)* Waveforms.

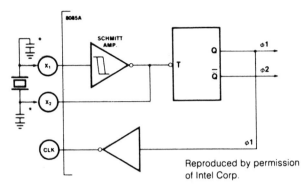

*EXTERNAL CAPACITORS REQUIRED ONLY FOR CRYSTAL FREQUENCIES ≤ 4 MHz.

Figure 9.3 8085 internal-clock logic.

8080/8085 TIMING CYCLES

Like its human counterpart, a computer is a creature of repetition. One instruction after the other is fetched and executed—just like the recurring theme of a melody. It follows that if we understand in detail the processing of one instruction, the others will be similar.

The longest processing cycle found in the 8080/8085 is the *instruction cycle,* which represents the time required to fetch and execute one complete instruction. Instruction-cycle times can vary widely, depending on the speed of the clock and the complexity of the instruction. A typical 8080/8085 instruction cycle requires approximately 3 microseconds, allowing an average of some 330,000 instructions to be processed every second.

An instruction cycle in turn is made up of 1 to 5 *machine cycles. A machine cycle is required every time a data byte is transferred between a peripheral and the 8080/8085 microprocessor.* Obviously, a machine cycle is closely associated with the where/when data-transfer operation (see Figure 9.4).

Let us work with a specific case and identify the machine cycles of the familiar OUT-port instruction. How many machine cycles are contained within the OUT port's instruc-

tion cycle? Remember, that is the same as asking: how many data transfers take place between 8080/8085 and external components? The answer is three. Can you identify them?

1. First is the operation-code fetch to the instruction register. Of course, all instructions require an op-code fetch, and therefore all instruction cycles must consist of at least one machine cycle.

2. Under direction of the OUT-port instruction's microprogram, the operand address is fetched to the WZ register pair—another data transfer, another machine cycle.

3. The execution portion of the OUT-port instruction is also a data transfer, requiring yet another machine cycle to carry out the transfer of data from accumulator to selected output port.

Therefore, the OUT-port instruction cycle consists of three machine cycles to carry out the three data transfers.

We are not quite done with our study of timing cycles, for the machine cycle itself can be further subdivided into three to five *states* (six for the 8085). We can expect no further subdivisions, *for a state is defined as one clock cycle,* and a clock cycle—determined by dividing the external crystal frequency—is the smallest unit of time possible. On an 8080 system (driven by an 18-MHz crystal), a state lasts for 0.5 microseconds; on an 8085 system (driven by a 6-MHz crystal), a state lasts for $\frac{1}{3}$ of a microsecond.

Basically, the first three states, known as T_1, T_2, and T_3, are involved in the actual where/when data-transfer process. The final three states, if present at all, are reserved for internal operations within the 8080/8085 chip. If no internal operations are required, the last three states will not be present.

The state sequence for the OUT-port instruction is shown in Figure 9.5. Note that the operation-code fetch is the only machine cycle requiring four states. This is because state T_4 is reserved for internal operation-code decoding. The final two machine cycles are pure data transfers and do not require more than the first three states. (The machine-cycle/state

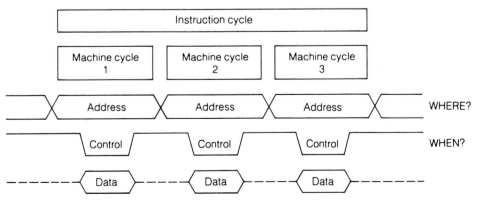

Figure 9.4 Typical instruction-cycle/machine-cycle timing, showing where/when data-transfer processes.

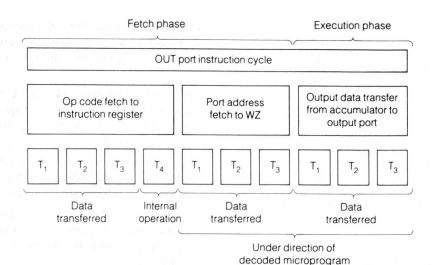

Figure 9.5 OUT-port instruction-cycle/maching-cycle/state timing.

breakdown for all 72 instruction types appears in Appendix III.) Also note in Figure 9.5 that all operations following the first machine cycle—the op-code fetch—are under direction of the decoded microprogram.

THE WAIT AND HOLD STATES

The WAIT Request and READY

Primary memory has one major duty: to keep pace with the CPU. In other words, it should be quick enough to react within the timing requirements of the processor's read and write operations. However, that is not always possible. As a case in point, we saw in Chapter 5 that the 2186A integrated RAM (iRAM) must occasionally suspend a read or write operation in order to attend to a critical refresh cycle.

A more common problem is encountered when selecting primary memory RAM or ROM chips to populate a large memory board. For example, according to the memory-read specifications for a high-speed 8085, approximately 250 nsec after a RAM address has been sent out by the CPU, valid data must appear at the data input lines (see Figure 9.6). Since one version of the 2114A RAM has a maximum access time of 250 nsec, it looks like a perfect match. Unfortunately, it is not. The problem is that the address signal may be required to pass through several decoders on its way to the RAM chip. If we are using 8205 decoders, as we did in Chapter 5, each decoder introduces approximately 20-nsec delay into the address signal. When valid data finally arrive at the data input lines of the CPU, they can be up to 40 nsec too late. One answer is to simply select a faster version of the 2114A. However, you must be willing to absorb the added cost of the faster RAM.

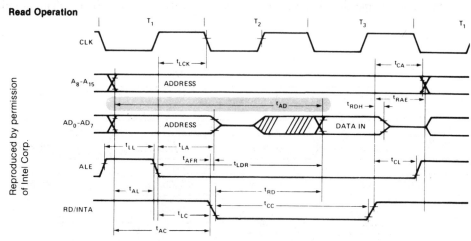

Figure 9.6 *Address valid to valid data in* (t_{AD}) *maximum allowed time period for 8085 CPU.*

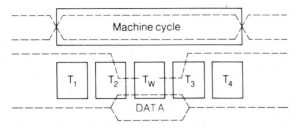

Figure 9.7 Control time "stretching" by adding one or more Tw states.

As a solution to these problems, the 8080/8085 system includes the WAIT request. Basically, the WAIT request—if honored—stretches the time the control line is active by inserting one or more special WAIT states (T_W) between states T2 and T3 (see Figure 9.7). *During these special WAIT states, all address, data, and control lines remain active.*

Referring to Figure 9.8*a*, the WAIT request is initiated in a similar way for both 8080 and 8085 systems—by placing a low on the READY input (so that the processor is NOT READY). In 8080 systems, however, the WAIT request must first be passed through the 8224, where it is synchronized with the system clock. And only on the 8080 is the WAIT request acknowledged by a high on the WAIT output pin.

As long as READY remains low, WAIT states will be continuously added between states T_2 and T_3. When READY

goes high, the processor will exit the WAIT state and continue on to state T_3. When interfacing slow memories to an 8085 system, Figure 9.8*b* shows how to add a single WAIT state to each 8085 machine cycle.

The DMA Request

In the study of computers, *throughput* is the key indicator of computer performance. Throughput is the amount of material processed by a computer system in a given period.

Consider a block transfer of data from one memory area to another. To cycle the data through the accumulator by computer action is relatively slow (instructions must be fetched and address pointers incremented). If the data could be transferred directly between the two storage areas, with the microprocessor totally bypassed, the entire transfer process could be significantly accelerated. To accomplish this direct transfer of data, the 8080/8085 microprocessor must relinquish its control over the bus system—a process known as *direct memory access* (DMA).

Basically, the DMA (HOLD) request—if honored—stops processor action after the current machine cycle is completed and floats its address, data, and control lines. An external DMA controller then takes over control of the system bus and transfers information directly between source and destination at a high rate of speed. When the DMA

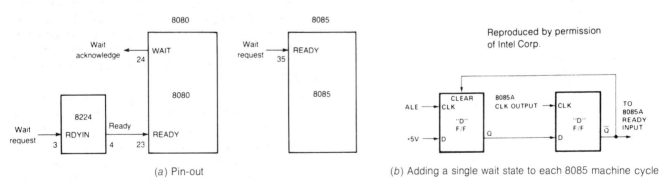

Figure 9.8 The WAIT state: *a)* 8080/8085 WAIT request pin-out. *b)* Adding a single wait state to each 8085 machine cycle.

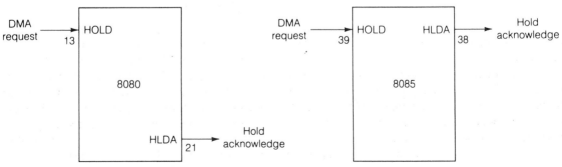

Figure 9.9 8080/8085 DMA request pin-out.

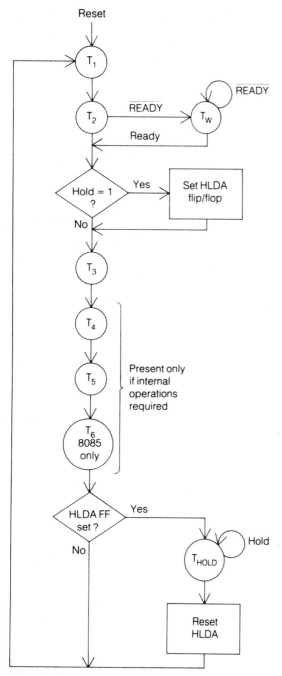

Figure 9.10 8080/8085 WAIT/HOLD-state transition diagram.

State-Transition Diagram

Figure 9.10 flowcharts a simplified state-transition diagram, valid for both the 8080 and 8085 processors. Each pass through the transition diagram completes one machine cycle.

Both processors check for a WAIT request by sampling the READY input pin during state T_2 of each machine cycle. If READY is low, one or more T_w states are inserted between states T_2 and T_3. When READY is raised high, the processor returns from the T_w state. It next checks the HOLD input pin for the active-high condition. If a DMA request is not pending, it moves on to state T_3.

If the DMA condition has been requested, it sets an internal HOLD flip-flop before proceeding on to state T_3. States T_3, T_4, T_5, and T_6 are completed as required. (Remember, states T_4, T_5, and T_6 are present only if internal operations are required.) At the end of the final state, the processor checks the state of the HOLD flip-flop. If set, the processor enters the HOLD mode, floating the bus lines and stopping computer action. When released from the HOLD mode (or the last T state has been completed), action returns to the beginning of the state-transition diagram to sequence through the next machine cycle.

Cycle Stealing

Suppose we could perform DMA-type direct data transfers between memory units while the 8080/8085 continued normal operation at full speed. Although such a feat seems impossible, it really isn't. The process is called *cycle stealing,* and anyone can do it. Simply transfer information on the bus lines during states T_4, T_5, and T_6, when the processors are involved in internal operations and the bus lines are not required.

In the worst case, every instruction cycle will have at least one internal operation state (the T_4 state of the op-code fetch, used for internal op-code decoding). Even with a relatively fast clock, 300 nsec are available every instruction cycle. Since 250,000 instructions can be processed every second, a cycle-stealing data-transfer rate of 100,000 bytes/sec is very realistic.

MULTIPLEXING

Time multiplexing, as we saw in Chapter 2, is a powerful technique for simplifying the hardware of a computer system. Modern calculators make effective use of multiplexing concepts to increase the number of functions performed, without an increase in the number of pushbuttons. Microprocessors have adopted this time-sharing (multiplexing) concept to increase the number of functions that can take place within the limited 40-pin format.

transfer of data is complete, the processor regains control of the bus system.

All aspects of the DMA request are the same on the 8080 and 8085 systems. As shown in Figure 9.9, the DMA request is initiated by placing a high on the HOLD input. The DMA request is synchronized internally and can be requested at any time. Both processors acknowledge the DMA state by placing a high on the HLDA (hold acknowledge) output pin.

For both the 8080 and 8085 microprocessors, it is the data pins that are time-multiplexed. The reason is simple: according to the basic data-transfer waveforms studied earlier, the data bus appears to be unused during the early portion of every machine cycle (see Figure 9.4). Although both the 8080 and 8085 processors multiplex the data lines, the exact application is quite different.

8080 Systems

In an 8080 system, *status* information shares the data lines (see Figure 9.11a) and flows from the eight data pins during states T_1 and T_2. The 8-bit status word identifies the type of machine cycle under way. Figure 9.11b reveals the ten categories of machine cycles found on an 8080-based system.

A status word is used during each machine cycle to generate the control signals that will go active later in the same machine cycle. Consequently, the status signals must be latched in place. (Remember, when a control line goes active, these same eight pins—now outputting status information—will be used to carry true data.) Referring to Figure 9.12, here is how it is done: During states T_1 and T_2, status infor-

mation flows from the data-output pins and is latched into the 8228 system controller chip by the STSTB signal. This latched status information is changed into true control information by the actions of the 8080 control outputs DBIN (Data Bus-IN) and $\overline{WR}$ (write). DBIN controls the input process, and $\overline{WR}$ controls the output process. (Figure 9.12 is an equivalent circuit and is not necessarily the precise logic used with the 8228 chip.) Figure 9.13 shows the complete 8080-based CPU module; Figure 9.14 depicts a complete 8080-based microcomputer system.

The combined effects of timing cycles and multiplexing are demonstrated in the complete set of waveforms for the familiar OUT-port instruction cycle of Figure 9.15. To review the entire sequencing/ multiplexing process, begin at the left side of the OUT-port waveforms and follow all signals through the diagrams of Figures 9.13, 9.14, and 9.15 (also refer to Appendix III).

8085 Systems

In an 8085 system, address rather than status information shares the data lines and flows from the eight data pins

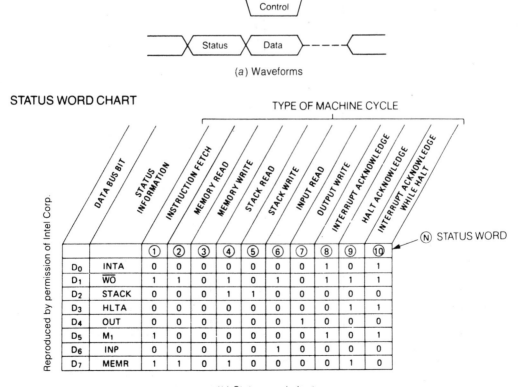

(a) Waveforms

STATUS WORD CHART

TYPE OF MACHINE CYCLE

Data Bus Bit	Status Information	① Instruction Fetch	② Memory Read	③ Memory Write	④ Stack Read	⑤ Stack Write	⑥ Input Read	⑦ Output Write	⑧ Interrupt Acknowledge	⑨ Halt Acknowledge	⑩ Interrupt Acknowledge While Halt
D_0	INTA	0	0	0	0	0	0	0	1	0	1
D_1	$\overline{WO}$	1	1	0	1	0	1	0	1	1	1
D_2	STACK	0	0	0	1	1	0	0	0	0	0
D_3	HLTA	0	0	0	0	0	0	0	0	1	1
D_4	OUT	0	0	0	0	0	0	1	0	0	0
D_5	M_1	1	0	0	0	0	0	0	1	0	1
D_6	INP	0	0	0	0	0	1	0	0	0	0
D_7	MEMR	1	1	0	1	0	0	0	0	1	0

Ⓝ STATUS WORD

Reproduced by permission of Intel Corp.

(b) Status-word chart

Figure 9.11 The 8080 status word.

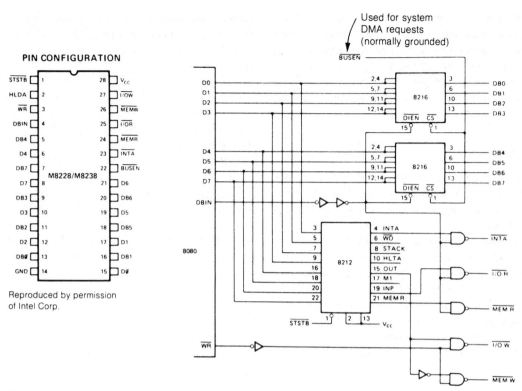

Figure 9.12 8228 pin-out and equivalent circuit.

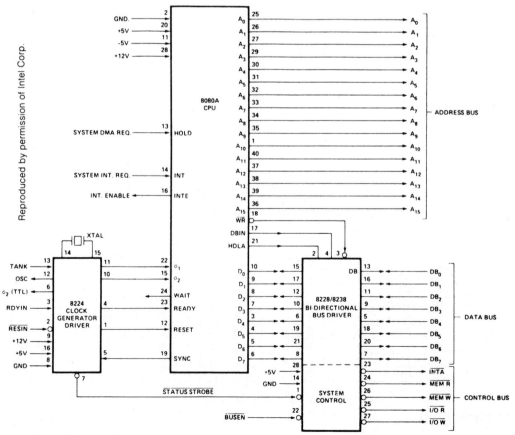

Figure 9.13 8080 CPU module.

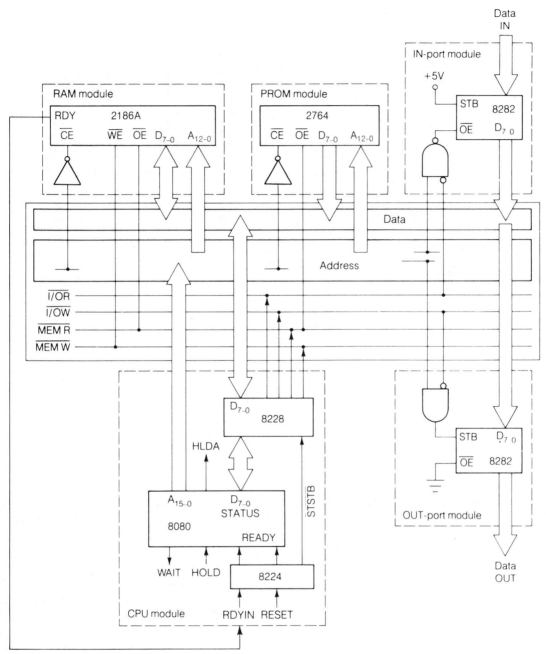

Figure 9.14 8080-based microcomputer system.

during states T_1 and T_2. As illustrated in Figure 9.16, the address/data timing of the 8085 is similar to the status/data timing of the 8080.

Early in each machine cycle the CPU outputs low-order address information on pins AD_0 through AD_7. Since the where/when data-transfer process demands that the address information remain valid throughout the entire machine cycle, it must be saved within a latch before it disappears and the AD pins are taken over by data information. To strobe this low-order address information into a latch, the 8085 provides the Address Latch Enable (ALE) signal early in each machine cycle (Figure 9.17).

When the ALE signal goes active high, the address information flows through the latch. When ALE goes low, the address information is safely latched in place and available throughout the remaining machine-cycle time. (On some 8085-based peripheral chips, the low-order latch is provided within the peripheral chip.) To complete the full 16-bit address, remember that the high-order address from pins 21 through 28 and the IO/$\overline{M}$ signal from pin 34 are output in the normal manner.

Machine-cycle identification is handled differently in an 8085-based system. Since some peripherals can benefit from a knowledge of the type of machine cycle under way, the

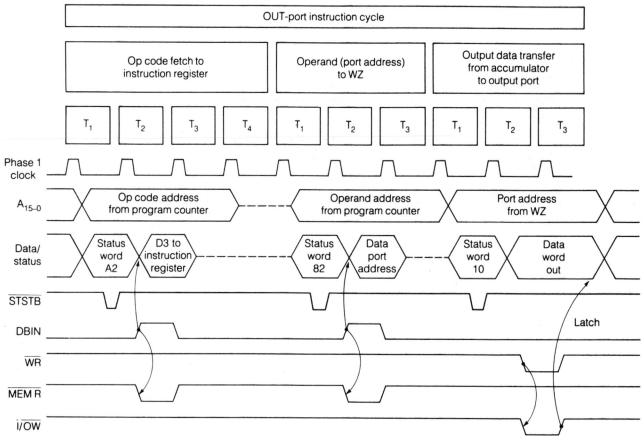

Figure 9.15 OUT-port instruction-cycle waveforms (8080).

8085 provides this information by way of pins 29 and 33 (labeled S_0 and S_1). The S_0 and S_1 signals are active for the same period of time as the IO/$\overline{M}$ and address lines, and are combined with the IO/$\overline{M}$ signal to provide status information according to the following chart:

	Status		
	IO/$\overline{M}$	S_1	S_0
Memory write	0	0	1
Memory read	0	1	0
I/O write	1	0	1
I/O read	1	1	0
Op-code fetch	0	1	1

A complete 8085-based microcomputer system is shown in Figure 9.18. When the low-order address lines are demultiplexed by the 8282 latch, as shown, any peripheral used by an 8080-based system can be matched to an 8085-based system.

If we take advantage of the special 8085-based peripheral chips used by the SDK-85 single-board computer (Figure 9.19), the component count is considerably reduced. Since the low-order address bits are latched within the peripherals by the action of the ALE signal, an external address latch

is not required. In addition, these *programmable peripheral devices* provide for a number of fully integrated I/O ports (programmable peripheral chips are the subject of Chapter 19).

The combined effects of timing and multiplexing for an 8085-based system are demonstrated in Figure 9.20 for the familiar OUT-port instruction cycle. To review the entire sequencing/multiplexing process, begin at the left side of the OUT-port waveforms and follow all signals through the system diagram of Figure 9.18. A summary and comparison of 8080/8085 timing and multiplexing are given in Figure 9.21.

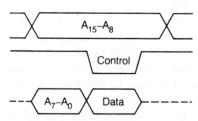

Figure 9.16 Where/when waveforms showing low-order address-information sharing 8085 data lines.

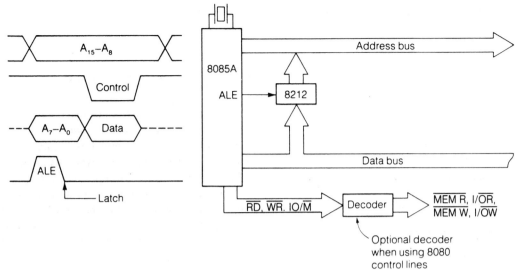

Figure 9.17   8085 address/data-bus interface and timing.

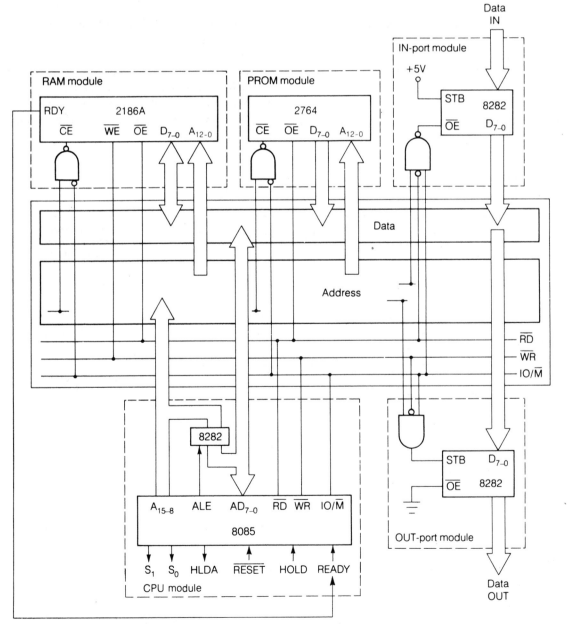

Figure 9.18   8085-based microcomputer system.

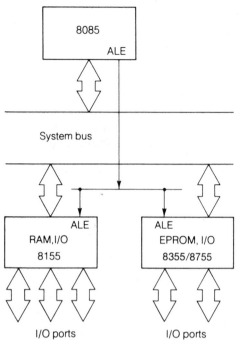

Figure 9.19   Special 8085 peripheral chips latch low-level address lines internally.

INTELLIGENT-MACHINE UPDATE

Our knowledge of basic computer anatomy—its hardware—is now complete, and we have studied its actions as it spoke its first word. As demonstrated by Figure 9.22, our intelligent machine has developed beyond its infancy.

Fully equipped to learn, our computer can now be sent back to school, where it will expand its vocabulary and be taught many new skills. In other words, starting with the next chapter, the emphasis will shift from hardware and processing action to software and program development.

QUESTIONS AND PROBLEMS

1. Based on Figure 9.2, describe how the RESET input is synchronized.
2. If both 8080 and 8085 microprocessors are driven by crystals of the same frequency, how much faster is the 8085's clock frequency over the 8080's?
3. What major operation occurs in each machine cycle?
4. Why do operation-code fetch machine cycles require at least four states?

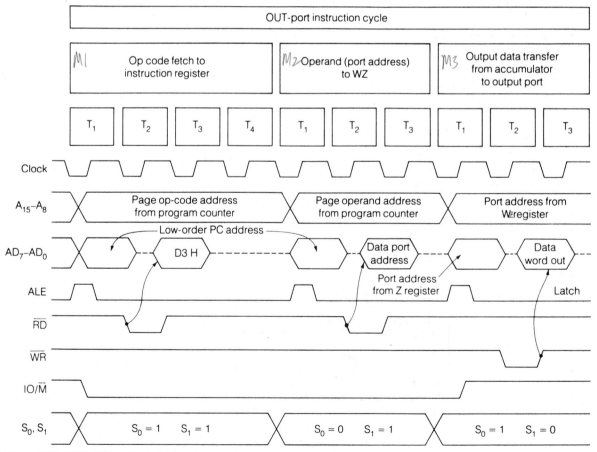

Figure 9.20   8085 OUT-port instruction-cycle waveforms.

MCS-80™ System Bus

The basic timing of the MCS-80 BUS for a READ CYCLE is as follows:

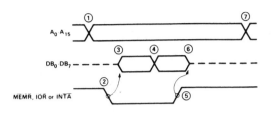

The MCS-80 first presents the address ① and shortly thereafter the control signal ②. The data bus, which was in the high impedance state, is driven by the selected device ③. The selected device eventually presents the valid data to the processor ④. The processor raises the control signal ⑤, which causes the selected device to put the data bus in the high impedance state ⑥. The processor then changes the address ⑦ for the start of the next data transfer.

The basic timing of the MCS-80 BUS for a WRITE CYCLE is as follows:

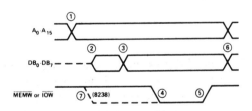

The MCS-80 first presents the address ①, then enables the data bus driver ②, and later presents the data ③. Shortly thereafter, the MCS-80 drops the control signal ④ for an interval of time and then raises the signal ⑤. The MCS-80 then changes the address ⑥ in preparation for the next data transfer. The advance write signal of the 8238 is also shown ⑦.

Figure 9.21 8080/8085 timing and multiplexing comparison. *Reproduced by permission of Intel Corp.*

MCS-85™ System Bus

The basic timing of the MCS-85 BUS for a READ CYCLE is as follows:

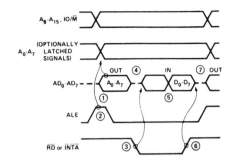

At the beginning of the READ cycle, the 8085A sends out all 16 bits of address ①. This is followed by ALE ② which causes the lower eight bits of address to be latched in either the 8155/56, 8355, 8755A, or in an external 8212. $\overline{RD}$ is then dropped ③ by the 8085A. The data bus is then tri-stated by the 8085A in preparation for the selected device driving the bus ④; the selected device will continue to drive the bus with valid data ⑤, until $\overline{RD}$ is raised ⑥ by the 8085A. At the end of the READ CYCLE ⑦, the address and data lines are changed in preparation for the next cycle.

The basic timing of the MCS-85 BUS for a WRITE CYCLE is as follows:

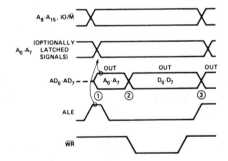

The timing of the WRITE CYCLE is identical to the MCS-85 READ CYCLE with the exception of the AD_0-AD_7 lines. At the beginning of the cycle ①, the low order eight bits of address are on AD_0-AD_7. After ALE drops, the eight bits of data ② are put on AD_0-AD_7. They are removed ③ at the end of the WRITE CYCLE, in anticipation of the next data transfer.

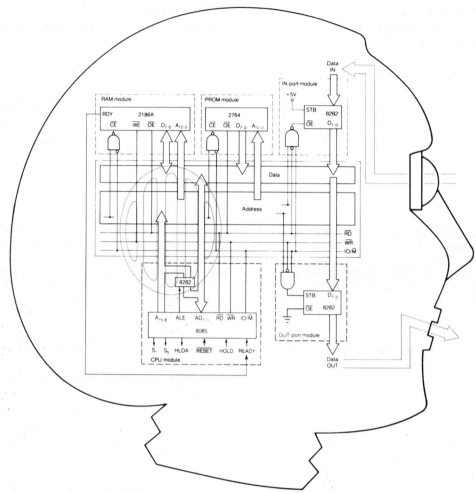

Figure 9.22 Fully functional 8085-based thinking machine.

5. Under what conditions is a WAIT request issued?

6. When a WAIT request is honored, what state does the CPU assume?

7. Under what conditions is a DMA request issued?

8. When a DMA request is honored, what state does the CPU assume? How do we know the DMA request has been honored?

9. What are the two major differences between the WAIT and HOLD states?

10. Why are the data pins of an 8080/8085 microprocessor multiplexed?

11. Using Figure 9.12, describe how an operation-code fetch results in the MEM R control line going active.

12. What signal in an 8085 system latches the low-order address information?

13. On an 8085 system, what three signals are used to identify an operation-code machine cycle?

14. For an 8080 processor, draw a complete set of waveforms for the IN-port instruction cycle similar to those in Figure 9.15. For an 8085 processor, draw a complete set of IN-port waveforms similar to those in Figure 9.20.

15. Why do you think the 8080 WAIT pin (READY acknowledge) was left off the 8085?

16. Referring to Figure 9.10, why does the processor wait until the end of a machine cycle to enter the HOLD state (rather than entering it in the middle of a machine cycle, as for the WAIT state)?

part III

Software:
The Spark of Life

System hardware, whether the cells of the human mind or the pieces of a chess board, has no motion or action about it, no life or direction—it simply exists. But add software and the whole scene springs to life. It is software, the sequential flow of actions, that animates the hardware system.

Our intelligent machine now has a working vocabulary of only two words, the familiar IN port and OUT port, and with these two words it can perform only the simple mimic task. Clearly, if our computer is ever going to grow into a skilled and useful intelligent machine, its vocabulary must be enlarged.

A computer's vocabulary is known as its *instruction set*. When a variety of instructions are arranged into a program, it is known as *software*. In Part III we will be looking at most of the 72/74 types of instructions that make up the 8080/8085's instruction set. To expand the working vocabulary of our intelligent machine, Part III will introduce many specific examples in the use of the 8080/8085 instructions.

chapter 10

The Data-Transfer Group

Data transfer is a subject we are familiar with, for seeing, hearing, and speaking are little more than data-transfer operations using the IN- and OUT-port instructions from group 5.

But what about memory-related data-transfer operations ("remembering" and "recalling" information to and from memory)? These data-transfer operations will require a great deal more flexibility than simple input and output.

Another reason why we need a powerful group of data-transfer instructions is the array of general-purpose internal registers you see between the program counter and the WZ register pair (see Figure 10.1). We have not introduced them before because they were not needed for the simple mimic process. Certainly, we can expect the data-transfer group to move information to and from these six internal registers.

DATA-TRANSFER VERBS

Below are listed three familiar English instructions, in verb/object format:

Verb	Object
load	supplies
add	fuel
move	truck

In each case, is not the verb portion the operative part of the instruction, and does not the verb alone reveal what action the instruction will take? Therefore, let us begin by listing the four verbs that make up the data-transfer group of instructions:

> Move
> Load
> Store
> Exchange

In practice, all four verbs refer to the same basic process: the transfer of data from source to destination. However, each verb really means more than this. The verb *store,* for example, commands the remembering process, when data are transferred from one of the seven internal registers to a memory location. (The accumulator is known as the A register and is grouped with the other six internal registers.) And when we see the verb *load,* we will know the recall process is to be carried out, and data transferred from memory to one of the seven internal registers. The verb *move* is a little more general. All we know for sure is that an 8-bit word, rather than a 16-bit word, is involved in the data transfer. The last verb, *exchange,* is the simplest of all and commands a swapping of the DE and HL register pairs.

The verb *exchange* reveals something special about the six general-purpose internal registers, B through H. These registers can be referred to as pairs as well as individually. The reason is simple: sometimes the internal registers will be holding 16-bit address information rather than 8-bit data information, and only a register pair will do.

As we can see, the verb content (op code) of each instruction will seldom be difficult to comprehend. It is the object (operand) portion of each instruction, though, that will give us the greatest difficulty—at first at least.

DATA-TRANSFER ADDRESSING MODES

Recall from our discussions of the IN- and OUT-port instructions the two ways in which the operand of an instruction can be specified. The instruction can contain the data (load *supplies*), or it can tell us where the data are located by supplying an address (load *contents of warehouse 2040H*). These same two operand categories are found in the data-transfer group. What complicates the situation are the three possible addressing techniques within the second category. Thus the total number of ways the operand can be specified is four. Each of these is known as an *addressing mode* and is defined as:

1. Immediate—The instruction contains the data. } WHAT ARE THE DATA?

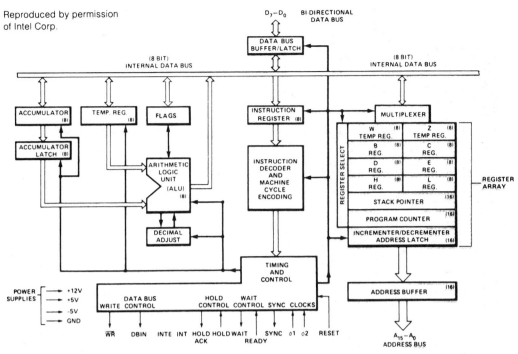

Figure 10.1 8080 CPU functional block diagram showing general-purpose internal registers B through L (8085 diagram similar).

2. Direct—Bytes 2 and 3 of the instruction contain the exact memory address of the data.

3. Register—The instruction gives the internal register or register-pair address where the data are located.

4. Register indirect—The instruction specifies a register pair that contains the memory address where the data are stored.

WHERE ARE THE DATA?

As we familiarize ourselves with each mode of addressing, concentrate on two questions: what is the source of the data transfer, and what is the destination? Each data-transfer instruction must in some manner supply this information.

Immediate Addressing Mode

The *immediate* form of addressing is perhaps the easiest to understand, because we have seen it before (load *supplies*). If the instruction contains the actual data, it is an immediate type of instruction.

A specific example will show how easy it is to work with the immediate form of addressing. Scan through the 13 instruction types composing the data-transfer group in Appendix I. What is the first type of instruction you encounter that uses immediate addressing? The letter "I" in the mnemonic is the giveaway, for it stands for "Immediate." The *move immediate* instruction is the first one to use this mode of addressing (Figure 10.2*a*).

According to the instruction summary, the second byte contains the actual data, and when the instruction is processed,

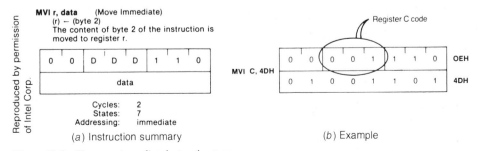

(a) Instruction summary

(b) Example

Figure 10.2 The *move immediate* instruction type.

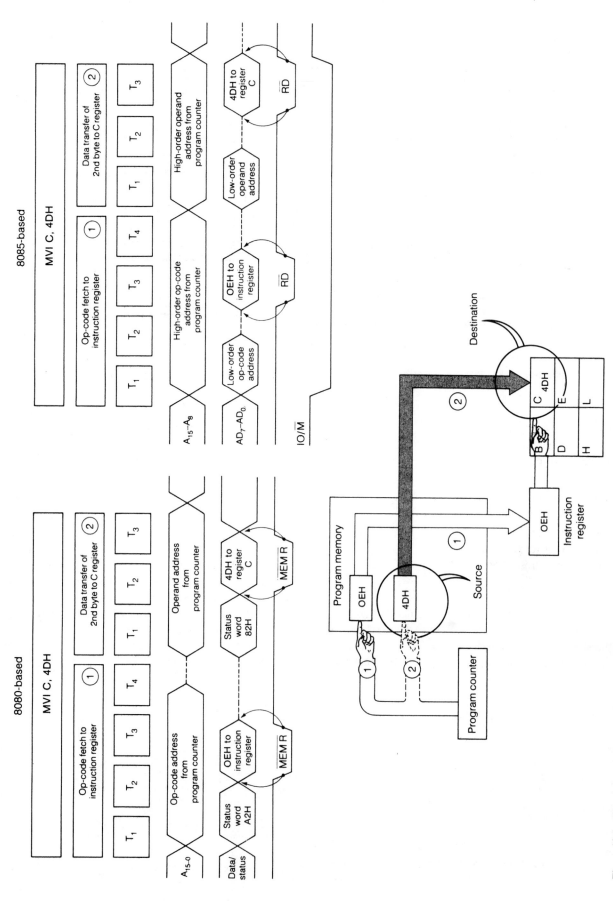

Figure 10.3 Waveform/machine-cycle analysis of MVI C,4DH instruction.

this information will be moved to one of the seven internal registers within the 8080/8085 microprocessor chip. But which internal register is to serve as the destination? It is up to the programmer. Any of the seven internal registers can be selected as the destination by coding bits D_3, D_4, and D_5 of the first byte according to the following address chart of internal registers:

DDD or SSS	Register name
111	A
000	B
001	C
010	D
011	E
100	H
101	L

For the *move immediate* type of instruction, can you now answer the two important questions: what is the source of the data transfer, and what is the destination? The source is memory—it is the second byte of the *move immediate* instruction. The destination is one of the seven internal registers—to be selected by the programmer.

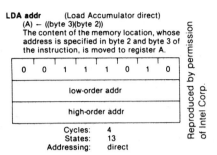

LDA addr   (Load Accumulator direct)
(A) ← ((byte 3)(byte 2))
The content of the memory location, whose address is specified in byte 2 and byte 3 of the instruction, is moved to register A.

0	0	1	1	1	0	1	0

low-order addr

high-order addr

Cycles: 4
States: 13
Addressing: direct

Reproduced by permission of Intel Corp.

Figure 10.4   The *load accumulator direct* instruction type.

To test our knowledge of the *move immediate* type of instruction, let us write the complete binary instruction for moving data byte 4DH to register C. As shown in Figure 10.2b, just code the destination bits with the binary register address 001, and place the data to be transferred in the second byte of the instruction. Note how we also update the mnemonic to reflect this specific example.

Incidentally, do you now see the value of the mnemonic notation? Once you know the mnemonic format, a quick glance will tell you exactly what the instruction is to accom-

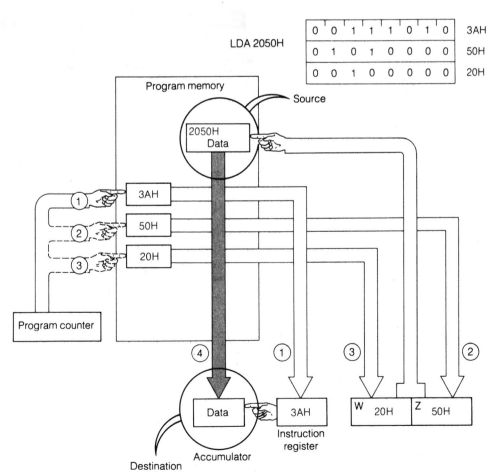

Figure 10.5   The LDA 2050H instruction and machine-cycle diagram.

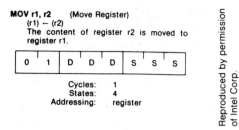

MOV r1, r2 (Move Register)
(r1) ← (r2)
The content of register r2 is moved to register r1.

| 0 | 1 | D | D | D | S | S | S |

Cycles: 1
States: 4
Addressing: register

Reproduced by permission of Intel Corp.

Figure 10.6 The *move register* instruction type.

plish—a feat not possible with the binary formulation. We will see other advantages of using the mnemonic notation in a later chapter.

To see how the MVI C, 4DH instruction is processed, and to review the material of Chapters 8 and 9, Figure 10.3 shows both the 8080-based and 8085-based instruction-cycle waveforms, along with a diagram of the data-transfer process (also see Appendix III).

The three remaining addressing modes are not as simple as the immediate form of addressing, for they specify the data by telling *where* they are rather than *what* they are. Let us take a look at each of these addressing modes.

Direct Addressing Mode

Again, scanning through the 13 data-transfer instructions, we locate the *load accumulator direct* instruction, the first

one making use of the *direct* mode of addressing (Figure 10.4).

The most striking feature of a direct addressing instruction is its three bytes of information—as many as any instruction. The reason is that a full 16-bit address must be specified directly by the instruction, and that requires two memory locations. As the instruction summary clearly reveals, the source of the data transfer is a memory location given directly by bytes 2 and 3, and the destination is the accumulator. The same source/destination information is implied, as always, by the mnemonic in shorthand form.

The machine-cycle diagram of Figure 10.5 shows how the contents of memory location 2050H can be moved to the accumulator directly. (Note that the low-order memory address goes in the second byte and the high-order memory address in the third byte.) A waveform analysis (similar to Figure 10.3) is left as an exercise.

Register Addressing Mode

The word *register,* in this mode of addressing, refers to the seven internal registers within the 8080/8085 chip. The very first instruction type in the data-transfer group uses this mode (Figure 10.6).

This simple instruction, which moves data from one internal register to another, is the only instruction type in the data-transfer group that allows the programmer to select *both* the source and the destination by directly coding bits of the

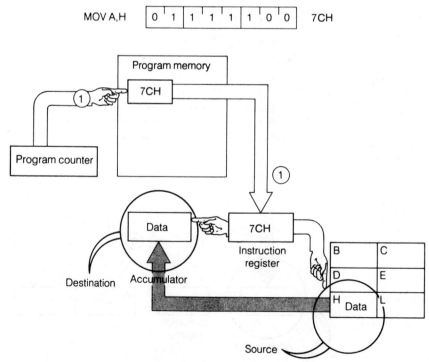

Figure 10.7 The MOV A,H instruction and machine-cycle diagram.

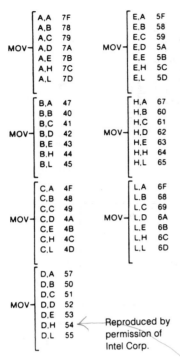

Figure 10.8 Addressing combinations of the *move register* instruction type.

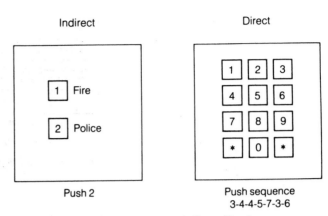

Figure 10.9 Example of direct versus indirect addressing.

instruction. This is possible because the seven internal registers—being few in number—do not require large binary addresses.

Figure 10.7 shows how the *move register* instruction would be coded to transfer data from register H to register A.

The *move register* instruction type clearly demonstrates why we have been using the term *type of instruction* for each of the 72 commands in the instruction set. The reason is that, within the *move register type* of instruction, there are nearly 50 combinations of source and destination addresses selectable by the programmer (Figure 10.8). The only bits remaining unchanged are bits D_6 and D_7. In other words, this one instruction type encompasses nearly 50 combinations of binary numbers and uses up nearly 20% of the available 256-word instruction space.

To summarize, the instruction set consists of five groups of instructions. Within the five groups are 72 (74) *types* of instructions, consisting of 244 (246) binary combinations. (The ten "secret" binary op codes not advertised by Intel do perform functions, as revealed in Appendix IV.)

Indirect Addressing Mode

An everyday example of *indirect addressing* will help to set the stage for this rather involved instruction type. An automatic telephone-dialing system is a popular commercial device making use of the indirect addressing concept. Consider a simple system, consisting of just two buttons, labeled "1"

and "2." When button 1 is pushed, the fire department is automatically called, and when button 2 is pushed, the police are automatically summoned. In this case, the numbers "1" and "2" are both *indirect* addresses. If we assume an arbitrary number for the police department, Figure 10.9 compares the direct and indirect methods of placing the call.

The advantage of the indirect method shows up at a glance: the instruction is shorter, more easily coded, and is processed more quickly. (Of course, the actual phone number must have previously been stored within the automatic dialing system.) The *load accumulator indirect* instruction (Figure 10.10a) indirectly addresses a memory location in the same manner.

By coding bits D_4 and D_5, the *load accumulator indirect* instruction specifies the address of either register pair BC or DE. Within the specified register pair is the 16-bit memory address pointing to the data. Figure 10.10b summarizes the indirect addressing process.

Suppose memory address 2045H has previously been stored in register pair BC. Making use of the following register-pair addressing table, can you properly code the *load accumulator indirect* instruction to transfer data from memory location 2045H to the accumulator?

RP	Register pair
00	BC
01	DE
10	HL
11	SP

If you coded the two address bits according to the data-transfer diagram of Figure 10.11, you are correct. Note that it is common practice to place only the letter "B" in the mnemonic, even though the instruction refers to the BC register pair. This practice simply saves time—the mnemonic, remember, is designed as a shorthand tool.

A special case of indirect addressing should be highlighted because it is used so often. Also using register-indirect addressing, it blends features of both indirect and reg-

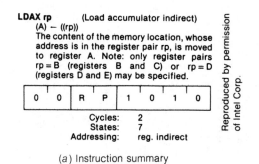

(a) Instruction summary

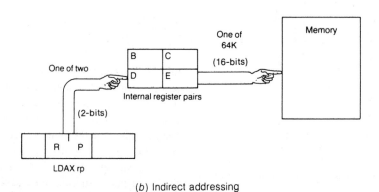

(b) Indirect addressing

Figure 10.10 The *load accumulator indirect* instruction.

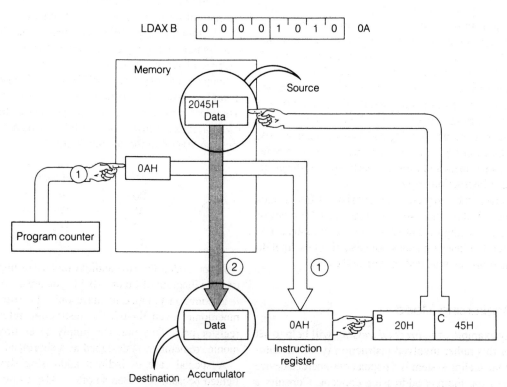

Figure 10.11 The LDAX B instruction and machine-cycle diagram.

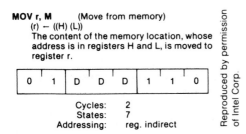

MOV r, M   (Move from memory)
(r) — ((H) (L))
The content of the memory location, whose address is in registers H and L, is moved to register r.

0	1	D	D	D	1	1	0

Cycles: 2
States: 7
Addressing: reg. indirect

Reproduced by permission of Intel Corp.

Figure 10.12   The *move from memory* instruction type.

ister addressing modes. This technique is found in the very powerful *move from memory* instruction (Figure 10.12).

It differs from the reg. indirect addressing instruction of Figure 10.10 in two ways: (1) the HL register pair is automatically used as a memory pointer (you have no choice, the HL register pair must be used); and (2) the programmer is free to select the destination register.

Putting it into source/destination terms, the source of the data transfer is the memory location pointed to by the HL register pair, and the destination is given by filling in the destination register address in the operation code. For example, suppose you wish to move from memory the data located at memory location 2032H to register E. As shown in Figure 10.13, it is necessary only to code the instruction with the E register binary address. No code is required to specify the source, because the HL register pair automatically points to the source. (A quick way to preset the HL pointer is with

the LXI rp—*load register pair immediate*—data-transfer instruction of Figure 10.14.)

As we move on to new instruction groups, we will find a whole class of instruction types automatically making use of the HL register pair as a memory pointer.

A DATA-TRANSFER EXAMPLE

We have now completed our study of the three basic data-transfer verbs (*move, load,* and *store*) and have studied the four available addressing modes (*immediate, direct, register,* and *indirect*). To test our knowledge of the data-transfer instructions and addressing modes, let's write a "checkers" program in which a data byte is commanded to "hop" between various computer locations. The task is shown in Figure 10.15. Each leg of the journey is labeled with the desired addressing mode. Let's write the program that will complete the round trip from input to output.

- *Leg 1:* We begin by transferring our data byte from the "outside world" to the accumulator. Since we are already quite familiar with the IN-port technique, let's adopt the *immediate* addressing method:

  MVI A,data   3EH,data

- *Let 2:* To transfer the data from the accumulator to memory location 2030H, we use direct addressing:

  STA 2030H   32H,30H,20H

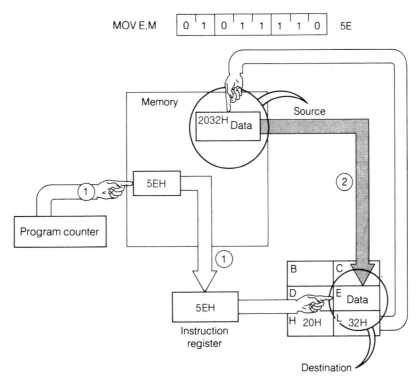

Figure 10.13   The MOV E,M instruction and machine-cycle diagram.

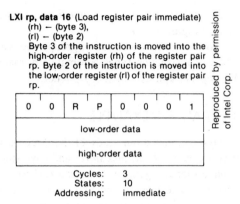

LXI rp, data 16 (Load register pair immediate)
(rh) ← (byte 3),
(rl) ← (byte 2)
Byte 3 of the instruction is moved into the
high-order register (rh) of the register pair
rp. Byte 2 of the instruction is moved into
the low-order register (rl) of the register pair
rp.

0	0	R	P	0	0	0	1

low-order data

high-order data

Cycles: 3
States: 10
Addressing: immediate

Reproduced by permission of Intel Corp.

Figure 10.14   The *load register pair immediate* instruction type.

- *Leg 3:* Next, for variety, *register-indirect* addressing is used to transfer the data to register B. First, we load the HL register pair with the memory address (2030H) using the *load immediate* addressing mode:

LXI H,2030H   21H,30H,20H

We then use the *move from memory* instruction to carry out the transfer:

MOV B,M   46H

- *Leg 4:* Leg 4 uses *register* addressing to carry out a simple transfer from register B to the accumulator:

MOV A,B   78H

- *Leg 5:* Using the familiar OUT-port instruction, we output the data from port 22H:

OUT 22H   D3H,22H

ADDITIONAL STUDY

We have looked in detail at most of the thirteen instruction types composing the data-transfer group and have reviewed all four addressing modes. By performing the exercises in the Questions and Problems for this chapter, the remaining data transfer instruction types can be included in your working vocabulary with a minimum of effort.

INTELLIGENT-MACHINE UPDATE

In addition to its sensory and speaking abilities, our intelligent machine can now learn, recall, and remember. If it wishes to recite poetry, give a speech, or sing at the "Met," these are essential traits. But what if it wants to become an architect, or an engineer, or a navigator? What is missing is

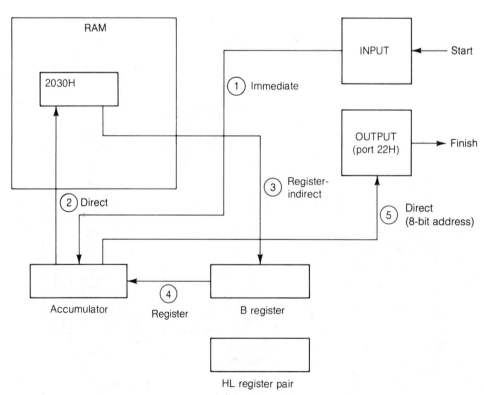

Figure 10.15   Diagram for the "checkers" data-transfer program.

the ability to perform simple arithmetic. The group 2 instructions of the next chapter will expand its vocabulary into this vital area.

QUESTIONS AND PROBLEMS

1. What is the difference between the data-transfer "verbs" *load* and *store*?

2. When using the *immediate* form of addressing, where is the source of the data and where is the destination?

3. What two special *direct*-addressing instructions use an 8-bit address?

4. When you are using the *register indirect* form of addressing, where can the memory address be found?

5. What is the binary address of register D? Of register pair DE?

6. Write a modified MIMIC program that stores and updates all incoming data in memory location 2030H.

7. What *single byte* instruction transfers a byte of data from register B to a memory location?

8. Why are the internal registers sometimes addressed as pairs?

9. Why do you think the verb *copy* is a valid term to apply to all data-transfer operations?

10. For one or more of the examples of Figures 10.5, 10.7, 10.11, and 10.13, draw the instruction-cycle waveforms similar to those of Figure 10.3.

11. For the instruction shown here (stored at RAM location 2008H), complete the waveform diagram. Choose the 8080 or 8085 processor, or both.

12. Why are five machine cycles required to carry out the LHLD addr instruction?

13. The MVI M, data instruction is a combination of what two addressing modes?

14. Data byte 77H is to be moved to the memory location whose address is presently stored in memory locations 2020H and 2021H. Using the LHLD addr and MVI M,data instructions, perform this operation.

15. For each of the following data transfer instructions, what 16-bit register is pointing to the data?
    a. MVI A,03H
    b. LDA 2030H
    c. MOV C,M
    d. LDAX B

16. What does "M" used in the *move from memory* instruction (MOV r,M) refer to?

17. Can we transfer a data byte directly from one memory location to another without going through an internal register?

18. We wish to transfer a byte of data from one memory location to another. Register pair HL contains the source address and register pair DE contains the destination address. Using the MOV r,M, MOV M,r, and XCHG instructions, perform the operation.

19. Write a "checkers" program corresponding to the following data transfer sequence:
    a. "Outside world" to memory location 2040H (immediate)
    b. Memory to E register (register-indirect)
    c. E register to A register (register)
    d. A register to memory location 2030H (direct).

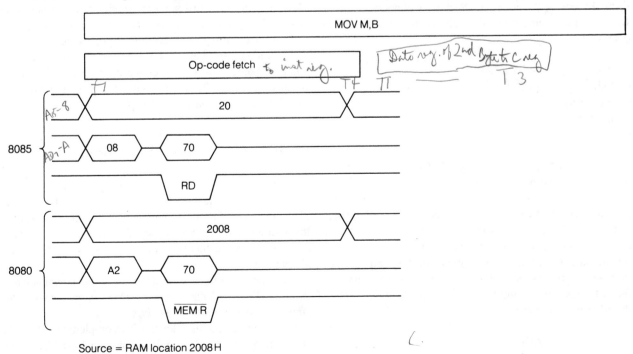

Source = RAM location 2008 H
Destination = Instruction register

chapter 11

The Arithmetic Group

"What's one and one and one and one and one and one and one and one and one and one?"

"I don't know," said Alice. "I lost count."

"She can't do addition," said the Red Queen. (Lewis Carroll, *Through the Looking Glass*.)

The Red Queen would never have tried to ridicule a computer the way she did Alice, for she picked the one feat at which computers truly excel: high-speed repetitive tasks. This chapter introduces the group 2 arithmetic instructions and generally restricts operations to addition and subtraction of small integers. Chapter 17 refines the arithmetic processes to include many other instructions, data structures, and arithmetic operations.

THE GROUP 2 VERBS

As before, let us begin with a simple listing of the group 2 verbs. Except for the last verb, which we will not be involved with for quite some time, they all command well-known operations:

- Add   *no carry*   *no double add.*
- Subtract   *no borrow*
- Increment *& INX*
- Decrement *& DCX*
- Decimal Adjust

no There are 20 mnemonics or types of instructions falling within the five verbs (see Appendix I). To whittle down the list, let us ignore for now the *Add register pair* (DAD) and *Decimal Adjust* (DAA) instructions, and set aside all instruction types with a C (for carry) or a B (for borrow). These operations will be discussed in a later chapter. The remaining mnemonics, mostly involving simple addition and subtraction, should be easy to add to our working vocabulary, for they all make use of the familiar addressing modes introduced in the last chapter:

ADD r	INR r
ADD M	INR M

ADI data	DCR r
SUB r	DCR M
SUB M	INX rp
SUI data	DCX rp

That leaves only two possible sources of confusion to clarify. Consider the following simple problem in subtraction. In any subtraction, at least three numbers are involved—the two numbers to be subtracted and the result:

$$\text{SUB} \quad \begin{array}{r} +3 \\ +5 \\ \hline -2 \end{array}$$

The first problem is, *How can we locate three numbers with only one address bus?* The answer is: Assign two of them to an accumulator. That is, one of the two numbers to be subtracted is always stored in the accumulator and the result of the subtraction is always placed back into the accumulator. Only the third number remains to be located—an easy task for any addressing mode. Figure 11.1 diagrams the basic data flow during arithmetic processing.

The second problem is, How do we deal with negative values? In other words, How do we distinguish positive from negative numbers? To find the answer, we are going to have to delve into some basic number theory.

POSITIVE AND NEGATIVE NUMBERS

To distinguish positive from negative, our computer takes advantage of a subject that seems to border on sheer magic: *2's complement*. Through the magic of 2's complement, both the addition and the subtraction of positive as well as negative numbers are handled automatically. Just obey a few simple rules.

First, let us define 2's complement. *Two's complement is equal to 1's complement plus 1. (One's complement is the simple inversion of all binary bits.)*

For example, let us take the 2's complement of 7. As shown here, the result certainly does not look like 7, but when using magic, things are not always as they appear:

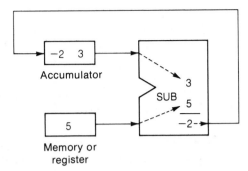

Figure 11.1 Arithmetic-processing flow diagram.

The signed-number convention is demonstrated below using the numbers ± 5 and ± 7:

Number	Sign bit	Magnitude
+5	0	0000101
−5	1	1111011
+7	0	0000111
−7	1	1111001

When using 8-bit signed numbers, the range of values is from −128 (10000000B) to +127 (01111111B).

Before → 00000111	7
Step 1 11111000	1's complement of 7
Step 2 11111000 + 1	ADD 1
After → 11111001	2's complement of 7

Next we will take a look at the rules you must obey in order to make 2's complement arithmetic work.

Signed Numbers

All 2's complement operations must use *signed* numbers. To "sign" a number, place a 0 in the most significant bit position (the leftmost position) if the number is positive and a 1 in the most significant position if the number is negative.

The remaining bits are used to specify the magnitude of the number. They are also governed by rules:

• If the number is positive, the magnitude is entered in true form, as usual.
• If the number is negative, the magnitude is entered in 2's complement form.

It follows that whenever a signed number has a 1 in the most significant position, the remaining magnitude bits are always in 2's complement form.

Addition and Subtraction of Signed Numbers

To add two signed numbers, simply perform a straightforward binary addition using any of the ADD instructions. If the answer is negative, the result will automatically be in 2's complement form. For example:

	+7 0 0000111		−7 1 1111001
ADD	−5 1 1111011	ADD	+5 0 0000101
	+2 0 0000010		−2 1 1111110

Note that all negative numbers are entered in 2's complement form, and all negative answers will automatically appear in 2's complement form. (To verify the negative answers, convert the magnitude to true form by reversing the 2's complement process. Or take the 2's complement again. Either method will give the magnitude in true form.)

To subtract two signed numbers (here is where more magic comes in), take the 2's complement of the subtrahend and add! *Subtraction, then, is performed by 2's complement addition.*

Figure 11.2 shows what happens when +7 is subtracted from +2. Since both numbers are positive, they are entered in true form. *Inside the ALU*, the +7 is converted to 2's complement and added to the +2. And (just like pulling a

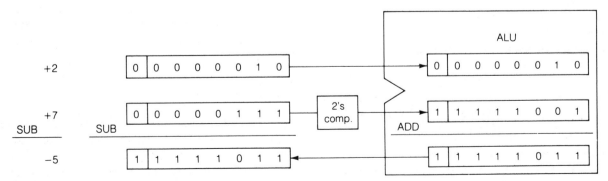

Figure 11.2 Subtracting signed numbers by 2's complement addition.

rabbit from a hat) we obtain −5, properly signed with a 1 and with its magnitude in 2's complement form.

Of course, for the magic to work, we must make sure the result of the addition or subtraction does not overflow the −128/+127 signed-number bounds (the carry out of the magnitude bits would enter the sign bit, causing an erroneous sign change).

A Signed-Number Problem

Once you know the rules, signed numbers are as easy to handle as unsigned numbers. For example, using *immediate* addressing, the following program will successively subtract +7, −9, and −5 from the accumulator:

Mnemonic		Hexadecimal
SUI	7	D6,07H
SUI	F7H (−9)	D6,F7H
SUI	FBH (−5)	D6,FBH

If the accumulator held −6 initially, processing action will proceed as follows:

	Math operations		Operations within ALU
	−6		11111010B
SUB	+7 (00000111)	ADD	11111001B
	−13		11110011B
SUB	−9 (11110111)	ADD	00001001B
	−4		11111100B
SUB	−5 (11111011)	ADD	00000101B
	+1		00000001B

Sign-Magnitude Entry

Using 2's complement arithmetic, all negative numbers must be entered into the computer already in 2's complement form, and all negative answers are automatically reported in 2's complement form. Since this system is awkward for human beings, we may wish to adopt the *sign-magnitude* convention. Using this convention, all numbers are signed, as before, but all magnitudes (negative as well as positive) are entered in true form. The following chart compares 2's complement with sign magnitude for two arbitrary numbers:

Number	2's complement	Sign magnitude
+6	00000110	00000110
−8	11111000	10001000

Since the computer *must* process all numbers in 2's complement form, we program the computer to automatically convert all sign-magnitude entries to 2's complement form.

Also, before answers are outported, all negative numbers are converted to sign-magnitude form. Since a decision is involved (is the number positive or negative?), the conversion program is left as an exercise for Chapter 14.

ARITHMETIC INSTRUCTION EXAMPLES

Three arithmetic problems, each requiring a different addressing mode, are all the practice we will need to include the group 2 instructions in our working vocabulary. Chances are, because we are familiar with both the verbs and the addressing modes, we will be able to quickly select the correct instruction type—including the correct addressing mode—to solve each arithmetic problem.

Problem 1

The contents of register C are to be added to the contents of the accumulator. The result, of course, will be found in the accumulator. Can you select the correct type of instruction and properly code the operand to carry out the addition process?

We know the verb is "add" and the mode of addressing is "register." Therefore, the *add register* instruction type is the correct choice (Figure 11.3*a*). Fill in the binary code for the source register C, update the mnemonic to conform to the specific problem at hand, and the instruction is complete (Figure 11.3*b*).

Problem 2

Write an instruction to add the contents of memory location 2040H to the accumulator. Again the result will automatically go back to the accumulator.

The *add memory* instruction type of Figure 11.4*a* will solve the problem. According to the instruction summary, the *add memory* instruction belongs to that important group automatically making use of the HL register pair as a memory pointer. In other words, it uses register-indirect addressing, the same addressing mode as the MOV r,M data-transfer instruction. As revealed by Figure 11.4*b*, no address coding is required within the instruction. Simply run the 86H op code and the problem is solved (LXI H, 2040H will preset the HL pointer).

Problem 3

Suppose we plan to subtract −7 from the accumulator but do not wish to set up any memory pointers or preload any registers. Then, as shown in Figure 11.5*a*, use the *immediate* form of addressing; it is often the quickest and most direct way to get the job done.

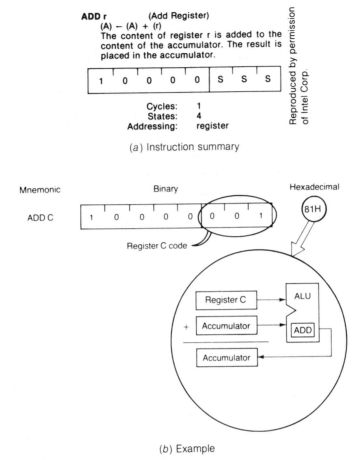

ADD r   (Add Register)
(A) ← (A) + (r)
The content of register r is added to the
content of the accumulator. The result is
placed in the accumulator.

| 1 | 0 | 0 | 0 | 0 | S | S | S |

Cycles: 1
States: 4
Addressing: register

Reproduced by permission
of Intel Corp.

(a) Instruction summary

Mnemonic   Binary   Hexadecimal

ADD C | 1 | 0 | 0 | 0 | 0 | 0 | 0 | 1 | 81H

Register C code

Register C → ALU

+ Accumulator → ADD

Accumulator

(b) Example

Figure 11.3 The *add register* instruction.

To solve our specific problem, place -7 (*in 2's complement form*) in the second byte of the instruction, update the mnemonic, and problem 3 is complete (Figure 11.5b). (Note that subtracting -7 is the same as adding $+7$.)

THE INCREMENT AND DECREMENT INSTRUCTION TYPES

The increment and decrement instructions (Figure 11.6) are special because they afford the programmer the option of affecting either individual registers or register pairs. (An "X" in the mnemonic means the instruction refers to a register pair rather than a single 8-bit register.)

To illustrate the use of the increment/decrement instructions, Figure 11.7a shows how to increment the D register, and Figure 11.7b commands the decrement HL register-*pair* operation.

AN ARITHMETIC PROGRAM

Including the new arithmetic processes, our intelligent machine now has a working vocabulary of approximately 25 instruc-

tions and should be able to perform some useful exercises. To see what it can do, let us teach it a simple task: to look at any date on the calendar (except the last) and tell us what the following date will be. If it looks at the third day of the month, for example, it will say "4." Having already taught our computer the mimic task, we know what the learning procedure will be.

The first step is to produce a flowchart. Figure 11.8a shows how the task is implemented by simply inserting an "ADD 1" block in the middle of the MIMIC program. The new "ADD 1" block, the only one we are not familiar with, looks simple enough, but actually it is complicated by the number of ways the process can be fulfilled. We will look at several of them.

Perhaps the most obvious choice is to use the *increment register* instruction (Figure 11.8b). Since we are incrementing the accumulator, the destination bits are all 1. You may wish to determine for yourself that 3C is the proper hex code. Of course, as shown by Figure 11.8c, we can add 1 to the accumulator immediately.

And finally, if we want to adopt a real roundabout method, Figure 11.8d shows us how. Preset the HL pointer to any available RAM location (such as 2030H) and load a "1" in

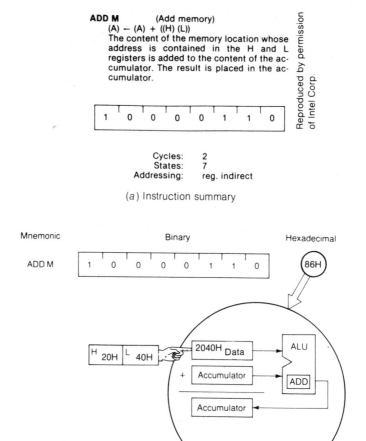

Reproduced by permission of Intel Corp.

ADD M (Add memory)

(A) — (A) + ((H) (L))

The content of the memory location whose address is contained in the H and L registers is added to the content of the accumulator. The result is placed in the accumulator.

| 1 | 0 | 0 | 0 | 0 | 1 | 1 | 0 |

Cycles: 2
States: 7
Addressing: reg. indirect

(a) Instruction summary

| Mnemonic | Binary | Hexadecimal |

ADD M

| 1 | 0 | 0 | 0 | 0 | 1 | 1 | 0 |

86H

H 20H L 40H

2040H Data

+ Accumulator

Accumulator

ALU

ADD

(b) Example

Figure 11.4 The *add memory* instruction.

that location using the *move to memory immediate* instruction. Then follow up with the *add memory* instruction to add 1 to the accumulator.

Three ways to carry out the same task—which one should we choose? Usually the best choice is the simplest, and that is normally the method requiring the least amount of memory. In addition, the shortest program is usually the fastest to run. The first technique—using the increment instruction—is therefore the best choice. It requires only six stored-program locations—the fewest of any of the three techniques.

For additional practice in writing programs involving various combinations of arithmetic and data-transfer instructions, and the four addressing modes, turn to the Questions and Problems section at the end of the chapter.

is to save memory space. Instructions using *direct* addressing are 3 bytes long, while those using *indirect* (or *register-indirect*) addressing take up only a single byte. As if to demonstrate the greater power of indirect addressing, note that the arithmetic group does not include the direct mode of addressing.

To show off the power of *indirect* addressing, the "add 5 numbers" program of Figure 11.9 makes good use of the INX/ADD-M combination to efficiently scan through the sequence of locations, adding together the contents. A comparison of the same program written using *direct* addressing for all memory accesses is saved for an exercise. In Chapter 14, we will see how *indirect* addressing is used within program loops to provide another powerful programming tool.

DIRECT VS INDIRECT ADDRESSING

If *direct* addressing can access any memory location, what is the reason for providing *indirect* addressing? One reason

THE ADDITION PROCESS

It is interesting to learn to what extent microprocessor designers will go to save a microsecond or two. A technique known

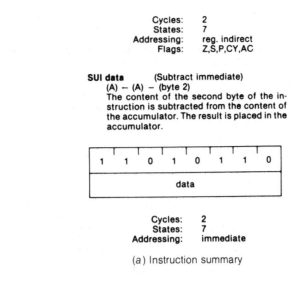

Cycles: 2
States: 7
Addressing: reg. indirect
Flags: Z,S,P,CY,AC

SUI data   (Subtract immediate)
(A) ← (A) − (byte 2)
The content of the second byte of the instruction is subtracted from the content of the accumulator. The result is placed in the accumulator.

| 1 | 1 | 0 | 1 | 0 | 1 | 1 | 0 |

data

Cycles: 2
States: 7
Addressing: immediate

(a) Instruction summary

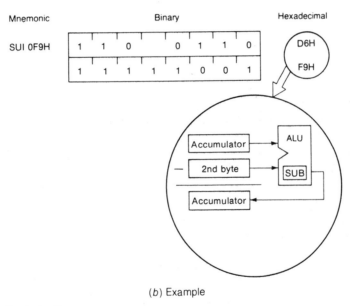

(b) Example

Figure 11.5 The *subtract immediate* instruction.

as *overlapping* is used by most of the arithmetic instructions to shorten the instruction-cycle time. Overlapping takes advantage of the ALU dead time during an op-code fetch machine cycle. (The ALU cannot be required by the *present* instruction during an op-code fetch because the instruction has yet to be decoded.) To make the process clear, let us go through the entire sequence, step by step, for the *add register* instruction (refer to Figure 11.10 and Appendix III). Remember, using this instruction, the contents of the accumulator will be added to the contents of an internal register.

1. First, the *add register* op code is fetched to the instruction register and is decoded during state T_4. Also during state T_4 the contents of the accumulator move to the *accu-mulator latch* (ACT), and the contents of the selected register move to the *temporary register* (TMP).

2. The op code of the *next* instruction (the one following the *add register* instruction) is fetched to the instruction register (remember, the *add register* instruction is a single-byte instruction). During state T_2 of the *next* op-code fetch, the addition takes place: the contents of the accumulator latch and the contents of the temporary register move to the ALU and are added together; the result is moved back to the accumulator.

By overlapping the ALU operation into the next instruction cycle, at least one clock cycle is saved. Saving time here is an especially important design goal, for register-to-

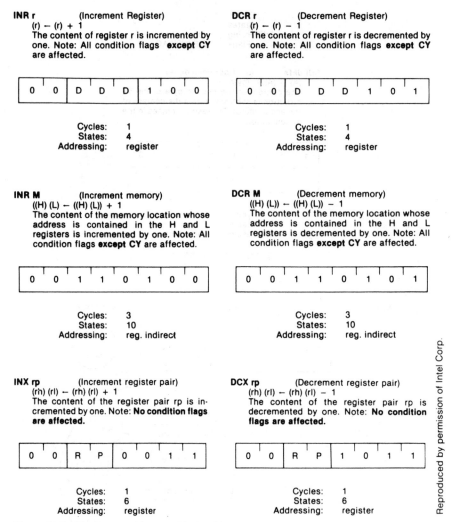

INR r   (Increment Register)
(r) ← (r) + 1
The content of register r is incremented by one. Note: All condition flags **except CY** are affected.

| 0 | 0 | D | D | D | 1 | 0 | 0 |

Cycles: 1
States: 4
Addressing: register

INR M   (Increment memory)
((H) (L) ← ((H) (L)) + 1
The content of the memory location whose address is contained in the H and L registers is incremented by one. Note: All condition flags **except CY** are affected.

| 0 | 0 | 1 | 1 | 0 | 1 | 0 | 0 |

Cycles: 3
States: 10
Addressing: reg. indirect

INX rp   (Increment register pair)
(rh) (rl) ← (rh) (rl) + 1
The content of the register pair rp is incremented by one. Note: **No condition flags are affected.**

| 0 | 0 | R | P | 0 | 0 | 1 | 1 |

Cycles: 1
States: 6
Addressing: register

DCR r   (Decrement Register)
(r) ← (r) − 1
The content of register r is decremented by one. Note: All condition flags **except CY** are affected.

| 0 | 0 | D | D | D | 1 | 0 | 1 |

Cycles: 1
States: 4
Addressing: register

DCR M   (Decrement memory)
((H) (L)) ← ((H) (L)) − 1
The content of the memory location whose address is contained in the H and L registers is decremented by one. Note: All condition flags **except CY** are affected.

| 0 | 0 | 1 | 1 | 0 | 1 | 0 | 1 |

Cycles: 3
States: 10
Addressing: reg. indirect

DCX rp   (Decrement register pair)
(rh) (rl) ← (rh) (rl) − 1
The content of the register pair rp is decremented by one. Note: **No condition flags are affected.**

| 0 | 0 | R | P | 1 | 0 | 1 | 1 |

Cycles: 1
States: 6
Addressing: register

Reproduced by permission of Intel Corp.

Figure 11.6   The increment/decrement instructions.

register addition time is often used as a means of estimating overall computer speed, and may be used as part of a *benchmark routine* (a program used to compare the relative performance of different microprocessors).

Mnemonic	Binary	Hexadecimal
INR D	0 0 0 1 0 1 0 0	14

(a) Increment D register

| DCX H | 0 0 1 0 1 0 1 1 | 2B |

(b) Decrement HL register pair

Figure 11.7   Increment/decrement instruction examples.

The machine-cycle sequence for the *add register* (ADD C) instruction is diagrammed in Figure 11.11.

HIGH-LEVEL AND LOW-LEVEL FLOWCHARTING

Referring to Figure 11.8*d*, we see that the "ADD1" flowchart block, unlike the other blocks in the program, represents more than one machine-level instruction. In fact, carrying this idea to the extreme, it is possible for a flowchart to be written in which each block corresponds to many thousands of instructions (see Figure 11.12). Such a flowchart, called a *high-level* or *system* flowchart, is often the first stage of program evolution, when the most general and overall aspects of the program are under development. (Obviously, a system flowchart need not be written with a particular microprocessor in mind.)

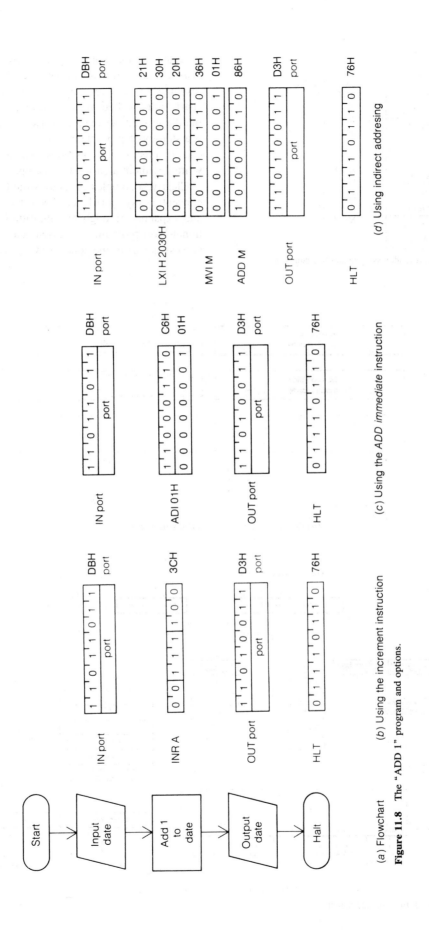

Figure 11.8 The "ADD 1" program and options.

(a) Flowchart

(b) Using the increment instruction

(c) Using the ADD immediate instruction

(d) Using indirect addresing

2030H		MVI	A,0
Data 1		LXI	H,2030H
2031H		ADD	M
Data 2		INX	H
2032H		ADD	M
		INX	H
Data 3		ADD	M
2033H		INX	H
Data 4		ADD	M
		INX	H
2034H		ADD	M
Data 5		INX	H
2035H		MOV	M,A
Answer		HLT	

Figure 11.9 Using indirect addressing to add five numbers.

At the other end of the spectrum, we find the *low-level* or *instructional* flowchart in which each flowchart block corresponds to very few instructions. A *medium-level* flowchart, often called an *algorithm* flowchart, occupies the middle ground between these two extremes. (An algorithm is a step-by-step problem-solving procedure that can be likened to a recipe in a cookbook. An algorithm also is usually written without a particular microprocessor in mind.)

Clearly, a complex program would first be written at the conceptual (system) level. Then it would be broken down and expanded through the algorithm level to the instructional-level program. (As discussed in Chapter 22, such a process is part of the concept of *top-down programming*.)

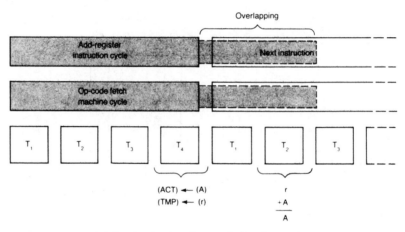

(a) Overlapping into the next instruction cycle

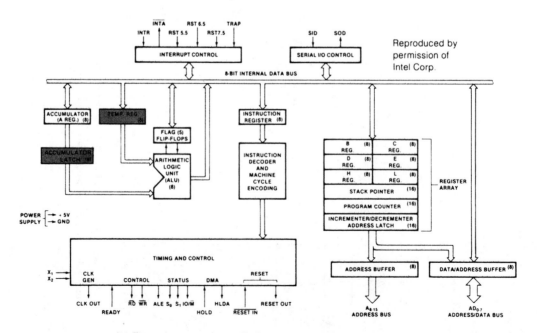

(b) The temporary register (TMP) and accumulator latch (ACT)

Figure 11.10 The addition process.

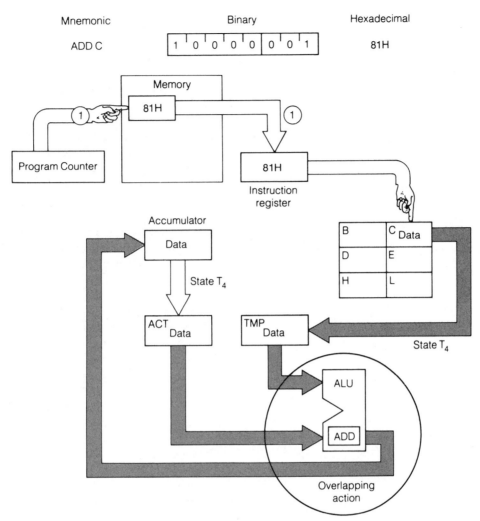

Figure 11.11   The *add C* instruction and machine-cycle diagram.

INTELLIGENT-MACHINE UPDATE

As if riding a time machine forward, our android is chasing its human creators through their evolutionary past. With the development of arithmetic abilities, it has at last entered the era of recorded history. From here on, as it moves into the higher-level thought processes, its progress will accelerate.

QUESTIONS AND PROBLEMS

1. What mode of addressing is not used by the arithmetic group?
2. What role does the accumulator play in the addition and subtraction processes?
3. Write the instruction (in both mnemonic and hexadecimal form) that will add -5 to the accumulator.
4. By making a small change to the program of Figure 11.9, write a program that will add the contents of memory locations 2020H through 2024H and place the result in memory location 2025H.
5. Convert the following decimal numbers to binary using signed-number rules: -27, $+10$, -127. Repeat using sign-magnitude rules.
6. What does an "X" in the mnemonic usually mean?
7. Based on the "ADD 1 immediately" program of Figure 11.8c, *exactly* when does the addition take place in the ALU? How is your answer related to the concept of *overlapping*?
8. In a *system-level* flowchart, how many machine-level instructions may correspond to a single flowchart block?
9. During arithmetic processing, why are the accumulator contents moved to the accumulator latch (ACT) before the ALU process?
10. Complete a waveform diagram (see Figure 10.3) for each of the following instructions. Use the 8080 or 8085 processor, or both, and assume that the op code of each instruction is stored at memory location 200AH:

Moon Program

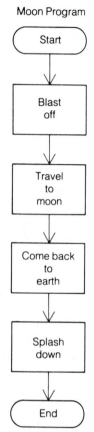

Figure 11.12 Conceptual-level flowchart.

a. Add M (number stored in RAM location 2050H)

b. ADI 07H

11. Rewrite the "add 5 numbers" program of Figure 11.9 using *direct* addressing to access memory (remember that direct addressing is found only in the data transfer group).

12. What is the purpose of each of the two machine cycles of the ADD M instruction?

13. Using the INR M and INX H instructions, write a routine that adds one to all memory locations between 2050H and 2055H.

14. Using a combination of data transfer and arithmetic instructions, involving all four address modes, write a program to accomplish the following sequence:

a. Subtract 7 from memory location 2060H.

b. Add the result to register E and place the final answer in location 2052H.

15. We wish to add the contents of register C to a selected memory location in page 20H. The low-order address of the selected memory location is entered from port 21H. Write a program to accomplish the task.

16. We wish to add together the contents of the memory location pointed to by the BC register pair to the contents of the memory location pointed to by the HL register pair, then place the answer in the memory location pointed to by the DE register pair. *Using only three instructions,* accomplish the task.

17. Which of the following addressing modes will allow the memory address to be changed *during execution*:

- Direct
- Indirect

chapter 12

The Logical Group

Sherlock Holmes was a master of deduction. Our intelligent machine, on the other hand, is presently incapable of even the simplest logical analysis. The reason is that the data-transfer and arithmetic-group instructions—the only instructions it presently knows—do not contain the elements of deductive logic. These elements are contained within the third major group of instructions—the logical group—and are the subject of this chapter.

THE ELEMENTS OF LOGIC

Consider the following logical situation (based on a famous Sherlock Holmes episode):

If the moon is full *or* lightning is flashing, *and* the dog did *not* bark, then the suspect is nearby.

This is simple deductive logic—arguing from a premise to a logical conclusion. (If the dog did *not* bark at the moon or the lightning, then the suspect must be nearby, *quieting the dog*.) The key elements of deductive logic may surprise you. They are the simple terms *and, or,* and *not*—all present in our mystery. In fact, according to George Boole, the inventor of symbolic logic, all deductive logic is based on combinations of the terms *and, or,* and *not*. Therefore, to turn our computer into a master sleuth, it appears we should expand its vocabulary to include these terms.

THE GROUP 3 VERBS

Looking over the seven verbs that constitute the logical group, we find the Boolean terms *and, or,* and *not* (*complement* performs the *not* function), along with several miscellaneous operations.

$$\left.\begin{array}{l} \text{And} \\ \text{Or} \\ \text{Exclusive or} \\ \text{Complement} \end{array}\right\} \quad \begin{array}{l} \text{Boolean} \\ \text{operations} \end{array}$$

$$\left.\begin{array}{l} \text{Rotate} \\ \text{Set} \\ \text{Compare} \end{array}\right\} \quad \begin{array}{l} \text{Miscellaneous} \\ \text{operations} \end{array}$$

Logic designers may be surprised to find that the universal logic gates (NAND and NOR) are not provided directly in the instruction set. The reason is straightforward: one of the major advantages of NAND and NOR gates in hardware design (their lower cost) simply evaporates in software design. In software, the "cost" is time, and all Boolean operations take up the same amount of processing time.

The *exclusive or* function is included in the logical group just for convenience and to save processing time, for as we all know, the *exclusive or* operation can itself be developed from the basic *and, or,* and *not* terms.

The reason for including the *rotate* instruction type in the logical group will be clear shortly. However, the *compare* and *set* instruction types are purely flag oriented, and therefore will be saved for Chapter 14 when flags and decision making are introduced.

Once again, the verb content of the group 3 instructions is easy to understand. This time, however, the operand portion is also second nature, for the addressing modes are the same as for the arithmetic group. Furthermore, the logical instructions are processed in the same manner as the arithmetic instructions. One of the logical inputs and the result of the Boolean operation reside in the accumulator; the other logical input resides in memory or an internal register and is located by way of the immediate, register, or indirect addressing modes. As with the arithmetic instructions, the actual combination of the logical variables within the ALU overlaps into the following instruction.

BOOLEAN OPERATIONS

There is one big difference between the arithmetic and logical operations, however, and it shows up when we try to simulate a simple 2-input OR gate on the computer. The question is: how can *two* 8-bit *registers* simulate *one* 2-input OR gate?

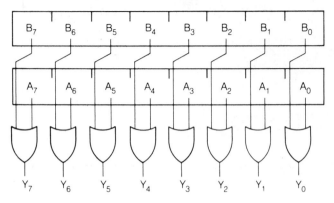

(a) Bit positions ORed together eight at a time

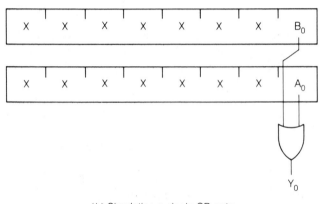

(b) Simulating a single OR gate

Figure 12.1 The OR process.

The answer is very simple: *each bit position is OR'ed together independently of all the others*. When the OR instruction is run, up to eight 2-input OR gates are simulated simultaneously (Figure 12.1a).

If we wish to simulate only one 2-input OR gate rather than the possible eight, we simply select any one of the eight available bit positions and run the OR instruction. All other bit positions are simply "don't care" values (Figure 12.1b).

On the other hand, as shown in Figure 12.2a, if the two variables to be OR'ed together are in unlike bit positions, they may not be combined as they stand. The variables must first be aligned in the same bit position.

The *rotate* instructions (Figure 12.2b) will solve the problem by allowing the programmer to line up the variables in a like bit position before logical processing. (It is left as an exercise to determine the difference between the two types of rotate instructions.)

To summarize the actions of the Boolean instructions, up to eight 2-input gates can be simulated with a single Boolean instruction. How then would we simulate a 3-input gate? The answer is: it must be broken down into a sequence of 2-input gates and the Boolean instruction run twice. Figure 12.3 illustrates the process using the AND instruction.

SOLVING THE MYSTERY

To solve the case of the "dog that did *not* bark," we will build a logic machine to process the clues. The machine will have three input variables (moon, lightning, and bark) and one output variable (suspect nearby). When these three clues are logically combined, they will indicate whether our suspect is close by.

With our three input variables, there are eight possible combinations of clues. For some of the combinations the output will reveal "suspect nearby" (logic 1); for others it will show "suspect not nearby" (logic 0). When all possible combinations are listed (Figure 12.4), this array of clues becomes the familiar *truth table*. (Verify for yourself the logical conclusion to each clue combination.) The next step is to design a machine to simulate the conclusions of the truth table.

Logic-Machine Design

There are two ways to design a logic machine. Referring to Figure 12.5a, we can use the older combinational-logic method; or, referring to Figure 12.5b, we can make use of a "sequential logic machine" (a computer), simulating the logic by way of software. Let us complete the computer design.

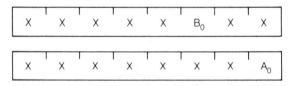

(a) Variables in unlike bit positions cannot be logically combined

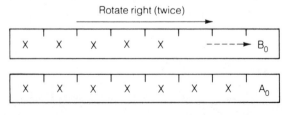

RRC—Rotate right
RLC—Rotate left
RAR—Rotate right through carry
RAL—Rotate left through carry

(b) The rotate instructions align variables in like bit positions

Figure 12.2 Aligning Boolean variables.

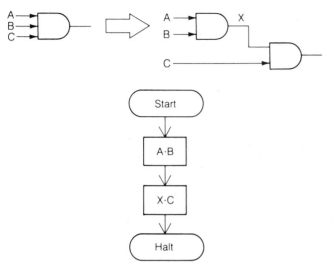

Figure 12.3 Simulating gates with more than two inputs requires consecutive Boolean instructions.

Moon	Lightning	Bark	Suspect nearby
0	0	0	0
0	0	1	0
0	1	0	1
0	1	1	0
1	0	0	1
1	0	1	0
1	1	0	1
1	1	1	0

Figure 12.4 Mystery truth table listing all combinations of clues.

Conventional Logic Design vs Computer Design

Solving the case of the "dog that did not bark" gave us an opportunity to contrast the older, more conventional combinational-logic method (Figure 12.5a) with the newer sequential methods of the microprocessor (Figure 12.5b). Clearly the older technique—at least in this case—is simpler and less expensive. What, then, is the advantage of using a computer and of writing software? The advantage is basic: when our thinking machine solves the present case and moves on to a new one, requiring a new logical sequence to solve, it is necessary only to change the program in memory—a quick, simple, and inexpensive process. To accomplish the same changeover in hardware would require a time-consuming rewiring of the circuit.

The important point to make is this: computers, like human beings, can easily be adapted to new situations. Simply send them back to "school" to be reprogrammed. Imagine what an advantage this is during the early development stages of an electronic system. Furthermore, as the conventional arrays become larger and larger, the parts count of the computer solution can be many times fewer (remember, software takes

Since we are confronted with a typical design problem, we will approach it in a formal manner. First of all, computer design requires a hardware/software balance. In this case, as shown in Figure 12.5b, the hardware is very simple: just input the three variables from a DIP switch feeding an input port and view the results on an LED fed by an output port.

Software design, on the other hand, is where most of our time will be spent. As always, software design begins with a high-level flowchart. As shown in Figure 12.6a, the process involves four steps.

The instructional-level flowchart and completed program are presented in Figure 12.6b. (To simplify program documentation, only the mnemonic form of each instruction has been listed.) To verify the routine, trace the flow of data through the program and see if the correct results are given as required by the truth table of Figure 12.4.

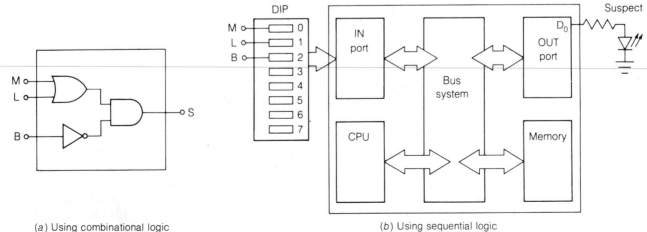

(a) Using combinational logic   (b) Using sequential logic

Figure 12.5 Logic-machine design.

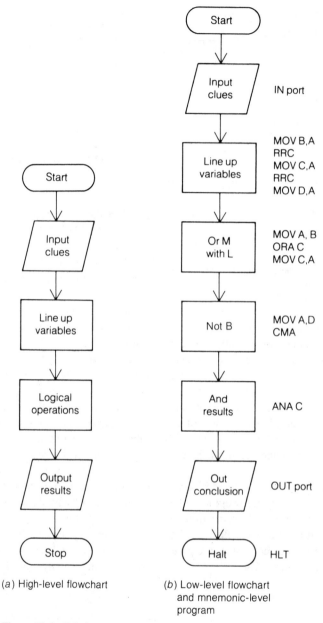

(a) High-level flowchart

(b) Low-level flowchart and mnemonic-level program

Figure 12.6 Solution to mystery program.

the place of hardware.) The threshold is reached for a conventional circuit of approximately 30 or more chips. No wonder microprocessors are replacing more and more conventional circuit arrays.

There are two disadvantages to the software technique, however, and they become apparent when speed and reliability are critical. Using conventional logic, for example, how long does it take to solve the case of the "dog that did not bark"? The answer is: probably no more than 50 nanoseconds—the time it takes the signal to propagate through two levels of gates. Compare that to the software technique, which requires 14 instruction cycles, 18 machine cycles, and 69 states—more than 20 microseconds, easily some 500 times longer. And when we compare reliability, combinational-logic circuits cannot get "out of sync" and will automatically recover from glitch-induced errors. Glitches in a microcomputer system, on the other hand, can cause a change in program execution, resulting in a complete system crash. Nevertheless, the computer usually is sufficiently fast and reliable for most applications, and is often the wiser choice.

BIT MANIPULATION

The second important duty performed by the logical group is called *bit manipulation*. An everyday application will reveal what we mean by bit manipulation (also known as *masking*).

A certain large hotel has eight electrical motors located around the building to control air conditioning and heating. To keep all parts of the building under environmental control, it is essential that these eight motors be independently controlled. Can a computer be assigned the task, especially one with a single 8-bit output port? (What we really need are eight 1-bit ports.) It does look possible to make use of a single 8-bit port, because, after all, don't the Boolean instructions operate independently on each bit? Let us tie in the eight motors to our single output port and test our theory with an example (Figure 12.7).

Suppose, because of a sudden influx of heat through an open window, we must turn on motor 2 but leave all others unchanged. That is, if some of the other motors are on, leave them on. If they are off, leave them off. The only motor we want to change is motor 2 (Figure 12.7*a*).

The key to the operation lies in several fundamental Boolean axioms. If we want to force a particular bit position to 1, OR that position with a 1. If we want to leave a bit position unchanged, OR that position with a 0.

$$A + 1 = 1 \text{ (force to 1)}$$
$$A + 0 = A \text{ (leave unchanged)}$$

The solution now becomes very easy. If we assume the accumulator is holding the present states of the motors, then, to turn on motor 2 but leave all others unaffected, simply OR immediate the accumulator with 04H and outport the result to the bank of motors (Figure 12.7*b*).

When the routine is tested on an arbitrary profile of motor states, it does give the desired results (Figure 12.7*c*). Only motor 2 has been changed—in this case, forced to turn on.

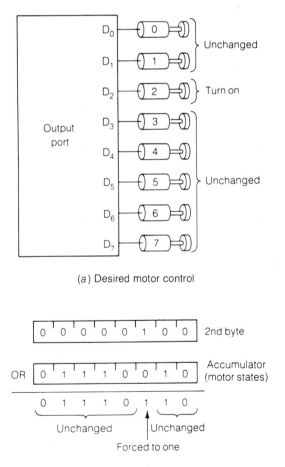

(a) Desired motor control

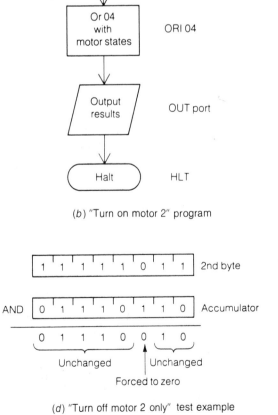

(b) "Turn on motor 2" program

(c) "Turn on motor 2 only" test example

(d) "Turn off motor 2 only" test example

Figure 12.7 Example of bit manipulation.

Of course, after motor 2 has been turned on for some time and the heat dissipated, it will have to be turned off—again without affecting the other seven motors.

This time we will take full advantage of several axioms involving the AND process. We just AND a 1 to those positions we wish to save and a 0 to those we wish to force to 0.

$$A \cdot 1 = A \quad \text{(leave unchanged)}$$
$$A \cdot 0 = 0 \quad \text{(force to 0)}$$

As illustrated in Figure 12.7d, AND immediate the accumulator with FBH, outport the results, and the process is reversed: motor 2 is turned off without affecting any of the other seven motors.

Clearly, with an OR/AND sequence (or an AND/OR sequence), the eight motors can be turned on, turned off, or left unchanged in any combination we wish.

Given the ability to manipulate individual bits, we can think of one 8-bit register as equivalent to eight 1-bit registers, or two 4-bit registers, or any combination we wish.

BIT CHANGE OF STATE

If the AND and OR processes are useful for changing the state of individual bits, then the Exclusive OR instruction is useful for *determining* individual bit changes of state.

Suppose our air-conditioned hotel is also fitted with eight burglar alarm sensors (Figure 12.8a), some normally open (NO) and usually sending a logic 0, while the others are normally closed (NC) and usually sending a logic 1. Therefore, as shown in the diagram, 01101011 represents the normal condition. The routine of Figure 12.8b inputs the sensor states, checks for changes, and outputs a 1 in any bit position where the present sensor state differs from the normal (bit 5 in this case).

INTELLIGENT-MACHINE UPDATE

The logical group is largely completed, and our intelligent machine can now examine a set of clues and solve a mystery

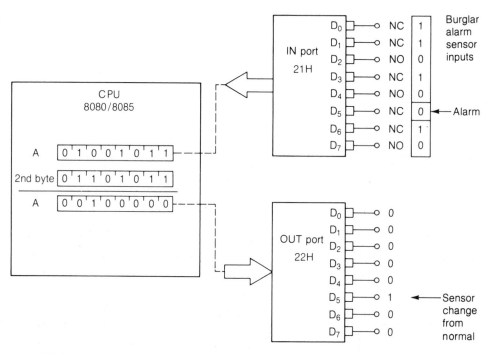

(a) Eight sensor states inported, exclusive ORed with normal condition, and results outported

(b) Change-of-state bit detection routine

Figure 12.8 Example of change-of-state bit detection.

using purely logical techniques. Also it can individually manipulate the digits of each hand by properly sequencing AND or OR instructions. For our intelligent machine, hand and eye and brain are coming together, just as they did for the human species many millions of years ago.

QUESTIONS AND PROBLEMS

1. What 8080/8085 instruction type performs the NOT operation?
2. What role does the accumulator play in the processing of the OR, AND, and EXCLUSIVE OR operations?
3. In a logical operation, do the various bit positions have any relationship *to each other?*
4. Why are the rotate instructions included in the logical group?
5. Referring to Appendix I, list the two categories of *rotate* instructions and state the difference. (The *carry flag* is a one-bit flip-flop, and will be explained fully in Chapter 14.)
6. Write a program to simulate a 3-input NAND gate. Assume the inputs are bit positions D_0, D_1, and D_2 of the input port, and the output is bit position D_0 of the output port.
7. What Boolean operation is used to blank out selected bit positions? To set selected bit positions high?
8. Write a program that will turn on outport bit positions D_0 and D_7, turn off positions D_3 and D_4, and mimic the remaining bit positions.
9. Explain how you would simulate six 2-input OR gates on your 8080/8085 system.
10. Explain how you would simulate one 5-input OR gate.
11. When simulating an 8-input AND gate on the 8080/8085 computer, what is the minimum number of times that the AND instruction would have to be used? (*Hint:* The answer is less than 7, but greater than 2.)
12. The four most significant bits (MSBs) of register B are to be combined with the four least significant bits (LSBs) of register C. Making use of logical instructions, how can this be accomplished?
13. What masking instruction placed before the out conclusion block of Figure 12.6 will ensure that all unused bit positions (D_1 through D_7) will always be blanked out?
14. What will be the result when we operate on the bank of motions of Figure 12.7*a* with the XRI FFH instruction?
15. For the XRA M instruction, complete the waveform diagram following the format of Figure 10.3. Assume that data to be combined with the accumulator is stored at RAM location 2060H.
16. By changing the order of the input variables, can the program of Figure 12.6*b* be shortened?
17. Using the *8080/8085 Assembly-Language Reference Card* from Appendix V, convert each mnemonic instruction of Figure 12.6*b* into hexadecimal machine code.
18. Explain how the rotate instructions can be used to multiply and divide by factors of two.
19. What is the difference between *shift* and *rotate?* What 8080/8085 rotate instructions can perform the shift process? (Research may be required.)

chapter 13

Loops and Jumps: Introduction to Assembly-Language Programming

We are creatures of repetition. To keep every cell in our bodies continuously awash with a fresh supply of oxygen and nutrients, our hearts may beat well over 3 billion times. Does it not follow that our memories must hold at least 3 billion instructions in order to keep our hearts active throughout our life span?

Of course, if that were true, life as we know it would not be possible. Instead, we have a special way of handling routines that repeat themselves over and over again: we place them into a *loop*.

LOOPS AND JUMPS

A loop is a circle. The MIMIC program developed earlier is presently a straight line (it starts and stops). To turn the process into a repetitive loop, we need a special command that will automatically cause the processor to go back to the IN-port instruction and repeat the mimic process—over and over again. The *jump* instruction is such a command (Figure 13.1).

When the jump instruction is substituted for the *halt* instruction, the program is placed into a repetitive loop (Figure 13.2). Note the flowchart arrow leading from the jump block to the return location.

When the MIMIC program is placed into a loop, only seven memory locations are required—no matter how many times the mimic process is repeated. The saving in memory space is enormous.

The jump instruction introduces the *branch group,* probably the most powerful and versatile instruction group available to the computer programmer. *The branch group alters normal sequential program flow.*

Fortunately, the jump instruction is rather easy to master. In Figure 13.1, the mnemonic of the instruction contains the expected action *jump* and reference to a 16-bit address. This address, of course, is the location to which the program is to jump. On completion of this instruction, the program counter is effectively changed to the value specified in byte 3 and byte 2 of the jump instruction. Using the jump instruction the program can branch to any of the 65,536 memory locations. When the program jumps back to a previous location, it usually forms a loop.

JMP addr   (Jump)
(PC) — (byte 3) (byte 2)
Control is transferred to the instruction whose address is specified in byte 3 and byte 2 of the current instruction.

1	1	0	0	0	0	1	1

low-order addr

high-order addr

Cycles: 3
States: 10
Addressing: immediate

Reproduced by permission of Intel Corp.

Figure 13.1   The jump instruction.

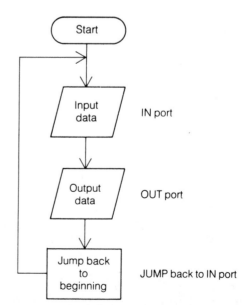

Figure 13.2   Mimic program placed into loop.

142

Jump Instruction Processing

The jump instruction uses the technique of *overlapping* to carry out the process of branching from one stored-program location to another. As we sequence through the process, follow the machine-cycle diagram of Figure 13.3, and note how smoothly the computer "passes the baton" from one program sequence to another. (Also refer to Appendix III.)

1. The jump-instruction op code is fetched to the instruction register and decoded.

2. The jump microprogram updates the program counter and directs the transfer of instruction bytes 2 and 3 to the Z and W registers respectively.

3. When the three machine cycles of the jump instruction are completed, the processor initiates the op-code fetch

sequence for the *next* instruction. However, rather than releasing the PC contents onto the address bus, the WZ register-pair contents are fed to the address bus.

4. Simultaneously, the WZ register is incremented to look ahead to the next machine cycle and is loaded into the program counter.

Based on these four steps, the actual jump takes place when the contents of WZ are fed to the address bus rather than the contents of the program counter. This action takes place during the first machine cycle *following* the jump instruction (the jump instruction therefore overlaps into the next instruction).

Any of the programs from previous chapters can be placed into a loop, thereby eliminating the need to reset the computer after each program run. (See Figure 13.4.)

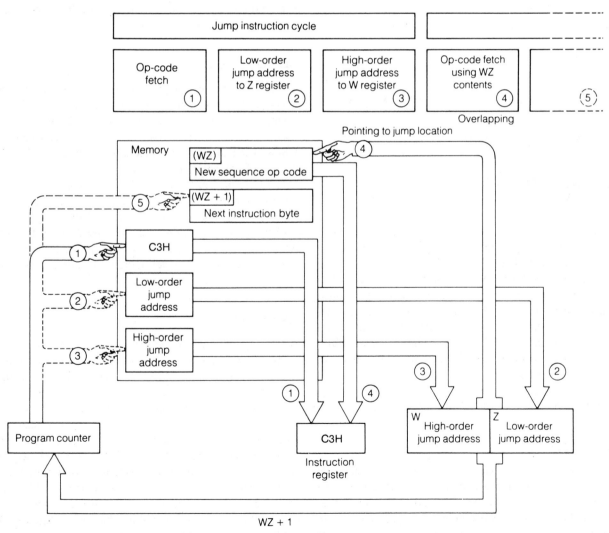

Figure 13.3 Jump-instruction timing and machine-cycle diagram.

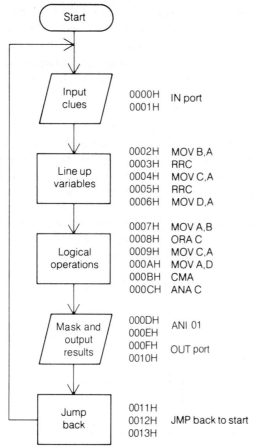

Figure 13.4 shows the flowchart with the following elements:

Start

| Input clues | 0000H 0001H | IN port |

| Line up variables | 0002H 0003H 0004H 0005H 0006H | MOV B,A RRC MOV C,A RRC MOV D,A |

| Logical operations | 0007H 0008H 0009H 000AH 000BH 000CH | MOV A,B ORA C MOV C,A MOV A,D CMA ANA C |

| Mask and output results | 000DH 000EH 000FH 0010H | ANI 01 OUT port |

| Jump back | 0011H 0012H 0013H | JMP back to start |

Figure 13.4 Mystery program placed into loop.

ASSEMBLY-LANGUAGE PROGRAMMING

Looking over the routine of Figure 13.4, we have apparently developed the natural habit of listing just the instruction mnemonics rather than the pure binary or hexadecimal machine-language formulation. Clearly binary or hexadecimal numbers just do not convey the same meaning as short-hand English statements. For that reason the list of mnemonics often is developed before the actual binary machine-language program; it is called *assembly-language programming.* Such a mnemonic-based program is easy to write, interpret, and correct.

An assembly-language program, called a *source listing,* is arranged in four columns, called *fields* (see Figure 13.5).

Code Field

By its very name the *code field* is closely related to the operation code of each instruction, and is basically the list of mnemonic verbs. ORG, which stands for *origin,* serves merely to identify the very beginning of the program. Origin is known as a *pseudo-instruction,* since it is not actually part

Source Listing

Label	Code	Operand	Comments
	ORG	2000H	Starting location of routine
START:	IN	port	Input clues to accumulator
	MOV	B,A	Place "moon" into B register
	RRC		Rotate clues right
	MOV	C,A	Place "lightning" into C register
	RRC		Rotate clues right
	MOV	D,A	Place "dog" into D register
	MOV	A,B	Place "moon" into accumulator
	ORA	C	OR "moon" with "lightning"
	MOV	C,A	Store M or L in C register
	MOV	A,D	Move "dog" to accumulator
	CMA		Complement "dog"
	ANA	C	AND "dog" with M or L
	ANI	01	Mask $D_1 \sim D_7$
	OUT	port	Give result
	JMP	START	Place into loop

(handwritten annotations: "OPcode" pointing to Code header; "memory location" pointing to Label column)

Figure 13.5 Mystery routine programmed in assembly language.

of the program but serves to supply information necessary for final program development.

Operand Field

As expected, the *operand field* is the list of instruction operands—in mnemonic form. As always, the letter "H" following all numbers indicates a hexadecimal number (octal numbers are identified with an "O" or "Q," binary numbers with a "B," and decimal numbers with either a "D" or the absence of any letter designation).

The last entry in the operand column represents one of the most important features of assembly-language programming. What kind of an operand is "start"? *Start is a symbolic representation of an address* (in this case 2000H). But why use a symbol—why not just use the numerical address directly? After we introduce the label field in the source listing, the reason will be clear.

Label Field

The *label field* is where the memory addresses would normally be. Surprisingly, it is mostly blank. Rather than a sequence of hexadecimal addresses, there is a single English word (START).

The label concept arose because some very practical questions were asked during the early development stages of programming. Perhaps the most obvious question is: why should I list all memory addresses if most are merely sequential? Does it not follow from this that the only time I need worry about addresses is at the very beginning of the program and wherever a program branch is involved? And finally, why should I use hexadecimal numbers when English-like symbols greatly improve program development and read-

```
ASM80 :F1:MYSTRY.SRC


ISIS-II 8080/8085 MACRO ASSEMBLER, V4.1          MYSTER    PAGE    1


  LOC  OBJ          LINE          SOURCE STATEMENT
                      1              NAME   MYSTERYPROGRAM
                      2
                      3   ; This is our first machine assembler printout.
                      4
                      5   ; This program (as well as all programs in this text
                      6   ; presented as list file printouts) is compatible
                      7   ; with the SDK-85 singleboard computer.  Any special
                      8   ; instructions required for SDK-85 operation are
                      9   ; tagged in the comment field with "SDK-85".  See
                     10   ; the SDK-85 User's Manual, Appendix II, and Chapter
                     11   ; 19 for proper operation of the SDK-85.
                     12
 2000                13              ORG    2000H  ; Starting location of routine
 2000 3E0E           14              MVI    A,OEH  ; SDK-85 (define 8155A mode)
 2002 D320           15              OUT    20H    ; SDK-85 (write to mode register)
 2004 DB21           16   START:     IN     21H    ; Input clues to accumulator
 2006 47             17              MOV    B,A    ; Place "MOON" into B register
 2007 0F             18              RRC           ; Rotate clues right
 2008 4F             19              MOV    C,A    ; Place "LIGHTNING" into C register
 2009 0F             20              RRC           ; Rotate clues right
 200A 57             21              MOV    D,A    ; Place "BARK" into D register
 200B 78             22              MOV    A,B    ; Place "MOON" into accumulator
 200C B1             23              ORA    C      ; OR "MOON" with "LIGHTNING"
 200D 4F             24              MOV    C,A    ; Store "M OR L" in C register
 200E 7A             25              MOV    A,D    ; Move "BARK" to accumulator
 200F 2F             26              CMA           ; Complement "BARK"
 2010 A1             27              ANA    C      ; AND "BARK" with "M OR L"
 2011 E601           28              ANI    01     ; Mask out D1 through D7
 2013 D322           29              OUT    22H    ; Give result
 2015 C30420         30              JMP    START  ; Place into loop
                     31              END


PUBLIC SYMBOLS

EXTERNAL SYMBOLS

USER SYMBOLS
START  A 2004

ASSEMBLY COMPLETE,    NO ERRORS
```

Figure 13.6   Machine-assembly printout of mystery program (list file).

ability? In answer to these and other questions, assembly language programming developed the label field and the *symbolic address*.

Start in our program is a symbolic address (a label) and stands for the location to which the program branches when the jump instruction is executed. No other labels are required because all other addresses are sequential (as shown, all labels end with a colon). Clearly, the use of labels greatly speeds up initial program development when concepts, rather than details, are important.

Comment Field

The last field is the *comment field*, and here there are no hard and fast rules: any comment helping to document the program and to aid others in understanding its intent are proper. However, the programmer should avoid the temp-

tation to repeat information that is obvious from the presence of the instruction itself.

PROGRAM ASSEMBLY

Once the assembly-language program is written, most of the work is done. But certainly the program is not ready to enter into the computer. It must be assembled into the proper hexadecimal or binary sequence of numbers, known as the *object program*. Of course, all symbolic addresses must be fully identified.

For very complex programs, the assembly process is accomplished by a computer under the direction of a program called an *assembler*. For simple programs, or when an assembler is not available, all programs are hand-assembled.

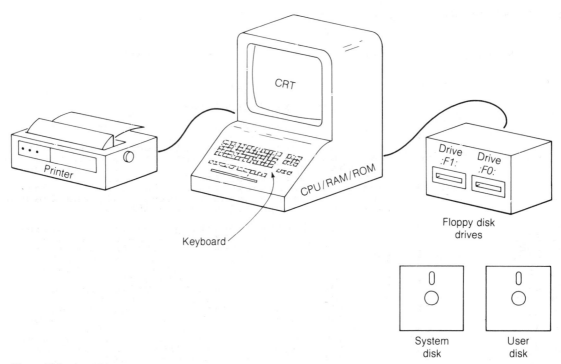

Figure 13.7   A machine-assembly system.

Machine Assembler

When a machine assembler is available, the art of assembly-language programming takes on new dimensions. For example, there are nearly a dozen different ways in which to specify an operand, and even arithmetic computations may be included. Furthermore, a machine assembler is programmed to recognize a great number of pseudo-instructions, including *macros*. (A macro is a single-line pseudo-instruction that stands for a group of instructions previously defined.)

The assembly process is usually performed in two passes over the source program (a two-pass assembler). The first pass expands macros, substitutes relative addresses for symbols, and writes the program into a temporary storage space (a file in a floppy). During the second pass all symbolic op codes and operands are assigned numeric values and an object program is generated.

As an example of the machine assembly process, Figure 13.6 shows our mystery program of the previous chapter coded by a machine assembler. Let's see how this assembled program was generated.

The hardware required for machine assembly is shown in Figure 13.7, and consists of a computer (with internal RAM and ROM), a video monitor, two disk drives, a printer, and system and user floppy disks. The software is stored as files (a program with a name) on the system disk, and includes an operating system, word processor, and assembler.

A typical machine-assembly process begins by "booting up" (transferring) the operating system from the system disk to the computer's internal RAM (the "boot" routine is stored in ROM within the computer). Running under the operating system, the user commands the word processor file to be transferred into internal RAM and executed. Using the facilities of the word processor, the user types in the source program in assembly language. When the user is satisfied with the program as written (it may later require corrections and modifications), the program is transferred to the user floppy disk and becomes a file. A typical file name might be :F1:MYSTERY.SRC (:F1: is the disk drive identification number).

Using an operating system command (such as ASM80 :F1:MYSTERY.SRC), the 8080/8085 macroassembler is evoked and the program mnemonics are automatically converted to machine code. During the assembly process a *location counter* keeps track of the address where the assembled code is to be placed. To initialize the location counter, we use the ORG directive, which sets the location counter to the value specified by the operand expression. As shown in Figure 13.6, we usually place the ORG directive at the beginning of the program to specify the starting address.

When completed, the assembly process generates two new files on the user's disk: an *object* file (MYSTERY.OBJ) and a *list* file (MYSTERY.LST). The object file (Figure 13.8*a*) is the binary machine-language code represented by ASCII characters and printer commands and is ready to run on an

>S [!GOWx10z/!fS"C   svq

(a) Interpretion of binary code by printer

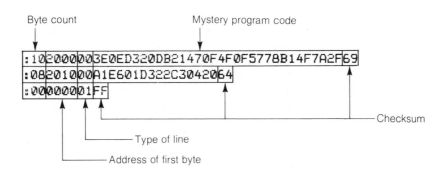

(b) MYSTERY.HEX—binary code converted to hexadecimal format

Figure 13.8   Mystery program object code.

8080/8085-based system. The object file obviously is of little use to the programmer for the purpose of documentation or program debugging.

However, if we convert the binary object file to hexadecimal (accomplished by an operating-system utility program), we can at least determine what is contained in MYSTERY.OBJ. Examining the result (MYSTERY.HEX of Figure 13.8b), we see that the hex converter added format information to the mystery program code. Each line starts with a count of the number of bytes of program data in that line (i.e., there are 10H or 16D bytes of program code in the first line). Next is placed the address of the first byte of program code (2000H), followed by the type of line ("00" is a code line; "01" is a termination line). At the end of each line a checksum byte is used to verify that the conversion to hexadecimal was made without error.

The list file (MYSTERY.LST) of Figure 13.6 is, however, of great use to the programmer during the development process. The list program is a listing of hexadecimal machine code placed side by side with the source program. Note that all addresses—including the branch address—have been filled in automatically. As an added bonus most assemblers will notify the operator if certain types of syntax errors were made in the source listing. Since none was found in the program of Figure 13.6, it prints "no errors" at the bottom of the sheet.

Note that all symbols are fully identified at the bottom of the list file. As shown, START is the symbolic address (A) for memory location 2004H. (PUBLIC and EXTERNAL symbols will be introduced in Chapter 20.)

If syntax errors are found, they are identified in the list file (the assembler, of course, cannot check for errors in

programming logic). For example, the mystery program of Figure 13.9—as indicated—contains five errors. To help identify the type and location of an error, a variety of error codes are printed on the same line as the statement in error: "Q" indicates an op code/operand combination that is not valid, "E" indicates that an expression has been constructed erroneously, and "U" indicates an undefined symbol (symbolic name in argument field which has never appeared in label field). Identifying the five errors is left as an exercise.

Entire books are written on assembly-language programming techniques, and many systems are on the market. If you have access to a machine assembler, it would be wise to consult the manufacturer's literature in order to fully realize the power of the system. Because of the increased availability of machine assemblers, we will introduce a number of advanced features in the chapters to follow.

Hand Assembly

When a machine assembler is not available, most manufacturers provide an "assembly language reference card" to aid the process of hand assembly (see Appendix V). The mnemonics are conveniently arranged in instruction groups and all possible addressing combinations provided, thereby eliminating the need for coding.

INTELLIGENT-MACHINE UPDATE

When placed into a loop, our intelligent machine seems much more alive. No longer does it function in bursts from reset to halt, but now processes continuously. Is it the pres-

```
ASM80 :F1:ERROR.SRC


ISIS-II 8080/8085 MACRO ASSEMBLER, V4.1          MYSTER     PAGE     1


   LOC   OBJ          LINE          SOURCE STATEMENT

                        1          NAME   MYSTERYPROGRAM
                        2
                        3  ; This is our first machine assembler printout.
                        4
   2000                 5          ORG    2000H ; Starting location of routine
   2000  3EOE           6          MVI    A,OEH ; SDK-85 operation
   2002  D320           7          OUT    20H   ; SDK-85 operation
   2004  DB21           8 START:   IN     21H   ; Input clues to accumulator
 Q 2006  40             9          MOV    B     ; Place "MOON" into B register
   (   O)
   2007  OF            10          RRC          ; Rotate clues right
 E 2008  8A9COO        11          MOV    C,A   ; Place "LIGHTNING" into C register
   (   9)
   200B  OF            12          RRC          ; Rotate clues right
   200C  57            13          MOV    D,A   ; Place "BARK" into D register
   200D  78            14          MOV    A,B   ; Place "MOON" into accumulator
 Q 200E  0100          15          OR     C     ; OR "MOON" with "LIGHTNING"
   (  11)
   2010  4F            16          MOV    C,A   ; Store "M OR L" in C register
   2011  7A            17          MOV    A,D   ; Move "BARK" to accumulator
 Q 2012  B56100        18          CMA    A     ; Complement "BARK"
   (  15)
   2015  A1            19          ANA    C     ; AND "BARK" with "M OR L"
   2016  E601          20          ANI    01    ; Mask out D1 through D7
   2018  D322          21          OUT    22H   ; Give result
 U 201A  C30000        22          JMP    BEGIN ; Place into loop
   (  18)
                       23          END


PUBLIC SYMBOLS


EXTERNAL SYMBOLS


USER SYMBOLS
START   A 2004

ASSEMBLY COMPLETE,     5 ERRORS (   22 )
```

Figure 13.9 Mystery program list file showing 5 errors.

ence of loops that gives us continuous life? It seems like a reasonable theory.

The many program loops working to keep our bodies functioning were developed millions of years ago, and they certainly are not the higher-level thought processes that give our species the almost unique ability to reason. Is it the ability to reason and to make decisions that will allow us at last to part company with our intelligent machine?

Not at all, for as we will see in the next chapter, even the ability to reason affords the human being no real sanctuary from our rapidly developing machine.

QUESTIONS AND PROBLEMS

1. Bytes 2 and 3 of the *jump* instruction contain what information?
2. If a *jump* instruction is stored at memory location 2040H (through 2042H), what range of numbers placed into bytes 2 and 3 will place the processor into a loop?
3. What role does the WZ register play in the jump process?
4. How many of the 64K memory locations can the JMP addr instruction branch to? Can we jump forward as well as backward?
5. The memory location to which the processor jumps should always contain what kind of information?
6. List several advantages of assembly-language programming over machine-language programming.
7. List and briefly describe each of the four fields of assembly-language programming.
8. What are *source, object,* and *list* programs?
9. What are *symbolic* addresses, and why were they developed?
10. Why are symbolic addresses (labels) placed in the label field?
11. What is an *assembler?* What is a *two-pass* assembler?
12. Using the jump instruction (and page 0 ROM), how can RESET (which clears the program counter) result in processing a program starting at location 2000H?
13. Using the *8085A CPU instructions in operation code*

sequence table from Appendix I, *disassemble* (convert from hex to mnemonics) the following program (be sure to use the ORG statement and labels).

Address	Code
2000H	0EH
2001H	0FH
2002H	79H
2003H	C6H
2004H	02H
2005H	32H
2006H	30H
2007H	20H
2008H	C3H
2009H	00H
200AH	20H

14. What is the purpose of the ANI 01 instruction near the end of our mystery program (Figure 13.6)? (Also see question 13 in Chapter 12.)

15. Referring to Figure 13.6, what address would START correspond to if we place the ORG 10C0H directive at the start of our program?

16. What is wrong with the comments given in this MIMIC program:

```
        ORG    2000H   ; Start at 2000H
START:  IN     21H     ; Input to port 21H
        OUT    22H     ; Output to port 22H
        JMP    START   ; Jump to symbol START
        END
```

chapter 14

Reasoning: The Conditional Jump

Leonardo da Vinci could reason. A caveman could reason. And you and I can reason. But can a computer reason? Many people say no. A computer, they argue, can only do what it is told to do—what it is programmed to do. But the catch is: that is also true of us. We reason because we are programmed to reason, and so can a computer be programmed to reason.

THE ELEMENTS OF REASONING

First of all, let us reduce the elements of reasoning to more concrete terms; reasoning, after all, is a very abstract concept.

> To *reason* is to *decide*.
> To *decide* is to *choose*.

So reasoning is decision making, and it is choosing—something we do every day. We *choose* to stop at the intersection if the light is red; otherwise we ignore the signal and go on through. We *choose* to go to the beach if the sun is shining; otherwise we stay at home.

These two examples of decision making have several features in common. First, each involves a branch concept—the sort of action you take when coming to a fork in the road. When you arrive at the branch point, you must make a decision—a choice. You can go straight ahead, or you can branch away. And what determines if a branch should be made or ignored? In the first case the traffic signal determines our course of action, and in the second case it is the sun. When these *signs* are consulted, the correct decisions are made.

Based on these simple ideas, the process of decision making can be flowcharted as a two-step process (Figure 14.1):

1. The signs are set. For example, the sun comes out.

2. A branch is made—or ignored. It all depends on the sun. (Note the flowchart symbol for branching and how it resembles a fork in the road. There is only one way in, but two ways out.)

And that is how we make a decision—such as going to the beach. *A computer makes a decision in exactly the same way.* In a computer, however, the *signs* are called *flags,* and the branch can still be called a *branch* or it can be called a *jump*—either term will do. To teach our computer to make decisions we will have to locate the right instructions to carry out each of the two flowchart blocks in the decision-making process.

The Flag-Setting Block

For us, almost anything can be a *flag* or sign, including a flag itself. The 8080/8085 microprocessor, on the other hand, uses only five flags—electronic flags—each one a single flip-flop:

- Zero (Z) flag
- Carry (CY) flag
- Sign (S) flag
- Parity (P) flag
- Auxiliary Carry (AC) flag

The last three, the sign, parity, and auxiliary carry flags, will not be covered until later in the book, allowing us to

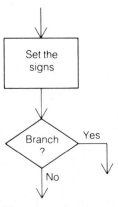

Figure 14.1   The two-step decision-making process.

concentrate in this chapter on the two flags that are used most often: the zero and carry flags.

Like the sun, which is either shining or not shining (in a two-valued system), each flag is also two-valued, and can be set to a 1 or reset to a 0. *It is the purpose of the flag-setting instructions to translate the state of the system on which decisions are based (sun out?) into flag values.* Most of the flag-setting instructions come from the arithmetic or logical group. It works like this: when an arithmetic or logical instruction is run, the flags are set or reset, *depending on the numerical outcome of the operation.* It follows that the set-flags block of our two-step decision-making process is usually an arithmetic or logical instruction.

As an example of a flag-setting instruction, let us see how the simple *add register* instruction affects the carry and zero flags (see Figure 14.2a). As shown, we have included flag information in our instruction summary for the first time. Whichever flags are listed are those affected by the *add register* instruction. Since all are listed, the *add register* instruction affects all five flags.

When the *add register* instruction is processed, the Z and C flags will tell you something about the result:

- If the result of the *add register* process produces a zero sum, the Z flag goes to "1." Otherwise, if the result is nonzero, the Z flag goes to "0."

- If the result of the *add register* process produces a carry, the CY flag goes to "1." Otherwise, the CY flag goes to "0."

Figure 14.2b shows the results of adding 64_{10} and 192_{10}.

The Branch Block

Once the flags are set or reset by one or more arithmetic/logic instructions, it is the job of the branch block to see that the correct path is taken. To jump or not to jump—that is the question. The flags will provide the answer.

Obviously, the branch block is processed by a jump-type instruction. But it certainly cannot be the unconditional jump that we learned about in the last chapter. The unconditional jump says you must jump (you must go to the beach, even if the sun is hidden).

The *conditional jump* instruction of Figure 14.3 is the answer. The conditional jump is one of the most powerful instruction types in the entire instruction set, and will allow the computer to reason, to make a choice—to jump or not to jump.

Think of the *conditional jump* instruction as asking a question (is the sun shining?), except that this time, since the computer is doing the asking, it must be in terms of flags. For example, is the carry flag set? If the answer is yes, the jump is made. If the answer is no, the jump is ignored. *The design logic of the 8080/8085 demands that, whenever the answer is yes, we must jump; we have no choice.* Because of this constraint, there may be a need to ask the question in a negative manner: is the carry flag *not* set? Again, if the answer is yes (it is zero), 8080/8085 logic design demands that the jump be made; if the answer is no (it is set), the jump is always ignored. In other words, *jump on yes; ignore on no.*

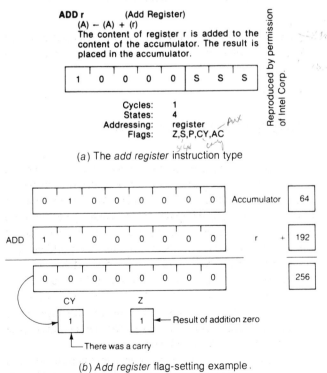

(a) The *add register* instruction type

(b) Add register flag-setting example.

Figure 14.2   A flag-setting instruction.

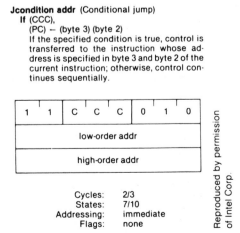

Figure 14.3   The *conditional jump* instruction.

Mnemonic	Condition	CCC	Question based on flags	Question based on math or logic result
JNZ	NZ Not zero	000	Is the Z flag not set?	Is the result not zero?
JZ	Z Zero	001	Is the Z flag set?	Is the result zero?
JNC	NC No carry	010	Is the CY flag not set?	Was there *no* borrow, carry or rotate into carry?
JC	C Carry	011	Is the CY flag set?	Was there a borrow, carry, or rotate into carry?
JPO	PO Parity odd	100	Is the P flag not set?	Did the operation produce odd parity?
JPE	PE Parity even	101	Is the P flag set?	Did the operation produce even parity?
JP	P Plus	110	Is the S flag not set?	Is the MSB of the result zero?
JM	M Minus	111	Is the S flag set?	Is the MSB of the result one?

Figure 14.4 The eight conditional jumps.

Because there are four flags (the *auxiliary carry* flag is not used for conditional jumps), and because each question can be asked in either a negative or a positive manner, there are eight possible questions that we can program the conditional jump instruction to ask:

Is the *zero* flag set?

Is the *zero* flag *not* set?

Is the *sign* flag set?

Is the *sign* flag *not* set?

Is the *parity* flag set?

Is the *parity* flag *not* set?

Is the *carry* flag set?

Is the *carry* flag *not* set?

We program the computer to ask the correct question from this list of eight by coding the condition bits in the first byte of the instruction (refer to Figure 14.3). Although CCC stands for *condition*, it could just as well stand for *question*. Jump when the answer to the question is yes, or jump when the condition is true; they both mean the same thing.

From Figure 14.4, select the question you would like to have the computer ask at the branching point, and simply place the proper 3-bit binary code in the CCC position. Assembly-language programmers will note the mnemonic form of the various conditional jump questions.

Summary of the Two-Step Decision-Making Process

And that is how decisions are made. For people or for machines, it is the same two-step process: set flags based on the state of the system, and jump *if* the flag condition is true. As shown in Figure 14.5, the set-flags operation usually is performed with a math or logical operation, while the branch process is accomplished with one of the conditional branch instructions.

Therefore, when writing programs involving decision making, each decision will require the programmer to:

1. Select the correct flag-setting instruction.
2. Select the correct conditional branch instruction.

Nearly every program developed in the remainder of this book will involve one or more of these two-step decision-making processes.

A DECISION-MAKING EXAMPLE

To put the decision-making process to work, let us write a modified mimic program to mimic only the year in which you were born and blank out all others. We know a decision is involved, for the computer must decide if the inported number is the correct year, then pass on the one correct number and zero out all others. To make the problem specific, let us assume you were born in "52" (1952).

The first step, as always, is a flowchart. Do you see how the strategy of Figure 14.6 will solve the problem? If the incoming number is 52 (34H in hexadecimal), simply jump around the clear block; otherwise, the number must pass through the clear block and be blanked out.

The next task is to select the proper instructions to carry out each flowchart block. As we develop the assembly-language program, we will allow a software error (bug) to find its way into the routine. If you haven't found the bug when

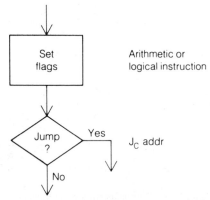

Figure 14.5 The two-step decision-making process for a computer.

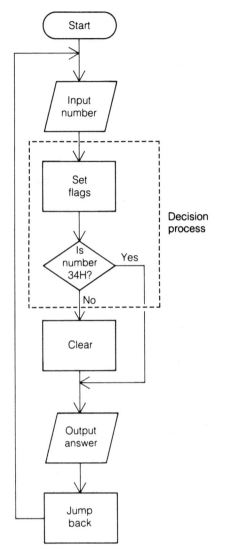

Figure 14.6 "Mmimic birthday" program flowchart.

(XRI 34H) instruction to search for a match. When a match is found, the Z flag will go high. *In other words, the set-flags block has translated a unique physical condition (number equal to 34H) into a unique flag condition (Z flag high).*

The set-flags block completed, we move on to the second part of decision making, the conditional branch.

The Conditional Branch Block

The set-flags block, using the *exclusive OR immediate* instruction, guarantees us the following: whenever the imported number is 34H, the Z flag will be set (otherwise it will be reset). The branch block must now ask the right question (or set the right condition). The two choices are: *jump on zero* (JZ), or *jump on not zero* (JNZ). Often the best way to proceed is simple trial and error. Choose one, go through the process mentally, and if it works, we have our answer. If not, the other choice must be correct. To save time, we will make the correct choice to begin with (jump on zero) and follow the process through the decision-making block. If the inported number is indeed 34H, the exclusive OR operation gives a result of zero, and the zero flag goes to one (indicating the *result* of the operation was zero). Since we jump on zero (jump if result of operation is zero), we jump around the clear block and outport the number 34H unchanged. On the other hand, if the inported number is *not* 34H, the exclusive OR operation gives a nonzero result, the Z flag is reset to zero, and we do not jump, but pass through the clear block and outport a zero. (Because the Z flag goes to a *one* only when the result of the operation is *zero*, the Z flag is often tricky to work with and may require some practice.)

Just complete the remaining blocks with well-known instructions, and the "birthday" program is complete (Figure 14.7a).

But will the program work? No, it will not, for as promised there is a software error in the routine. The problem is this: when we set the flags using the XRI 34H instruction, we also destroy the inported information when a match is found. Therefore, as written, the program always outports a zero. One solution, shown in Figure 14.7b, is to save the inported number in an internal register and restore it to the accumulator after the set-flags instruction.

When the program is written in assembly language, note how easy it is to make corrections. We simply add or delete instructions at will, paying no attention to the increased program length—the addresses and labels will not be set until the final assembly process.

A list file (MIMIC.LST) of our mimic birthday program is shown in Figure 14.8. Access to a machine assembler here is greatly appreciated, since we have two symbolic addresses to decode—and address calculations are one of the most frequent sources of error during the hand assembly process.

we are finished, we will show how programming in assembly language allows for quick and easy program corrections.

The Flag-Setting Block

Passing by the familiar input block, we move to the set-flags block, where the decision-making process begins. How are we going to set the flags to determine if the inported number is equal to 34H? Here is where we learn that programming is an art as well as a science. Like playing the game of chess, we must rely largely on *heuristics* to solve the problem. (Heuristics is a method of education in which the student proceeds along empirical lines, using rules of thumb, to find answers.) One fact looks promising: when two numbers are exclusive ORed, the result is zero only when they are equal. And only when the result is zero will the Z flag go high. Therefore, the set-flags block will use the Exclusive OR

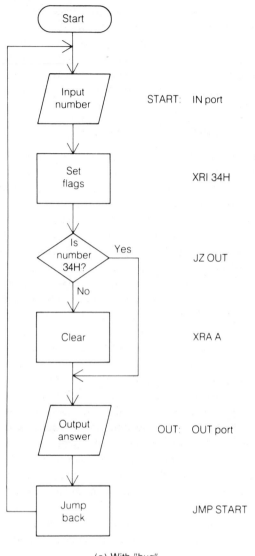

(a) With "bug"

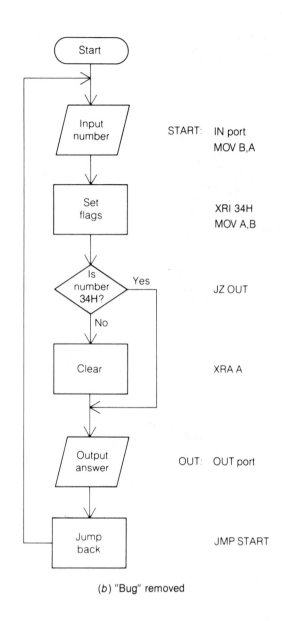

(b) "Bug" removed

Figure 14.7 "Mimic birthday" program.

MACHINE-ASSEMBLY UPDATE—I

It is convenient here to present our first "machine-assembly update," in which we introduce the more commonly used features of a machine assembler that greatly improve program efficiency, readability, and error correction. *Many of the features will be useful even if the program is to be hand assembled.*

A good rule for writing source programs is: the more humanlike, the better. Therefore, as shown in Figure 14.8 (line 13), we are allowed to write the date (52) in the more convenient decimal form. The assembler—which only can work on binary/hexadecimal—will perform the necessary translation from decimal to hexadecimal *automatically* (note the hexadecimal code corresponding to XR1 52). As with

address calculations, letting the machine do the work saves time and reduces the chances of error.

GREATER-THAN/LESS-THAN DECISIONS

Suppose we assign our computer the task of mimicking certain numbers, as before, but this time, rather than passing on only the number 34H, it is to mimic all numbers *less than* 34H and blank out all numbers 34H *or greater*. Can our computer handle this task as easily as it did the first assignment?

Yes, but only after we introduce the *compare* instruction—an instruction type designed to handle *greater-than/*

```
ASM80 :F1:BRTHDY.SRC


ISIS-II 8080/8085 MACRO ASSEMBLER, V4.1        MIMICB    PAGE    1


 LOC   OBJ        LINE        SOURCE STATEMENT
                     1            NAME MIMICBIRTHDAY
                     2
                     3    ; This program only mimics numbers equal to 52.
                     4    ; This program also demonstrates the automatic
                     5    ; conversion from decimal (52) to hexadecimal
                     6    ; (34H) during assembly.
                     7
 2000               8            ORG  2000H
 2000 3E0E          9            MVI  A,0EH   ; SDK-85 (define 8155A mode)
 2002 D320          10           OUT  20H     ; SDK-85 (write to mode register)
 2004 DB21          11   START:  IN   21H     ; Input test date
 2006 47            12           MOV  B,A     ; Store away
 2007 EE34          13           XRI  52      ; Test for match
 2009 78            14           MOV  A,B     ; Move back
 200A CA0E20        15           JZ   OUTPUT  ; Jump if match
 200D AF            16           XRA  A       ; Blank out
 200E D322          17   OUTPUT: OUT  22H     ; Give answer
 2010 C30420        18           JMP  START   ; Place into loop
                     19           END


PUBLIC SYMBOLS


EXTERNAL SYMBOLS


USER SYMBOLS
OUTPUT A 200E     START  A 2004

ASSEMBLY COMPLETE,    NO ERRORS
```

Figure 14.8 Mimic-birthday program list file.

CMP r   (Compare Register)
(A) − (r)
The content of register r is subtracted from the accumulator. The accumulator remains unchanged. The condition flags are set as a result of the subtraction. **The Z flag is set to 1 if (A) = (r). The CY flag is set to 1 if (A) < (r).**

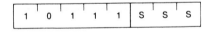

| 1 | 0 | 1 | 1 | 1 | S | S | S |

Cycles: 1
States: 4
Addressing: register
Flags: Z,S,P,CY,AC

CMP M   (Compare memory)
(A) − ((H) (L))
The content of the memory location whose address is contained in the H and L registers is subtracted from the accumulator. The accumulator remains unchanged. The condition flags are set as a result of the subtraction. **The Z flag is set to 1 if (A) = ((H) (L)). The CY flag is set to 1 if (A) < ((H) (L)).**

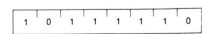

| 1 | 0 | 1 | 1 | 1 | 1 | 1 | 0 |

Cycles: 2
States: 7
Addressing: reg. indirect
Flags: Z,S,P,CY,AC

CPI data   (Compare immediate)
(A) − (byte 2)
The content of the second byte of the instruction is subtracted from the accumulator. The condition flags are set by the result of the subtraction. **The Z flag is set to 1 if (A) = (byte 2). The CY flag is set to 1 if (A) < (byte 2).**

| 1 | 1 | 1 | 1 | 1 | 1 | 1 | 0 |
| data |

Cycles: 2
States: 7
Addressing: immediate
Flags: Z,S,P,CY,AC

Reproduced by permission
of Intel Corp.

Figure 14.9 The *compare* instructions.

less-than/equal-to decision making. As usual, it comes in various addressing modes (Figure 14.9).

Using the *compare immediate* addressing mode as an example, the accumulator is compared to the second byte of the instruction and placed into one of three categories, depending on whether it is less than, equal to, or greater than the second byte of the instruction. (Actually, the compare process is basically a subtraction. In this case, the second byte of the compare immediate instruction is subtracted from the accumulator and the flags are set according to the result.)

The carry flag handles the greater-than/less-than requirements of the instruction, for if the second byte is bigger than the accumulator, a borrow is required, which sets the carry flag. If the second byte is equal to or less than the accumulator, no borrow is required and the carry flag resets. Only when the two numbers are exactly equal will the result be zero and the Z flag set. As shown here, a particular combination of the carry and zero flags uniquely identifies the three categories:

Data less than accumulator	*Data equal to accumulator*	*Data greater than accumulator*
CY = 0	CY = 0	CY = 1
Z = 0	Z = 1	Z = 0

There is, however, one important difference between the *compare* and *subtract* processes. The compare process inhibits the answer from being placed in the accumulator, and is often called an *invisible subtraction*. In other words, the original number in the accumulator is not changed as a result of the compare process—only the flags are affected. *Obviously, the compare instruction is exclusively a flag-setting instruction and is always used for greater-than/less-than/equal-to decision making. It has no other purpose.*

The complete solution to our problem is given in Figure 14.10. Trace through the program and convince yourself that all input numbers less than 34H will be mimicked and all numbers 34H or greater will be blanked out. As noted, the Z flag has no role in the decision-making process because the carry flag uniquely defines the numbers to be mimicked. Figure 14.11 shows the program coded by a machine assembler for SDK-85 operation (see Appendix II).

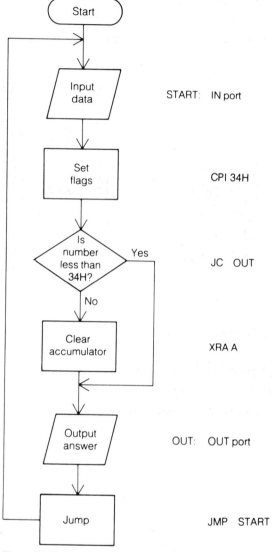

Figure 14.10 Program for mimicking numbers less than 34H.

By extending this process to any number of flag-setting instructions, we see that the decision-making ability of a computer is not at all hampered by an increased number of choices.

MULTIPRONGED FORKS IN THE ROAD

Decisions often involve more than a simple choice between two alternatives. Suppose we have three options to choose from—a three-pronged fork in the road. Can our computer pick out the correct path from the three choices? Figure 14.12 shows how it is done: just make two 2-valued decisions in a row. There is one way in, but three ways out.

THE DELAY LOOP

To a computer, one second is a very long period of time, for it can easily process 200,000 instructions in a single second. Yet, to human beings, a second is a very brief period of time. Because of this discrepancy, there often is a need to delay the processing action at various points in the program. This slowdown is made possible by the *time-delay*

```
ASM80 :F1:LESS52.SRC


ISIS-II 8080/8085 MACRO ASSEMBLER, V4.1        MIMICL    PAGE    1


    LOC   OBJ        LINE          SOURCE STATEMENT
                      1             NAME MIMICLESSTHAN52
                      2
                      3   ; This program only mimics numbers less
                      4   ; than 52.
                      5
    2000              6             ORG   2000H
    2000  3E0E        7             MVI   A,0EH     ; SDK-85 operation
    2002  D320        8             OUT   20H       ; SDK-85 operation
    2004  DB21        9   START:    IN    21H       ; Input test date
    2006  FE34       10             CPI   52        ; Test for match
    2008  DA0C20     11             JC    OUTPUT    ; Jump if < 52
    200B  AF         12             XRA   A         ; Blank out
    200C  D322       13   OUTPUT:   OUT   22H       ; Give answer
    200E  C30420     14             JMP   START     ; Place into loop
                     15             END


PUBLIC SYMBOLS


EXTERNAL SYMBOLS


USER SYMBOLS
OUTPUT A 200C    START   A 2004

ASSEMBLY COMPLETE,    NO ERRORS
```

Figure 14.11 Machine-generated list file for program "mimic less than 52 (34H)."

loop, a routine making use of the conditional jump instruction. Here is how it works:

1. A number is loaded into one of the internal registers (or memory).

2. The computer decrements the register and, using the Jcondition instruction, checks to see if it is zero.

3. If it is not zero, the computer jumps back to the decrement instruction for another pass. If it is zero, the computer continues to the next instruction.

Clearly, the number of cycles the computer loops through is directly proportional to the size of the number loaded into the register, which in turn is approximately proportional to the magnitude of the delay time span. Figure 14.13 shows the delay-loop flowchart and program.

NESTING

Although the computer can be forced to circle the delay loop up to 256 times, this still gives a delay of barely one millisecond. Many applications may require delays of many seconds, or minutes, or hours, or even days. To produce these longer delay times, two or more delay loops can be *nested* (one delay loop placed inside another). Figure 14.14 shows how it is done for a double-nested loop.

Delay numbers are loaded into two registers (or memory locations), corresponding to the inner loop and the outer loop. Let us assume that the inner delay-loop number is 10_{10} and is loaded into register B, and the outer delay-loop number is 15_{10} and is loaded into register C.

When the processor decrements the inner-loop register (register B) down to zero and drops out of the inner delay loop, it enters the outer loop. After decrementing the outer-

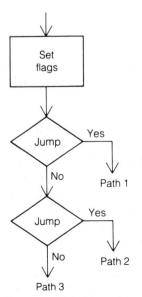

Figure 14.12 Three-pronged decision-making flowchart.

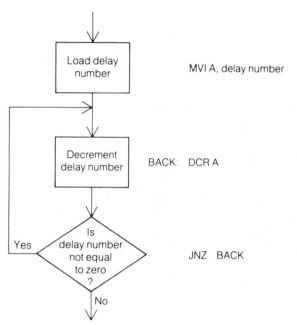

Figure 14.13   Delay-loop flowchart and program.

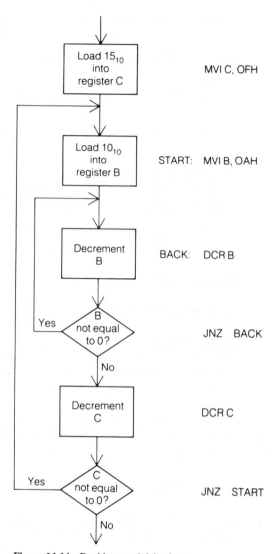

Figure 14.14   Double-nested delay loop.

loop register (register C) by one, it jumps back to the start of the program. Before reaching the inner loop again, however, 10 is reloaded into register B. Therefore, each time the processor passes around the outer loop, it is forced to spin around the inner loop 10 more times. Since the processor circles the outer loop 15 times before decrementing the C register down to zero and dropping out of the double-nested delay loop entirely, the inner loop is circled 150 times during one pass through the entire delay routine.

Using a double-nested delay loop, delay times of approximately ⅓ sec can be developed. Obviously this nesting process can be continued indefinitely, producing delay times as long as you wish.

PROGRAM TIMING

A crystal-controlled digital system offers yet another advantage over a purely analog system: all times and events can be specified exactly—all we have to do is count states, where each state is equal to one clock period. Figure 14.15 shows the results of counting the states for an updated version of our "birthday" program, when processed on an 8085 system running at 3 MHz. (The number of states required to process each instruction is included with each instruction summary in Appendix I.) As we see, the total processing time depends on which path is taken through the decision-making process. (Be aware that when the condition for jumping is not met, only the first two machine cycles—or seven states—of the Jcondition instruction are processed.)

As a second example of program timing, let's write a program to provide a delay of 1 second. Of course, with a digital machine, we will not be able to delay *exactly* 1 second, but let's get as close as we can. To shorten the program and at the same time provide a high degree of accuracy, we will resort to a couple of tricks.

Referring to Figure 14.16, our first trick is to use the 16-bit HL register pair to hold the delay number. Able to count down from 65,536 (256 × 256), the HL register pair will simulate a double-nested loop using 8-bit registers. Since the DCX H instruction does not affect the flags, we OR together the H and L registers to set the Z flag when both are empty. The second trick is to include four-state NOP (No OPeration) instructions both inside and outside the loop to fine-tune the delay time. Of course, to save memory locations, the fewer NOPs the better.

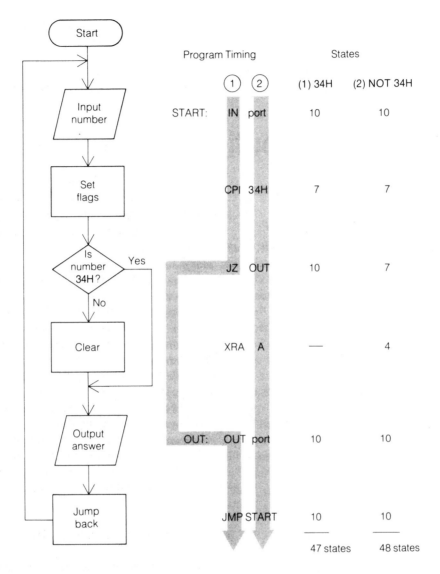

(1) 47 states × ⅓ μs/state = 15.7 μs
(2) 48 states × ⅓ μs/state = 16.0 μs

Figure 14.15 "Mimic birthday" program timing.

First of all, for a 3 MHz clock, convince yourself that the formula of Figure 14.17*a* relates the overall delay time to the delay number and number of NOPs.

After considerable trial-and-error juggling, we find that a delay number of 62,500, with six NOPs inside the loop and zero NOPs outside the loop, will generate a delay of 1.000003 seconds (see Figure 14.17*b*).

LOOPS AND INDIRECT ADDRESSING

In previous chapters we learned that register-indirect addressing—which requires only a single byte to address

any memory location—can often shorten a program. Now, with the introduction of conditional jumps in this chapter, we will find that indirect addressing and loops can team up to provide another powerful program-shortening tool. The key lies with the ability to manipulate the HL register pair with various instructions from the arithmetic group, most notably *increment HL register pair* (INX H) and *decrement HL register pair* (DCX H).

As shown in Figure 14.18, our "add 5 numbers" program of Figure 11.9 has been shortened from 16 to 13 memory locations. In fact, the size of the program is nearly independent of the number of integers to be added. In the next section, we will put loops, indirect addressing, and delays into action and generate a sequence of notes (a song!).

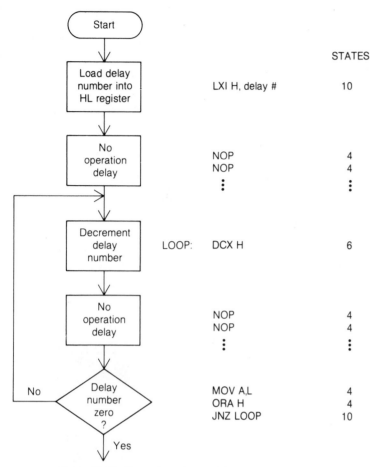

Figure 14.16 Generating a 1-second delay.

COMPUTER MUSIC

As a final application of decision making, Figure 14.19*a* is a program listing for generating a simple one-note-at-a-time melody.

Basically a melody is nothing more than a sequence of notes, each with its own frequency, duration, and (optional) rest parameters. These parameters are stored in sequential memory locations and are pulled from memory as the melody progresses. An analysis of the program is left as an exercise.

Figure 14.19*b* is a listing of the frequency and duration parameters required to play the old English folk song "Greensleeves."

MACHINE-ASSEMBLY UPDATE—II

Our next machine-assembly update introduces the EQU (equate) directive. Referring to Figure 14.20, a modified mimic routine with a double-nested delay between input and output, we note the following assembler directive:

DELAY   EQU 200

When DELAY is equated to 200, it means we can use the more descriptive English-like "DELAY" anywhere in the program instead of the number 200. The EQU directive is especially useful when an item *that may be modified in the future* appears many times in a program. Rather than modify the item wherever it appears, we merely modify its value in the declaration, and every reference to it will reflect the change. As shown, we even can perform mathematical calculations within the program (note that 64H is properly generated from the *expression* DELAY − 100). Since DELAY is a symbol, just like LOOP and OUTER, it is fully identified in the *symbol table* at the bottom of the listing (since EQU always yields a value in the range 0–65,535, DELAY is identified as an address).

INTELLIGENT-MACHINE UPDATE

In one brief chapter, our intelligent machine has passed through the age of reason. No longer is it a mere puppet to its human

$$\text{Delay time} = 1/3\ \mu s\ [N_0\ (24 + (N_1 \times 4)) + (N_2 \times 4) + 10]$$

N_0 = delay number
N_1 = NOPs inside loop
N_2 = NOPs outside loop

(*a*) General formula

$$1.000003\ \text{seconds} = 1/3\ \mu s\ [62{,}500\ (24 + (6 \times 4)) + (0 \times 4) + 10]$$

(*b*) Generating a 1-second delay

Figure 14.17 Calculating delay times.

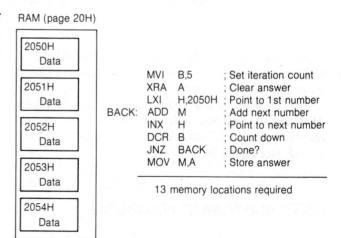

Figure 14.18 Combining loops and indirect addressing to dramatically shorten repetitive routines.

ASM80 :F1:MUSIC.SRC

ISIS-II 8080/8085 MACRO ASSEMBLER, V4.1   MUSIC   PAGE   1


```
LOC   OBJ         LINE        SOURCE STATEMENT

                   1              NAME MUSIC
                   2
                   3    ; This program processes note information stored
                   4    ; in memory. Each note consists of two bytes, the
                   5    ; first for duration and the second for frequency.
                   6    ; There are no rest periods between notes.
                   7
2000               8              ORG   2000H
2000  3E0E         9              MVI   A,0EH      ; SDK-85
2002  D320        10              OUT   20H        ; SDK-85
2004  1E49        11    START:    MVI   E,73       ; Place number of notes in reg E
2006  213020      12              LXI   H,2030H    ; Load HL with start address
2009  DB21        13    LOOPS:    IN    21H        ; Input outer D loop dur num
200B  57          14              MOV   D,A        ; Move D delay num to D register
200C  4E          15    OUTER:    MOV   C,M        ; Load dur num of present note
200D  23          16              INX   H          ; Point to freq num of pres note
200E  46          17    DURTN:    MOV   B,M        ; Place B freq num into B reg
200F  05          18    FREQCY:   DCR   B          ; Decrement B freq number
2010  C20F20      19              JNZ   FREQCY     ; If B not 0, decrement again
2013  3C          20              INR   A          ; Increment A to generate note
2014  D323        21              OUT   23H        ; Output note change
2016  0D          22              DCR   C          ; Decrement C duration number
2017  C20E20      23              JNZ   DURTN      ; If C not 0, reload B
201A  15          24              DCR   D          ; Decrement outer D delay number
201B  2B          25              DCX   H          ; Point back to C delay number
201C  C20C20      26              JNZ   OUTER      ; If D not 0, reload B and C
201F  23          27              INX   H          ; Point to B num of present note
2020  23          28              INX   H          ; Point to C delay num next note
2021  1D          29              DCR   E          ; Decrement note register
2022  C20920      30              JNZ   LOOPS      ; If E not 0, generate next note
2025  C30420      31              JMP   START      ; Repeat song
                  32              END
```

PUBLIC SYMBOLS

EXTERNAL SYMBOLS

USER SYMBOLS
DURTN A 200E   FREQCY A 200F   LOOPS A 2009   OUTER A 200C   START A 200 4

ASSEMBLY COMPLETE,   NO ERRORS

Figure 14.19 Computer music—program and note information: *a)* Program.

creators, for now it can make decisions on its own. Does our computer now have free will? Can it learn by experience and be capable of high-level thought processes? It is simply too early to say.

QUESTIONS AND PROBLEMS $1 \rightarrow 19$

1. When human beings make decisions, we consult "signs" (e.g., sun or traffic light). In a computer, what are analogous to signs?
2. What are the two general steps in the decision-making process?
3. Most of the flag-setting instructions are from what two groups?

4. At the present time the accumulator is holding 200_{10}. Trace the states of the Z and CY flags through the program below:

```
               Z  CY
   ADI   55_10
   INR   A
   MOV   B,A
```

5. Why is it necessary for the *conditional jump* instruction to ask questions in a negative manner? For example, is the carry flag *not* set?
6. Write a program that will scan through ten consecutive memory locations looking for the <u>first occurrence</u> of FFH and print its location when found. (Note: Assume the ten locations hold at least one FFH).

Note	Data	Note	Data	Note	Data	Note	Data
A	05 6B	and	05 6B	ny	18 6B	sleeves	11 3B
las	OB 5A	I	OB 5A	Green	19 3B	was	08 3F
my	06 50	have	06 50	sleeves	19 3B	my	OE 47
love	15 47	loved	15 47	——	08 3F	heart	OD 50
——	08 3F	——	08 3F	was	OE 47	of	05 5E
you	OE 47	you	OE 47	all	OD 50	gold	OD 79
do	OD 50	oh	OD 50	my	05 5E	——	05 6B
me	05 5E	so	05 5E	joy	OD 79	and	OA 5E
wrong	OD 79	long	OD 79	——	05 6B	who	OB 5A
——	05 6B	——	05 6B	——	OA 5E	but	OA 5E
to	OA 5E	de	OA 5E	Green	OB 5A	my	09 6B
cast	OB 5A	light	OB 5A	——	05 6B	la	09 71
me	05 6B	——	OA 5E	sleeves	OE 6B	——	04 7F
off	OD 6B	ing	09 6B	——	04 79	dy	09 71
——	04 79	in	09 71	was	09 6B	Green	20 6B
dis	09 6B	——	04 7F	my	OA 5E	sleeves	48 6B
cour	OA 5E	your	09 71	de	04 79		
teous	04 79	com	09 6B	light	13 90		
ly	07 90	pa	05 6B	Green	19 3B		

(b) Note information

Figure 14.19b   Computer music—program and note information (*continued*)

```
ASM80 :F1:EQUATE.SRC

ISIS-II 8080/8085 MACRO ASSEMBLER, V4.1        EQUATE   PAGE    1

   LOC  OBJ        LINE         SOURCE STATEMENT
                     1           NAME  EQUATE
                     2
                     3   ; This machine assembly update (based on a
                     4   ; double-nested delay loop) introduces the
                     5   ; EQU directive and expressions.
                     6
   00C8              7   DELAY   EQU   200        ; Delay = 200
                     8
   2000              9           ORG   2000H
   2000 3E0E        10           MVI   A,0EH      ; SDK-85
   2002 D320        11           OUT   20H        ; SDK-85
   2004 DB21        12   LOOP:   IN    21H        ; Input
   2006 0EC8        13           MVI   C,DELAY    ; Load outer delay num
   2008 0664        14   OUTER:  MVI   B,DELAY-100 ; Load inner delay num
   200A 05          15   GOBACK: DCR   B          ; Dec inner number
   200B C20A20      16           JNZ   GOBACK     ; Loop if inner <> 0
   200E 0D          17           DCR   C          ; Dec outer number
   200F C20820      18           JNZ   OUTER      ; Loop if outer <> 0
   2012 D322        19           OUT   22H        ; Mimic
   2014 C30420      20           JMP   LOOP       ; Repeat
                    21           END


PUBLIC SYMBOLS

EXTERNAL SYMBOLS

USER SYMBOLS
DELAY  A 00C8    GOBACK A 200A    LOOP   A 2004    OUTER  A 2008

ASSEMBLY COMPLETE,   NO ERRORS
```

Figure 14.20 Machine-assembly update—using the EQU directive to create an expression.

7. Modify the above program to print (outport) the number of times FFH is found.

8. Rewrite Figure 14.10 to mimic numbers *greater* than 34H (*Hint:* Reverse the order of the numbers in the compare process).

9. Why do you think the carry flag was designed not to be affected by the DCX and INX instructions?

10. Write a program that will mimic only odd numbers (blanking out even numbers).

11. How does a computer use decision making to choose the right path among three possible choices?

12. Write a "bandpass" program that passes (mimics) only numbers between 32 and 64 (base 10).

13. By nesting delay loops ten deep, what is the maximum delay period that can be produced? (*Hint:* Your answer will show why you should not attempt to perform this experiment in the laboratory.)

14. Simulate a double-nested delay loop by decrementing the BC register *pair.* (*Hint:* see Figure 14.16.)

15. There are two common ways to determine when to end a loop: *loop counting* and *event detection*. Using a flowchart and assembly-language programming, give an example of each.

16. Rewrite the program of Figure 14.13, decrementing a memory location rather than a register location.

17. Write a program that will search a list of numbers for a particular *sequence* of two numbers (a *string*), outporting the location of the first number.

18. Write a modified MIMIC program that will mimic only number sequences that increase or stay the same, blanking out decreasing number sequences. (Using a delay loop, provide time for inputting the numbers from the DIP).

19. Write a program that produces as close as possible the musical note A (880 Hz).

20. Write a program that produces a square-wave tone whose pitch (frequency) is approximately proportional (inversely) to an inported number.

21. Write a reaction-time program that turns on an LED and then outports in tenths of seconds the time required to react and throw an input-port switch.

22. What delay numbers placed into the program of Figure 14.14 will result in the longest possible delay? (*Hint:* The answer is not all FFs.)

23. Making use of *indirect* addressing, write an "add 5 numbers" program in which the data are spaced 10H (16) locations apart in memory. The answer should be outported.

24. Write a conversion program that inports all signed numbers between -128 and $+127$, converting them

to sign-magnitude form. Also, write a routine to reverse the process.

25. For the music program of Figure 14.19a, why should the frequency delay number times the duration delay number be a constant for all notes of equal duration (that is, quarter note, half note)?

26. In general terms, how would you add volume control for each note to the music program of Figure 14.19a?

27. Based on the format of Figure 14.19b, derive the note information for a song of your choice. Summarize how you derived your note information.

28. How would the 1-second delay calculation of Figure 14.17 change if we took into account the small factor that when using an 8085 the final Jc instruction (when the jump is not made) requires 7 rather than 10 states?

29. Write a "warble" program in which a tone steadily increases in pitch (frequency), falls instantly to a base note, and repeats.

30. Write a program in which the tempo of a repeating note is varied via the input port. (*Hint:* Tempo is increased as duration of note/rest/note sequence decreases.)

31. Write a program that generates five notes of equal duration, each one an octave higher. (*Hint:* An increase of one octave is produced by doubling the frequency.)

32. Write a program to implement the game of *Sumo wrestling*. Output 1s to LEDs 3 and 4 (representing the two wrestlers). When the LEDs go off after a certain amount of time, the player able to throw the corresponding switch first (DIP bit D_0 for player A and bit D_7 for player B) wins, and the two LEDs move over one position in the proper direction and reappear. The process continues until one "wrestler" is pushed off the "mat."

33. Modify the *Sumo wrestling* program of question 32 so that the period of time in which the players wait for the LEDs to go off is semirandom. (*Hint:* Reaction time is semirandom.)

chapter 15

Calls, Subroutines, and Stacks

A minstrel, performing a medley of popular songs, must learn long passages of words and music. Our intelligent machine, with its ability to remember and recall information, seems to possess all the required skills. Unfortunately, its concert debut is unsuccessful, for part way into the first ballad it runs out of memory. What our computer requires is a method of storing long program sequences in limited amounts of memory—a feat that seems impossible at first glance. How do we pour 5 quarts of water into a 4-quart container? The answer is: parts of the 4-quart container are used more than once.

This chapter introduces subroutines, a powerful new technique for shortening programs. When our study is complete, we will discover an important side benefit: our programs will be easier to write.

SUBROUTINES

A technique from the world of music will show us how to make more effective use or our computer's limited memory capacity.

A typical musical composition may consist of four verses. Following each verse is the *chorus, a routine that remains unchanged.* If this musical score is placed into the computer's memory, four memory locations, each storing the chorus, will have precisely the same sequence of instructions. And that results in wasted memory space—lots of it.

A solution is found in many popular musical scores. To save space, *the chorus of the song is written once but used many times.* When performing the song, we simply jump back and forth between the chorus and the three verses as required. This is precisely the technique we will use to reduce our computer's memory requirements. That is how we will pour 5 quarts of water into a 4-quart container.

In computer terminology, the chorus is known as a *subroutine,* and the three verses of the ballad make up the *main program.* As shown in Figure 15.1, the chorus subroutine is stored in only one place in memory and is accessed by the *jump* instruction. And just that simply our major goal has been achieved: we have saved memory space—in this

case an amount of memory equal to approximately three chorus routines.

Unfortunately, it is not that simple. There is no problem with jumping *to* the chorus subroutine whenever it is needed; a simple unconditional jump will suffice. The problem is, how do you get *back* to the proper verse when the chorus is over? It could be verse 2 or verse 3 or verse 4 or the end of the song.

We could solve the problem in a number of ways. We might make use of the *jump H and L indirect* instruction (Figure 15.2). Each time the chorus subroutine is used, a counter is updated and used to indirectly set the program counter to the correct return address.

Another method might involve the *conditional jump* instruction and some clever flag setting. But these methods are unwieldy at best, and fortunately are not required at all.

THE CALL INSTRUCTION

To process subroutines, computer designers have given us the CALL instruction (see Figure 15.3). It looks compli-

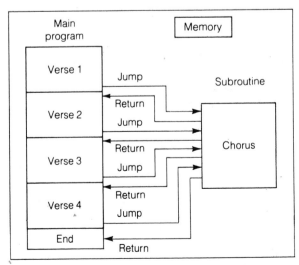

Figure 15.1 The repetitive chorus becomes a subroutine.

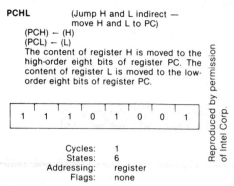

PCHL   (Jump H and L indirect —
                  move H and L to PC)
(PCH) ← (H)
(PCL) ← (L)
The content of register H is moved to the
high-order eight bits of register PC. The
content of register L is moved to the low-
order eight bits of register PC.

| 1 | 1 | 1 | 0 | 1 | 0 | 0 | 1 |

Cycles: 1
States: 6
Addressing: register
Flags: none

Figure 15.2   The *jump indirect* instruction.

Reproduced by permission of Intel Corp.

cated, but it handles subroutines like magic. First of all, a CALL is basically a jump with an extra twist thrown in. That extra twist involves some new terms that we should explain.

The Stack and Stack Pointer

The *stack* is a special block of memory. Theoretically, it could be any available memory location. However, a given computer will often require a specific stack location.

The *stack pointer* is a register pair—known as the SP register pair—placed between the HL register pair and the program counter in the 8080/8085 internal block diagram. The stack pointer points to a location in the stack, in much the same way the HL register pair points to any location in memory.

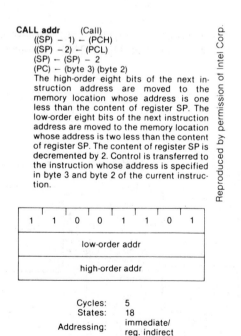

CALL addr   (Call)
((SP) − 1) ← (PCH)
((SP) − 2) ← (PCL)
(SP) ← (SP) − 2
(PC) ← (byte 3) (byte 2)
The high-order eight bits of the next instruction address are moved to the
memory location whose address is one
less than the content of register SP. The
low-order eight bits of the next instruction
address are moved to the memory location
whose address is two less than the content
of register SP. The content of register SP is
decremented by 2. Control is transferred to
the instruction whose address is specified
in byte 3 and byte 2 of the current instruction.

| 1 | 1 | 0 | 0 | 1 | 1 | 0 | 1 |

| low-order addr |

| high-order addr |

Cycles: 5
States: 18
Addressing: immediate/
              reg. indirect
Flags: none

Figure 15.3   The CALL instruction.

Reproduced by permission of Intel Corp.

Call vs Jump

Now that we have been introduced to the stack and the stack pointer, what is that extra twist separating a CALL from a simple jump? It is this: *the return location*—the place in the main program where we would like to return after the sub-routine is complete—is stored in the stack. And what location would we like to return to? The answer is: *the very next location following the CALL.* The process is much like marking a road map with our present position before retiring for the night (CALLing our sleep routine). When we arise the next morning, a quick glance at the map will tell us where we are on the main route and allow us to pick up precisely where we left off.

Figure 15.4 illustrates the main ideas. Using arbitrary memory locations from page 20H, three memory areas are involved in the CALL process: the main program, the subroutine, and the stack. These three areas can be placed anywhere as long as they don't overlap or interfere with the operation of the computer.

To get a better idea of what is involved, let us go through the five machine cycles of the CALL process (Figure 15.5). Remember what to look for: a jump with an extra twist (to place the return address on the stack).

The first three machine cycles are the jump part of the CALL instruction, and are nearly the same as the three machine cycles of a jump instruction. The only difference finds the stack pointer decremented during the op-code fetch and pointing to the next lowest stack location (the next available stack location).

The final two machine cycles give us that extra twist, when the main-program return address (2003H) is placed on the stack. The process is particularly easy, for the return address—the address of the next instruction following the CALL—just happens to be the *present* contents of the program counter. (Remember, the program counter is updated during state T_2 of the third machine cycle and always looks ahead to the next instruction to be fetched.) During the fourth machine cycle, the high-order contents of the program counter are "pushed" onto the stack location pointed to by the stack pointer. The stack pointer is decremented, and during the fifth and last machine cycle, the low-order contents of the program counter are "pushed" onto the stack. ("Push" is the technical term for placing data onto the stack.)

The Return

Once the CALL instruction has been executed, the computer continues along, processing the subroutine. But when it arrives at the end of the subroutine, how does it use the return address in the stack to get back to the main program? Another instruction—the *return* instruction (Figure 15.6)—will enable it to complete the round trip back to the main program.

The return instruction simply reverses the CALL process, and (using the stack pointer as a guide) "pops" the return

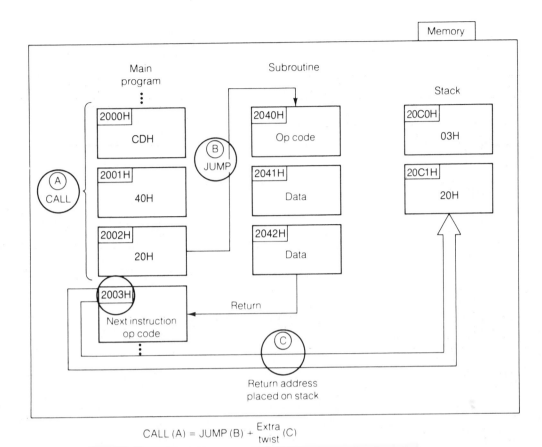

$$\text{CALL (A)} = \text{JUMP (B)} + \frac{\text{Extra}}{\text{twist}} \text{(C)}$$

Figure 15.4   A CALL is basically a jump, but with the return address stored on the stack.

information off the two top positions of the stack and places them back into the program counter by way of the WZ register pair. ("Pop" is the technical term for removing data from the stack.) Like the CALL instruction, the return instruction is basically a jump—except the return address comes from the stack rather than the WZ register pair. During the return process the stack pointer is incremented twice to again point to the bottom of the stack.

When the return instruction is added to the end of the subroutine (Figure 15.7), our musical program is complete and ready to run. Clearly, the CALL and return instructions always appear together as a pair. Figure 15.8 reviews the CALL/return process.

Stack Rules

During the CALL/return operation, automatic increment and decrement processes make sure the stack pointer obeys the following important rule: *The stack pointer always points to the last item added to the stack or the next item to be removed from the stack.* In other words, the stack pointer always points to the top of the stack.

Another rule obeyed by the stack goes by the name of FILO (or LIFO). All data bytes are added to or removed

from the stack on a *First In/Last Out* (FILO) or a *Last In/ First Out* (LIFO) basis. The process is similar to stacking dishes: the last dish added to the stack must be the first one removed.

A SUBROUTINE EXAMPLE

To put what we have learned so far to work, Figure 15.9a is a subroutine demonstration program called MIMIC-DELAY: our familiar mimic program with a DELAY subroutine inserted between the input and output. Note that simple labels link the subroutine to the main program. Figure 15.9b shows how the ORG pseudo-instruction (or *directive*) specifies both the main program and the subroutine locations for machine assembly. (For SDK-85 operation, the stack pointer normally is preset by way of the keypad.)

NESTING SUBROUTINES

Referring back to Figure 15.7, CALLing the chorus portion of our four-verse ballad has saved a great deal of stored-

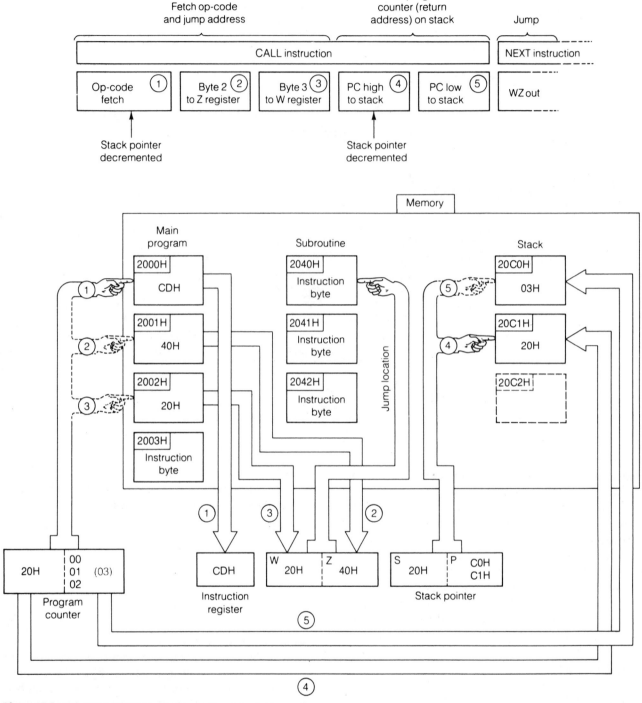

Figure 15.5 The CALL instruction machine-cycle sequencing.

program space. Unfortunately, there still is insufficient memory space to store a second ballad. Is there a way we can make even more efficient use of our limited memory? There is, and the good news is that it still involves the CALL process.

Zoom in on the chorus subroutine of our musical score (Figure 15.10) and note that a particular phrase is repeated

three times. This is more wasted memory space of the same kind we saw before.

Therefore, the solution is the same as before (Figure 15.11). Turn the subroutine phrase into a sub-subroutine, and CALL it whenever needed. In so doing we have placed a subroutine within another subroutine. Or, to use a more familiar term, we have *nested* subroutines.

RET   (Return)
(PCL) ← ((SP));
(PCH) ← ((SP) + 1);
(SP) ← (SP) + 2;
The content of the memory location whose
address is specified in register SP is moved
to the low-order eight bits of register PC.
The content of the memory location whose
address is one more than the content of
register SP is moved to the high-order eight
bits of register PC. The content of register
SP is incremented by 2.

1	1	0	0	1	0	0	1

Cycles: 3
States: 10
Addressing: reg. indirect
Flags: none

Reproduced by permission
of Intel Corp.

Figure 15.6   The return instruction.

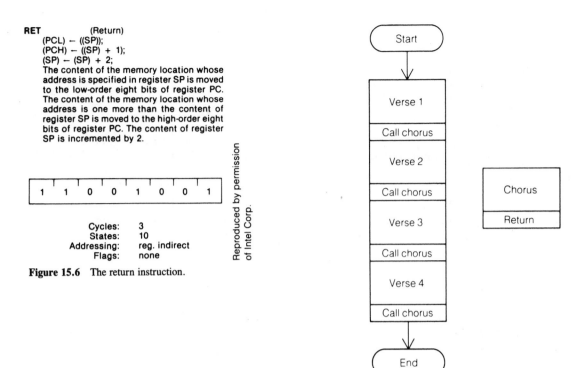

Figure 15.7   Complete musical program using chorus subroutine.

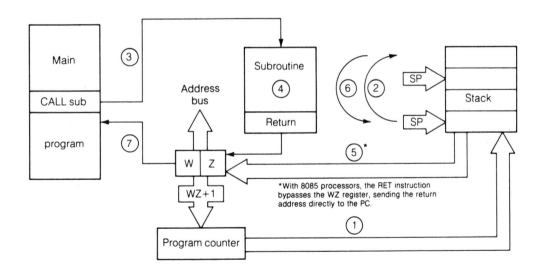

CALL
(1) Place the return address onto the stack.
(2) Move the stack pointer up two positions to the top of the stack.
(3) Jump to the subroutine.
(4) Process the subroutine.

RETURN
(5) Transfer the return address at the top of the stack to the WZ register pair.
(6) Move the stack pointer down two positions.
(7) Output WZ, update the program counter with WZ+1, and return to the main program.

Figure 15.8   The seven steps of the CALL/return process.

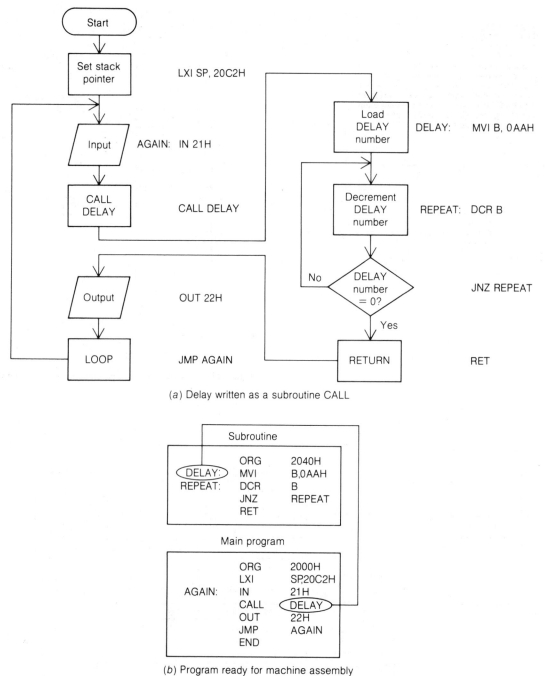

(a) Delay written as a subroutine CALL

(b) Program ready for machine assembly

Figure 15.9 The Delay-Mimic program.

In fact, it is nesting that demonstrates the real power of the CALL process. First of all, this nesting process can go on indefinitely. (Within a sub-subroutine it is possible to have repetitive data blocks made into a sub-sub-subroutine and called several times during the sub-subroutine.) When subroutines are deeply nested, the real beauty of the CALL process is revealed, for as we go into and out of our routines and subroutines, the return addresses are automatically sorted on the stack, leaving almost nothing for the programmer to worry about. As we go deeper and deeper into the nested subroutines, the stack grows, and as we come out of them, it shrinks (see Figure 15.12).

THE PUSH AND POP INSTRUCTIONS

One problem with subroutines is the possible internal register tug-of-war set up between routines and subroutines. At

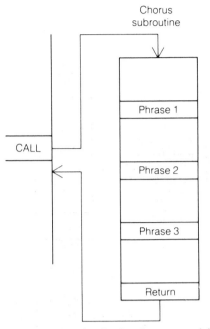

Figure 15.10 Chorus subroutine showing phrase repeated three times.

the point a CALL is made from the main program, suppose all internal registers and flags are holding crucial main-program information that cannot be lost. The problem is that more than likely the subroutine also makes use of these same internal registers and flags. When the action returns to the main program, the original register and flag information will be lost. In other words, both the main program and the subroutine are competing for the same registers and flags.

The solution lies with the stack. Consider the stack to be a safe, whose purpose is to store away for safekeeping all crucial main-program information before a jump to the subroutine. When the subroutine is completed, the main-program information is taken from the "safe" and used to restore the original main-program conditions.

To store and retrieve register and flag information, the PUSH and POP instructions have been provided (Figure 15.13). You PUSH register and flag information onto the stack and you POP it off, two bytes at a time.

Any of the seven internal registers and flags can be PUSHed onto the stack. Once the information is safely stored on the stack, these registers and flags are completely free to be used by the subroutine. Of course, to keep the stack pointer aimed at the top of the stack, each two-byte information push will automatically decrement the stack pointer by two. The POP instructions will reverse the process and restore the register and flag information so the main program can continue where it left off. During a POP, the stack pointer is incremented twice. Therefore, as shown in Figure 15.14, a typical CALL process may involve from one to four PUSH/POP pairs. Following the FILO rule, the register and flag data are POPed off the stack in reverse order to being PUSHed onto the

stack. Figure 15.15 illustrates the machine-cycle action of a typical PUSH process. (The machine-cycle action of the POP process is left as an exercise.)

WHEN TO CALL

The CALL process should be considered whenever memory space is saved. (The CALL process itself does introduce a tiny loss of speed.) To put it another way, the more times subroutines are called, the larger they are; and the greater the depth of nesting, the greater the need.

Another factor to consider is software development cost. Using CALLs, all or part of a main program can be written in block form. That is, the program can consist of software blocks (modules) arranged and linked together by the proper sequence of CALLs. In addition, the software blocks can be divided among several programmers, and in fact may already be available in a software library. This idea—related to the concept of top-down modular design—represents the software counterpart of using LSI blocks to create the computer hardware system. Using software blocks, programs are usually easier to write and to interpret.

For example, let's select the familiar mystery program of Chapter 12 and apply the lessons of top-down modular design. Figure 15.16 shows the result. The main program is nothing but calls! *But it is easy to read*—like the table of contents

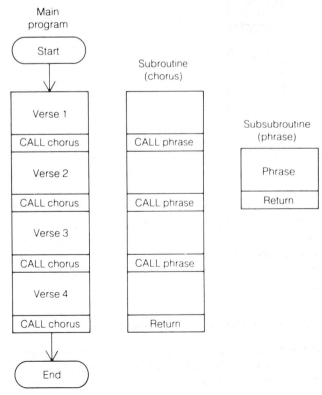

Figure 15.11 Subroutine nesting.

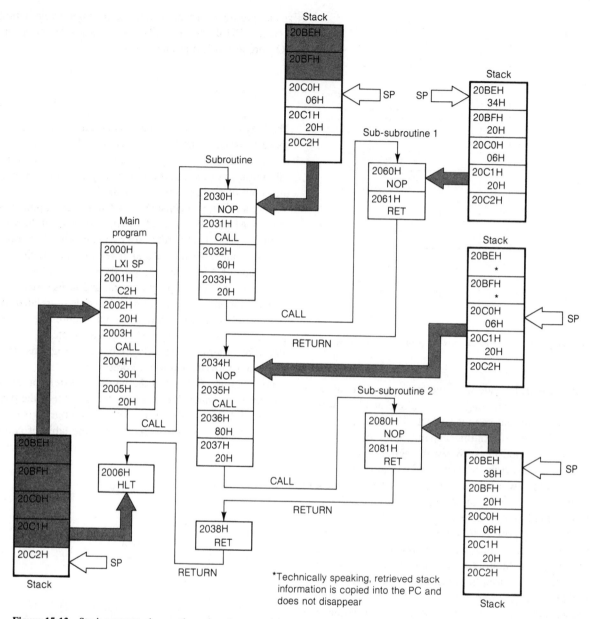

Figure 15.12   Stack contents when nesting subroutines.

*Technically speaking, retrieved stack information is copied into the PC and does not disappear

of a book—because the program is summarized in general terms without the low-level programming details clouding its overall intent. We will return to the subject of top-down *modular* design in Chapter 22 and see how program modules (called *procedures*) are implemented in high-level structured languages.

THE CALL AND RETURN CONDITIONS

In the process of decision making, to jump or not to jump was the question. Then why not to CALL or not to CALL? After all, a CALL is basically a jump (with the extra twist thrown in).

Therefore, it was entirely natural to blend the decision-making features of the *jump condition* instruction with the subroutine-processing ability of the CALL instruction to produce the powerful *CALL condition* instruction, perhaps the most complex instruction in the entire 8080/8085 instruction set (Figure 15.17*a*).

The CALL *condition* instruction is fetched and executed just like the *jump condition* instruction, except with the added twist (the return address is pushed onto the stack). There is even a *return condition* instruction to provide decision making for the return process (Figure 15.17*b*).

When using the CALL condition process during critical timing routines, be aware that if the CALLing condition is

PUSH rp   (Push)

$((SP) - 1) \leftarrow (rh)$
$((SP) - 2) \leftarrow (rl)$
$((SP) \leftarrow (SP) - 2$

The content of the high-order register of register pair rp is moved to the memory location whose address is one less than the content of register SP. The content of the low-order register of register pair rp is moved to the memory location whose address is two less than the content of register SP. The content of register SP is decremented by 2. **Note: Register pair rp = SP may not be specified.**

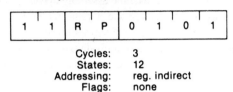

| 1 | 1 | R | P | 0 | 1 | 0 | 1 |

Cycles: 3
States: 12
Addressing: reg. indirect
Flags: none

PUSH PSW   (Push processor status word)

$((SP) - 1) \leftarrow (A)$
$((SP) - 2)_0 \leftarrow (CY) , ((SP) - 2)_1 \leftarrow X$
$((SP) - 2)_2 \leftarrow (P) , ((SP) - 2)_3 \leftarrow X$
$((SP) - 2)_4 \leftarrow (AC) , ((SP) - 2)_5 \leftarrow X$
$((SP) - 2)_6 \leftarrow (Z) , ((SP) - 2)_7 \leftarrow (S)$
$(SP) \leftarrow (SP) - 2$ X: Undefined.

The content of register A is moved to the memory location whose address is one less than register SP. The contents of the condition flags are assembled into a processor status word and the word is moved to the memory location whose address is two less than the content of register SP. The content of register SP is decremented by two.

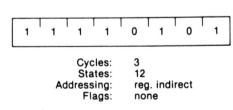

| 1 | 1 | 1 | 1 | 0 | 1 | 0 | 1 |

Cycles: 3
States: 12
Addressing: reg. indirect
Flags: none

Reproduced by permission of Intel Corp.

POP rp   (POP)

$(rl) \leftarrow ((SP))$
$(rh) \leftarrow ((SP) + 1)$
$(SP) \leftarrow (SP) + 2$

The content of the memory location, whose address is specified by the content of register SP, is moved to the low-order register of register pair rp. The content of the memory location, whose address is one more than the content of register SP, is moved to the high-order register of register rp. The content of register SP is incremented by 2. **Note: Register pair rp = SP may not be specified.**

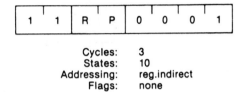

| 1 | 1 | R | P | 0 | 0 | 0 | 1 |

Cycles: 3
States: 10
Addressing: reg.indirect
Flags: none

POP PSW   (Pop processor status word)

$(CY) \leftarrow ((SP))_0$
$(P) \leftarrow ((SP))_2$
$(AC) \leftarrow ((SP))_4$
$(Z) \leftarrow ((SP))_6$
$(S) \leftarrow ((SP))_7$
$(A) \leftarrow ((SP) + 1)$
$(SP) \leftarrow (SP) + 2$

The content of the memory location whose address is specified by the content of register SP is used to restore the condition flags. The content of the memory location whose address is one more than the content of register SP is moved to register A. The content of register SP is incremented by 2.

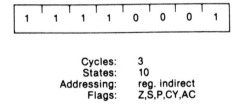

| 1 | 1 | 1 | 1 | 0 | 0 | 0 | 1 |

Cycles: 3
States: 10
Addressing: reg. indirect
Flags: Z,S,P,CY,AC

Figure 15.13 The PUSH/POP instructions.

not met (the subroutine is not CALLed), the last two machine cycles—whose purpose is to PUSH the return address onto the stack—are skipped (indeed, they *must* be skipped). The same is true of the *return condition* instruction. When the condition for returning is not met, the two machine cycles that return stack contents to the program counter must be skipped.

PARAMETER PASSING

The top-down modular design concepts of the last section are especially vital when large, complex, "real-world" pro-

grams are to be written. If the program requires one worker-year to write, and the product must be released to market in 4 months, clearly the problem must be broken up into "bite-size" modules and parceled out among several programmers. *For efficiency, each module should be independent of the others*. However, quite often data will have to be transmitted back and forth between modules. How can the various modules maintain independence and still communicate with each other? They pass *parameters*.

A *parameter* is a piece of data generated by one module and used by another. A number of techniques are used to maintain independence as the parameters cross the border from one module to another.

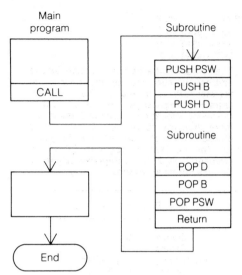

Figure 15.14 PUSH/POP processing to store and retrieve register and flag data.

The simplest method is to place the parameters in one or more registers accessible to both modules. However, when the number of parameters exceeds the number of registers, this technique breaks down.

For multiple parameters, a popular technique is to place the actual parameters (called the *parameter list*) in a section of RAM and pass the *address* of this list to the subroutine in the HL register pair. (An example of this technique will be given in this chapter's first *machine-assembly update*.)

Advanced third-generation microprocessors, such as the 8088, often use the stack as the parameter-passing medium. Special return instructions and special modes of addressing simplify the job of sorting the parameters on the stack.

MACHINE-ASSEMBLY UPDATE—I

This chapter's first machine assembly update gives us a bonus: not only will we cover one popular method of passing multiple parameters from main program to subroutine, we also will learn how the assembly-language programmer works with blocks of pure *data*, apart from executable program code.

Let's write a program in which subroutine ADD receives two numbers to be added together and the result outported. The two numbers (known as *actual parameters*) will be sent to subroutine ADD as a *parameter list* stored in memory. Using 8 and 10 for the two numbers, we first create the parameter list using the *data definition* directive:

LIST: DB   8,10

The DB (Data Byte) directive stores the two data bytes in consecutive memory locations, starting with the current set-

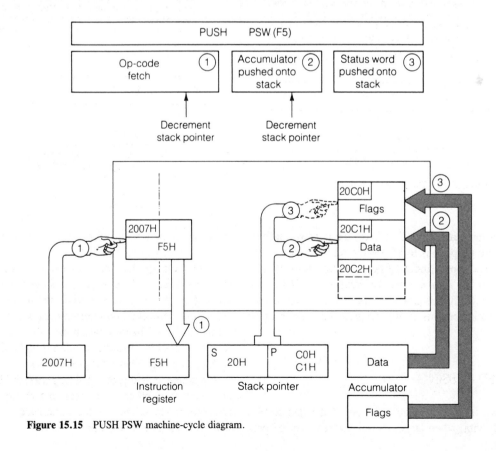

Figure 15.15 PUSH PSW machine-cycle diagram.

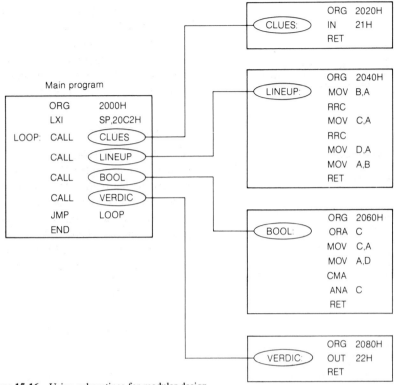

Figure 15.16 Using subroutines for modular design.

ting of the location counter (set by the ORG directive). Symbolic address LIST (a label) refers to the *address* of the first data byte in the list (the location where the 8 is stored). *It is this first location address in the parameter list that we pass to subroutine ADD via the HL register pair.*

Figure 15.18 shows us how it is done for program ADD-TWONUMBERS. As shown, we make use of the ORG directive to specify the exact memory locations for the two numbers (2040H and 2041H). To pass the actual parameters 8 and 10 to subroutine ADD we use the LXI H, LIST instruction to place the starting address of the parameter list in the HL register pair. To retrieve the parameters, the subroutine scans the parameter list using the INX H instruction, and pulls the parameters from the list using the MOV r,M instruction.

The advantage of this technique is that we can store any number of two-number parameter lists (LIST1, LIST2, LIST3, etc.) in memory and correctly pass parameters by simply loading the correct label into the HL register pair. Of course this same technique can be used to pass parameter lists of any length.

MACHINE-ASSEMBLY UPDATE—II

Our next machine-assembly update is a natural for this chapter because it introduces MACROs, a concept similar to subroutine CALLs.

A MACRO is a single-line assembly-language statement which stands for a group of assembly-language instructions. Based on this definition, a MACRO and a subroutine CALL seem identical. Of course, they are not, and here is the difference: A MACRO "calls" a sequence of assembly-language instructions *during assembly;* a subroutine CALL calls a group of machine-language instructions *during execution.*

Both MACROs and CALLs lend themselves to the block-structured, modular design concepts of the last section. So—which is best? The answer is, there is a tradeoff involved, and most programs will involve a combination of both MACROs and CALLs. To get a better idea of how MACROs are used, let's examine the structure of a MACRO using a simple "tone" program.

Macro Demonstration Program

As we learned in Chapter 14, a simple musical tone is generated by an increment/delay/output sequence placed into a loop. Since the details of how a delay is produced are unimportant, it is a natural for a MACRO. The program is:

```
DELAY   MACRO
        MVI     B, 0AH    ; Load delay number
LOOPS:  DCR     B         ; Decrement delay number
        JNZ     LOOPS     ; Branch if <> 0
        ENDM
```

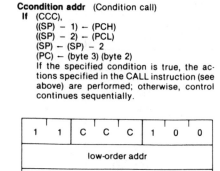

Ccondition addr   (Condition call)
If (CCC),
((SP) − 1) ← (PCH)
((SP) − 2) ← (PCL)
(SP) ← (SP) − 2
(PC) ← (byte 3) (byte 2)
If the specified condition is true, the actions specified in the CALL instruction (see above) are performed; otherwise, control continues sequentially.

1	1	C	C	C	1	0	0

low-order addr

high-order addr

Cycles: 2/5
States: 9/18
Addressing: immediate/
             reg. indirect
Flags: none

(a) The CALL condition instruction

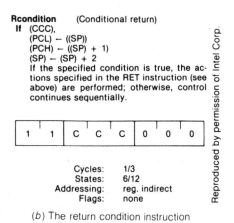

Rcondition   (Conditional return)
If (CCC),
(PCL) ← ((SP))
(PCH) ← ((SP) + 1)
(SP) ← (SP) + 2
If the specified condition is true, the actions specified in the RET instruction (see above) are performed; otherwise, control continues sequentially.

1	1	C	C	C	0	0	0

Cycles: 1/3
States: 6/12
Addressing: reg. indirect
Flags: none

(b) The return condition instruction

Figure 15.17   Instructions for conditional subroutine processing.

Reproduced by permission of Intel Corp.

```
         ORG     2000H
START:   INR     A          ; Toggle note
         DELAY              ; Call MACRO DELAY
         OUT     23H        ; Generate tone
         JMP     START      ; Generate forever
         END
```

The three instructions making up MACRO DELAY are bracketed by the reserved words MACRO and ENDM (End Macro). The MACRO name ("DELAY") is written before the word MACRO in the label column. As shown the MACRO is "called" by writing its name in the main program.

Now let's look at the list program of Figure 15.19 and see how the assembler processed the MACRO. When the assembler arrived at the MACRO name "DELAY" in the main program, it *substituted* the three instructions making up the

body of the MACRO for the MACRO name, just as if the three instructions were written in the original program (note the three " + " signs). *Observe that no subroutine CALLs were generated!* Subroutine CALLs would appear in the program only if they were written into the body of the MACRO or the main program to begin with.

Adding Parameters

A MACRO is a program module, and program modules should be independent. Therefore, it should come as no surprise to learn that MACROs communicate by way of parameters. Our tone routine is a natural for passing a parameter, because it can be used many times during a program—each time generating a different tone frequency. Therefore, each time the MACRO is called, we might send it a different delay number. The process is shown below:

```
DELAY    MACRO   PR1       ; Declare MACRO with
                             parameter
         MVI     B,PR1     ; Load delay number
LOOPS:   DCR     B         ; Decrement delay
                             number
         JNZ     LOOPS     ; Branch if <> 0
         ENDM

         ORG     2000H
START:   INR     A         ; Toggle note
         DELAY   0AH       ; Call MACRO & send
                             parameter
         OUT     23H       ; Generate note
         JMP     START     ; Generate forever
         END
```

Looking at the assembled printout (Figure 15.20), we see that parameter 0AH (the *actual parameter*) follows the MACRO name (DELAY). The actual parameter is sent to MACRO DELAY by way of the *formal parameter* (PR1). The parameter value (0AH) is then substituted for the formal parameter wherever it appears in the body of the MACRO (that is, MVI B,PR1).

Macros vs Subroutines

To summarize, parameters allow MACROs to be written and modified independently of other MACROs and to operate upon different sets of data. Still, we haven't answered our original question: Which is better, MACROs or subroutine CALLs? A difficult question, for as we have seen, our tone program can be written either way. Let's look at the advantages and disadvantages of each.

The MACRO version (Figure 15.20) executes faster and uses less memory than the subroutine version (Figure 15.21) because there are no subroutine CALLs in the final assem-

```
ASM80 :F1:ADD2.SRC MACROFILE


ISIS-II 8080/8085 MACRO ASSEMBLER, V4.1        ADDTWO    PAGE    1


    LOC  OBJ           LINE           SOURCE STATEMENT
                         1             NAME    ADDTWONUMBERS
                         2
                         3  ; In this parameter-passing demonstration
                         4  ; program we place parameters 8 and 10 at
                         5  ; symbolic locations LIST and LIST + 1 (2040H
                         6  ; and 2041H).
                         7  ; Note that we have the option of placing the
                         8  ; main program before the subroutine.
                         9
                        10  ; Main program
                        11
    2000                12             ORG     2000H
    2000 3E0E           13             MVI     A,0EH      ; SDK-85
    2002 D320           14             OUT     20H        ; SDK-85
    2004 31C220         15             LXI     SP,20C2H   ; Load stack pointer
    2007 214020         16             LXI     H,LIST     ; Pass address parameter
    200A CD2020         17             CALL    ADD2
    200D 76             18             HLT
                        19
                        20  ; Create parameter list
                        21
    2040                22             ORG     2040H
    2040 08             23  LIST:  DB     8,10
    2041 0A
                        24
                        25  ; Subroutine ADD
                        26
    2020                27             ORG     2020H
    2020 7E             28  ADD2:  MOV     A,M        ; Fetch 1st parameter
    2021 23             29             INX     H          ; Point to 2nd parameter
    2022 46             30             MOV     B,M        ; Fetch 2nd parameter
    2023 80             31             ADD     B          ; Perform addition
    2024 D322           32             OUT     22H        ; Give results
    2026 C9             33             RET
                        34             END


PUBLIC SYMBOLS

EXTERNAL SYMBOLS

USER SYMBOLS
ADD2   A 2020    LIST   A 2040

ASSEMBLY COMPLETE,    NO ERRORS
```

Figure 15.18 The parameter list technique of passing parameters.

bled object program. (A subroutine CALL uses up time in storing and retrieving data from the stack and in making the jump.) However, if the DELAY routine were needed many times, then code would be generated each time. Clearly, in this case, subroutine CALLs—although slightly slower—would use far less memory space. Therefore, it follows that *the ideal use of MACROs is in conjunction with subroutines.* Subroutine CALLs can be used to improve program readability and to save memory space. MACROs can also be used to simplify the coding of programs—with no loss in execution speed. Both MACROs (via formal and actual parameters) and CALLs (via the registers, lists, or the stack) will support parameter passing.

The modular-oriented programs developed in this chapter have been relatively simple. In contrast, imagine a large, complex program containing numerous nested MACROs and CALLs, each sending different actual parameters using a variety of parameter-passing techniques. It is clear that many of the techniques used in assembly-language programming that seem cumbersome in small programs are critical when the program assumes real-world dimensions. Without a doubt, assembly-language programming is a skilled art.

PUTTING IT ALL TOGETHER

Program DEMONSTRATION of Figure 15.22 includes many of the features of subroutine and MACRO processing covered in this chapter, including the CALL condition, MACROs, nested subroutines, PUSH/POP storage, and parameter passing.

```
ASM80 :F1:MACRO.SRC MACROFILE


ISIS-II 8080/8085 MACRO ASSEMBLER, V4.1          MACROD     PAGE     1


   LOC   OBJ          LINE          SOURCE STATEMENT

                       1            NAME  MACRODEMONSTRATION
                       2
                       3    ; A tone consists of a repeating increment/
                       4    ; output/delay algorithm.  In this program,
                       5    ; the three instructions comprising a simple
                       6    ; delay loop are written as the MACRO DELAY.
                       7
                       8  DELAY   MACRO
   -                   9          MVI     B, OAH ; Load delay number
   -                  10  LOOPS:  DCR     B      ; Decrement delay number
   -                  11          JNZ     LOOPS  ; Branch if <> 0
                      12          ENDM
                      13
   2000               14          ORG     2000H
   2000  3EOE         15          MVI     A,OEH  ; SDK-85
   2002  D320         16          OUT     20H    ; SDK-85
   2004  3C           17  START:  INR     A      ; Toggle note
                      18          DELAY          ; Call MACRO
   2005  060A         19+         MVI     B, OAH ; Load delay number
   2007  05           20+LOOPS:   DCR     B      ; Decrement delay number
   2008  C20720       21+         JNZ     LOOPS  ; Branch if <> 0
   200B  D323         22          OUT     23H    ; Generate tone
   200D  C30420       23          JMP     START  ; Do forever
                      24          END


PUBLIC SYMBOLS


EXTERNAL SYMBOLS


USER SYMBOLS
DELAY  + 0000     LOOPS  A 2007     START   A 2004

ASSEMBLY COMPLETE,    NO ERRORS
```

Figure 15.19 The TONE program list file with the DELAY routine written as a MACRO.

Looking to the main program, all inported numbers are mimicked. However, for all numbers less than 10H, a tone is generated at a frequency inversely proportional to the size of the inported number. A detailed analysis of the program is left for the Questions and Problems section.

THE SDK-85's SPECIAL MONITOR SUBROUTINES

For convenience, the SDK-85's monitor routine (burned into its 8355 ROM) includes several subroutines that are fully accessible to the programmer. The three most useful are:

- CALL 036EH sends the contents of A to the data field of the display as a hexadecimal character. (All registers and flags are affected and must be saved on the stack if their contents are vital).

- CALL 02E7H inputs a character from the keyboard to the A register. (Registers A, H, L, and the flags are affected.) Note: Unmask RST 5.5 (see Chapter 16).

- CALL 05F1 creates a delay proportional to the size of the number in register pair DE. (Registers A, D, E, and the flags are affected.)

INTELLIGENT-MACHINE UPDATE

Through the use of nested subroutines, our intelligent machine finally is able to squeeze the entire ballad into its available memory space and to successfully complete its concert debut. Our intelligent machine will remember the lesson it learned: the clever use of software can save hardware. In later chapters, it will find the reverse also to be true: the clever use of hardware can save software.

QUESTIONS AND PROBLEMS

1. A CALL is basically a *jump,* but with an extra twist thrown in. What is that extra twist?

main prog return address is placed on stack

```
ASM80 :F1:PARAM1.SRC MACROFILE


ISIS-II 8080/8085 MACRO ASSEMBLER, V4.1          PARAME    PAGE     1


  LOC  OBJ          LINE           SOURCE STATEMENT
                      1             NAME  PARAMETERSANDMACROS
                      2
                      3  ; In this program, delay number (0AH) is passed to
                      4  ; MACRO DELAY as a parameter.
                      5
                      6  DELAY    MACRO  PR1      ; Declare MACRO with parameter
       -              7           MVI    B,PR1    ; Load delay number
       -              8  LOOPS:   DCR    B        ; Decrement delay number
       -              9           JNZ    LOOPS    ; Branch if <> 0
                     10           ENDM
                     11
  2000               12           ORG    2000H
  2000  3E0E         13           MVI    A,0EH    ; SDK-85
  2002  D320         14           OUT    20H      ; SDK-85
  2004  3C           15  START:   INR    A        ; Toggle note
                     16           DELAY  0AH      ; Call MACRO & send parameter
  2005  060A         17+          MVI    B,0AH    ; Load delay number
  2007  05           18+LOOPS:    DCR    B        ; Decrement delay number
  2008  C20720       19+          JNZ    LOOPS    ; Branch if <> 0
  200B  D323         20           OUT    23H      ; Generate note
  200D  C30420       21           JMP    START    ; Do forever
                     22           END


PUBLIC SYMBOLS

EXTERNAL SYMBOLS

USER SYMBOLS
DELAY  + 0000    LOOPS  A 2007    START  A 2004

ASSEMBLY COMPLETE,   NO ERRORS
```

Figure 15.20 Sending a delay parameter (0AH) to MACRO DELAY.

2. Does the stack grow toward smaller locations or toward larger locations?

3. When a CALL instruction is processed, what information is placed onto the stack?

4. Why are five machine cycles required to process the CALL instruction?

5. All subroutines must be terminated with what instruction?

6. The stack pointer always points to what part of the stack?

7. What does the term FILO stand for, and how does it relate to the use of the stack?

8. The stack pointer is presently holding 20BCH when the CALL instruction is processed. At what stack location is the return address placed?

9. Under what conditions are PUSH/POP pairs used during subroutine processing?

10. A program can be constructed from software blocks linked together by a series of CALL instructions. Why is such a program easy to write and to interpret?

11. What is the difference between a *return* and a *jump?*

12. Draw a machine-cycle diagram for the POP PSW process (similar to Figure 15.15).

13. For the program shown, complete the 8085 timing diagram for the CALL instruction on the next page.

14. Why is the following program statement guaranteed to overflow the stack?

START: CALL START

15. Rewrite the mystery program of Figure 15.16 using MACROs rather than CALLs. Why does the MACRO version execute faster than the CALL version?

16. Why is accumulator and flag information POPed from the stack in reverse order to being PUSHed onto the stack?

17. Referring to Figure 15.9, show the contents of the stack and the position of the stack pointer while in the delay loop.

18. If a subroutine CALL is to be nested four deep (a main

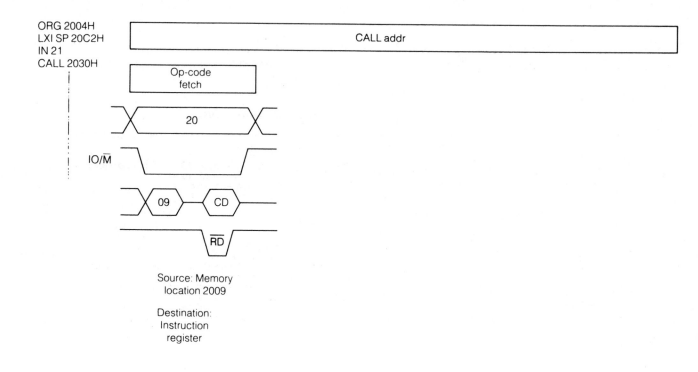

```
ORG 2004H
LXI SP 20C2H
IN 21
CALL 2030H
```

CALL addr

Op-code
fetch

20

IO/M̄

09   CD

R̄D̄

Source: Memory
location 2009

Destination:
Instruction
register

ASM80 :F1:PARAM2.SRC

ISIS-II 8080/8085 MACRO ASSEMBLER, V4.1   PARAME   PAGE   1

```
    LOC  OBJ           LINE          SOURCE STATEMENT
                        1           NAME     PARAMETERSANDCALLS
                        2
                        3    ; This tone program uses the B register to
                        4    ; pass delay parameter from main program to
                        5    ; subroutine.
                        6
    2040                7           ORG      2040H
    2040 05             8  DELAY:   DCR      B         ; Receive parameter
    2041 C24020         9           JNZ      DELAY
    2044 C9            10           RET
                       11
    2000               12           ORG      2000H
    2000 3EOE          13           MVI      A,OEH
    2002 D320          14           OUT      20H
    2004 31C220        15           LXI      SP,20C2H
    2007 3C            16  START:   INR      A
    2008 060A          17           MVI      B,OAH     ; Send parameter
    200A CD4020        18           CALL     DELAY
    200D D323          19           OUT      23H
    200F C30720        20           JMP      START
                       21           END
```

PUBLIC SYMBOLS

EXTERNAL SYMBOLS

USER SYMBOLS
DELAY A 2040   START   A 2007

ASSEMBLY COMPLETE,   NO ERRORS

Figure 15.21 The TONE program list file with the DELAY routine written as a subroutine CALL.

ASM80 :F1:DEMO1.SRC MACROFILE

ISIS-II 8080/8085 MACRO ASSEMBLER, V4.1   DEMONS   PAGE   1

```
  LOC   OBJ         LINE          SOURCE STATEMENT
                      1           NAME    DEMONSTRATION
                      2
                      3   ; This Chapter 15 demonstration program uses
                      4   ; MACROs, parameters, nested subroutines, and
                      5   ; conditional CALLS.
                      6
                      7   ; All input numbers are mimicked.  If the number
                      8   ; is less than 10H, a tone is also created whose
                      9   ; frequency is inversely proportional to the size
                     10   ; of the inported number.
                     11
                     12   ; MACRO SDK
                     13
                     14   SDK      MACRO   PAR
  -                  15            ORG     2000H       ; Set starting address
  -                  16            MVI     A,PAR       ; SDK-85
  -                  17            OUT     20H         ; SDK-85
  -                  18            LXI     SP,20C2H ; SDK-85
                     19            ENDM
                     20
                     21   ; Main program
                     22
                     23            SDK     OEH         ; Para OEH to MACRO DELAY
2000                 24+           ORG     2000H       ; Set starting address
2000 3E0E            25+           MVI     A,OEH       ; SDK-85
2002 D320            26+           OUT     20H         ; SDK-85
2004 31C220          27+           LXI     SP,20C2H ; SDK-85
2007 DB21            28   AGAIN:   IN      21H         ; Input number
2009 47              29            MOV     B,A         ; Pass parameter
200A FE10            30            CPI     10H         ; Num < 10H?
200C DC2020          31            CC      TONE        ; If so, gen tone
200F D322            32            OUT     22H         ; mimic
2011 C30720          33            JMP     AGAIN       ; loop
                     34
                     35   ; Subroutine TONE
                     36
2020                 37            ORG     2020H
2020 F5              38   TONE:    PUSH    PSW         ; Save mimic number
2021 0C              39            INR     C           ; Toggle note
2022 79              40            MOV     A,C         ; Ready note
2023 D323            41            OUT     23H         ; Generate tone
2025 CD3020          42            CALL    DELAY       ; CALL DELAY sub
2028 F1              43            POP     PSW         ; Restore mimic num
2029 C9              44            RET
                     45
                     46   ; Sub-subroutine
                     47
2030                 48            ORG     2030H
2030 05              49   DELAY:   DCR     B           ; Delay
2031 C23020          50            JNZ     DELAY       ; B <> 0, repeat
2034 C9              51            RET
                     52            END
```

ISIS-II 8080/8085 MACRO ASSEMBLER, V4.1   DEMONS   PAGE   2

PUBLIC SYMBOLS

EXTERNAL SYMBOLS

USER SYMBOLS
AGAIN   A 2007   DELAY A 2030   SDK   + 0000   TONE   A 2020

ASSEMBLY COMPLETE,   NO ERRORS

Figure 15.22 Chapter 15 demonstration program.

program and three nested subroutines), and register B and the flags are to be saved on the stack each time, how much memory must be reserved for the stack?

19. What is a *parameter?* What is the difference between the *actual parameter* and the *formal parameter?*

20. To increase the delay time of our delay-mimic routine of Figure 15.9, CALL another delay loop from within the present subroutine loop. Is the total delay time generated equivalent to a double-nested delay loop (Figure 14.14)?

21. When a subroutine is to be CALLed many times, why is it more efficient to place any required PUSH/POP pairs in the subroutine rather than the main program?

22. Program *patching* is the addition or deletion of a group of instructions without going through the process of reassembly. In general terms, how could a patch be implemented using subroutines?

23. Show the contents of the stack and the position of the stack pointer at each of the points shown:

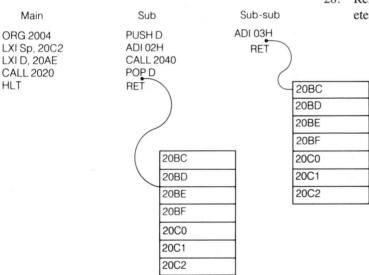

24. The following questions all refer to the MIMIC-DELAY demonstration program of Figure 15.22.
    a. What actual parameter is sent to MACRO SDK?
    b. What technique is used to pass the delay parameter to sub-subroutine DELAY?
    c. Why is the PUSH/POP PSW set included in the subroutine?
    d. How much memory should be reserved for the stack?
    e. What advantage would there be in making subroutine delay a MACRO?

25. Both TONE programs of Figure 15.20 and 15.21 use identical delay numbers. Nevertheless, why should the MACRO version (Figure 15.20) result in a higher frequency tone than the CALL version of Figure 15.21?

26. Using the three special subroutines available in the SDK-85's monitor (input, output, and delay), write a MIMIC-DELAY program.

27. Rewrite any of the programs of Chapter 14 using any combination of MACROs and CALLs.

28. Referring to Figure 15.19, why must AH (the parameter) be preceded by a zero?

chapter 16

Interrupts

Able to call subroutines, and thereby make efficient use of its available memory, our intelligent machine can generate long and complex programs. But what does it do when the power suddenly fails?

Able to learn and recall duties, it can be programmed to be an obedient butler. But what does it do when the phone rings?

In each of these cases our intelligent machine is helpless, and for a very basic reason: it has no means at all for reacting to the unexpected. Power failures and phone calls are all natural but unexpected events, and it is essential for computers as well as human beings to be able to handle them.

In computer terminology, the unexpected is known as an *interrupt* and these interrupts are the subject of this chapter.

AN EVERYDAY EXAMPLE

A phone call is a good place to begin our study of interrupts, for all the major elements of interrupt processing are found there.

First of all, a question: Are those unexpected events that will trigger an interrupt really a complete surprise? Not at all, for we know the power can fail and phones can ring. The point is, we do not know precisely when, or even if, unexpected events will occur. Nevertheless, we had better prepare ourselves with contingency plans, just in case they are needed. For a computer, each contingency plan is known as an *interrupt-service routine* (or *interrupt-handling routine*), and usually is placed in the computer's permanent memory.

The next step is to enable the interrupt system so it will function when needed. For us, that simply means remaining within earshot of the phone.

Contingency program in place and interrupt system enabled, we go about normal duties. Suddenly, unexpectedly, the phone rings. In essence, an interrupt is requested. We respond by finishing our immediate task and branching to the contingency plan (which causes the phone to be answered).

When finished with the phone call, we return to the original main program and take up where we left off.

The major elements of interrupt processing contained in our telephone example are condensed into the following four steps (assume the interrupt-service routine is already deposited in memory):

1. Enable the interrupt system.
2. Request an interrupt.
3. CALL and perform the interrupt-service routine.
4. Return to the main program.

Further condensing these four steps into a single sentence:

AN INTERRUPT IS AN UNEXPECTED
SUBROUTINE CALL.

Because an interrupt involves a subroutine CALL, many of the steps will be familiar. But, because an interrupt is unexpected, many of the steps will be new. Our next task is to apply these four basic elements of interrupt processing to an 8080/8085 system, paying particular attention to what is new.

8080/8085 INTERRUPT PROCESSING

The need for interrupts generally falls into three categories:

* Input/output data transfers from peripheral devices
* Input signals to be used for timing purposes
* Emergency situations

Focusing on the third category, if the unexpected is considered to be an emergency (panic) situation, then naturally a "panic button" is required. On the 8080 it is pin 14, the *interrupt* (INT) input; on the 8085 it is pin 10, the *interrupt request* (INTR) input (Figure 16.1).

Using the INT or INTR input, interrupt processing on an 8080/8085 system follows the same four-step sequence as our earlier telephone example.

Step 1—Enable the interrupt system After system reset, the INT and INTR interrupts are automatically disabled

183

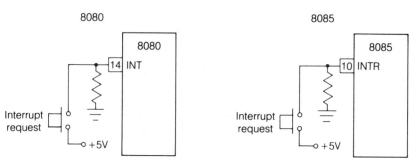

Figure 16.1   8080/8085 general-purpose, interrupt-request inputs.

(masked out). In general, masking is used to prevent unwanted interrupts. For example, the processor may be involved in a critical timing loop or I/O operation, and an interrupt would add an unwanted time increment to the processor's programmed operations.

To give the programmer control over interrupt operations, the 8080/8085 provides the *interrupt enable* and *interrupt disable* instructions (Figure 16.2), which set or reset an internal interrupt-enable flip-flop.

In practice, the programmer would bracket those portions of the program in which an interrupt is allowed with the *interrupt enable/interrupt disable* pair. In those cases where the entire program can be safely interrupted, the *interrupt enable* instruction would be placed early in the main program.

Step 2—Request an interrupt   As shown in Figure 16.1, an interrupt is requested by driving INT (8080) or INTR (8085) high. This can be done asynchronously (any time). During the last stages of the present instruction cycle, an internal interrupt latch is set and the interrupt system is armed. (To maintain the integrity of the main program, the instruction in progress is allowed to complete.) The INT and INTR inputs are known as "level active," and must remain high throughout the last stages of the present instruction cycle.

Step 3—CALL and perform the interrupt-service routine   At the completion of the present instruction, the CPU checks the state of the interrupt flip-flop. If an interrupt has been requested, the processor breaks away from the main program and sets in motion a special *interrupt-acknowledge* machine cycle. This machine cycle is very similar to an ordinary op-code fetch—except INTA (interrupt acknowledge), rather than MEM R (RD), goes active low. In general, it is up to external circuitry to use this special INTA control signal in order to place a special operation code onto the data bus. This special op code automatically flows to the instruction register (is *jammed* into the instruction register); the op code is decoded and the instruction is carried out in the usual way.

The complete hardware system for processing an interrupt request is shown in Figure 16.3. Its function is to transfer the special operation code from interrupt input port to the instruction register in response to an interrupt request. (Since a system contains only one interrupt port, no interrupt port address is required—and none is generated.)

Only one question remains to be answered. What operation code will be jammed into the instruction register when INTA goes active? The answer is: any instruction we wish. For example, to shut down computer action in the event of an emergency, we might use the *halt* instruction. The use of halt is simple because it is a single-byte instruction. Should we choose to jam a two- or three-byte instruction into the system (such as *load accumulator direct*), it would be up to the external circuitry to jam each additional byte onto the data bus at just the right time—a very difficult task. In practice, however, neither of these examples reflects how interrupts are normally used. Usually, *an interrupt is processed as an unexpected CALL.* That is, it causes a branch to an interrupt-service routine and return to the main program when the job is done. We know the CALL instruction can perform such a service, but CALL is a three-byte instruction.

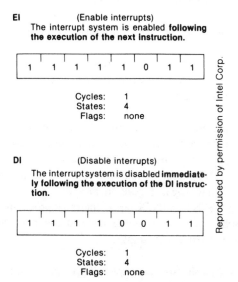

Figure 16.2   The *enable interrupt/disable interrupt* instructions.

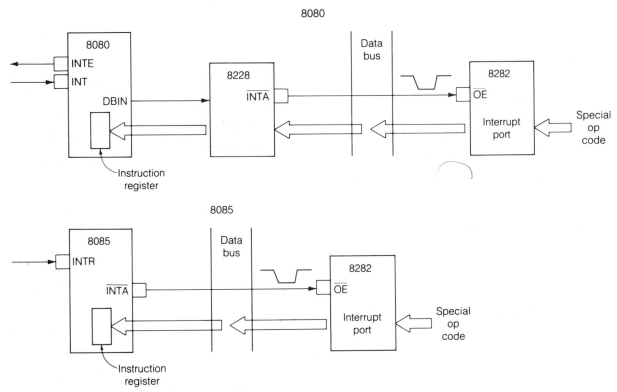

Figure 16.3   8080/8085 general-purpose interrupt system.

Again, the designers of the 8080/8085 foresaw the problem and provided a solution—*a special one-byte CALL* (Figure 16.4*a*).

The type of coding (NNN) used by the *RST n* instruction means we can call subroutines beginning at the locations shown in Figure 16.4*b*. Because the program is "vectored" (directed) to one of eight specific locations, the process is called a *vectored interrupt*.

An interrupt-service routine can be placed at any of the vectored interrupt locations. However, since space is limited at the RST n locations (they are spaced eight locations apart), long interrupt-service routines can be reached by placing a jump at the proper RST n location. (Vectored interrupt processing on an actual microcomputer—the SDK-85—is discussed at the end of this chapter.)

Also, during the interrupt-request stage, the interrupt system is automatically disabled, and will remain disabled until the EI instruction is processed again. This prevents an external device (perhaps the same external device) from interrupting the processor out of the present interrupt-service routine. As with all CALL processes, the interrupt-service routine may include PUSH/POP pairs so internal register usage may be shared between main program and interrupt-service subroutine.

Step 4—Return to the main program   Since *restart* performs the same functions as a CALL, we return to the main

program by placing the *return* instruction at the end of the interrupt-service routine, as shown in Figure 16.5. To reenable the interrupt system upon return to the main program, we place the EI instruction just before the return instruction. To prevent the processor from being interrupted after the completion of the EI instruction and before the *return* instruction is processed, the EI instruction will enable the interrupt system only *after the execution of the next instruction* (See Figure 16.2).

Special Interrupt Processing for Small Systems

By coding the RST n instruction, up to eight interrupt vectors can be processed. Although the technique is straightforward, we pay a penalty in the need for external hardware. For small systems, therefore, both the 8080 and 8085 provide for a simplification.

8080   For 8080-based systems in which only one interrupt vector is required, the 8228 system controller provides a special feature. It can automatically insert an RST 7 instruction onto the data bus at the proper time. To arm the system to provide this feature, simply tie the $\overline{\text{INTA}}$ output to the + 12-volt supply through a 1K-ohm resistor. Then, when an interrupt is acknowledged, the 8228 (rather than external

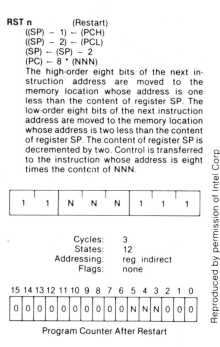

RST n (Restart)
((SP) − 1) ← (PCH)
((SP) − 2) ← (PCL)
(SP) ← (SP) − 2
(PC) ← 8 * (NNN)

The high-order eight bits of the next instruction address are moved to the memory location whose address is one less than the content of register SP. The low-order eight bits of the next instruction address are moved to the memory location whose address is two less than the content of register SP. The content of register SP is decremented by two. Control is transferred to the instruction whose address is eight times the content of NNN.

| 1 | 1 | N | N | N | 1 | 1 | 1 |

Cycles: 3
States: 12
Addressing: reg. indirect
Flags: none

15	14	13	12	11	10	9	8	7	6	5	4	3	2	1	0
0	0	0	0	0	0	0	0	0	0	N	N	N	0	0	0

Program Counter After Restart

(*a*) The *restart* instruction
(a single-byte CALL)

Reproduced by permission of Intel Corp.

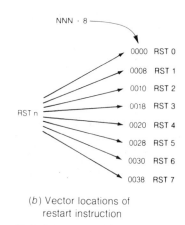

(*b*) Vector locations of restart instruction

Figure 16.4 Interrupt vectoring.

circuitry) automatically jams an RST 7 instruction into the instruction register. The hardware is shown in Figure 16.6.

8085 Besides the INTR (interrupt request), which is identical in function to the 8080's INT, the 8085 provides four additional interrupt pins that *automatically* insert RST instructions into the instruction register. (These four additional pins were made available by multiplexing the lower-order address lines.) (See Figure 16.7.)

These four interrupt requests are special because, unlike the interrupt request we studied earlier, no external hardware is required—no input port and no interrupt-acknowledge control signal. Everything is integrated within the 8085 chip.

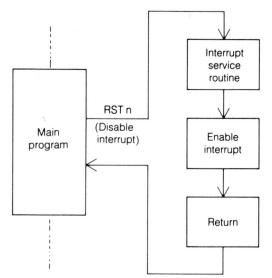

Figure 16.5 A vectored interrupt responds like a subroutine CALL.

The pin and vector assignments of these four special interrupt requests are as follows:

Pin	Name	Restart address (hex)
6	TRAP	0024
9	RST 5.5	002C
8	RST 6.5	0034
7	RST 7.5	003C

When activated, each of these four special interrupt pins automatically initiates an RST machine cycle, and CALLs a location equal to eight times the RST number. For example, if the RST 6.5 pin were driven active high, the processor would automatically call a memory location equal to 6.5 times 8, or 52 (0034 in hexadecimal).

Briefly, the following points should be known concerning this *multilevel* RST interrupt structure:

• Each of the three *restart* inputs—5.5, 6.5, and 7.5—has a programmable mask (inhibit) through the SIM (Set

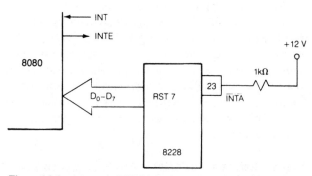

Figure 16.6 Automatic RST 7 injection circuitry for 8080 systems.

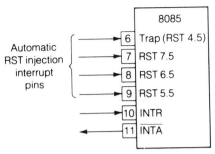

Figure 16.7 Complete six-pin 8085 interrupt system.

Interrupt Masks) instruction and the ability to determine interrupt status through the RIM (Read Interrupt Masks) instruction. To set (disable) or reset (enable) interrupt masks, first load the accumulator with the proper command word, according to the format of Figure 16.8a, then run the SIM instruction.

To determine interrupt status, first run the RIM instruction, then locate status information in the accumulator according to Figure 16.8b. The RIM instruction also can determine whether any RST interrupts are pending and whether the interrupt system is enabled.

- Once an interrupt cycle is set in motion, all future interrupts (except TRAP) are disabled until an EI instruction is executed.

- RST 5.5 and RST 6.5 are high-level-sensitive only, meaning the inputs must be high during the next to the last clock cycle of the present instruction in order for the interrupt requests to be honored (INT and INTR also are level-sensitive).

- The RST 7.5 input is rising-edge-sensitive, and a short pulse is sufficient to set an internal flip-flop, which in turn generates the internal interrupt request. The flip-flop remains set until the request is serviced, whereupon it resets automatically. The flip-flop can also be reset by way of the SIM instruction (Figure 16.8a).

- TRAP is not affected by any mask or enable instruction (TRAP cannot be disabled and is known as a *nonmaskable interrupt,* or NMI). TRAP is both edge- and level-sensitive. The input must go high and remain high to be acknowledged, but cannot again be recognized until it completes another low-to-high transition.

The complete 8085 interrupt system is summarized in Figure 16.9. By activating these five interrupt pins, and including the proper external hardware, we can vector to one of 12 memory locations, which means—using these techniques—an 8085-based computer can service the interrupt needs of up to 12 peripheral devices.

SDK-85 INTERRUPT PROCESSING

When we look at interrupt processing on the SDK-85 single-board microcomputer, two facts are presently in apparent contradiction. First of all, all 12 interrupts vector to page 0. But page 0 is reserved for the monitor ROM (the program that runs the keyboard). How can we ever hope to get to our service routines—which are placed in RAM at page 20H?

The answer is related to a well-known Olympic sport, the *hop, step, and jump.* That is, we *hop, step, jump* to the interrupt-service routine. Using the RST 6.5 interrupt as an example, and referring to Figure 16.10, here is how it works:

- The hop—When the RST 6.5 vectored interrupt is initiated, we "hop" to location 0034H in page 0.

- The step—At that location in the monitor ROM, we find a jump instruction, telling us to "step" to word location C8H in page 20H. (The branch to location 20C8H was placed into the monitor ROM at the factory.)

- The jump—At reserved location 20C8H in RAM, we find a jump instruction to finally carry us to the interrupt-

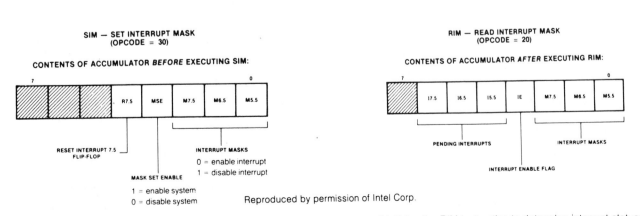

(a) Using the SIM instruction to set RST masks

(b) Using the RIM instruction to determine interrupt status

Figure 16.8 The RIM and SIM instructions.

8085 INTERRUPT STRUCTURE

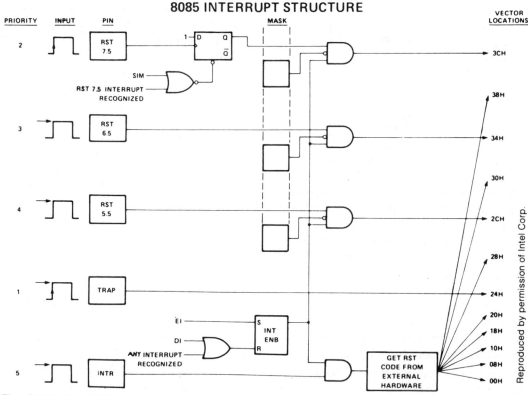

Figure 16.9 Total 8085 interrupt structure.

service routine. (It is the responsibility of the programmer to place the final jump instruction at location 20C8H before the interrupt is initiated.)

In order for a vectored interrupt to be allowed, the monitor ROM must contain the *step* to page 20H. Of the 12 vectors available, the SDK-85 has made provisions for only RST vectors, 5, 6, 7, 6.5, and 7.5.

A SIMPLE INTERRUPT TEST PROGRAM

For a simple test of the vectored interrupt process (on the SDK-85), let's make the familiar MIMIC program an interrupt-service routine (ISR); each time an interrupt is requested, the contents of input port 21H are transferred to output port 22H. The software design is given by Figure 16.11. When the program is executed, the following happens:

1. The stack pointer is set to RAM location 20C2H by the LXI SP,20C2H instruction (not necessary if the stack pointer is preset by way of the front keypad).

2. The overall interrupt system is enabled by the EI instruction, and the RST 6.5 interrupt input is enabled (unmasked) by the MVI A,0DH and SIM combination.

3. The RST 6.5 pin is pulled high and an interrupt is requested.

4. After completion of the present JMP instruction sequence, the processor stores (PUSHes) the next instruction address (200BH) on the stack, disables the interrupt system (does not affect the RST masks), and transfers control to the interrupt service routine by the *hop, step, jump* process.

5. The mimic process is performed.

6. The interrupt system is re-enabled by the EI instruction (the enable takes place only *after* the RET instruction has been processed).

8. We return to the main program by POPing the return address off the stack and jamming it into the program counter.

ADDITIONAL INTERRUPT CONSIDERATIONS

When peripherals are serviced by way of interrupts, the I/O processes are entirely asynchronous and no longer under complete control of the processor. A number of considerations therefore arise when devices are interfaced by way of interrupts.

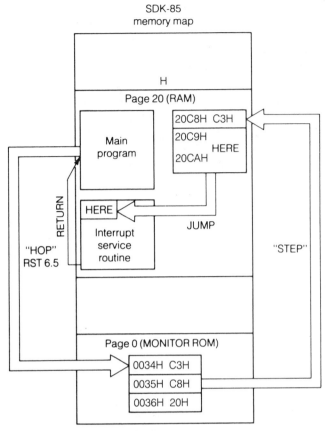

Figure 16.10 "Hop, step, jump" interrupt processing on the SDK-85.

Priority and Multiple Interrupts

A telephone is only one type of interrupting device found in everyday life. In general, your home or office will have many such interrupting devices: a doorbell, an auto horn, the bark of a dog, or a fire alarm. In addition, these multiple inputs are often given priority according to importance. That is, if more than one interrupt is requested simultaneously, the one with the highest priority would be recognized (i.e., the fire alarm).

Considering the many peripheral devices available, it is more than likely that any computer system will also interface with many peripheral devices on a priority basis.

When multiple devices communicate with the CPU via interrupts, the basic purpose of the interrupt system is to jam into the program counter the starting service-routine address of the highest-priority device requesting service.

As illustrated by Figure 16.12, three general methods are available for making sure the right service-routine address gets placed into the program counter.

Scanned In the *scanned* interrupt system, the multiple external devices are ORed to a single interrupt line. When one or more devices requests an interrupt, the computer must scan (poll) the devices to determine which one is requesting service. Priority is automatically provided by the order in which the devices are scanned. Any number of peripherals can be serviced using this technique. The circuit of Figure 16.12a shows one possible scanned configuration. When an interrupt is requested, the interrupt-service routine inports the status word. Using masking or rotate instructions, the highest-priority interrupting device can easily be determined and the proper interrupt-service routine address generated. The scanned technique is usually a *single-level* interrupt system, since only a single interrupt vector is in use.

Vectored A vectored interrupt system is one in which the highest-priority device requesting service causes a direct branch (vector) to the proper service routine. The microcomputer does not need to poll the devices to determine which one caused the interrupt. With each device tied to a separate interrupt line, the number of devices serviced is limited to the available vectored interrupt levels. Priority is automatically determined by hardware, both internal and external to the CPU. An 8080/8085-based vectored interrupt system is shown in Figure 16.12b. When one or more of the inputs to the priority encoder are pulled active low, an output line goes high and generates the interrupt-request signal. The 3-bit code corresponding to the highest-priority interrupt request is combined with the RST n operation code (all ones) and fed to an input port. During the interrupt op-code fetch, INTA reads the restart instruction into the instruction register, and the processor vectors to the proper interrupt-service routine. For 8085 systems with their added RST interrupt inputs, overall priority is determined by circuitry hardwired within the 8085 chip. The five interrupt inputs are ranked as follows, with the highest priority at the top (for the INTR input, priority of up to eight vectors is determined by an external priority encoder):

TRAP
RST 7.5
RST 6.5
RST 5.5
INTR

Vectored interrupt systems can be either single level, with only one interrupt vector in use, or *multilevel,* with up to 12 interrupt vectors readily available (with an 8085-based system).

Daisy chain In a single-level *daisy-chain* interrupt system, a device is identified through an acknowledge signal hardware-propagated through the peripheral devices. The daisy-chain (or *serial-priority*) technique is intermediate in speed between the scanned and vectored interrupt methods.

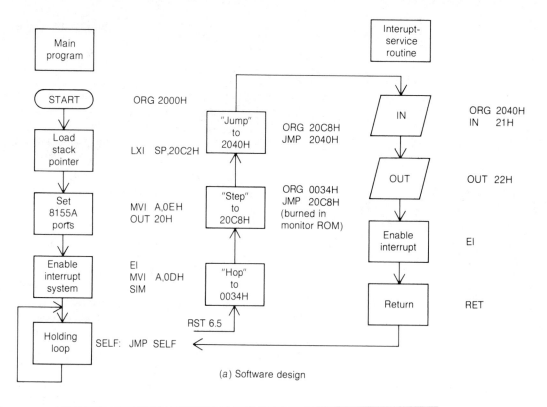

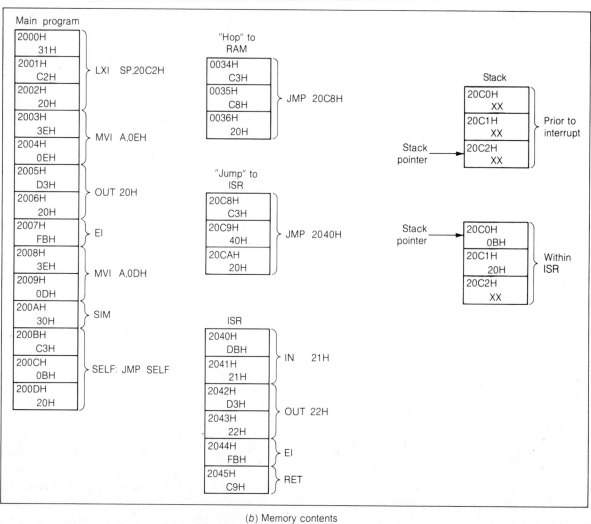

(b) Memory contents

Figure 16.11 Interrupt test system using mimic interrupt-service-routine (ISR).

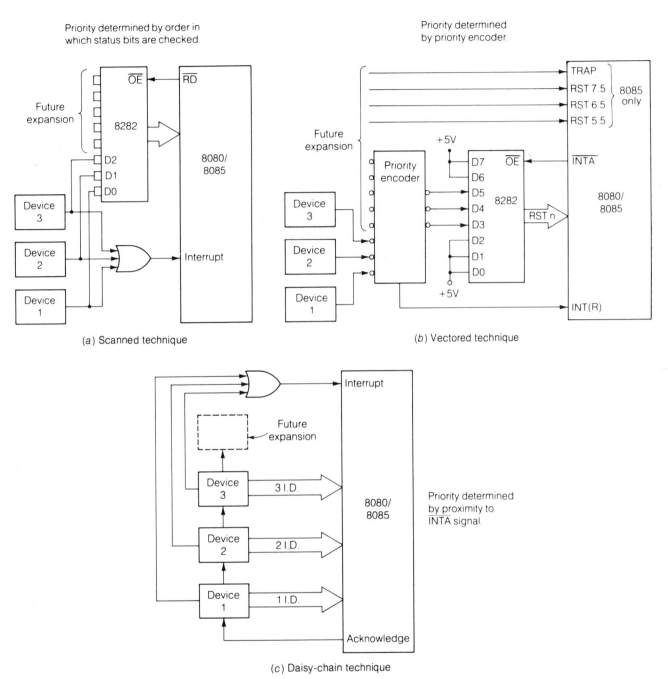

Figure 16.12 The three basic interrupt techniques for multiple-prioritized interrupt systems.

As illustrated in Figure 16.12c, an interrupt request by one or more peripherals will drive the processor into a service routine. This service routine generates an interrupt-acknowledge signal that is hardware-propagated (and therefore at high speed) through the peripheral devices. When the first interrupting device is found, the propagating acknowledge signal is halted, and the device places its identification number (address) on the data bus. This ID number is read by the microprocessor and used to generate the address

of the interrupt-service routine. Priority is automatically established by the order of the peripherals.

Nested Interrupts

When the processor is in one interrupt-service routine, can another interrupt pull the processor from this service routine into another, perhaps of higher priority? Generally, the answer is no. In fact, as we have seen, when any interrupt is recognized, the entire interrupt system is disabled (except, of course, for TRAP) just to prevent such an occurrence. Stack overflow is the problem. Each time the processor is pulled from an interrupt-service routine by another vectored interrupt (or the same vectored interrupt), two additional bytes are added to the stack. Eventually, if this were allowed to continue, the stack would overflow.

Nevertheless, interrupts can be nested if the proper debouncing and stack-overflow provisions are met. To nest interrupts it will be necessary to place the enable-interrupt instruction near the beginning of each interrupt-service routine.

However, when using nested subroutines and interrupts, we should be alert to a possible danger. If, for example, we are within a multiply subroutine when interrupted, and the same multiply subroutine is "reentered" within the interrupt subroutine (the interrupt service routine called the same multiply subroutine), much of the original multiplication data stands to be destroyed. The solution is to use a *reentrant* multiply subroutine.

A subroutine is said to be reentrant if it can be interrupted at any time and called again within the interrupt-service routine without affecting the interrupted calculation. To make a subroutine reentrant, simply arrange to have all registers and memory locations holding vital data pushed onto the stack when an interrupt occurs. The interrupt-service routine can then safely reuse the multiply subroutine. After the interrupt service routine, the original partial results can be pulled from the stack and the original multiplication continued.

Masking Interrupts

When interrupts are nested, it is logical that only interrupts of higher priority be allowed to pull the processor from its present ISR. Figure 16.13 shows how the scanned circuit of Figure 16.12a is modified to include masking. A 3-bit mask (perhaps corresponding to the present ISR) is written to the mask register (an output port). Only if the 3-bit code from the priority encoder is greater than the mask data will an interrupt be generated. In the Questions and Problems section you will be asked to redesign the circuit to *individually* mask out the interrupt inputs.

In Chapter 19 we will see how the 8259A *Programmable Interrupt Controller* implements multiple/vectored/prioritized/maskable interrupts with far less hardware than any of the schemes presented in this chapter.

Debouncing

The 8085-based system of Figure 16.14 is designed to count up by one each time a push-button switch is activated. To work properly, we must *call* the interrupt-service routine once and only once for each pressing of the push-button switch.

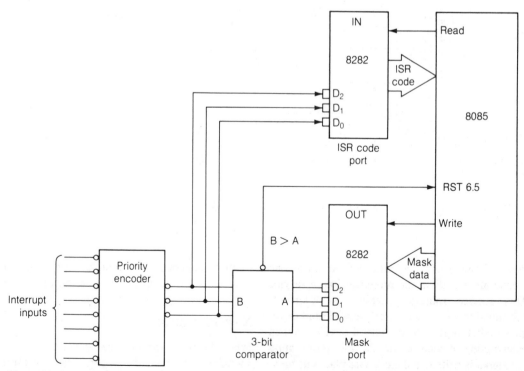

Figure 16.13 Adding priority encoding and masking to the basic scanned technique.

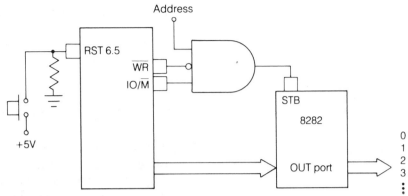

Figure 16.14   Interrupt-based count system.

Using this design, we run into trouble, for all mechanical switches bounce (they bounce when you make contact, and they bounce when you break contact). Because of switch bouncing, a single activation of the push-button switch will initiate multiple counts. Even the type of interrupt input will not matter, for we encounter trouble with all of them.

To solve the problem of mechanical switch bouncing, we have at our disposal both software and hardware techniques.

Hardware debouncing   For level-activated interrupt inputs, the circuit of Figure 16.15a will solve the problem. The $\overline{\text{INTA}}$ (interrupt acknowledge) signal may be automatically generated by the CPU, or it may be generated and outported by the interrupt-service routine. If the processor is currently involved in an interrupt-service routine, the interrupt request will be stored until action returns to the main program.

If an interrupt-acknowledge signal is not readily available, the one-shot of Figure 16.15b also will debounce the level-active lines. The monostable time must be long enough to assure that an interrupt will be requested (the worst case is when the request occurs at the beginning of a five-machine-cycle instruction), yet short enough to assure that the interrupt input line will be low when action returns to the main program.

For rising-edge-sensitive inputs (TRAP), only the feedback-debounce portion of the circuit is required. (It is not necessary for the interrupt signal to be low when the processor returns to the main program.)

Software debouncing   The simplest way to software debounce an interrupt line is to add a delay loop to the interrupt-service routine. After vectoring to the interrupt-service routine, we simply wait for the switch to stop bouncing before returning. For 8085 systems, another interesting technique combining software and hardware is shown in Figure 16.16. The RIM instruction continually checks the

status of the RST 6.5 line. Only when the line has returned low is action allowed to return to the main program.

And finally, for RST 7.5 interrupts, the SIM instruction can reset the interrupt-service flip-flop while in the interrupt-service routine.

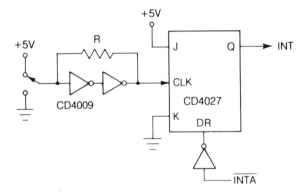

(a) Flip-flop debouncing

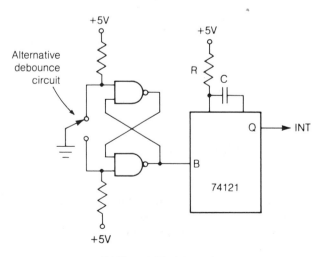

(b) Monostable debouncing

Figure 16.15   Hardware debouncing of level-active interrupt requests.

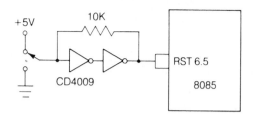

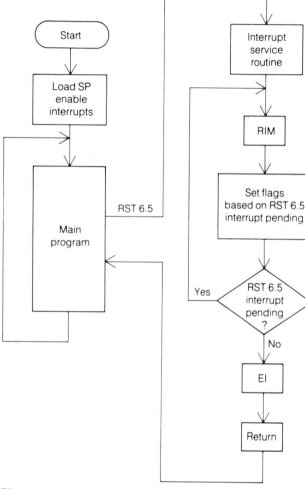

Figure 16.16 Combined hardware/software debouncing using the RIM instruction to check RST 6.5 interrupt-pending status.

MACHINE-ASSEMBLY UPDATE I

Our next machine-assembly update is primarily a reminder: an interrupt-service routine (ISR) is handled nearly the same as a subroutine. The only difference is that the last two legs of our "hop-step-jump" process must be accounted for by the programmer.

The counter circuit of Figure 16.17a is a case in point. It uses a timer-initiated interrupt and software debouncing to count from 0 to 255 at the rate of 1 hertz. The list file printout

of Figure 16.17b shows that the "step" and "jump" segments are established by way of the ORG directive. As a review exercise, follow through one complete cycle until all facets of interrupt processing included in the system are clear.

MULTITASKING VIA INTERRUPTS

Computers as well as people are notoriously single-minded. *Multitasking,* or the ability to perform several tasks at once, is generally a difficult process. However, through the use of multiple interrupts, we can simulate a multitasking environment.

As a simple case in point, let's take three tasks we have seen before and carry all of them out "simultaneously" (within a single program identify). The three routines are listed below, along with the multitasking technique used by each:

- TONE (main program)
- MIMIC (RST 7.5)
- COUNT (RST 6.5)

The solution to our multitasking problem is given in Figure 16.18. The hardware design of Figure 16.18a shows that no debouncing is required on the RST 7.5 line because routine MIMIC is immune to multiple requests for each switch activation. Routine COUNT, however, is sensitive to switch bouncing, and we have chosen the combined hardware/software debouncing technique of Figure 16.16.

Looking to the software solution of Figure 16.18b (designed to run on the SDK-85), program TONE—the main program—will be "free running," and a steady TONE will be generated whose frequency is inversely proportional to an inported number. Routine MIMIC, called whenever an RST 7.5 interrupt is requested, will transfer the contents of port 21H to port 22H. Routine COUNT, the third independent task, is also an interrupt service routine that increments the output port when an RST 6.5 interrupt is requested.

MACHINE-ASSEMBLY UPDATE II

A *variable* is a quantity that can change—like the outside temperature (an analog variable) or the state of a light switch (a Boolean variable). Our mystery program of Chapter 12 involved four Boolean variables (MOON, LIGHTNING, BARK, SUSPECT). To store and process the four variables we relied completely on the six internal registers (plus accumulator). One rather obvious problem with this technique for storing variables is: what do we do when the number of variables exceeds the number of available registers? Another problem is readability—register names are not at all descriptive of the information they contain.

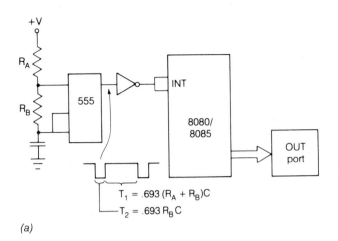

$$T_1 = .693 (R_A + R_B)C$$
$$T_2 = .693 R_B C$$

(a)

```
ASM80 :F1:COUNT.SRC MOD85


ISIS-II 8080/8085 MACRO ASSEMBLER, V4.1          COUNT     PAGE    1


  LOC  OBJ          LINE          SOURCE STATEMENT
                      1           NAME    COUNT
                      2
                      3   ; This COUNT program uses the software
                      4   ; technique to debounce the RST 6.5 input
                      5   ; line.   The RST 6.5 input pin is polled
                      6   ; via the RIM instruction.   Only when
                      7   ; low does the program exit the ISR.
                      8   ; Since the STEP from location 0034H to
                      9   ; 20C8H is built-in to the SDK-85 monitor,
                     10   ; it is not included in the program.
                     11
                     12   ; Jump to subroutine
                     13
  20C8               14           ORG     20C8H       ; SDK-85 ("step" location)
  20C8 C34020        15           JMP     COUNT       ; SDK-85 (jump to ISR)
                     16
                     17   ; Interrupt Service Routine
                     18
  2040               19           ORG     2040H
  2040 04            20   COUNT:  INR     B
  2041 78            21           MOV     A,B
  2042 D322          22           OUT     22H
  2044 20            23   LOOP:   RIM                 ; Poll RST 6.5 pending
  2045 E620          24           ANI     20H         ; Mask all but RST 6.5
  2047 C24420        25           JNZ     LOOP        ; Loop if still high
  204A FB            26           EI
  204B C9            27           RET
                     28
                     29   ; Main program
                     30
  2000               31           ORG     2000H
  2000 3E0E          32           MVI     A,0EH
  2002 D320          33           OUT     20H
  2004 0600          34           MVI     B,00H       ; Initialize count
  2006 31C220        35           LXI     SP,20C2H
  2009 FB            36           EI
  200A 3E0D          37           MVI     A,0DH       ; Create mask data
  200C 30            38           SIM                 ; Enable RST 6.5
  200D C30D20        39   TOSELF: JMP     TOSELF      ; Wait for interrupt
                     40           END


PUBLIC SYMBOLS

EXTERNAL SYMBOLS

USER SYMBOLS
COUNT  A 2040    LOOP    A 2044     TOSELF A 200D

ASSEMBLY COMPLETE,   NO ERRORS
```

(b)

Figure 16.17 Interrupt demonstration program: *a)* Hardware design. *b)* List file showing software debouncing.

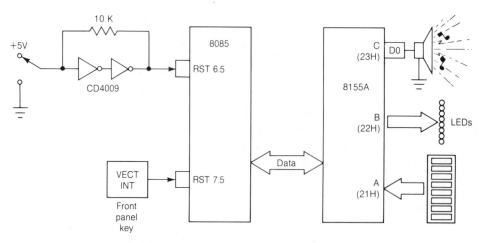

(a) Hardware design (SDK-85)

```
ASM80 :F1:MULTI.SRC MOD85


ISIS-II 8080/8085 MACRO ASSEMBLER, V4.1          MULTIT    PAGE    1

   LOC   OBJ         LINE         SOURCE STATEMENT

                       1           NAME    MULTITASKING
                       2
                       3    ; This multitasking demonstration program
                       4    ; carries out 3 independent tasks using a
                       5    ; single stored program.
                       6
                       7    ; JUMP to COUNT
                       8
   20C8                9           ORG     20C8H    ; SDK-85 ("step" location)
   20C8 C33020        10           JMP     COUNT    ; SDK-85 (jump to ISR)
                      11
                      12    ; JUMP to MIMIC
                      13
   20CE               14           ORG     20CEH    ; SDK-85 ("step" location)
   20CE C34020        15           JMP     MIMIC    ; SDK-85 (jump to ISR)
                      16
                      17    ; Task COUNT (RST 6.5)
                      18
   2030               19           ORG     2030H
   2030 04            20   COUNT:   INR     B
   2031 78            21           MOV     A,B
   2032 D322          22           OUT     22H
   2034 20            23   LOOP:    RIM              ; Read Interrupts pending
   2035 E620          24           ANI     20H      ; Mask all but RST 6.5
   2037 C23420        25           JNZ     LOOP     ; Loop if pending
   203A FB            26           EI
   203B C9            27           RET
                      28
                      29    ; Task MIMIC (RST 7.5)
                      30
   2040               31           ORG     2040H
   2040 DB21          32   MIMIC:   IN      21H
   2042 D322          33           OUT     22H
   2044 FB            34           EI
   2045 C9            35           RET
                      36
                      37    ; Task TONE (Main program)
                      38
   2000               39           ORG     2000H
   2000 3E0E          40           MVI     A,0EH    ; SDK-85
   2002 D320          41           OUT     20H      ; SDK-85
   2004 31C220        42           LXI     SP,20C2H ; SDK-85
   2007 0600          43           MVI     B,00H
   2009 FB            44           EI
   200A 3E09          45           MVI     A,09H    ; Unmask RST 6.5,7.5
   200C 30            46           SIM
   200D DB21          47   REPEAT:  IN      21H
   200F 3D            48   DELAY:   DCR     A
   2010 C20F20        49           JNZ     DELAY
   2013 0C            50           INR     C
   2014 79            51           MOV     A,C
   2015 D323          52           OUT     23H
   2017 C30D20        53           JMP     REPEAT
                      54           END
```

(b) Software design

Figure 16.18 Multitasking program.

One popular solution to all these problems is to combine the data definition directive with direct addressing. Looking to Figure 16.19, we have rewritten our mystery program using this new method of handling multiple variables. First, we define and label the four variables *symbolically* using the DB (define byte) directive, and we initialize them to specific values (rather than inporting the variables as we have done in the past). Clearly, the number of variables that we can define is limited only by the available memory. The variables are then conveniently accessed within the program by using their symbolic names in the LDA and STA direct addressing instructions.

INTELLIGENT-MACHINE UPDATE

Now able to react to the unexpected, our intelligent machine has fully matured. Its anatomy (hardware) and vocabulary (software) have fully developed, and it seems to possess all the tools required to enter the real world. Still, to this purely digital machine, the outside world is an alien and unfamiliar environment. Before our machine can leave the "nest," it must learn to interact with the world about it.

QUESTIONS AND PROBLEMS

1. On an 8080-based computer, how is an *interrupt* initiated?
2. During a normal interrupt process using the *restart* instruction, at what times is the interrupt system enabled and at what times is it disabled?
3. What is special about an interrupt machine cycle?
4. Precisely *when* and *how* is the restart instruction jammed into the instruction register in response to an interrupt?
5. What is a *vectored* interrupt?
6. What is special about the 8085's TRAP interrupt?
7. What memory location does the RST 7.5 instruction vector to?
8. Using the SIM instruction, explain precisely how you

```
ASM80 :F1:VAR.ASM


ISIS-II 8080/8085 MACRO ASSEMBLER, V4.1          MODULE    PAGE    1


   LOC  OBJ         LINE            SOURCE STATEMENT

                      1 ; MYSTERY PROGRAM USING VARIABLES
                      2
                      3 ; When storing variables in internal registers
                      4 ; becomes unwieldy, store them in memory
                      5 ; locations using symbolic names.  Be sure
                      6 ; to start execution at 2004H.
                      7
                      8 ; Define variables
                      9
   2000              10         ORG   2000H
   2000 01           11 MOON:   DB    01        ; Moon is out
   2001 00           12 LIGHT:  DB    00        ; No lightning
   2002 00           13 BARK:   DB    00        ; No barking
   2003 00           14 SUSPECT: DB   00        ; Create answer location
                     15
                     16 ; Mystery program
                     17
   2004 3A0020       18         LDA   MOON      ; Bring in Moon
   2007 47           19         MOV   B,A       ; Store away
   2008 3A0120       20         LDA   LIGHT     ; Bring in lightning
   200B B0           21         ORA   B         ; Moon OR lightning
   200C 47           22         MOV   B,A       ; Store away
   200D 3A0220       23         LDA   BARK      ; Bring in bark
   2010 2F           24         CMA             ; Create NOT bark
   2011 A0           25         ANA   B         ; NOT B AND M OR L
   2012 E601         26         ANI   01        ; Mask out D1-D7
   2014 320320       27         STA   SUSPECT   ; Store answer
   2017 CF           28         RST   1         ; SDK-85
                     29         END


PUBLIC SYMBOLS


EXTERNAL SYMBOLS


USER SYMBOLS
BARK   A 2002    LIGHT  A 2001    MOON   A 2000    SUSPEC A 2003

ASSEMBLY COMPLETE,    NO ERRORS
```

Figure 16.19   Using memory to store variables.

would enable RST 5.5 but mask out RST 6.5 and RST 7.5.

9. What interrupt-related information does the RIM instruction provide?

10. Using a single interrupt input, how can ten interrupting devices be serviced?

11. Can interrupts be nested? Why is the EI instruction required when nesting interrupts?

12. Explain one hardware debouncing technique and one software debouncing technique.

13. Why is the daisy-chain method of multiple-interrupt processing faster than the scanned technique, but generally slower than the vectored technique?

14. Under what conditions might you disable the interrupt system?

15. For the circuit of Figure 16.12a, how would you determine which peripheral requested service?

16. By adding a latching output port and AND gate inputs to Figure 16.12a, design into the scanned interrupt technique the ability to individually mask out the interrupt inputs.

17. By researching the 8085 User's Manual, list all the actions that take place when the 8080/8085 is RESET.

18. By what process does the 8080/8085 make sure the interrupt system is not enabled until the processing action returns to the main program (unless nesting is desired)?

19. Referring to Figure 16.11b, which of the five blocks of code are stored in RAM (page 20H), and which are stored in ROM (page 0)?

20. Using the VECT INTR (RST 7.5) key on the SDK-85, write a program in which a low frequency tone is sounded. Each time the VECT INTR key is pressed, the tone increases one octave in frequency. On the 9th press, it returns to the original low frequency and the cycle repeats. (*Note*: Be sure to reset the RST 7.5 flip-flop at the end of each ISR.)

21. Write program SKEET SHOOT: a light (clay pigeon) moves rapidly from LED D0 to LED D7 of port 22H. As soon as the player (the shooter) sees the clay pigeon, he or she activates the VECT INTR key as quickly as possible. The quicker the player reacts, the more points earned (8 points for D0, 7 points for D1, etc.). The play continues 10 times, with the cumulative score displayed on the SDK-85 hex display. (Use the special call routine UPDDT.)

22. Modify the program in problem 21 so:
   a. The speed of the pigeon starts slow and gradually increases.
   b. The time interval between shots is semirandom. (*Hint:* Reaction time is semirandom.)

part IV

Applications and Interfacing: Living in a Real World

The final stage of human development, based on the imaginative prose of the futurists, is pure thought—a formless world of light and energy, completely self-contained and isolated from its surroundings.

The human species, of course, has not yet reached this final stage of development, and neither have the computers we create. In other words, we do not build computers so they may merely contemplate their existence. Indeed, our actions are as basic as they can be: we build computers to be slaves!

Consequently, a computer must interact and communicate with its environment, and it must perform useful tasks—all at our command. This we will teach our computer to do in Part IV of this book.

chapter 17

Mathematical Refinement

A digital computer helped guide the Apollo 11 spacecraft to the moon. If our intelligent machine, in its present state of development, attempted to repeat the flight of Apollo 11, the mission would be quickly aborted, and for a number of good reasons.

How can our intelligent machine undertake trips of 240,000 miles when it can handle numbers no larger than 255? Even more basic, how does it determine distance at all when it cannot multiply velocity times time? Even descending to the surface of the moon is presently out of the question, for the velocity is negative when landing, and our computer cannot efficiently process negative numbers. And, what action should the pilot take when the landing altimeter flashes 1CFA? We are used to readouts in the decimal number system, so we could not quickly determine the descent distance to the surface of the moon.

Before our intelligent machine can help us explore space, we must solve these and other arithmetic problems—the subject of this chapter.

MULTIPLE-PRECISION NUMBERS

Using the decimal number system, we require only six digits to specify the distance to the moon. Convert that same number to binary, however, and an incredible 18 digits are required:

$$Decimal \qquad\qquad Binary$$
$$240{,}000_{10} = \underbrace{00000011}\ 10101001\ 10000000_2$$
$$\text{Zeros added to complete byte}$$

Such numbers are known as *triple-precision numbers* because 3 bytes of data are required to describe them. *Double-precision* numbers require 2 bytes of data; numbers of 2 or more bytes are generalized as *multiple-precision* numbers.

Triple-precision numbers are easy enough to store—just use three memory locations. The real question is: Can they be operated on by the instructions of the arithmetic group? That is, can we add and subtract triple-precision numbers? The real problem lies in the generation of carries and borrows from one byte to the next. This really turns out to be

no problem at all, for the arithmetic group already includes a set of special add and subtract instructions specifically designed to handle carries and borrows (Figure 17.1).

To see how these instructions process multiple-precision numbers, we will set up a simple exercise. We have traveled 54,000 miles into space, and our on-board computer indicates we have another 186,000 miles to go to reach the moon. We will instruct our computer to add the two numbers together and see if they total 240,000. First, all numbers must be converted to hexadecimal or binary. Hexadecimal is usually chosen because it is more convenient.

Decimal	Hexadecimal
186,000	02 D6 90
+ 54,000	+ D2 F0
240,000	03 A9 80

In preparation for the addition, all numbers are stored in memory. The exact memory locations chosen are not important, for the HL pointer can quickly be "aimed" at any memory location.

The addition begins as if we were doing it on paper, with the least significant bytes added first using the simple *ADD memory* instruction. Since a carry is generated from the answer, the simple ADD M instruction cannot be used to calculate the total of the middle bytes (it would ignore the carry).

The *ADD memory with carry* instruction (Figure 17.1), however, does include the carry and will give us the right answer. Of course, the final addition of the most significant bytes must also use the *ADD memory with carry* instruction to account for a possible carry from the middle bytes. Figure 17.2 summarizes the triple-precision addition operation. (Multiple-precision subtraction is left as an exercise.)

Incidentally, the DAD rp instruction of Figure 17.3 allows the 8-bit 8080/8085 to perform double-precision addition, and for one brief moment to take on the 16-bit properties of its 8088/86 big brother. As we will see in the Questions and Problems section, the DAD rp instruction can be used to manipulate the HL pointer.

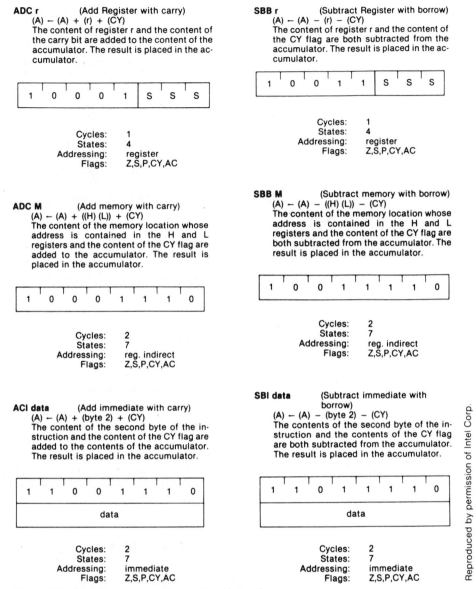

Figure 17.1 Multiple-precision add and subtract instructions.

MULTIPLICATION

How can the Apollo 11 spacecraft determine its distance from the earth? In the emptiness of space there is no way to *directly* measure distance traveled or velocity attained. The only motion that can be sensed directly is acceleration. But acceleration is really enough—providing you have the ability to multiply—for velocity is equal to acceleration times time, and distance in turn is equal to velocity times time. After the two multiplication processes, you have the distance. (Actually, since acceleration and velocity would in general be variables, a double *integration* would be required. However, it is not necessary to introduce such a complica-

tion here. The concept of integration will be discussed in Chapter 24.)

Unfortunately, the instruction set of the 8080/8085 does not contain a multiply instruction. It does not have to because multiplication really is successive addition—and addition is something our computer can do very well. The multiplication process involves a *test/shift/add* algorithm. The simple 6 times 5 binary multiplication problem of Figure 17.4 will reveal the steps involved.

The process is initialized by clearing the *cumulative total register* (a name assigned to any one of the internal registers). First we test the lowest multiplier position. Since it is 1, we add the multiplicand to the cumulative total register.

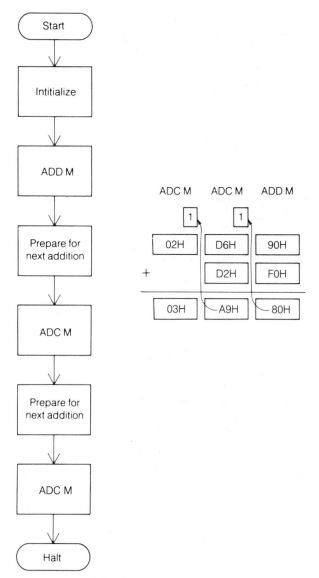

Figure 17.2 Complete triple-precision addition operation.

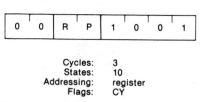

DAD rp (Add register pair to H and L)
(H) (L) — (H) (L) + (rh) (rl)
The content of the register pair rp is added to the content of the register pair H and L. The result is placed in the register pair H and L. Note: **Only the CY flag is affected.** It is set if there is a carry out of the double precision add; otherwise it is reset.

| 0 | 0 | R | P | 1 | 0 | 0 | 1 |

Cycles: 3
States: 10
Addressing: register
Flags: CY

Figure 17.3 The DAD rp instruction summary.

For multiplications involving 8-bit numbers and 16-bit results, it is more convenient to rotate the partial products right, rather than the multiplicand left. The technique is left as an exercise.

DIVISION

Binary division is basically the reverse of the multiplication process. As with multiplication, division proceeds along the same lines as it does on paper. A high-level flowchart and example problem are presented in Figure 17.6.

Since most later-generation microprocessors (such as the 8086) include multiply and divide instructions in their instruction set, and since they can be coupled with powerful LSI math processor chips (such as the 8087), *the need to write basic mathematical algorithms is rapidly disappearing.*

PROCESSING NEGATIVE NUMBERS

The second-generation 8080/8085 lacks many of the signed-number features found on the next generation 8088/86. These include the *overflow flag,* which detects an overflow into the sign bit, and an assortment of signed-number conditional branch instructions.

Nevertheless, through various programming techniques, the 8080/8085 can handle most any signed number problem.

Next we rotate the multiplicand left to prepare for the next cycle.

The process is repeated for the next highest multiplier-bit position. Since this position is 0, we delete the addition step. The multiplicand is again rotated left one position and the final multiplier bit tested. The 1 tells the program to add the twice-rotated multiplicand to the cumulative total register. All multiplier-bit positions tested, the contents of the cumulative total register are reported as the answer. For numbers as large as the distance to the moon, the successive additions and rotations would be triple precision.

Figure 17.5 shows the assembly-language program and flowchart for the multiplication process. The program assumes that both the multiplier and the multiplicand are brought in from separate ports.

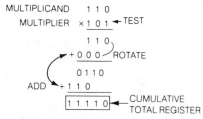

Figure 17.4 Binary multiplication routine.

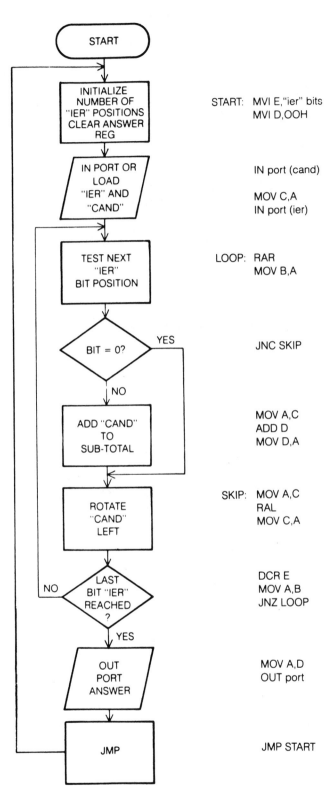

START:	MVI E,"ier" bits
	MVI D,OOH
	IN port (cand)
	MOV C,A
	IN port (ier)
LOOP:	RAR
	MOV B,A
	JNC SKIP
	MOV A,C
	ADD D
	MOV D,A
SKIP:	MOV A,C
	RAL
	MOV C,A
	DCR E
	MOV A,B
	JNZ LOOP
	MOV A,D
	OUT port
	JMP START

Figure 17.5 Binary multiplication flowchart and program.

Let's consider two examples, both based on our familiar mimic format.

Problem 1: Write a modified mimic routine that mimics only negative numbers.

For this case, the 8080/8085 directly provides all the tools that are needed, for it offers the *sign* flag. As shown in Figure 17.7a, we merely set the sign flag with the compare instruction and jump on minus (JM).

Problem 2: Write a modified mimic routine that mimics all numbers greater than -5 (-4 is greater than -5).

For this more difficult problem, we must do some programming "slight of hand." Looking to Figure 17.7b, we capitalize on two facts: 1. All positive signed numbers will be less than 128 (zero in the most significant position). 2. The numbers -1, -2, -3, and -4, when written as signed numbers (FFH, FEH, FDH, and FCH) are greater than FBH. (Another technique would be to convert all incoming numbers to sign magnitude form and check for magnitudes less than 5.)

BCD MATHEMATICS

The next mathematical refinement, strangely enough, is due to an accident of nature, when our distant ancestors evolved 10 fingers and relegated us to the decimal number system. In a sense, however, computers were "born" with 2 fingers, for they prefer the binary number system. As we all know, computer and human beings got together, compromised, and developed *binary coded decimal* (BCD). If two 4-bit BCD numbers are combined in one byte, it is known as a *packed* BCD number (an *unpacked* BCD number contains only a single BCD digit per byte).

The storage of BDC numbers is no problem—but the addition and subtraction are. If we attempt to add or subtract in the normal manner, using any of the ADD or SUB instructions, we will not arrive at the correct answer. The solution is to *adjust* the incorrect result back to BCD by using the Decimal Adjust (DAA) instruction.

BCD Addition

Carefully following the example of Figure 17.8a, the DAA process for BCD addition involves adding $+6$ to both the high-order and low-order nibbles of the result of the addition process. After the DAA process, the number is back in BCD form.

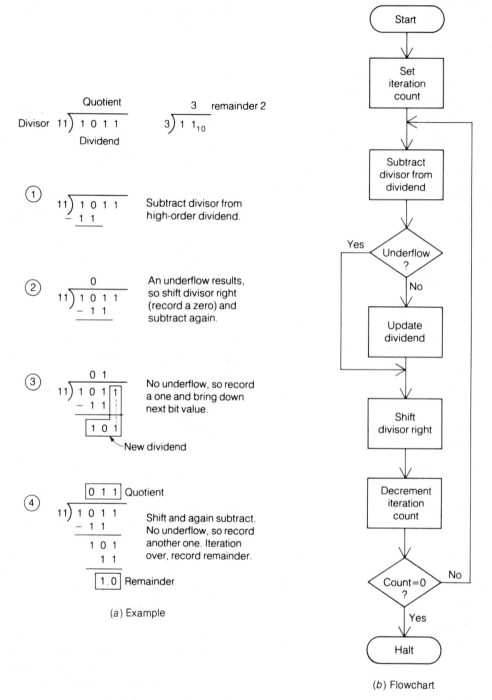

Figure 17.6 The binary division process.

BCD Subtraction

Through the use of a mathematical "trick," BCD subtraction is nearly as simple as BCD addition. The trick is this: to subtract two BCD numbers, we add the 10s complement of the subtrahend to the minuend prior to the DAA process. The process works because the 10s complement (100 − subtrahend) is equal to the 9s complement plus one (99 − subtrahend + 1)—*and any BCD number subtracted from 99 does not require adjusting!* The sample problem of Figure 17.8b (25 subtracted from 54 to give 29) should make the process clear. (Converting the algorithm of Figure 17.8b into a program is left as an exercise.)

ASM80 :F1:MINUS1.SRC

ISIS-II 8080/8085 MACRO ASSEMBLER, V4.1   MIMICN   PAGE   1


```
    LOC   OBJ          LINE          SOURCE STATEMENT
                         1            NAME    MIMICNEGATIVE
                         2
                         3    ; This program uses the sign flag to
                         4    ; mimic only negative numbers.
                         5
    2000                 6            ORG    2000H
    2000  3E0E           7            MVI    A,OEH   ; SDK-85
    2002  D320           8            OUT    20H     ; SDK-85
    2004  DB21           9    BEGIN:  IN     21H
    2006  FE00          10            CPI    0       ; Set flags
    2008  FA0C20        11            JM     AROUND  ; Jump if minus
    200B  AF            12            XRA    A       ; Clear reg A
    200C  D322          13    AROUND: OUT    22H
    200E  C30420        14            JMP    BEGIN
                        15            END
```


PUBLIC SYMBOLS

EXTERNAL SYMBOLS

USER SYMBOLS
AROUND A 200C   BEGIN A 2004

ASSEMBLY COMPLETE,   NO ERRORS

(a)

ASM80 :F1:MINUS2.SRC

ISIS-II 8080/8085 MACRO ASSEMBLER, V4.1   MINUSF   PAGE   1


```
    LOC   OBJ          LINE          SOURCE STATEMENT
                         1            NAME    MINUSFIVE
                         2
                         3    ; This program uses the fact that all
                         4    ; positive numbers (when written in signed
                         5    ; number convention) will be less than 128,
                         6    ; and all numbers greater than -5 (but not
                         7    ; positive) will be greater than FBH.
                         8
    2000                 9            ORG    2000H
    2000  3E0E          10            MVI    A,OEH   ; SDK-85
    2002  D320          11            OUT    20H     ; SDK-85
    2004  DB21          12    BEGIN:  IN     21H
    2006  FE80          13            CPI    128     ; Set flags for neg
    2008  DA1120        14            JC     MIMIC   ; Jmp if positive
    200B  FEFC          15            CPI    OFCH    ; Set flags for >-5
    200D  D21120        16            JNC    MIMIC   ; Jmp if >-5
    2010  AF            17            XRA    A       ; Clear
    2011  D322          18    MIMIC:  OUT    22H
    2013  C30420        19            JMP    BEGIN
                        20            END
```


PUBLIC SYMBOLS

EXTERNAL SYMBOLS

USER SYMBOLS
BEGIN   A 2004   MIMIC A 2011

ASSEMBLY COMPLETE,   NO ERRORS

(b)

Figure 17.7 Processing negative numbers: *a)* Mimic only negative numbers. *b)* Mimic only greater than −5.

DAA   (Decimal Adjust Accumulator)
The eight-bit number in the accumulator is adjusted to form two four-bit Binary-Coded-Decimal digits by the following process:

1. If the value of the lease significant 4 bits of the accumulator is greater than 9 **or** if the AC flag is set, 6 is added to the accumulator.

2. If the value of the most significant 4 bits of the accumulator is now greater than 9, **or** if the CY flag is set, 6 is added to the most significant 4 bits of the accumulator.

NOTE: All flags are affected.

```
EXAMPLE

   59
+  78
-----
  D1   (AC FLAG SET)
+   6
-----
  D7   (MOST SIGNIFICANT 4 BITS GREATER THAN 9)
+   6
-----
 137
```

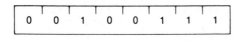

0	0	1	0	0	1	1	1

Cycles: 1
States: 4
Flags: Z,S,P,CY,AC

Reproduced by permission of Intel Corp.

(*a*) The DAA instruction and addition example

Problem		Solution	
54	(minuend)	54	
− 25	(subtrahend)	ADD [(99 − 25) + 1]	(10s complement of 25)
29	(answer)	C9 H	
		DAA + 6	(most significant 4 bits > 9)
		29	(ignore carry)

(*b*) BCD subtraction

Figure 17.8   BCD mathematics. (*Note*: The AC flag detects overflow from bit positions D3 to D4.)

Remember, the DAA instruction does not convert binary numbers to BCD numbers; it adjusts the result of adding or subtracting two numbers already in BCD format.

ASCII MATHEMATICS

Quite often numbers are passed to and from a computer for processing using the following ASCII representations for the decimal digits:

Digit	ASCII
0	00110000
1	00110001
2	00110010
3	00110011
4	00110100
5	00110101
6	00110110
7	00110111
8	00111000
9	00111001

After the most significant 4 bits are stripped away, we are left with *unpacked* BCD. As shown by the following sample problem, for the addition of 8 and 9, the adjustment process is similar to that for packed BCD numbers.

```
          00001000     (8)
ADD       00001001     (9)
        -----------
          00010001     (AC flag set)
DAA            0110     (ASCII adjust for addition)
        -----------
        1 00010111     (CY flag set)
ANI       00001111     (Zero high-order half-byte)
        -----------
        1 00000111     (Answer)
```

Third generation processors, such as the 8088/86, offer the programmer a wide range of packed and unpacked BCD and ASCII instructions, for multiplication and division as well as addition and subtraction.

FRACTIONS

Weighted number systems (decimal, binary, hexadecimal) handle fractions through a very old and clever invention—the decimal point. Numbers 1 or greater are to the left of the decimal point, and numbers less than 1 are to the right. In binary, each position to the left is weighted by increasing powers of 2, and each position to the right is weighted by negative increasing powers of 2.

Decimal
point
↓
_ _ _ _ _ _ _ _

$\leftarrow 2^3\,2^2\,2^1\,2^0 \bullet 2^{-1}\,2^{-2}\,2^{-3}\,2^{-4} \rightarrow$

The following examples demonstrate that signed numbers with fractions are added and subtracted using the same procedures as whole numbers. (Generally, we are free to place the decimal point between any two bit positions.)

Example 1:

		Sign bits
	− 5.25	1 1010.110
ADD	+ 7.50	0 0111.100
	+ 2.25	0 0010.010

Example 2:

	− 4.875
SUB	+ 6.250
	− 11.125

		Sign bits
	− 4.875	1 1011.001
ADD	− 6.250	1 1001.110
	− 11.125	1 0100.111

FLOATING-POINT NUMBERS

Computers are useful in areas ranging from microbiology to astronomy. Consequently, number magnitudes vary from very large to very small, and even multiple-precision techniques are impractical. To handle numbers that vary widely in magnitude, computers have adopted the *floating point,* a technique related to scientific notation.

The floating-point format of Figure 17.9a—an ANSI (American National Standards Institute) FORTRAN stan-

dard—is typical of those used throughout the computer industry. The 32-bit format is divided into two parts: a fraction (often called the *mantissa*) and an exponent. The fraction requires 25 bits and is in sign-magnitude form. The exponent uses the remaining 7 bits and is in (excess 64) 2's complement form.

Starting from bit 0 (see Figure 17.9a), the format is as follows:

1. Bit 0 is the sign bit for the fraction. A "1" is negative; a "0" is positive.
2. Bits 1 through 7 specify the exponent in 2's complement. However, the sign bit is inverted (excess 64 notation). A "1" indicates a positive exponent, a "0" a negative exponent. *The exponent is a power of 16.*
3. Bits 8 through 31 specify the magnitude of the fraction. The decimal point is assumed to be to the left of the most significant bit.

The ANSI FORTRAN floating-point format handles numbers from $.1 \times 16^{-64}$ to $.FFFF \times 16^{+64}$ (approximately 10^{-79} to 10^{+76}). The examples of Figure 17.9b should make the coding process clear.

Although multiplication and division of floating-point numbers are simplified by the property of adding and subtracting exponents, addition and subtraction are quite involved.

LSI MATHEMATICAL PROCESSORS

Many real-time process-control and signal-processing operations require number crunching beyond the capability of even the fastest microprocessors. However, specialized LSI arithmetic-processing chips, designed from the ground up to handle fixed or floating-point mathematical operations, are giving microcomputers a second chance at complex control and signal-processing applications.

In addition to basic addition, subtraction, multiplication, and division, these chips perform many complex operations such as square roots and logarithmic and trigonometric operations.

Compared to microcomputers, the processing speed is quite remarkable and can easily represent a hundredfold improvement in throughput. Sixteen-bit fixed-point addition can be polished off in a mere 8 μs (2 MHz clock), and a 16×16-bit multiplication can be performed in as little as 45 ns. Using GaAs technology, an 8×8-bit multiplication has been performed in an incredible 5 ns!

A typical programmable math chip may have 30 to 40 arithmetic instructions. The host CPU will write an instruction into the device, followed by the data. The math chip, a microprocessor in its own right, carries out the command by performing a sequential operation directed by a microprogram within its built-in ROM. When the operation is

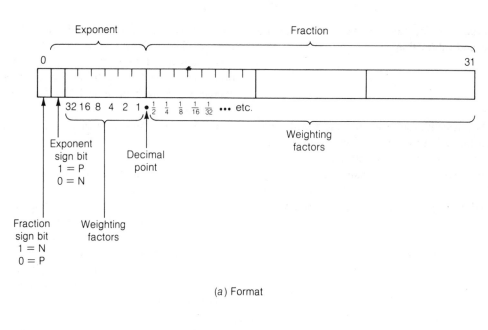

(a) Format

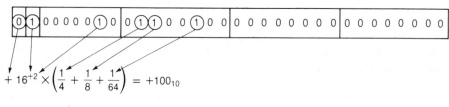

$$+ 16^{+2} \times \left(\frac{1}{4} + \frac{1}{8} + \frac{1}{64}\right) = +100_{10}$$

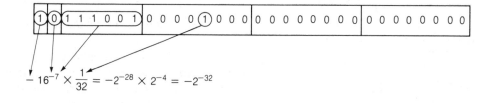

$$- 16^{-7} \times \frac{1}{32} = -2^{-28} \times 2^{-4} = -2^{-32}$$

(b) Examples

Figure 17.9 The ANSI FORTRAN floating-point standard.

over, an "end of execution" pulse signals the CPU to read out the answer.

DATA STRUCTURES

A data structure is simply a way of classifying data. Technically speaking, simple integers (1, 2, etc.) and real numbers (+1.25, −7.9, etc.) are data structures. However, the term usually is reserved for *organized collections of data*. By grouping or associating a number of data elements together, we may form the following data structures:

- *Table*—a collection of data in which each item is uniquely identified by a label or by its relative position to other items
- *List*—an ordered set of items

- *Array*—a collection of data in multidimensional matrix form
- *Vector*—an ordered set containing a fixed number of items, all of the same type
- *Tree*—data arranged in a pyramid structure, such as a family tree

Because data structures are so common, the computer programmer must be able to handle them efficiently. Searching, sorting, and table lookup are three examples of typical mathematical operations performed on various data structures.

Searching

Suppose a series of consecutive memory locations are storing the batting averages of a major-league baseball team:

Address	Average
2030H	234
2031H	167
2032H	253
2033H	200
2034H	247
2035H	207

We may wish to search this table for the value of the highest batting average. Using two decision-making blocks, the flowchart of Figure 17.10 shows how it is done. The first value (234) is moved to an accumulator and compared with the second value (167). Since the first value is larger than the second, it remains in the accumulator. Next we compare the accumulator value with the next number in line (253). Since the next number is greater than the accumulator value, it replaces the accumulator value. The process continues through all six numbers, and the largest number found is outported.

Sorting

Suppose we wish to arrange (sort) the batting averages of the preceding section in ascending order from lowest to highest.

Before-sort process		**After-sort process**	
Address	*Average*	*Address*	*Average*
2030H	234	2030H	167
2031H	167	2031H	200
2032H	253	2032H	207
2033H	200	2033H	234
2034H	247	2034H	247
2035H	207	2035H	253

A familiar sorting technique is called *bubble sort,* because the smaller values tend to "bubble up" toward one end of the list. The process requires a number of passes through the list of numbers. During each pass, each two adjacent numbers are compared, and if they are out of order they are interchanged. After the first pass, the largest value is at the end of the list. Each successive pass places the next largest value in the next position. After $n - 1$ passes (n = length of list), the numbers are sorted.

Translating the bubble sort algorithm to an assembly-language program is left as an exercise.

Table Lookup

Suppose we wish to design a temperature transducer around the inexpensive thermistor (resistance is a function of temperature). The problem is that the thermistor is not a linear device but obeys the curve of Figure 17.11*a*. If the ther-

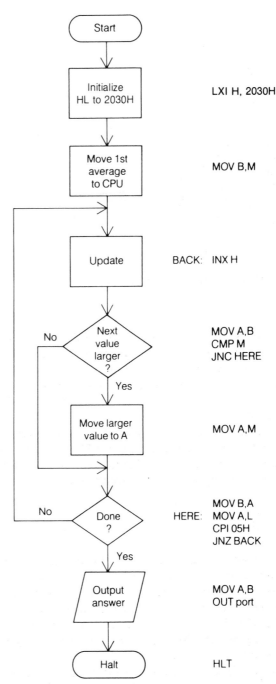

Figure 17.10 Searching a table for the largest value.

mistor controls the current into a simple inverting amplifier (current to voltage transducer of Figure 17.11*b*), the resulting inverted scaled voltage (to be sent to the analog-to-digital or A/D converter) also obeys this nonlinear curve. How are we going to convert the voltage inputs to corresponding temperature values?

One method always is open to us: we can derive an equation relating temperature and resistance, and program the computer to solve the equation for each inported voltage.

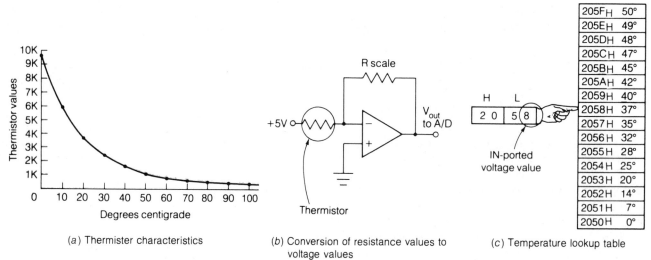

Figure 17.11 Performing a calculation by table lookup.

However, we have an alternative—to use the inported voltage as an address to "point to" a location in a sequence of memory locations (a table). If we are using a 16-level A/D system, the table would resemble that shown in Figure 17.11*c*. (The voltage input becomes the lowest-order nibble of the HL register pair.)

Since no calculations are required, the table method is simpler to implement, but becomes unwieldy as the need for accuracy and the number of table entries increase (note the inaccuracy of the table at low temperatures).

STRINGS

More complex operations are required when the data are in the form of *strings,* or sequences of data bytes regarded as a single entity. For example, each name in a list of names is a string, since each letter in each name must be converted to ASCII and stored in an individual memory location. Searching for a specific name means searching for a given *sequence* of letters (a string).

As we will see in Chapters 23 and 25, many microprocessors (for example, Zilog Z80 and Intel 8088) include instructions specifically designed to streamline the processing of data structures and strings.

LINKED LISTS

Instead of the short list of only six batting averages, as we have been working with so far, suppose instead our list contains 100,000 names—all the entries in the phone book of a large city. To insert a new name (a string) in this list of *sequentially allocated* strings is a time-consuming process,

for all the names below the insertion point must be moved down one memory location.

The solution is to store the names as a *linked list.* When storing elements in a linked list, each element is followed by a pointer (address) to the next element in the list. Using this *linked allocation* approach, the elements of the list need not be physically adjacent in memory. For example, Figure 17.12*a* shows how four names are stored as a linked list (NULL is a special value denoting the last element in the list).

As demonstrated by Figure 17.12*b,* inserting a new name in a linked list is trivial. We simply modify the pointers of both the new element and the previous element to include the new name. Since no data has been moved (only pointers have been reassigned) the process is quick and efficient.

MACHINE-ASSEMBLY UPDATE

Our next machine-assembly update will expand on the theme of this chapter and demonstrate several techniques for handling data structures. In particular, let's see how the assembly-language programmer may process an *array* of data (an *array,* remember, is a collection of data in multidimensional matrix form).

As a case in point, five people have purchased varying numbers of lottery tickets in the new state lottery. There are 25 tickets available, numbered from 1 through 25, and *all 25 tickets are always purchased.* Our task is to write a program that searches this *data base* for the winning number. Because of the complexity of our data base, we should adopt a technique that aids readability.

Using the data definition directive, we define the data base in a way that is clear to both assembler and human:

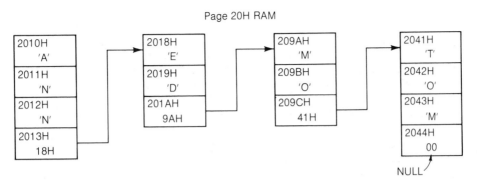

(a) Linked list of four names

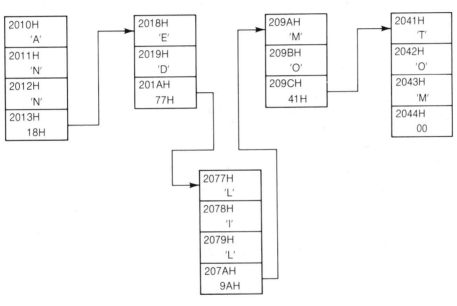

(b) Adding a name to the linked list

Figure 17.12   Linked lists.

```
LIST:    DW    NAME1
         DW    NAME2
         DW    NAME3
         DW    NAME4
         DW    NAME5

NAME1:   DB    25,22,0
NAME2:   DB    1,2,8,10,14,19,20,6,18,0
NAME3:   DB    5,0
NAME4:   DB    3,4,7,9,12,13,15,16,17,11,0
NAME5:   DB    21,23,24,0
```

LIST is a symbolic address specifying a word memory location (two consecutive bytes) that holds the *address* corresponding to NAME1. Location NAME1, in turn, holds the first data byte (25).

Since the number of tickets that can be purchased by any individual varies, we end each row of numbers with a *ter-minator,* a number that cannot appear in the data base (there is no lottery ticket corresponding to 0).

To see how our array of numbers is scanned for the winning number, let's examine the list file solution of Figure 17.13. We first load the *address* corresponding to LIST (2040H) into the HL register pair, and then fetch the *contents* of LIST (204AH, which corresponds to symbol NAME1) to the DE register pair. By entering a loop that increments the DE register pair and fetches data by way of the LDAX D indirect addressing instruction, we scan through the numbers for the given name. When we reach the end of a row (a 0 is detected), we go to the next name. When the winning number (8) is detected, we divide the L register by two (to generate the correct name number) and report the winner.

Incidentally, while we are discussing unique uses for data definition, another convenience feature is the ability to load and manipulate a data *string* (a sequence of ASCII characters). For example, the following DB directive loads the

```
          NAME   LOTTERY
    ; This program uses list processing techniques to
    ; search for the winning number in an array of 25
    ; numbers held by 5 people.  The person holding
    ; the winning number is identified by an outported
    ; number from 1 to 5.
    ; Since we are guaranteed that the winning number
    ; is present, there is no need to check for the
    ; final end of search.
    ; Using the EQU statement, we have chosen 8 as the
    ; winning number.

    WIN    EQU    8

           ORG    2040H
    LIST:  DW     NAME1
           DW     NAME2
           DW     NAME3
           DW     NAME4
           DW     NAME5

    NAME1: DB     3,7,9,14,22,23,25,0
    NAME2: DB     2,4,11,17,0
    NAME3: DB     1,5,0
    NAME4: DB     6,8,12,13,19,20,24,0
    NAME5: DB     10,15,16,18,21,0

           ORG    2000H
           MVI    A,OEH       ; SDK-85 operation
           OUT    20H         ; SDK-85 operation
           LXI    SP,20C2H    ; SDK-85 operation
           LXI    H,LIST      ; Load NAME1 address into HL
    NEXT:  MOV    E,M         ; Get low-order address of name
           INX    H           ; Point to high-order address
           MOV    D,M         ; Get high-order address of name
           INX    H           ; Point to next name
    AGAIN: LDAX   D           ; Bring in next array number
           CPI    WIN         ; Winning number?
           JZ     DONE        ; If yes, go to DONE
           INX    D           ; Point to next number
           CPI    0           ; Last number in row?
           JNZ    AGAIN       ; If not, try next number
           JMP    NEXT        ; Go to next name
    DONE:  MOV    A,L         ; Bring in low-order name address
           RRC                ; Divide by 2 to get name number
           ANI    07H         ; Mask out upper 5 bits
           OUT    22H         ; Report winning name number
           HLT
           END
```

Figure 17.13 Program LOTTERY source file.

ASCII equivalents for "JULY" into four consecutive memory locations.

Label	Opcode	Operands	Assembled Code
MONTH:	DB	'JULY'	4A554C59

Because a label always refers to the first element in a string, label *MONTH* refers to the location of the letter "J."

INTELLIGENT-MACHINE UPDATE

Number crunching (processing numbers at high speed) is an area in which computers quickly surpassed their human creators. Even ENIAC, the world's first electronic computer, could process numbers far faster than human beings. When mathematical refinements are included, along with ultrafast processing speeds, the number-crunching ability of the computer is truly superhuman. Our intelligent machine makes good use of its high-speed mathematical abilities to compensate for the lack of the sophisticated analog- and parallel-processing abilities of the human mind.

QUESTIONS AND PROBLEMS

1. In an 8080/8085 system, how large can an unsigned triple-precision number be?
2. What is the difference between the ADD r instruction and the ADC r instruction?
3. Write the assembly-language division program corresponding to the flowchart of Figure 17.6.
4. Using the subtract with borrow instructions, write a program to subtract 54,000 (base 10) from 186,000 (base 10). All numbers are in memory.
5. What range of value (positive to negative) can a single-precision signed number have? A double-precision signed number?

6. If BCD numbers 97 and 44 are added together, explain how the DAA instruction adjusts the answer back to BCD.

7. Based on the BCD subtraction algorithm of Figure 17.8*b*, subtract the packed BCD number 17 in register B from the packed BCD number 80 in register C and output the answer to port 22H.

8. What are several advantages of table lookup over direct calculations? Disadvantages?

9. An arithmetic operation results in a number whose magnitude appears in 2's complement form. What is the state of the sign flag?

10. How many bytes are required to store away the distance to the moon (240,000 miles) using *packed* BCD? Using *unpacked* BCD?

11. Based on the ANSI FORTRAN format of Figure 17.9*a*, convert the following numbers to floating-point standard: (a) 200, (b) -2^{-4}.

12. Rewrite the multiplication program of Figure 17.5 by rotating the partial products right rather than the multiplicand left.

13. Using a table, write a program that converts the binary numbers 0000 (0H) to 1111 (FH) to BCD.

14. Explain how table lookup can be used to convert Celsius (centigrade) to Fahrenheit. The formula is:

$$°F = (9/5)°C + 32$$

15. When -103 is added to -64, why does the operation give an erroneous sign change?

16. What instruction will toggle (correct) the sign bit but leave the magnitude unchanged?

17. Referring to Figure 17.12, how would a new name be added to the end of a linked list?

18. What is the difference between an integer and a real number?

19. Referring to the section in this chapter that describes the bubble sort technique, write an assembly-language program that sorts the six batting averages from lowest to highest.

20. Using the DAD rp instruction to update the HL pointer, write a program that adds together 10 numbers spaced 100 (64H) bytes apart in memory. (*Note:* To test the program on the SDK-85, the spacing of the numbers will have to be considerably reduced.)

21. Write a program that multiplies two numbers by successive addition (answer does not exceed 255). What is the disadvantage of this technique compared to that of Figure 17.5?

22. Write a program that divides two numbers by successive subtraction (all numbers less than 256). What is the disadvantage of this technique compared to that of Figure 17.6?

23. Write a program that acts as a frequency counter for frequencies between 1 and 99 Hz. (Input the signal to bit D0 of port 21H, and output the resulting frequency value to port 22H or the front panel display.) (*Hint:* So your program works for signals of any duty cycle, count the number of signal transitions in ½ second.)

chapter 18

Basic I/O and Interfacing Techniques: Parallel I/O

When we leave our familiar home base and travel throughout the world, we are confronted with a wide variety of languages and communication techniques. When the computer leaves its comfortable and precise digital environment and enters the real world, it too is confronted with an incredible variety of peripheral components, each with its own interfacing and I/O requirements.

However, regardless of the diversity, data exchange for both human and computer can be divided into two major categories: short distance and long distance. Over short distances, data is efficiently transferred in *parallel,* a byte or a word at a time. However, for long distance data exchanges (known as *data communication*), we must reduce the number of interconnecting lines and will switch to a *serial* mode that transfers one bit at a time.

In this chapter we will introduce the basic I/O and interfacing concepts and the terminology used throughout Part IV, and we will concentrate on short-distance parallel I/O techniques. In Chapter 21, we will turn to the long-distance serial techniques of data communication.

SYNCHRONOUS VS ASYNCHRONOUS

When we are interfacing components to a computer system, perhaps the most basic question we can ask is: Is the transfer of information *synchronous* or *asynchronous?*

First of all, let us paint the difference between synchronous and asynchronous in broad strokes:

- Synchronous is predictable (clocked) transfer of data.
- Asynchronous is unpredictable (unclocked) transfer of data.

In a synchronous data transfer or I/O operation, all transfer events are tied to a common system clock and are usually under the direction and control of the CPU. If the data transfer or I/O process is asynchronous, however, the information transferred is not tied to a common system clock but can come at any time and at irregular rates and intervals. In addition, asynchronous data transfers often are initiated by external devices, such as a printer.

The choice between synchronous and asynchronous transfer of information often depends on the type of peripheral device to be added to the system. For example, if the device is a fast RAM with well-known timing characteristics, then all transfers can be tied to the system clock. On the other hand, if the device is mechanical, such as a printer, then the data words may be transferred at irregular rates and intervals, and asynchronous techniques may have to be employed.

Up to now, all of our data transfers have been synchronous, and we are quite familiar with that process. Therefore, as the first major topic of this chapter, let's turn our attention to the asynchronous transfer of parallel data.

REQUIREMENTS OF ASYNCHRONOUS TRANSMISSION

During asynchronous data transfers, we must find some means of regulating the flow of information between source and destination. The most general technique, known as *handshaking,* consists of a separate set of synchronizing signals used to coordinate the data transfers. These handshaking signals can be completely separate from the data and use separate signal pathways, or can be included *along with the data* (time multiplexed on the same line). The second method—designed to reduce the number of interconnecting lines—is a data-communication technique and will be covered in Chapter 21. In this chapter, all handshaking signals will be in parallel with the data.

HANDSHAKING

Handshaking refers to a set of back-and-forth "hand" signals coordinating the flow of data between computer and peripheral. The terminology is appropriate because handshaking signals occur in a given sequence and often consist of a request followed by an acknowledge. *That is, each event is*

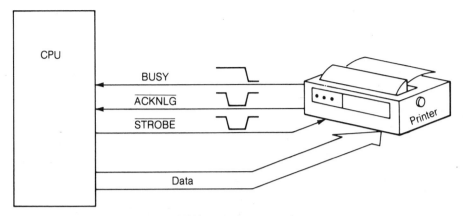

(a) CPU/printer interconnections

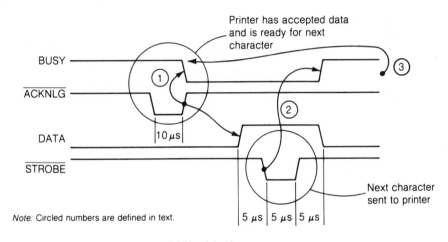

Note: Circled numbers are defined in text.

(b) Handshaking sequence

Figure 18.1   The Centronics printer interface standard.

initiated (request) *as a result of a signal indicating completion of a previous operation* (acknowledge).

A printer is a common peripheral often requiring handshaking signals, for such a mechanical device can in no way keep up with the maximum rate at which a computer can spew out characters.

Using the popular *Centronics* handshaking standard as a specific example, handshaking consists of the three signals shown in Figure 18.1a. The three-step handshaking "conversation" for transferring a single byte of data to the printer follows that of Figure 18.1b.

① The printer says, "I'm done, send me the next character," by sending an ACKNLG (acknowledge) pulse and pulling BUSY low.

② The CPU reacts to the printer's request by placing the next character at the output pins to the printer. When the data character is stable, the CPU says, "Here is the data," by issuing the STROBE pulse. The STROBE pulse automatically causes the printer to set BUSY high. ("Thanks, I received the character.")

③ The printer performs the function indicated by the data, and when done, again issues ACKNLG and BUSY ("I'm ready for the next character")—and the three-step sequence is repeated.

Why did the printer send both ACKNLG *and* BUSY when requesting the next character? The signals seem to be redundant, since both are conveying the same information ("I'm ready for the next character"). The answer is flexibility. As we will see in the following sections, the ACKNLG/BUSY combination offers the designer a variety of handshaking schemes.

PROGRAMMED I/O VS INTERRUPT I/O

A handshaking signal to the CPU—such as the Centronics standard BUSY signal of the last section—can be accepted in one of two ways: it can be inported or it can initiate an interrupt.

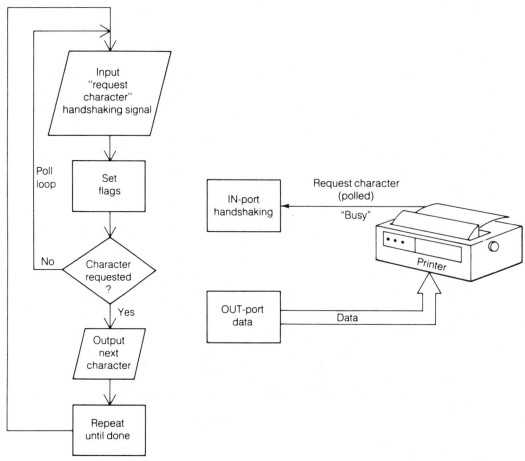

Figure 18.2 The programmed I/O technique.

The first technique is known as *programmed I/O* (or *polling*), since the sampling of the request signal takes place under main-program control. Usually the computer is placed into a wait loop, where it continuously *polls* the request-handshaking signal via an input port. Only when the request signal (or external flag) is detected does it exit the loop and send the next character to the printer (Figure 18.2). As shown, the BUSY handshaking signal is designed for polled operation because it is level active; that is, it stays active until recognized.

Since the request signal is initiated by the printer and can occur at any time and at irregular intervals, handshaking is an asynchronous technique (although the *exact* time of data transfer may be under CPU control and synchronous with the system clock). Using an ordinary input port to poll the status of the printer, programmed I/O minimizes the use of hardware at the expense of software.

When more than one I/O device interfaces the system, the program polls the devices in order, looking for a request signal. For example, the three output devices of Figure 18.3 are sequentially polled by inporting the status flags and checking each bit in turn. When a bit is found to be active,

it is used to generate the address of the service routine. The devices are ranked in priority according to the order in which they are polled. Many software priority schemes are possible.

Although simple to implement, the polling technique has several drawbacks. First of all, polling—the continuous checking of status bits—can take up all of the computer's time (all peripheral devices must be checked, even when servicing is not required). Second, the response time can be slow, for the sequential polling process as well as the software time used to generate the address of the service routine can consume a great deal of time.

Interrupt I/O, the second major I/O technique, is designed to largely overcome these two drawbacks of programmed I/O. In interrupt I/O, the request-handshaking signal becomes an interrupt request. When interrupted, the computer branches (vectors) directly to the interrupt-service routine and sends the next character to the printer.

As discussed in Chapter 16, interrupt I/O can service the needs of multiple-prioritized I/O devices by way of the scanned, priority, or daisy-chain techniques (see Figure 16.12). Under interrupt I/O control, the computer services the peripherals only when necessary and is free to process

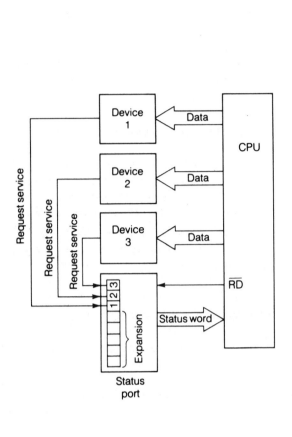

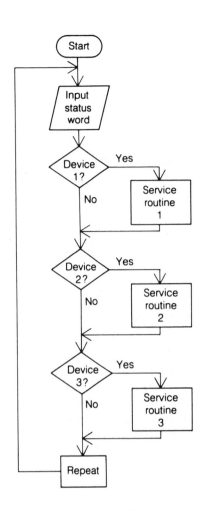

Figure 18.3   Multiple-device programmed I/O technique.

other information during its spare time. In general, using interrupt I/O improves the response time. However, the need for PUSH/PULL register storage on the stack introduces an often significant delay.

In Chapter 19 we will use both programmed I/O and interrupt I/O in order to drive a Centronics interface printer with an 8155A RAM/I/O programmable chip.

DMA I/O

Direct Memory Access (DMA), first introduced in Chapter 9, is a different form of I/O process. A DMA request (hold) allows a peripheral device to gain access to memory without going through the microprocessor at all. By eliminating the processor "middleman," memory transfers are greatly accelerated. To see why, consider the following simple routine, used to inport and transfer data from a peripheral device to system RAM:

```
BACK:   IN port
        MOV M,A
```

```
        INX H
        DCR B
        JNZ BACK
```

Driven by a 3-MHz clock, one transfer loop uses up approximately 12 μsec, which translates to a data-transfer rate of slightly more than 80,000 bytes/sec. Under DMA control, on the other hand, the processor's address, data, and control lines are floated (tristated) and the CPU is completely out of the picture. The DMA device issues its own sequential addresses and can oversee the transfer of data as quickly as the access times of the peripheral device and RAM allow. If we assume a 500-nsec transfer time, the data-transfer rate jumps to nearly 2 megabyte/sec—more than 20 times faster!

A simplified DMA system is shown in Figure 18.4 in which high-speed block transfers between floppy disk and RAM are under DMA control. The sequence is as follows: The disk requests a DMA operation. The DMA controller acquires control of the system bus by way of the hold signal to the CPU. After receiving an acknowledge, the DMA controller initiates a block-transfer operation, generating in

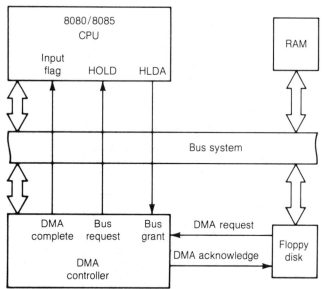

Figure 18.4   Simplified DMA-controller block diagram.

sequence the where/when waveforms required for direct read or write operations between peripheral and memory. When the specified number of data bytes has been transferred, the DMA controller informs the CPU that the DMA operation is complete, thereby handing control back to the processor. Many DMA controllers are programmable, single-chip devices.

MEMORY-MAPPED I/O VS ISOLATED I/O

A memory-mapped system treats I/O ports as if they were memory locations. The diagram of Figure 18.5, using 8085 control signals, depicts the change from a conventional system (known as an *isolated I/O* system) to a memory-mapped system. Note how the separate I/O port space and memory space of the isolated I/O system blend together in the mem-

ory-mapped system. In other words, with memory mapping the 64K address space is shared by both memory and I/O ports. In a memory-mapped system, with no distinction between memory locations and port locations, each memory and port location must have a unique address. There are, as usual, advantages to both systems.

Advantages to Memory Mapping

- All instructions that operate on ordinary memory locations can now be used with I/O ports (for example, MOV r,M). Greater overall flexibility and speed as well as reduced program size are two immediate results.
- The number of processor pins can be reduced without relying on multiplexing. (Or, conversely, the number of features that can be placed within a 40-pin chip is increased.)

Advantages to Isolated I/O

- I/O transfers are conceptually easier since only the accumulator and IN- or OUT-port instructions are involved.
- It is often easier to assign port addresses, since compatibility with memory is not required.
- The full 64K address space is in no way affected by I/O addressing.

Figure 18.6 shows one popular technique for converting from an isolated I/O to a memory-mapped configuration. We split the available memory space in half and assign the lower 32K to memory locations and the upper 32K to I/O ports.

DIGITAL-TO-ANALOG CONVERSION

The real world is largely an *analog* world in which the various parameters—temperature, pressure, mass—can assume

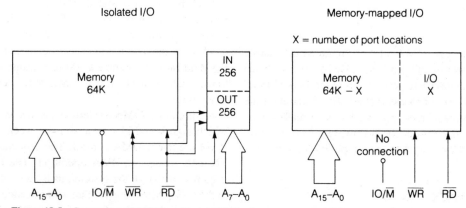

Figure 18.5   Comparison of 8085-based isolated I/O and memory-mapped I/O.

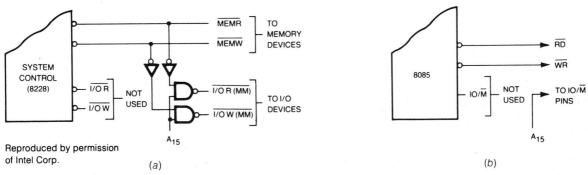

Reproduced by permission
of Intel Corp.

(a)   (b)

Figure 18.6   Memory-mapped I/O by splitting memory space in half: *a)* 8080 system. *b)* 8085 system.

a continuous range of values. In order for a digital computer to "speak" to this analog world, a translator is required—a digital-to-analog converter (DAC). The simplest digital-to-analog configuration is the ladder network of Figure 18.7*a*. Using the superposition principle, it can be demonstrated that the contribution of each input is weighted in an 8-4-2-1 manner from bit D_3 to bit D_0. The high-impedance voltage amplifier scales and buffers the output.

An alternative configuration that also provides weighted inputs, buffering, and amplification is the current-summing

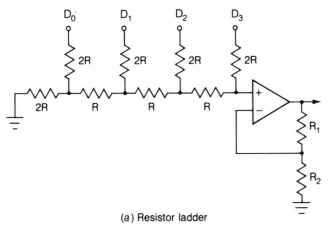

(a) Resistor ladder

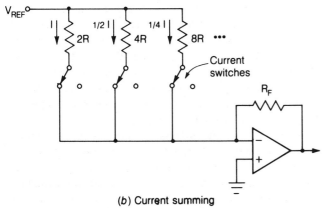

(b) Current summing

Figure 18.7   Digital-to-analog techniques.

method of Figure 18.7*b*. Here current is weighted in an 8-4-2-1 pattern by selecting proper resistor values. The feedback resistor (R_F) provides the overall scaling factor.

For the ultimate in convenience, the designer can select from the many single-chip (monolithic) DACs on the market. Shown in Figure 18.8*a* is the AD558 8-bit digital-to-analog converter. By means of the voltage-switching technique, it offers a settling time (input to stable output) of 1 μs.

Interfacing the AD558 to the 8080/8085 (Figure 18.8*b*) is a simple process. When a digital word is written to the AD558, its analog equivalent is available at the output line 1 μs later.

External jumpers from V_{out} (pin 16) to a selected feedback resistor (pins 13, 14, and 15) provide a choice of voltage gain values.

ANALOG-TO-DIGITAL CONVERSION

It is easier to convert from digital to analog (D/A) than from analog to digital (A/D)—that is, it is easier for a computer to "speak" to us than to "listen" to us. Analog-to-digital conversion is a *sampled* data process: the incoming analog signal is sampled at regular intervals and each voltage converted to a parallel digital word (Figure 18.9).

There are four well-known techniques for A/D conversion:

- Counter
- Successive approximation
- Ramp method
- Flash technique

(The simple counter technique is saved for an exercise.)

Successive-Approximation A/D Conversion

Successive approximation is the most popular method of A/D conversion. To see how successive approximation works, consider the following puzzle: Buried treasure is located in one of four quadrants on an island. By asking just two ques-

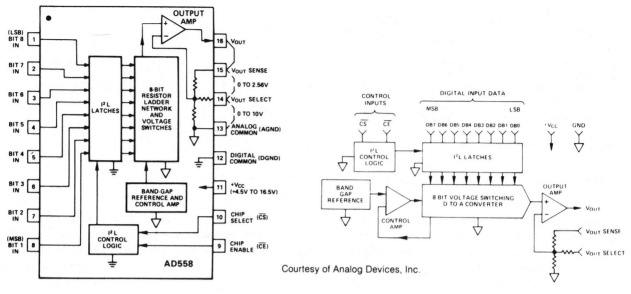

Courtesy of Analog Devices, Inc.

(a) AD558 architecture

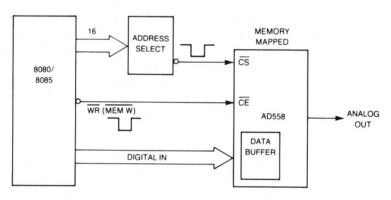

(b) Interfacing the AD558 to the 8080/8085

Figure 18.8   The AD558 single-chip DAC.

tions, can you determine the proper quadrant? Here is how it is done:

- *First question:* Is the treasure located in the north half or the south half of the island? *Answer:* It is located in the north half.

- *Second question:* Is the treasure located in the upper or lower part of the northern half of the island? *Answer:* It is located in the lower part.

We have homed in on the correct spot by successively cutting in half the space where the treasure can lie (Figure 18.10a). To see how a computer uses this technique to home in on the correct analog input voltage, let us follow through a single sampling event (for example, when the analog input voltage is 10.4 volts).

Referring to Figure 18.10b, note how each successive-approximation iteration sets the next bit position, starting with the most significant bit (MSB). (For greater accuracy, we have extended the process to four iterations.)

Successive approximation is a trial-and-error process. The routine begins by placing a logic 1 in the most significant position. This test voltage is compared to the input voltage. If the input voltage is greater, the 1 is kept. If the input voltage is less, the 1 is masked out. A logic 1 is then placed in the next most significant position and another comparison test is made with the input voltage to determine if this logic 1 should be kept. The process continues through an "elimination pyramid," with each iteration determining the next most significant bit, until the correct slot is found among the 16 possibilities. The process is as simple as finding buried treasure; we home in on the input voltage by successively cutting in half the space where the answer lies.

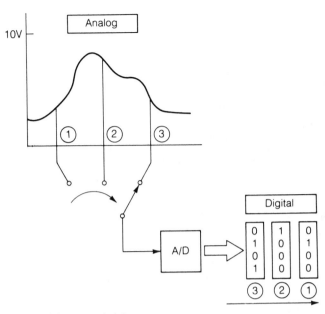

Figure 18.9   A sampled-data system.

Clearly we could continue the process any number of additional steps, driving our test voltage closer and closer to the true analog input voltage and thus reducing the error.

Successive-approximation analog-to-digital conversion is popular because it arrives at the answer very quickly. For example, with just four iterations of the test routine, we have placed the actual voltage within a 1-volt slot out of a possible 16-volt range, giving the answer to within $6\frac{1}{4}\%$ of full-scale voltage. Each additional iteration cuts the error in half. After eight successive subdivisions, we know the answer to within 0.4%.

Only two pieces of hardware are required to build the converter system: a digital-to-analog converter to send out the test voltages and a comparator to determine if the test voltage is greater than or less than the input voltage (Figure 18.11a).

It is the job of the software to send out the proper sequence of test voltages, based on the comparator output at each test point. Figure 18.11b is a high-level flowchart of the successive-approximation routine. The program is left as an exercise.

The Ramp Technique

The *ramp technique* for A/D conversion, also known as the *integration* or *slope method*, is often used in digital voltmeters. It is slower than successive approximation, but more accurate. Referring to Figure 18.12, we measure the time it takes a capacitor to charge under the unknown analog input voltage. Then we discharge the capacitor under a known reference voltage. The ratio between our known and unknown voltages is equal to the ratio of the two time measurements.

If implemented by a microcomputer, it is the job of the software to switch between the unknown and reference voltages and to measure the times involved and compute the unknown voltage.

Flash Converters

For superfast conversion rates, the iteration process of the successive-approximation method and the capacitive charging time of the ramp method are too slow, and we must switch to pure hardware techniques. Figure 18.13 depicts the simultaneous method (also known as the *flash* technique). Conversion speed is a function only of the propagation delay of the circuitry. For example, TRW's TDC1029J 6-bit flash converter provides 100 million samples per second, while an experimental 6-bit Josephson A/D flash converter has achieved a conversion rate of 2 billion samples per second!

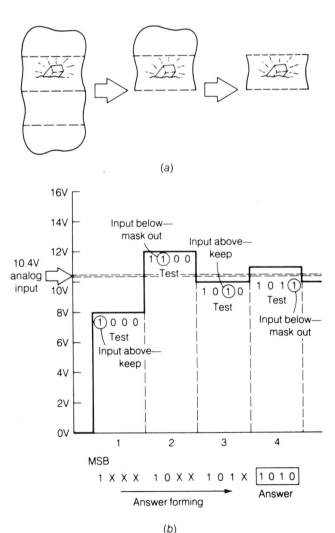

Figure 18.10   Successive-approximation A/D conversion: *a)* Locating buried treasure. *b)* Computer equivalent.

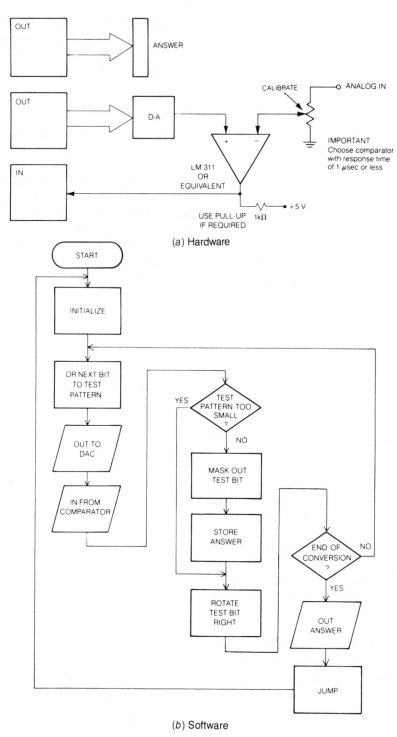

Figure 18.11 Successive-approximation A/D technique.

A/D Parameters

When selecting the correct A/D converter to meet your needs, the following criteria should be considered:

- *Range*—the input voltage span over which the converter will work

- *Linearity*—the degree to which all voltage steps are the same size
- *Resolution*—the number of states into which the signal can be divided (equal to the value of the LSB)
- *Absolute accuracy*—the difference between measured and ideal full-scale output

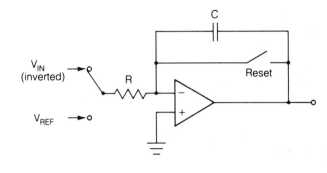

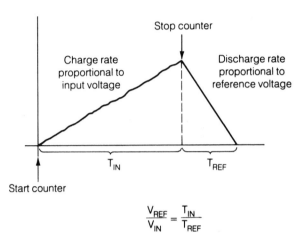

$$\frac{V_{REF}}{V_{IN}} = \frac{T_{IN}}{T_{REF}}$$

Figure 18.12   The dual-slope method of A/D conversion.

Single-Chip A/D Converters

As with DACs, A/D converters are also available in single-chip form, using all the standard technologies (bipolar, MOS, CMOS, TTL).

The AD574, shown in Figure 18.14*a*, is a typical state-of-the-art precision, successive-approximation, 12-bit A/D

converter, performing a complete conversion in 25 μs—corresponding to a 40 kHz sample rate.

The complete A/D process involves two steps:

* Analog-to-digital *conversion*
* A microprocessor *read* of the converted digital word

The timing for both the *conversion* and *read* actions is displayed in Figure 18.14*b*. Basically, to initiate conversion, $\overline{CS}$ and R/$\overline{C}$ are both pulled low; status (STS) goes high to indicate conversion under progress. When the conversion process is complete—after 10 to 40 μs—STS goes low, signaling *end of conversion*. By driving $\overline{CS}$ low and R/$\overline{C}$ high, the output pins will come out of their floating state and allow the data to be read in by the microprocessor.

KEYBOARD INPUT

For many applications, a keyboard is the most convenient method for entering information into the computer system. The two most common keyboard configurations are hexadecimal and ASCII. A hexadecimal keypad includes 16 input keys (0 through F) and several control keys. An ASCII keyboard closely resembles a typewriter keyboard and includes approximately 60 keys (the shift key doubles the number of possible inputs).

The keypad is organized into rows and columns, with each row and column fed by a conducting line. Pressing a key causes a contact between the corresponding row and column, thereby identifying the active key by coincident selection. Because of this technique, a large number of keys can be serviced with only a small number of interfacing lines.

Figure 18.15*a* shows the design for a small-scale four-key system. Pressing a key makes contact between the cor-

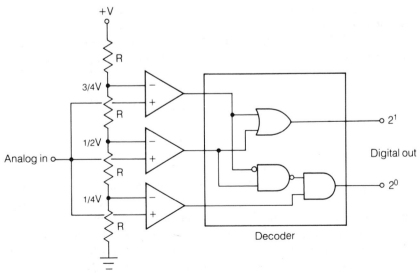

Figure 18.13   Two-bit simultaneous (flash) A/D converter.

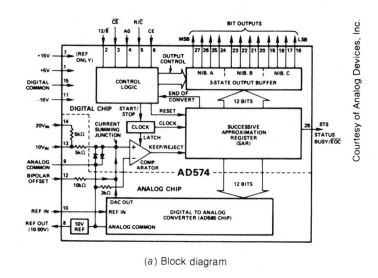

(a) Block diagram

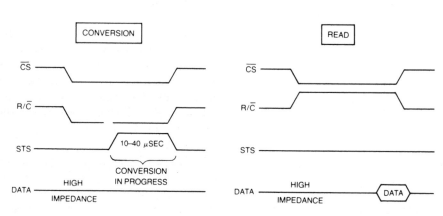

(b) Conversion and read timing

Figure 18.14 The AD574 analog-to-digital converter.

responding column and row. As each column is activated (scanned), row information is input and checked for a logic high. Debouncing is normally accomplished using software techniques (such as a delay loop). In the Questions and Problems section, we will design a simple four-tone organ based on our scanned keyboard configuration.

Display Multiplexing

The concept of scanning (multiplexing) also reduces the hardware requirement of multiple character displays. As shown in Figure 18.15b, the technique is similar to keyboard scanning.

Seven-segment information is sent to all displays simultaneously. However, only one of the seven-segment displays—the one to be illuminated—is grounded by port 2. By grounding the segments in sequence, and sending synchronized BCD information to the display array, we drive

the system. (Display flicker is reduced to acceptable levels as the scanning rate is increased.)

As we will see in Chapter 19, Intel's 8279 *Programmable Keyboard/Display Interface* chip provides automatic keyboard scanning and display refreshing, and operates in the more efficient interrupt I/O mode.

TOUCH-SCREEN DISPLAYS

A favorite "user-friendly" I/O device is the *touch-screen display*. Using familiar lightpen techniques, as well as various exotic techniques such as infrared light beams, surface-wave acoustics, and conductive membranes, we can determine the position of an object (finger, lightpen, pencil) in front of the CRT screen.

The lightpen—the oldest and most common screen-position device—is basically a pulse-detection device. As the electron beam scans past the pen, the pulse is detected and an interrupt is issued. Since the electron-beam position is

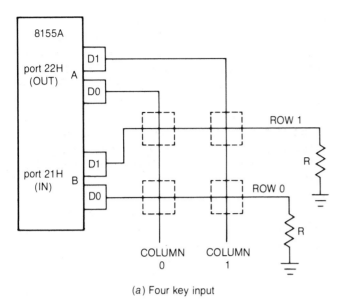

(a) Four key input

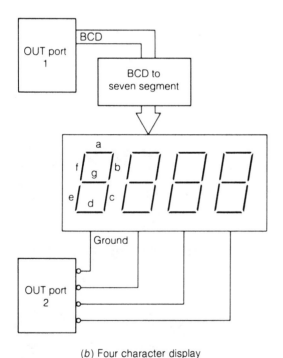

(b) Four character display

Figure 18.15 The scanned I/O technique.

always "known," the lightpen position can easily be determined within the ISR by reading row and column registers.

THE MOUSE

The latest in computer ergonomics (the science of adapting working conditions to suit the workers) is called the *mouse*. Developed in the early sixties, the mouse is a handheld input device that slides along the desk, translating hand motion to cursor movement on the video screen. When the cursor is at the proper position on the screen, a simple press of a button located on the mouse will initiate the selected action. The mouse is slated to become a popular and widely used input device because of two key features:

1. It allows quick and accurate cursor location without the necessity to shift eyes from the screen.
2. It frees the user from issuing potentially confusing command sequences from the keyboard.

MONITOR PROGRAMS

Single-board computers that use scanned keyboards and multiplexed seven-segment displays always include a ROM with a built-in program called a *monitor*. It is the monitor program (the program the computer automatically runs when RESET) that the computer "wakes up" into.

A monitor program performs two fundamental tasks: (1) basic housekeeping duties such as keyboard and display interfacing, and (2) the acceptance and execution of simple commands issued by way of the keyboard. Typical commands accepted by the SDK-85 single-board computer include:

- Display and modify internal registers and memory locations
- Enter, examine, and execute programs
- Perform single stepping
- Set breakpoints (As detailed in Chapter 22, a *breakpoint* stops computer action at a specific point.)

When more advanced computers (such as Apple II, IBM PC) entered the scene, the simple monitor program grew into a full-fledged *operating system,* able to both carry out the more complex housekeeping operations required for floppy disk drives, video monitors, and printers, as well as accept very high level commands issued by the operator via the keyboard. We will continue our discussion of operating systems in Chapter 22.

VIDEO DISPLAY

A video monitor is the most popular method for displaying large numbers of ASCII characters. A video monitor is similar in operation to an ordinary television set.

Basic Television Operation

A video monitor "paints" an image onto a monitor screen by sweeping an electron beam rapidly across the face of the screen. The on-off pattern of the electron beam produces the ASCII characters.

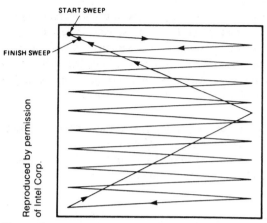

Figure 18.16 CRT monitor raster.

Starting at the upper-left corner of the screen (Figure 18.16), the beam sweeps horizontally from left to right, laying down one line of the image for each pass. When the beam reaches the right side of the screen, it is blanked out and quickly returned to the left side. The beam is deflected downward a small amount for each pass, so the second line is traced out slightly below the first. The scanning continues back and forth until the bottom of the screen is reached. The beam then returns to the upper-left corner and the process is repeated.

For displaying ASCII characters, the screen is subdivided into a number of character spaces. The simplest format allows for 16 lines of 32 rows, for a total of 512 characters. Again using the simplest format, each character space is in turn divided into a 5×7 matrix. As the electron beam scans through the dot matrix, each dot is either illuminated or left blank. From the many dot-matrix patterns possible, all ASCII characters can be generated. Typically, two horizontal dot positions and three vertical positions are left blank to provide spacing between the characters. Figure 18.17 shows a dot-matrix pattern holding the letter R.

Generating the Characters

Let us assume a 512×8 RAM is presently holding the 512 characters to be displayed on the CRT screen. We must devise a method of transferring the RAM information into a dot-matrix pattern generated by the serial tracing of an electronic beam.

This seemingly difficult task is actually made quite simple once we accept one crucial fact: since the electron beam is controlled by digital circuitry (counters), we know at all times precisely at which of the 35,000 dots the electron beam is pointing. Furthermore, the display circuitry contains only one circuit we have not seen before: the *character generator*.

The character generator is really a preprogrammed ROM, with the address inputs divided into four row-select and seven ASCII-code inputs. As shown in Figure 18.17, when an

ASCII code is entered (for example, the code for R), the proper dot matrix is generated as the rows are sequenced.

The first step in understanding the total operation of the system is to visualize each of the 512 RAM locations as corresponding to a like 7×10 character position on the CRT screen (known as *character mapping*). As the character spaces are scanned on the CRT, like RAM locations are also scanned (addressed) simultaneously and in synchronization.

Figure 18.18 is a simplified block diagram of the display system. It works as follows: At the present time, let us assume the line and character counters are arbitrarily addressing the second line, sixth character (holding an R). The ASCII code for R appears at the output lines of the RAM and is fed into the character generator. Also, we assume the row-select counter feeding the character generator is set to the second row (the top of the letter). Therefore, 0111100 appears at the output of the character generator (refer back

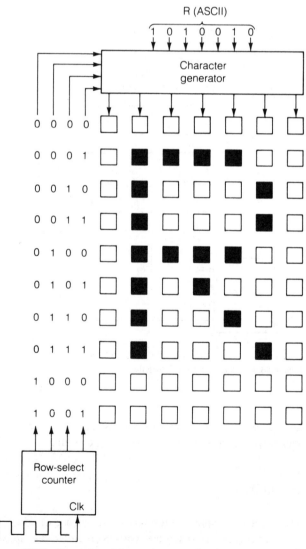

Figure 18.17 Generation of dot-matrix pattern for "R."

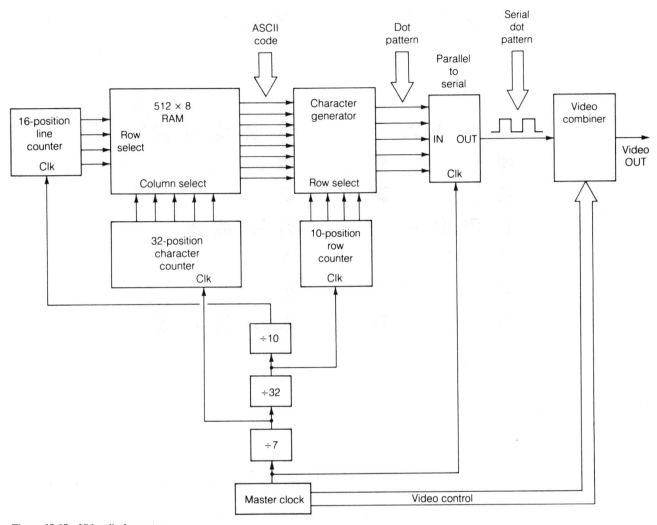

Figure 18.18 Video display system.

to Figure 18.17) and enters the parallel-to-serial shift register. The seven dots in the top row of the letter R are clocked out in serial, combined with necessary video information, and fed to the CRT. After seven clock pulses of the master clock, the top of the letter R is traced onto the CRT screen.

The divide-by-7 counter overflows and clocks the character counter to address the next RAM location in the same row. The process is repeated seven more master clock cycles, and the top of the next character is traced onto the screen. Assuming the next character is an E, Figure 18.19a shows the result.

After the top row of all 32 characters has been traced out on the CRT, a divide-by-32 counter clocks the character generator's row-select counter, and the next row of each letter is selected. After all 10 rows are traced out, the 2 characters fully appear (Figure 18.19b).

When the tenth row of the last character is traced out, a pulse increments the RAM line counter, and it addresses the

next line of characters stored in RAM. The entire process is then repeated. As always, a number of video LSI controller chips are available to ease the design task.

GRAPHICS

When the character-generation concepts of the last section are expanded and coupled with VLSI technology, we move from simple character generation to *graphics*—the ability to display any figure on the CRT screen (limited only by resolution).

Especially promising are the new text processors (such as Intel's 82730 *text coprocessor*). By modifying a table of pointers (linked list) to update the display (rather than moving data from one location to another), speed is greatly enhanced. In addition, by including a huge library of characters on chip (15,000) and allowing characters to be rede-

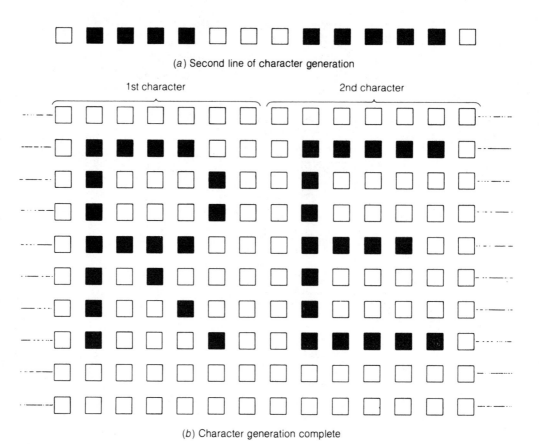

(a) Second line of character generation

(b) Character generation complete

Figure 18.19 Generation of two ASCII characters.

fined "on the fly" (by software), a flexible high-resolution graphics system can be implemented.

However, at present, most graphics systems are based on the concept of *bit mapping* rather than character mapping. Interestingly, bit-mapping technology is not new; such graphics display systems are relatively late bloomers because they consume vast amounts of high-speed primary memory—a commodity only recently available in large quantities at low prices.

Bit-Mapping

To understand bit-mapping, imagine a CRT screen divided into 320 by 200 dots (see Figure 18.20). Each dot, which can be illuminated by the electron beam, is called a *picture element* (or *pixel*). Further imagine each dot to correspond to a single bit in a 64K $\times$ 1 RAM array called a *bit plane* ($320 \times 200 = 64{,}000$). If a 1 is stored in a particular bit location, the corresponding pixel is turned on (white); if a 0 is stored, the corresponding pixel is blank (black). It is the responsibility of the video refresh circuitry to translate the pattern of 1s and 0s in the bit plane to whites and blacks on the CRT screen. To avoid tying up software for such a routine operation, video refreshing is now performed by a sophisticated *video interface chip,* or VIC. (This is how the Commodore VIC computer got its name.)

For flexibility, video interface chips and boards are available to drive two types of video displays: *raster scan* and *vector.* Raster scan is the technique used by television (see Figure 18.16), whereas the vector technique is found on oscilloscopes. Each technique has its advantages. The raster scan (the most popular) updates the screen at a constant rate (usually 30 or 60 Hz) and therefore avoids flicker. However, a straight line is seldom perfectly straight, for it must be drawn in increments from one fixed pixel to the next in staircase fashion. The vector method, which is able to move the electron beam to anywhere on the screen at any time, draws perfectly straight lines, but is subject to flicker if too many lines are on the screen at one time. Perhaps the most important difference between the two display technologies is that color-based graphics are accomplished more readily with raster scan.

High-Resolution Displays

Our 320 $\times$ 200 pixel graphics display, although more versatile than a character-generation system, is still rather crude by state-of-the-art standards. It is medium resolution at best

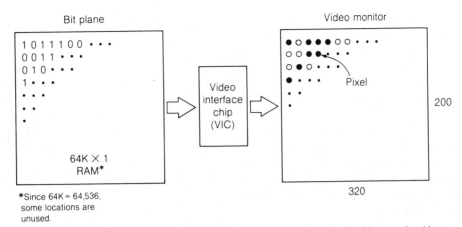

Figure 18.20 Correspondence of memory bit positions in the bit plane to like pixel positions on the video monitor.

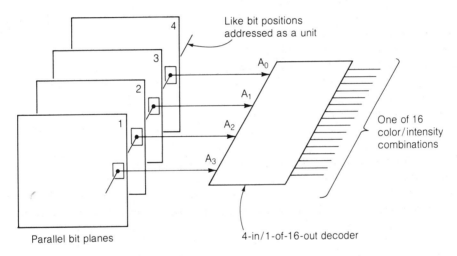

Figure 18.21 Four-bit-plane graphics storage system.

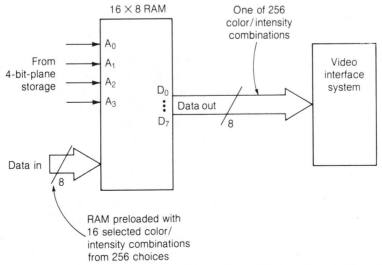

Figure 18.22 Technique for providing 256 color/intensity combinations—but only 16 at a time.

and offers only one color or shade of gray (on or off). Clearly, to provide various colors and intensities, each pixel must be represented by more than 1 bit. Four bits per pixel, for example, gives us 16 combinations of color and intensity. And, to improve resolution, let's go to a 364 × 720 pixel screen. To support such a system requires over 1 megabit of high-speed RAM (364 × 720 × 4 = 1,048,320). Moving further up the scale brings us to state-of-the-art 2048 × 2048 pixel resolution, with 16-megabit requirements—and we begin to see why graphics is so dependent on low-cost, large-scale primary memory. (With character mapping, each 7 × 10 pixel character space requires only a single byte, accounting for its greatly reduced memory requirements when compared to bit-mapping.)

Figure 18.21 shows us how to visualize the bit-mapped RAM for our high-resolution system. Each like position in the four bit planes is accessed (addressed) as a unit. The 4 bits (one from each plane) are then used to set the color/intensity combination of the selected pixel.

If we wish to have 256 color/intensity combinations, clearly we can expand the number of bit planes to 8. However, even though primary memory is relatively inexpensive, it is not free. So, for such a system, a compromise is in order. We can still select from among 256 color/intensity combinations; but to save bit planes, we select only 16 at any one time. The hardware of Figure 18.22 shows how the compromise is implemented. We preload the 16 8-bit registers with the selected 16 color/intensity combinations from our "palette" of 256 selections. For each pixel, our four-bit-plane RAM array selects one of the 16 registers, which in

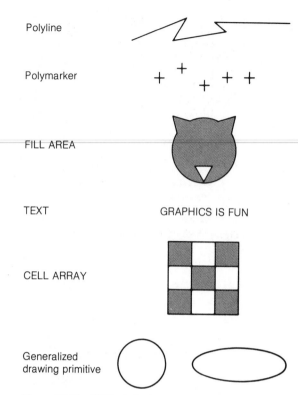

Figure 18.24   GKS's six basic output primitives.

turn sends the 8-bit (one-of-256) color/intensity information to the video interface system.

Clearly we can expand the size of our 16 8-bit registers to give us a larger selection (16-bit registers will allow us to select from 65,536 combinations of intensity and color). It is even possible to mix graphics with character generation by assigning one or more bit planes to text and the rest to graphics.

Software

Once the bit-mapped RAM array and video interface chips are in place, graphics generation is all software. The question is, What information is written to the bit-plane array to produce the desired graphics display? Since the answer is quite complex—even for a geometric figure as simple as a straight line—we must take full advantage of block-structured, modular design principles. Recall from our *machine-assembly updates,* that whenever we write a basic routine that we expect to use many times, we make it a subroutine and call it whenever needed—passing any necessary parameters. In high-level-language programming, these subroutines are called *procedures.*

Putting block-structured techniques into action for our straight-line problem, we begin by writing low-level software "primitives" to control individual pixels. To draw a straight line, we must identify each pixel and write information to its corresponding bit-map position (most graphics

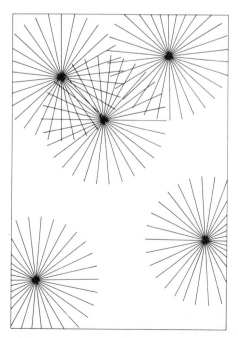

Figure 18.23   The "fireworks" display using turtle graphics.

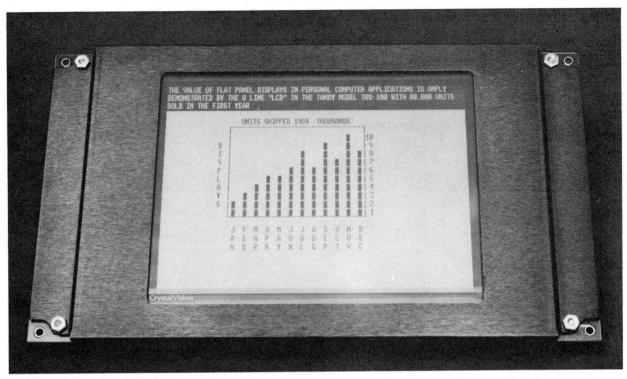

Figure 18.25 The liquid crystal display.
(Courtesy Crystal Vision.)

systems generate figures by combinations of straight-line segments).

The next level of software might generate a line by specifying only its end points, calling and sending parameters to the necessary low-level primitives as needed. As shown below, such a line routine can be written in Pascal, a high-level language to be discussed in Chapter 22.

```
PROCEDURE LINE (x1,y1,x2,y2,value : integer);
VAR x,y,dx,dy,slope : real;
BEGIN
    if x1 <> x2 THEN
      Begin
        dy := y2 − y1;
        dx := x2 − x1;
        slope := dy/dx;
        FOR x := x1 to x2 DO
          BEGIN
            WRITETOPIXEL (x,ROUND(y),value);
            y := y + slope;
          END
      END
    ELSE
        IF y1 = y2 THEN
            WRITETOPIXEL (x1,y1)
        ELSE ERROR:
END;
```

Procedure *Linedraw* then becomes a subroutine to be called from a still higher level of software. Turtle graphics, a software system that provides a vehicle to create simple line and figure graphics, is a perfect case in point.

Turtle graphics Turtle graphics is a collection of midlevel movement commands (procedures) based on the polar and Cartesian coordinate systems. Using these commands, the "turtle" lays down a track, like a spider spinning a web. For example, to draw a simple line requires the following four procedures:

$$
\begin{aligned}
&\text{MOVETO(140,95);}\\
&\text{PENCOLOR(white);}\\
&\text{TURNTO(30);}\\
&\text{MOVE(10);}
\end{aligned}
$$

When these four procedures are sequenced in a program, the turtle performs the following actions:

1. When procedure MOVETO is called and center-of-screen parameters (140,95) are sent, the turtle will move to the center of the screen.
2. Procedure PENCOLOR is called and parameter *white* turns on the turtle (makes its track visible when it moves).
3. Procedure TURNTO receives parameter 30 and the turtle "faces" 30 degrees.

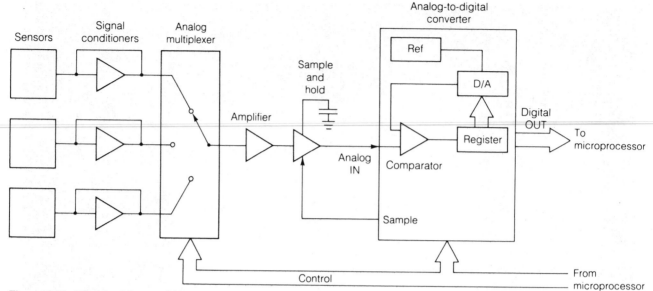

Figure 18.26 Block-level data-acquisition system.

4. Parameter 10 is sent to procedure MOVE, and the turtle moves across the screen from its present position 10 units at an angle of 30 degrees, laying down a visible track.

By including such midlevel turtle-graphics language procedures in a Pascal program, we can create graphics that fall into the realm of simple art. For example, the program below (using Apple Pascal) will create the "fireworks" display of Figure 18.23.

```
PROGRAM FIREWORKS;
USES TURTLEGRAPHICS, APPLESTUFF;
VAR A,B,N : INTEGER;


BEGIN
  INITTURTLE;
  REPEAT
    A := RANDOM MOD 278;
    B := RANDOM MOD 195;
    MOVETO(A,B) ;
    PENCOLOR(WHITE);
    FOR N := 1 TO 30 DO
      BEGIN
        MOVE(100);
        TURN(12);
        MOVETO(A,B);
      END;
    PENCOLOR(NONE);
  UNTIL KEYPRESS;
END.
```

Even with turtle graphics we are far from state of the art. To generate 3-D and surfaces, we are into *computer-aided design* (CAD), where 16-bit computers and high-level graphics languages are found. Add solid figures, and we are into advanced computer art, where only 32-bit mainframe computers have the required power. Clearly, the field of computer graphics has many surprises in store for us as hardware and software technology advances.

Graphics Standards

To simplify program development and to allow graphics software to run on any machine (portability), several graphics standards are now nearing completion. Two leading contenders vying for international recognization are *Graphical Kernel System (GKS)* and *North America Presentation Level Protocol Syntax (NAPLPS)*.

As an example of the type of information comprising a standard, Figure 18.24 shows the six basic output primitives specified by the GKS standard. Using these six primitives, nearly any object can be generated in graphics. Modularization and top-down design are also represented in the GKS standard, for using *combinations* of these six primitives, the operator can generate a graphics *segment,* which can be named and manipulated as a single entity.

By coding graphics primitives in an ASCII-like format, high-resolution graphics can be sent over standard communications lines.

The advantages of a graphics standard are the same as for all standards: the programmer is free to concentrate on the application at hand, without being concerned with the details of the graphics device.

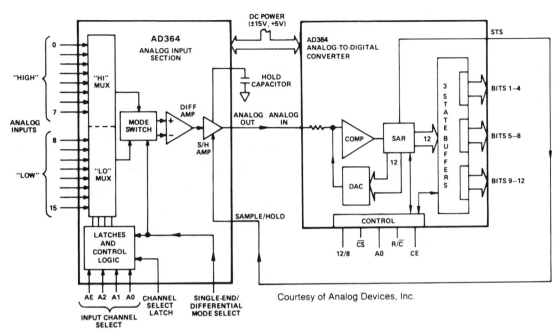

Figure 18.27 The AD364 data-acquisition system.

Advanced Graphics Memory Systems

Graphics memory systems are a beehive of activity, for display-update information must continuously enter the RAM, while screen refreshing data must continuously exit the RAM—at an output bit rate of over 80 MHz. To overcome the bottleneck created by these clashing requirements, Intel has endowed its 51C64 CMOS 64K × 1 dynamic RAM with *ripple mode access*. During ripple mode access an entire row of information can be clocked out at a data rate up to 15.3 million bits per second.

Going one step further, Texas Instruments' TMS4161 multiport video RAM includes two ports, one for display update and one for screen refreshing. After a 256-bit row is dumped into a shift register, the RAM array and shift register disconnect. While the shift register is sending screen refresh data through its own port, the CPU has sole access to the RAM for updating.

THE LIQUID CRYSTAL DISPLAY

The CRT display, one of the most enduring electronic components ever invented, may finally give way to newer technology—the *liquid crystal display*. Long simmering in the research laboratory, the nagging problems of speed, size, and cost are gradually being solved.

When we look at the characteristics of a typical liquid crystal display, such as CrystalVision's CV 640/250 PD-01

shown in Figure 18.25, we see why it is nearly the perfect display solution for the graphics-oriented portable computer. First of all, it is a solid-state device, with interfacing characteristics similar to a RAM with ripple-mode access (the address is presented in parallel, and the data entered in serial).

Furthermore, the screen is based on a bit-mapped format, offering 160,000 pixel dots. When using the companion controller board, it will produce full-screen graphics and alphanumerics with equal ease. To these features, add a wide-angle 8-inch diagonal screen, an 11-inch profile, high-contrast image, antiglare coating, and a nonvolatile image (meaning only pixel rows with new information need be written to).

As screen size and refresh speed improve, and as full color becomes available at low cost, the CRT—which is approaching the limits of its capabilities—may fade from the scene.

DATA ACQUISITION

Over the years, computers have become more "sociable," leaving the purely mathematical world of data processing and number crunching to enter the real world, where most of the data to be collected and analyzed consist of physical parameters of an analog nature (pressure, acceleration, temperature). To exist in this multisensor analog world, the computer clothed itself in a *data-acquisition system* (DAS). A typical system (Figure 18.26) consists of sensors and transducers sending analog data to an analog-acquisition signal processor. The analog processor samples (multiplexes) the

```
ASM80 :F1:IN.SRC


ISIS-II 8080/8085 MACRO ASSEMBLER, V4.1          INMODU     PAGE      1

   LOC  OBJ          LINE            SOURCE STATEMENT
                      1              NAME    INMODULE
                      2
                      3   ; Using the CSEG directive to produce IN.LST
                      4   ; in relocatable code.   The expression START
                      5   ; after the END directive tells the linker
                      6   ; that this is the main module (the one to
                      7   ; which the other modules are linked), and
                      8   ; identifies (symbolically) the starting
                      9   ; location of the linked program.
                     10
                     11              CSEG            ; Relocatable code
   0000 3EOE         12   START:     MVI   A,OEH     ; SDK-85
   0002 D320         13              OUT   20H       ; SDK-85
   0004 DB21         14              IN    21H
   0000        C     15              END   START

PUBLIC SYMBOLS

EXTERNAL SYMBOLS

USER SYMBOLS
START   C 0000

ASSEMBLY COMPLETE,   NO ERRORS
```

(a)

```
ASM80 :F1:DELAY.SRC


ISIS-II 8080/8085 MACRO ASSEMBLER, V4.1          DELAYM     PAGE      1

    LOC  OBJ         LINE            SOURCE STATEMENT
                      1              NAME    DELAYMODULE
                      2
                      3   ; Using the CSEG directive to produce
                      4   ; DELAY.LST in relocatable code
                      5
                      6              CSEG
   0000 5F            7              MOV   E,A       ; Save A
   0001 0100F0        8              LXI   B,OFOOOH  ; Load delay num
   0004 0B            9   LOOP:      DCX   B         ; Decrement
   0005 78           10              MOV   A,B       ; Set up OR
   0006 B1           11              ORA   C         ; Set flags
   0007 C20400    C  12              JNZ   LOOP      ; Continue delay
   000A 7B          13              MOV   A,E       ; Restore A
                     14              END

PUBLIC SYMBOLS

EXTERNAL SYMBOLS

USER SYMBOLS
LOOP    C 0004

ASSEMBLY COMPLETE,   NO ERRORS
```

(b)

Figure 18.28 Relocatable list program for task mimic-delay: *a)* IN.LST. *b)* DELAY.LST. *c)* OUT.LST.

```
ASM80 :F1:OUT.SRC


ISIS-II 8080/8085 MACRO ASSEMBLER, V4.1          OUTMOD    PAGE    1


    LOC   OBJ        LINE         SOURCE STATEMENT
                       1             NAME    OUTMODULE
                       2
                       3  ; Using CSEG to produce OUT.LST
                       4  ; in relocatable code.
                       5
                       6             CSEG
    0000  D322         7             OUT     22H
    0002  CF           8             RST     1    ; SDK-85
                       9             END


PUBLIC SYMBOLS

EXTERNAL SYMBOLS

USER SYMBOLS

ASSEMBLY COMPLETE,    NO ERRORS
```
(c)

analog inputs, holds the signal steady, amplifies the signal if necessary, and feeds each analog voltage to a high-speed A/D converter. Acquisition is complete when a microcomputer accepts, categorizes, and stores the digital information.

If data is measured, acquired, and sorted automatically, the DAS is known as a *data logger*. Data loggers are often CMOS, battery-operated systems, suitable for remote, unattended data-gathering applications.

The data-acquisition system is also available in highly integrated form. Figure 18.27 shows a two-package hybrid DAS specifically designed for microprocessor interfacing. The first package is the analog section and holds the programmable 16 single-ended (or 8 differential) analog multiplexer, buffer, and sample-and-hold amplifier. The microprocessor selects the 1-of-16 analog inputs by way of the input channel select (AE, A2, A1, and A0). The second section is a conventional 12-bit analog-to-digital converter.

MACHINE-ASSEMBLY UPDATE

Our next machine-assembly update brings us back to modular programming. In particular, we emphasize the desirability (indeed, necessity) of dividing up a large program into smaller "bite size" modules—*independent of each other.*

True independence means that each module should be separately assembled, debugged, and tested before they are combined into one main program. But how can we assemble a module when we don't know precisely at what absolute addresses it will be stored in memory? And how can we combine all these separately assembled object modules into one large program? (We can't use MACROs, for they are eliminated *during* assembly.) The answer is, by using two new utility programs: LINK and LOCATE.

As usual, for clarity, let's direct the discussion toward a specific example. We have just been assigned the task of writing the mimic delay program (MIMDEL for short), which simply adds a timespan between input and output. To simplify our job, program MIMDEL is composed of code we are already quite familiar with.

Following good modular concepts, we break up the program into three blocks (modules)—IN, DELAY, and OUT—and assign each to a separate programmer. The results of their activity (each is well aware of the LINK and LOCATE utilities) are shown in Figure 18.28. Note that each programmer has preceded the modules with the CSEG (Code SEGment) directive. The CSEG directive is the key to modular programming, for it commands the assembler to generate *relocatable* code—code which is "floating" and not tied down to absolute memory locations (the code is *position independent*). (As shown, the ORG directive is not given since each module is *temporarily* assumed to start at 0000.)

The next step is to LINK together the three separately compiled (and presently independent) object modules into a single object module, just as if the entire program had been written and compiled as a single block. The LINK command is given as follows:

LINK :F1:IN.OBJ,:F1:DELAY.OBJ,:F1:OUT.OBJ TO :F1:MIMDEL.LNK MAP

The linker will blend together the three object modules, arranging the code in the order in which the modules are listed (that is, the first instruction of DELAY.OBJ follows the last instruction of IN.OBJ). The optional attribute "MAP"

```
ISIS-II OBJECT LINKER V3.0 INVOKED BY:
-LINK :F1:IN.OBJ,:F1:DELAY.OBJ,:F1:OUT.OBJ &
**TO :F1:MIMDEL.LNK MAP PRINT(:LP:)

LINK MAP OF MODULE MIMDEL
WRITTEN TO FILE :F1:MIMDEL.LNK
MODULE IS A MAIN MODULE

SEGMENT INFORMATION:
START   STOP LENGTH REL NAME

             14H  B   CODE

INPUT MODULES INCLUDED:
 :F1:IN.OBJ(INMODU)
 :F1:DELAY.OBJ(DELAYM)
 :F1:OUT.OBJ(OUTMOD)
```
(a)

```
ISIS-II OBJECT LOCATER V3.0 INVOKED BY:
-LOCATE :F1:MIMDEL.LNK CODE(2000H)
MAP PRINT(:LP:)

MEMORY MAP OF MODULE MIMDEL
READ FROM FILE :F1:MIMDEL.LNK
WRITTEN TO FILE :F1:MIMDEL
MODULE START ADDRESS 2000H

START   STOP LENGTH REL NAME

2000H   2013H   14H  B   CODE
2014H   201FH    CH  B   STACK
2020H   F6BFH  D6A0H  B   MEMORY
```
(b)

Figure 18.29 Machine-assembler link and locate maps: *a)* Module MIM-DEL link map (generated by LINK process). *b)* Module MIMDEL memory map (generated by LOCATE process).

directs the linker to generate the MIMDEL MAP file of Figure 18.29*a,* which lists both the linked input modules and the name and length of the output module.

The linker output file (:F1:MIMDEL.LNK) is still object code in relocatable format. To establish absolute addresses, we evoke the LOCATE command:

LOCATE :F1:MIMDEL.LNK CODE (2000H)   MAP

The LOCATE utility scans through file MIMDEL.LNK converting all branch addresses to correspond to a starting location of 2000H (rather than the temporary *relocatable* starting location of 0000H).

We now have a single program module called MIMDEL (no extension), with 2000H as its starting location—and ready to run! The attribute MAP generates the memory map of Figure 18.29*b,* which shows that 20 (14H) bytes of code were generated to run from locations 2000H through 2013H. Since no stack or data locations were specified in the LOCATE directive, those shown are default values. Converting MIM-DEL to hexadecimal, Figure 18.30 shows precisely what the link and locate utilities accomplished (compare Figure 18.30 with Figures 18.28*a, b,* and *c*).

Incidentally, modules IN and OUT—each containing no more than three instructions—may seem too small to qualify as independent modules. However, on the basis of modular design, this approach can be justified. For example, suppose we upgrade the output circuits from the simple LED array we are presently using to seven-segment displays. We need only redesign the output module, without touching modules IN and DELAY. When larger modules are divided into many smaller modules, they are given more "room to grow," and stand a better chance that they will be improved and modified.

Breaking up a large programming task into smaller modules, writing and assembling relocatable code, linking together the modules to form one main program, and locating the program at absolute addresses are elements of the general industry-wide technique for generating large complex programs. In Chapter 22, we will renew the process using high-level languages.

INTELLIGENT-MACHINE UPDATE

Once completely a digital device, unable to function in an analog world, our intelligent machine has clothed itself in layers of I/O and interfacing circuitry and is now at home in the real world. It is becoming a truly social, well-behaved machine, and it will soon be easy to forget that at its core lies a purely digital, two-valued system.

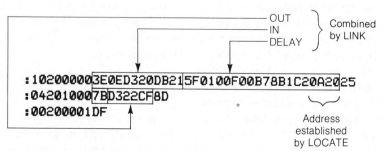

Figure 18.30 Program MIMDEL hex file showing results of LINK and LOCATE processes.

QUESTIONS AND PROBLEMS

1. What are some of the characteristics that make human conversation normally an asynchronous information transfer process?

2. Why is handshaking not normally required when we are reading data from primary memory?

3. The Motorola 68000 *does* use handshaking to interface primary memory. What advantage does this *asynchronous* technique have over the conventional *synchronous* technique employed by Intel?

4. What is the major advantage of interrupt I/O over programmed I/O?

5. When we are interfacing multiple devices, why is interrupt I/O generally faster than programmed I/O?

6. Why is DMA I/O an especially fast I/O process?

7. Give one advantage (a) of memory mapping; (b) of isolated I/O.

8. In memory-mapped systems, why can output ports occupy the same addresses as ROM locations?

9. Design a 2-bit DAC, using the weighted-current technique.

10. Complete the successive-approximation A/D program of Figure 18.11*b*.

11. What is the accuracy of a 12-bit A/D system?

12. Why must ultra-high-speed A/D converters use the simultaneous (flash) method?

13. What is the major advantage of the scanned method of keyboard entry?

14. Using scanned methods to access the four keys of Figure 18.15*a*, write an *organ* program in which each key generates a different tone (note continues when key is pressed; stops when key is released). Attach a speaker to bit position D0 of port 23H (the 8155A's port C).

15. Flowchart a method of driving the multiplexed display of Figure 18.15*b*.

16. What are the three major components of a data-acquisition system?

17. What is a *character generator*?

18. Write a program to implement the "counter" technique of A to D conversion (the output test voltage is a staircase. When the voltage level reaches the input analog level, exit the loop and report the number of steps required to reach the level). How would you calibrate the system using an external potentiomenter?

19. What is a *pixel?*

20. How much bit-mapped RAM would be required to support an 8000 × 8000 pixel display, each having a full 256 color/intensity variations?

21. To prove that high-level programming languages are "English-like," analyze the Pascal program that generated the fireworks display of Figure 18.23 and summarize how it was done (don't be concerned if you have not learned Pascal).

22. Why do display systems based on bit-mapping require so much more memory than those built around character mapping? What is the difference between bit-mapping and character mapping?

23. Although not covered directly in this text, how would you use a transistor to buffer the output lines of MOS or CMOS components to drive a high-current LED?

24. What is *relocatable* code?

25. Program modules can be "linked" during assembly by using MACROs, or after assembly by using the LINK command. What is the advantage of the second method?

26. Since an independent module of relocatable code is incomplete, how can it be tested?

27. Comparing Figure 18.28*a, b,* and *c* with Figure 18.30, exactly what did the LOCATE process perform?

28. What is a *liquid crystal?* (Research will be required.)

29. More realism could be obtained for the fireworks display of Figure 18.23 by erasing "old" bursts as "new" ones are produced. In general terms, how might you modify the fireworks program listed in the text to include this feature?

30. Following up on Question #29 above, even more realism would result from tracing the path of the rocket to the burst point. Again in general terms, how might this be accomplished?

chapter 19

Programmable Peripheral Chips: the SDK-85 Single-Board Computer

All animals that share this planet—as well as human beings—are a blend of hardware and software characteristics. The high-order animals are rich in software properties; they are adaptable and can be "programmed" to meet new situations. The lower-order animals, on the other hand, have few software properties; their actions are "hardwired" and primarily instinctive. When facing the challenges of the real world, each property has its advantages as well as its drawbacks.

Animals with a high degree of programmability (software-oriented) can modify their behavior, and—given the flexibility of learning—have a reduced need for specialized anatomy. However, the process of learning new tasks is often slow and agonizing, and once learned, the tasks are often performed slowly, inefficiently, and unreliably.

Animals that rely on hardware have developed highly specialized anatomy and instincts to best fit their particular niche in the environment; they have advantages in speed, efficiency, and reliability—*provided the task they are doing is one for which they are inherently suited.* (All the specialized "tools" they have acquired over the generations can turn against them should the environment change too suddenly.)

Today, computers are in a similar situation: they are a blend of software and hardware. To design a system based primarily on software is to design a system that is flexible and adaptable—but one that requires a vast amount of programmer time, and in the end, one that may be too slow for the task at hand. Switch to a purely hardware system and we have a high-speed, reliable machine with no need for expensive software development—but one that is not easily modified, and exhibits no (artificial) intelligence. *Clearly the ideal computer system is a compromise.*

The *programmable peripheral chip*—the subject of this chapter—is designed with such a compromise in mind. Intended to link up with microprocessors—which are inherently software oriented—the programmable peripheral chip is primarily a hardware device. But, as we have seen, a purely hardware device lacks flexibility. So they made this chip programmable *to fit a range of related applications.*

Once nature discovered the benefits of a hardware/software blend, the animal kingdom flourished, each member

exhibiting the ideal blend of dedicated-anatomy (hardware) and adaptability (software) to prosper in its local environment. The computer world, now armed with the programmable peripheral chip, is once again merely following suit.

BASICS OF PROGRAMMABLE PERIPHERAL CHIPS

A programmable peripheral chip is a multimode integrated circuit, programmed by the user to match specific needs. In other words, a programmable peripheral chip is really many chips in one, and the user decides what configuration the chip will assume.

There are two general categories of programmable peripheral chips: those that are hardware-programmable, and—more important—those that are software-programmable.

Hardware-Programmable Chips

The popular 8282 8-bit input/output port (the "eyes" and "ears" of our intelligent machine) is an example of a chip

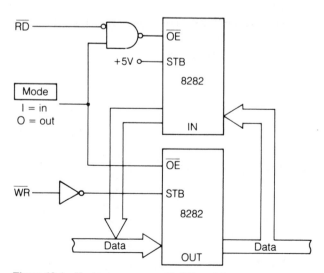

Figure 19.1 Hardware-programmable I/O module.

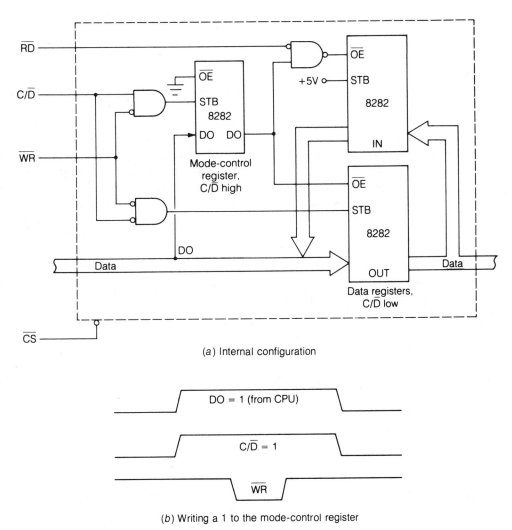

(a) Internal configuration

(b) Writing a 1 to the mode-control register

Figure 19.2   Software-programmable I/O module.

that can be hardware-programmed. The 8282 has a split personality, which is what makes it programmable. It can become either an input port or an output port—it all depends on the use of the $\overline{OE}$ and STB lines. By placing two 8282s side by side, one facing out and the other facing in (Figure 19.1), we have a true hardware-programmable I/O port module.

To program the module for input operations, tie "mode" high; for output operations, tie "mode" low. (When programmed for input operations, the output 8282 is tristated; when programmed for output operations, the input 8282 is tristated.)

There is also a big disadvantage to hardware programming. Once the chip is wired for one operation (say input-port operation), external circuitry changes are required to convert to an output-port operation (the mode line must be grounded).

Software Programmable Chips

The solution to this problem in hardware programming revolutionized the computer industry. Instead of *hardwiring* the "mode" line for either input or output operation, why not set this line with another latched output port? That way, the computer, by way of program action, will set the I/O module for either input or output operation. No hardware changes are required at all—the changes are made through software, *by the computer.*

Place both types of ports inside one chip, provide a means for addressing each, and you have the birth of a true programmable peripheral chip, one that is software-programmable (Figure 19.2a).

To configure this new chip for input operations, simply write a logic 1 to the mode-control port (or as it is now called, the *mode-control register*) by following the where/

when sequence of Figure 19.2*b*. The control/data (C/$\overline{\text{D}}$) input line is used to distinguish between control registers and data registers and will tie in to the address bus. If at a later time you would like to convert to output operation, write a logic 0 to the mode-control register.

You may even wish to include within the chip a special input-port register that will allow the computer to read in the mode status at any time. (Is the device presently configured for input operation or for output operation?) Such a register will be called the *status* register.

Although this simple programmable peripheral I/O chip we have developed does not really exist in integrated form, look for all programmable peripheral chips presently on the market to include the three types of internal registers shown in Figure 19.3: a data register to hold true data, a control register to set the mode of operation, and a status register to determine the internal state of the chip. Also, look for a method of addressing each register type, and expect the chip to operate in either the programmed I/O or interrupt I/O mode.

So powerful is the concept of software programmability that a veritable flood of programmable peripheral chips have flowed onto the market, and there is no end in sight:

- 8253 Programmable Interval Timer
- 8251A Programmable Communication Interface
- 8259A Programmable Interrupt Controller
- 8155A Static RAM with I/O ports and Timer
- 8207 DRAM Controller
- 8257 Programmable DMA Controller
- 8275 CRT Controller
- 8255A Programmable Peripheral Interface
- 8271 Programmable Floppy Disk Controller

In order of appearance, these ten ICs are the most frequently used support chips in microprocessor-based equipment. The first four on the list will be covered in detail in this and future chapters. (These first four have recently been incorporated into a single device—the 8256 "Combo Chip.")

This chapter is divided into two sections. In the first section of this chapter we will take a close look at three special programmable chips—all found aboard Intel's SDK-85 singleboard computer, and together forming the backbone of this popular laboratory system. In the final section, we will review-by-application two additional programmable chips which can easily be interfaced to the SDK-85 system. *For a complete description of all programmable chips used in this chapter, consult the appropriate Intel handbook.*

THE SDK-85 SINGLE-BOARD COMPUTER

The SDK-85 single-board computer (shown in Chapter 5, Figure 5.15*b*) is an example of a system build around the programmable peripheral chip. This versatile laboratory computer includes three programmable chips:

- The 8155 256 × 8 RAM with I/O and Timer
- The 8355 2K × 8 ROM with I/O
- The 8279 Programmable Keyboard/Display Interface

The SDK-85 also offers two expansion sockets, allowing an additional 8355/8755 and an additional 8155A to be added to the system.

The SDK-85 functional block diagram of Figure 19.4 reveals how each of these chips is used in the overall system. The use of programmable chips makes the SDK-85 considerably more versatile than a system built of dedicated chips exclusively. Remember, from Chapter 9 (Figure 9.19) that the 8155 and 8355 contain an internal address latch and are designed to interface directly with the 8085's multiplexed address/data bus.

Let's now examine each of these three chips as they are used on the SDK-85 single-board computer. Keep in mind that, since all programmable peripheral chips have a great deal in common, mastery of several representative examples will help you to understand the theory and use of all programmable peripheral chips.

THE 8355 ROM WITH I/O

The 8355 ROM with I/O is a multifacet chip containing 2K × 8 of factory-programmed ROM, and two general-purpose 8-bit I/O ports—with each port bit individually programmable as input or output. The 8355's multiplexed

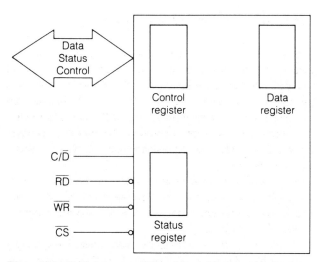

Figure 19.3 Typical programmable peripheral-chip, internal-register types and bus interfacing.

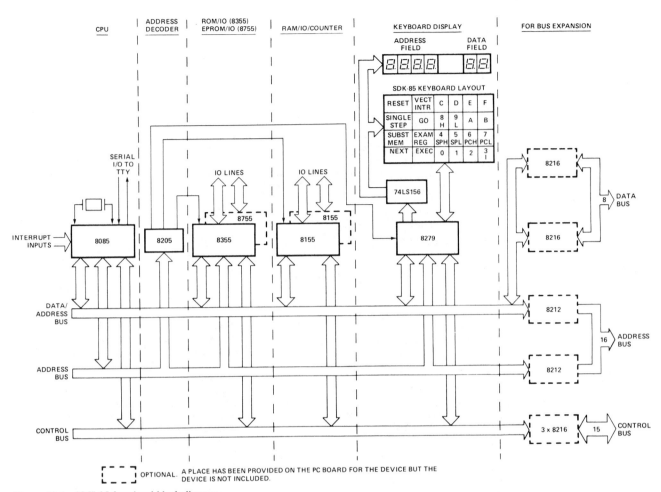

Figure 19.4 SDK-85 functional block diagram.

address/data bus and internal address latch allow it to directly interface to the 8085.

We select the 8355 ROM with I/O first because of its basic simplicity, and because the "personality" of the SDK-85 is determined by the *monitor program* firmware within its internal, factory-programmed ROM. (When the computer is reset, it "wakes up" in the monitor.) As we learned earlier, a monitor routine is the precursor of an *operating system;* it manages the resources of the system (that is, the 8279), and issues a prompt (a hyphen) and waits for a command. Commands are available for loading and examining memory, running a program, single-stepping, and loading and examining internal registers. For a full listing and explanation of the commands and features available under the monitor consult the *SDK-85 User's Manual*.

The 8355's vital statistics are given by Figure 19.5. Looking inside the 8355 (Figure 19.5a) we find the 2K × 8 ROM block, two 8-bit ports, and two data direction registers (DDR). The data direction registers are what make the 8355 programmable. *By writing various control words to the two DDRs, each pin of the two ports can be individually programmed as input or output* (0 for input; 1 for output). As

the DDRs cannot be read, there are no status registers within the 8355.

The 8355 is interfaced to the SDK-85 bus following the block diagram of Figure 19.6 (developed on Apple's MacIntosh computer). Since the 8355 contains an internal address latch, the low-order address bits are latched within the peripherals by the action of the ALE signal, and an external address latch is not required.

An analysis of the memory/port addressing follows along conventional lines: high-level versus low-level. An individual ROM location within the 2K × 8 memory array is addressed by an 11-bit low-level address (A0 through A10), and an I/O port or DDR is addressed by the latched value of *low-level* lines AD0 and AD1 according to the chart of Figure 19.7. (Remember that IO/$\overline{\text{M}}$ differentiates between a memory and a port operation.) The *high-level* lines (A11 through A15) also follow standard practice: they are decoded and sent to the 8355's chip enable (CE) input. An analysis of the addresses yields the memory/port maps of Figure 19.8. A more detailed analysis of the 8355's memory and port addressing scheme is left for the Questions and Problems section.

PIN CONFIGURATION

BLOCK DIAGRAM

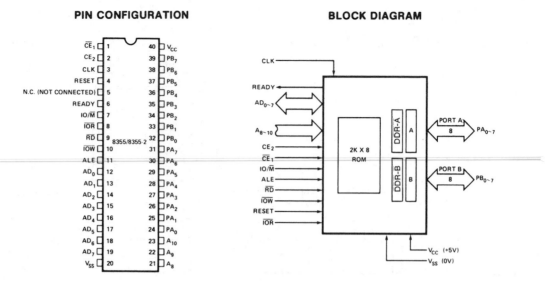

(a) Internal structure and pin-out

Symbol	Function
ALE (Input)	When ALE (Address Latch Enable is high, AD_{0-7}, $IO/\overline{M}$, A_{8-10}, CE, and $\overline{CE}$ enter address latched. The signals (AD, $IO/\overline{M}$, A_{8-10}, CE, $\overline{CE}$) are latched in at the trailing edge of ALE.
AD_{0-7} (Input)	Bidirectional Address/Data bus. The lower 8-bits of the ROM or I/O address are applied to the bus lines when ALE is high. During an I/O cycle, Port A or B are selected based on the latched value of AD_0. If $\overline{RD}$ or $\overline{IOR}$ is low when the latched chip enables are active, the output buffers present data on the bus.
A_{8-10} (Input)	These are the high order bits of the ROM address. They do not affect I/O operations.
$\overline{CE}_1$ CE2 (Input)	Chip Enable Inputs: $\overline{CE}_1$ is active low and CE_2 is active high. The 8355 can be accessed only when BOTH Chip Enables are active at the time the ALE signal latches them up. If either Chip Enable input is not active, the AD_{0-7} and READY outputs will be in a high impedance state.
$IO/\overline{M}$ (Input)	If the latched $IO/\overline{M}$ is high when $\overline{RD}$ is low, the output data comes from an I/O port. If it is low the output data comes from the ROM.
$\overline{RD}$ (Input)	If the latched Chip Enables are active when $\overline{RD}$ goes low, the AD_{0-7} output buffers are enabled and output either the selected ROM location or I/O port. When both $\overline{RD}$ and $\overline{IOR}$ are high, the AD_{0-7} output buffers are 3-state.
$\overline{IOW}$ (Input)	If the latched Chip Enables are active, a low on $\overline{IOW}$ causes the output port pointed to by the latched value of AD_0 to be written with the data on AD_{0-7}. The state of $IO/\overline{M}$ is ignored.

Symbol	Function
CLK (Input)	The CLK is used to force the READY into its high impedance state after it has been forced low by $\overline{CE}$ low, CE high and ALE high.
READY (Output)	Ready is a 3-state output controlled by $\overline{CE}_1$, CE_2, ALE and CLK. READY is forced low when the Chip Enables are active during the time ALE is high, and remains low until the rising edge of the next CLK (see Figure 6).
PA_{0-7} (Input/ Output)	These are general purpose I/O pins. Their input/output direction is determined by the contents of Data Direction Register (DDR). Port A is selected for write operations when the Chip Enables are active and $\overline{IOW}$ is low and a 0 was previously latched from AD_0. Read operation is selected by either $\overline{IOR}$ low and active Chip Enables and AD_0 low, or $IO/\overline{M}$ high, $\overline{RD}$ low, active chip enables, and AD_0 low.
PB_{0-7} (Input/ Output)	This general purpose I/O port is identical to Port A except that it is selected by a 1 latched from AD_0.
RESET (Input)	An input high on RESET causes all pins in Port A and B to assume input mode.
$\overline{IOR}$ (Input)	When the Chip Enables are active, a low on $\overline{IOR}$ will output the selected I/O port onto the AD bus. $\overline{IOR}$ low performs the same function as the combination $IO/\overline{M}$ high and $\overline{RD}$ low. When $\overline{IOR}$ is not used in a system, $\overline{IOR}$ should be tied to V_{CC} ("1").
V_{CC}	+5 volt supply.
V_{SS}	Ground Reference.

(b) Pin descriptions

Figure 19.5   8355 specifications.

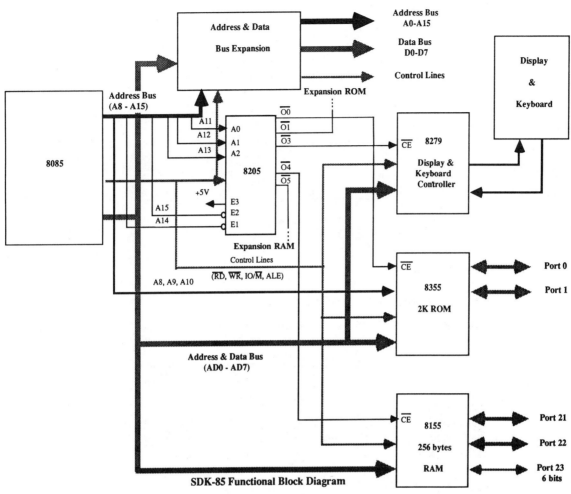

Figure 19.6 SDK-85 bus interfacing.
(Thanks to Rick Hoiberg).

As always, after a brief overview, the best way to further our study is by example. When looking at examples of the 8355—as well as other programmable peripheral chips—consider each chip the way a skilled make-up artist looks at the human face—as many faces, depending on the needs of the script (the program).

8355 Example One

Our first assignment is to redesign our mimic machine of part one around the 8355 rather than two 8282s. Adding a DIP switch to port A (port 0) and LEDs to port B (port 1), our hardware design is complete (Figure 19.9a).

AD₁	AD₀	Selection
0	0	Port A
0	1	Port B
1	0	Port A Data Direction Register (DDR A)
1	1	Port B Data Direction Register (DDR B)

Figure 19.7 8355 port addressing.

The next step is to program the data direction registers for proper I/O operation. Reviewing the address chart of Figure 19.7, we simply write all 0s to DDR-A (port 2) and all 1s to DDR-B (port 3). Our final software design is given in Figure 19.9b.

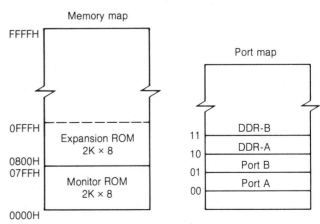

Figure 19.8 8355 memory and port maps for SDK-85 operation.

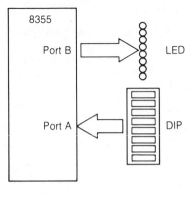

(a) Hardware

```
ASM80 :F1:P8355.SRC


ISIS-II 8080/8085 MACRO ASSEMBLER, V4.1          MIMIC     PAGE     1


    LOC   OBJ          LINE          SOURCE STATEMENT
                        1             NAME  MIMIC
                        2
                        3 ; 8355 EXAMPLE ONE
                        4 ; This routine programs the 8355's
                        5 ; port 0 as input and port 1 as
                        6 ; output, and enters a mimic loop
                        7
    2000                8             ORG   2000H
    2000 3E00           9             MVI   A,O       ; Generate DDRA data
    2002 D302          10             OUT   2         ; Program DDRA
    2004 3EFF          11             MVI   A,OFFH    ; Generate DDRB data
    2006 D303          12             OUT   3         ; Progam DDRB
    2008 DB00          13 LOOP:       IN    0         ; Input data
    200A D301          14             OUT   1         ; Mimic data
    200C C30820        15             JMP   LOOP      ; Repeat
                       16             END


PUBLIC SYMBOLS


EXTERNAL SYMBOLS


USER SYMBOLS
LOOP   A 2008

ASSEMBLY COMPLETE,   NO ERRORS
```

(b) Software

Figure 19.9   8355 example one design.

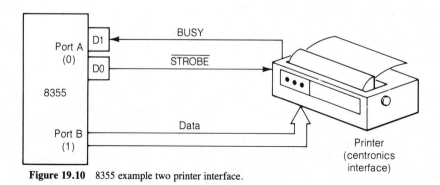

Figure 19.10   8355 example two printer interface.

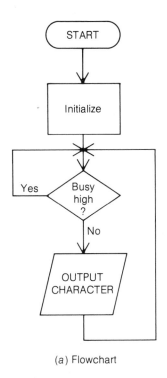

(a) Flowchart

```
ASM80 :F1:H8355.SRC

ISIS-II 8080/8085 MACRO ASSEMBLER, V4.1          SOFTWA     PAGE     1

LOC  OBJ          LINE          SOURCE STATEMENT
                   1            NAME    SOFTWAREHANDSHAKING
                   2
                   3     ; This program uses the the ability to
                   4     ; individually program each 8355 port bit
                   5     ; as input or output to set up port A
                   6     ; (address 0) as a handshaking port to
                   7     ; a printer.
                   8
2000               9            ORG     2000H
2000 3E01         10            MVI     A,01     ; Generate DDRA data
2002 D302         11            OUT     2        ; Program DDRA
2004 3EFF         12            MVI     A,OFFH   ; Generate DRRB data
2006 D303         13            OUT     3        ; Program DDRB
2008 DB00         14  LOOP:     IN      0        ; Input BUSY
200A E602         15            ANI     02H      ; Mask out all but BUSY
200C C20820       16            JNZ     LOOP     ; If BUSY high, loop
200F 3E41         17            MVI     A,'A'    ; Generate print char.
2011 D301         18            OUT     1        ; Send 'A' to printer
2013 3E00         19            MVI     A,0      ; Generate STROBE edge1
2015 D300         20            OUT     0        ; Send STROBE edge1 to P
2017 3E01         21            MVI     A,01     ; Generate STROBE edge2
2019 D300         22            OUT     0        ; Send STROBE edge2 to P
201B C30820       23            JMP     LOOP     ; Repeat
                  24            END

PUBLIC SYMBOLS

EXTERNAL SYMBOLS

USER SYMBOLS
LOOP    A 2008

ASSEMBLY COMPLETE,    NO ERRORS
```

(b) List file

Figure 19.11 Example two software solution.

8355 Example Two

Our next assignment is considerably more challenging: to continuously output a given character to a printer. As shown in Figure 19.10, we have chosen port 0 for our Centronics handshaking signals, and port 1 for the output to the printer. In our design, we have taken full advantage of our ability to program each bit as input or output. Since only a single task is involved, we will adopt programmed I/O (the CPU can devote full attention to polling the BUSY signal). The flowchart and completed assembly-language program appear in Figure 19.11. We will have an opportunity to analyze the program in the Questions and Problems section.

THE 8155A 256 × 8 RAM WITH I/O PORTS AND TIMER

The 8155A RAM with I/O ports and timer (also known as a *Programmable Peripheral Interface* or *Peripheral Interface Adapter*) is perhaps the most common type of programmable peripheral chip in use today, and consequently has been selected for more detailed study.

The 8155 is a three-port general-purpose I/O-timer device, designed to interface peripheral equipment to the system bus, and to provide a small amount of byte-wide RAM.

Looking over the 8155 specifications (Figure 19.12), we find the three expected types of registers—data, command, and status—along with two 8-bit ports, one 6-bit port, a timer, and 256 bytes of RAM. By writing various control words to the command register, and determining the state of the chip by reading the status register, a number of basic modes of operation can be selected under program control (see Figure 19.13).

The 8155 is interfaced to the SDK-85 bus as shown in Figure 19.6. An analysis of the low-level/high-level addressing scheme reveals that the one page of RAM is located at page 20H and is folded back over the next seven pages. Consulting the port and timer addressing chart of Figure 19.14, we find that the six port and internal registers are located at port addresses 20H through 25H (drawing the memory/port map is left as an exercise).

8155 Example One

Our first example involves the internal 14-bit timer. Our assignment is to divide the TIMER IN signal (pin 3) by 1,000 and send the result to the $\overline{\text{TIMER OUT}}$ line (pin 6). Once again, our hardware design is simple (see Figure 19.15).

Our software design begins by writing 1 to bit positions 6 and 7 of the command register (all other bit positions are don't care). Referring back to Figure 19.13a, this operation starts the timer output immediately after loading the timer register. Examining the timer format specifications of Figure 19.16a allows us to generate the timer data of Figure 19.16b. The software solution follows immediately (Figure 19.17).

8155 Example Two

Now that we have gained considerable experience in the use of I/O-related peripheral chips, let's carry our printer example one step further—by introducing multitasking.

Here is our design assignment: to output parallel data to a printer at the maximum possible rate, but still allow the computer to *simultaneously* generate a fixed tone. We conclude immediately that *our printer interface must be of asynchronous design using handshaking signals in the interrupt I/O mode*. The steady tone, of course, is best generated by the main program. The design consists of the following three phases:

- Programming the mode of operation
- Interfacing the 8155 to the printer and to the speaker
- Writing and testing the output routine

Phase 1—Programming the mode of operation Before we can program the 8155, we must first determine the proper mode of operation. The question is this: what mode of operation will set up the system for asynchronous output using interrupt I/O?

Looking at the available options (Figure 19.13a), we see that alternatives 3 and 4 provide for *automatic* handshaking control via port C. In other words, when programmed in alternatives 3 or 4, the pins of port C take on *dedicated* handshaking functions. Since the two sets of handshaking signals provided by alternative 4 (one set for port A and the other for port B) are not required, we will select alternative 3. Within alternative three, if port A is programmed as output we automatically enter the *strobed output mode*.

As diagrammed in Figure 19.18, we complete the job of programming the command register by enabling the port A interrupt and setting ports A and B as output ports.

Phase 2—Interfacing the 8155 to the printer By matching the two handshaking signals to the corresponding Centronics printer signals and sending the interrupt output to the CPU (through the bus expansion buffers), phase 2 of our design is quickly completed (see Figure 19.19). As noted, the 8155's *buffer full* (BF) signal is active high, while the printer's corresponding signal—STROBE—is active low. The inverter attached to line PC1 will make the signals compatible.

Phase 3—Writing and testing the output routine Before we write the output routine and test our system, it is crucial that we understand the *strobed-output* mode of the 8155. The purpose of the strobed-output mode is to automatically allow the fastest possible flow of data to the printer. Since the strobed-output handshaking sequence is a little involved, an analogy will help to explain the process.

Strobed-Output-Mode Analogy In the game of baseball, a player going to bat must sequence through three locations: the *dugout,* the *on-deck circle,* and the *plate.* The on-deck circle, specifically created to speed up the game, works like this: when the player presently on deck goes to bat, another player leaves the dugout and goes on deck. Since the long walk from dugout to on-deck circle takes place when a player is at bat, the game is greatly speeded up. Using computer terminology, the on-deck circle is known as a *buffer.*

The handshaking sequence of the 8155 speeds data to the printer in precisely the same way. Figure 19.19 shows the

PIN CONFIGURATION

BLOCK DIAGRAM

8155/8155-2 = $\overline{CE}$, 8156/8156-2 = CE

(a) Internal structure and pin-out

Symbol	Function	Symbol	Function
RESET (input)	Pulse provided by the 8085A to initialize the system (connect to 8085A RESET OUT). Input high on this line resets the chip and initializes the three I/O ports to input mode. The width of RESET pulse should typically be two 8085A clock cycle times.	ALE (input)	Address Latch Enable: This control signal latches both the address on the AD_{0-7} lines and the state of the Chip Enable and $IO/\overline{M}$ into the chip at the falling edge of ALE.
AD_{0-7} (input)	3-state Address/Data lines that interface with the CPU lower 8-bit Address/Data Bus. The 8-bit address is latched into the address latch inside the 8155/56 on the falling edge of ALE. The address can be either for the memory section or the I/O section depending on the $IO/\overline{M}$ input. The 8-bit data is either written into the chip or read from the chip, depending on the $\overline{WR}$ or $\overline{RD}$ input signal.	$IO/\overline{M}$ (input)	Selects memory if low and I/O and command/status registers if high.
		$PA_{0-7}(8)$ (input/output)	These 8 pins are general purpose I/O pins. The in/out direction is selected by programming the command register.
		$PB_{0-7}(8)$ (input/output)	These 8 pins are general purpose I/O pins. The in/out direction is selected by programming the command register.
CE or $\overline{CE}$ (input)	Chip Enable: On the 8155, this pin is $\overline{CE}$ and is ACTIVE LOW. On the 8156, this pin is CE and is ACTIVE HIGH.	$PC_{0-5}(6)$ (input/output)	These 6 pins can function as either input port, output port, or as control signals for PA and PB. Programming is done through the command register. When PC_{0-5} are used as control signals, they will provide the following:
$\overline{RD}$ (input)	Read control: Input low on this line with the Chip Enable active enables and AD_{0-7} buffers. If $IO/\overline{M}$ pin is low, the RAM content will be read out to the AD bus. Otherwise the content of the selected I/O port or command/status registers will be read to the AD bus.		PC_0 — A INTR (Port A Interrupt) PC_1 — ABF (Port A Buffer Full) PC_2 — $\overline{A\ STB}$ (Port A Strobe) PC_3 — B INTR (Port B Interrupt) PC_4 — $\overline{B\ BF}$ (Port B Buffer Full) PC_5 — B STB (Port B Strobe)
		TIMER IN (input)	Input to the counter-timer.
$\overline{WR}$ (input)	Write control: Input low on this line with the Chip Enable active causes the data on the Address/Data bus to be written to the RAM or I/O ports and command/status register depending on $IO/\overline{M}$.	$\overline{TIMER\ OUT}$ (output)	Timer output. This output can be either a square wave or a pulse depending on the timer mode.
		V_{CC}	+5 volt supply.
		V_{SS}	Ground Reference.

(b) Pin descriptions

Figure 19.12 8155A specifications.

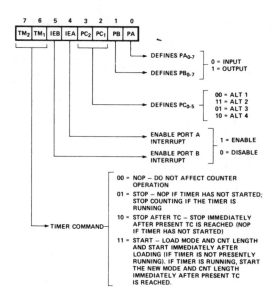

Pin	ALT 1	ALT 2	ALT 3	ALT 4
PC0	Input Port	Output Port	A INTR (Port A Interrupt)	A INTR (Port A Interrupt)
PC1	Input Port	Output Port	A BF (Port A Buffer Full)	A BF (Port A Buffer Full)
PC2	Input Port	Output Port	A $\overline{STB}$ (Port A Strobe)	A $\overline{STB}$ (Port A Strobe)
PC3	Input Port	Output Port	Output Port	B INTR (Port B Interrupt)
PC4	Input Port	Output Port	Output Port	B BF (Port B Buffer Full)
PC5	Input Port	Output Port	Output Port	B $\overline{STB}$ (Port B Strobe)

(a) Command register format

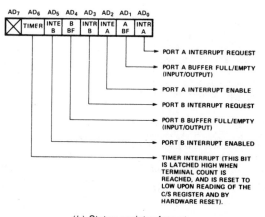

(b) Status register format

Figure 19.13 8155 command/status programming formats.

I/O ADDRESS†								SELECTION
A7	A6	A5	A4	A3	A2	A1	A0	
X	X	X	X	X	0	0	0	Interval Command/Status Register
X	X	X	X	X	0	0	1	General Purpose I/O Port A
X	X	X	X	X	0	1	0	General Purpose I/O Port B
X	X	X	X	X	0	1	1	Port C — General Purpose I/O or Control
X	X	X	X	X	1	0	0	Low-Order 8 bits of Timer Count
X	X	X	X	X	1	0	1	High 6 bits of Timer Count and 2 bits of Timer Mode

X: Don't Care.
†: I/O Address must be qualified by CE = 1 8156 or $\overline{CE}$ = 0 8155 and IO/$\overline{M}$ = 1 in order to select the appropriate register.

Figure 19.14 8155 I/O port and timer addressing scheme.

"dugout," "on deck," and "at bat" locations of the computer system. (In computer terminology, the process is known as *double-buffering,* and the "on-deck" location is generally known as a *buffer register.*)

To show how the strobed-output mode works, we will pick up the action when the printer has just finished with data word 1 and is ready to fetch data word 2 from the 8155 buffer register (go from "on deck" to "at bat"). Refer to Figure 19.19 as the sequence unfolds.

1. The printer sends a low $\overline{ACK}$ (acknowledge) pulse to indicate that it has accepted a byte of data and is ready for more.
2. The $\overline{ACK}$ pulse does two things: it pulls the BF (buffer full) line low, and it causes an interrupt to be requested via the INTR line (PC0).
3. The CPU responds and writes the next data word to the buffer. The write pulse to the 8155A also causes two things to happen: the interrupt request line is returned low and the buffer full (BF) line is driven high.
4. The printer reads in the data, issues an $\overline{ACK}$, and the cycle is repeated.

The waveforms of the strobed-output mode are given in Figure 19.20. To reinforce your understanding of the strobed-out mode, repeat the four steps of the output process while following the waveforms from left to right.

What makes the strobed-output process so useful is that most of the housekeeping tasks required to feed data to the printer at the fastest possible rate are handled by the 8155. The workload on the CPU is considerably reduced—and so is the workload of the programmer. As shown by the flow-

chart of Figure 19.21, the handshaking sequence is invisible to the CPU, and consequently the program is a very straightforward interrupt output routine. The completed list file program is given in Figure 19.22.

If a polled (programmed I/O) rather than an interrupt operation is desired, a simple polling of status bit 1 (port A buffer empty) will inform the CPU when the next data word is to be written to the 8155's buffer register (see Figure 19.13b).

THE 8279 PROGRAMMABLE KEYBOARD/DISPLAY INTERFACE

The third and final of the three programmable chips of the SDK-85 is the most complex of the three, offering nearly

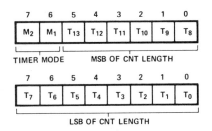

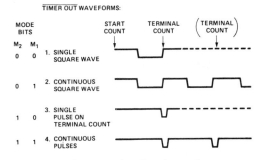

(a) Format and modes of operation

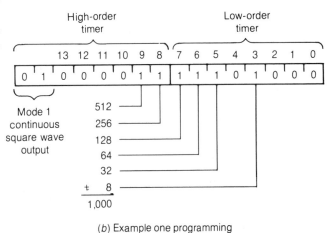

(b) Example one programming

Figure 19.16 8155 timer.

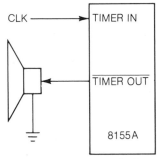

Figure 19.15 8155 example one hardware design.

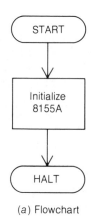

(a) Flowchart

```
ASM80 :F1:T8155A.SRC


ISIS-II 8080/8085 MACRO ASSEMBLER, V4.1          DIVIDE   PAGE    1

    LOC  OBJ        LINE        SOURCE STATEMENT
                      1            NAME  DIVIDEBYTIMER
                      2
                      3    ; This sample program sets up the 8155A timer
                      4    ; to divide by 1,000.  The TIMER-IN signal is
                      5    ; divided by 1,000 and sent to the TIMER-OUT line.
                      6    ; Since on the SDK-85, the TIMER-IN and TIMER-OUT
                      7    ; signals only available via the expansion 8155A,
                      8    ; the port addresses shown below correspond to the
                      9    ; expansion 8155A addresses.
    2000             10
    2000 3EC0        11            ORG   2000H
    2000 3EC0        12            MVI   A,0C0H  ; Generate CMD data
    2002 D328        13            OUT   28H     ; Enable the timer
    2004 3EE8        14            MVI   A,0E8H  ; Low-order timer data
    2006 D32C        15            OUT   2CH     ; Load low-order data
    2008 3E43        16            MVI   A,43H   ; High-order timer data
    200A D32D        17            OUT   2DH     ; Load high-order data
    200C CF          18            RST   1       ; SDK-85
                     19            END

PUBLIC SYMBOLS

EXTERNAL SYMBOLS

USER SYMBOLS

ASSEMBLY COMPLETE,   NO ERRORS
```

(b) List file

Figure 19.17   8155 example one software solution.

40 bits of programmable control, and many modes of operation. However, unlike the 8855 and 8155, in which all programming modes are available to the user, the 8279 is set by the monitor program for a specific mode of operation. *To simplify our discussion, we will concentrate on the modes of operation used by the SDK-85 single-board computer.*

SDK-85 Keyboard/Display Design

Using a simplified block diagram, Figure 19.23 illustrates the roll of the 8279 within the SDK-85 overall design. As shown, the 8279 consists of two major sections: keyboard and display. When we zoom in more closely on the keyboard/display interfacing (Figure 19.24), we see that the 8279

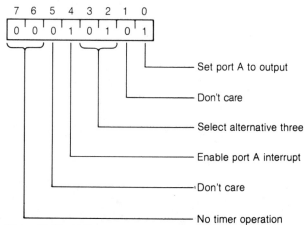

Figure 19.18   8155 example two command word.

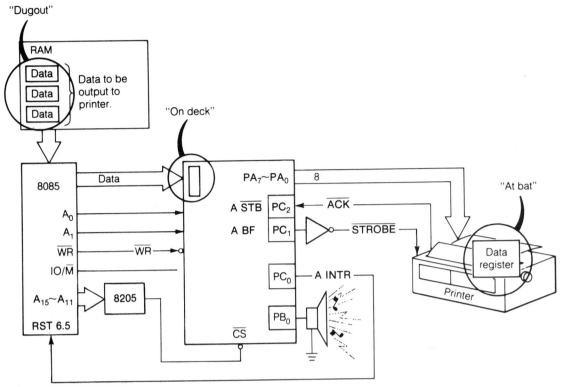

Figure 19.19 8155 example two hardware design.

adopts the keyboard-scanning and display-multiplexing techniques of Chapter 18.

Access to the 8279's command and data registers is by way of memory mapping to locations 1900H (command) and 1800H (data). Command words are distinguished from data words by way of the A0 input line (high for control; low for data). On the SDK-85, A0 on the 8279 is connected to bus line A8. It is left as a problem to explain how this addressing scheme results in address 1800H/1900H operation.

Software Initialization

As with all programmable chips, the CPU must initialize its configuration and control its operation through command and status words.

The 8279 offers only a single address (1900H) for writing command words—yet there are eight command registers within the 8279. The solution to this dilemma is revealed by Figure 19.25a. Each command word has three "op code"

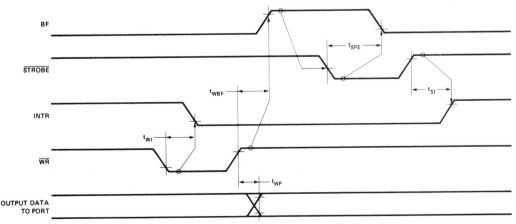

Figure 19.20 Strobed output mode timing.

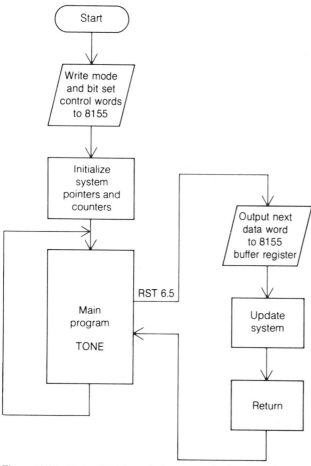

Figure 19.21 To the CPU the strobed-output routine is a simple interrupt I/O output sequence to a port.

bits (D5, D6, and D7) for routing the control word (containing the remaining 5 bits) to the correct internal command register.

To see how the 8279 works in a real-world situation, let's go inside the SDK-85's monitor program (listed in Appendix A of the SDK-85 user's manual) and look at two examples of how the 8279 is initialized by control words and how data is transferred between CPU and 8279:

Example 1: Setting the basic mode of operation SDK-85 operation begins when the CPU is RESET and we enter the monitor routine at location 0000 (RESET clears the program counter). At that location we find our first 8279 initialization process:

```
0000 3E00   MVI A,KMODE ; GET CONTROL
                        ; CHARACTER
0002 320019 STA CNTRL   ; SET KEYBOARD/
                        ; DISPLAY MODE
```

When we analyze these two instructions, we see that command data 00H is written to location 1900H (the 8279's

command register). Since the control word op code is 000B (B = binary), we are writing to the keyboard/display command register. The format for the keyboard/display command word is given in Figure 19.25b. As shown, we have selected the KKK = 000 and DD = 00 mode of operation. The 8-bit character-display (left entry) option (DD = 00) turns the display into an eight-position shift register. Entering characters from position 0 causes the display to fill from the left automatically. When programmed with the encoded scan-keyboard option (KKK = 000) the output scan lines count in binary and must be externally decoded to provide up to 8 keyboard scan lines and up to 16 display scan lines (as shown in Figure 19.24). Two-key lockout is a debouncing scheme that ensures that the first key pressed enters its coded key position into the sensor RAM.

Example 2: Reading the keyboard Our next example turns the keypad of the SDK-85 into an input port. The technique involves the use of a CALL to a special monitor routine instead of the familiar IN-port and OUT-port instructions. Anywhere in our program we wish to input a character from the keypad we simply write:

Hex code   Mnemonic
CDE702H   CALL   RDKBD (where RDKBD = 02E7H)

The called program waits in a loop for information to be written to memory location 20FEH (called the *input buffer*). When a key is pressed and an RST 5.5 interrupt is issued, we exit the wait loop and a character corresponding to the activated key (see Figure 19.25c) automatically flows to the FIFO/SENSOR RAM. Moving to monitor location 002CH (the RST 5.5 entry point), we find a jump to location 028EH. Passing over several PUSHs to store away vital information, we finally arrive at the critical instruction sequence (within the RST 5.5 interrupt service routine):

```
0290 210019 LXI  H,CNTRL  ; ADDRESS FOR
                          ; CONTROL CHAR OUT
0293 3640   MVI  M,READ   ; OUT CONTROL CHAR
                          ; FOR READ KEY
0295 25     DCR  H        ; ADDRESS FOR CHAR
                          ; INPUT
0296 7E     MOV  A,M      ; READ A CHARACTER
0297 E63F   ANI  3FH      ; ZERO TWO HIGH
                          ; ORDER BITS
0299 32FE20 STA  IBUFF    ; STORE CHAR IN
                          ; INPUT BUFFER
```

First we load the HL register pair with the address of the 8279's control location (1900H). We then output control character 40H. Referring to Figure 19.25d, this control word sets up the 8279 for a read of the FIFO/Sensor RAM. (Since we are in the scanned keyboard mode, the auto-increment

```
ASM80 :F1:H8155A.SRC MOD85


ISIS-II 8080/8085 MACRO ASSEMBLER, V4.1        HARDWA     PAGE    1

   LOC  OBJ        LINE         SOURCE STATEMENT
                     1             NAME  HARDWAREHANDSHAKING
                     2
                     3  ; This interrupt-I/O program makes use of the
                     4  ; strobed-output mode of the 8155A for automatic
                     5  ; handshaking to a printer.  The program outputs
                     6  ; a constant stream of 'A's.  To determine the
                     7  ; effect of constant interruptions, the main
                     8  ; program generates a steady tone (use output PC3).
                     9
                    10  ; Main program
                    11
   2000             12             ORG   2000H
   2000 3E15        13             MVI   A,15H     ; Generate CMD word
   2002 D320        14             OUT   20H       ; Write to CMD reg.
   2004 31C220      15             LXI   SP,20C2H  ; Set stack pointer
   2007 FB          16             EI              ; Enable INT system
   2008 3E0D        17             MVI   A,0DH     ; Load mask word
   200A 30          18             SIM             ; Unmask RST 6.5
   200B 0C          19  LOOP:      INR   C         ; Toggle note
   200C 79          20             MOV   A,C       ; Ready for output
   200D D323        21             OUT   23H       ; Generate note
   200F 0618        22             MVI   B,18H     ; Load delay number
   2011 05          23  TONE:      DCR   B         ; Delay
   2012 C21120      24             JNZ   TONE      ; If <> 0, repeat
   2015 C30B20      25             JMP   LOOP      ; Stay in loop
                    26
                    27  ; RST 6.5 Interrupt vector
                    28
   20C8             29             ORG   20C8H
   20C8 C34020      30             JMP   SEND       ; SDK-85 operation
                    31
                    32  ; Interrupt service routine
                    33
   2040             34             ORG   2040H
   2040 3E41        35  SEND:      MVI   A,'A'      ; Load character 'A'
   2042 D321        36             OUT   21H        ; Send to printer
   2044 FB          37             EI
   2045 C9          38             RET
                    39             END


PUBLIC SYMBOLS

EXTERNAL SYMBOLS

USER SYMBOLS
LOOP    A 200B     SEND    A 2040     TONE    A 2011

ASSEMBLY COMPLETE,    NO ERRORS
```

Figure 19.22 The strobed output mode list file.

flag and the RAM address bits are irrelevant.) We then decrement the H register to point to 1800H (the data location) and read the character stored in the FIFO/Sensor RAM to the accumulator. We then blank out the two highest-order bits, corresponding to the state of 8279 pins 36 and 37 (which are not used by the SDK-85) and store the result to memory location 20FEH (the INPUT BUFFER). We return from the RST 5.5 ISR to the RDKBD CALL routine. Since a POP PSW to restore the flags also destroyed the input data in the accumulator, we transfer the contents of IBUFF to the accumulator and return to the main program.

INTERFACING ADDITIONAL PROGRAMMABLE CHIPS TO THE SDK-85 SYSTEM

Although the three programmable chips introduced so far (the 8155A, 8355, and 8279) are the only chips built-in to the SDK-85 system, there are several others that can easily be interfaced via the expansion buffers. These include the 8253 *Programmable Interval Timer* and the 8259A *Programmable Interrupt Controller*—the subjects of this section. To keep our discussion brief, let's interface and program each for a specific task.

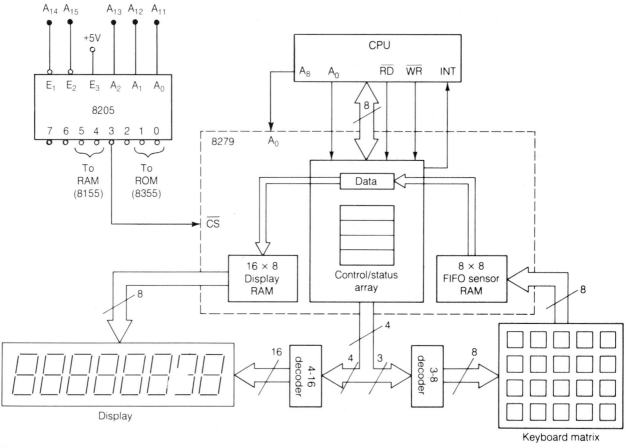

Figure 19.23 The 8279 as used by the SDK-85.

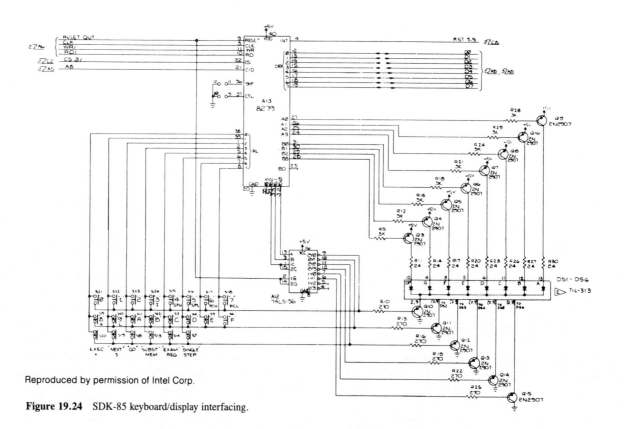

Reproduced by permission of Intel Corp.

Figure 19.24 SDK-85 keyboard/display interfacing.

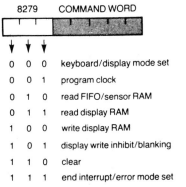

(a) A three-bit op code routes each command word to the proper internal register

Keyboard/Display Mode Set

MSB							LSB

Code: | 0 | 0 | 0 | D | D | K | K | K |

Where DD is the Display Mode and KKK is the Keyboard Mode.

DD

0	0	8 8-bit character display — Left entry
0	1	16 8-bit character display — Left entry*
1	0	8 8-bit character display — Right entry
1	1	16 8-bit character display — Right entry

KKK

0	0	0	Encoded Scan Keyboard — 2 Key Lockout
0	0	1	Decoded Scan Keyboard — 2-Key Lockout
0	1	0	Encoded Scan Keyboard — N-Key Rollover
0	1	1	Decoded Scan Keyboard — N-Key Rollover
1	0	0	Encoded Scan Sensor Matrix
1	0	1	Decoded Scan Sensor Matrix
1	1	0	Strobed Input, Encoded Display Scan
1	1	1	Strobed Input, Decoded Display Scan

(b) The keyboard/display mode set format highlighting the DD = 00 and KKK = 000 mode of operation

FIFO sensor RAM key position code word

Cntl key	Shift key	Scan key	Line position	Return key	Line position

(c) Scanned-keyboard data format

Read FIFO/sensor RAM command word

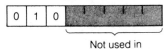

Not used in keyboard mode

(d) Preparing for sensor RAM read

Figure 19.25 Programming the 8279.

Reproduced by permission of Intel Corp.

The 8253 Programmable Interval Timer

Our task is to use an 8253 timer chip to generate in continuous succession the three notes making up the chord of C (C, E, and G).

First let's dispense with the basics. Turning to the block and pin diagram of Figure 19.26, we see that the 8253 consists of three 16-bit counter/timers and three control registers to set each counter's mode of operation. Each of the three 16-bit counters is independent and can be separately programmed with any one of six modes of operation diagrammed in Figure 19.27.

The mode of operation for each counter and the desired value to be loaded into each counter are determined by the system software in a two-step process (Figure 19.28a). To configure all three timers, six software-directed operations would be required. The mode-control format is given by Figure 19.28b. As shown, the mode word channels the control information to the correct mode control register, programs the counter with the desired mode, selects a BCD or binary loading format, and determines the sequence in which the count values are loaded. (The loading of the count values follows the loading of the mode-control word.)

Referring to Figure 19.26, each counter has two inputs (CLK and GATE) and one output (OUT). The GATE input enables the counting process (count when high; disable count when low). As diagrammed in the waveforms of Figure 19.27, the system clock (the 2 MHz clock of the SDK-85) is normally the input, and the output is the processed result.

Armed with an overview of the 8253's architecture and operation, let's complete our task. First, we will interface the hardware to the SDK-85; second, we will determine the mode control word; and third, we will write and test the software.

Interfacing the 8253 to the SDK-85 As with most programmable peripheral chips, the hardware interface is straightforward. To make several needed signals readily available without additional hardware, we have removed the expansion 8155A and 8355/8755 (if present) in order to expose the socket pins. In particular, as shown in Figure 19.29, we have used the on-board decoder chip-select of the missing (expansion) 8155A to place our 8253 at memory-mapped location 28XXH (the same as our expansion 8155A, were it in place). Also, we have tapped the clock signal off pin 3 of the 8355 expansion socket.

Also shown in Figure 19.29 is an address chart to complete the addressing description of the nine internal registers.

Writing to the mode and count registers Looking to Figure 19.27, it is clear that mode 3 will give us our desired continuous waveform output by dividing the incoming signal by the number loaded into counter 0. We then complete the

PIN CONFIGURATION

BLOCK DIAGRAM

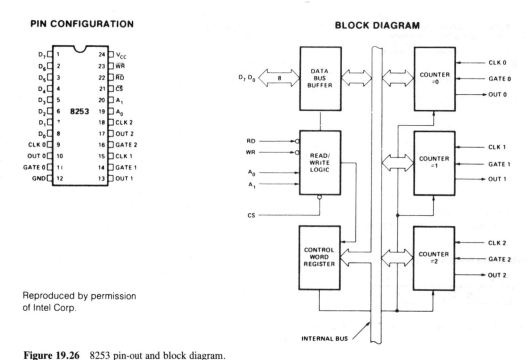

Reproduced by permission
of Intel Corp.

Figure 19.26 8253 pin-out and block diagram.

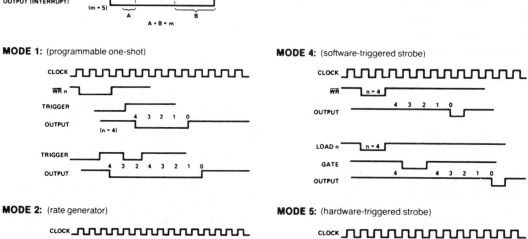

MODE 0: (interrupt on terminal count)

MODE 3: (square-wave rate generator)

MODE 1: (programmable one-shot)

MODE 4: (software-triggered strobe)

MODE 2: (rate generator)

MODE 5: (hardware-triggered strobe)

Reproduced by permission of Intel Corp.

Figure 19.27 8253 timing diagrams for the six modes of operation.

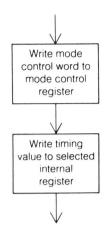

(a) Programming each counter is a two-step process

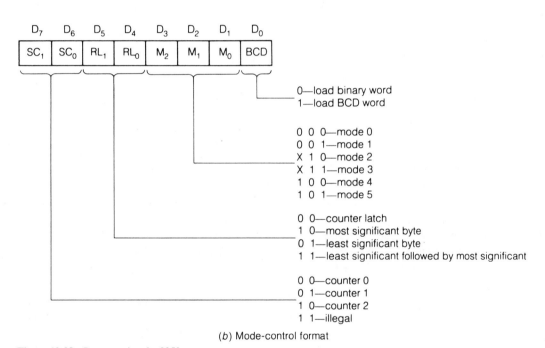

(b) Mode-control format

Figure 19.28   Programming the 8253.

mode word definition according to the format of Figure 19.28b, selecting the BCD input format for convenience, and loading the full 16-bit counter to get as close as we can to the desired frequencies corresponding to the notes of C, E, and G.

Researching the musical literature we find that the frequencies corresponding to the notes of C, E, and G are as follows:

C = 261.63 Hz   E = 329.63 Hz   G = 392.00 Hz

When each of these is divided into our clock frequency (6.144 Mz ÷ 3), we generate the required numbers to be loaded into counter 0 as each note is played in succession:

C = 7,828   E = 6,213   G = 5,224

Software design   Figure 19.30 gives our complete software design. We have used list processing techniques and a subroutine to considerably shorten the code. A detailed analysis of the program will be left to the Questions and Problems section.

The 8259A Programmable Interrupt Controller

Our task is to use the 8259 interrupt controller, *along with the 8253 timer*, to design an electronic organ that will play the note of C, E, or G continuously whenever the corresponding key is momentarily tapped. Each key will initiate an interrupt that in turn will write the correct tone-generation data into the 8253.

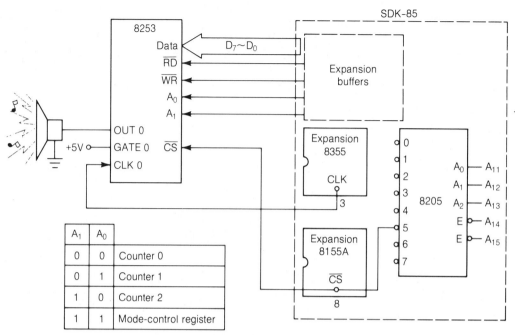

Figure 19.29 Task chord-of-C hardware design and register addressing.

A₁	A₀	
0	0	Counter 0
0	1	Counter 1
1	0	Counter 2
1	1	Mode-control register

As usual, we will become generally familiar with the 8259A interrupt controller before we begin our design. Our first look at the 8259A will be its pin and block diagram of Figure 19.31. Following the normal sequence of events during an interrupt will help us understand its overall operation:

1. Up to 8 interrupts are requested on the IR0 through IR7 input lines. All lines in which the corresponding bit in the *interrupt mask register* are 0 are allowed to pass. All others are masked out.
2. The *interrupt request register* (IRR) stores all unmasked inputs. If any exist, an interrupt is sent to the INTR (interrupt request) input of the 8085 via the INT output.
3. The CPU responds with an INTA (interrupt acknowledge) return signal.
4. The *priority resolver* selects the highest priority interrupt and strobes it into the *interrupt service register*. The corresponding IRR bit is reset. Simultaneously, the 8259A releases a CALL op code onto the data bus, which flows to the 8085's instruction register.
5. The CPU will generate two more INTA pulses (at the machine cycle rate) to fetch the 16-bit call address from the 8259A (least significant call address, followed by most significant).
6. The ISR bit is automatically reset (normally), and the process repeats for the next interrupt cycle.

To program the chip, and especially to determine the location of the 8 possible interrupt vectors (CALL addresses), we examine the *initialization command word format* of Figure 19.32*a,* and the *operation command word format* of Figure 19.32*b.* As shown, to initialize the 8259A, up to seven control words are available. In the case of the initialization command words (ICWs), all but the first command word location is determined by the order in which they are written. (The leftmost bit position, labeled A0, specifies the state of the A0 input pin when addressing a particular internal register.)

Carefully examining the ICWs of Figure 19.32*a* (good for both the 8085 and 8088 CPUs), we see that the programmer (via ICW words 1 and 2) determines the higher order bits of the interrupt vector (call address), while the lower-order bits are determined by the interrupt level (0 through 7). We also have the option (bit D2 of ICW1) of placing the vector locations 4 or 8 bytes apart. The final vector addresses fetched to the 8085 during the INTA sequence follow the format of Figure 19.33.

We now have enough general information to complete task *electronic organ.* We will follow the same design sequence as with the 8253 timer task: interface the 8259A to the SDK-85, determine the initialization and operation command words, and write and test the program.

Interfacing the 8259A to the SDK-85   Our hardware design is shown in Figure 19.34. Again, to save on hardware, we have used the on-board decoder to place out 8259A at memory-mapped location 080XH. The A0 line will help distinguish between the various control registers.

Writing to the command words   Figure 19.35 shows how we configured the initialization and operation words to match

ASM80 :F1:CHORD1.SRC

```
ISIS-II 8080/8085 MACRO ASSEMBLER, V4.1          CCHORD    PAGE    1

   LOC  OBJ        LINE          SOURCE STATEMENT
                     1           NAME   CCHORD
                     2
                     3    ; This program generates in sequence the
                     4    ; three notes making up the chord of C
                     5    ; (C,E, and G).
                     6    ; All addressing to the 8253 is via memory
                     7    ; mapping to expansion 8155A location 28XXH
                     8
   2000              9           ORG    2000H
   2000 37          10  LIST:    DB     37H,28H,78H
   2001 28
   2002 78
   2003 37          11           DB     37H,13H,62H
   2004 13
   2005 62
   2006 37          12           DB     37H,24H,52H
   2007 24
   2008 52
                    13
   2009 0603        14  START:   MVI    B,03H    ; Load iteration count
   200B 210020      15           LXI    H,LIST   ; Point to LIST
   200E 7E          16  AGAIN:   MOV    A,M      ; Bring in CONT word
   200F 320328      17           STA    2803H    ; Write MODE word
   2012 23          18           INX    H        ; Point to LS count
   2013 7E          19           MOV    A,M      ; Bring in LS count
   2014 320028      20           STA    2800H    ; Load LS count
   2017 23          21           INX    H        ; Point to MS count
   2018 7E          22           MOV    A,M      ; Bring in MS count
   2019 320028      23           STA    2800H    ; Load MS count
   201C 23          24           INX    H        ; Next list item
   201D CD2720      25           CALL   DELAY
   2020 05          26           DCR    B
   2021 C20E20      27           JNZ    AGAIN    ; Next note
   2024 C30920      28           JMP    START    ; Do again
                    29
   2027 11FFFF      30  DELAY:   LXI    D,0FFFFH
   202A 1B          31  LOOPS:   DCX    D
   202B 7B          32           MOV    A,E
   202C B2          33           ORA    D
   202D C22A20      34           JNZ    LOOPS
   2030 C9          35           RET
                    36           END
```

PUBLIC SYMBOLS

EXTERNAL SYMBOLS

USER SYMBOLS
AGAIN A 200E   DELAY A 2027   LIST A 2000   LOOPS A 202A   START A 200
9

ASSEMBLY COMPLETE,   NO ERRORS

Figure 19.30 Task chord-of-C software design.

our electronic organ project. Looking over our choices, we note the following:

- ICW1—Since we plan to use simple jumps to our interrupt service routines, we placed our vector locations only 4 bytes apart.
- ICW2—Along with ICW1, we select A5 to A15 to match vector addresses 2020H (C), 2024H (E), and 2028H (G).
- ICW3—Since we have not cascaded 8259As (placed them in master/slave configuration to increase the number of vectors up to 64), we do not use ICW3.

- ICW4—We use ICW4 to program the 8259A for the 8085 mode and to enable the automatic end-of-interrupt (in service bit automatically reset after each interrupt).
- OCW1—We mask out unused interrupt inputs IR3 to IR7. The other OCW words involve advanced modes of operation not required by our task.

Software design Figure 19.36 is our electronic organ software solution. As shown, the main program consists almost entirely of 8259A initialization words. The 8253, of course, is initialized during each ISR. Note the jumps placed at the

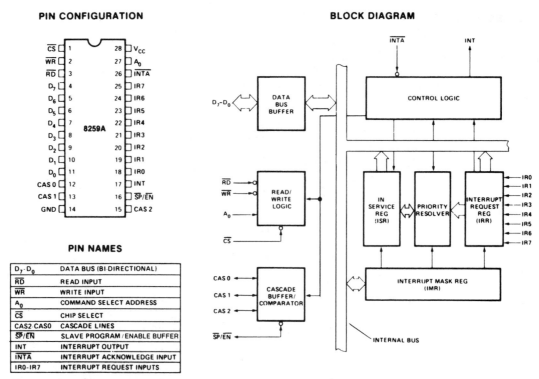

Figure 19.31   8259A pin and block diagrams.

three vector locations to branch to each ISR. A brief analysis of Figure 19.36, which is left to the student, should make the process clear.

MACHINE-ASSEMBLY UPDATE

Our next machine assembly update is placed in this Chapter because it involves *conditional assembly*—the software counterpart of the programmable peripheral chip. That is, using conditional assembly, we can write a single program that is really many programs in one.

As a simple case in point, let's write a single mimic source program that is really two programs. One program (called PROG 1) is designed to use the ports on the 8155A, while the other program (called PROG 2) is designed to use the ports on the 8355. From a single source program we will use conditional assembly to generate the desired program. Figure 19.37 shows us how it is done.

To enable the assembler to select one of the two possible versions of the mimic program, we "program" the source code using the PROG EQU statement and the IF/ELSE directive. As demonstrated by the list files of Figure 19.38, equating the label PROG to equal 8155, will generate the 8155 version (Figure 19.38*a*), while equating PROG to 8355 (anything else) will generate the 8355 version (Figure 19.38*b*).

By nesting IF-ENDIF directives, we can write very generalized source programs that will generate a wide range of customized versions.

A FINAL WORD

Although we have configured specific programmable chips for specific operations, we have learned a number of lessons common to nearly all programmable peripheral chips:

- Look for one or more control/mode registers to configure the system for a specific task.

- Expect a programmable peripheral chip to offer both interrupt and polled operation.

- Expect a wide variety of ways to distinguish between the various data/control/status registers.

- Expect the software to be simplified when switching over to programmable peripheral chips. (Programmable peripheral chips add hardware to eliminate software.)

- Expect a system to include many types of programmable peripheral chips. (Figure 19.39 shows a typical bank-teller intelligent terminal employing seven types of programmable peripheral chips.)

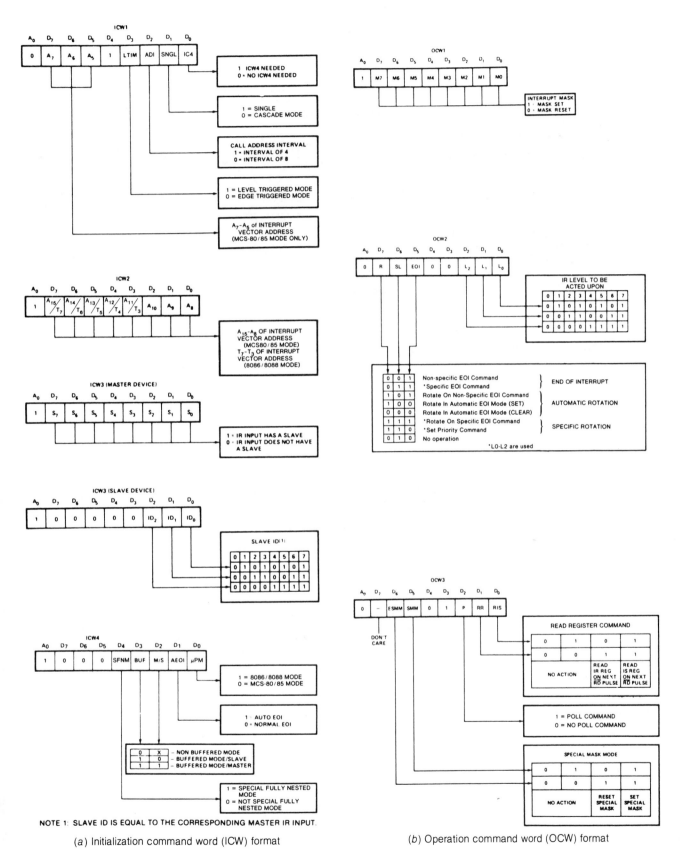

(a) Initialization command word (ICW) format

(b) Operation command word (OCW) format

Figure 19.32 8259A programming formats.

Content of First Interrupt Vector Byte

	D7	D6	D5	D4	D3	D2	D1	D0
CALL CODE	1	1	0	0	1	1	0	1

Content of Second Interrupt Vector Byte

IR	Interval = 4							
	D7	D6	D5	D4	D3	D2	D1	D0
7	A7	A6	A5	1	1	1	0	0
6	A7	A6	A5	1	1	0	0	0
5	A7	A6	A5	1	0	1	0	0
4	A7	A6	A5	1	0	0	0	0
3	A7	A6	A5	0	1	1	0	0
2	A7	A6	A5	0	1	0	0	0
1	A7	A6	A5	0	0	1	0	0
0	A7	A6	A5	0	0	0	0	0

IR	Interval = 8							
	D7	D6	D5	D4	D3	D2	D1	D0
7	A7	A6	1	1	1	0	0	0
6	A7	A6	1	1	0	0	0	0
5	A7	A6	1	0	1	0	0	0
4	A7	A6	1	0	0	0	0	0
3	A7	A6	0	1	1	0	0	0
2	A7	A6	0	1	0	0	0	0
1	A7	A6	0	0	1	0	0	0
0	A7	A6	0	0	0	0	0	0

Content of Third Interrupt Vector Byte

D7	D6	D5	D4	D3	D2	D1	D0
A15	A14	A13	A12	A11	A10	A9	A8

Figure 19.33 8259A interrupt vector (CALL instruction) 3-byte format.

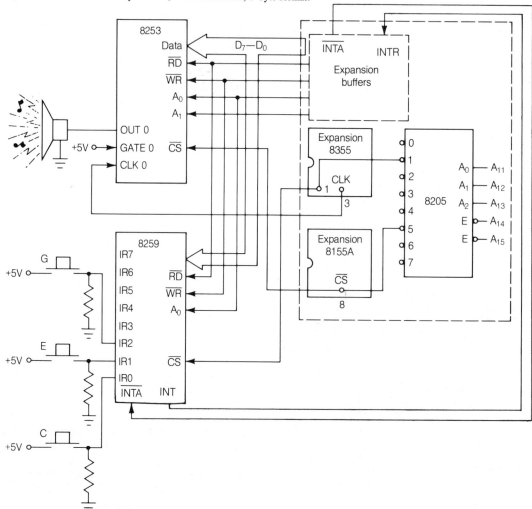

Figure 19.34 Task electronic organ hardware design.

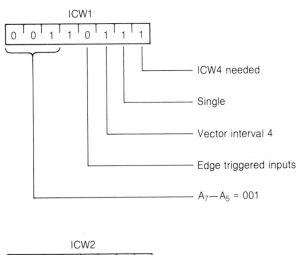

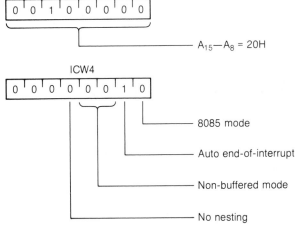

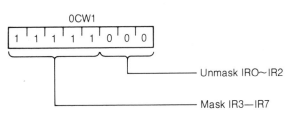

Figure 19.35 Programming the initialization and operation control words for task electronic organ.

INTELLIGENT-MACHINE UPDATE

When using programmable peripheral chips, computers are displaying a high-order trait that human beings cannot match: computers can change their configuration to match their environment. Human beings—creatures who adapt very slowly—must instead change their environment to match their needs. Computers, therefore, unhampered by our biological shackles, can expand into areas where human beings cannot go. The intelligent machine of tomorrow, it seems, may be as different from us as we are from the dinosaurs—creatures that could not adapt to a changing environment.

QUESTIONS AND PROBLEMS

1. What is the major advantage of software programming over hardware programming?

2. What are the three types of registers normally found in programmable peripheral chips?

3. Based on the 8355 design of Figure 19.6, write a mimic program in which the low-order four bits of port 0 are input and sent to the highest four bits *of the same port*.

4. Referring to Figure 19.6, the SDK-85 contains a socket for an expansion 8355/8755, with CE attached to output 1 of the 8205 decoder. What are the port and memory addresses of this *expansion* ROM?

5. Referring to Figure 19.5, what is the purpose of the 8355's READY output?

6. Why does the 8355 contain both a $\overline{RD}$ and an $\overline{IOR}$ input?

7. In an 8355, how are the ports and data-direction registers addressed?

8. Modify the program of Figure 19.9*b* so the roles of ports A and B are reversed.

9. What technique is used by Figure 19.11*b* to generate a $\overline{STROBE}$ signal?

10. Referring to Figure 19.6, what are the addresses of the RAM, timer registers, command register, and ports of the expansion 8155A?

11. How large a number can a 14-bit timer store?

12. Which three bus lines determine the address of the timer and port registers within the 8155A?

13. Referring to Figure 19.19, why is it best to drive the printer (rather than generate the steady tone) via interrupt I/O?

14. Regarding the *strobed output mode* sequence of Figure 19.20, rearrange the following 8155A signals in their proper sequence:

    - INTR
    - BF
    - $\overline{STB}$

15. What major CPU keyboard/display operations does the 8279 do?

16. How do we select one of the eight possible commands to the 8279?

17. How is the 8279 informed that a key has been activated?

18. How can the CPU write a data word to a specific location of the write display RAM?

19. By entering addresses 1800H and 1900H into the circuitry of Figure 19.23, show how the 8279's command and data ports are addressed.

20. What technique is used by the 8253 to distinguish between the three mode control registers (one for each counter)?

21. Which of the 8253's modes of operation could be used to initiate an interrupt?

ASM80 :F1:CHORD2.SRC

ISIS-II 8080/8085 MACRO ASSEMBLER, V4.1   ORGAN   PAGE   1


```
LOC  OBJ          LINE         SOURCE STATEMENT
                  1              NAME    ORGAN
                  2
                  3    ; This program generates the three notes
                  4    ; making up the chord of C via interrupts
                  5    ; on the 8259A. All addressing to the 8259A
                  6    ; is via memory mapping to expansion 8755
                  7    ; location 080XH.   Stack pointer is set
                  8    ; via SDK-85 monitor.
                  9
2000              10             ORG     2000H
2000 3E37         11             MVI     A,37H   ; ICW1
2002 320008       12             STA     0800H   ; Load ICW1
2005 3E20         13             MVI     A,20H   ; ICW2
2007 320108       14             STA     0801H   ; Load ICW2
200A 3E02         15             MVI     A,02    ; ICW4
200C 320108       16             STA     0801H   ; Load  ICW4
200F 3EF8         17             MVI     A,0F8H  ; OCW1
2011 320108       18             STA     0801H   ; Load OCW1
2014 FB           19             EI              ; Enable int system
2015 C31520       20  SELF:      JMP     SELF    ; Wait for interrupt
                  21
2020              22             ORG     2020H
2020 C32B20       23             JMP     CHORDC  ; Generate C routine
2024              24             ORG     2024H
2024 C33C20       25             JMP     CHORDE  ; Generate E routine
2028              26             ORG     2028H
2028 C34D20       27             JMP     CHORDG  ; Generate G routine
                  28
202B 3E37         29  CHORDC:    MVI     A,37H   ; Generate MODE
202D 320328       30             STA     2803H   ; Load MODE
2030 3E28         31             MVI     A,28H   ; Generate LS
2032 320028       32             STA     2800H   ; Load LS
2035 3E78         33             MVI     A,78H   ; Generate MS
2037 320028       34             STA     2800H   ; Load MS
203A FB           35             EI
203B C9           36             RET
203C 3E37         37  CHORDE:    MVI     A,37H
203E 320328       38             STA     2803H
2041 3E13         39             MVI     A,13H
2043 320028       40             STA     2800H
2046 3E62         41             MVI     A,62H
2048 320028       42             STA     2800H
204B FB           43             EI
204C C9           44             RET
204D 3E37         45  CHORDG:    MVI     A,37H
204F 320328       46             STA     2803H
2052 3E24         47             MVI     A,24H
2054 320028       48             STA     2800H
2057 3E52         49             MVI     A,52H
2059 320028       50             STA     2800H
205C FB           51             EI
205D C9           52             RET
                  53             END
```


ISIS-II 8080/8085 MACRO ASSEMBLER, V4.1   ORGAN   PAGE   2

PUBLIC SYMBOLS

EXTERNAL SYMBOLS

USER SYMBOLS
CHORDC A 202B   CHORDE A 203C   CHORDG A 204D   SELF   A 2015
ASSEMBLY COMPLETE,   NO ERRORS

Figure 19.36 Task electronic organ software solution.

```
        NAME    MIMICCHOICE
; This program uses conditional assembly
; to generate one of two MIMIC programs,
; one using the 8155A and the other using
; the 8355.
; THIS PROG IS SET TO ASSEMBLE 8155A VERSION

PROG    EQU     8155
        ORG     2000H
        IF   PROG EQ 8155
        MVI     A,OEH   ; PROG 8155A
        OUT     20H
LOOP:   IN      21H
        OUT     22H
        JMP     LOOP
        ELSE
        MVI     A,O      ; PROG 8355
        OUT     2
        MVI     A,OFFH
        OUT     3
LOOP:   IN      O
        OUT     1
        JMP     LOOP
        ENDIF
        END
```

(a)

```
        NAME    MIMICCHOICE
; This program uses conditional assembly
; to generate one of two MIMIC programs,
; one using the 8155A and the other using
; the 8355.
; THIS PROG IS SET TO ASSEMBLE 8355 VERSION

PROG    EQU     8355
        ORG     2000H
        IF   PROG EQ 8155
        MVI     A,OEH   ; PROG 8155A
        OUT     20H
LOOP:   IN      21H
        OUT     22H
        JMP     LOOP
        ELSE
        MVI     A,O      ; PROG 8355
        OUT     2
        MVI     A,OFFH
        OUT     3
LOOP:   IN      O
        OUT     1
        JMP     LOOP
        ENDIF
        END
```

(b)

Figure 19.37 Conditional assembly source programs: *a)* Programmed for
8155A assembly. *b)* Programmed for 8355 assembly.

22. What would happen to the square-wave signal corresponding to mode three of the 8253 if the GATE input were grounded?

23. Once a counter's mode register has been programmed, can the number in the count register be changed at any time (on the fly)?

24. In general terms, how would you modify the hardware/software designs of Figure 19.29 and 19.30 so each time a key was pressed it generated a full chord (three notes simultaneously)?

25. What does a set bit in the in-service register (ISR) indicate?

26. When using the 8259A, how is a vector address generated?

27. How does the 8259A distinguish between the four *initialization command words*?

28. Why are jumps usually placed at the vector locations when using an 8259A?

29. Based on the conditional assembly technique demonstrated in Figures 19.37 and 19.38, write a single program that generates code to produce one of three steady tones (*Hint:* The entire program need not be conditionally assembled).

```
ASM80 :F1:COND1.SRC


ISIS-II 8080/8085 MACRO ASSEMBLER, V4.1         MIMICC    PAGE     1

    LOC   OBJ          LINE          SOURCE STATEMENT
                        1            NAME    MIMICCHOICE
                        2
                        3  ; This program uses conditional assembly
                        4  ; to generate one of two MIMIC programs,
                        5  ; one using the 8155A and the other using
                        6  ; the 8355.
                        7  ; THIS PROG IS SET TO ASSEMBLE 8155A VERSION
                        8
    1FDB                9  PROG    EQU     8155
    2000               10          ORG     2000H
                       11          IF  PROG EQ 8155
    2000  3E0E         12          MVI     A,0EH  ; PROG 8155A
    2002  D320         13          OUT     20H
    2004  DB21         14  LOOP:   IN      21H
    2006  D322         15          OUT     22H
    2008  C30420       16          JMP     LOOP
                       17          ELSE
                       18          MVI     A,0     ; PROG 8355
                       19          OUT     2
                       20          MVI     A,0FFH
                       21          OUT     3
                       22  LOOP:   IN      0
                       23          OUT     1
                       24          JMP     LOOP
                       25          ENDIF
                       26          END


PUBLIC SYMBOLS

EXTERNAL SYMBOLS

USER SYMBOLS
LOOP    A 2004     PROG    A 1FDB

ASSEMBLY COMPLETE,    NO ERRORS
```

(a)

```
ASM80 :F1:COND2.SRC


ISIS-II 8080/8085 MACRO ASSEMBLER, V4.1         MIMICC    PAGE     1

    LOC   OBJ          LINE          SOURCE STATEMENT
                        1            NAME    MIMICCHOICE
                        2
                        3  ; This program uses conditional assembly
                        4  ; to generate one of two MIMIC programs,
                        5  ; one using the 8155A and the other using
                        6  ; the 8355.
                        7  ; THIS PROG IS SET TO ASSEMBLE 8355 VERSION
                        8
    20A3                9  PROG    EQU     8355
    2000               10          ORG     2000H
                       11          IF  PROG EQ 8155
                       12          MVI     A,0EH  ; PROG 8155A
                       13          OUT     20H
                       14  LOOP:   IN      21H
                       15          OUT     22H
                       16          JMP     LOOP
                       17          ELSE
    2000  3E00         18          MVI     A,0     ; PROG 8355
    2002  D302         19          OUT     2
    2004  3EFF         20          MVI     A,0FFH
    2006  D303         21          OUT     3
    2008  DB00         22  LOOP:   IN      0
    200A  D301         23          OUT     1
    200C  C30820       24          JMP     LOOP
                       25          ENDIF
                       26          END


PUBLIC SYMBOLS

EXTERNAL SYMBOLS

USER SYMBOLS
LOOP    A 2008     PROG    A 20A3

ASSEMBLY COMPLETE,    NO ERRORS
```

(b)

Figure 19.38 Conditional assembly list files: *a)* 8155A version. *b)* 8355 version.

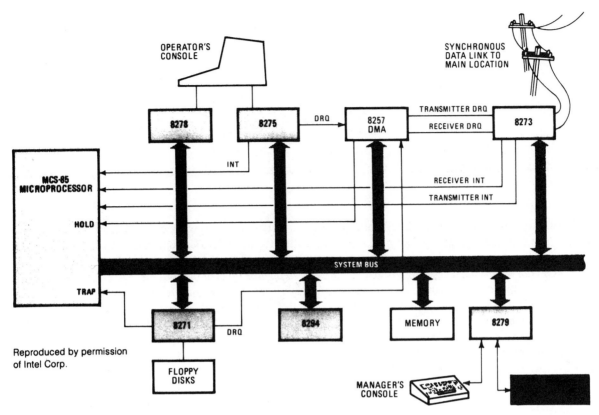

Figure 19.39   Intelligent bank terminal using programmable peripheral chips.

chapter 20

Controllers

Like all warm-blooded animals, we are able to hold our body temperature to within 1 or 2 degrees of normal, even when the ambient environment fluctuates widely over many tens of degrees. Of course, this amazing ability is no accident of nature, for temperature control is just one of the many precision *cybernetic* control systems operating in the human body. In this chapter we will examine the computer as a cybernetic control system, and we will introduce the single-chip microcomputer, a device specifically designed for control applications.

CYBERNETICS

Cybernetics is the science of communication and control. Although cybernetics encompasses many disciplines, most cybernetic systems have one element in common: a circular motion or closed loop in which an action initiates a reaction—which in turn *feeds back* and alters the original action.

It is *feedback,* then, that is the central feature of cybernetic control systems. As illustrated in Figure 20.1, however, there are two ways in which the reaction can be fed back:

- Positively, by aiding the original action
- Negatively, by opposing the original action

Positive feedback usually leads to runaway or explosive situations, such as snowballing. (The faster a snowball rolls downhill, the more snow it gathers. But the more snow it gathers, the faster it travels. The effect quickly builds and soon we have a full-scale avalanche.) Since positive feedback leads to unstable situations, it is of little use in control systems.

Negative feedback, on the other hand, does lead to stability and control, and is at the heart of all control systems.

To begin with, how does negative feedback so accurately maintain our body temperature near 98.6°F? As expected, the process is a cybernetic, closed-loop, negative-feedback control system. Step outside on a cold winter day, and that action quickly leads to a slight lowering of the body temperature. This lowered temperature is sensed, and the body reacts by increasing its metabolism—which in turn drives the temperature back to normal. When we step back inside the warm house, another closed-loop, negative-feedback sequence is set in motion. Our increased metabolism causes our body temperature to rise slightly. This increased temperature is sensed, which leads to a lowering of the metabolism and increased perspiration—which pulls the body temperature back to normal again. Negative feedback, then, is the magic process allowing our body temperature to remain stable amid large fluctuations in air temperature (see Figure 20.2).

When we put the concept of control into the simplest possible terms, a *negative-feedback control system* compares where you are with where you want to be and sends out an error signal whose purpose is to drive where you are to where you want to be. To bring the design needs more in focus, we diagram the process in block form (Figure 20.3). The most basic form of control is called *dual position.* If the actual state is below the desired state, the error signal is full positive; if above the desired state the error signal is full negative.

Damping

When using dual position control, often a degree of built-in inertia causes the actual state to swing past the desired state.

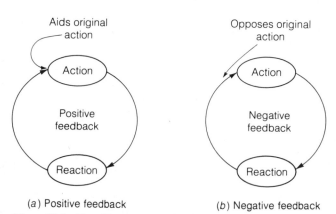

(a) Positive feedback   (b) Negative feedback

Figure 20.1 Closed-loop cybernetic feedback system.

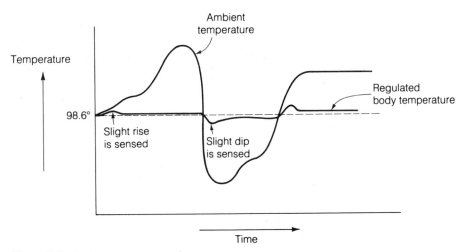

Figure 20.2 Body-temperature control.

For example, the fight-control system of a rocket is a negative-feedback control system. If the actual pitch of the rocket is different from the desired pitch (sent by guidance), steering thrust will be applied to rotate the rocket toward the desired state. If the thrust is maintained until the actual and desired states are just equal, the inertia of the rocket will carry it beyond the desired pitch in the other direction. Again, opposite thrust is applied to bring it back, and again inertia causes it to swing past the desired point. The result is an oscillating motion. If the swings become too large, the system can go completely out of control.

To cure the problem, we must *damp* the system. When the system is properly damped, the actual state will quickly settle into the desired state, with little or no overswing. Damping can be achieved in a number of ways. Perhaps the most popular closed-loop control technique is called PID, and is actually three methods rolled into one: *proportional, integral,* and *differential.*

Proportional control means that the correction signal is proportional to the error signal (actual state is subtracted from the desired state). However, as the error signal goes to zero, the correction signal also goes to zero and the actual state is usually *offset* slightly from the desired state. When we add integral control, the offset error is *accumulated* over time, and we are assured that small errors will gradually build up and eliminate the offset. However, like straight dual-position control, *integral damping* also tends to generate oscillations about the desired state. The solution is to add *derivative control,* which responds to *changes* in the error signal. That is, if the system is moving rapidly toward the desired state, decrease the net error signal to avoid overswing; if not moving at all, transmit the full error signal to the "steering" device; and if moving in the opposite direction, away from the desired point, enhance the basic error signal with negative rate information.

When PID control is added to our basic negative feedback loop, we have a control system that is both responsive and smoothly operating. Clearly, as shown in Figure 20.4, most of the steps in our control system can be handled by a computer. To see how it is done, we will design a simple computerized cybernetic temperature-control system. Because we can tolerate a small offset error, we will employ PD (proportional/derivative) control only.

A COMPUTERIZED TEMPERATURE-CONTROL SYSTEM

Here is our assignment: Design a computerized control system to maintain a gallon of water to within two degrees of a selected temperature.

The hardware design, given in Figure 20.5, consists of a resistive heater and thermoelectric heat pump, both fed by digital-to-analog converters. (A thermoelectric heat pump is a solid-state device that pumps heat from one side of the device to the other when driven by suitable electric current.) Also included is a temperature transducer feeding an A/D converter. To simplify the software, the A/D converter is a monolithic chip (such as the AD574 of Figure 18.14). The signal conditioner buffers and scales the output of the tem-

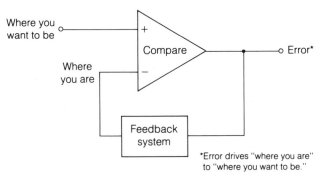

Figure 20.3 Negative-feedback, closed-loop system.

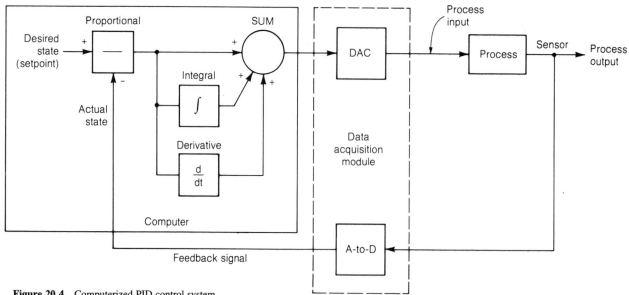

Figure 20.4   Computerized PID control system.

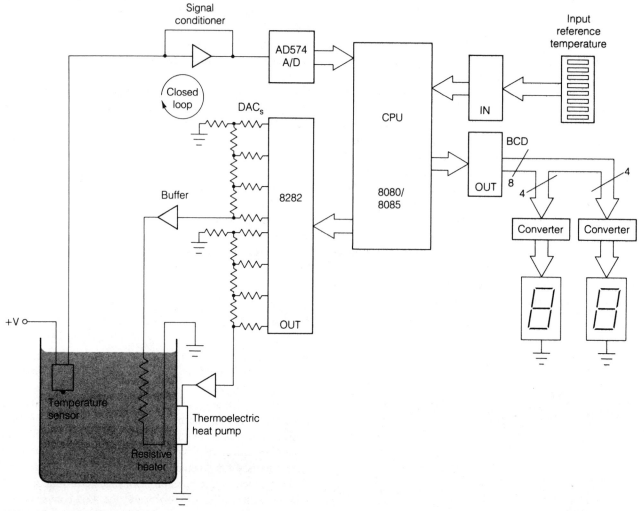

Figure 20.5   8080/8085-based, temperature-control system.

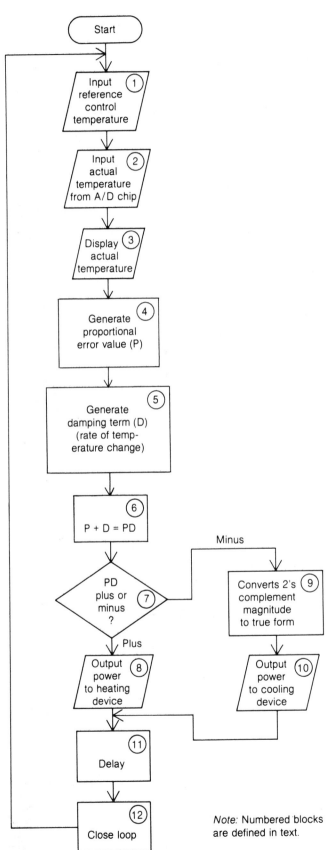

Figure 20.6 Closed loop, temperature-control routine, including damping.

perature probe, so the expected voltage range of the transducer corresponds to the acceptable voltage range of the A/D converter. The output port displays the actual temperature so that the performance of the system can be monitored.

The high-level flowchart of Figure 20.6 reflects the closed-loop concept:

- Block ① inputs the reference temperature (the goal) from the DIP switch.
- Block ② inputs the actual temperature (the present temperature of the water) from the A/D converter.
- Block ③ converts the actual temperature to BCD and sends the result to the displays. (With only two seven-segment displays, multiplexing is not necessary.)
- Block ④ generates the signed number proportional error signal (P) by subtracting the input present temperature from the desired temperature reference (+ if water is too cold; − if too hot).
- Block ⑤ generates the signed number derivative damping term (D) by subtracting the present actual temperature from the previous actual temperature (the greater the result, the greater rate of change).
- Block ⑥ sums the proportional error term (P) with the derivative damping term (D) to generate the PD error signal to be sent to the "steering" system.
- Block ⑦ determines if the PD error signal is positive or negative (check the sign bit).
- Block ⑧ is processed if the PD error signal is positive. Since a positive signal generally indicates that the water is too cold, the heating device will be activated. (It is possible for the derivative term to overwhelm the proportional term, indicating the water is too hot but cooling off very rapidly—in fact so rapidly that, paradoxically, the heating element is activated to "head off" a possible overswing.)
- Block ⑨ converts the negative PD error term to true form prior to transmission to the steering system.
- Block ⑩ powers the cooling device at a rate proportional to the magnitude of the PD error signal.
- Block ⑪ adds a delay in order to give the system time to change so reasonable rate information can be generated by block ⑤.
- Block ⑫ closes the feedback loop.

When our temperature-control system is activated, it should closely simulate temperature control in the human body (refer to Figure 20.2). Of course, if the outside temperature varies too quickly or over too wide a range, the regulation system will be unable to maintain control.

Our temperature-control system is an example of a *real-time process*. A real-time process is one in which the input parameters reflect the present state of the system, and the results of processing are required immediately for the control

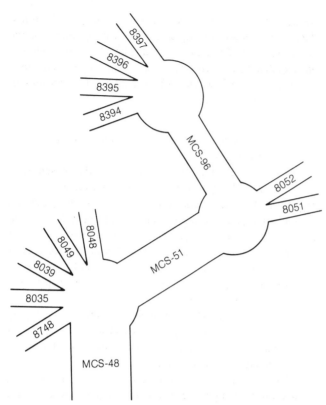

Figure 20.7   The Intel single-chip microcontroller family tree.

process. Most industrial *process-control* systems (manufacturing steps controlled by a computer) are real-time systems.

SINGLE-CHIP MICROCONTROLLERS: INTELLIGENT MACHINES ON A CHIP

Our temperature-regulation system of the last section is an example of a low-end control process. That is, the design is relatively simple and only small amounts of program ROM, data RAM, and I/O ports are required. Suppose all memory and ports could be placed on a single microprocessor chip. We would then have a computer on a chip—a *microcontroller,* ideally suited for control applications and unmatched for reliability, low cost, and ease of use.

When we look at the Intel microcontroller family tree (Figure 20.7), we see three major spurts of growth:

- The MCS-48 group
- The MCS-51 group
- The MCS-96 group

In this section, let's take a close look at the baseline MCS-48 group, and follow-up with a brief look at the enhancements offered by the newer MCS-51 and MCS-96 groups.

The 8048 Branch

The 8048 is the flagship of the MCS-48 group. The overall architecture and major characteristics of the 8048 are summarized in Figure 20.8. The other four branches of the MCS-48 trunk are all derivatives of the basic 8048, differing only in the type and size of their memory systems:

$$8048—1K \text{ ROM}, 64 \times 8 \text{ RAM}$$
$$8049—2K \text{ ROM}, 64 \times 8 \text{ RAM}$$
$$8039—\text{No ROM}, 128 \times 8 \text{ RAM}$$
$$8035—\text{No ROM}, 64 \times 8 \text{ RAM}$$
$$8748—1K \text{ EPROM}, 64 \times 8 \text{ RAM}$$

Each of these derivatives of the 8048 is pin-compatible, which means that the 8748, with its EPROM for prototype development, can be replaced by the low-cost, factory-programmed 8048 in the production phase.

Control applications were uppermost in the minds of the designers of the 8048, and its architecture and instruction set reflect this emphasis. Since bit manipulation, BCD operations, conditional branching, and table lookup figure heavily in control applications, the instruction set is tailored to these areas. (The 8048 instruction set is provided in Appendix VI.) The 8048 can directly set and reset individual lines of its I/O ports, and can test individual bits within the accumulator. Also available are three test inputs that can cause program branching when tested by conditional jump instructions. To help the programmer compress the entire control routine into the available ROM, special attention has been given to code efficiency. More than 70% of the instructions are a single byte long and all others are only two bytes long. Along with shorter instructions are shorter execution times, with 50% of all instructions executed in a single machine cycle (placing the memory and I/O ports on chip greatly reduces the need for machine-cycle external data transfers).

The 16 I/O lines making up ports 1 and 2 offer a special quasi-bidirectional feature. Special circuitry allows each line to serve as an input, an output, or both (even though outputs are latched).

The 8048 contains an 8-bit *interval timer/event counter* in order to generate accurate time delays and count external events without placing a software burden on the processor (or resorting to the addition of an 8253 programmable timer chip). All timer/counter actions are software-controlled, and all external events are counted by way of the T_1 input pin. Other features include an interrupt input, also testable with conditional jump instruction, and a single-step input to provide the user with troubleshooting capability (single stepping is covered in Chapter 22).

Should the on-chip features of the 8048 be insufficient to meet your requirements, the 8048 allows for easy expansion. Figure 20.9 shows how additional program memory can be added to the system. Note the 8085-type multiplexed data bus and the use of port 2 to supply high-order addressing.

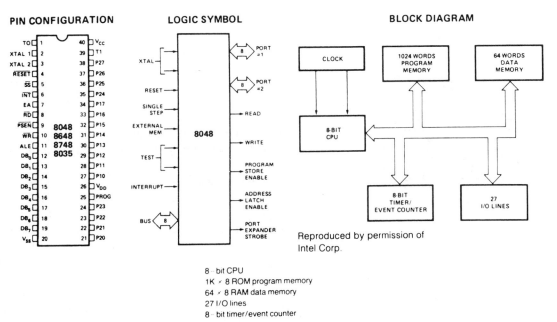

Figure 20.8 Basic architecture, pin-out, and major features of the 8048.

The MCS-51 Branch

The 8051 of Figure 20.10 is the newest member of the 8-bit single-chip family. As revealed by the block diagram of Figure 20.10b, most of the 8051's features are enhancements of its 8048 predecessor, and only the serial I/O feature is completely new. The 8051's major improvements include:

- 32 programmable I/O lines
- Full-duplex UART operation (the UART is explained in the next chapter).

- Two 16-bit timer/event counters.
- A special Boolean processor, in addition to the ALU.
- Multiply and divide instructions, requiring only 4 usec.
- 4K bytes of ROM or EPROM (8751).
- Expandable memory to 64K for both RAM and ROM.
- Multiple addressing modes.
- High-speed operation (over half of the instructions execute in 1 microsecond).
- Five-source, two-priority nested interrupts.
- A CHMOS version (the 80C51) for low-power operation.

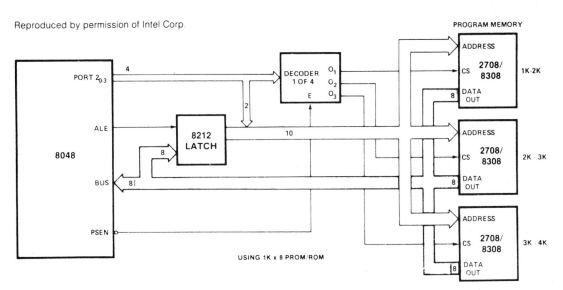

Figure 20.9 Expanding the program memory of the 8048.

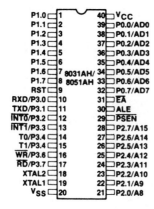

(a) Pin-out

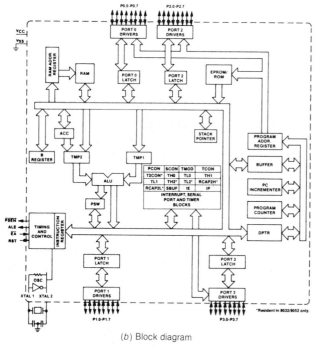

(b) Block diagram

Figure 20.10 The MCS-51 system.

The MCS-96 Branch

As revealed by the comparison chart of Figure 20.11, the 16-bit MCS-96 group enhances the 8-bit MCS-51 group and provides four new features. Let's briefly take a look at each of these new areas (see Figure 20.12):

High-speed I/O The four high-speed inputs are used in conjunction with the built-in timer to record the exact time a particular external event occurred. The high-speed output unit is used to trigger events at specific times through its 6 external high-speed output lines.

Ten-bit A/D The fully integrated A/D unit takes one of 8 input analog channels and uses successive approximation to generate a 10-bit digital result.

PWM (Pulse Width Modulation) output The PWM unit is basically a digital to analog conversion device, in which the *duty cycle* of the output waveform is proportional to the size of the number in the internal PWM register. A PWM output is useful for driving a common type of motor.

Watchdog timer If a computer system crashes due to a software error, usually a reset pulse re-cycles the system back to normal operation. That is how the 16-bit watchdog timer works. If it receives regular "all's well" (clear timer) commands from properly-functioning software, it will never overflow. However, if the software crashes, the commands will stop, and the watchdog timer will overflow and reset the system. Since the watchdog timer is incremented every state time, a software malfunction can exist for no longer than 16 mS (12 MHz clock).

STEPPER MOTOR

A *stepper motor* is a precision motor device that allows the rotor to be accurately incremented in precise steps (typically varying from 3.75° to 90°) *without the use of feedback.* When we remove the *acknowledge* aspect of the feedback signal, however, an important assumption must be made: When the computer issues a command to the stepper motor (for example, rotate 5°), we must assume the command will be carried out precisely.

The technique that allows the rotor to be turned by a predetermined amount (in this case, 90°) is shown in Figure 20.13. Two well-known properties of magnetic fields are involved: (1) like poles repel and unlike poles attract; and (2) a magnetic pole can be created by sending a current through a coil of wire (reverse the current and the pole direction reverses). There are two center-tapped stator coils and therefore four windings (labeled W_1, W_2, W_3, and W_4). The purpose of the center tap is to allow the direction of current to change in each of the two coils by proper grounding of the winding outputs (thereby allowing each of the windings to be driven by a current-sinking transistor). A motor employing this winding scheme is known as a *four-phase stepper motor.* (Stepping in increments smaller than 90° is entirely a function of the number of rotor and stator poles designed into the motor. In a realizable four-phase system, the number of windings remains constant, with each winding activating many stator poles.)

From Figure 20.13 we can also see how the rotor can be turned in precise 90° increments. By grounding W_1 and W_4, we have created side-by-side south poles that hold the rotor in place as shown by magnetic attraction. If the grounds on

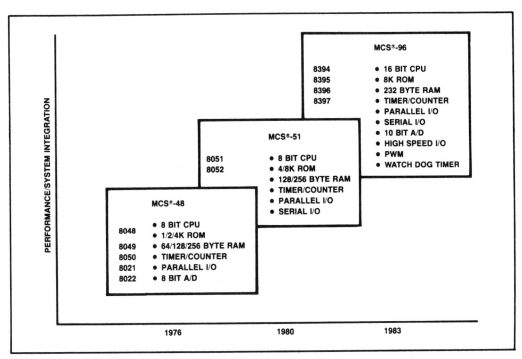

Figure 20.11   The evolution of microcontrollers at Intel.

W_1 and W_4 were rotated clockwise to W_2 and W_4, it is clear that the rotor also would rotate clockwise 90°, following the new south-pole orientation. When this rotating pair of grounds is diagrammed (Figure 20.14), we note a simple rotate pattern—a pattern easily produced by an 8080/8085 system. We simply copy the bit pattern into both nibbles of the accumulator and use the Rotate Left (for clockwise rotation) and Rotate Right (for counterclockwise rotation) instructions.

Using the 8155A RAM/IO chip to drive the motor, Figure 20.15 summarizes our hardware/software stepper-motor design. (The diodes are for back EMF protection). Motor direction is determined by an inported flag bit, and motor speed depends on size of inported number transferred to the delay loop. Our final software solution of Figure 20.16 allows control of both speed and direction via the SDK-85's input port 21H. A stepper motor will be used in Chapter 24 to implement a microcomputer application.

MACHINE-ASSEMBLY UPDATE—I

Our next machine-assembly update is important because it refines the *linkage* process—the key to modular programming. Linkage, remember, is a combination of two or more independently assembled, relocatable program modules.

As a case in point, refer back to Figure 18.28c. Instead of ending the MIMIC-DELAY program with a simple halt (RST 1), suppose we wish to place the program into a continuous loop. Proceeding as we have in the past, we replace the RST instruction in module OUT with a JMP REPEAT instruction. And to complete the loop we place the symbol REPEAT in the label field near the beginning of module IN. Clearly this time we have a problem. How will the assembler handle labels that cross module boundaries (known as *global symbols*)? Any symbol used in the operand field but not defined in the label field will be tagged as an error.

The solution rests with two new directives: PUBLIC and EXTRN (external). For each label that appears in two or more modules we must ask the following question: Is the label *defined* (declared) in the present module and *used* elsewhere, or is it *used* in the present module and *defined* elsewhere? Referring to Figure 20.17a and c, we find that:

- Label REPEAT is *defined* in module IN2 (that is, it appears in the label field), so we make it accessible to external programs by listing it after the PUBLIC directive.
- Label REPEAT is *used* by module OUT2 (that is, it appears in the operand field), so we use the EXTRN directive to tell the assembler and linker that label REPEAT is *defined* in another module.

With label REPEAT now properly accounted for, modules IN2 and OUT2 can be assembled. Again looking to the list files of Figure 20.17 we see that label REPEAT is listed as a PUBLIC symbol in module IN2, and as an EXTERNAL symbol in module OUT2. The assembler now accepts symbol REPEAT, confident that its address will be fully established after the LINK and LOCATE processes.

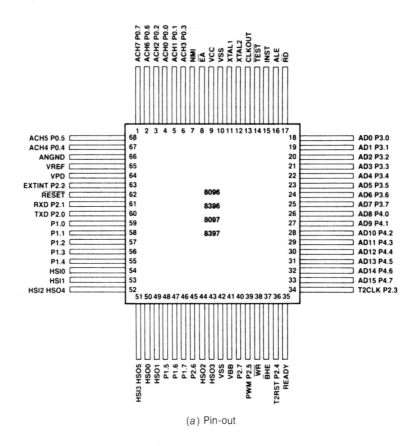

(a) Pin-out

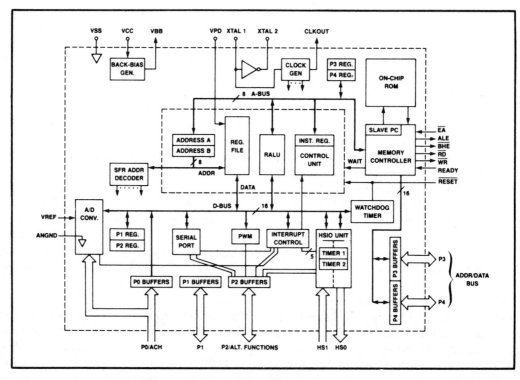

(b) Block diagram

Figure 20.12   The MCS-96 system.

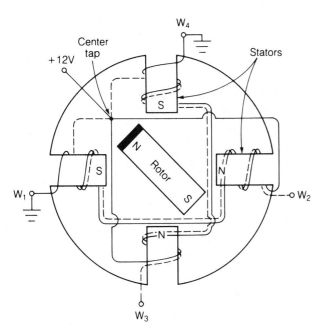

Figure 20.13 Stepper motor mechanical design.

After the three modules are linked and located, we examine the HEX file of Figure 20.18 and note that the correct jump address was generated.

ROBOTICS

A *robot* is a specialized controller that simulates one or more simple human functions. As simulation improves, the robot may someday evolve into an *android,* a machine that closely resembles a human.

A Robotic System

The simplest kind of robotic system is shown in Figure 20.19. It is a basic cybernetic system consisting of a sensor and a movable arm, all under program control. Sensors are the "eyes" of the robot, servomechanisms are the "muscles" of the robot, and the stored program is the "brains" of the robot. Let's take a look at each of these areas.

Sensors Robots can be fitted with devices (sensors) that simulate the five human senses: sight, hearing, touch, smell,

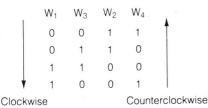

Figure 20.14 Shift-register pattern of four-phase, stepper-motor rotation.

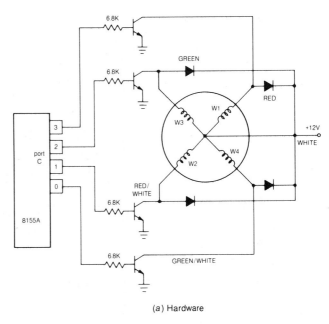

(*a*) Hardware

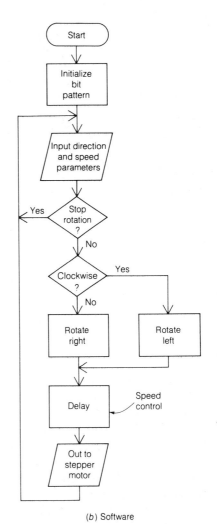

(*b*) Software

Figure 20.15 Computer-driven, stepper-motor design with variable speed and direction.

```
ASM80 :F1:MOTOR.SRC


ISIS-II 8080/8085 MACRO ASSEMBLER, V4.1        STEPPE    PAGE    1

  LOC  OBJ         LINE          SOURCE STATEMENT
                     1           NAME    STEPPERMOTOR
                     2
                     3  ; This stepper motor program allows control of
                     4  ; both motor speed and direction by way of input
                     5  ; port 21H.  Direction is controlled via bit 7
                     6  ; and speed is controlled via bits 0 through 6.
                     7  ; We assume the control number is entered in sign
                     8  ; magnitude form (bits 0 through 6 always positive).
                     9
  2000              10          ORG     2000H
  2000 3E0E         11          MVI     A,0EH   ; SDK-85
  2002 D320         12          OUT     20H     ; SDK-85
  2004 0666         13          MVI     B,66H   ; Initialize motor position
  2006 2E00         14          MVI     L,00H   ; Clear register L
  2008 DB21         15  REPEAT: IN      21H     ; Input speed and dir param
  200A 67           16          MOV     H,A     ; Store in H
                    17
                    18  ; Determine direction
                    19
  200B 07           20          RLC
  200C 0F           21          RRC             ; Set C flag with bit 7
  200D 78           22          MOV     A,B     ; Bring in motor position
  200E DA1520       23          JC      LEFT    ; Jump if bit 7 = 1
  2011 0F           24          RRC             ; Step right
  2012 C31620       25          JMP     OVER
  2015 07           26  LEFT:   RLC             ; Step left
  2016 D323         27  OVER:   OUT     23H     ; Perform step
  2018 47           28          MOV     B,A     ; Store motor position
                    29
                    30  ; Determine speed
                    31
  2019 7C           32          MOV     A,H
  201A 17           33          RAL             ; Mask & delay x two
  201B 67           34          MOV     H,A     ; Put back into H
  201C 2B           35  LOOP:   DCX     H       ; Decrement delay counter
  201D 7C           36          MOV     A,H
  201E B5           37          ORA     L       ; HL zero?
  201F C21C20       38          JNZ     LOOP    ; If not, stay in loop
  2022 C30820       39          JMP     REPEAT  ; Keep motor running
                    40          END


PUBLIC SYMBOLS

EXTERNAL SYMBOLS

USER SYMBOLS
LEFT    A 2015    LOOP    A 201C    OVER    A 2016    REPEAT A 2008

ASSEMBLY COMPLETE,    NO ERRORS
```

Figure 20.16 Program for controlling speed and direction of stepper motor.

and taste. They even can be endowed with *extrasensory perception* (ESP) by sensing such stimuli as magnetic fields, which humans cannot detect.

Robots "hear" through microphones. When speech recognition is added (Chapter 21), they can be given high-level commands verbally.

Robots "feel" by way of strain gauges. By using a piezoelectric crystal within a resonant LC circuit, for example, pressure can be converted to frequency. Placed in the "fingers" of a robot, these tiny flat crystals can provide the feedback necessary to close the cybernetic loop when the robot lifts an object.

Robots "taste" and "smell" through the science of chemistry. For example, the presence of ammonia in the atmosphere will cause clouding of an HCl solution. An LED/phototransistor combination can easily detect the change from transparency to opaqueness.

The "eyes" of the robot   It is the "eyes" of the robot that are receiving the greatest attention.

ASM80 :F1:IN2.SRC

ISIS-II 8080/8085 MACRO ASSEMBLER, V4.1   INMODU   PAGE   1

```
    LOC  OBJ        LINE           SOURCE STATEMENT
                       1           NAME    INMODULE2
                       2
                       3  ; By declaring label REPEAT to be
                       4  ; PUBLIC, the assembler is notified
                       5  ; that this independently-compiled
                       6  ; IN2 module defines a label (REPEAT)
                       7  ; which is used by another module.
                       8
                       9           CSEG
                      10           PUBLIC  REPEAT
    0000 3E0E         11  START:   MVI     A,0EH   ; SDK-85
    0002 D320         12           OUT     20H     ; SDK-85
    0004 DB21         13  REPEAT:  IN      21H
    0000      C       14           END     START
```

PUBLIC SYMBOLS
REPEAT C 0004

EXTERNAL SYMBOLS

USER SYMBOLS
REPEAT C 0004   START   C 0000

ASSEMBLY COMPLETE,   NO ERRORS

(a)

ASM80 :F1:DELAY.SRC

ISIS-II 8080/8085 MACRO ASSEMBLER, V4.1   DELAYM   PAGE   1

```
    LOC  OBJ        LINE           SOURCE STATEMENT
                       1           NAME    DELAYMODULE
                       2
                       3  ; Using the CSEG directive to produce
                       4  ; DELAY.LST in relocatable code
                       5
                       6           CSEG
    0000 5F           7           MOV     E,A      ; Save A
    0001 0100F0       8           LXI     B,0F000H ; Load delay num
    0004 0B           9  LOOP:    DCX     B        ; Decrement
    0005 78          10           MOV     A,B      ; Set up OR
    0006 B1          11           ORA     C        ; Set flags
    0007 C20400   C  12           JNZ     LOOP     ; Continue delay
    000A 7B         13           MOV     A,E      ; Restore A
                     14           END
```

PUBLIC SYMBOLS

EXTERNAL SYMBOLS

USER SYMBOLS
LOOP   C 0004

ASSEMBLY COMPLETE,   NO ERRORS

(b)

Figure 20.17 Using the PUBLIC/EXTRN pair to handle lables that cross modular boundries: *a)* INM routine with label REPEAT declared PUBLIC. *b)* DELAY module. *c)* OUTM module with REPEAT declared EXTRN, on next page.

```
ASM80 :F1:OUT2.SRC


ISIS-II 8080/8085 MACRO ASSEMBLER, V4.1        OUTMOD    PAGE    1


      LOC   OBJ          LINE           SOURCE STATEMENT
                           1              NAME    OUTMODULE
                           2
                           3   ; By declaring label REPEAT to be
                           4   ; EXTRN, the assembler is notified
                           5   ; that this independently-compiled
                           6   ; OUT2 module uses a label (REPEAT)
                           7   ; that is defined by another module.
                           8
                           9              CSEG
                          10              EXTRN   REPEAT
     0000 D322            11              OUT     22H
     0002 C30000     E    12              JMP     REPEAT
                          13              END

PUBLIC SYMBOLS

EXTERNAL SYMBOLS
REPEAT E 0000

USER SYMBOLS
REPEAT E 0000

ASSEMBLY COMPLETE,    NO ERRORS
```
(c)

A typical imaging system uses a solid-state, charge-coupled-device camera that recognizes objects by a technique known as "training by showing" (comparing an object with images of known objects shown earlier). More advanced systems offer "bin-picking" capability, in which a robot can recognize parts that are randomly positioned atop one another. As with graphics, vision technology labors under an inherent handicap: human vision is massively parallel, while today's computers are primarily serial. Even to begin to simulate human sight, a vision system must process a 100×100 pixel image in under 100 ms—still only a designer's dream.

The muscles of a robot   At the present time, most industrial robots are equipped with a single "arm." To simulate human movement requires several degrees of freedom. The polar coordinate system of Figure 20.20 is a popular method of achieving three degrees of freedom (plus gripper action). For simple movements, each degree of freedom is controlled by a stepper motor (nonservo). For accurate positioning and high speed, the arm movements must be servo-controlled (using feedback). A servomechanism is a cybernetic control system designed for mechanical activation (a "muscle").

For large-scale systems, the arm must be damped to avoid oscillations and to allow rapid but smooth arm motion. Using the same PD technique as our water temperature control system, we damp the robotic arm by adding rate (derivative) information to the proportional error signal (see Figure 20.21a). The mathematics of the system is summarized by Figure 20.21b. By adjusting the damping coefficient (K) and

gain characteristics (A) of a system with a given moment of inertia (I), we can achieve the ideal critically damped motion. Of course, in a realizable system all the required mathematics would be implemented in software, rather than hardware (note that d/dt is a calculus term that means rate of change).

The brains of a robot   In the last 2,400 years, ever since Hippocrates located the seat of the intellect inside the skull, we have made only modest inroads into understanding the human brain—that electrochemical intelligent machine that far outclasses today's computers.

Nevertheless, we can simulate some actions of the human mind, and endow our robot with a very crude form of intelligence. Let's look at several areas in which there is a degree of similarity between computer brain and human brain. In general, the brains of a robot are the software routines stored in program memory.

The Chain-of-Command Concept

Human actions follow a hierarchical goal-directed behavior: a pyramid structure, with a high-level goal at the top (say, ride bicycle), triggering a number of subgoals (such as, move pedals), until the original goal is translated into the numerous "primitive" actions (such as, tense ankle muscles) required to carry out the original high-level goal. Such a hierarchical "chain of command" is the basis of controlling any complex structure, such as a government or a military organization.

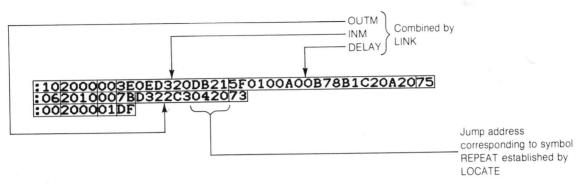

Figure 20.18   Proper jump address generated for label REPEAT.

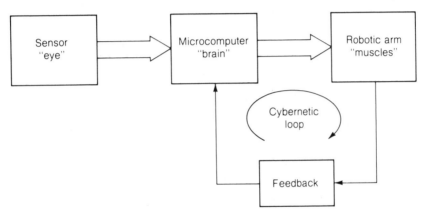

Figure 20.19   Basic robotic system block diagram—a specialized cybernetic control system.

A hierarchical control system limits the complexity of any action (module) to manageable limits regardless of the complexity of the overall system.

How can this hierarchical goal-directed behavior—exhibited by humans—be implemented on a computer? We recognize immediately the principles of top-down modular design! The chain of command in top-down design is represented by levels of software, with the higher levels calling the lower-level subroutines when needed.

First we define a set of midlevel commands (procedures), specifically designed for robot actions. For example, listed below are a few of the commands from the programming language VAL. They are essentially a set of elemental-move commands, passing parameters to lower-level subroutines:

> MOVE(parameters)
> GRASP(parameters)
> OPEN(parameters)
> CLOSE(parameters)

As always, these elemental robot-oriented movement commands can be combined to implement a task:

> PROCEDURE: PICKUP
>   FOR N = 1 to 10
>   MOVE(N)
>   GRASP(N)
> END

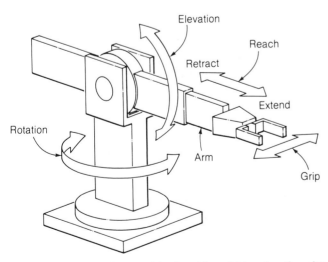

Figure 20.20   Three degrees of freedom (plus grip) based on the polar coordinate system.

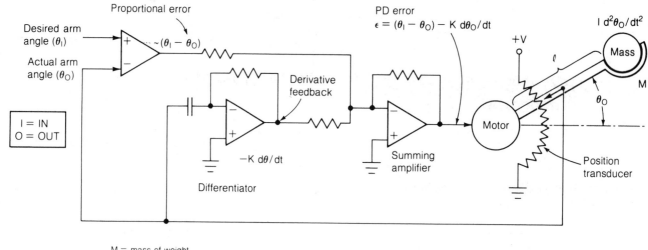

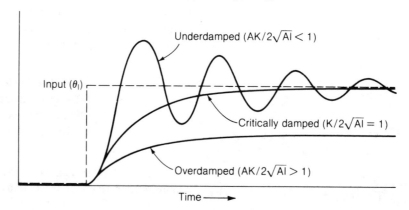

M = mass of weight
ℓ = length of arm
θ_I = input (desired) arm angle
θ_O = output (actual) arm angle
A = motor gain characteristics
K = damping coefficient
I = moment of inertia (I = $M\ell^2$ for massless arm)
$d\theta_O/dt$ = rate of change (speed) of arm angle (angular velocity)
$d^2\theta_O/dt^2$ = angular acceleration
ϵ = damped error signal sent to motor

(a) Damping circuitry added to basic servomechanism

Input torque		Resulting motion
$A\epsilon$	=	$I\, d^2\theta_O/dt^2$
$A[(\theta_I - \theta_O) - K\, d\theta_O/dt]$	=	$I\, d^2\theta_O/dt^2$

or

$$I\, d^2\theta_O/dt^2 + AK\, d\theta_O/dt - A(\theta_I - \theta_O) = 0$$

(b) Equation of motion and resulting step-input response for various degrees of damping

Figure 20.21 The robotic arm as a servomechanism.

ASM80 :F1:STEPR.SRC

ISIS-II 8080/8085 MACRO ASSEMBLER, V4.1   STEPRI   PAGE   1

```
   LOC   OBJ          LINE            SOURCE STATEMENT
                        1             NAME    STEPRIGHT
                        2
                        3      ; This robotics instruction (subroutine) steps
                        4      ; right a number of times equal to the value of
                        5      ; the formal parameter stored in register D.
                        6      ; Register B holds the motor position.
                        7
                        8             CSEG
                        9             PUBLIC STEPR
   0000 78             10  STEPR:  MOV    A,B       ; Bring in motor position
   0001 OF             11          RRC              ; Rotate right once
   0002 47             12          MOV    B,A       ; Store motor position
   0003 E6OF           13          ANI    OFH       ; Mask out upper bits
   0005 D322           14          OUT    22H       ; Perform step right
   0007 2100FF         15          LXI    H,OFFOOH  ; Load delay number
   000A 2B             16  BACK:   DCX    H         ; Count down
   000B 7C             17          MOV    A,H
   000C B5             18          ORA    L         ; HL zero?
   000D C20A00   C     19          JNZ    BACK      ; If not, jmp back
   0010 15             20          DCR    D         ; Last step?
   0011 C20000   C     21          JNZ    STEPR     ; If not, step again
   0014 C9             22          RET
                       23          END
```

PUBLIC SYMBOLS
STEPR C 0000

EXTERNAL SYMBOLS

USER SYMBOLS
BACK   C 000A   STEPR C 0000

ASSEMBLY COMPLETE,   NO ERRORS

(a)

ASM80 :F1:STEPL.SRC

ISIS-II 8080/8085 MACRO ASSEMBLER, V4.1   STEPLE   PAGE   1

```
   LOC   OBJ          LINE            SOURCE STATEMENT
                        1             NAME    STEPLEFT
                        2
                        3      ; This robotics instruction (subroutine) steps
                        4      ; left a number of times equal to the value of
                        5      ; the formal parameter stored in register E.
                        6      ; Register B holds the motor position.
                        7
                        8             CSEG
                        9             PUBLIC STEPL
   0000 78             10  STEPL:  MOV    A,B       ; Bring in motor position
   0001 07             11          RLC              ; Rotate left once
   0002 47             12          MOV    B,A       ; Store motor position
   0003 E6OF           13          ANI    OFH       ; Mask out upper bits
   0005 D322           14          OUT    22H       ; Perform step left
   0007 2100FF         15          LXI    H,OFFOOH  ; Load delay number
   000A 2B             16  BACK:   DCX    H         ; Count down
   000B 7C             17          MOV    A,H
   000C B5             18          ORA    L         ; HL zero?
   000D C20A00   C     19          JNZ    BACK      ; If not, jmp back
   0010 1D             20          DCR    E         ; Last step?
   0011 C20000   C     21          JNZ    STEPL     ; If not, step again
   0014 C9             22          RET
                       23          END
```

PUBLIC SYMBOLS
STEPL C 0000

EXTERNAL SYMBOLS

USER SYMBOLS
BACK   C 000A   STEPL C 0000

ASSEMBLY COMPLETE,   NO ERRORS   (b)

Figure 20.22 Program RADAR using subroutines as independently-assembled modules: *a)* Robotics instruction STEPR. *b)* Robotics instruction STEPL.
c) Main program RADAR, on next page.

```
ASM80 :F1:RADAR.SRC


ISIS-II 8080/8085 MACRO ASSEMBLER, V4.1        RADAR     PAGE    1

        LOC  OBJ        LINE            SOURCE STATEMENT
                          1             NAME   RADAR
                          2
                          3   ; This is the main program.  It calls robotics
                          4   ; instructions STEPL and STEPR to carry out
                          5   ; process RADAR.   Actual parameters 4 and 3
                          6   ; are passed via registers D and E.    Register B
                          7   ; is a global register holding the motor position.
                          8   ; The motor is attached to the low-order nibble of
                          9   ; port 22H (use a buffer for large motors).
                         10
                         11             CSEG
                         12             EXTRN STEPR,STEPL
        0000 3E0E        13   BEGIN:    MVI   A,0EH   ; SDK-85
        0002 D320        14             OUT   20H     ; SDK-85
        0004 0666        15             MVI   B,66H   ; Initialize motor position
        0006 110304      16   LOOP:     LXI   D,0403H ; Pass actual parameters
        0009 CD0000   E  17             CALL  STEPR   ; Robotics instruction
        000C CD0000   E  18             CALL  STEPL   ; Robotics instruction
        000F C30600   C  19             JMP   LOOP    ; Repeat
        0000          C  20             END   BEGIN   ; ID 1st exec. inst

PUBLIC SYMBOLS


EXTERNAL SYMBOLS
STEPL  E 0000    STEPR  E 0000

USER SYMBOLS
BEGIN  C 0000    LOOP    C 0006    STEPL  E 0000    STEPR  E 0000

ASSEMBLY COMPLETE,    NO ERRORS
```

(c)

The robot will raise its arm while closing its gripper in 10 short movements. Of course, procedure PICKUP can now be included in still higher-level routines. When a useful task is written at any level, it can be included in a library of procedures and "linked" to the main program whenever needed. (Note the similarity of our robotics routines to the turtle graphics programs of Chapter 18.)

By including IF-THEN conditional branching and WHILE-DO looping in our high-level programs, the robot can select from one of several different program pathways and continue or break off repetitive tasks depending on sensed conditions. Using EE-PROMs, it can also modify its behavior in response to external conditions, thereby exhibiting a crude form of learning. (Incidentally, procedure PICKUP is written in *pseudocode,* an informal English-like language, similar to a high-level programming language, that allows the program logic to be initially expressed without obeying all the coding rules of a formal computer language.)

Parallel Processing

Another important human characteristic is the ability to process information in parallel at many hierarchical levels. When we touch a hot surface, the reflex action must take place quickly and independently, without passing up through higher thought levels. The same is true of a robot. Low-level data—such as servo feedback information—requires very little processing, but must be done quickly. Analysis of high-level

verbal commands using speech recognition, on the other hand, is at a higher level and requires considerably more processing—but at a slower rate.

When a full range of sensory feedback at all possible levels is considered, even structured programming, with its layers of subroutines, cannot handle the simultaneous actions required. Image processing, in particular, is dependent on a highly parallel organization (such as the human vision system). One solution is to offload parallel tasks to special-purpose peripheral chips (replacing slower-speed software with higher-speed hardware). A *servo-controller* chip, for example, could handle the low-level feedback processing at high speed, while receiving midlevel commands as necessary, and offering midlevel status information when needed. Communication between processing modules is done through a common memory, known as the *mail box.*

Even more exciting are the new fifth generation computers—computers that will break out of the serial-processing constraints of von Neumann machines. Instead of a sequential list of instructions operating upon a separately located data bank, these new parallel machines operate simultaneously on "chunks" of data and instructions (called *packets*).

To match the hardware of these new parallel machines—promising to be 100 times faster than a von Neumann machine—new "declarative" languages such as LISP have been created. Based on formal deductive logic and set theory, they allow a complex task to be subdivided into many simpler tasks *that can be executed in parallel.* (The subtasks created using Pascal, on the other hand, are designed to be executed in series.)

Still we are a long way from true artificial intelligence. To think like a human, a robot must plan and it must problem solve; it must understand language (not just recognize speech); and finally, it must be able to compose music or write a novel, and *know that it has done so.*

MACHINE ASSEMBLY UPDATE—II

Our next machine assembly update brings us closer to home—to a robotics language, an ideal example of modularized programming. In particular, how do we handle independent modules that are *subroutines* (perhaps the most common form of modularized programming)?

Let's have a design goal clearly in mind: using a robotics language consisting of two stepper motor instructions (STEPR and STEPL), write a main program module that continuously steps right four times and left three times. Since our motor scans back and forth continuously as well as gradually turning to the right, we call our program RADAR.

Figure 20.22 shows the three modules that make up our software solution:

- Robotics instruction (subroutine) STEPR (step right).
- Robotics instruction (subroutine) STEPL (step left).
- Main program RADAR.

Notice how the PUBLIC/EXTRN directives handle the problem of labels (STEPR and STEPL) that cross modular boundaries. Parameters 4 and 3 are passed from the main program to the subroutines by way of registers D and E, and the motor position (a global variable) is stored in register B. The label BEGIN after the END directive identifies module RADAR as the main module, and MVI A,0EH as the first executable instruction. With the details of the step-right and step-left processes removed, note how main program RADAR is so much more readable.

After the LINK and LOCATE processes, the three modules are properly linked together and all branch addresses established.

INTELLIGENT-MACHINE UPDATE

The science of cybernetics is often associated with robots and androids—for good reason. The human body requires literally thousands of cybernetic feedback systems in order to regulate the multitude of physical and chemical actions going on continuously. Without feedback systems we would be unable to maintain control—of our environment as well as ourselves.

When parallel processing and declarative languages are combined with cybernetics, our intelligent machine will take control of the physical world. Precisely how much control it takes away from us remains to be seen.

QUESTIONS AND PROBLEMS

1. Give several everyday examples of positive feedback and how it leads to instability.
2. Why is a control system said to be a *closed-loop* system?
3. In a feedback system, to what is the error signal equal?
4. What is the usual result if a negative-feedback system is not damped?
5. How does a PD control system differ from a PID system?
6. What is a *real-time* process?
7. What are the major features of the 8048 single-chip microcomputer that make it ideal for control applications?
8. What features of the 8048 instruction set make it highly code-efficient?
9. How does the 8748 differ from the 8048, and how does this difference relate to product development?
10. When an 8048 system is expanded with additional memory, how are the high-level address lines produced?
11. Referring to Figure 20.11, what feature of the MCS-51 microcontroller group is not found in the MCS-48 group? In turn, what features of the MCS-96 group are not found in the MCS-51 group?
12. Why is feedback not necessary when driving a stepper motor?
13. Under what conditions do we use the PUBLIC and EXTRN directives in a program module?
14. Using robotics instructions STEPL and STEPR (Figure 20.22*a* and *b*), write main program DRUMROLL in which the stepper motor rotates back and forth at ever smaller angles (initialize to 90 degrees).
15. What is a *transducer?* (Consult a dictionary.)
16. How does the RAL instruction (line 33) of Figure 20.16 mask out the direction bit *and* double the delay time?
17. What is *pseudocode?*
18. By starting with an elemental command set (of procedures) for running a lap, construct a high-level routine (using pseudocode) for running a mile (four laps).
19. What are the three major blocks of a robotic system?
20. Why is parallel processing so crucial for sophisticated robotic action?
21. Rather than generating derivative feedback electronically as shown in Figure 20.21, could we achieve the same effect mechanically by adding a "shock absorber" to the robotic arm? What is the advantage of the electronic method?

chapter 21

Data Communication: Serial I/O

With the invention of the drum, our early ancestors discovered a great deal about communication at a distance. Information could best be sent asynchronously in serial form, coded in pulses, and modulated by a hollow log. Today, communication at a distance also often involves the techniques of conversion, coding, modulation, and asynchronous transmission.

Today's communication systems, however, must do a great deal more, for microcomputers are increasingly being linked together in distributed processing networks, or accessed from remote terminals over telephone lines, or called on to transmit data at ultrahigh rates.

Because data communication implies information transfer at a distance, there is a strong need to reduce the number of interconnecting lines. Therefore, unlike the parallel interfacing techniques discussed in Chapter 18, serial format is most often used for data transmission, and address/control/sync information is time multiplexed with the data (rather than sent on separate lines). For human beings, the ear is a serial, one-word-at-a-time data-communication system, while the eye is massively parallel. Although "a picture is worth a thousand words," over long distances it often is more convenient to transmit the spoken word.

SYNCHRONOUS VS ASYNCHRONOUS

As with the simple I/O and interfacing considerations of Chapter 18, the most basic question we can ask about data communication is: Is it synchronous or asynchronous? Clocked or unclocked?

- To communicate asynchronously is to transmit data words one at a time at irregular intervals and rates. The arrival of the data is *unpredictable*.

- To communicate synchronously, both receiver and transmitter are driven at the same clock rate and phase, and data flow occurs precisely in step with this common clock. The arrival of the data is *predictable*.

Asynchronous transmission, known as *start/stop* transmission, is the less sophisticated of the two. Generally used with human-machine interfaces (where the transmission is irregular), asynchronous transmission is reserved for data-transfer rates below 10,000 b/s. In asynchronous transmission systems, the clocks of receiver and transmitter are unmatched and may differ slightly in frequency and phase. Since data characters come at irregular rates (any time), the necessary timing and synchronization information is derived *from each character transmitted*. To assure proper reception of data, each serial byte of a TTY (teletype) bit stream is bracketed (framed) by synchronizing information called *start* and *stop* bits (Figure 21.1).

In the idle condition, when information is not being transmitted, the serial line is high (marking time). To signal the start of transmission, the transmitter precedes each byte with a logic 0 start bit. The negative-going (leading) edge of this start bit is used by the receiver to synchronize *each character*. By the time the last bit is read in, the receive clock will be slightly out of phase (skewed) from the transmitted bits—but not enough to prevent proper capture of the byte. The stop bits at the end of each character set up the negative-going start bit and allow a short "breathing space" when characters are being transmitted at the maximum rate. (If spaces exist between characters, the stop bits are indistinguishable from the idle state.) The start and stop bits rep-

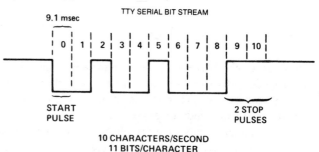

Reproduced by permission of Intel Corp.

Figure 21.1 TTY asynchronous serial-transmission format (110 baud).

286

resent a timing overhead that can take up to 20% of the total transmission time.

When high data-transfer rates are required, above approximately 20,000 b/s, the more complex synchronous method is adopted. Synchronous transmission, usually reserved for machine-to-machine communication, sends information in *packets* (blocks) rather than individually. For each block, receiver and transmitter are matched initially by the transmission of a special sync pattern consisting of one or more synchronization characters. Special error-checking words at the end of each packet provide built-in error checking. Since synchronization must be maintained over a fairly long stream of data, the transmitter and receiver clocks must be precisely matched. The simplest method is to apply the same external clock signal to both transmitter and receiver. Because a separate clock signal requires a separate line, more often clock pulses are mixed in (multiplexed) with the data on the same line. The receiver recovers (demultiplexes) the clock signal from the information stream and phase-locks its clock to that of the transmitter. Quite often the data itself provides all the required clocking information. (Special coding formats assure that sufficient signal transitions occur to maintain phase lock.) With synchronous systems the timing pulse overhead is only about 1 percent. Figure 21.2 compares synchronous with asynchronous serial data transmission.

Asynchronous transmission is the more common of the two because the majority of microcomputer applications involve low-speed terminals and small computer systems. We will be taking a closer look at both synchronous and asynchronous data communication techniques later in this chapter. First, let's look at several features that are common to both.

SIMPLEX/DUPLEX TRANSMISSION

Physically, communication between the CPU and peripheral can take place in one of the three basic modes shown in Figure 21.3. As diagrammed, *simplex* transmission is unidirectional (one direction only), *half-duplex* is bidirectional (one direction at a time), and *full duplex* is simultaneous bidirectional (both directions at the same time). Which of these three modes of communication is chosen depends on a number of factors, many of which are covered in this chapter.

TRANSMISSION CODES

Providing that each character is first converted into an alphanumeric code, a computer can, in a sense, speak in English. When using an alphanumeric code, each letter or symbol is converted into a unique sequence of binary bits.

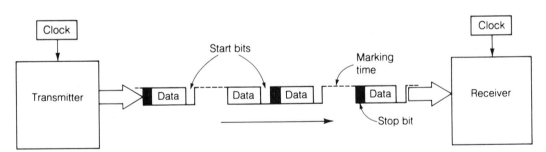

(*a*) Asynchronous system—data flow at irregular rates and intervals, requiring each data word to be synchronized by the receiver

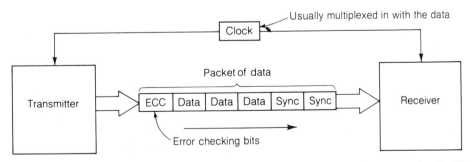

(*b*) Synchronous system—data flow at regular rates; once receiver and transmitter are synchronized by the initial sync words, data (or additional sync characters) flow continuously

Figure 21.2 Asynchronous/synchronous comparison.

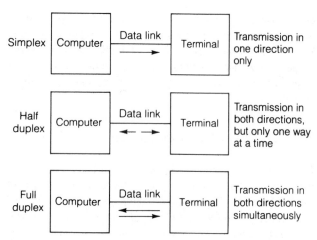

Figure 21.3 Simplex, half-duplex, and full-duplex communications.

In response to the need for standardization, the American National Standards Institute has published an American Standard Code for Information Interchange (known as the *ASCII code*). ASCII, now widely used in the computer industry, uses 7 bits in its code to provide 128 combinations

for coding letters, numbers, and symbols (see Figure 21.4). When sent in serial form, ASCII adds an extra parity bit. Extended Binary-Coded Decimal Interchange Code (EBCDIC), a 9-bit code giving 256 combinations, is the standard language of IBM equipment.

As we learned in Chapter 18, the North American Presentation Level Protocol Syntax (NAPLPS), an extension (a superset) of ASCII, provides a communication standard for the exchange of text and graphical information among computers.

BUS AND COMMUNICATION STANDARDS

Imagine a world of intercommunications without standards—without uniform guidelines for transferring information from point to point. For each new product, the designer would create a unique interface from scratch. For every 100 systems there would be 100 new cables and 100 new documentation packages.

b_4	b_3	b_2	b_1	COLUMN / ROW	0 0 0 / 0	0 0 1 / 1	0 1 0 / 2	0 1 1 / 3	1 0 0 / 4	1 0 1 / 5	1 1 0 / 6	1 1 1 / 7
0	0	0	0	0	NUL	DLE	SP	0	@	P	`	p
0	0	0	1	1	SOH	DC1	!	1	A	Q	a	q
0	0	1	0	2	STX	DC2	''	2	B	R	b	r
0	0	1	1	3	ETX	DC3	#	3	C	S	c	s
0	1	0	0	4	EOT	DC4	$	4	D	T	d	t
0	1	0	1	5	ENQ	NAK	%	5	E	U	e	u
0	1	1	0	6	ACK	SYN	&	6	F	V	f	v
0	1	1	1	7	BEL	ETB	'	7	G	W	g	w
1	0	0	0	8	BS	CAN	(	8	H	X	h	x
1	0	0	1	9	HT	EM	)	9	I	Y	i	y
1	0	1	0	A	LF	SUB	*	:	J	Z	j	z
1	0	1	1	B	VT	ESC	+	;	K	[	k	{
1	1	0	0	C	FF	FS	,	<	L	\	l	|
1	1	0	1	D	CR	GS	–	=	M	]	m	}
1	1	1	0	E	SO	RS	.	>	N	^	n	~
1	1	1	1	F	SI	US	/	?	O	_	o	DEL

Hex | Machine commands | Numbers and symbols | Uppercase | Lowercase

Figure 21.4 American Standard Code for Information Interchange (ASCII).

Often, however, a scheme proposed by one manufacturer proves to be successful and is adopted by other manufacturers—a standard is born. Instead of hundreds of bus schemes, there is a mere handful, each designed to satisfy the needs of a particular area of data communication. Shown in Figure 21.5 are six popular existing and proposed communication bus standards. In general, they are categorized according to distance and rate of transmission, as well as parallel or serial. (Although a parallel standard, the IEEE488 interface bus is primarily used as a communication link and is therefore included in this chapter.)

Serial Standards

RS-232C In terms of the present computer and communications world, the Electronic Industries Association (EIA) RS-232C is *the* standard; therefore it deserves most of our attention.

The full title of the RS-232C standard is, "Interface Between Data Terminal Equipment and Data Communication Equipment Employing Serial Binary Data Interchange." *Data Terminal Equipment* (DTE) refers to any device that transmits or receives information, and *Data Communication Equipment* (DCE) refers to any device that "passes on" information. Computers and CRT terminals belong in the DTE category, while modems (which connect telephone circuits to computers) fall in the DCE category (modems are covered later in this chapter).

The RS-232C serial communication standard was one of the first serial standards developed, and in fact predates integrated circuits. Therefore, the logic levels are not defined in terms of the standard +5 volt IC levels. Instead, the RS-232C standard defines a space or logic 0 as a voltage level from +3 to +25, and a mark or logic 1 as a voltage level from −3 to −25. Since these voltages are wholly incompatible with +5 volt microcomputer systems, special interfacing circuitry is required. Figure 21.6 shows the use of an MC1489 and MC1488 driver/receiver pair to effect communication to an old-style CRT.

Although not defined in the RS-232C standard, the 25-pin connector (DB-25 of Figure 21.7a) has become the defacto standard for the mechanical interface. However, some manufacturers (notably IBM) use a different connector on much of their equipment.

Glancing over the RS-232C line assignments of Figure 21.7a, it is clear that the 25-pin standard was originally intended for use with telephones and modems. However, in today's computer oriented world, most serial data communication is simple data transfer, without the need for the numerous supervisory, control, or handshaking signals provided. Therefore, the minimum system of Figure 21.7b is also the most common. Note that pins 2 and 3 must be crossed if both pieces of equipment fall into the same category.

Just remember when using RS-232C that the standard was specifically designed for telephone facilities and not as a general serial input/output port. Therefore, when applying the standard to printers and other similar peripherals some pin modifications may be required.

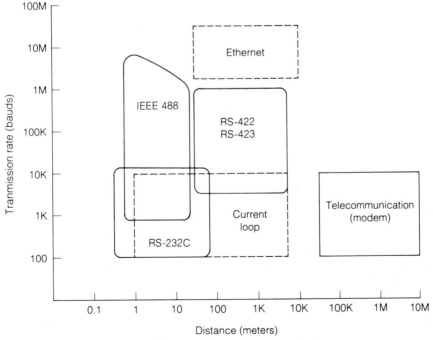

Figure 21.5 Microcomputer parallel and serial communication standards.

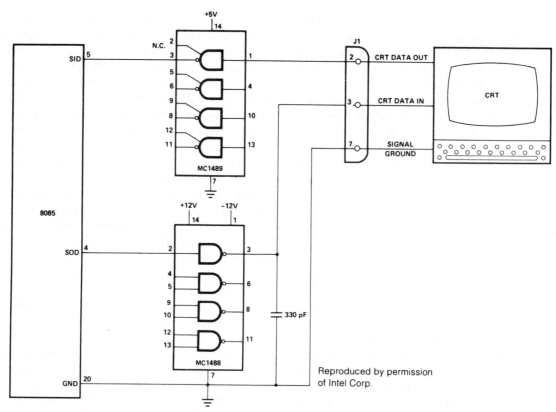

Figure 21.6   RS-232C/computer interface.

Unfortunately, the high-impedance, single-ended termination restructed the line length to about 50 feet and the data transmission rate to 20 kilobauds. For distances of up to several miles, the signal can be amplified by line drivers and a terminal can be connected to the computer over twisted pair wires.

RS-442A   By using differential signals and low-Z drivers for improved noise rejection, the RS-442A standard extends the transmission rate to 10 megabauds and the transmission distance to more than 5,000 feet (see Figure 21.8). Widespread acceptance of RS-232C has decreased the popularity of the more advanced RS-442A and other similar standards (RS-423A and RS-449).

20/60 mA current loop   Teletypewriters (TTY), introduced in the early 1960s, are responsible for the popularity of the current loop. A current loop is a closed circular path connecting transmitter with teletype (Figure 21.9a). The return path is often replaced with a common ground. A logic 1 is represented by a flow of 20 mA (or 60 mA), and a logic 0 is represented by no flow of current.

By using current rather than voltage as the logic standard, the voltage drops and noise that normally would occur on a long transmission line are suppressed. The standard transmission rate for TTY is also 110 bauds. Often, systems

requiring current loops can also make use of the standard RS-232C connector format. Although the current loop is still a common form of data transmission, its use is decreasing.

To interface a TTY to the 8085, the transistor is often used as the current source. The send/receive current loop is created as shown in Figure 21.9b.

Parallel Standards—IEEE 488

The IEEE 488 standard (also known as the *general-purpose interface bus*—or GPIB) provides a communication link between the CPU and a wide variety of programmable peripherals and instrumentation systems. Following the need to keep the number of interconnecting lines to a minimum, the GPIB standard multiplexes the data, address, and control information on the same set of eight lines.

The 24 lines composing the GPIB bus consist of three types of signals: eight data/address/control bus lines, three handshake lines, and five bus-interface management lines (see Figure 21.10). The remaining lines are used for grounding and shielding.

With one controller, up to eight devices can be interconnected using the format of Figure 21.11. Each device can be any combination of talker (transmitter), listener (receiver), and controller. The maximum cable length is 20 meters, with

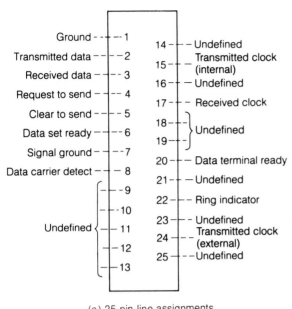

(a) 25 pin line assignments

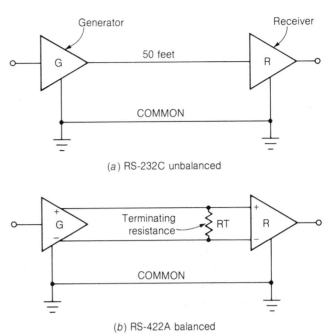

(a) RS-232C unbalanced

(b) RS-422A balanced

Figure 21.8 Balanced and unbalanced circuits.

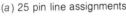

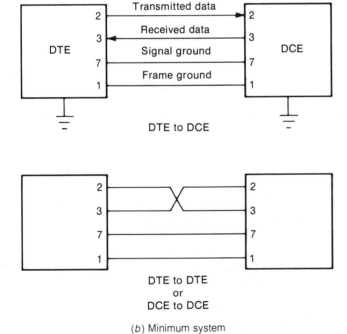

(b) Minimum system

Figure 21.7 Interfacing to the RS-232C standard.

no more than 2 meters per device. (New GPIB "extenders" increase the maximum cable length to 1000 meters.)

With the help of the five bus-management lines, data are transferred at up to 1 Mbyte/s using any of the three basic I/O techniques: programmed I/O, interrupt I/O, and DMA I/O. For example, if device D is to transmit (talk) onto the bus (Figure 21.11), the controller (computer) first must program D as a "talker." This is accomplished by transmitting

a special command byte to device D while ATN is low. (Bits D_0 through D_4 are D's address; bits D_5 and D_6 program D as a "talker.") When ATN is high, device D can transmit data onto the bus using a handshake sequence (programmed I/O).

To cause device B to listen, the sequence is similar. Device B is addressed and programmed as a "listener" by a special command word sent by the controller (ATN low). When ATN goes high, data are sent to device B by way of handshake signals.

The IEEE 488 system has been successful because it interfaces equally well with most instrumentation systems and most microprocessors.

SID AND SOD

To provide a single line of serial I/O, without tying up an 8-bit I/O port, the 8085 microprocessor reserves pins 4 and 5 for the SID (serial in data) and SOD (serial out data) I/O lines (see Figure 21.6). Sounding much like a nursery rhyme, SID and SOD are serviced by instructions RIM and SIM. Recall from Chapter 16 that instructions RIM (read interrupt mask) and SIM (set interrupt mask) were also used for enabling interrupts and for determining interrupt status. Instructions RIM and SIM, therefore, are dual purpose.

Referring to Figure 21.12, here is how the serial I/O process is accomplished:

• Each time a RIM instruction is executed, the status of the SID pin is read into bit 7 of the accumulator.

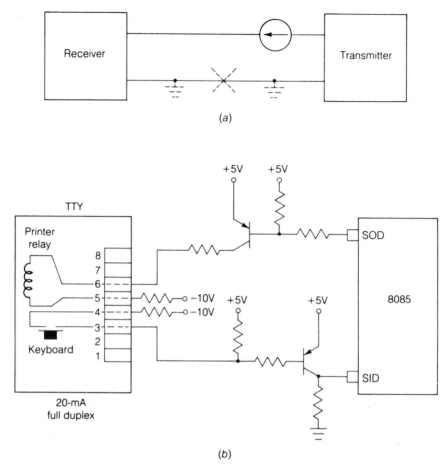

Figure 21.9 Communication by current loop: *a)* Current-loop configuration. *b)* 8085 20-mA current-loop/TTY communication.

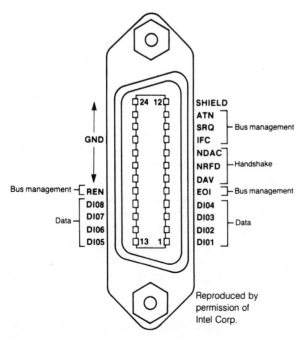

Figure 21.10 GPIB connector and signal categories.

- Each time a SIM instruction is executed, bit 7 of the accumulator is latched into the SOD output (providing that enable bit 6 of the accumulator is set to 1).

In the Questions and Problems section, we will have an opportunity to write a program that uses the SID and SOD single-bit I/O lines.

THE 8251A PROGRAMMABLE COMMUNICATION INTERFACE (USART)

As an application of several of the data-communication topics introduced so far, Figure 21.13 illustrates one of the simplest and most common forms of data communication: simplex, asynchronous, 110-baud, point-to-point (two-station), serial transmission of data to a printer. We assume the printer is close enough to the CPU to warrant direct RS-232C or current-loop interconnections. Timing and identification of data are done asynchronously, by way of the start-and-stop bit format of Figure 21.1. Because of the slow rate

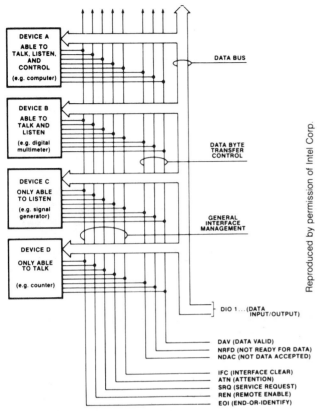

Reproduced by permission of Intel Corp.

Figure 21.11 GPIB interfacing and bus structure.

of transmission, handshaking is not required. (We assume the receiver can accept and "digest" the data at 110 bauds. If it cannot, information will be lost.) The Universal Synchronous/Asynchronous Receiver/Transmitter (USART) is the most common device for implementing such a system.

Basic Description

The 8251A *Programmable Communication Interface* (or USART) is basically a parallel-to-serial/serial-to-parallel converter that is at home in either asynchronous or synchronous environments. (A UART—Universal Asynchronous Receiver/Transmitter—operates in the asynchronous mode only.)

The internal block diagram of the 8251A is given in Figure 21.14. Within the various blocks are found parallel and serial buffers, and control and status registers. (The C/$\overline{D}$ line differentiates between control/status and data registers.) Also shown are software-serviced 1-bit I/O ports ($\overline{CTS}$, $\overline{RTS}$, $\overline{DSR}$, $\overline{DTR}$), which are provided for controlling various external hardware in certain applications. These 1-bit I/O ports will not be required by our TTY system.

Adding simplified versions of the 8251A block diagram to our asynchronous CPU-to-TTY communication system, we arrive at the design of Figure 21.15.

The next step is to configure the USART by writing the correct words to the two control registers (mode and command).

Control-Word Format

The 8251A is software-programmed for asynchronous transmission by writing the two control words of Figure 21.16*a* into the internal control registers. Basically, the *mode-control word* sets the overall configuration, and the *command word* refines the operation within that configuration. (The CPU differentiates between a mode word and a command word by the order in which they are written. After system reset, the next input to the 8251A must be a mode word. All control words written after that will automatically be interpreted as command words.)

To match our requirements for asynchronous transmission, the mode and command words take on the configuration of Figure 21.16*b*. We have arbitrarily chosen the baud rate to equal the clock rate (the baud rate also can be programmed to equal $\frac{1}{16}$ or $\frac{1}{64}$ the clock rate), 8-bit characters, even parity, and one stop bit. Note that selecting the baud-rate factor also automatically selects the asynchronous mode of operation.

Status-Read Format

If we adopt the polled (programmed I/O) mode of operation, it will be necessary to determine when various data registers are empty and to check error flags. By reading this information from the 8251A status register of Figure 21.17, we can implement the polled mode of operation.

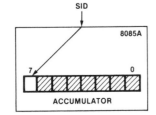

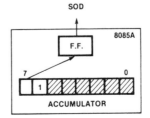

Figure 21.12 Effect of RIM and SIM instructions.

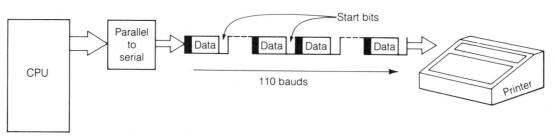

Figure 21.13 Simplex, asynchronous, serial data flow to a printer.

Completed Hardware/Software Design

Our final system design is revealed in Figure 21.18a (interrupt I/O) and 21.18b (programmed I/O).

Briefly, the operation of the system is as follows: under polled or interrupt control, the CPU writes the next word to be transmitted into the *parallel* buffer using the where/when waveforms of Figure 21.19. Whenever the *serial* transmit buffer becomes empty, this next data word is immediately (and automatically) transferred from the parallel buffer to the serial buffer. The start, stop, and parity bits are automatically added and the bits are "walked out" of the TxD pin in serial format at the rate controlled by the TxC (transmit clock) input (start bit followed by least significant bit).

As soon as the parallel buffer is again empty, an interrupt is automatically generated by the TxRDY (transmit ready) pin, and the CPU writes the next word into the parallel buffer (giving the 8251A the same "on deck/at bat" double-buff-

ered feature as the 8155A). For the polled operation of Figure 21.18b, the CPU continuously reads the state of the TxRDY status flag, looking for the "parallel register empty" condition.

On the receiving end, a "print character" operation begins when each start bit is detected and mechanical operation is initiated. When all data, start, stop, and parity bits have been received (number of bits times 9.09 msec/bit), a character is struck. The stop bits give the printing mechanism time to prepare for the next start bit.

On many serial communications systems, the receiving end is also a USART (or UART), programmed for serial reception of data (Figure 21.20). As before, each transmitted word is synchronized by the high-to-low transition of each start bit. To assure a valid start bit, the receive USART automatically rechecks the state of the input line approximately $\frac{1}{2}$-bit period after the high-to-low transition. If the input is still low, a valid start bit—rather than a glitch—is assumed, and the bits are clocked into the RxD (receive data)

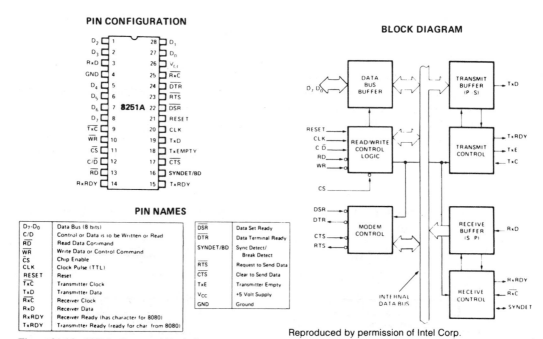

Figure 21.14 8251A pin-out and block diagram.

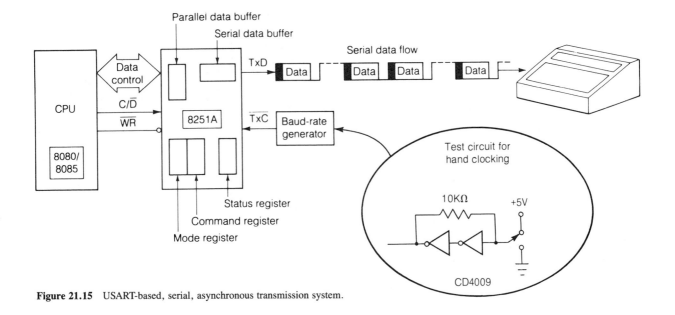

Figure 21.15 USART-based, serial, asynchronous transmission system.

pin at a rate controlled by the RxC (receive clock) input pin. When a full word is strobed into the serial buffer, it is stripped of its parity, start, and stop bits and transferred to the parallel buffer. The receiving device is immediately notified of the "parallel buffer full" condition by way of the RxRDY interrupt pin or a polling of the RxRDY status flag. A read operation removes the word from the 8251A's parallel buffer.

Software-accessible status flags within the receive 8251A (see Figure 21.17) are set to detect parity, overrun (printer does not read in a character before the next one becomes available), or framing (valid stop bit not detected) errors. (Without the 8251A, errors would have to be detected using the parity flag within the 8080/8085.)

Once again we find the work load on the CPU considerably reduced by the use of a programmable peripheral chip. To the CPU the transmit and receive operations are nothing more than interrupt or programmed I/O operations to and from a parallel register. All other aspects of asynchronous serial transmission are handled automatically by the 8251A.

SYNCHRONOUS COMMUNICATION PROTOCOLS

Now let's turn our attention back to *synchronous* serial communication, where machines talk to machines over data links and networks at a high rate of data transmission.

The printer of our previous example is known as a *dumb terminal* because it merely displays data just as it receives it. A dumb terminal cannot check for errors, cannot be combined with other terminals on the same line and addressed, cannot ask for retransmission of data should an error occur, and cannot operate synchronously.

Smart terminals, on the other hand, contain internal processing capability (intelligence) and can perform all of these functions and more. Therefore, smart terminals (also known as *intelligent terminals*) require communication protocols.

A *communication protocol* is a set of rules governing information flow in a "smart" (synchronous) data-communication system. The earliest protocols, which generally specified only the data link portion of the overall communications picture, are known as *data link control protocols*.

The Data Link Control Protocol

A *data link* includes the modems, serial communications interfaces, and the communication channel—and nothing else. The data link does not include the computers, terminals, and other I/O devices at each end of the line. The *data link control protocol* is further broken down into three basic categories:

- Character oriented
- Byte oriented
- Bit oriented

The character oriented protocol—the first to appear on the scene—is best represented by IBM's *BInary SYNchronous Communications* protocol (BISYNC). As seen by the transmission format of Figure 21.21a, BISYNC uses special characters to synchronize transmitter and receiver and to indicate the beginning and end of the header and text portions of the message.

Its most serious flaw is that the need for constant acknowledgment limited its operation to half-duplex. In addition, a

MODE INSTRUCTION FORMAT, ASYNCHRONOUS MODE

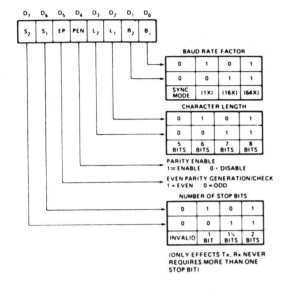

COMMAND INSTRUCTION DEFINITION

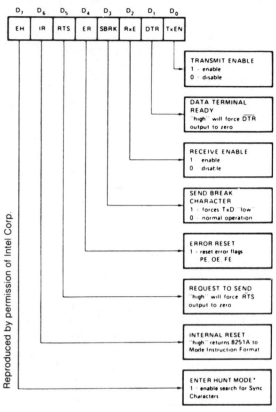

Reproduced by permission of Intel Corp.

(a) Format

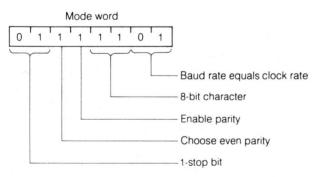

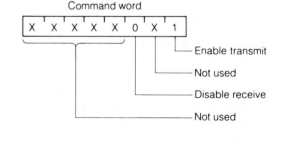

(b) Programmed for asynchronous transmission

Figure 21.16   8251A mode and command words.

character oriented protocol is not inherently *transparent*. That is, the special bit sequences making up the various control characters can appear in the data field. We must take care to ensure that data and control information is properly interpreted.

One solution to the problem was the *byte oriented* protocol. By including in the header the number of bytes contained in the data field there is no possibility of confusion.

However, the added length of the header made byte oriented protocols rather inefficient.

The *bit oriented* protocol, the latest and most advanced of the three, uses a rather novel method to achieve transparency. As shown by IBM's *Synchronous Data Link Control* (SDLC) of Figure 21.21b, the opening and closing flags consist of a 01111110 sequence. To prevent this unique flag

STATUS READ DEFINITION

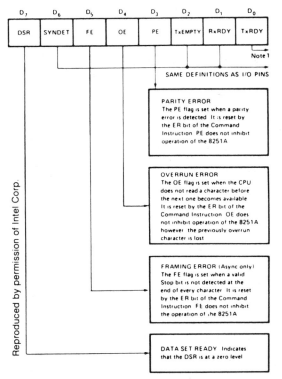

Figure 21.17 8251A status-word format.

word from appearing anywhere in the text, a binary zero bit is automatically inserted after five contiguous ones are detected. The inserted zeroes are automatically deleted in the received bit stream. This technique results in full-duplex operation based on one standard frame format for all types of messages. The data field can vary in length and can be configured in any code structure—binary, BCD, ASCII, etc. Error checking is via the well-known cyclic redundancy-check characters, also used in magnetic storage protocols.

LSI Protocol-Control Chips

Because of the complexity of synchronous protocols, the housekeeping details often are best handled by specialized programmable peripheral chips (hardware) rather than programming action (software). The 8273 is a typical example.

The 8273 *Programmable HDLC/SDLC Protocol Controller* (shown in simplified form in Figure 21.22a) handles the HDLC and SDLC bit-oriented protocols, and does for "smart" terminals what the 8251A does for "dumb" terminals. When information is sent to a secondary station, the 8273 helps to assemble an HDLC or SDLC frame for transmission and to disassemble a frame upon reception. As with the 8251A, it can be used in either synchronous or asynchronous applications.

The 8273 can also handle loop-mode SDLC data links, popular because of a drastic reduction in hardware and software requirements. In the loop mode, the substations (slave stations) are daisy-chained on a single line (a loop) as shown in Figure 21.22b. The data frames sent out on the loop by the 8273 loop controller (master) are relayed from station to station. Any secondary station finding its address in the address field inputs the data from that frame. Future protocol chips will be multilingual and will feature automatic protocol recognition in order to provide transparent communication (operator need not be aware of protocol used).

MULTIUSER SYSTEMS AND LOCAL AREA NETWORKS (LANs)

When the simple data link between two terminals is expanded to include a multiuser/multifunction collection of terminals that share data and peripherals, it is known as a *shared resource* system. The two alternatives are *multiuser* systems and *local area networks* (LANs). The two approaches are diagrammed in Figure 21.23.

In a typical multiuser system (Figure 21.23a), each workstation is an inexpensive dumb terminal, with its own processor in the main cabinet instead of within each workstation. The reduced cost of each work station greatly reduces the cost of the overall system. A multiuser system, however, is usually limited in the number of work stations it can support (typically a dozen).

If our system requires a large number of workstations, or we have already acquired a number of microcomputers, then a LAN may be the best approach. Furthermore, as shown in Figure 21.23b, a LAN offers three basic *topologies* (configurations). The star configuration is used for systems requiring centralized control. The string and loop configurations are often found in distributed control systems, where the cable acts as a bus and each terminal can gain network control as the need arises. In the more common star and bus configurations, a central *file server* usually controls the distribution and storage of data.

The final stage of network evolution will produce the *dispersed* processing network. Rather than the top-down hierarchically (master/slave) oriented distributed system, the processing capability is parceled out (dispersed) among many equally accessible multifunction/multiprotocol information stations, all in direct communication.

Channel Access

Channel access to a network (Who gets to use the common line?) is by way of *polling* or *contention* techniques such as token passing and collision detection.

Token passing *Token passing,* often associated with ring networks, is a polling process in which a special "token"

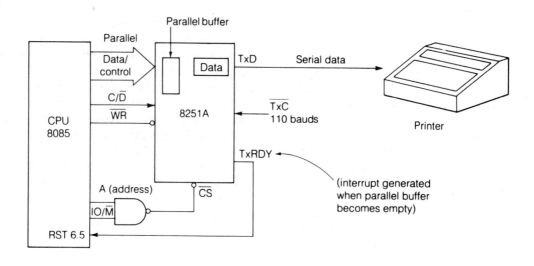

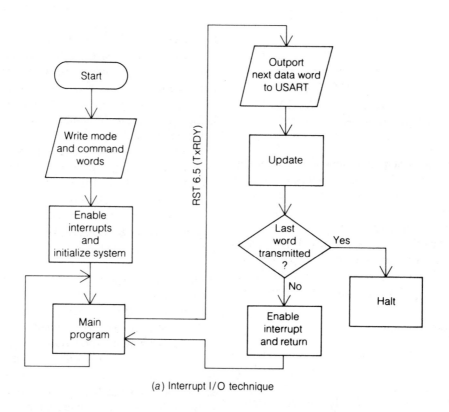

(a) Interrupt I/O technique

Figure 21.18   USART-based asynchronous transmission to TTY.

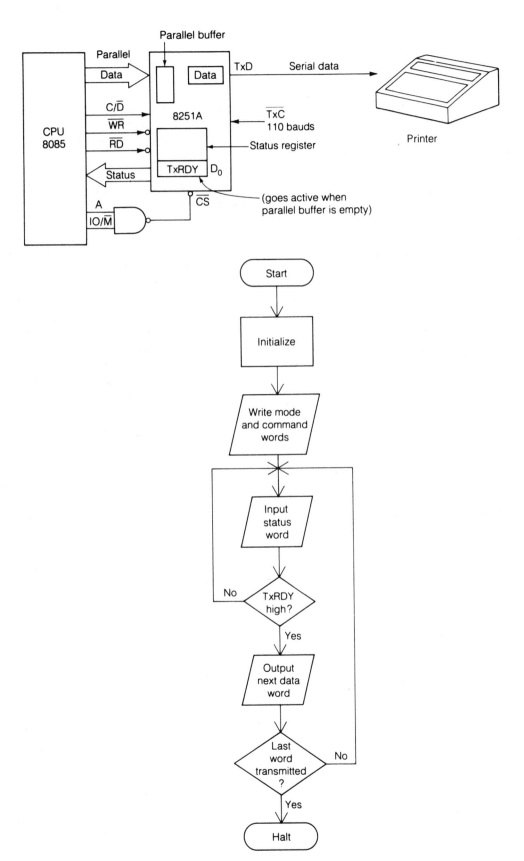

(*b*) Programmed I/O technique

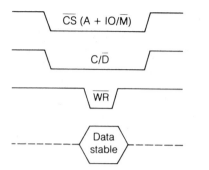

Figure 21.19 8085 waveforms for writing next data word to parallel buffer.

word circulates around the loop from node to node. When a node wishes to transmit, it captures and holds the token, giving it exclusive right to the channel. When finished sending its message, the token is placed back into circulation. Because token-passing networks are deterministic (all events can be predetermined by a control algorithm), they are ideally suited for real-time application like process control.

Collision detection *Collision detection* is a random access arbitration technique built into the CSMA/CD (carrier-sense, multiple-access with collision detection) protocol. Collision detection gives each node the ability to detect traffic on the channel. As soon as the channel is quiet, any of the nodes can transmit (known as *listen-before-talking*). On those rare occasions when two nodes attempt to begin transmission simultaneously, the messages will collide, resulting in a change in channel energy. When the collision (energy burst) is detected, both transmitters withhold activity for a random period of time, then attempt to transmit again. Because access to the network is "probabilistic" (based on random access), it is not useful for real-time operations, but is highly efficient in an office environment.

Layered Protocols

When the simple data link control protocols—which basically specify the data format between two communication nodes—are expanded to handle communication networks, we create the *layered* protocol. A layered protocol expands to include all aspects of network communication, from the highest-level *application* layer to the lowest-level *physical* layer.

The goal of the layered protocol is to avoid the chaos of a Tower of Babel—to promote universal communication between any and all brands of computers (worldwide!). To help develop a model for this *open-systems interconnection,* the International Standards Organization (ISO) recommended the seven-layered protocol shown in Figure 21.24. The seven layers of the ISO model are designed to include all aspects of network communication, and are based on the modularized, hierarchical (general-to-specific) concept that is also the basis of software development and robotics.

To help understand the layered approach, imagine the process of communication between ships at sea. Logically, communication between ships takes place at the captain level (the highest layer). However, in reality all communication must take place at the lowest layer because that is where the physical link between ships is specified. When communication takes place between captains, the high-level message issued by one captain must filter down through the various layers to the bottom physical layer. It is then sent over the physical link to the receiving station, where the message works it way up to the captain level.

Briefly, based on this analogy:

- The *physical* layer includes the ship-to-ship communication hardware, such as light beam modulation.

- The *data-link* layer (analogous to the older data link control protocol) specifies the data format (Morse code) between two ships (nodes) and provides for error checking.

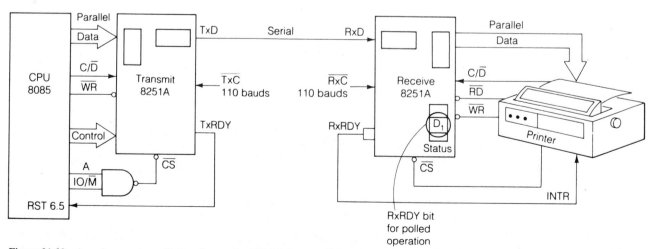

Figure 21.20 Asynchronous transmission using receive USART (interrupt I/O).

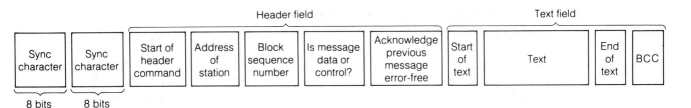

(a) Binary SYNchronous Communications (BISYNC) protocol frame

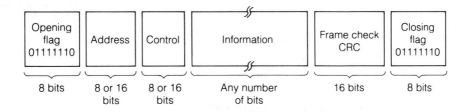

(b) Synchronous Data-link Control (SDLC) frame

Figure 21.21 Two popular serial communication protocols.

- The *network control* layer controls the flow of messages between *all* the ships in the network. For example, if a message sent from ship A to ship C must pass through ship B, how does ship B relay the message?

- The *transport* layer takes care of matters involved in verifying that the message got from ship A to ship C (perhaps no one on ship B was watching to relay the message).

- The *session* layer is under control of the communication officer who establishes and terminates *sessions* (specific periods of communication) between ships. It is also the responsibility of this layer to ensure that all messages are complete before relaying them on to the next higher layer.

- The *presentation* layer is where the first officer resides. It is his responsibility to translate the encoded data from Morse code to English and *present* it to the captain.

- The *applications* layer is at the captain level. In cooperation with other captains, and acting on orders sent by a higher authority (the *user*), this layer carries out a specific task. This layer is also responsible for overall systems management (that is, how functions are to be distributed among the various ships in the fleet).

The layered modular approach—in which each layer is relatively independent of the others—allows the network system to be flexible and to easily adapt to new technology and changing standards. For example, any one layer can be replaced without changing the entire design.

The Local Area Network Landscape

At first glance, the LAN marketplace, with its many varieties of hardware and software, may seem hopelessly fractured. In reality, however, they all occupy one of the following three tiers: mainframe networks, which exchange data at ultrahigh speeds; minicomputer "backbone" networks, with their reduced but still high-speed (10 Mbps) data exchanges, and personal computer "department cluster" networks, with their low-cost and moderate speed (1 Mbps) requirements. LANs can even be nested, with clusters of PC LANs linked together along a tier two backbone. *Ethernet* is the defacto standard for the minicomputer tier, and *Starlan* is vying for the same honor in the PC tier.

Ethernet *Ethernet* is a local serial data-communication network that is equivalent to layers 1 and 2 of the seven layer ISO model. Under joint development by Xerox, Digital Equipment, and Intel, Ethernet uses collision detection to arbitrate the transmission of data packets. (*Collision detection* is part of the data link layer).

Figure 21.25 depicts a typical medium-scale Ethernet configuration, in which eight peripherals communicate over a 50-ohm coaxial cable system at a data rate of 10 million b/s. Each of the two segments, interconnected by a repeater, can be as long as 500 meters. As many as 100 transceivers per segment can be accommodated, with a maximum separation of 2.5 kilometers.

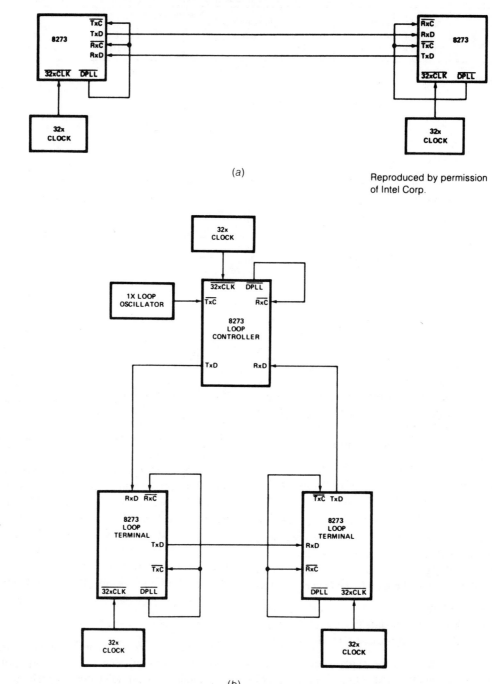

Asynchronous — No Modems — Duplex or Half Duplex

(a)

Reproduced by permission
of Intel Corp.

(b)

Figure 21.22 Serial communication using the 8273 protocol controller: *a)* Direct string mode. *b)* Loop mode.

Starlan Starlan, a tier three office-environment LAN based on collision detection, helps to reduce costs by tapping into the installed telephone system network. Special VLSI chips (the 82588 LAN controller) reduce the cost of each network node. LAN software, designed to implement all seven layers of the ISO model, will soon result in a complete LAN package.

TELECOMMUNICATIONS

The global telephone network is the most extensive and readily available communication system presently in use. It is only natural for computers to look to the telephone system for communication with remote locations.

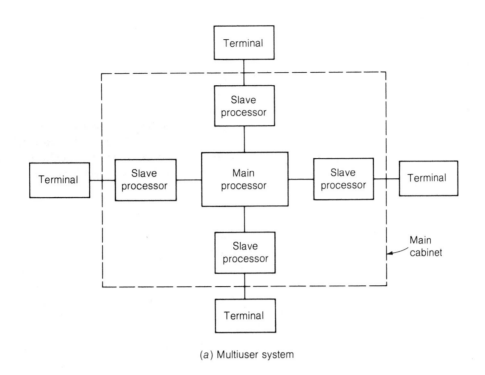

(a) Multiuser system

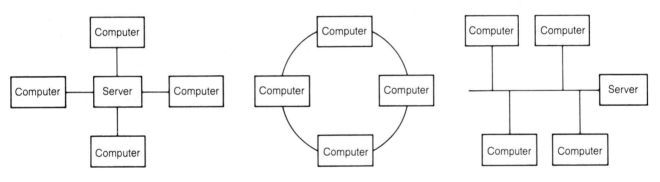

(b) The star, ring, and bus topologies of local area networks

Figure 21.23   A comparison of multiuser vs LAN systems.

Modems

The problem with the existing telecommunication network is that the phone lines were developed for human communication—which means analog information within a bandwidth of 300 to 3.3 kHz. To condition the signals to flow properly within these limitations, the digital information must first be sent through a *modem* (*mo*dulator/*dem*odulator). A modem is an electronic device for converting digital information to analog form (modulation) for transmission over the telephone network, and to reverse the process upon reception (demodulation).

Using modems, a simple two-station telecommunication system takes on the configuration of Figure 21.26.

Modems use the incoming digital signal to modulate a sine-wave carrier frequency and to demodulate the signal at

the other end. As shown in Figure 21.27, modulation can take any of three basic forms: amplitude, frequency, or phase.

Figure 21.28 depicts the two most common telecommunication transmission standards. The Bell 103/113 uses frequency multiplexing to achieve full-duplex operation. If the modem originates the call, it transmits in the 1070/1270 Hz channel and receives in the 2025/2225 Hz channel. However, the narrow bandwidth for each channel limits the transmission rate to approximately 300 bauds. The Bell 202 transmits at a higher baud rate (up to 1800 bauds), but the larger bandwidth limits operation to half-duplex.

Higher-speed modems go beyond the simple *frequency-shift-keying (FSK)* techniques of Figure 21.28 to *phase-shift keying (PSK)*. The most popular PSK variation—widely used in 1200 b/s modems—is called *quadrature amplitude modulation* (QAM). This sophisticated technique blends

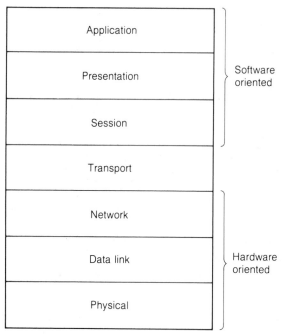

Figure 21.24 The ISO seven-layer model for Open Systems Interconnection (OSI).

both amplitude and phase modulation to encode 2 bits of data in every state transition. (Since the term *baud* is usually reserved for number of transitions of state, the baud rate of our QAM system is half the bit rate.)

Modems for use in a synchronous environment must time-multiplex timing information in with the data, and must include phase lock hardware to maintain synchronization.

When interfaced to a computer and supplied with *terminal software,* a modem becomes "intelligent" and can automatically dial numbers and answer messages.

Digital Telecommunications

Until recently, information and voice transmission over telephone lines was entirely an analog operation. However, with the evolution of digital technology and the many advantages it brings—ease of design, precision, low cost, and speed—it was only natural for digital techniques to slowly infiltrate the previously all-analog telephone system. Unfortunately, the high investment in the present analog lines means they cannot be replaced overnight with the more efficient digital channels. Especially hard to replace are the long-distance, narrow-bandwidth voice highways. Therefore, the first digital communication systems have been developed primarily for short distances: toll lines connecting offices, private branch exchanges (PBX), local communication networks (Ethernet), and in general wherever it is economically feasible. Using a technique called *submultiplexing,* in which a voice slot is further subdivided into data-carrying fields, these

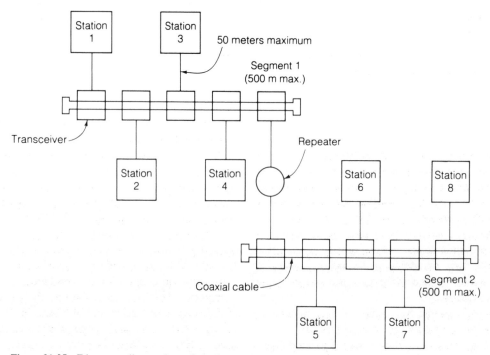

Figure 21.25 Ethernet medium-scale configuration.

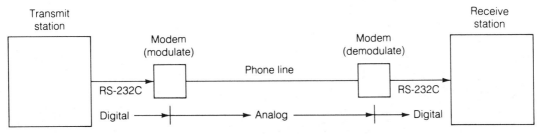

Figure 21.26 The use of modems to communicate by way of phone lines.

systems will allow both voice and digital communication on the same line.

Pulse-code modulation (PCM)   The type of modulation used by digital telecommunication systems is called *pulse-code modulation*. As shown in Figure 21.29, an input signal is sampled at regular intervals, and each analog voltage is converted to an 8-bit word. The sequence of 8-bit words becomes the serial data stream. Special coding (companding) processes allow 8 bits to represent a full 72 dB of dynamic range.

If 24 analog signals (phones) are sampled in a time-multiplexed scheme, with synchronization and signaling (control) added, you have the basic PCM carrier format of Figure 21.30. This sequence of PCM words, known as the *T1 PCM*

carrier format, was developed primarily for interconnecting switching offices. It allows the transmission of 24 time-multiplexed serial channels over a single twisted-pair line. Note that control information for each of the 24 channels is sent by reserving the eighth bit of every sixth frame for signaling; an extra bit is added to each frame to maintain synchronization.

The Codec and PCM filter   To efficiently implement the 24-channel T1 PCM carrier format, a new LSI chip has evolved. Known as the 2913/2914 *Codec/Filter Combochip* (see Figure 21.31), it places both *co*der/*de*coder and *PCM line filter* functions on a single chip. Divided into XMIT

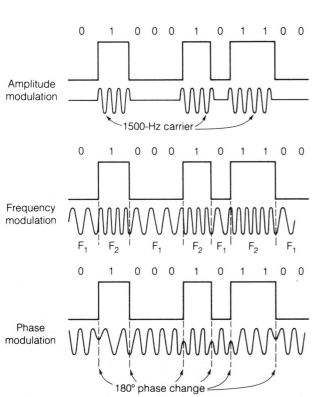

Figure 21.27 Basic telecommunication signal-modulation techniques.

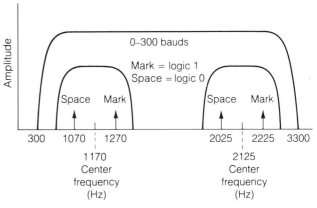

(a) Bell 103/113 channel assignments for full-duplex operation

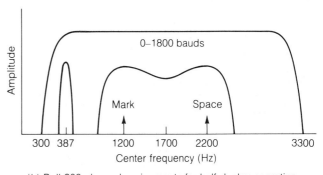

(b) Bell 202 channel assignments for half-duplex operation

Figure 21.28 Bell serial, binary, asynchronous telecommunication standards based on frequency-shift-keying (FSK) modulation.

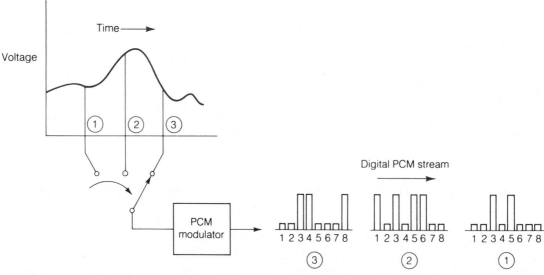

Figure 21.29   Sampled analog voltages converted to serial stream of PCM words.

(transmit) and RCV (receive) sections, it is the function of the combochip to convert an analog voice signal to a digital PCM bit stream (xmit section) and to reverse the process at the other end of the line (rcv section).

Using the 2913/2914 combochip, a simple two-station telecommunication link takes on the configuration of Figure 21.32a.

The transmit filter, called an *antialiasing filter,* is used to remove high-frequency components in order to minimize the distortion noise caused by the sampling process. The receive filter, called the *reconstruction filter,* is used at the receive end to reconstruct (smooth out) the digital "staircase-like" signal sent from the transmitter.

The codec (coder/decoder) portions of the combochip performs analog-to-digital and digital-to-analog conversions, PCM formatting, companding (nonlinear conversion between analog and digital), and timing.

Reproduced by permission of Intel Corp.

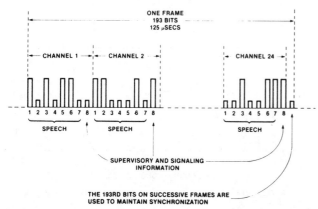

Figure 21.30   PCM carrier format.

A typical PCM link and associated waveforms (both time and frequency domain) are shown in Figure 21.32b. Since satisfactory voice reproduction does not require frequency components above approximately 4 kHz, we may safely sample at 8 kHz. (According to sampling theory, if we sample at twice the highest frequency of interest, essentially no information will be lost.)

From transmitter to receiver, the following operations take place:

1. Before transmission begins, an 8-bit word written to the control registers of both transmit and receive codecs assigns the data link to a particular transmit-and-receive time slot.

2. An arbitrary voice signal, consisting of a 2 kHz low-frequency component and a 5 kHz high-frequency component, is transmitted from a telephone set. (As previously stated, the 5 kHz component is unnecessary for adequate voice reproduction and is included simply to determine its effect.)

3. By counting clock cycles relative to the incoming transmit-and-receive frame sync pulse, the codec is able to determine the correct time slot among the 24 channels to transmit a PCM word.

4. Once synchronized to its assigned time channel, the analog signal is filtered to remove the unnecessary 5 kHz component and sampled at the 8 kHz rate. Each sample is held in the sample-and-hold block for A/D conversion. (Note that the sum and difference 6 kHz and 10 kHz sidebands produced by the 8K sampling process do not fold back into the 300 Hz to 4 kHz signal band. However, the 5 kHz incoming component, if it had not been removed by the antialiasing filter, would have appeared

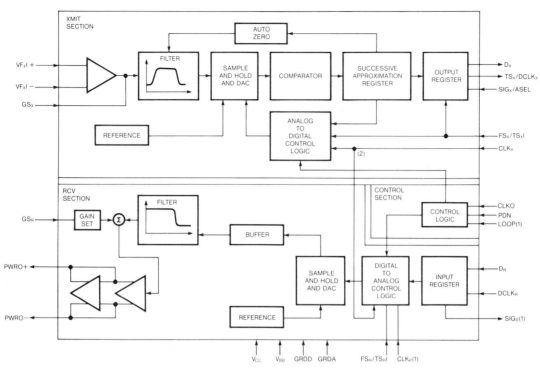

Figure 21.31   The 2913/14 codec/filter combochip.

at 3 kHz in the signal band, causing distortion noise that could not have been removed.) Analog-to-digital conversion is initiated and the corresponding digital word is generated in the appropriate time slot.

5. Every sixth frame the combochip automatically inserts a special signal bit in the eighth bit position (used for control functions such as dialing information) and a special sync bit following the entire 24 frames (used for frame identification). (The signal and sync information is obtained from the SIG_x and FS_x input pins to the 2913/14).

6. The digital information is sent out on the PCM highway and blended in with up to 23 other PCM streams, each assigned to its own unique time slot.

7. When the receive codec at the other end detects the proper time slot, the 8-bit data word is shifted into a serial register. When the register is full, a digital-to-analog operation is performed.

8. The resulting analog signal level is held in a sample-and-hold circuit until released by timing.

9. The "squared off" output of the receive codec is passed through the reconstruction filter where the 6K and 10K aliasing components are removed.

10. The original analog signal is recreated (without the unnecessary 5 kHz component, of course) and passed on to the receive telephone.

Figure 21.33 shows how an array of combochips is used to produce a complete intelligent switching system, able to handle up to 256 input phone lines (only 24 can be transmitting simultaneously). When the microprocessor detects an "off-hook" condition, it assigns that codec to an available time slot (by writing an 8-bit code into the codec). At the end of conversation, the codec is taken off the line and placed into a standby condition.

In the future, we can expect the present analog-based phone system to give way gradually to an all-digital network.

FIBER-OPTIC DIGITAL HIGHWAYS

The ever-expanding requirements of modern communication systems are one reason for the development of newer high-speed technologies (silicon on sapphire, Josephson junction). The T1 PCM system can transmit information at a respectable 1.5 million bits per second (Mb/s). However, transmission by lightwave carrier over fiber-optic lines can take place at more than 250 Mb/s, with 200 gigabits per second demonstrated in the laboratory (1 gigabit = 10^9 bits).

This wider bandwidth means that a single inexpensive fiber cable can carry as much information as 1000 pairs of copper wire—with high resistance to erosion and total freedom from electromagnetic interference and short circuits.

New low-loss fiber-optic cables, coupled with special high-radiance LEDs (Figure 21.34*a*), allow repeater stations to

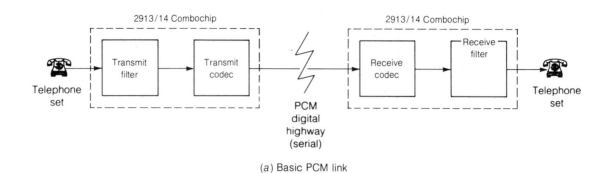

(a) Basic PCM link

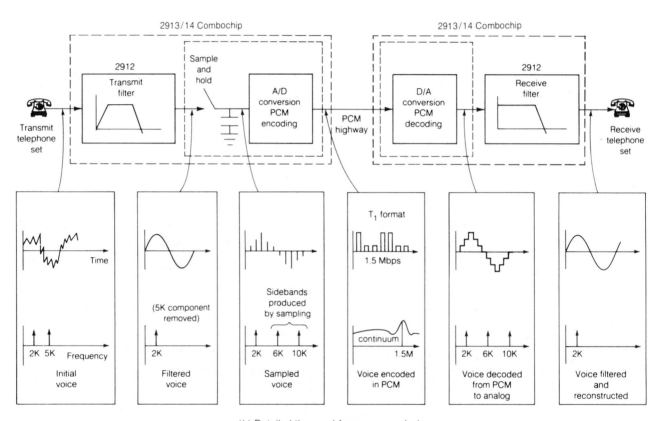

(b) Detailed time and frequency analysis

Figure 21.32 A single PCM telephone link using the 2913/14 combochip.

be extended from the conventional 1 mile to more than 100 miles.

By the use of the electro-optic effect to modify the refractive index of a Lithium Niobate substrate (Figure 21.34b), these fiber-optic signals can be electrically switched. This high-speed routing and multiplexing ability will soon give us an all optical communication system.

SPEECH SYNTHESIS

The 1980s will also be the decade of the talking computer. As the techniques of speech synthesis reach maturity, a vast

array of consumer, industrial, and military products will be communicating with us by way of the spoken word.

At first glance, speech synthesis appears to be a very simple process. Just sample the spoken word at twice the highest frequency of interest (the Nyquist rate) and store the digitized words in memory for later playback. Unfortunately, this direct recording technique is not practical, for synthesizing only a single second of speech would require some 100,000 bits of stored information. Therefore, the race for practical speech synthesis becomes a race to reduce the storage requirements—to store in memory only that information absolutely necessary for the realistic reproduction of speech. As we will see, by eliminating unnecessary infor-

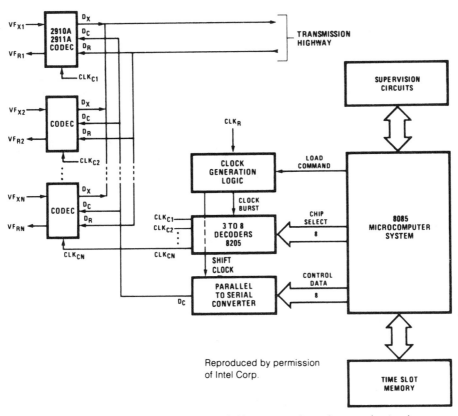

Figure 21.33 Multiplexed telecommunications switching system using codec transmitter/receivers.

mation in the speech pattern, we can produce one second of human speech with only 400 to 2,000 bits of information. Two general techniques are available for the synthesis of human speech:

- Time-domain synthesis
- Frequency-domain synthesis

The first method is more straightforward. We simply compress and digitize speech wave patterns in the time domain, and store the information sequentially in ROM for later playback through a DAC. The process is diagrammed in Figure 21.35a. The speech waveform is sampled at the Nyquist rate, digitized by an A/D converter, and passed through four digital compression processes, eliminating information that is not required for faithful sound reproduction.

The first compression process removes redundant speech elements, and the second process removes absolute amplitude information, leaving only relative amplitude data. Phase (direction) components—which the ear cannot detect—are removed by the third process, and the fourth process removes all low-amplitude components. The hardware for carrying out waveform digitization and compression is simple and straightforward, with little need for sophisticated mathematical calculations and number crunching.

The second method operates in the frequency domain and is true speech synthesis, not merely a modified (compressed) recording of real speech. The most popular frequency-domain technique is called *linear predictive coding* (LPC). To speak a word using LPC, either periodic pulses (for voiced sounds such as "a") or white noise (for unvoiced sounds such as "f" or "s") is generated and passed through a multipole digital filter (Figure 21.35b), whose coefficients are sequentially controlled by parameters stored in ROM.

The filter parameters are obtained from a linear equation that models the human voice tract, allowing a speech sample to be predicted from previous ones and thereby eliminating redundancies.

Another frequency-domain technique reconstructs speech from stored spectral bands of frequencies (called *formants*). Each formant corresponds to a major band of resonant frequencies. An especially promising technique is called *phoneme* synthesis, in which the spectral patterns are derived from basic word sounds. A phoneme represents a simple elemental speech sound, of which there are 38 to 40 in the English language.

Programmable speech-synthesis chip sets are now available from a variety of manufacturers. For example, the Digitalker™ from National Semiconductor (Figure 21.36) uses the compression technique to store up to 256 words of natu-

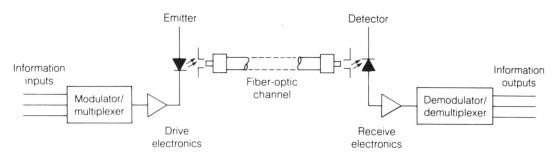

(a) Fiber-optic communication link

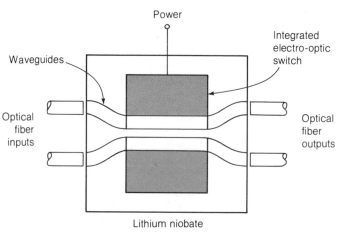

(b) Electro-optic switch

Figure 21.34 Fiber-optics.

ral-sounding speech. It is designed to interface easily with any popular microprocessor.

Although speech recognition is considerably more difficult than speech synthesis, progress is occurring on this front also. In one technique, the speaker's voice is sampled some 20,000 times a second. The samples are grouped into blocks of approximately 1,000 and each block is converted to the frequency domain (a spectral profile) by a Fourier transformation. The spectral waveform is then compared with samples previously recorded and stored in ROM. Since each spectral block may be compared with thousands of stored patterns, the process is slow, taking some 100 times longer than speech synthesis. However, real-time speech recognition probably will become a reality in this decade.

MACHINE-ASSEMBLY UPDATE

Our final machine assembly update puts the finishing touch on modularized programming. To see what is missing, let's expand our simple robotics example of the last chapter to

the real world, where a high degree of complexity is the norm. More than likely a real-world robotics language will consist of hundreds of robotics instructions, linked together to perform a very complex series of motions. Typing 100 file names after the LINK heading each time we generate the main program seems out of place in a development process optimized for efficiency.

The solution is to place our separately compiled object modules in a *library*. During linkage, the LINK utility automatically scans the library, linking the desired modules to the main program. To see how it is done, let's go back to our simple RADAR example of the last Chapter.

As before, the first step is to assemble all of our source programs to relocatable object code. We then enter the library routine using the command:

LIB <CR>

Within the library utility program we create a library called ROBOT:

CREATE :F1:ROBOT.LIB

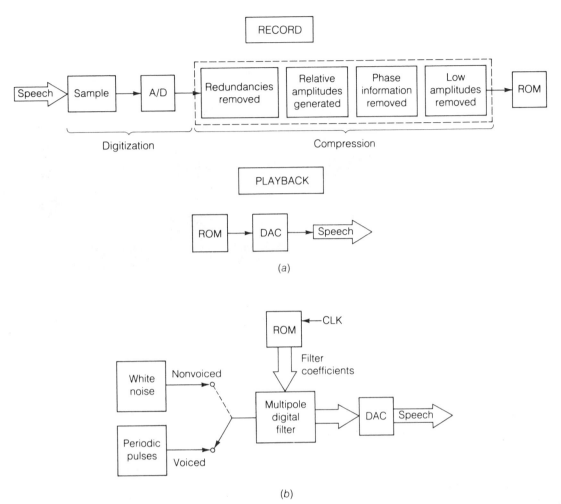

Figure 21.35 Two popular speech-synthesis techniques: *a)* Time-domain waveform compression. *b)* Frequency-domain filter control.

To add our two robotics instructions to the library, we type:

ADD :F1:STEPR.OBJ,:F1:STEPL.OBJ TO :F1:ROBOT.LIB

With STEPR.OBJ and STEPL.OBJ now included in our ROBOT library, the link operation simplifies to:

LINK :F1:RADAR.OBJ,:F1:ROBOT.LIB

The LINK utility will automatically search library ROBOT for all required object modules, no matter how many modules are stored in the library.

If we compare the link map (Figure 21.37) with that of the previous chapter (when the library was not used) we would see that the resulting object code is identical.

With this, our final machine assembly update, we pave the way for the next chapter, when our machine assembler

expands into a full-fledged *development system,* designed not just to streamline the writing of programs in assembly language, but to nurture a product from the first stages of conception to the final stages of testing.

INTELLIGENT-MACHINE UPDATE

Having mastered the techniques of data communication, our intelligent machine will soon be able to communicate accurately and reliably, using a variety of languages and formats, with any computer in the world. When the human species first developed this ability, it quickly revolutionized our social structure. What an intelligent machine—capable of learning and making decisions—will do with instant access to unlimited information can only be imagined.

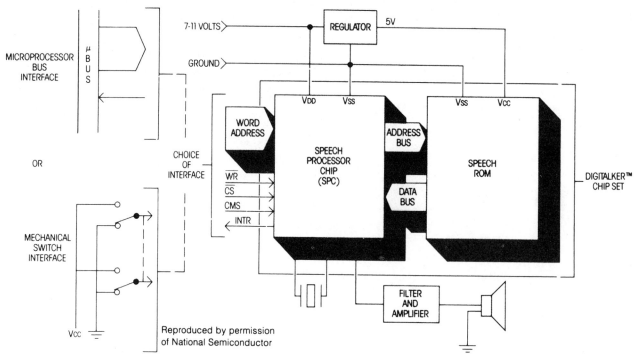

Figure 21.36 The National Semiconductor Digitalker.

```
ISIS-II OBJECT LINKER V3.0 INVOKED BY:
-LINK :F1:RADAR.OBJ,:F1:ROBOT.LIB &
**TO :F1:RADAR.LNK MAP PRINT(:LP:)

LINK MAP OF MODULE RADAR
WRITTEN TO FILE :F1:RADAR.LNK
MODULE IS A MAIN MODULE

SEGMENT INFORMATION:
START  STOP LENGTH REL NAME

          38H  B  CODE

INPUT MODULES INCLUDED:
 :F1:RADAR.OBJ(RADAR)
 :F1:ROBOT.LIB(STEPRI)
 :F1:ROBOT.LIB(STEPLE)
```

Figure 21.37 Link map for program RADAR, showing the use of the library.

QUESTIONS AND PROBLEMS

1. What are the major characteristics of *asynchronous* communications? Of *synchronous* communications?
2. Compare *simplex, half-duplex,* and *full-duplex* transmission.
3. What is the ASCII code sequence for the word STOP?
4. When using RS-232C, how is the logic-1 state determined?
5. What is the advantage of using a current loop for communication?
6. Based on the IEEE 488 standard, how does a peripheral transmit data?
7. Describe the five major registers within the 8251A and state the function of each.
8. On the 8251A, what is the purpose of the $C/\overline{D}$ input?
9. Write a program to generate the asynchronous data stream of Figure 21.1 without the use of the USART (the serial data stream is emitted directly from the SOD output of the 8085).
10. Develop the assembly-language programs corresponding to the flowcharts of Figure 21.18.
11. When the TxRDY signal goes signal goes active, what condition of the 8251A is indicated?
12. What are the major characteristics of a synchronous protocol?
13. When using the SDLC bit-oriented protocol, how do we make sure the transmission is *transparent* (the flag word does not appear anywhere in the text)?
14. When using the Binary Synchronous Communication protocol (BISYNC), how does the receiver determine start of transmission?
15. What is a *modem,* and what is it used for?
16. What type of multiplexing does the Bell 202 format use?
17. What are some of the advantages of communicating in digital rather than analog?
18. How are data encoded when using *pulse-code modulation* (PCM)?

19. When using the T1 PCM carrier format, how many people may use a single digital highway at the same time?

20. What kind of multiplexing does the T1 system use?

21. How does the T1 system detect the "phone off hook" condition?

22. What are the inputs and resulting outputs to a *codec?*

23. What is the purpose of the transmit-and-receive filters within the 2913/14 combochip?

24. Redraw the waveforms of Figure 21.32*b,* using 3K- and 6K-Hz input signals from the transmit phone.

25. What is the major advantage of a fiber-optic digital highway?

26. Name several components of human speech that are unnecessary for faithful reproduction of the spoken word.

27. Describe how the parity flag might be used in serial transmission to detect errors.

28. Write a modified mimic program that mimics only even numbers of odd parity.

29. Modify the routine of question 9 to include an even parity bit in the "8" position.

30. Into which layer of the 7-layer ISO protocol model would each of the following fit?

    a. An end-of-message flag.
    b. Receipt of message acknowledge.
    c. The metal connectors at each end of the transmission link.
    d. The purpose of the communication.

31. What is the difference between a general network and a local area network (LAN)?

32. What form of channel access uses random arbitration means?

33. What was the Tower of Babel and how does it relate to the goal of the layered protocol? (Research may be required).

34. *Ethernet* is equivalent to what layers of the 7-layer ISO model?

35. How is synchronization maintained when using synchronous data transmission techniques?

36. How does the use of a *library* speed up the process of linkage?

37. Compare the *counsel output* (CO) built-in monitor routine of the SDK-85 (at location 05C4H) with your answer to question 9 (See the *SDK-85 User's Manual* for the code listing).

38. Is the 8251A double-buffered?

chapter 22

Product Development

The ultimate purpose in the game of chess—at least in tournament play—is to win the game. The ultimate purpose of studying microcomputers is to help bring microprocessor-based products to market.

A number of steps are involved in product development, from initial conception to final packaging. Only two, however, are of primary interest to the engineer and technician, and they will be the subjects of this chapter: hardware/software development and troubleshooting.

As shown in Figure 22.1, a great deal of interaction between hardware design, software design, and troubleshooting must take place before the final product is perfected and released to the market.

HARDWARE/SOFTWARE DEVELOPMENT

Software on Silicon

To become adept at the "hardware" of chess (the chess pieces and the board) requires perhaps only a day or two. To become adept at the "software" of chess (playing the game) requires a lifetime. Today, hardware/software development is in much the same state. Although hardware costs have dropped dramatically, software costs—because of increased program complexity—have risen just as dramatically. It can easily cost $100,000 of software development time to fill $100 worth of memory.

One solution to the problem is to increase the complexity of the hardware—*to place the software on silicon*. The first salvos in the battle to swallow up software with complex LSI circuits began with the programmable peripheral chips introduced in Chapter 19. The process began in earnest, however, with the development of the 8086 and its coprocessors (the 8086 system is covered in Chapter 25) and will be carried still further with the new 32-bit systems.

Therefore, perhaps the first step in hardware/software development is to take full advantage of the sophisticated support chips presently on the market. A few typical examples are (those near the top of the list we have already covered):

- 8155A Programmable Peripheral Interface
- 8253 Programmable Interval Timer
- 8251A Programmable Communications Interface
- 8279 Programmable Keyboard/Display Timer
- 8273 Programmable HDLC/SDLC Controller
- 2653 Polynomial Generator Checker (Signetics)
- 2652 Multiprotocol Communications Controller (Signetics)
- SCU-1 Serial Control Unit (Mostek)
- MT8860 Digital Decoder (Mitel)
- SC-01 Speech Synthesizer (Votrax)
- MC6859 Data-Encryption Chip (Motorola)

Each of these chips can greatly reduce the software load of both the CPU and the programmer. In the future, we can expect VLSI technology to place even more software on silicon, eventually integrating the operating system and the high-level language into the hardware.

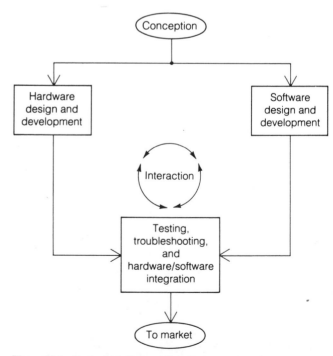

Figure 22.1 Product-development flowchart.

314

The feature that makes VLSI a "sky's the limit" technology and that gives it such an exciting potential is the new computer-aided-design (CAD) workstations, which are rapidly approaching the designer's dream: a slab of purified sand (silicon) and tiny amounts of doping material are entered into one end of the system and, after several sessions at the computer keyboard, a fully functional and tested VLSI custom chip flows from the other end (see the section on CAD/CAM later in this chapter). Not all the system and applications software can be placed on silicon, of course, so sooner or later we must turn to software development.

Software Development

Program design and coding is both an art and a science. In the early days the process was very much an individual effort (an art). However, as programs grew in scope and complexity, this "artistic" approach produced programs that were unreliable and difficult to modify and maintain. Although there is still room in programming for the unique inspirations and insights of the individual, today we approach programming in a systematic and disciplined manner (as a science).

In this section, we will review the software development process from a historical perspective, and we will see how a number of innovations took program design from the art of the 1960s to the science of the 1980s. Since the learning process is always enhanced by following a specific example, we will focus on our familiar three-step mimic-delay process (input, delay proportional to size of number, output).

The Flowchart

From the late 1940s to the mid-1960s, the primary program design tool was the *flowchart,* the technique used throughout the previous 21 chapters of this text. However, for programs of any complexity, conventional flowcharting produced a patchwork mosaic that was difficult to read, understand, and modify. As shown by the mimic-delay flowchart of Figure 22.2, the problem was the numerous criss-crossing transfers of control (jumps) to various parts of the program.

Structured Programming

The first major breakthrough came in the mid-1960s when Corrado Bohm and Guiseppe Jacopini published their *structure theorem.* According to the structure theorem, any programming logic, no matter how complex, can be implemented using only three basic control structures: *sequence, alternation,* and *repetition.* Looking to Figure 22.3, the sequence handles events that occur immediately after one another, alternation is provided by the *if-then-else* decision-making concept, and repetition follows a *while-do* looping pattern.

Especially important is that each of these three control structures has a single entry point and a single exit point, *a feature that is maintained when the three constructs are combined and nested to generate highly-complex structured flowcharts.* As demonstrated by Figure 22.4a, our mimic-delay *structured* flowchart is now easy to read, understand, and modify, since the confusing branches from one program location to another have been eliminated.

Because structured flowcharts are time-consuming, especially if an error is made, many programmers advocate the use of pseudocode. *Pseudocode* is a logical representation of a program using English-language versions of the three constructs of structured programming. Comparing the pseudocode version of our mimic-delay program (Figure 22.4b) with the structured flowchart version (Figure 22.4a), the choice between the two is clearly one of personal preference.

Top-Down Structured Design

To solve any complex problem, such as forming a government or traveling to the moon—or writing a large program—there is only one reasonable way to approach the task: the overall responsibility must be subdivided into smaller and smaller parcels until each is at a manageable level. This *modularization* concept is at the heart of *top-down structured design.* Two major developments that supported top-down design were *structure charts* and *Warnier-Orr diagrams.*

Structure charts As shown in Figure 22.5a, a structure chart modularizes our mimic-delay program into a pyramid structure. Starting at the top of the chart, the program is broken down into smaller and smaller modules until each is at a manageable size.

Although both a structure chart and a flow chart use boxes to represent portions of a program, they are not the same. A flowchart shows the decisions and operations *within* a module; a structure chart shows the relationship *between* modules, and generally would be used earlier in the top-down process.

Note the use of special symbols to indicate such inter-module relationships as decision making and nesting.

The Warnier-Orr diagram Somewhat below the structure chart in modularization level, the Warnier-Orr diagram is a useful technique for modularizing an entire program or each block within a structure chart.

Figure 22.5b shows how the mimic-delay program is broken down (modularized) by Warnier-Orr diagramming. Going from left to right, the program is subdivided hierarchically into smaller and smaller blocks by the use of left-hand braces (the right-hand braces would be redundant). As shown, the IF-THEN-ELSE construct is diagrammed by the use of the exclusive-OR and NOT Boolean symbols, and the WHILE-DO construct by writing the number of loops to be performed in parentheses below the block title. Nesting is automatically handled by the placement of the blocks.

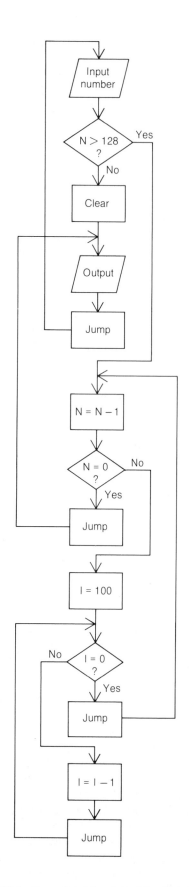

Figure 22.2   Conventional flowchart of the mimic-delay program.

In summary, structured design consists of two major concepts:

- Modularization, from the top-down.
- The exclusive use of sequence, alternation, and repetition.

In a real-world programming environment, a structure chart might be the first step taken. Each block of the structure chart might then be further broken down using structured flowcharts or Warnier-Orr diagramming. After the final step, the generation of pseudocode, we are ready for the coding process—the use of a programming language to translate each module into a sequence of statements or instructions. As we will see in the next section, special block-structured languages were developed to match perfectly with the concepts of top-down structured design.

Programming Languages

All three software routines in Figure 22.6 are identical. We can see at a glance that the ease of writing and interpreting the programs is ranked from left to right—from high-level to low-level languages (those who are totally unfamiliar with Pascal can probably understand the intent of the single program statement).

Pascal is a high-level language. That is, each statement of a high-level program is formulated to resemble plain conversational English or traditional mathematical symbols and corresponds to several lines of assembly or machine code (typically 8 to 12 lines). We already know the advantages of writing programs in assembly language. A high-level language simply extends the benefits further. When using a high-level language, we can concentrate fully on program concepts and not be concerned at all with hardware-management details. In fact, when writing programs in high-level language, we do not even need to know what microprocessor will ultimately run the program. High-level routines are compact, reliable, easy to modify, and simple to read and understand.

Many types of high-level languages are available. As shown in Figure 22.7, the higher the level, the more they resemble natural human languages. For software development purposes, we will divide all high-level languages into one of two groups: *structured or nonstructured*. At the present time, Pascal is the best-known structured language, and BASIC is the most prominent nonstructured language. (The trend is toward applying structured concepts to normally nonstructured languages.)

Structured/nonstructured programming   Pascal, PL/M, Ada, and FORTRAN 77 are riding the current wave of popularity for structured programming. In the broadest possible terms, *structured programming* is simply a set of rules yielding programs that are particularly easy to write, test, modify,

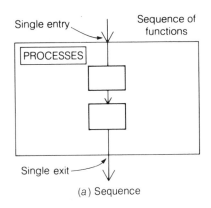

(a) Sequence

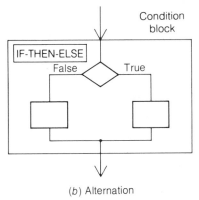

(b) Alternation

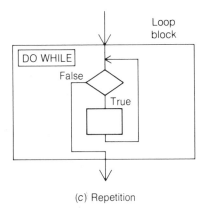

(c) Repetition

Figure 22.3   The three basic control structures of structured programming.

and read. In other words, a structured program is reliable, readable, and maintainable. More specifically, the term refers to the same two properties we have seen before: subdividing a large problem into smaller modules and using the three basic constructs (sequence, alternation, and repetition) to eliminate the need for jumps (GOTOs) between modules. (Structured programming is often called "GOTO-less" programming, even though the concept involves a great deal more.) Programs written in structured format are known as *proper* programs.

One way to contrast structured with nonstructured programming is to make two listings of the same program, one using BASIC, a nonstructured language, and the other using Pascal, a structured language. Based on the very familiar mimic-delay program, such a comparison is shown in Figure 22.8.

The MIMIC-DELAY Pascal program   Turning to the structured version first (Figure 22.8a), we see that modularization is handled by *procedures* (subroutines) and structuring is accomplished by nesting the three basic constructs.

Turning our attention to the main program, we see that it is a sequence of four procedure calls, each sending an actual

parameter to its corresponding procedure for processing. Unlike the DELAY procedure, which we wrote, procedures WRITE, READLN, and WRITELN are built-in (intrinsic) and need not be included in our source program.

Briefly, here is how execution proceeds. We begin at the main program block (bracketed by BEGIN/END) and enter a continuous loop (WHILE TRUE DO). The first statement calls intrinsic procedure WRITE, sending actual parameter "GIVE ME A NUMBER" to the CRT screen. Intrinsic procedure READLN waits in a loop, and when the operator responds (types in a number), places the number into variable NUMBER. Procedure DELAY sends actual parameter NUMBER to formal parameter N for processing. If N is greater than 128, a delay is created; otherwise the number is cleared. We return to the main program and write the number contents to the CRT screen.

An important feature of structured programming is declaration statements. All variables (memory locations into which data can be placed) must be declared before they can be used. For example, VAR NUMBER : INTEGER "creates" a symbolic memory location called NUMBER and states that only whole numbers (such as 1, 4, 234) can be stored within it.

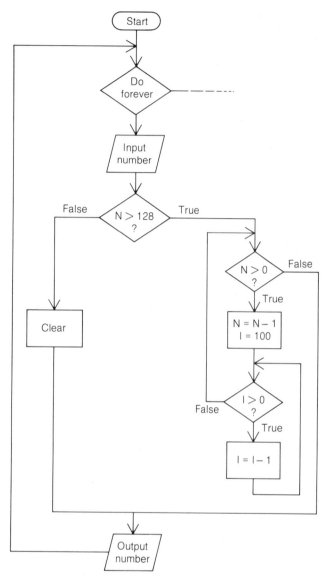

(a) Structured flowchart

```
Start
DO forever
  Read number
  IF number > 128
    Decrement number
    Set I = 100
    DO while I > 0
      Decrement I
    END DO
  ELSE
    Number = 0
  Write number
END DO
Stop
```

(b) Pseudocode

Figure 22.4 Structured programming design methods.

By declaring variable NUMBER in the main program block, it becomes a *global* variable, accessible by all procedure and program modules. By declaring N and I within procedure DELAY, they become *local* variables, accessible only from within procedure DELAY. By making all variables as local as possible, we ensure that during software development, changes and modifications in one procedure module will not ripple through the program, causing unwanted changes elsewhere, and that during execution, one procedure's operations will not cause inadvertent changes in another procedure's data.

The structured version is easy to follow because it reads like a book—*it is English-like, it is modular, and it flows from one construct to the next*. Would you like a brief high-level summary of the program's intent? Look to the main program and there you will find a "Table of Contents," a descriptive list of "Chapter Titles" (procedures) arranged in sequence.

Comparing the structured Pascal program with the nonstructured BASIC program (Figure 22.8b), it is obvious at a glance that the structured program is easier to follow, troubleshoot, and maintain. Nonstructured programming, with its numerous jumps (GOTOs) back and forth, is often compared to a plate of spaghetti; structured programming, with its smooth, sequential flow, is like a string of pearls. (To be fair, we should mention that the BASIC program of Figure 22.8b is designed to demonstrate nonstructured programming and is not necessarily the way a skilled BASIC programmer would code the problem.)

Of course, this simple mimic-delay program uses only a tiny fraction of the available power and versatility of the full Pascal language. Numerous textbooks and courses are available on this and other block-structured languages if you want additional information.

Bottom-Up Programming

Even though top-down design is clearly the best overall approach, we should mention that there is also room in any large scale project for *bottom-up* activity. Bottom-up programming is essentially *tool-building*. If it is known at the outset that certain low-level routines will ultimately be needed, they might as well be written immediately (perhaps by less-experienced programmers). A program that grows from the bottom up as well as the top down can shorten the time to completion.

Object-Oriented Programming

The next step in structured design is represented by the new object-oriented high-level languages, such as Ada.

Rather than simply modularizing program code in the form of procedures, an object-oriented language modularizes *groups*

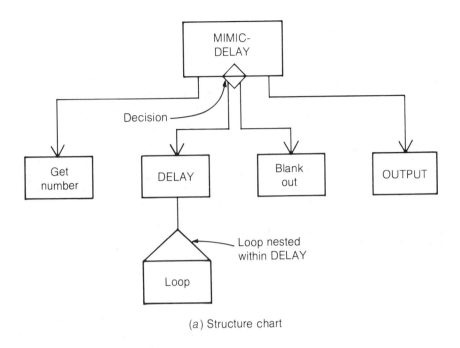

(a) Structure chart

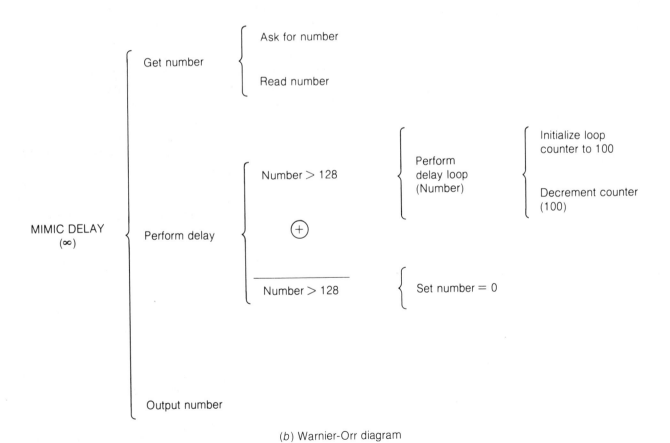

(b) Warnier-Orr diagram

Figure 22.5   Techniques of top-down structured design.

BENEFITS OF A HIGH LEVEL LANGUAGE
REDUCED DEVELOPMENT COSTS THRU
FEWER STATEMENTS

PASCAL	ASSEMBLY LANGUAGE		MACHINE CODE
IF X > Y THEN	LDA	Y	3A
Z := X	LXI	H, X	FF
ELSE Z := Y ;	CMP	M	01
	JC	GO	21
	MOV	A, M	D3
	GO: STA	Z	00
			BE
			DA
			43
			01
			7E
			32
			88
			01

**MORE TIME CAN BE SPENT ON PROGRAM LOGIC
AND LESS ON HARDWARE MANAGEMENT DETAILS.**

Reproduced by permission of Intel Corp.

Figure 22.6 High-level, assembly, and machine-language comparison.

Natural human languages	Humanlike ↑
LISP	
APL	
Ada	
C	
Pascal	
ALGOL	
COBOL	
FORTRAN	
BASIC	
Forth	
Assembly	
Machine	Machinelike ↓

Figure 22.7 The computer language scale from machine to human.

of procedures, *and their associated data structures* in a single unit (called an *object* or *package*). Each object is treated as a software "black box" (similar to objects in real life such as a TV set or an automobile), providing a service or function to the outside world with the internal design—the data structures and algorithms—invisible and inaccessible.

A specification or contract defines the interface between objects. *As long as the contract is upheld, changes can be made freely to objects on either side of the interface.*

By clustering both the procedures and their common data structures and specifying only the information required to interface the objects, program design and debugging are greatly enhanced.

Compiler vs Interpreter

Programs written in high-level languages are like poetry because they can be written down as fast as our inspirations come. The computer, however, is a single-minded machine able to absorb commands only in its native tongue of binary. Since translation from high-level statements to binary machine code is a repetitive process following exact rules, it is tailor-made for a computer. The program that accomplishes the translation, known as a *compiler,* is similar in concept to the assembler program used to translate assembly code to machine code. Of course, a compiler is a more complex and sophisticated program, particularly for the structured languages.

There are times, however, when assembly-language programming is preferable to high-level programming. The problem with high-level languages is that the generated code is not as compact as it could be (human beings, given enough time, can usually write more efficient programs consuming less memory space). For example, if a program must fit into the available 2K of ROM space aboard an 8048 single-chip microprocessor, it may be necessary to resort to assembly-language programming to squeeze down a program of 2,055 words into the available 2,048 memory locations. On the other hand, if there is memory to spare (remember, memory space is relatively inexpensive when compared to software development costs), a high-level language can generate code up to 10 times faster and therefore at lower cost. (Using modular techniques, it is possible to code some modules in assembly language and the remaining in a high-level language. Each module can be separately compiled and linked together to form one main program module.) Processing speed is also a factor in the choice between high-level and assembly-level programming. If an assembled program is shorter than a compiled program, it runs faster—an especially important factor in the fields of telecommunications and real-time process control.

An *interpreter* is closely related to a compiler and often used to execute BASIC. An interpreter translates and executes *each line* of a high-level language program *as it is running;* the compiler translates the *entire* high-level pro-

```
(*  This modified mimic program delays all input numbers > 128 by
an amount equal to the inported number.   All numbers <= 128  are
blanked out (set to zero) *)

PROGRAM MIMICDELAY;
VAR NUMBER : INTEGER;

PROCEDURE DELAY (N : INTEGER);
VAR I : INTEGER;
BEGIN
  IF N > 128 THEN
    WHILE N > 0 DO
    BEGIN
      N := N - 1;
      I := 100;
      WHILE I > 0 DO
        I := I - 1;
    END
  ELSE
    NUMBER := 0;
END;

BEGIN (* MAIN PROGRAM *)
  WHILE TRUE DO
  BEGIN
    WRITE('GIVE ME A NUMBER ');
    READLN(NUMBER);
    DELAY(NUMBER);
    WRITELN(NUMBER);
  END;
END.
```

(a) Structured Pascal

```
10   REM This modified mimic program delays all input numbers
20   REM > 128 by an amount equal to the inported number.
30   REM All numbers <= 128 are blanked out (set to zero).
40   PRINT "Give me a number"
50   INPUT NUM
60   N = NUM
70   IF N > 128 THEN GOTO 100
80   NUM = 0
90   GOTO 160
100  IF N = 0 THEN GOTO 160
110  N = N - 1
120  I = 100
130  IF I = 0 THEN GOTO 100
140  I = I - 1
150  GOTO 130
160  PRINT NUM
170  GOTO 40
```

(b) Nonstructured BASIC

Figure 22.8   The MIMIC-DELAY high-level program.

gram to object code before execution. Giving instantaneous results, an interpreter is interactive with the programmer and allows for easy program development and error correction. However, it slows down the execution of programs. (In a loop, for example, each line of code would have to be translated on each pass.) Furthermore, since an interpreter must be stored in memory at the time of execution, it requires a great deal more memory than a compiler.

There even exists an in-between system, called a *P-system*. To bring down the expense of writing a separate compiler for each microprocessor on the market, why not partially compile the high-level language *just short of the point where it becomes processor dependent?* This "partially digested" code is called *P-code*. The final translation of the universal P-code (which will run on any machine) down to machine code (which will run on only a specific processor) is done by a relatively inexpensive and simple interpreter— which is unique to each machine. A P-system—partly compiled and partly interpreted—is intermediate in speed between fully compiled code and purely interpreted code. The best-known P-system is UCSD Pascal.

The choice between a compiler, a P-system, or an interpreter, then, depends on the application. If you are using your computer as an intelligent calculator, in which quick answers are a must, an interpreter would be the logical choice. On the other hand, if you are developing a high-speed telecommunication program to load into a 2764 EPROM, the routine would have to be compiled into machine language. Some languages—such as BASIC—even offer the user a choice between an interpreter or a compiler.

Due to the popularity and relative simplicity of BASIC, the BASIC interpreter is often included in an on-board ROM (software on silicon). For example, the 8052AH member of the 8051 microcontroller family stores a basic interpreter in its 8 kilobytes of integrated ROM. When speed is not critical and program complexity does not justify the use of assemblers and compilers, the 8052AH-BASIC allows for fast and easy program development.

The Artificial-Intelligence (AI) Languages

LISP, Logo, and *PROLOG,* the languages of artificial intelligence, are successfully casting off their reputations as mere "toys for thinktanks." In areas such as VLSI design, graphics, and digital signal processing, programming in such languages as LISP or PROLOG can greatly improve productivity. Still, the AI languages are best known for their association with artificial intelligence. Such tasks as theorem proving, natural language processing, and symbolic mathematics can best be done using an AI language.

LISP is one of the oldest AI languages. As the name implies, *LISP* is a *list processing language*—and that is the

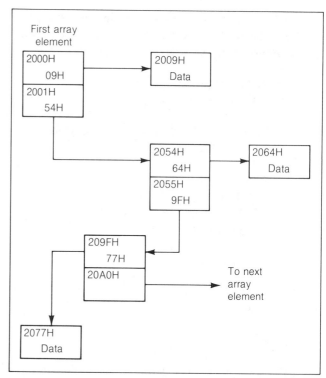

Figure 22.9 The linked list storage representation of the AI language LISP.

source of its power. As demonstrated by Figure 22.9, both programs *and* data are stored in memory as *linked lists*. Each element in the linked list consists of two memory locations, one to point to the data or program and another to point to the address of the next list element. Using linked lists, program and data elements can be placed anywhere in memory, rather than in sequence as with Pascal and other conventional languages.

An immediate benefit is ease of program modification. To add a line of code to a Pascal program means the entire program must be recompiled and relinked. By comparison, adding an array element (line of code) to a LISP program amounts to changing two addresses and allocating two new memory locations. Recompiling and relinking take place almost instantaneously. Of course the price you pay for storing programs and data as linked lists is an increased memory requirement and slower execution speed.

Another major benefit of list processing is the ability to create *objects* (known in LISP as *flavors*). When an object is created, the programmer hides the details from view, specifying only the information needed to interface with other flavors. In true modular fashion, you can build complex flavors from other flavors. By using flavors the programmer can break up a complex project into many small modules.

The characteristic that gives the linked list its artificial intelligence properties is the equivalence of programs and data. *This means that the AI languages can write programs for themselves to execute.* In other words, LISP can write its own program, execute it, and examine the results. As more information is received, it can modify the program and re-execute it. Given this characteristic, it is not hard to imagine a chess-playing computer—a common application of AI—modifying its program *as it plays*.

Taking yet another step toward the artificial intelligence goal of programming directly using logical constructions is PROLOG (PROgramming in LOGic). Unlike conventional programming languages such as BASIC and PASCAL, PROLOG solves problems using a database of facts and rules between the facts. It exhibits a surprising degree of artificial intelligence because it can *infer* facts that are not expressly in the database.

Programming in PROLOG involves the following three steps:

1. *Facts* are entered into the database.
2. *Rules* between the facts are entered into the database.
3. *Questions* are asked about the facts and their relationships.

For example, step one of a medical diagnosis *expert* system may involve adding the following facts to your database:

1. has(mary,fever).
   has(mary,aches).
   is(mary,tired).

   These facts are interpreted as: Mary has a fever, Mary has aches, and Mary is tired.

2. We then add the following rule (perhaps already in the data base):

   has(Patient,flu) : −
   has(Patient,fever),
   has(Patient,aches),
   is(Patient, tired),

   The rule means, any patient has the flu *if* (: −) the patient has a fever, *and* (,) the patient has aches, *and* (,) the patient is tired. (A capitalized word, such as Patient, is a variable). By adding such *if-then* rules, we have created a simple *expert* system.

3. Finally, we ask the question, "Mary has what disease?"

   has(mary,Whatdisease)?

PROLOG searches the data base for a match, and responds:

   Whatdisease = flu

Chosen as the core language for the Japanese Fifth Generation Computer project, PROLOG is rapidly gaining in popularity as an alternative to LISP.

TROUBLESHOOTING

It is not unusual for troubleshooting and program debugging to take up 50% of product development time. Troubleshooting, therefore, should be placed on an equal footing with system design. As expected, a number of tools and techniques are available—some designed primarily for software debugging, others aimed at hardware troubleshooting.

First of all, there are very few troubleshooting techniques that do not require a knowledge of the system under test. Random substitution and replacement of parts (known as "shotgunning") is the exception. Although such a technique can be effective in small systems using a limited number of LSI parts (such as the SDK-85 single-board computer), it generally is time-consuming, expensive, and unproductive. At the onset, therefore, we will assume a basic rule of troubleshooting: *To effectively troubleshoot a microcomputer system, we require a fundamental knowledge of microcomputer architecture and processing action.* Quite often, when armed with a good knowledge of the computer system, a simple description of the problem will quickly bring to mind a number of probable causes.

In this chapter we will introduce seven basic troubleshooting techniques, all requiring a knowledge of the system under test. Each technique has its advantages and disadvantages, of course, and part of the troubleshooting art is in selecting the proper tools and techniques to best debug the system at hand. These seven techniques are:

- Static testing
- Software diagnostics
- Single stepping
- Breakpointing
- Signature analysis
- Logic analysis
- In-circuit emulation

(In-circuit emulation will be covered in the section on development systems.)

Static Testing

Static testing involves the use of dc voltages to stimulate the circuit. It is aimed primarily at locating faults in circuits and components. Since the microprocessor is the controlling device for the system under test, static testing begins with removing the microprocessor and substituting static signals for those normally produced by the microprocessor. By manipulating the dc signals, we can stimulate any state or action of the microprocessor (but, of course, at much reduced speed). We can trace signals from the CPU socket to the system peripherals, and we can simulate memory and I/O read and write processes. (Static testing is really a form of dc *emulation,* in which we are emulating the actions of the microprocessor.)

The major advantages of static testing are its simplicity and low cost. Testing static voltages is easier than testing dynamic signals, and requires less expensive equipment. Because all signals hold steady, certain types of faults in the circuitry are more easily located. However, static testing cannot uncover timing problems—these require a dynamic analysis of the system, often when running at full speed. Also, static testing is limited in its ability to uncover software-related problems.

Software Diagnostics

Under certain conditions, the computer itself can locate faults within the system (self-diagnostics). A popular use of diagnostic programs is to test the system RAM using a diagnostic program stored in ROM. A simple RAM diagnostic routine is shown in Figure 22.10. All ones are written to each cell under test, and then read back out. If an error is found (a zero), the location of the fault is outported. If the RAM system passes the ones test, it is repeated using all zeros. Many instruments and computer systems (the IBM PC, for example) perform self-diagnostics upon power up.

Single Stepping

Single stepping is a way of slowing down computer action for close scrutiny. The operator steps, at any desired speed, from one program-processing location to the next, carefully examining the state of the system (comparing the present state with the expected state). The operator normally has the option of single stepping through the program by machine cycles or by instruction cycles.

Single stepping by machine cycles is a form of static testing, although the microprocessor is in the system and fully functional. During machine-cycle single stepping, the computer system under test is "frozen" in the wait state of each machine cycle (see Chapter 9), allowing the technician or engineer to directly access the state of each data-transfer operation during its most active period (see Figure 22.11).

Single stepping from one wait state to the next requires the add-on hardware circuit of Figure 22.12*a.*

Single stepping by machine cycle is useful for both software and hardware troubleshooting. Figure 22.12*b,* for example, depicts a typical troubleshooting situation. We are "frozen" in the third machine cycle of the IN-port instruction, but the port is not enabled ($\overline{OE}$ is high). Looking at the circuit diagram, it is clear to us that both IO/$\overline{M}$ and

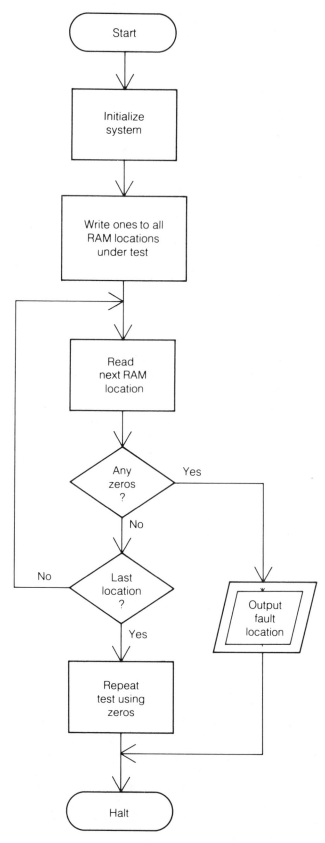

Figure 22.10 High-level diagnostic flowchart for testing RAM.

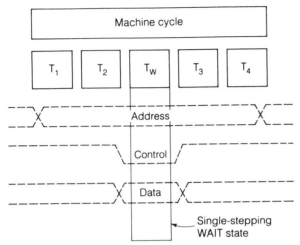

Figure 22.11 Machine-cycle single-stepping by way of the WAIT state.

address line A_5 should be high, and $\overline{RD}$ should be low. Testing the system, we find that $IO/\overline{M}$ and $\overline{RD}$ have the proper states, but address line A_5 does not—it is low. Therefore, we have a hardware problem in the A_5 line, the CPU chip, or the 8282 I/O port; or we used the incorrect port address in the IN-port instruction and have a software problem.

Single stepping by instruction cycles rather than machine cycles is usually done by way of the built-in monitor program in ROM. After each instruction is processed, the op code and address location are typically displayed. Many systems, such as the SDK-85, allow the operator to examine and modify all register and memory locations at each single-step location. Instruction-cycle single stepping streamlines software troubleshooting, but is largely ineffective at locating hardware faults. And single stepping in general has its limitations. It would be impractical, for example, to single step through a triple-nested delay loop.

Breakpointing

The technique of breakpointing also "freezes" computer action, but only at certain predesignated program locations (called *breakpoints*). Between breakpoints, the processor runs at full speed. Breakpointing, therefore, gives the operator a method of quickly homing in on the problem. Once the problem is localized, single stepping may prove productive.

Typically, a breakpoint is installed in a program by substituting a *call* (or *restart*) instruction at a point where an error is expected to appear. When the processor arrives at the breakpoint, it ceases main-program action and branches to a breakpoint routine, giving the operator an opportunity to examine the system.

Installing a breakpoint can be as simple as the "home-made" technique shown in Figure 22.13. The program shown

is designed to produce a musical tone whose pitch is proportional to the size of the inported number. Instead, the routine is generating a constant high-frequency tone, regardless of the number inported. Since the decision-making block is the most crucial, we will place a breakpoint following the conditional branch to check on the state of the system at that point. The breakpoint routine is very simple, and reflects our interest in only the contents of the A register (which should be holding a zero at the breakpoint).

When the program is run, from the start to the breakpoint, the breakpoint routine tells us the accumulator is holding a number one less than the value of the inported number—meaning the routine passed through the delay loop only once. Immediately we see the answer: instead of jumping on zero, we should be jumping on *not* zero. When the change is made, the program operates as intended.

Many computer systems offer built-in breakpoint capability. On the SDK-85 single-board computer, for example, breakpoints are set with the RST 1 (warm start) instruction. When the processor arrives at the first breakpoint, it calls the RST 1 routine. Within the breakpoint routine, all internal registers are stored at reserved locations in RAM (called *image locations*). The operator is now free to use the front panel keys to examine and set memory locations and registers, and to single step through the program. When troubleshooting is complete at the first breakpoint location, the system can be commanded to resume main-program action until the second breakpoint is reached. When debugging is complete, all breakpoints are removed (they can be replaced with NOP instructions).

Signature Analysis

The signature analyzer of Figure 22.14 is a simple, easy-to-use test instrument for verifying the performance of and locating bugs in a complex microcomputer or digital system.

The idea behind signature analysis is to absorb a long string of serial digital data from a circuit node and then compress it into a short 4-digit "signature." The signature corresponding to each node in the circuit could be labeled on the schematic as shown in Figure 22.15a. A field-service engineer would simply backtrack through a circuit, checking signatures until an error is found. Signature analysis is a portable, field-service technique, especially useful in circuits employing LSI chips, where internal operations are inaccessible.

The technique for compressing a long string of data into a short code we have seen before; it is the cyclic-redundancy-check character (CRCC), borrowed from the telecommunications field. We produce a CRCC by dividing a specified data stream by a polynomial and retaining the remainder. Based on a rather complex mathematical proof, it turns out that feeding data into a pseudorandom binary sequence (PRBS)

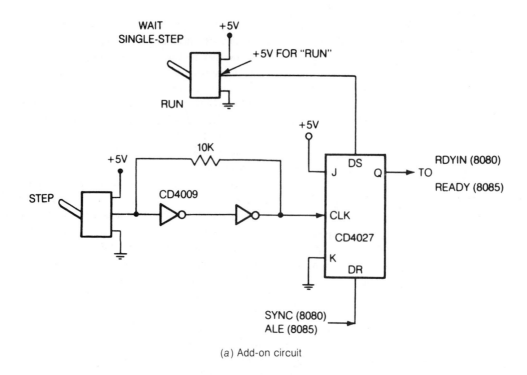

(a) Add-on circuit

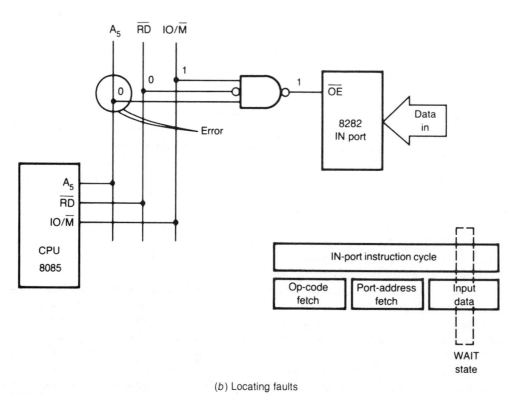

(b) Locating faults

Figure 22.12 Machine-cycle single-stepping.

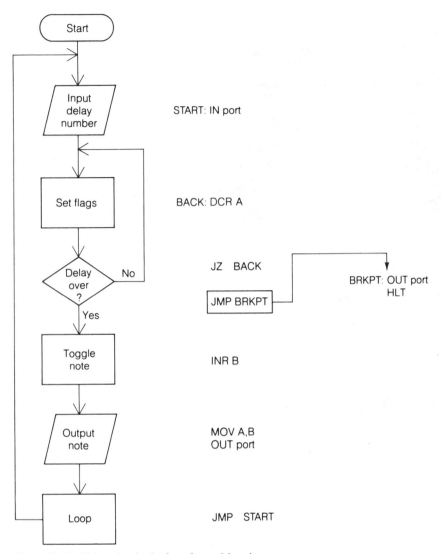

Figure 22.13 Using a breakpoint for software debugging.

generator is the same as dividing the data by the characteristic polynomial of the generator. Figure 22.15*b* shows how a PRBS corresponding to a characteristic polynomial is generated by modulo 2 addition of taps on a 16-bit shift register. When the PRBS is combined with the external data stream, a 4-character CRCC signature is produced.

Figure 22.15*c* demonstrates the acquisition sequence. Start and stop signals are taken from the system under test, and they provide the data-collection "window" or measurement time period. The start and stop signals can be taken from address or control lines, output ports, or any signals that bracket a unique data stream. During the acquisition sequence, incoming data are sampled at each rising edge of the clock.

The one drawback to signature analysis is that the stimulus required to produce the streams of data had to be designed into the product. However, external-stimulus devices are now coming onto the market to provide the field-service technician with the necessary external-stimulus signals.

Logic Analyzers

As microcomputer systems become more complex, even the most sophisticated oscilloscopes lack the power to ferret out a well-entrenched "bug." Consequently, microcomputer hardware/software debugging has been turned over to the *logic analyzer,* a test instrument specifically designed to operate in the parallel digital environment of the microcomputer.

Basic principles The logic analyzer is to the digital world what the oscilloscope is to the analog world. As with all test

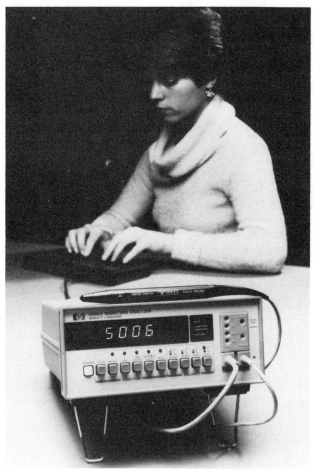

Figure 22.14 The Hewlett-Packard 5006A fully programmable signature analyzer, used for field troubleshooting of complex microprocessor-based circuits. *Courtesy of Hewlett-Packard Co.*

instruments, logic analysis is a two-step process: acquisition of data followed by display of data.

In both acquisition and display, a number of basic factors are common to all logic analyzers. Where the various logic analyzers differ is in their *exact* acquisition and display techniques. Using 4-bit data words, Figure 22.16 shows the three facets of data acquisition common to all logic analyzers: threshold detection, clocking and triggering, and sequential storage.

Unlike an oscilloscope, the logic analyzer displays logic states (1s and 0s), not continuous analog signals. The threshold-detection circuits classify each bit of an incoming data word as either a logic 0 or a logic 1, depending on its voltage level relative to a threshold. When the threshold is user selectable, data can be acquired from all the popular logic families—TTL, CMOS, ECL.

The clock-trigger section is responsible for strobing the data into the sequential storage medium and for issuing a trigger to either start or end data collection, for viewing either pretrigger or posttrigger information. (When the trig-

ger *initiates* data collection, acquisition is automatically halted when the display RAM is filled.) The trigger is generated by constantly comparing the incoming parallel data words with a user-selectable trigger word. By including a clocked delay in the trigger line, acquisition can be stopped a specific number of clock cycles *after* the trigger word is detected, allowing the trigger word to be positioned anywhere in RAM. Using this delay-trigger feature, we can select the desired ratio of pre- to post trigger information to be viewed.

The clock circuit determines the rate at which data are acquired and strobed into the sequential storage medium. The operator can select between two clock sources: a synchronous source from the system under test, or an asynchronous source from an internal clock generator. Generally speaking, logic *state* analysis—in which data words are displayed as sequences of binary, octal, or hexadecimal numbers—requires synchronous sampling; logic *timing* analysis—in which the data words are displayed as continuous waveforms—requires asynchronous sampling. The reason is fundamental. To make sense from a sequence of binary, octal, or hexadecimal numbers, and to avoid skipping or repeating data, those numbers must be correlated with the system under test by way of clock-cycle timing. When viewing waveforms, on the other hand, we must provide good resolution and we must be able to capture randomly occurring glitches. Therefore, we should sample the data asynchronously three to ten times faster than the system under test.

Sequential storage, the final element in data acquisition, is usually accomplished by a high-speed RAM addressed by a counter. In practice, most analyzers store anywhere from 64 to 2,048 words.

Figure 22.17*a* illustrates the display of data, the second and final step in the logic-analysis process. When data acquisition is complete, the information stored in the sequential-access RAM is displayed in one of two major formats: *state* and *timing*.

The state display, usually generated from information captured synchronously, displays sequential data words in binary, octal, hexadecimal, and sometimes even in mnemonics. The timing display, usually generated from information captured asynchronously, displays the data waveforms in parallel, using up to 16 or more channels.

Occasionally logic analyzers display information pictorially, in the form of a graph or a map (Figure 22.17*b*). The graph mode plots the binary weight of each word in memory on the Y axis and the position in RAM on the X axis. Since the data are displayed from left to right in the order of collection, the graph highlights the data-flow sequence.

Similar to the graph mode, the map mode breaks down each memory word into two sections, one section forming the X value on the CRT screen; and the other, the Y value. The map mode is often the starting point for troubleshooting a system, since it presents the widest possible overview of

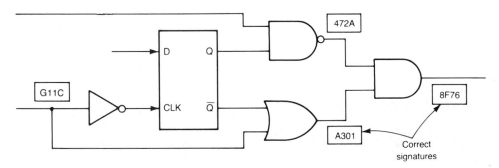

(*a*) Documenting a schematic for signature-analysis troubleshooting

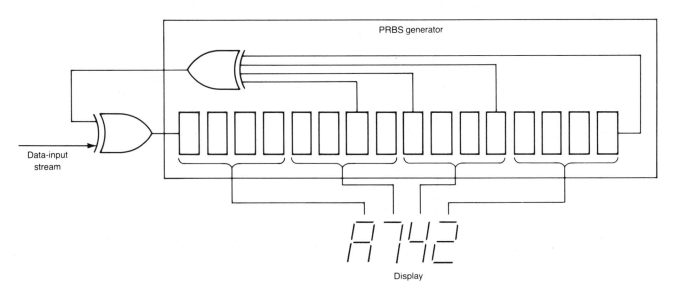

(*b*) A CRCC signature produced by overlaying the input-data stream with the PseudoRandom Binary Sequence (PRBS) generator

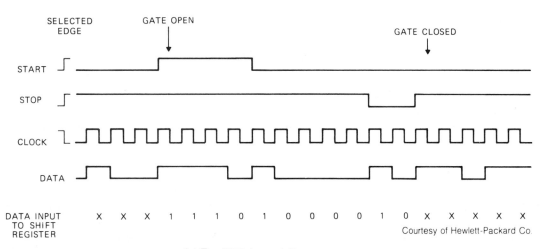

(*c*) The 5006 A acquisition sequence

Figure 22.15 The signature-analysis technique.

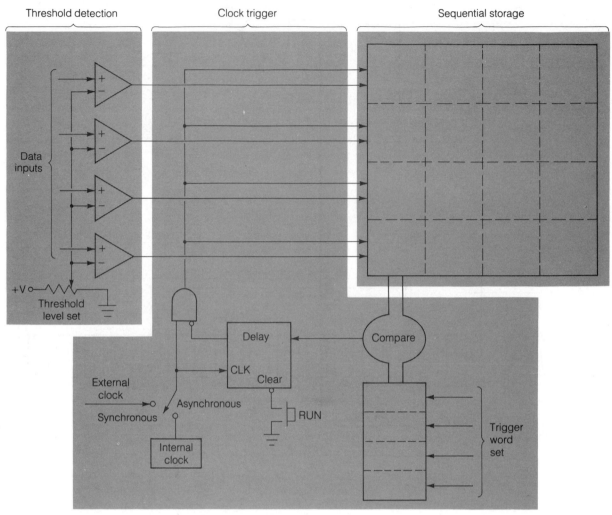

Figure 22.16 The three basic acquisition sections of a logic analyzer.

system activity. The operator quickly learns the map characteristics of a properly functioning system, and any changes are readily apparent. As we home in on the problem, we may go from map to graph to state to timing modes, each display mode narrowing down the problem area and presenting a more detailed picture of a specific area of program activity.

Now that we are acquainted with the basics of logic analysis, it is time to examine a real-world logic analyzer to see how it has refined the two-step acquisition/display process to a high level of sophistication.

The Hewlett-Packard 1630G Logic Analyzer The Hewlett-Packard 1630G (Figure 22.18) is a 65-channel (16 for timing), 100 MHz, synchronous/asynchronous logic analyzer, featuring 1K of storage RAM, sophisticated glitch detection, and simultaneous state and timing measurements. The 1630G, like all modern logic analyzers, is a multifunctional "menu" analyzer. A menu analyzer allows the user to

select acquisition and display parameters by positioning a cursor on the CRT. After a quick overview of the timing and state analysis capabilities, we will see what really sets the 1630G apart from earlier logic analyzers: *performance analysis*.

By pressing front panel keys, we bring up the timing menu and are able to enter powerful and flexible triggering conditions. For example, to a 16-channel trigger pattern we can AND each channel with a positive or negative edge condition.

After the system is run, the captured data is displayed in a simple format (see Figure 22.18). The waveforms can be magnified (expanded) and on-screen cursors provide easy time-interval measurements.

In the state mode (the "reflection" of Figure 22.18), *sequential* triggering (events must follow in a set pattern) allows us to track complex operations within the program. Features that improve analysis of data include the presentation of state information in relocatable format (for direct comparison with our list files), and the display of informa-

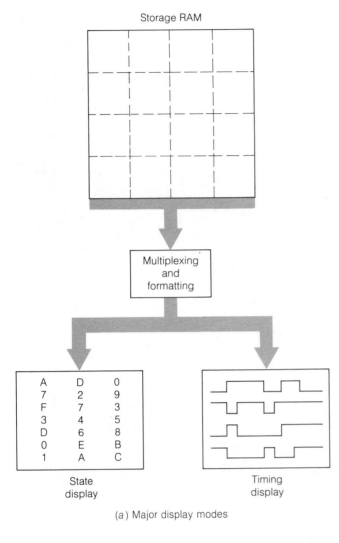

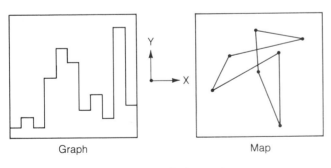

(b) Additional display modes

Figure 22.17 Logic-analysis display.

portions of code (a *histogram* is a graphic representation of a frequency distribution). For example, suppose we have a multitasking system in which six different routines access the disk drive as a shared resource. By keeping track of calls to the disk-handling routine from each of the six tasks, the 1630G generates the occurrence histogram of Figure 22.19a. (A *link* is a start/stop event pair.) As shown, most of the disk requests come from the ARCHV task.

To gain further information about event ARCHV, we run a time histogram (Figure 22.19b), in which the horizontal axis is time and the vertical axis is the number of calls to the disk-handling routine. Since most disk requests are made at the start of the ARCHV routine, the other five tasks are forced to wait until disk access is over. By spreading out the calls over time (Figure 22.19c), the other five tasks are given more favorable access to the disk and overall system performance is improved.

We can expect future logic analyzers to become even more sophisticated as they strive to meet the needs of the more complex microprocessing systems of the near future.

DEVELOPMENT SYSTEMS

A *development system* is a machine that gives the programmer development leverage. *Development leverage* refers to the use of any device that performs the low-level specific tasks, leaving the high-level conceptual tasks to humans. The higher the level of task performed by the device, the higher the degree of leverage. In today's competitive market, the *development system* is our most important development leverage tool.

As shown in Figure 22.20, a development system is a complete computer system, designed to aid product development, and usually includes a video terminal, floppy or Winchester disk drives, line printer, processing unit, user-available RAM, several serial and parallel I/O ports, and a number of support programs (usually offered on floppy disk). Although the development system cannot help in the conception of the product, it can greatly aid the remaining aspects of product development (refer to Figure 22.1).

The development system offers a complete computer system on which to write, compile, and store programs. An option—the in-circuit emulator (ICE)—allows us to test and troubleshoot the hardware and to integrate our hardware/software design (the system of Figure 22.20 includes ICE51). By sharing resources with the development system, software/hardware debugging and integration can take place *while the prototype system is under development.*

Software Development

Since we are using the development system to perform software-design tasks that would otherwise have to be per-

tion in assembly language mnemonics (the 1630G performs inverse assembly automatically).

Performance analysis, the newest feature of state-of-the-art logic analyzers, is an indication of the importance placed on software performance. Using histograms, the 1630G measures the times or occurrence distribution of selected

Figure 22.18 The Hewlett-Packard 1630G logic analyzer. *Courtesy Hewlett-Packard.*

formed by the human brain, it follows that we must load the computer's memory with various programs designed to carry out those development tasks. Such a software-development package includes the following routines:

- Monitor system
- System supervisor
- Editor
- Assembler or compiler
- Library
- Link
- Locate
- UPM (PROM programming)
- ICE (In-circuit emulator)

Based on these development system routines, Figure 22.21 flowcharts the product development sequence. Moving from left to right, we proceed as follows:

1. When the system is turned on, it "wakes up" in the *monitor* routine (contained within a built-in ROM). Using the monitor routine, the operator loads ("bootstraps") the *system supervisor* from the *system disk* (the disk that holds the development system routines). The major function of the system supervisor is to recognize commands issued by the operator. The system supervisor, along with its collection of utility programs, is often called an *operating system*. The system supervisor and each utility is stored on disk as a *file* (a named program).

2. The operator commands the system supervisor to bring in the *text editor* file from the system disk. The text editor is similar to a word processor in that it allows the programmer to create, modify, and correct source programs (files) from the terminal.

3. Once the prototype source program has been written (and stored away on the *user* disk), it must be compiled or assembled into a binary *object* program. The operator enters the compile or assemble command, and the compiler or assembler utility program translates the source code into relocatable binary object code (*relocatable*, remember, means that all addresses are symbolic or rel-

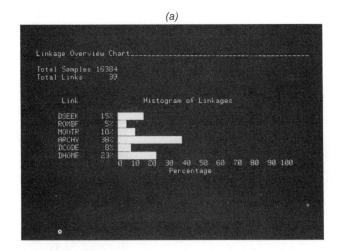

(a)

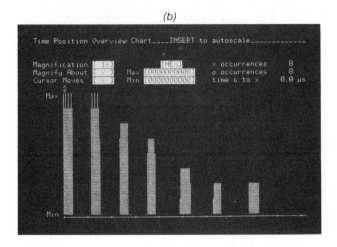

(b)

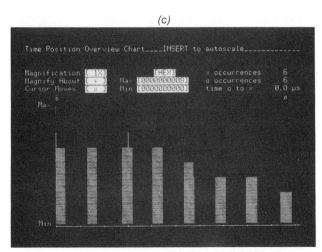

(c)

Figure 22.19 Software performance histograms: *a)* Disc-access occurrence histogram. *b)* Time-access histogram (before software modification). *c)* Time-access histogram (after software modification).
Courtesy Hewlett-Packard.

ative and the program can be adjusted to run from any address location).

Also generated by the compilation or assembly process is the LIST (LST) file. For example, a list file generated from our familiar mimic-delay program written in PLM-86 (an Intel-developed structured high-level language similar to Pascal) is shown in Figure 22.22*a*. All source statements are numbered and a nesting level (how deeply is a given instruction nested within an IF-THEN or DO-WHILE construct) assigned to each. As shown, the compiler has uncovered two syntax errors. When the errors are corrected (Figure 22.22*b*), we are ready to proceed. (Identification of the two errors is left as an exercise.)

4. If our object program is an independently compiled procedure module, at this point we have the option of storing it in a *library* (See the machine-assembly update of Chapter 21).

5. Once an error-free object file is created, the system supervisor calls on the *link* routine to combine all library and separately compiled programs into a single object program. (Remember, a block-structured language—such as Pascal—encourages large programming tasks to be broken up into several modules and written individually.)

6. The operator directs the system supervisor to activate the *locate* utility, and the operator specifies the exact RAM and ROM locations to be reserved for program code, data, and stack operations.

A machine-language program now exists. With the help of the system supervisor, it can be burned into PROM or downloaded into the hardware system under test. For programs and systems of any complexity, it would be very rare indeed if the software were error-free and the hardware devoid of bugs. The next step in the product-development process is to troubleshoot the system and merge the hardware and software efforts.

In-Circuit Emulation is a development-system option that allows hardware/software development to proceed interactively. To accomplish emulation, the microprocessor of the product is removed, and in essence the entire development system is substituted by plugging in a 40-pin cable (see Figure 22.20).

To test the product, the program is run on the product hardware, just as if the original microprocessor were in place. (As far as the product is concerned, the development system/ emulator combination acts just like the original microprocessor.) However, the in-circuit emulator does much more than the original microprocessor: it gives the operator a "window" to look inside the system; to examine and alter CPU registers, main memory, and flag values; and to automatically collect and store address, data, and status information for future reference.

Figure 22.20 The Intel Series IV Development System with ICE51. *Courtesy Intel Corporation.*

A "trace" (block of collected real-time program information) can be displayed as disassembled mnemonics and compared with the LIST file.

Using in-circuit emulation, your program can be single-stepped. Within the single-step mode, the in-circuit emulator runs your program and collects information one instruction cycle at a time. All register and status information may be displayed at the end of each instruction cycle.

The in-circuit emulator can specify breakpoints, based on a number of different breakpoint conditions (for example, a specific address). When a breakpoint is encountered, you can display the last several instruction cycles executed and the contents of any memory or register.

Of special importance is the ability to use in-circuit emulation at any stage in product development. By borrowing the hardware resources of the development/emulator system, we can even begin testing software before any prototype hardware exists. As our prototype system develops, memory and I/O resources can be shared between emulator and prototype. In the final stages of design, when hardware and software integration is well along, the in-circuit emulator can run extensive diagnostics and product testing. In short, the in-circuit emulator is the "parent of a product," nurturing our prototype system from the earliest stages of implementation through the final phases of checkout.

In Chapter 25, we will review the entire development system process for a design based on the Intel 8088 16-bit microprocessor.

CAD/CAM

CAD/CAM stands for *computer-aided design/computer-aided manufacturing* and represents the full-scale invasion of the manufacturing industry by the computer.

Initially, CAD stood for little more than *computer-aided drafting*—a computer with two-dimensional graphics. Since then, it has spread into every facet of design, manufacturing,

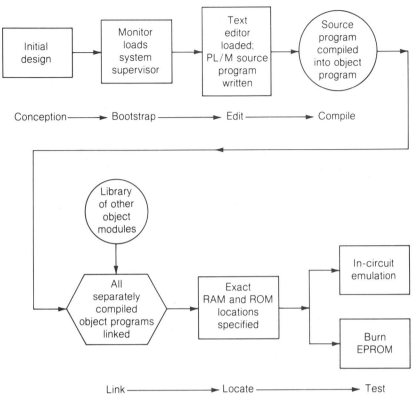

Figure 22.21 The major software design steps of a development system.

and engineering. CAD/CAM generally falls into one of two categories: mechanical or electrical.

Mechanical CAD/CAM

Although the state of the art in mechanical CAD is solids, the mainstay is the generation of a 3-D wire-frame model (see Figure 22.23). Since the wire-frame model is really a database stored in memory, the model can be mathematically moved, rotated, and manipulated in a variety of ways by simple software commands. Once a database exists, it can be tapped to support all areas of engineering, design, and manufacturing: the production of 2-D mechanical drawings by projection; the matching of separately created parts; the creation of a programmed "tool path" for numerically controlled machines; and the robotics control programs for assembly and manufacturing.

Even initial engineering functions are being integrated into the CAD/CAM process. Called *computer-aided engineering* (CAE), the computer will analyze the wire-frame model, perhaps calculating its mass and thermal properties. Using *finite element modeling* (FEM), in which a complex structure is broken up into a number of small solids, the computer can perform complex stress analysis. When ready for manufacturing, the CAD/CAM system can mathematically "unfold" the structure and develop the outlines for die stamping.

Electrical CAD/CAM

As with mechanical CAD/CAM concepts, its electrical counterpart started as an isolated incident—a computer digitizing printed-circuit artwork in order to aid the manufacturing process. From this simple beginning it spread rapidly in both directions, from initial engineering (CAE) to final manufacturing (CAM). The result is the *engineering workstation*. Using powerful software routines, coupled with a windowed high-resolution display (Figure 22.24), all activities from schematic design and chip layout to circuit simulation and testing becomes a CAD activity. Once a circuit is designed and photographic masks prepared, the database can be "post-processed" to control the drilling of holes in the printed-circuit board, as well as the insertion of components.

Beyond mechanical and electrical product development, CAE/CAD/CAM concepts are spreading into nearly every area of human activity: architecture and plant design, movies and art, and even mapping, where whole countries have been placed on a CAD/CAM system for analysis and planning.

The next logical step, already underway, is *CIM (Computer-Integrated Manufacturing),* where expert systems employing artificial intelligence will oversee all aspects of product development from design (CAE) to production (CAM). The future of CIM—in conjunction with graphics and robotics—is nothing short of awesome, for it will soon be hard

```
PL/M-86 COMPILER    MIMICDELAY
                            PAGE    1


ISIS-II PL/M-86 V2.1 COMPILATION OF MODULE MIMICDELAY
OBJECT MODULE PLACED IN :F1:ROY.OBJ
COMPILER INVOKED BY:   PLM86 :F1:ROY.SRC



     1              MIMIC$DELAY:
                    DO;
     2    1           DECLARE NUMBER BYTE;

     3    1           DELAY:
                      PROCEDURE (N);
     4    2             DECLARE (N,I) BYTE;
     5    2             IF N > 128D THEN
     6    2               DO WHILE N > 0;
     7    3                 N = N - 1;
     8    3                 I = 100;
     9    3                 DO WHILE I > 0;
*** ERROR #105, STATEMENT #9, NEAR 'O',    UNDECLARED IDENTIFIER, BYTE ASSUMED
    10    4                   I = I - 1;
    11    4                 END;
    12    3               END;
                        ELSE
    13    2               O = NUMBER;
*** ERROR #29, STATEMENT #13,    ILLEGAL STATEMENT
    14    2           END DELAY;

    15    1           NUMBER = INPUT(1);
    16    1           CALL DELAY(NUMBER);
    17    1           OUTPUT(2) = NUMBER;
    18    1         END MIMIC$DELAY;



MODULE INFORMATION:

     CODE AREA SIZE     = 0050H    80D
     CONSTANT AREA SIZE = 0000H     0D
     VARIABLE AREA SIZE = 0003H     3D
     MAXIMUM STACK SIZE = 0006H     6D
     24 LINES READ
     2 PROGRAM ERROR(S)

END OF PL/M-86 COMPILATION
```

(a) Two syntax errors found

Figure 22.22   The MIMIC-DELAY program LIST file written in PL/M: *a)* Two syntax error found. *b)* Errors corrected.

to imagine marketing a product that was not engineered, designed, and manufactured by a CIM system.

Silicon Compilation

Silicon compilation is the ultimate in development leverage. Just as a software compiler is a program that yields complex machine-language programs from high-level statements, a silicon compiler is a sophisticated program that yields VLSI solutions from high-level descriptions of the IC's architecture. All the in-between steps, such as circuit design, simulation, and layout, are eliminated.

As an example of silicon compilation, consider a circuit consisting of some 100,000 transistors. As shown by Figure 22.25, such a circuit is designed in hierarchical fashion, from the 20 high-level modules to the two million required

circuit geometries. Conventional CAD design techniques would require the designer to become involved to some degree at the cell, gate, and transistor levels. When using silicon compilation, on the other hand, all design activity below the block level is handled automatically by the compiler.

As with all hierarchical top-down techniques, silicon compilation promises to free the designer from the mundane and tedious in order to concentrate on the creative and abstract.

OPERATING SYSTEMS

In the world of software there are *applications* (users') programs and there are *system* (operating system) programs. In the simplest possible terms, an operating system controls the movement of information on your computer.

```
PL/M-86 COMPILER    MIMICDELAY
                               PAGE   1


ISIS-II PL/M-86 V2.1 COMPILATION OF MODULE MIMICDELAY
OBJECT MODULE PLACED IN :F1:ROY.OBJ
COMPILER INVOKED BY:   PLM86 :F1:ROY.SRC


   1              MIMIC$DELAY:
                  DO;
   2    1           DECLARE NUMBER BYTE;

   3    1           DELAY:
                    PROCEDURE (N);
   4    2             DECLARE (N,I) BYTE;
   5    2             IF N > 128D THEN
   6    2               DO WHILE N > 0;
   7    3                 N = N - 1;
   8    3                 I = 100;
   9    3                 DO WHILE I > 0;
  10    4                   I = I - 1;
  11    4                 END;
  12    3               END;
                      ELSE
  13    2               NUMBER = 0;
  14    2           END DELAY;

  15    1           NUMBER = INPUT(1);
  16    1           CALL DELAY(NUMBER);
  17    1           OUTPUT(2) = NUMBER;
  18    1           END MIMIC$DELAY;


MODULE INFORMATION:

    CODE AREA SIZE     = 005FH    95D
    CONSTANT AREA SIZE = 0000H     0D
    VARIABLE AREA SIZE = 0002H     2D
    MAXIMUM STACK SIZE = 0006H     6D
    24 LINES READ
    0 PROGRAM ERROR(S)

END OF PL/M-86 COMPILATION
```

(*b*) Errors corrected

Why are operating systems needed? Imagine the "simple" process of printing out a file of information from a floppy disk. Without the intervention of an operating system, the task would be unimaginably difficult and time-consuming for the average user. But with an operating system, one need only type in a high-level command (such as COPY PROG PRN) and the operating system will control all the movement of information required to carry out the command.

As introduced in Chapter 18, an *operating system* performs two major functions:

- It manages the resources of the computer system.
- It accepts and carries out high-level commands entered from a keyboard or other input device.

To carry out these two main functions, the operating system for a microcomputer is typically divided into four major categories:

- BIOS (Basic Input/Output System).
- BDOS (Basic Disk Operating System).
- CP (Command Processor).
- Utilities.

The BIOS program manages data transfer between the microprocessor and various peripherals; the BDOS program handles all operations associated with storing files on a disk; the CP (also known as the *system supervisor*) interprets commands from the keyboard; and the utilities group includes programs to manage files as well as develop programs.

Since resource management is automatic and therefore "invisible" to the user, the essence of an operating system boils down to the following:

AN OPERATING SYSTEM INTERPRETS AND
CARRIES OUT HIGH-LEVEL COMMANDS ISSUED
BY THE OPERATOR.

An operating system is therefore called a *command language*.

To logically tie together the whole process, each command name is also a utility program name. In other words, when a command is given, the command processor (CP) searches for a utility file of the same name. When the utility program is found, it is executed and the command carried out. When finished, control is returned to the command processor (the supervisor) to await the next high-level command.

Let us briefly review one of the more popular operating systems on the market and see what additional features it has to offer.

DOS

IBM's DOS (disk operating system), developed by Microsoft Corporation, is the most popular operating system on the market today.

DOS is actually a collection of programs (files) that reside on a *system diskette*. When the computer is turned on, the *resident monitor* in ROM automatically loads (*bootstraps*) the operating system software into internal RAM. The operating system then "takes over," issues the prompt (A>), and monitors the keyboard for high-level command. (A *prompt* is a symbol the system displays when ready for the next command, and the "A" in the prompt indicates that drive A is the *default drive*—the drive DOS automatically searches in response to a command.)

Since the primary function of DOS is to interpret and carry out high-level commands, let's begin by listing some of the commands that are available:

Internal commands	External commands
DIR	FORMAT
COPY	DISKCOPY
ERASE	COMP

Figure 22.23   CAD system for creating 3-D wire-frame models.

An *internal command* is one whose corresponding utility file is loaded into internal RAM during the bootstrap operation, and an *external command* is one that remains on the DOS disk until needed.

Let's review several of the above commands so we can learn to speak DOS's command language.

1. FORMAT (Initializes the disk).

   A>FORMAT B:

   Prepares the disk to accept DOS files by initializing the directory, file-allocation table, and system loader.

2. COPY (To transfer data between any of the system devices)

   A>COPY WHALE B:APPLES

   Copies file WHALE on default drive (A) to drive B and assigns it the new name APPLES.

3. DIR (Lists all the files stored on a disk).

   A>DIR

DOS Enhancements

Since the first disk operating system was introduced to the market, DOS has taken on a number of advanced features. A few of these are:

- I/O redirection: Under DOS the standard input device is the keyboard and the standard output device is the CRT screen. Using I/O redirection, the user can specify alternative devices for input and output. For example, the following command redirects the output of the DIR command to the printer rather than the CRT screen:

   A>DIR >PRN

- Filters: A filter is a program or command that reads data from a standard input device, modifies the data, then writes the result to a standard output device (the data has been "filtered"). DOS offers three on-disk filters: SORT, FIND, and MORE. The following command causes SORT

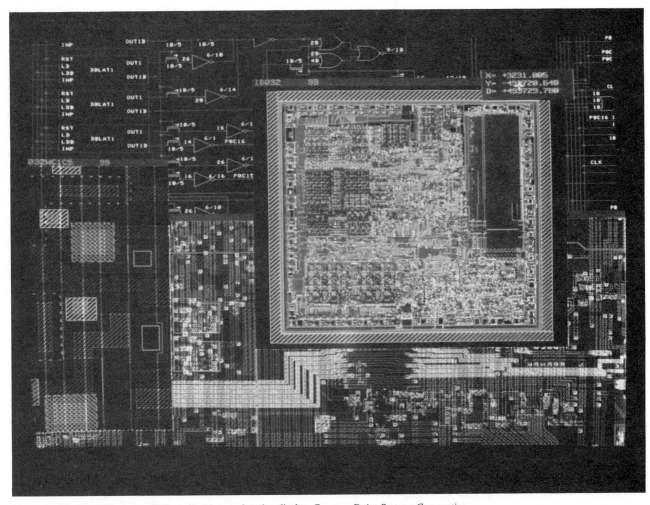

Figure 22.24   The Chipmaster (TM) engineering workstation display. *Courtesy Daisy Systems Corporation.*

to read file APPLES, sort the program, and send its output to the CRT screen:

A>SORT <APPLES

• Piping: Rather than redirect the output of the DIR command to another *device*, suppose we wish to send it to another *program*. For example, the command

A>DIR|SORT

would send the output of program DIR to the input of program SORT, and would generate a sorted directory listing. *Piping,* therefore, is the chaining of programs with automatic redirection of standard input and output. As shown, programs are chained by separating them by the vertical bar (|) character.

• Tree-structured directories: As shown in Figure 22.26, a tree-structured directory resembles an inverted tree and makes it possible to quickly locate a given file among thousands of files. To locate a particular file, we start at

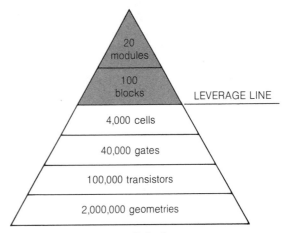

Figure 22.25   Silicon compilation leverage.

the top of the tree (the "root") and work our way down through the layers of file directories from general, broad-based categories to more and more specific categories until we locate the correct file.

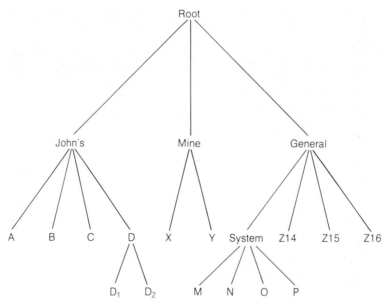

Figure 22.26 The inverted tree structure of the DOS file system.

- Wildcards: Suppose we wish to list on the CRT screen all files in the directory with an extension of ASM (regardless of the name of the file). As shown below, the wildcard symbol (∗) will carry out our wishes:

  A>DIR ∗.ASM

- Development system support: DOS offers an editor (EDLIN), linker (LINK), and emulator (DEBUG) for efficient writing and testing of programs.

- Batch files: Suppose that during development of a program you find yourself using the same sequence of commands over and over again (such as EDLIN, LINK, DEBUG). Why not let the computer "push the keys" instead of us? That is the purpose of a *batch file*. A batch file is a file containing one or more commands that DOS executes one at a time. Using such *subcommands* as GOTO, FOR, and IF, we can combine our command language with the loop and decision-making constructs of a programming language.

In addition to these features, the later versions of DOS (3.0 and 3.1) offer support for Winchester disk systems and for creating a RAM disk (see Chapter 6). For a full discussion of all the features of DOS, refer to the *IBM Disk Operating System User's Guide*.

Operating Environments

For some applications, the new *operating environments,* designed to simulate a real desk top, may make conventional operating systems obsolete.

By inputting information from "the mouse" and display-ing information in "windows" (separate sections of the CRT screen displaying different applications), new levels of task integration and user interfacing have been achieved. Via the mouse, the cursor is moved to an area on the screen; in this way, new windows can be opened and information can be shifted (as if shifting papers on a desk top) between windows without disturbing the operation of any programs they represent.

Requiring more than 128K of primary memory, operating environments are ambitious software systems, and many versions will battle for marketplace dominance in the coming years.

Real-Time Operating Systems

Operating systems that must respond rapidly to external events are known as *real-time* operating systems. Because external real-world events occur randomly and often simultaneously, interrupt handling and multitasking are primary attributes of a real-time operating system. To provide the necessary high-speed reaction times, many real-time operating system "primitives" (short standard routines) are "embedded" into ROM.

INTELLIGENT-MACHINE UPDATE

With the advent of the development system, computers are (in a sense) developing other computers. How long will it be before the initial *conception* block of Figure 22.1 is also carried out under computer control? Will the computer then be able to reproduce improved copies of itself, *without human intervention?*

QUESTIONS AND PROBLEMS

1. Why are duties normally assigned to software being taken over by a peripheral chips (hardware)?
2. What is a *high-level language?*
3. What are the advantages of *top-down programming?*
4. What task is performed by a *compiler?*
5. Why is *assembly-language programming* sometimes preferred over high-level language programming?
6. How does the *single-step circuit* of Figure 22.12a allow the operator to step from one machine cycle to the next?
7. How can the *breakpoint technique* home in on a problem area faster than single stepping?
8. Why do you think the SDK-85 computer stores the contents of all internal registers in memory at the beginning of the breakpoint routine?
9. With regard to signature analysis, what is a *signature* and how is it generated?
10. State the two steps involved in *logic analysis.*
11. Based on the simplified data-acquisition diagram of Figure 22.16, how is a *trigger* generated and what does it do?
12. How does the delay block of Figure 22.16 affect the position of the trigger word in the 4 × 4 RAM?
13. Why is *state analysis* usually a synchronous process, and *timing analysis* usually an asynchronous process?
14. What are combinational and sequential triggering?
15. How is information organized when using the *graph* mode of display?
16. What is a *menu* logic analyser?
17. What is a *histogram?*
18. List the hardware components of a development system.
19. What part of the development process is handled by the *in-circuit emulator?*
20. What is the *system supervisor* in a development system?
21. What is the purpose of the *text editor* file? the *locate* file? the *link* file?
22. During in-circuit emulation, how is the prototype product interfaced with the development system?
23. What are the three types of structures used by structured programs?
24. How is the instinctive intelligence of a newborn baby related to a *monitor* program?
25. Compared to a compiler, why is an interpreter inefficient when executing a program with many loops?
26. Replacing an existing ROM/PROM with a software diagnostic ROM/PROM is a popular means of troubleshooting. Write a simple diagnostic routine designed to "exercise" the system of Figure 9.22 (the diagnostic routine will be burned into a 2764 EPROM and substituted for the existing EPROM). Indicate what you would see on the various bus and I/O lines when they are probed by a scope.
27. What do the terms *CAD, CAM,* and *CAE* stand for?
28. In relation to CAD/CAM, what is "postprocessing"?
29. What are the two main functions of an *operating system?*
30. What occurs during a "bootstrap"?
31. In an operating system, what is the relationship between the "supervisor" and the "utilities"?
32. Is DOS intended for single-user or multiuser operation?
33. Why are files particularly easy to locate when using a hierarchical file structure (such as DOS offers)?
34. What is a *prompt?*
35. Related to DOS, what do the letters A and B stand for?
36. List the four major components of an operating system and state the functions of each.
37. Under the UCSD P-system, the Pascal program of Figure 22.8a runs in 8 seconds for an input of 129, and 16 seconds for an input of 255. In contrast, the interpreted BASIC program of Figure 22.8b requires 70 and 140 seconds, respectively, to run. Why is the BASIC program slower? How fast would a fully compiled program run?
38. In the Warnier-Orr diagram of Figure 22.5b, what is the meaning of the symbol "∞"?
39. Draw the Warnier-Orr diagram for a program that outputs a musical note whose frequency is proportional to an inported number.
40. By comparing Figures 22.22a and b, and using the error messages listed below (reprinted from the PL/M86 error message table), determine the two syntax errors of Figure 22.22a.

    ERROR # 29: ILLEGAL STATEMENT This may be due to misspelling or missing parts of an otherwise valid statement.

    ERROR #105: UNDECLARED IDENTIFIER Every identifier must be declared.

41. Referring to Figure 22.22b, how deeply nested is the high-level PL/M statement: I = I − 1;?
42. How does a *structure chart* differ from a *flow chart?*
43. Figure 22.9 shows a linked list consisting of three data bytes. Between the second and third bytes, add another byte of information at memory location 2030H.
44. In LISP, what is a *flavor?*
45. Which of the following is stored in a *library?*
    a. Source file.
    b. Relocated object file.
    c. Relocatable object file.
    d. Error free list file.
46. How does *silicon compilation* apply *development leverage?*

chapter 23

The 8-Bit Family
of Microprocessors

Biologically, the various species belonging to the same family of the animal kingdom exhibit many more similarities than differences. With a similar anatomy and physiology, experiments run on one family member often can be carried over to others.

The family of 8-bit microprocessors follows the same pattern. The many "species" of 8-bit microprocessors offered by various manufacturers are all different. Yet they all belong to the same family—the family of 8-bit microprocessors—and all have very similar architecture, processing action, and instruction set (indeed, some are direct descendants of others). Once we master a single member of the family—such as the 8080 or 8085—we have opened the door to all other 8-bit microprocessors, for only a slight change in focus will allow us to design and troubleshoot with almost any 8-bit microprocessor now on the market.

In this chapter we will take a brief look at two additional branches of the 8-bit microprocessor family tree (Figure 23.1), and we will point out how they differ from the Intel group in architecture, processing action, and instruction set.

THE ZILOG GROUP

After the 8080 was developed, the design team at Intel split—some staying at Intel to develop the 8085, and others moving to Zilog to develop the Z80. As expected, with similar architecture and instruction set, the 8085 and Z80 show the effects of their common 8080 ancestry.

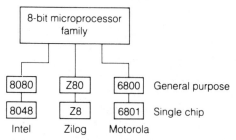

Figure 23.1 Popular members of the 8-bit microprocessor family tree.

The Z80 Basic Architecture

Figure 23.2 compares the basic architecture of the Z80 side by side with the 8085. As noted, the Z80 does not multiplex its address or data lines. Therefore, all 16 address and 8 bidirectional data lines are fully decoded and ready to tie directly into the system bus.

Like the 8085, the Z80 requires only a single 5-V dc supply. However, on Z80 systems the single-phase clock must be supplied externally, while the 8085 has integrated all clock circuitry, requiring only an external crystal.

As seen in Figure 23.2, the 8085 internal registers are a subset of the expanded Z80 register set. The basic register and flag set of the 8085 are duplicated to provide two sets of internal registers (register storage is often preferred over memory storage because of its faster access time). The interrupt-vector register (I), memory-refresh register (R), and index registers (IX and IY) are not found on the 8085 system.

Memory and I/O Control

The four control signals of the Z80 ($\overline{\text{MREQ}}$, $\overline{\text{IORQ}}$, $\overline{\text{RD}}$, and $\overline{\text{WR}}$) are designed to drive an isolated I/O system. Figure 23.3 shows the interfacing circuitry for each of the four basic data-transfer operations.

CPU and Bus Control

As shown in Figure 23.2, the CPU and bus-control signals $\overline{\text{WAIT}}$, $\overline{\text{BUSREQ}}$, $\overline{\text{BUSACK}}$, and $\overline{\text{RESET}}$ all have direct counterparts on 8085 systems (READY, HOLD, HLDA and RESET). $\overline{\text{HALT}}$ indicates the Z80 has executed a HALT instruction.

Interrupts

Two pins in the Z80 ($\overline{\text{INT}}$ and $\overline{\text{NMI}}$) are reserved for interrupt processing. All but one of the features of the interrupt system have counterparts in the 8085 system.

- $\overline{\text{NMI}}$ (Non-Maskable Interrupt)
  NMI is similar to the 8085's TRAP—it has the highest

342

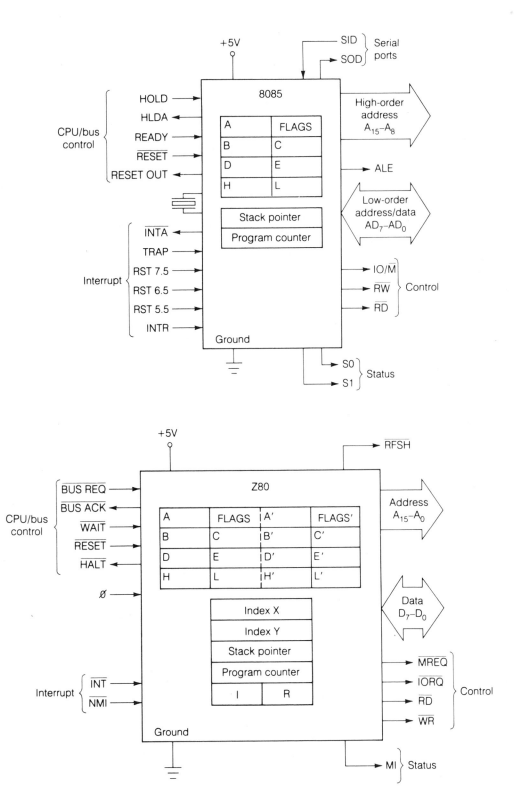

Figure 23.2 8085/Z80 hardware comparison.

priority and cannot be masked out or disabled. When NMI is recognized, it performs a restart vectored interrupt to location 0066H.

- $\overline{\text{INT}}$ (Interrupt)

With three possible modes of operation, the $\overline{\text{INT}}$ input of the Z80 is more complex than the INTR of the 8085. Each of the three modes is selected by software execution of the IM0, IM1, or IM2 instruction.

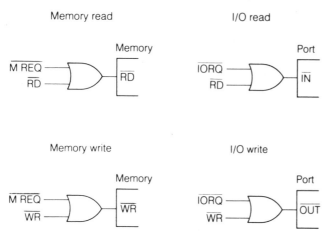

Figure 23.3 Z80 data-transfer control.

Mode 0 is similar to the INTR input of the 8085, and initiates a RESTART jam into the instruction register from external circuitry. Mode 1, set by the IM1 instruction, turns the $\overline{\text{INT}}$ input into an 8085-type RST 7 input, causing an automatic RESTART vector to location 0038H with no external circuitry required.

Mode 2, the most powerful of the three modes, is not represented on the 8085. Mode 2 allows up to 128 interrupt vectors to *anywhere* in memory. To form the 16-bit interrupt vector, the Z80 combines an 8-bit low-order address with an 8-bit high-order address supplied by the contents of the interrupt-vector register. Mode 2 is usually implemented by placing a vector table of up to 256 locations in memory at the page indicated by the I register. The table has up to 128 two-byte entries, with each entry representing the starting location of an interrupt-service routine. When a mode 2 interrupt is requested, the 8-bit value pulled from external circuitry is merged with the contents of the I register to point to a location within the vector table. The PC is loaded with the contents of the selected vector-table location, effectively causing a jump to the interrupt-service routine.

Memory Refresh

From the standpoint of the external circuitry, refreshing dynamic memory is basically a counting operation. A 6- or 7-bit row address is sent to the memory, along with a refresh-enable pulse. When that row of memory cells has been refreshed, the counter is incremented and the process repeated. In a Z80 system, the memory-refresh register (R) contains the 6- or 7-bit row address, while RFSH and MREQ (when both are simultaneously low) constitute the refresh-enable signal, informing the memory that the least significant 7 bits of the address bus contain the contents of the R register. Register R is automatically incremented after each refresh operation.

Z80 Timing

Driven by a 2.5–4-MHz clock, the basic clock speed of the Z80 is similar to the 8085. The basic state, machine-cycle, instruction-cycle breakdown is also very similar to that of the 8085, reflecting their common lineage.

Addressing Modes

The addressing modes available to the Z80 programmer exceed those available to the 8085 programmer. As shown in the following list, however, all but three (those starred) have counterparts in an 8085 system:

Z80/8085 counterpart

immediate/*immediate*
extended immediate/*16-bit immediate*
implied/*(present but undefined)*
register/*register*
register indirect/*register indirect*
extended/*direct*
modified page zero/*restart*
*relative
*indexed
*bit

Relative addressing can be explained with the help of an analogy: "Go three more houses beyond where you are right now." "Three more houses" is known as the *displacement*. To calculate the actual address, simply add the displacement to the present location. This process is known as *relative addressing* (the desired location is known *relative* to the present location). The Z80 uses relative addressing only for the JUMP group of instructions. The displacement is stored in the instruction as a signed number ranging from − 128 to + 127.

For *indexed addressing,* we will rewrite our analogy slightly: "Go three more houses beyond the church." The "church" has a known location or address (not related to the present location) and is called the *index.* Therefore, to calculate the actual address, simply add the displacement to the index. In Z80 systems, the index of the address is stored in either index register IX or index register IY. Indexed addressing is especially useful when processing tables or lists of data in memory. Figure 23.4 summarizes relative and indexed addressing.

Bit addressing can be used with any of the previous addressing modes to set, reset, or test any bit of any register or memory location.

The Z80 Instruction Set

The 158 instruction types making up the Z80 instruction set include the 8080 instruction set as a subset. Besides all the

Memory
map

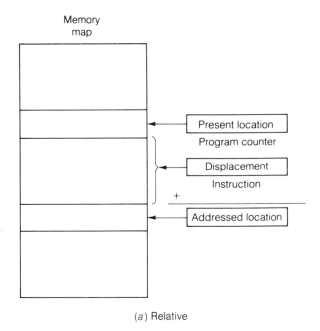

(a) Relative

Memory
map

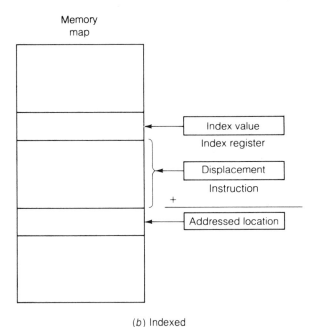

(b) Indexed

Figure 23.4   Special Z80 addressing modes.

8080 instructions, it features block transfers of data between memory and I/O, additional arithmetic instructions for efficient data processing, and bit operations on any location in memory. Although it is not possible to review all 86 new instructions, a few examples will show the extent of the Z80 instructions available.

Example 1   By entering into a repetitive loop, the load-increment-repeat (LDIR) instruction transfers a *block* of data

(from 1 to 64K bytes) from one area in memory to another area in memory, one byte at a time. Before using this instruction, three register pairs must be preset: register pair HL is initialized to the starting address of the source block, register pair DE to the starting address of the destination block, and register pair BC initialized to the number of bytes to be transferred. Assuming one page of data is to be transferred from memory page 20H to memory page 30H, Figure 23.5a shows the coded instruction and pertinent registers.

Example 2   The *negate accumulator* (NEG) instruction changes the sign of the contents of the accumulator by taking its 2's complement. Figure 23.5b shows how +7 is converted to −7.

Example 3   The RES b, (IX + d) instruction resets a selected bit within the contents of a memory location specified by indexed addressing. For example, if bit 5 of memory location 2040H is to be reset, the process is as shown in Figure 23.5c.

Example 4   The decrement and jump on nonzero (DJNZ e) instruction (Figure 23.5d) combines the decrement and JNZ processes, and implements a delay loop with just a single instruction. The DJNZ e instruction automatically decrements the B register, jumping to itself if the result is nonzero. When B is decremented to zero, control passes to the next instruction in sequence.

The Z8 Microcomputer

The Z8 is Zilog's entry in the single-chip field. Like the 8048, the Z8 emphasizes those features particularly well suited for real-time control applications: fast instruction execution, fast interrupt response, on-chip I/O ports, and a 47-member instruction set weighted in favor of bit manipulation, conditional branching, table lookup, and BCD operations.

Figure 23.6 reveals the major architectural features of the Z8. For stand-alone operation, it offers 2K of internal ROM, 128 bytes of RAM, 32 I/O lines, a 144-byte register file, and two timer/counters. Of special interest is the on-chip asynchronous receiver/transmitter (UART), designed to reduce the software overhead for serial data-communications applications.

Further enhancing its image as a single-chip microcomputer, the Z8 blends in features of the programmable peripheral chip. By designating 16 locations of the internal register file as status and control registers, the Z8 can be *self-programmed* to assume a number of configurations, ranging from a stand-alone microcomputer, to a traditional microprocessor with up to 124K of external memory, to a parallel processing element in a multiprocessing system. The four I/O ports, for example, can be configured under program

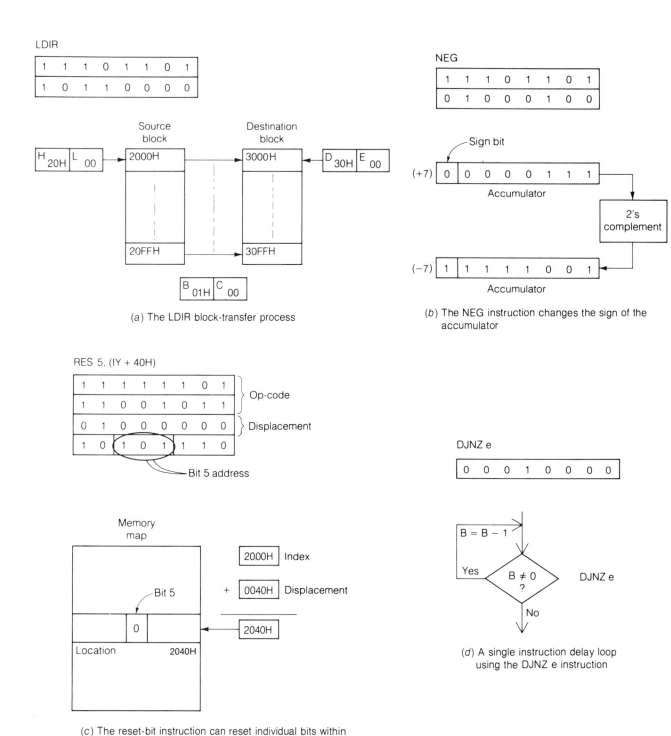

(a) The LDIR block-transfer process

(b) The NEG instruction changes the sign of the accumulator

(c) The reset-bit instruction can reset individual bits within any memory location

(d) A single instruction delay loop using the DJNZ e instruction

Figure 23.5   Typical Z80 instruction types not found in the 8080/8085 instruction set.

control to provide timing, status, address outputs (for system expansion), and serial or parallel I/O with or without handshake.

A number of versions of the Z8, including a 64-pin development version, complete the Z8 single-chip field.

THE MOTOROLA GROUP

Motorola offers a complete line of 8-bit microprocessors, from the popular 6800 to a full complement of single-chip configurations. The 6800 microprocessor, Motorola's first

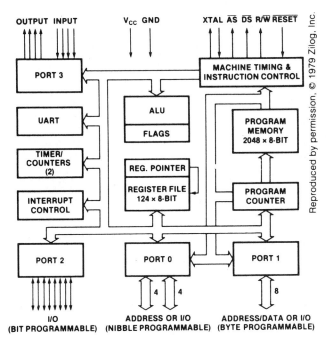

Figure 23.6 The Z8 internal block diagram.

offering, owes its popularity to two features: a basic simplicity in both hardware and software design, and a full complement of LSI support chips to interface the 6800 to a variety of peripheral devices.

6800 Architecture

Figure 23.7 compares the basic architecture of the 6800 side by side with the 8085 and Z80. Like the Z80, the 6800 does not multiplex its data or address lines, and all 16 address and 8 bidirectional data lines are available for direct tie-in to the system bus.

Only two general-purpose internal registers are available—accumulators A and B. The 6800 system is therefore a memory-oriented microprocessor. The index register, stack pointer, and program counter serve the same functions as their counterparts in the Intel/Zilog families. The C, Z, H, and N flags are equivalent to the 8085's C, Z, AC, and S flags. The V flag, called the *overflow* flag, is used (in conjunction with the N flag) for signed-number operations. The I flag is the interrupt mask for the $\overline{IRQ}$ (interrupt request) input.

Memory and I/O Control Signals

The 6800 uses memory mapping exclusively, with no distinction made between ports and memory. In a departure from Intel/Zilog designs, both the read and write processes are controlled by a single pin ($R/\overline{W}$). Normally high for a read operation, the $R/\overline{W}$ line goes low when a write operation is under way.

Reset and Bus Control

To allow the 6800 to vector to any location upon $\overline{RESET}$, the 6800 performs an action closely related to a vectored interrupt. A momentary low on the $\overline{RESET}$ input causes the contents of memory locations $FFFE and $FFFF to be loaded into the program counter. (A reset on the 8080/8085/Z80 causes the program counter to be cleared.) Note that Motorola designates hexadecimal numbers with a "$" before the number.

To allow a variety of DMA activities, the 6800 provides three input signals and one output-acknowledge signal related to three-state control:

- $\overline{HALT}$
- TSC (Three-State Control)
- DBE (Data Bus Enable)
- BA (Bus Available)

The $\overline{HALT}$ and BA pins serve the same function as the HOLD and HLDA pins on the 8080/8085. $\overline{HALT}$ also can be used for single stepping, in a manner similar to single stepping the 8080/8085 by way of the READY input. TSC places the address and R/W line in the high-impedance state, and DBE places the data bus into a high-impedance state. (DBE usually is tied to the $\phi2$ clock in order to time the flow of data and prevent bus contention.)

Interrupts

As listed in Figure 23.8, the 6800 provides three interrupt vectors—NMI (nonmaskable interrupt), $\overline{IRQ}$ (interrupt request), and a software-initiated interrupt by way of the SWI (software interrupt) instruction. (The RESET vector is also included.) In all cases, the action is similar:

1. An interrupt is requested by pulling $\overline{IRQ}$ or $\overline{NMI}$ low, or processing the SWI instruction.

2. When the present instruction is complete, the contents of all registers are automatically pushed onto the stack and the interrupt input is disabled ($\overline{NMI}$, like TRAP, cannot be masked out).

3. The data bytes stored at the vector locations hold the starting address of the interrupt-service routines and are automatically transferred to the program counter.

4. The return from interrupt (RTI) instruction, at the end of the service routine, recreates the preinterrupt conditions.

6800 Timing Cycles

As revealed by the comparison chart of Figure 23.9, the basic timing cycles of the 6800 differ considerably from the 8080/8085 standard. Perhaps the easiest way to compare the

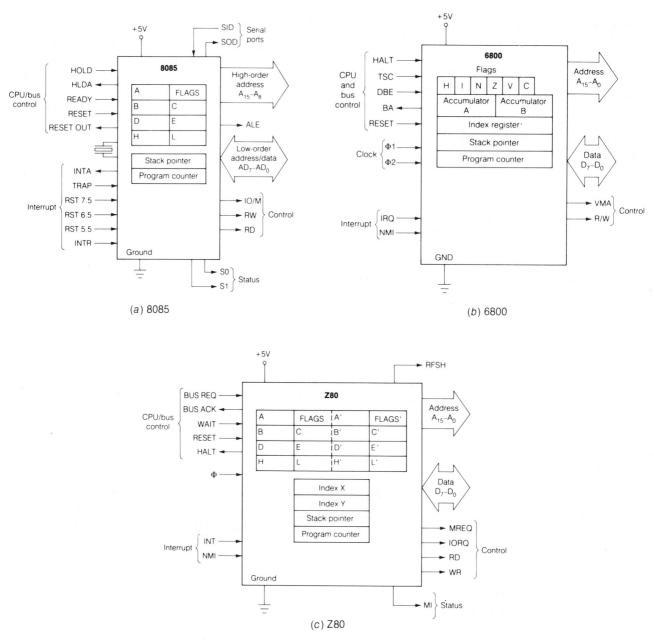

Figure 23.7 Comparison of 8085, 6800, and Z80 architecture.

waveforms is to note that the 8080/8085's *machine cycle* is equivalent to the 6800's *clock cycle*. The major purpose of a clock cycle, therefore, is to carry out one data transfer process.

In a 6800 system, the Φ1 and Φ2 clock periods are equal to the clock cycle period. By contrast it requires from 3 to 6 clock cycles to carry out one 8080/8085 machine cycle. Although the clock rate of the 8080/8085 is higher than the clock rate of the 6800, it does not translate into higher processing speed, since many clock cycles on the 8080/8085 are required to perform the operations carried out by a single

6800 clock cycle. The standard 6800 can operate at a clock frequency between 100 KHz and 1 MHz, and newer models can operate faster.

Processing Action Example

As a final review of the 6800 processing action, let's go through the familiar mimic sequence step by step, as we did for the 8080/8085 in Chapter 8.

The mimic program for the 6800 is shown in Figure 23.10. LDAA $2000 (load accumulator A with contents of mem-

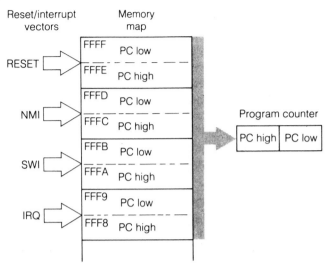

Figure 23.8 The 6800 interrupt and reset vectors.

ory/port location $2000), carries out the input process, while STAA $1000 (store accumulator A to memory/port location $1000) handles the output operation. WAI (wait for interrupt) essentially halts processor operation.

Placing an arbitrary data word (such as $BE) before the computer's "eyes," the action unfolds as follows (continued reference to Figure 23.11 should be helpful):

• *Step 1:* The starting address of the program ($0000) is placed into the program counter (this is accomplished by the *monitor* program in ROM—not shown).

• *Step 2:* The program counter points to the first memory location in the program ($0000), and a where/when operation fetches the LDAA $2000 operation code ($B6) to the instruction register.

• *Step 3:* The LDAA $2000 op code is decoded and the proper microprogram selected.

• *Step 4:* The microprogram directs the program counter to increment to $0001, and another where/when data transfer fetches the high-order port address ($20) to the high-order 8 bits of the MAR via the data bus.

• *Step 5:* The program counter increments to $0002, and the low-order port address ($00) is fetched to the low-order 8 bits of the MAR.

• *Step 6:* The fourth and final where/when data-transfer operation for the LDAA $2000 instruction begins with the port address ($2000) in the MAR "pointing to" the "eyes" of the computer, followed by the data word "$BE" INported from the outside world to accumulator A.

• *Step 7:* The first instruction complete, the controller/sequencer increments the program counter to $0003 and fetches the STAA $1000 operation code ($B7) to the instruction register.

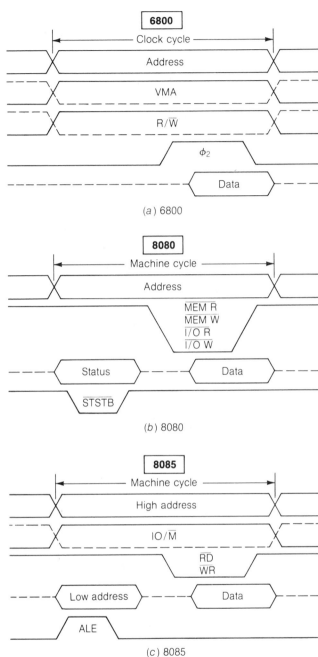

Figure 23.9 A comparison of typical where/when data-transfer waveforms.

• *Step 8:* Under direction of the decoded microprogram, the program counter is incremented to $0004 and $0005 as two consecutive data-transfer operations fetch the OUTport address ($1000) to the MAR.

• *Step 9:* The port address in the MAR ($1000) points to the "voice" of the computer, and the data in accumulator A ($BE) are transferred to the addressed output port and latched in place.

• *Step 10:* The second instruction complete, the operation

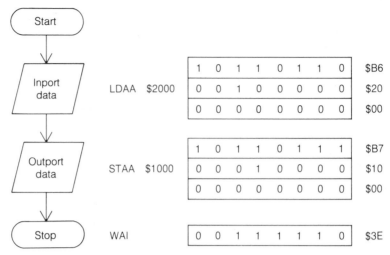

Figure 23.10 The complete mimic program.

code for WAIT ($3E) is fetched to the instruction register, decoded, and computer operation is stopped.

As with the 8080/8085, we exit the halt state and repeat the mimic process by resetting the microprocessor.

The Instruction Set

The instruction set for the 6800 is shown in Figure 23.12, arranged in the same five groups as the 8080/8085 instruction set.

The 6800 instructions are very similar to those of the 8080/8085—until you consider signed-number operations. Generally speaking, the 8080/8085 instruction set is not designed for efficient signed-number processing, and therefore is not suited for strictly data-processing applications. For example, unlike the 8080/8085, the 6800 contains a rich variety of signed-number conditional branch instructions, and a signed-number overflow-detection flag should the result of an arithmetic operation lie outside the $-128/+127$ signed-number bounds. Furthermore, the 6800 offers an arithmetic shift-right operation in which the original sign bit is preserved.

The 6800 instruction set contains five basic categories of addressing modes. As shown here, only the *relative* addressing mode has no counterpart in the 8080/8085 set.

Addressing Modes

6800	8080/8085
Immediate	Immediate
Extended, Direct	Direct
Indexed	Indirect
Implied/Inherent	Register/Not Specified
Relative	

The 6800 assembly-language mnemonics differ somewhat in structure from the Intel mnemonics. Unlike the 8080/ 8085, each 6800 addressing mode is uniquely specified only in the operand portion of the mnemonic. For example, contrast the following basic memory-transfer instructions using comparable addressing modes.

Addressing Mode	6800	8080/8085
Immediate	LDAA #data	MVI r, data
Direct	LDAA address	LDA address
Indirect/Indexed	LDAA address, X	MOV r,M

The 6801 Single-Chip Microcomputer

Referring to the following list of the 6801's major features, we find a number of similarities to the 8048 and Z8 single-chip microcomputers:

- Expanded M6800 instruction set
- Full-duplex serial-communications interface
- Upward-compatible with MC6800 source and object code
- 16-bit timer with three modes
- Single chip or expandable to 64K bytes
- 2K bytes of on-chip ROM
- 128 bytes of on-chip RAM
- 29 parallel I/O lines + 2 control lines
- Internal clock
- Interrupt capability (maskable and nonmaskable)

An important feature of all single-chip microcomputers is *flexibility,* the ability to be configured in a variety of modes to match the needs of the designer. The MC6801 provides three fundamental operating modes (see Figure 23.13):

- Single chip
- Expanded nonmultiplexed
- Expanded multiplexed

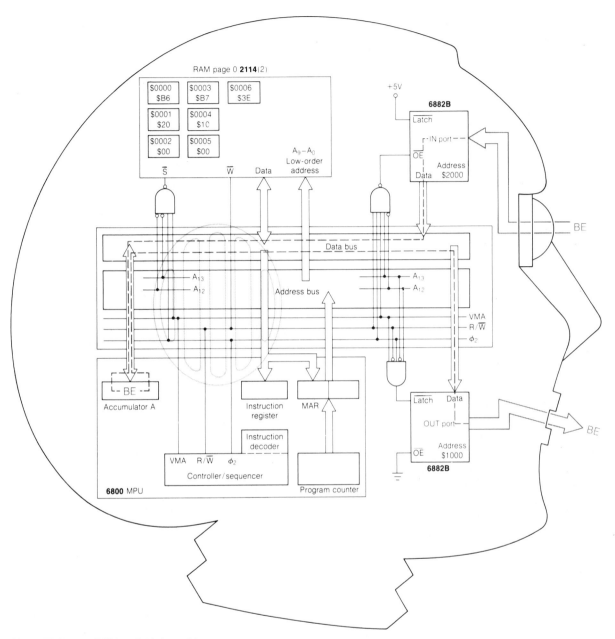

Figure 23.11 A 6800-based mimic machine.

The single-chip mode is for stand-alone applications, and it provides the maximum 29 I/O lines. The expanded non-multiplexed configuration uses port 4 to address an additional 256 external memory locations; in the expanded multiplexed mode, port 3 is multiplexed with address information and combined with port 4 to provide 16 bits of addressing, thereby allowing a full 64K of external memory to be added to the system.

In addition to the basic 72 instruction types of the 6800, the 6801 has eleven new instructions, giving increased arithmetic-processing power, including an 8-bit multiply.

Additional features include a serial-communications interface through three pins of port 2 (transmit, receive, and baud rate) and an internal 16-bit timer.

A 6803 version, which deletes the internal 2K × 8 ROM, and a 68701 version, which substitutes an EPROM for the ROM, round out the 6801 single-chip group.

BIT-SLICE PROCESSORS

Although not part of the 8-bit microprocessor family tree, bit-slice processors are mentioned because they represent an

DATA-TRANSFER GROUP

LDA	Load Accumulator
LDS	Load Stack Pointer
LDX	Load Index Register
STA	Store Accumulator
STS	Store Stack Register
STX	Store Index Register
TAB	Transfer Accumulators
TAP	Transfer Accumulators to Condition Codes Register
TBA	Transfer Accumulators
TPA	Transfer Condition Codes Register to Accumulator
TSX	Transfer Stack Pointer to Index Register
TXS	Transfer Index Register to Stack Pointer

LOGICAL GROUP

AND	Logical AND
ORA	Inclusive OR Accumulator
EOR	Exclusive OR
COM	Complement
CMP	Compare
CBA	Compare Accumulators
CPX	Compare Index Registers
LSR	Logical Shift Right
ROL	Rotate Left
ROR	Rotate Right
TST	Test
BIT	Bit Test

ARITHMETIC GROUP

ABA	Add Accumulators
ADC	Add with Carry
ADD	Add
SUB	Subtract
SBA	Subtract Accumulators
SBC	Subtract with Carry
DAA	Decimal Adjust
DEC	Decrement
DES	Decrement Stack Pointer
DEX	Decrement Index Register
INC	Increment

INS	Increment Stack Pointer
INX	Increment Index Register
ASL	Arithmetic Shift Left
ASR	Arithmetic Shift Right
NEG	Negate
CLR	Clear

BRANCH GROUP

JMP	Jump
JSR	Jump to Subroutine
BCC	Branch if Carry Clear
BCS	Branch if Carry Set
BEQ	Branch if Equal to Zero
BGE	Branch if Greater or Equal Zero
BGT	Branch if Greater than Zero
BHI	Branch if Higher
BLE	Branch if Less or Equal
BLS	Branch if Lower or Same
BLT	Branch if Less than Zero
BMI	Branch if Minus
BNE	Branch if Not Equal to Zero
BPL	Branch if Plus
BRA	Branch Always
BSR	Branch to Subroutine
BVC	Branch if Overflow Clear
BVS	Branch if Overflow Set
RTI	Return from Interrupt
RTS	Return from Subroutine
SWI	Software Interrupt

STACK AND MACHINE-CONTROL GROUP

PSH	Push Data
PUL	Pull Data
NOP	No Operation
CLC	Clear Carry
CLI	Clear Interrupt Mask
SEC	Set Carry
SEI	Set Interrupt Mask
SEV	Set Overflow
WAI	Wait for Interrupt
CLR	Clear

Figure 23.12 The 6800 instruction set.

alternative to the basic, general-purpose, fixed-word-size microprocessor (such as those discussed in this chapter).

The original impetus for a bit-slice configuration was the need for higher and higher speed. Ultra-high-speed proces-sors generally must be fashioned from bipolar or ECL tech-nology. However, these technologies are of low density and high power dissipation—properties that do not lend them-selves to large-scale integration. The solution is to construct

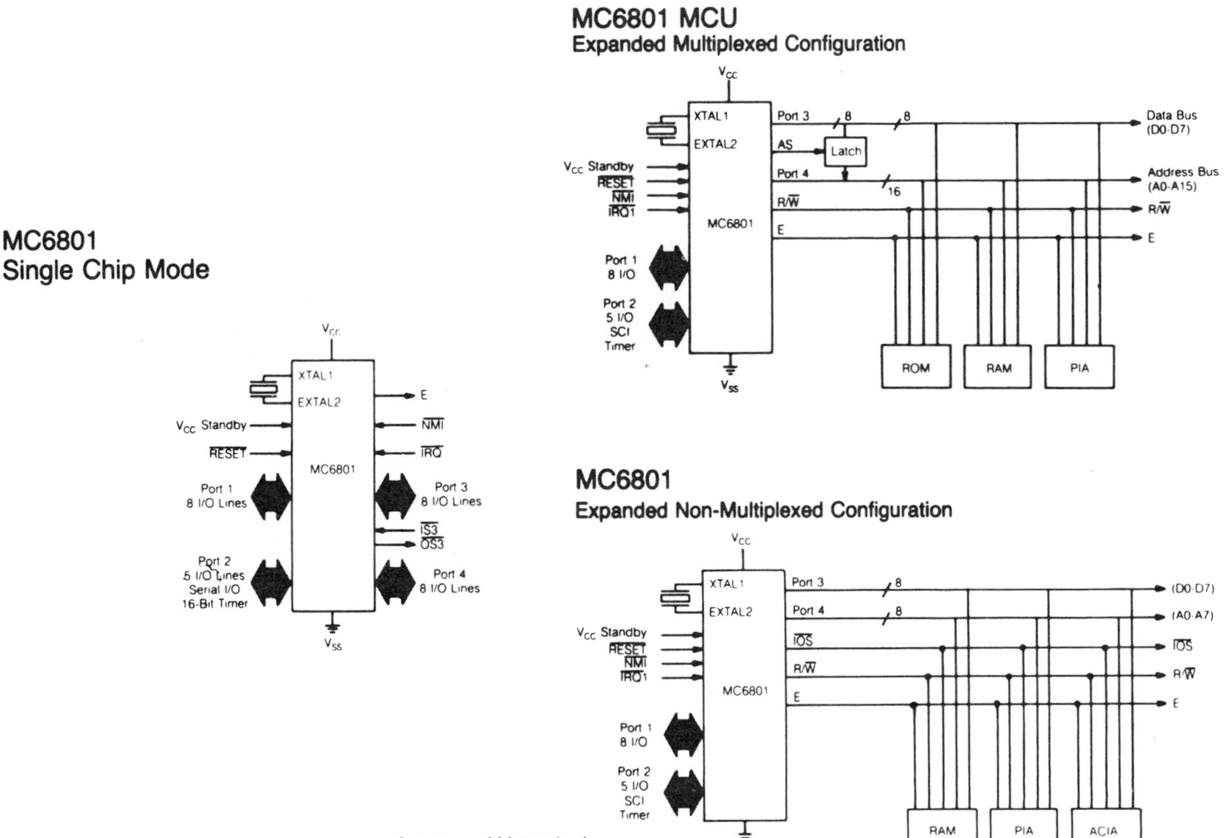

MC6801 MCU
Expanded Multiplexed Configuration

MC6801
Single Chip Mode

MC6801
Expanded Non-Multiplexed Configuration

Courtesy of Motorola, Inc.

Figure 23.13   The three basic modes of operation of the 6801.

the CPU from individual building blocks called *bit-slice chips*. Typically based on a 4-bit format, each bit slice is a section of a complete arithmetic/logic unit along with its multiplexers and data paths. The control logic and microinstruction ROM are provided separately. By combining these bit slices in parallel, a computer structure of nearly any word size can be constructed. Since bit-slice processors usually are dedicated to a specific task, the microprograms (and therefore the instruction set) are also custom-designed by the user.

Because of the availability and low cost of general-purpose microprocessors, few applications can justify the added expense of the bit-slice custom-design approach.

INTELLIGENT-MACHINE UPDATE

Showing a high degree of similarity, all 8-bit microprocessors belong to the same family. Although one particular member of the family may be better suited for a specific application, in general a system can be designed around any 8-bit microprocessor. But, as we have seen in this book, microcomputer and human being also show a great deal of similarity. As computer and medical technology improve,

will these two beings—microprocessor and human—gradually merge into a single life form?

QUESTIONS AND PROBLEMS

1. Name several hardware features that all microprocessors have in common.
2. Interface an 8282 input port to a Z80 bus system.
3. How do we set up the Z80 for DMA activities?
4. In a Z80 mode 2 interrupt, how is the starting address of the interrupt-service routine determined?
5. What is the difference between *relative* and *indexed* addressing?
6. What Z80 instruction combines both the flag setting and the conditional branch into a single instruction?
7. Why is the 6800 called a *memory-mapped* processor?
8. How is the 6800 RESET action related to a vectored interrupt?
9. Why is the 6800 called a *memory oriented* processor?
10. On the 6800, what is the purpose of the V flag?
11. A *clock cycle* on the 6800 is equivalent to what cycle on the 8080/8085?

12. On the 6800, what signal "qualifies" the read and write processes (on the 8080/8085, $\overline{\text{RD}}$ or $\overline{\text{WR}}$ qualifies the read or write process)?

13. Based on Figure 23.9a, what is the difference between a read and write set of waveforms for the 6800?

14. What mode of addressing is used by the LDAA $2000 and STAA $1000 instructions of Figure 23.10?

15. The MAR (memory address register) within the 6800 is comparable to what register within the 8080/8085?

16. The 6800 has a richer set of *signed number* instructions than the 8080/8085. From the instruction set listing of Figure 23.12, select several instructions that you feel are involved with signed number processing.

17. Why is ROM in a 6800 system placed at the top (highest memory locations) of the memory map (opposite from that of the 8080/8085)?

18. In general terms, how do the 6800 mnemonics distinguish one addressing mode from another? How does this compare to the 8080/8085?

19. When we are adding external memory to a 6801 single-chip microcomputer, how are the high-level address lines generated?

20. How can we tell by looking at the pinout of the 6800 that isolated I/O addressing is not possible? How can we tell the same by looking at the instruction set?

21. What is a *bit slice*?

chapter 24

Putting It All Together:
An Application

The human race has survived and prospered because it has used its unique tools—hands and brain—to overcome and shape the environment. From the wheel to the space shuttle, the application of our special structure has changed the way we live.

The computer must also prove its worth by application—by solving real-world problems and by performing a variety of tasks efficiently and reliably. Usually these are tasks that we do not wish to do at all or that a computer can do better. One such task is the subject of this chapter: a microprocessor-controlled lunar-landing simulator. Emphasizing control rather than data processing, the system will be taken from initial conception to block-level design, leaving the final hardware design and machine-language program as a laboratory project.

LUNAR-LANDING SIMULATOR

The computer is an ideal simulation device, for training can take place without expensive equipment or the threat of disaster if a mistake is made. Our project involves the simulation of a landing on the moon by controlling a small model of the lunar landing vehicle (LLV). This application will be more challenging than most, for the system must operate at moderate speed in real time and must perform some rather complex mathematical calculations.

Hardware Design

Our hardware design of Figure 24.1 makes use of techniques developed in previous chapters. Our throttle level is fed to the simple A-to-D converter of Chapter 18, and we use a stepper motor to control altitude without resorting to complex feedback paths. To simulate landing under various gravitational loads, the gravity level is stored in a memory location and preset to any value between one and six. A pink noise generator simulates the sound of thrust (in this case, the generation of thrust noise is more easily handled by hardware).

Software Design

Our moon-landing simulator program consists of two major parts:

- Calculation of velocity from input thrust and gravity
- Use of velocity parameters to generate the required stepper-motor waveforms

From Chapter 20, we know that, if the inputs to a four-phase stepper motor are properly matched to the bit positions of the output port, the generation of stepper-motor waveforms reduces to a simple series of rotate operations (Figure 24.2). The direction of rotation controls the direction of velocity (up or down), and the delay number sent to the delay loop controls the speed by specifying the time interval between rotate operations. By continually updating the velocity and direction parameters, the speed of the LLV can be controlled accurately (the parameters are passed from the math routine to the stepper-motor routine).

Generating the correct velocity parameters to send to the stepper-motor routine is more challenging, for simulating flight dynamics—even in one dimension—requires some advanced mathematics.

To convert thrust and gravity into altitude, we must process the steps indicated by Figure 24.3. The thrust of the lunar lander's engines is subtracted from the force of gravity (weight of the LLV), and, after the mass of the vehicle is divided out, the resulting net acceleration is *integrated* to give the velocity of the LLV. (If we normalize out the effects of mass during system calibration, the divide step is not required.)

To complete our software development, it is clear we must first understand the concept of integration.

Integration (a part of calculus) is closely related to *multiplication*. In fact, multiplication is a special form of integration. To see the difference, consider the following simple problem:

If we travel 50 mph for 3 hours, how far will we have gone?

The answer—150 miles—is obtained by the mathematical

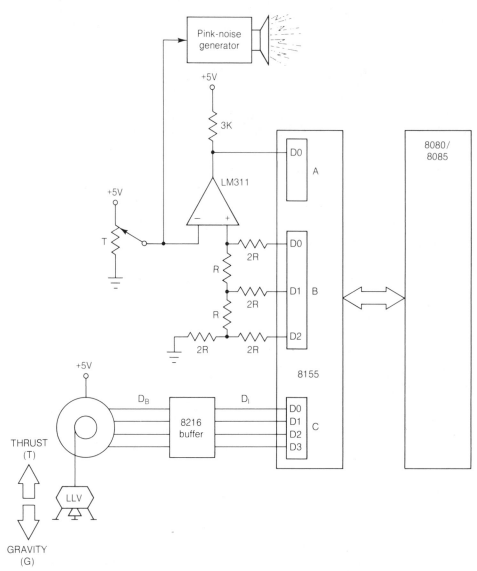

Figure 24.1   Initial hardware design of moon-landing simulator.

process of multiplication. That is, we multiply the speed (50 mph) by the time (3 hours) to obtain the distance (150 miles):

$$\text{Distance} = \text{velocity} \times \text{time}$$
$$150 \, \text{miles} = 50 \, \text{mph} \ \times 3 \, \text{hours}$$

The same problem can also be solved graphically as shown in Figure 24.4. If velocity and time are plotted as the y and x axis of a two-dimensional coordinate system, the solution to the problem (150) is represented by the area of the rectangle bounded by the 50-mph and 3-hour points. Or, to use more precise terminology, the answer is equal to the *area under the velocity curve*.

Now we will make one seemingly small change in the original problem, and the whole nature of the solution will change. This time, the velocity does not remain constant

over the 3-hour period, but becomes a *variable*. *How do we "multiply" velocity and time when velocity is a variable?* The answer is: we must *integrate*. Below we compare the symbolism of integration with that of simple multiplication. If velocity can be expressed as a mathematical function of time, the problem can be solved using the methods of calculus:

Multiplication	*Integration*
(velocity is a constant)	*(velocity is a variable)*
$D = V \times t$	
$150 = 50 \times 3$	$D = \int_{o}^{3} V(t) \, dt$

Fortunately, for those unfamiliar with the mathematical techniques of integration, there is an alternative: the graphical method using the area under the curve. If velocity varies

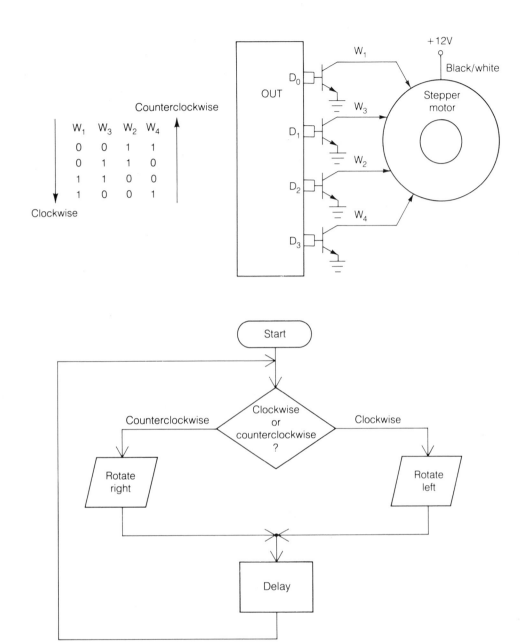

Figure 24.2 Stepper-motor control.

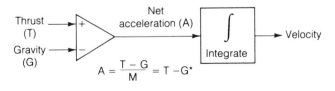

*Mass has been normalized to 1

Figure 24.3 Calculating velocity from thrust and gravity.

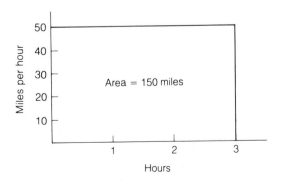

150 miles = 50 miles/hour × 3 hours

Figure 24.4 Graphical method of multiplying.

according to the curve of Figure 24.5a, what graphical quantity is equal to the distance traveled? The answer, of course, is *the area under the velocity curve*. When the velocity turns negative, as it does at the 3½-second point, then the gen-

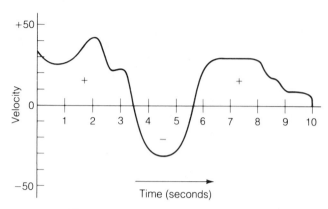

Distance = positive area minus negative area

(a) Calculating distance when velocity is a variable

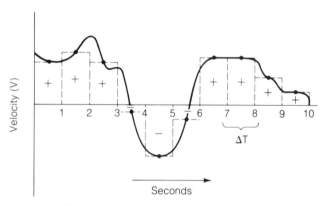

Distance = sum of elemental areas

$$D = \sum_{0}^{10} V\Delta T = \sum_{0}^{10} V$$

If $\Delta T = 1$

(b) Approximating the area under the curve
by summing incremental elements

Figure 24.5 Integration techniques for a computer.

erated area is also negative and must be subtracted from the positive area above the x axis. Since the velocity of our lunar lander will be both positive and negative, we will use signed numbers to handle the situation.

But how can we determine the area under an *analog* curve by calculations on a *digital* computer? Figure 24.5b shows us how—by approximating the curve with a series of thin rectangular elements. By adding the areas of the rectangular elements, we can approximate the area of the total curve.

If the points are sampled one second apart, as shown, then the area under a velocity/time curve (the distance) can be calculated by simply adding together the velocity values (height) of each elemental area. If we sample more often,

say four times per second, then the velocity values of each element must be divided by four (rotate right two times) in order to obtain the proper area. (The divide step can also be normalized out when the system is scaled and calibrated.) Again we subtract the negative elements (negative velocity) from the positive elements (positive velocity).

We now have all the mathematical expertise to calculate velocity from acceleration (rather than distance from velocity as we have been doing) and complete our velocity routine. By definition, *velocity is equal to acceleration multiplied by time;* but that is true only if acceleration is a constant. In our situation, since we can vary the thrust of the LLV, the net acceleration most certainly is not a constant—so we must integrate. But integration, we know, can be approximated by a summation (we sum together the small incremental elements of acceleration/time). The mathematical calculations are shown in Figure 24.6.

Converting the mathematics into a computer routine is easy, for we calculate the real-time velocity by keeping a running (cumulative) total of the sampled acceleration values. That is, as each thrust/gravitation reference level is sampled in real time, the calculated acceleration value is added to a *cumulative-total register.* The contents of the cumulative-total register at any time equals the present LLV velocity. (Effects of the sampling rate are normalized out during calibration.) Since we are using signed numbers, we automatically know both the direction and magnitude. Converting our ideas into a flowchart (Figure 24.7), the second major part of our moon-lander program is documented.

The final software-development task is to integrate (combine) the two software routines into a single processing sys-

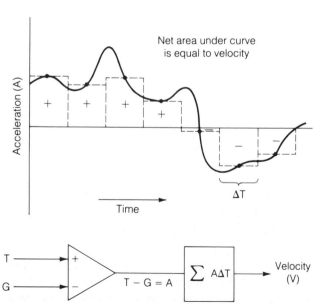

Figure 24.6 Approximating velocity from thrust and gravity.

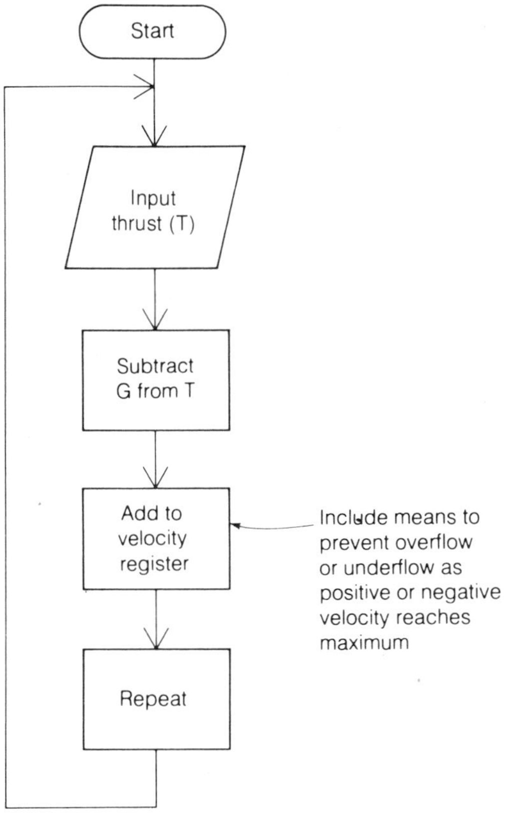
Start
Input thrust (T)
Subtract G from T
Add to velocity register
Include means to prevent overflow or underflow as positive or negative velocity reaches maximum
Repeat

Figure 24.7 Math-routine flowchart for calculation of velocity from thrust and gravity.

tem, remembering that each routine *independently* obeys strict timing standards:

- The stepper-motor routine must rotate the waveform outputs at a rate dependent on the velocity parameter sent to the delay block.
- The velocity routine—which calculates the velocity from the acceleration using the summation technique—requires the computer to sample the thrust and gravitational reference inputs at regular intervals (four times each second in our case).

The following are three ways in which we may approach the problem of processing the two independent routines on a single microcomputer system (Figure 24.8):

1. We may adopt a purely software approach, remaining in the stepper-motor routine and dropping out after each $\frac{1}{4}$ second to perform a single math routine (velocity update).
2. We can interrupt the stepper-motor routine at the 4-Hz rate, passing to the math routine at the required intervals.
3. We can turn over the stepper-motor processes to an 8041 slave processor, sending updated velocity information at the 4-Hz rate.

Method 1 would be difficult to implement because the amount of time spent in the stepper-motor routine would depend on the velocity parameter. Method 3 involves a programmable chip (the 8041) with which we are not all that familiar. Therefore, method 2—the interrupt method—appears to be the best choice.

Using the interrupt technique, a 555 timer, running at 4 Hz, will interrupt the computer and allow the thrust and gravitational reference values to be sampled at regular intervals and the velocity to be updated at the 4-Hz rate. (The small amount of interrupt time spent in the math routine will not significantly affect the stepper-motor timing.)

Our complete hardware/software design is given in Figure 24.9. The final system design is left as an exercise. (The instructor's guide contains the complete hardware/software design for the lunar-landing simulator.)

Modifications and Improvements

In real life an LLV has a limited amount of fuel aboard and must be landed before the fuel is expended. We assume the rate at which the fuel is consumed is proportional to the thrust. Therefore, to simulate the effects of fuel consumption, subtract the incremental thrust inputs (or fraction thereof) from a register holding an initial fuel value. When the fuel runs out, we inhibit the thrust input and the vehicle goes into free fall. In addition to varying the gravitational pull, we can allow the total amount of on-board fuel to be set at various levels to vary the skill factor. Of course, it would be helpful to display the fuel level as it is consumed.

As time goes by and fuel is consumed, the LLV becomes lighter and the thrust is more effective in producing acceleration. To simulate this action, we can add increasing values to the thrust input as the fuel is consumed (a high degree of simulation accuracy here requires advanced mathematics).

If we wish to output the LLV velocity at the time of impact (to determine the probable LLV damage and passenger injury), we may include a sensor at the surface impact point. An interrupt would cause the contents of the velocity register to be displayed at the time of impact. As an alternative, we could integrate the velocity to produce the distance. When the distance register equals zero, we would stop stepper-motor action and output the contents of the velocity register.

Many other modifications are possible—including two-dimensional motion—as we strive for greater and greater simulation accuracy.

INTELLIGENT-MACHINE UPDATE

By performing a variety of tasks—often more efficiently than its human counterparts—our intelligent machine has proven its worth. Like a band of sorcerers, microprocessors will now fan out across the land, taking each passive and

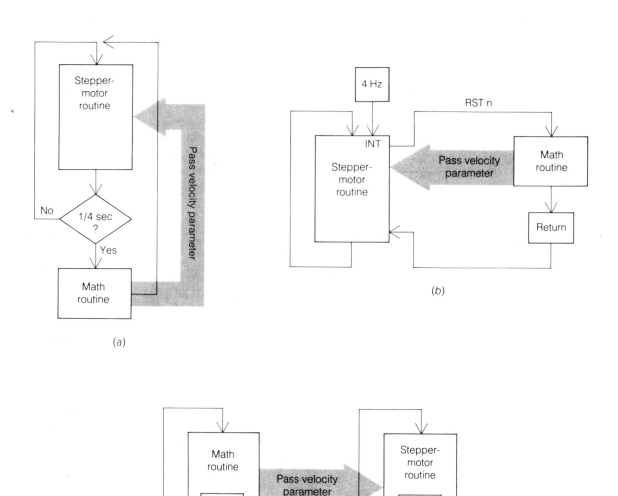

Figure 24.8 Three methods of processing two independent routines on a single processing system: *a)* Software method. *b)* Interrupt method. *c)* Slave processor method.

stoic machine they come across—from an airplane to a zoom lens—and infusing it with the magic of intelligence.

QUESTIONS AND PROBLEMS

1. Why did we choose to design our LLV system around a microprocessor rather than use combinational logic?
2. What are the two major components of a data-acquisition system?
3. Why does a stepper motor not require feedback?
4. Design a simple pink-noise generator circuit using the junction noise of a reverse-biased, open-collector transistor.
5. What is the difference between *multiplication* and *integration*?
6. What determines the theoretical accuracy of the summation approximation of an integral?
7. Why must the numbers used in our velocity calculation of the LLV be *signed* numbers?
8. What three techniques are available for combining two routines that have independent timing requirements?
9. Complete the hardware/software design of the lunar-landing simulator and test your design in the laboratory.

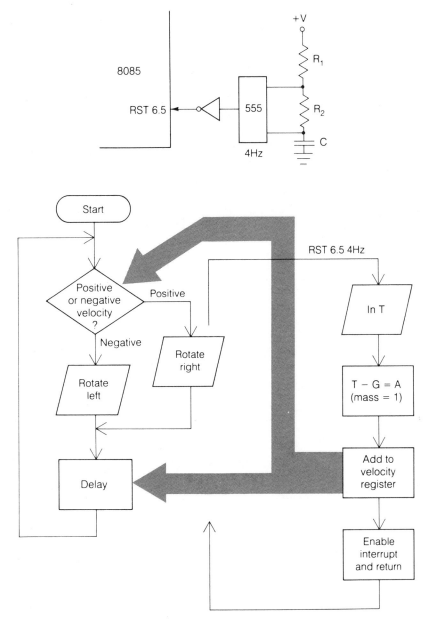

Figure 24.9 Complete moon-landing simulator software design.

Advanced Processors:
The Newest Generation

Human development has reached a nearly level stage, or plateau, in the history of life. The human brain has not changed, at least in gross size, in the past 100,000 years. However, development of *intelligence* has not ended on earth, for *artificial intelligence*—the intelligence of the computer—is growing at a staggering pace, and there is no natural limit in sight.

In Part V we will introduce several of the more recent products of computer evolution: the iAPX86, 186, 286, 386 16/32-bit microprocessor families, and the 2920 signal processor.

chapter 25

The 8086 16-Bit Microprocessor

The human mind is a living archaeological site. The deeper we go into the human brain, the farther back into history we travel—150 million years ago, to the oldest and most primitive brain structure, when mammals were just emerging. Such a system is hierarchical in nature. The outer, most recently developed cerebral cortex controls the higher-level abstract and more generalized processes, and sets system goals and priorities; the inner, most ancient levels handle the detailed and specific actions that carry out the system goals.

Sixteen-bit microprocessors are also hierarchical in nature. At the core of a 16-bit microprocessor we find remnants of the 8-bit architecture and instruction set. As we move away from the core, we find a complex multiprocessing system, specifically designed to operate from code generated by a high-level language. More than any other characteristic, *multiprocessing* is at the heart of the 16-bit microprocessor family.

MULTIPROCESSING

Multiprocessing is a technique that employs multiple processors, often in a hierarchical (master/slave) arrangement. Older multitasking systems, in contrast, usually rely on a single CPU to direct all operations by time-sharing. The human mind long ago adopted the multiprocessing concept, and the two major features of multiprocessing are found in both the human mind and in large-scale 16-bit microprocessor systems.

- *Distributed processing*—In any advanced system, overall system commands can be generated by a master processor; specific tasks can be given to special-purpose coprocessors, designed to perform certain tasks simply and efficiently. This is known as *distributed processing;* it not only increases system throughput, but also assures us that a failure in one part of the system has a limited effect on the system as a whole. (In the human mind, the holographic nature of memory gives us the same feature.)

- *Parallel processing*—Literally thousands of processes go on in the human body simultaneously (in parallel). Because of this, very high levels of performance can be achieved. In the computer world, using multiple processors executing in parallel, very high levels of system performance can be achieved.

In this chapter we will feature the 8086 16-bit microprocessor (the central processing unit of the iAPX86 family). We will find that the 8086 has achieved a quantum jump in overall performance, and has expanded into areas once the sole property of mini- and mainframe computers. The Zilog Z8000 and Motorola MC68000 are similar to the Intel 8086.

THE INTEL 8086

As expected, the architecture of the iAPX86 family is explicitly designed to encourage the development of distributed, parallel multiprocessing systems. Figure 25.1 depicts a typical multiprocessing system, consisting of three processing modules, all tied into a main bus system—called the *public system bus*. Within each processing module, one or more local processors can feed a *local bus*. The memory and I/O resources of the processing module feed a separate *private system bus*. Restricting the local bus to only processors and coprocessors allows them to share the same memory and I/O, resulting in greater efficiency. In addition, a separate private memory and I/O assures us that the public memory shared between all processor modules is not overtaxed and is available when needed. If system programs such as assemblers are written so that all users can share the same system program at the same location, the programs are said to be *reentrant*.

Obviously, a great deal of coordination must take place between the private, local, and system buses. The required bus arbitration may be performed by special bus-request/bus-grant logic contained within each processor, or by the 8289 bus-arbiter chip.

Reproduced by permission of Intel Corp.

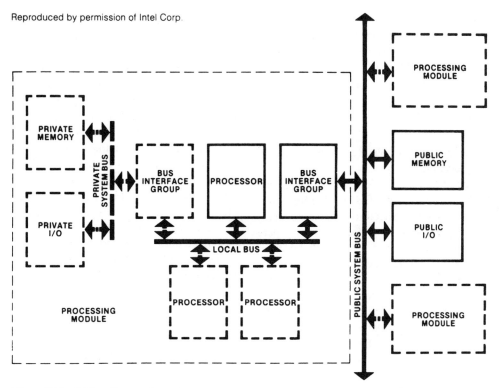

Figure 25.1   8086 mulitprocessing system.

Independent Processors and Coprocessors

Two types of processors feed the local bus within a given processing module: *independent processors* and *coprocessors*. An independent processor is a stand-alone device, fully capable of executing its own stored program. The 8086 and 8089 (I/O processor) are usually configured as independent processors (although the 8089 is usually slave to the 8086). A coprocessor, on the other hand, monitors the instructions fetched by the host; when it recognizes an instruction as its own, it executes the instruction. The 8087 numeric proces-

sor, usually hooked in as a coprocessor, operates as follows: when the 8086 master processor wishes to have the 8087 perform a mathematical operation, it simply allows the 8087 to capture an escape (ESC) instruction (placed onto the data bus by the master 8086). The 8087 begins its special numeric operation (see Figure 25.2) as specified by the escape instruction. Meanwhile, the 8086 continues processing activity until the result from the 8087 is required. It then "idles" in the WAIT state. When the 8087's result is available, the 8086 is notified by way of the TEST pin on the 8086. The numeric data are transferred to the 8086, and processing continues. The 8087 math processor in essence expands the instruction

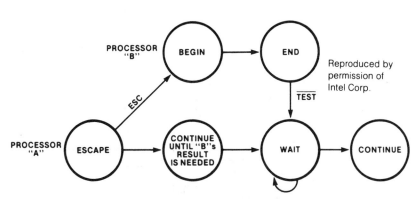

Figure 25.2   8087 coprocessor operation.

set of the 8086 to include 32- and 64-bit integer arithmetic, floating-point operations, and trigonometric and exponential operations, and it can increase the system throughput a hundredfold. In addition, by placing "software on silicon," the 8087 saves a great deal of programming time.

THE 8086 ARCHITECTURE

Figure 25.3 is a simplified internal block diagram and pinout of the 8086 microprocessor.

The internal architecture is divided into two separate processing units: the Execution Unit (EU) and the Bus Interface Unit (BIU). The BIU is arranged in a pipelined architecture that allows instructions to be prefetched during spare bus cycles. A queue line is established, meaning that instructions are "waiting in line" to be processed. Since little or no time is wasted on the instruction fetch operation, this technique greatly increases throughput. The EU pulls the instructions from the BIU's instruction queue as required and executes each instruction. If external data transfers are required in the course of execution, the EU commands the BIU to perform the necessary machine cycles.

Memory Segmentation

Many of the architectural features of the 8086 result from the concept of *memory segmentation,* a hardware feature designed to support high-level, block-structured programs and to encourage multitasking, multiuser configurations.

Using 20 address lines, the 8086 can directly address up to 1,048,576 (2^{20}) memory locations. The question is: how can a 16-bit microprocessor generate a 20-bit address?

The first step is to visualize within the 1-megabyte memory space a number of overlapping *segments,* each containing 64K of memory. Each segment begins at a memory address evenly divisible by 16—meaning the 4 least significant bits are all zero. Therefore, since only the 16 highest-level bits are needed to define a segment, the starting address of the various segments can conveniently be stored in a 16-bit register. These 16-bit registers are called *segment registers.* Once a segment is selected by specifying its starting address, we locate a byte within the selected 64K segment by specifying its 16-bit *offset,* or distance from the segment starting address (see Figure 25.4a).

The final 20-bit physical address is generated by adding the segment address and offset address as shown in Figure 25.4b.

Internal Registers

The 8086 contains more internal registers than the 8080/8085 (Figure 25.5), but perhaps not as many as you might have thought for a processor offering a quantum jump in overall performance. The reason can be traced back to the expected use of a high-level, *memory-oriented* language (such as PL/M), where variables are stored in memory as symbolic names. When using a memory-oriented language, the need for a large supply of internal registers is reduced.

Reproduced by permission of Intel Corp.

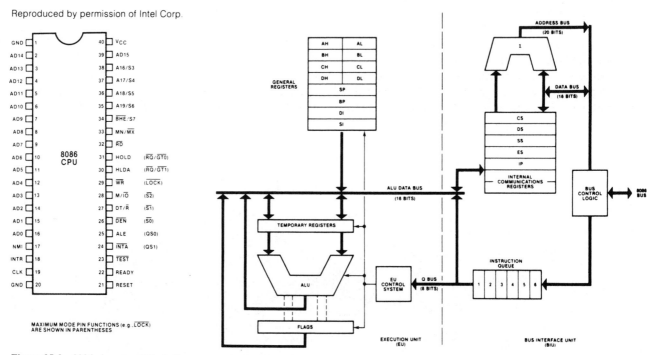

Figure 25.3   8086 pin-out and block diagram.

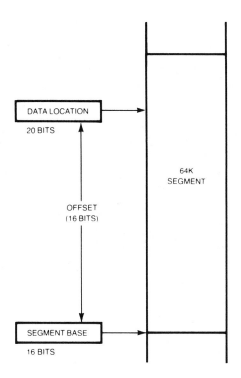

(a) Data is offset from segment base

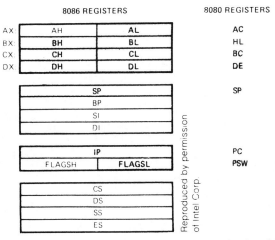

Figure 25.5   The 8086 internal register set compared to that of the 8080.

Figure 25.5 divides the internal registers into four categories. As with the 8080/8085, the eight general 8-bit registers (or four general 16-bit registers) are used for both general and specific purposes. In general, all registers are available to hold 8- or 16-bit temporary information (8-bit quantities are called *bytes,* and 16-bit quantities are called *words*). However, several of the registers are dedicated to specific uses. For example, the CX register is used by the block-transfer instructions to keep count of bytes transferred.

The pointer and index registers generally hold offset addresses for locating a byte or word within a segment. The base and stack pointers are used for stack operations, and the index registers are used for indirect addressing.

The four segment registers locate the four segments currently in use. Generally speaking, the code segment (CS) locates the current stored program segment, the data segment (DS) locates a segment holding data, the stack segment (SS) locates the stack portion currently in use, and the extra segment (ES) locates additional data.

The instruction pointer (IP) is similar to the program counter within the 8080/8085; it generally holds the code segment offset of the next instruction to be fetched. The flag register holds an extension of the 8080/8085 set of flags, and adds other features (for example, single step, interrupt enable).

Mode Selection

By strapping the MN/$\overline{\text{MX}}$ pin high or low, the user selects either the minimum or maximum mode of operation. The minimum mode provides standard control signals suitable for a small system. The maximum mode reassigns and expands the control pins to work in a multiprocessing environment. Figure 25.6 compares the external architecture of the minimum and maximum modes.

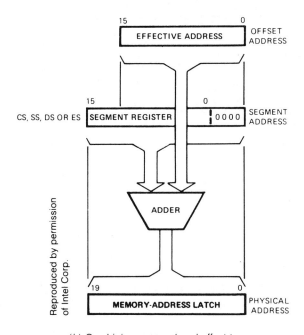

(b) Combining segment and offset to generate 20-bit physical address

Figure 25.4   The 8086 segmented addressing technique

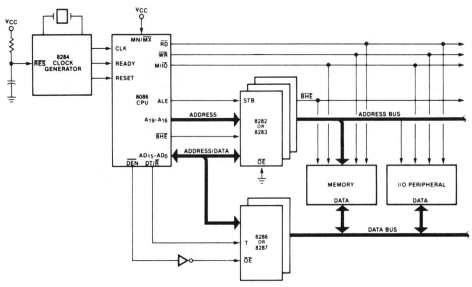

(a) Minimum mode (address bus demultiplexed)

Reproduced by permission of Intel Corp.

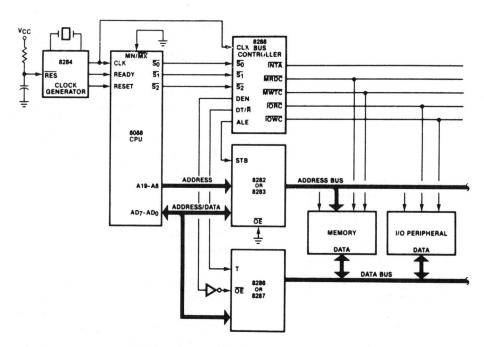

(b) Maximum mode (address bus demultiplexed)

Figure 25.6 8086 mode selection.

THE 8086 INSTRUCTION SET

The instruction set of the 8086 is built on equivalents to the 8080/8085 instruction set. The most important new operations include:

- Multiplication and division

- Move, scan, and compare *string* operations (a string operation is one performed on a sequence of bytes or words in memory)
- Nondestructive bit testing
- Software-generated interrupts
- Instructions to aid multiprocessing systems
- Complete set of signed arithmetic operations

The instruction set includes approximately 300 forms of machine-level instructions. These 300 instruction types are specifically chosen to translate efficiently into assembly or high-level code. For example, at the assembly level, there are only about 100 instruction types. As with the 8080/8085 instructions, we can get a fairly good idea of the instruction's intent by simply looking at the "verb" content of each mnemonic. These are listed below according to groups. Most of the 8086 instruction types are immediately recognizable from a knowledge of the 8080/8085 system.

Data transfer	Arithmetic	Logic
Move	Add	Invert
PUSH	Increment	Shift
POP	Adjust	Rotate
Exchange	Subtract	AND
INput	Decrement	TEST
OUTput	Change sign	OR
Translate	Compare	Exclusive OR
Load	Multiply	
Store	Divide	
	Convert	

String	Control transfer	Processor control
Repeat	CALL	Clear
Move	Jump	Complement
Compare	Return	Halt
Scan	Loop	Bus lock
Load	Interrupt	Set
Store		No operation
		WAIT
		Escape

To give you an idea of the increased scope of the 8086 instruction set, we will take a brief look at several instruction types that have no direct counterpart in the 8080/8085 repertoire of instructions:

- LEA (Load Effective Address) transfers the *address* of a memory byte to an internal register. LEA is useful for setting up pointers for string operations.
- MUL (MULtiply) performs 8- or 16-bit multiplications. For signed numbers, IMUL (Integer MULtiply) performs signed multiplication.
- SAR (Shift Arithmetic Right) provides a very quick and efficient way of dividing by a multiple of 2. SAR shifts a byte or word to the right the number of times specified by the operand. The sign bit is shifted in from the left and therefore preserved.

- TEST is a flag-setting instruction (like compare) that performs a logical AND operation, but inhibits the result from going to a register. As expected, the TEST instruction would most likely be followed by a conditional branch.
- SCAS (SCAn String) is a string instruction that searches a block of data for a given byte or word. Before the scan operation, the SI (Source Index) or DI (Destination Index) registers must be set up to address the first element in the string (LEA is useful for this purpose). When SCAN is processed, it successively subtracts each element of the string from the AL (Accumulator Low) register. The result of the subtraction is inhibited (as with the 8080/8085's compare process), and the flags are set as a result of the subtraction. SCAS can be prefixed with a *repeat*, which automatically causes the CX (Count) register to decrement each loop and checks the Z flag for a matching value. The scan process continues until CX is zero or a certain Z flag value occurs.
- JNBE (Jump on Not Below or Equal) simply extends the jump conditional concept to two simultaneous flag conditions.
- LOOPE/LOOPZ (LOOP while Equal and LOOP while Zero) performs an operation similar to the repeat prefix (REPE/REPZ) that can be added to the SCAS instruction: the loop continues until CX is zero or ZF is set.
- INTO (INTerrupt on Overflow) generates a software interrupt if the overflow flag is set. The overflow flag indicates a signed-number overflow from bit D_6 or D_{14} depending on the use of a byte or word. The carry flag, on the other hand, detects an unsigned overflow from bits D_7 or D_{15}.
- LOCK (bus LOCK) helps multiprocessor systems coordinate their activities when sharing a common resource such as memory. The LOCK instruction guarantees a processor that the next instruction will be processed with no interference from any other processor sharing the bus.

8086 ADDRESSING MODES

The two general methods of addressing data, first introduced in Chapter 11 for 8080/8085 systems, also hold for 8086-based systems:

- The instruction contains the data
- The instruction contains the location (address) of the data

As shown in the following list, however, the number of addressing modes in the second category is greatly expanded for 8086 systems:

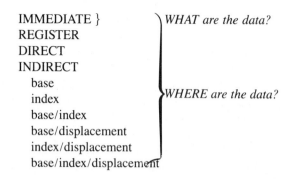

IMMEDIATE }
REGISTER
DIRECT
INDIRECT
  base
  index
  base/index
  base/displacement
  index/displacement
  base/index/displacement

WHAT are the data?

WHERE are the data?

It is the responsibility of the addressing mode (second category) to specify the *effective address* (also known as the *offset*). The effective address is made up of any combination of three components: the displacement, the base, and the index (remember that the 20-bit physical address is obtained by combining the effective address with the contents of a segment register). The displacement is contained within the instruction itself, and the base and index values are specified indirectly by way of the base and/or index registers. Figure 25.7 shows several addressing options (the MOD R/M portion of the operand indirectly specifies a base/index register).

To explain why there are so many memory-addressing modes, we must recall a major design goal of the 8086: the efficient translation of high-level language into machine code. For example, for the high-level statement C(J) = X (which means "Jth element in the C array becomes X"), it would be convenient to use the "index register + displacement"

mode of addressing. The index would point to the starting location of the array, and the displacement would locate the Jth element into the array.

INSTRUCTION CODING—AN EXAMPLE

Although an assembler or compiler will normally be called upon to form each machine-level instruction, we will hand-assemble one instruction to show what is involved.

Problem: Write a machine-language instruction to increment memory location 74AF2H. (We assume that 4AF0H is stored in the source index register and that the current code segment contains 7000H.)

The general form of this three-byte instruction is given in Figure 25.8, along with several tables that we will use to fill in the various fields of the instruction.

Figure 25.9a shows how the instruction is coded, and Figure 25.9b shows how the physical address (74AF2H) is calculated from the displacement, source index, and segment register contents. When the instruction is run, the contents of memory location 74AF2H will be incremented.

INTERRUPTS

8086 interrupts can be initiated by either software or hardware. This section deals with hardware interrupts.

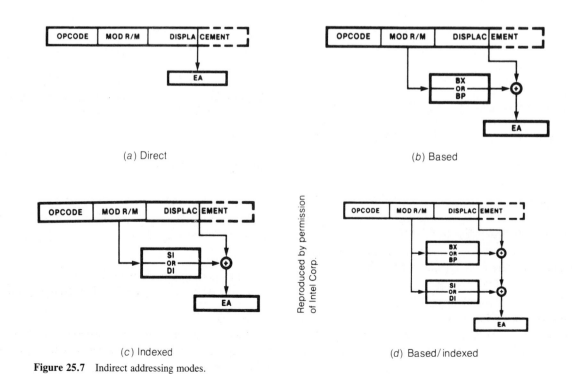

(a) Direct

(b) Based

(c) Indexed

(d) Based/indexed

Reproduced by permission of Intel Corp.

Figure 25.7 Indirect addressing modes.

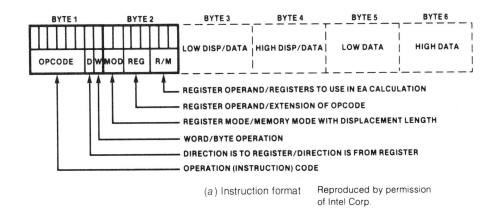

(a) Instruction format   Reproduced by permission of Intel Corp.

MOD = 11			EFFECTIVE ADDRESS CALCULATION			
R/M	W = 0	W = 1	R/M	MOD = 00	MOD = 01	MOD = 10
000	AL	AX	000	(BX) + (SI)	(BX) + (SI) + D8	(BX) + (SI) + D16
001	CL	CX	001	(BX) + (DI)	(BX) + (DI) + D8	(BX) + (DI) + D16
010	DL	DX	010	(BP) + (SI)	(BP) + (SI) + D8	(BP) + (SI) + D16
011	BL	BX	011	(BP) + (DI)	(BP) + (DI) + D8	(BP) + (DI) + D16
100	AH	SP	100	(SI)	(SI) + D8	(SI) + D16
101	CH	BP	101	(DI)	(DI) + D8	(DI) + D16
110	DH	SI	110	DIRECT ADDRESS	(BP) + D8	(BP) + D16
111	BH	DI	111	(BX)	(BX) + D8	(BX) + D16

(b) Register/memory field encoding

Figure 25.8   8086/88 instruction coding.

Note in Figure 25.3 that only three pins (INTR, NMI, INTA) are dedicated to external interrupts as compared to the six-pin interrupt structure of the 8085. Fewer inputs are needed because it is assumed the interrupt system will be driven by one or more 8259A priority interrupt controllers.

All interrupts, whether 8080, 8085, 8086, or software-based, result in the transfer of control to a new program location. In the 8086 system, up to 256 entry vectors are available and contained in absolute memory locations 0 through 3FFH (each vector specifies four bytes, so four pages are required overall).

As shown in Figure 25.10, many of the vectors are dedicated to specific functions and are not available for general use. Of special interest is vector location 2, reserved for the NMI input. The NMI input is similar to the 8085's TRAP interrupt, in that both cannot be disabled (masked out) and both are normally used for emergency situations (such as power failure).

Interrupt processing takes place in a manner similar to the INT and INTR requests of the 8080/8085. When one or more interrupts are received by the 8259A, it sends an interrupt signal to the 8086's INTR input. After the present instruction is complete (assuming the interrupt system is enabled), the 8086 sends back two INTA signals. The 8259A

responds by sending back information that points to the highest-priority vector location in the interrupt pointer table. The CPU pushes the current code segment, instruction pointer, and flag contents onto the stack, and loads the CS and IP vector values into the CS and IP registers. A return instruction at the end of the interrupt-service routine restores the original conditions.

THE 8089 INPUT/OUTPUT PROCESSOR

The 8089 I/O processor is a microprocessor in its own right, responding to more than 50 different types of instructions. Its only limitations are a design specifically tailored to I/O operations and a dependency on a master 8086 for general instructions. The 8089 pin-out and block diagram is shown in Figure 25.11.

The 8089 acts as a true slave, relieving the CPU of most of the overhead required for complex I/O operations and requiring only general commands. Figure 25.12 illustrates how the 8089 interfaces with three familiar programmable devices (introduced in previous chapters). The complex cycles required to carry out the simultaneous I/O operations are nearly invisible to the master CPU.

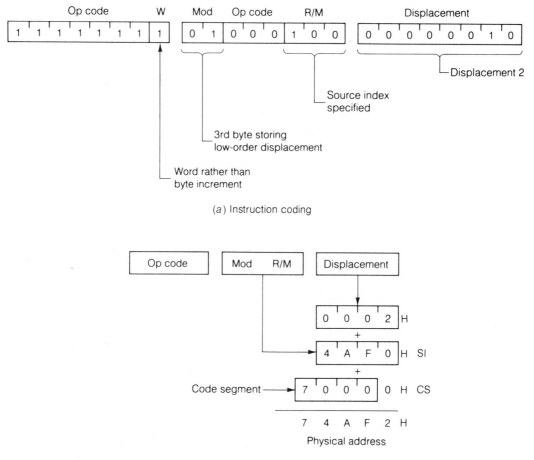

(a) Instruction coding

(b) Generating the physical address

Figure 25.9 "Increment memory location 74AF2" instruction example.

The 8089 can handle programmed, interrupt, or DMA I/O through two completely independent channels. Its instruction set is basically a subset of the 8086, retaining all commands oriented toward I/O operations.

Communication between master 8086 and slave 8089 is by way of a common memory. When the 8086 wishes to direct the 8089 to perform a task, it builds a complex "message" in memory. The 8089 is instructed to read the message and carry out the commands. When completed, the 8089 stores the requested information in memory and instructs the 8086 that the results are available. (This communication technique is called the *mail-box* system.)

THE 8088 8-BIT PROCESSOR

Although the 8086 is a more powerful processor than the 8085, certain byte-oriented applications such as word processors, telecommunication devices, and terminals require an 8-bit device to remain cost effective. To solve the problem, and to bring the computing power of the 8086 to the 8-bit world, the 8088 is offered. Except for the reduction in word length from 16 to 8 bits, there are very few differences between the 8086 and the 8088. With the 8088, the cost effectiveness of an 8-bit system can be retained while obtaining the very high performance of the 16-bit architecture and instruction set.

But won't speed be sacrificed when we move to an 8-bit system? Although it does require two cycles to fetch a 16-bit word, it does not require twice the time to execute a program. (Remember, most instructions are prefetched and are "waiting in line" in the instruction queue.)

To encourage present 8080/8085-based systems to upgrade to the power of the 8088, a utility program called CONV-86 will translate 8080/8085 programs into 8088 code.

8086/8088 Performance

Although the overall performance of any processor depends on the application and use of peripheral components, in general the 8086 offers a tenfold increase in system performance. The 16-bit processing ability, pipelined architecture (instruction prefetching), and compact instruction format are the three factors most responsible for the greatly improved performance of the 8086. The pipelined architecture also

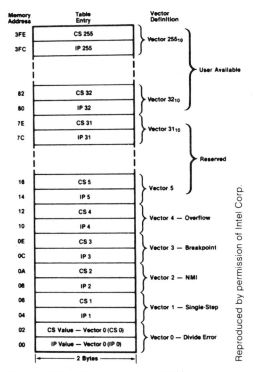

Figure 25.10 8086 interrupt-vector table.

provides a side benefit: since instructions can be fetched while execution of previous instructions is taking place, high-speed operation can be achieved with low-speed (low-cost) memories, with access times as low as 500 nsec.

THE 8088—AN APPLICATION EXAMPLE

To summarize the 8086/8088, and to review the product development material of the last few chapters, let's select a

specific task and follow through the development sequence from start to finish. To simplify the hardware, let's work with the 8088, and in order to concentrate on the development process, let's choose a task that is both familiar and simple: project TONE. In keeping with a 16-bit design environment, we have access to an Intel development system.

The Tone Task

Our task is to build an 8088-based "tone machine," in which the output frequency (pitch) is proportional (inversely) to an input number. Dividing our task into hardware and software efforts, we begin by configuring our system.

Hardware design   Selecting available components, we lay out our system according to the design of Figure 25.13. Since our design is small-scale, we choose the 8088's minimum mode, where interfacing is virtually identical with the 8085. Using 8205 decoders to select our RAM and ROM provides room for easy expansion. In the Questions and Problems section we will have an opportunity to determine the RAM, ROM, and port locations.

Software design   As is so often the case, most of our time will be devoted to software design. The process begins with the structure chart of Figure 25.14a. Based on the complexity of each module and on the nature of the task, we decide the following:

- Due to their small size, modules INPUT, TOGGLE, and OUTPUT will be placed in the main program. Due to its greater complexity, module DELAY will be a procedure.
- To improve software productivity, the main program will be written in PL/M86 (Intel's structured high-level language). Because of its strict timing requirements, module

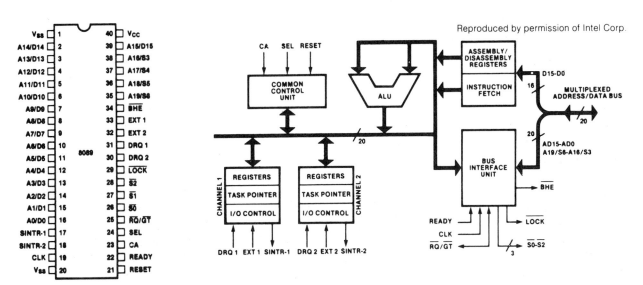

Figure 25.11   The 8089 I/O processor pin-out and block diagram.

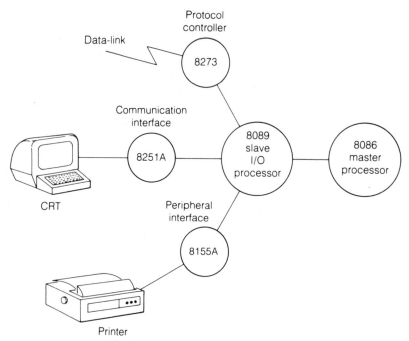

Figure 25.12 Typical 8089 application.

DELAY will be written in ASM86 (Intel's assembly language).
- To adopt parallel programming techniques, procedure DELAY will be independently assembled.

To implement parallel programming, we assign main module TONE and procedure DELAY to separate programmers. Under the ISIS II *(Intel Systems Implementation Supervisor)* operating system, each programmer enters CREDIT (a word processor utility) and generates the source programs of Figure 25.14b and c. Let's take a closer look at each of the two modules by scanning the program statements from top to bottom.

Main module TONE

- We name the program (TONE:) and enter the outermost DO/END block.
- We declare global variables A and NUMBER to hold bytes, and we declare procedure DELAY to be external.
- We initialize the 8155A.
- We enter the "DO forever" (DO WHILE 1) continuous loop.
- We input the delay value (NUMBER), and toggle the note variable (A).
- We CALL procedure DELAY, sending actual parameter NUMBER via the stack (passing parameters via the stack is the method automatically chosen by the compiler).
- We output the note variable, generating the sound.

- We bracket the DO WHILE 1 loop and the program with END statements.

Procedure DELAY

- We name the procedure (DELAY).
- To match the assignments automatically made by the compiler, we assign the code and data segments to groups CGROUP and DGROUP. (A *group* is a set of program regions combined so that they share a common segment base location.)
- Using the ASSUME statement, assign symbolic names to the code and data segments.
- We create the data segment and declare it to be PUBLIC, so it can be used by the main module. Within the data segment, we define variable I to be a word that is randomly initialized (the "?"). The attribute 'DATA' is the *class* name chosen to match that automatically selected by the compiler. (The purpose of the class name is to enable the locate utility to place all regions with the same class name next to each other in physical memory.)
- We create the code segment and declare it also to be PUBLIC. To match the compiler generated code, we give it the class name CODE.
- We declare symbolic procedure name DELAY to be PUBLIC, and we define DELAY to be a NEAR procedure (in the same segment as the main program).
- We move the stack pointer (initialized by the compiler)

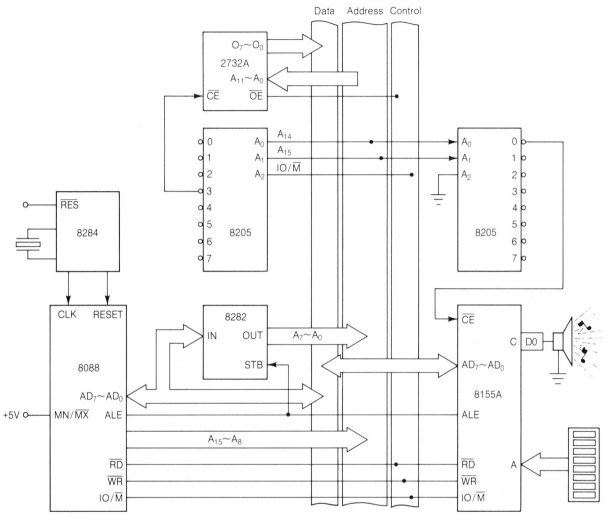

Figure 25.13 Project TONE hardware design.

to the base-pointer (BP) register, and we retrieve actual parameter NUMBER from the stack (parameter NUMBER was PUSHed onto the stack prior to the return address, so we increment the base pointer twice to point to the parameter).

- We transfer parameter NUMBER from the stack to the AL register.
- We move the delay parameter to variable I and enter the delay loop.
- When we have looped NUMBER times, we increment the stack pointer twice (to skip over the parameter and point to the return address) and return to the main program.
- We define the end of the segment (CODE ENDS) and END the module.

Using the proper ISIS II operating system utilities, source modules TONE.PLM and DELAY.ASM are compiled and assembled:

− PLM86 :F1:TONE.PLM
− ASM86 :F1:DELAY.ASM

generating the following files, holding relocatable object code:

- TONE.OBJ
- DELAY.OBJ

The LINK and LOCATE processes We combine the two independently-generated object modules using the LINK86 utility:

− LINK86 :F1:TONE.OBJ,:F1:DELAY.OBJ

and we locate the combined object module (TONE.LNK) using the LOC86 utility:

− LOC86 :F1:TONE.LNK AD(SM(CODE(0FFC00H),
    DATA(0),STACK(0C0H))) BS

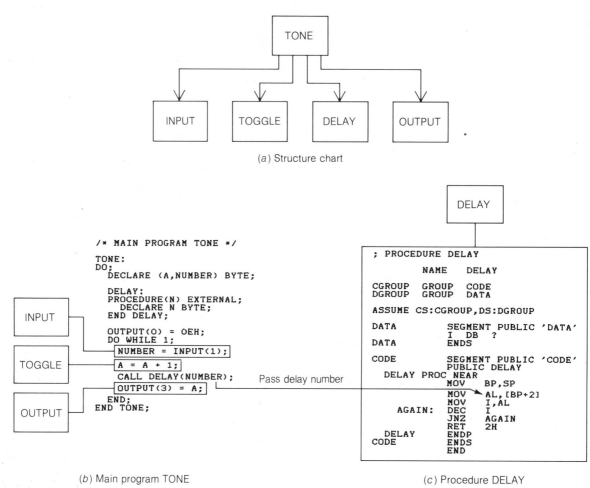

Figure 25.14   Project TONE software design.

The BS (bootstrap) attribute automatically generates the jump from reset location FFFF0H to the beginning of the program. The maps of Figure 25.15 summarize the LINK and LOCATE processes.

When we convert the located object code to hexadecimal (Figure 25.16) we can easily identify what was accomplished by the link and locate utilities. The final step is to burn a 2732A EPROM and test the system.

In-circuit emulation   To test both the hardware and software of our newly developed TONE machine, we turn to *in-circuit emulation* (ICE88).

The first step is to remove the 8088 from our prototype system and substitute the 40-pin socket leading from the external ICE module. A cable leading from the ICE module to a multibus board completes the connection between our prototype and the MDS system (see Figure 22.20).

We enter the ICE program by issuing the ICE88 command under the ISIS II operating system. ICE88 responds with the prompt "*". From here on, we have an interesting way of logging and documenting our ICE88 session. By entering

the LIST :LP: command we direct all ICE88 operations (anything that appears on the CRT) to the line printer.

Figure 25.17 is a record of our ICE88 session. The numbers beside each item correspond to the following numbered explanations:

1. We test our 8284 clock circuit by commanding the ICE88 module to obtain the clock signal from the external system rather than the ICE88 module. Since there is no response from ICE (other than the next prompt), our clock circuit is satisfactory.

2. We map the highest four pages in memory (FFC00H to FFFFFH) and the lowest four pages in memory (00000H to 003FFH) to the user system. This means that any memory access involving these address ranges will be from our *external* 2732A and 8155A. (As part of the *shared resource* feature of ICE, we could have mapped these locations to either the internal MDS RAM or the special 2K of RAM within the ICE88 module.)

3. We test the ports by first setting up the 8155A's command register. We input from port 1 and compare the

```
ISIS-II MCS-86 LINKER, V1.3, INVOKED BY:
LINK86 :F1:TONE.OBJ,:F1:DELAY.OBJ TO :F1:DELTON.LNK
LINK MAP FOR :F1:DELTON.LNK(TONE)

LOGICAL SEGMENTS INCLUDED:
LENGTH ADDRESS  SEGMENT           CLASS
  0051H ------  CODE              CODE
  0000H ------  CONST             CONST
  0011H ------  DATA              DATA
  0004H ------  STACK             STACK
  0000H ------  MEMORY            MEMORY
  0000H ------  ??SEG

INPUT MODULES INCLUDED:
:F1:TONE.OBJ(TONE)
:F1:DELAY.OBJ(DELAY)
```

(a) TONE.MP1

```
ISIS-II MCS-86 LOCATER, V1.3 INVOKED BY:
LOC86 :F1:DELTON.LNK AD(SM(CODE(OFFCOOH),DATA(O),STACK(OCOH))) BS

SYMBOL TABLE OF MODULE TONE
READ FROM FILE :F1:DELTON.LNK
WRITTEN TO FILE :F1:DELTON

BASE    OFFSET TYPE SYMBOL              BASE    OFFSET TYPE SYMBOL

FFCOH   0040H  PUB  DELAY

MEMORY MAP OF MODULE TONE
READ FROM FILE :F1:DELTON.LNK
WRITTEN TO FILE :F1:DELTON

MODULE START ADDRESS  PARAGRAPH = FFCOH  OFFSET = 0002H
SEGMENT MAP

START     STOP      LENGTH ALIGN NAME           CLASS

00000H    00010H    0011H  G     DATA           DATA
000COH    000C3H    0004H  W     STACK          STACK
00200H    00200H    0000H  W     CONST          CONST
00200H    00200H    0000H  G     ??SEG
FFCOOH    FFC50H    0051H  G     CODE           CODE
FFFFOH    FFFF4H    0005H  A     (ABSOLUTE)
FFFF6H    FFFF6H    0000H  W     MEMORY         MEMORY


GROUP MAP

ADDRESS  GROUP OR SEGMENT NAME
FFCOOH   CGROUP
         CODE
FFFFOH   DGROUP
         CONST
         DATA
         STACK
         MEMORY
```

(b) TONE.MP2

Figure 25.15 Project TONE link and locate maps.

```
:02000002FFC03D
:02000000FFFF00
:02000002FFC03D
:10000200FA2E8E160000BCD4008BEC161FFBB00E2D
:10001200E600B001D0D87203E91700E401880611A6
:10002200OOFE06100050E815008A061000E603E9FB
:04003200EOFFFBF4FC
:02000002000 1FB
:0100000000FF
:02000002FFC439
:10000000BBEC8A4602A22000FE0E200075FAC20286
:0100100000EF
:02000002FFFFFE
:05000000EA0200COFF50
:04000003FFC0000238
:00000001FF
```

TONE.OBJ } Combined
DELAY.OBJ } by LINK86

} Addresses
  established
} by LOC86

Bootstrap jump
(inter-segment direct
jump to FFC0:0002H)

Figure 25.16 Project TONE hex file.

```
1.  * CLO = EXT

2.  * MAP 0 = USER
    * MAP 1023 = USER

3.  * PORT 0 = 0E
    * PORT 1
    POR 0001H=0DH
    * PORT 3 = 0A

4.  * BYTE 0 = 55
    * BYTE FFFF:0 LEN 5
    BYT FFFF:0000H=EAH 02H 00H C0H FFH

5.  * GO FROM FFFF:0 FOREVER
    EMULATION BEGUN

6.  * GO FROM FFFF:0 TILL FFC0:45
    EMULATION BEGUN
    EMULATION TERMINATED, CS:IP=FFC0:0045H

7.  * PRINT -2
    FRAME ADDR      PREFIX        MNEMONIC     OPERANDS
    0165: FFC40H                  MOV          BP,SP
    0172: FFC42H                  MOV          AL,BYTE PTR [BP][+02]
           000C2H-R-    0DH-SS

8.  * MAP 1023 = ICE

9.  * LOAD :F1:TONE

10. * GO FROM FFFF:0 FOREVER

11. * EXIT
```

Figure 25.17   Project TONE ICE88 test session.

reported value to the DIP switch. We send information to port 3 and note the logic levels of the output lines.

4. We test RAM by sending 55H to location 00000H, and reading it back. No response indicates the RAM passed the test. We read from the first five locations of our ROM and note that these locations correctly hold the bootstrap jump.

5. We begin real-time emulation starting from location FFFF:0 (Segment FFFFH; offset 0000H). A special high-speed 8088 within the ICE88 system is now operating the prototype board. At the same time, information concerning each instruction is being stored in the internal MDS RAM. Since we hear the tone, and find it to be inversely proportional to the inported number, we conclude that the system is functioning properly. (FOR-EVER means to emulate continuously.)

6. For learning value, we set a breakpoint to location FFC0:45 (the location of the MOV AL,[BP+2] instruction).

7. We print to the screen information on the two instructions leading up to the breakpoint. Examining the print-

out, we note that 0DH was pulled from stack location 000C2H (0DH is the passed parameter, and should match the state of the DIP switch). (*FRAME* determines the instructions' position in the ICE storage RAM.)

8. To demonstrate the shared resource facility, we map the upper four pages of the memory map to the special high-speed RAM within the ICE module.

9. We then load our TONE program object code into these locations.

10. During emulation the instructions are now fetched from the RAM within the ICE module. *Our 2732A is totally bypassed.*

11. Satisfied that our system is working properly, we exit ICE88 and return to the ISIS II operating system.

Of course our simple ICE88 test sequence does not reveal the full power of the ICE88 system. For example, we can define MACROs (a single ICE88 command that stands for a series of ICE88 commands) and streamline the emulation process. In addition, we can use conditional branches and jumps to write an ICE88 automatic test sequence. Consult the *ICE88 User's Guide* for a full description of the ICE88 system.

INTELLIGENT-MACHINE UPDATE

When human beings developed a sophisticated language and learned to work together, dividing the tasks among the members of the social unit according to ability, the agricultural and industrial revolutions followed quickly.

Our intelligent machine has now entered the high-level language, multiprocessing, multitasking environment and is creating another revolution all its own. How long will it be before we look upon a computer complex of intelligent machines as a true social unit?

QUESTIONS AND PROBLEMS

1. What do the terms *distributed processing* and *parallel processing* mean?
2. In an 8086 multiprocessing system, what is the difference between the *public, local,* and *private* buses?
3. In an 8086 system, what is the difference between an *independent processor* and a *coprocessor*?
4. How is the 8087 *math processor* given a command?
5. How does *prefetching* increase the speed of the 8086?
6. In an 8086 system, how is the physical address calculated from the segment address and the offset?
7. What change occurs in pins 24 through 31 of the 8086 when MN/MX is strapped low?
8. How is the physical address determined when using *indexed* addressing?
9. In an 8086 system, where is the starting address of the interrupt-service routine stored?
10. For what types of operations is the 8089 processor particularly well suited?
11. Name several features of the 8086 that are responsible for its high performance (speed).
12. What additional features of interrupt processing are found in the 8086 as compared to the 8085?
13. For the system of Figure 25.13:
    a. Draw memory and port maps.
    b. Why must the 2732A be placed at the top of the memory map?
14. In Figure 25.14*b*:
    a. Identify the actual and formal parameters.
    b. Is N a local or a global variable?
    c. Identify the first executable instruction.
15. Referring to Figure 25.14*c*:
    a. What is the source and destination of the data moved by the MOV AL,[BP + 2] instruction?
    b. What information is defined by the ASSUME statement?
    c. What is the difference between a NEAR and a FAR procedure?
16. By eliminating the variable I and making use of the LOOP instruction (explained below), rewrite procedure DELAY of Figure 25.14*c* in a more compact form. (*Hint:* Is the data segment required?) Instruction LOOP decrements CX by 1 and transfers control to the target operand if CX is not 0; otherwise the instruction following LOOP is executed.
17. Referring to Figure 25.17, what is the purpose of each of the following ICE88 command words?
    a. CLO
    b. MAP
    c. PORT
    d. BYTE
    e. GO
    f. TILL
    g. PRINT
    h. LOAD

chapter 26

The iAPX186, 286, and 386 Advanced Processor Families

As civilization passed through the agricultural revolution, people gradually *integrated* their societies into central locations called towns, in which many activities could take place simultaneously. As information accumulated, they erected huge libraries and discovered many ingenious ways to store, retrieve, and protect data. As microprocessor technology matures, from the third generation iAPX86 to the fourth generation iAPX186, 286 and 386 families, we find a similar transformation.

THE 80186/88

When the design of the 8086/8088 CPU was well-established, Intel polled its customers and found that many were designing systems composed of at least the seven following functions:

- A central processing unit (CPU).
- A direct-memory-access unit (DMA).
- A timer.
- An interrupt controller.
- Bus interface circuitry.
- A clock generator.
- Chip-selection circuitry and a wait-state generator.

So, using state-of-the-art VLSI technology, Intel integrated all of these functions on a single chip—and called it the 80186/80188, the central processing unit of the iAPX186 family (see Figure 26.1). As with the 8086/88 family, the 80186 maintains a full 16-bit external data bus while the 81088 offers a hardware-saving 8-bit external data bus; that is the only difference. To maintain compatibility, the 80186/88 shares its architecture and instruction set with the 8086/88.

The Peripheral Control Block

All of the seven functional areas within the 80186/88 are controlled by sets of registers within each individual peripheral unit. They are addressed, however, as a single register block (the *peripheral control block*) that fills 256 contiguously addressed bytes (see Figure 26.2). For flexibility, the 256 byte block can be relocated to anywhere within the memory or I/O space. Here is how it is done.

After system reset, the peripheral control block is automatically located at the very top page of the I/O space—at addresses FF00H through FFFFH. The *relocation register* is therefore located at FFFEH and FFFFH. By writing a *base* address into the relocation register, we can relocate the peripheral control block on any 256 byte boundary within the processor's memory or I/O space. An individual control register is then located as an offset from the base value.

The Seven Functional Areas of the 80186/88

To complete our overview of the 80186/88, let's take a brief look at each of its seven functional blocks.

The CPU block Relatively few hardware and software enhancements separate the CPU block from an 8086/88 microprocessor chip. Most of the enhancements are related to speed. On the hardware side we have a three-fold increase in multiply and divide speed, faster effective (offset) address calculation, and full-speed string-move operations. On the software side are new block I/O operations, special instructions designed to streamline the passage of parameters via the stack, and new immediate-value multiply, shift, and pop instructions.

The DMA block The integrated DMA unit will perform transfers to or from any combination of I/O and memory space by either bytes or words. Each of the two high-speed DMA channels maintains independent 20-bit pointers to locate the source and destination of each data transfer (the DMA channels address the full 1 Mbyte address space as a linear array without segments). After each transfer, the pointers can be programmed to automatically increment, decrement, or remain constant. By maintaining a transfer count, each DMA channel can be programmed to terminate after the desired number of transfers.

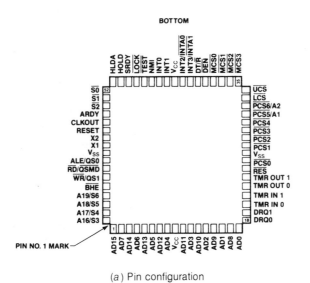

(a) Pin configuration

(b) Internal block diagram

Figure 26.1 The 80186 CPU. (Courtesy Intel Corporation)

Referring back to Figure 26.2, we control DMA operations by writing to offset locations C0H to DAH of the Peripheral Control Block.

The timer block To simulate the actions of the *8253 Programmable Interval Timer,* the built-in timer unit offers three independent 16-bit programmable timers. Timers 0 and 1 can be programmed to count external events, generate waveforms from either the internal CPU clock or an external clock, or to interrupt the CPU after receiving a specified number of "events." Timer 2, which only accepts CPU clock pulses as an input, can be used to generate CPU-dependent signals, such as regular DMA requests to the integrated DMA unit (remember to enable the DMA request-from-timer bit).

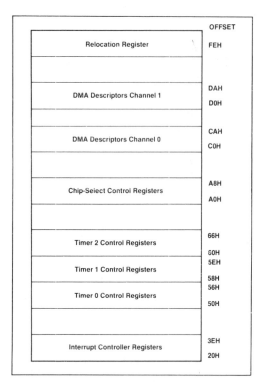

	OFFSET
Relocation Register	FEH
DMA Descriptors Channel 1	DAH
	D0H
DMA Descriptors Channel 0	CAH
	C0H
Chip-Select Control Registers	A8H
	A0H
Timer 2 Control Registers	66H
	60H
Timer 1 Control Registers	5EH
	58H
Timer 0 Control Registers	56H
	50H
Interrupt Controller Registers	3EH
	20H

Figure 26.2 The peripheral control block of the 80186/88.
(*Courtesy Intel Corporation*)

The interrupt controller To the basic features of an *8259A Priority Interrupt Controller,* the interrupt controller unit adds several useful features. Most notably, interrupts can be initiated via the internal timers and DMA channels, as well as the conventional external pins.

The chip-select and ready generation unit To reduce the need for external decoder chips, the on-board chip-select unit provides six output lines for memory addressing and seven for peripheral addressing.

The memory addressing lines are designed to enable the three major areas in a typical 8086 system: one upper range block for operating system code, one lower range block for interrupt vectors, and 4 midrange blocks for program code. The size of each of these regions is user-programmable.

The seven peripheral-selection lines address seven contiguous 128-byte blocks above a programmable base address. Each 128-byte block can be programmed for isolated I/O or memory-mapped operation.

To accommodate the needs of slow memory units, bits 0, 1, and 2 of each chip select control register are reserved for *wait state programming*.

Clock generator unit Integrating many of the functions of the 8284 timer chip is the function of the clock generator unit. Using only an external crystal, it provides a 50 percent duty-cycle CPU clock at half the crystal frequency. The clock generator also provides ready synchronization for the processor.

Summary

With its seven functional areas fully integrated on chip, the 80186/88 will find a ready home in workstations and personal computers. When combined with other advanced VLSI chips such as the 8274 serial controller, the 80150 CP/M 86 operating system kernel, and the 82586 Ethernet controller, systems of great power and complexity can be constructed from a mere handful of chips.

THE 80286/88

A single user performing a single task will generally find the power of an 8086/88-based system to be more than adequate. But move up to a multiuser, multitasking system, requiring memory protection and virtual-memory management, and a more powerful solution is needed. The 80286 of Figure 26.3 (the central processing unit of the iAPX286 family) was designed with such a need in mind.

Since memory management and protection are the most important features of the 80286/88, that is where we will begin our discussion.

Basic Modes of Operation

For those who wish to take advantage of the 80286/88's sixfold increase in throughput, but have no need for memory protection or management, the 80286/88 is placed in the *real* address mode. With a 1 Mbyte real (physical) address space, it will execute unmodified 8086/88 object code. The 80286/88 automatically enters the real address mode upon power-up.

However, when given the correct software instruction, the 80286/88 enters the *protected mode* and undergoes an amazing metamorphosis. As illustrated by Figure 26.4, the real address space expands to 16 megabytes (2^{24}), which in turn maps into a full gigabyte (2^{30}) of virtual memory *per task*. Most programs written for the 8086/88 require little or no modification to operate in the protected mode.

The Virtual (Protected) Address Mode

To generate a physical address, both the 8086/88 and 80286/88 start with the same basic data: a 16-bit segment and a 16-bit offset. However, the 8086/88 generates a 20-bit physical address, while the protected mode 80286/88 generates a 30-bit virtual address that maps into a 24-bit physical address. To see how the larger address of the protected mode 80286/88 is generated, we refer to Figure 26.5.

First, turning to Figure 26.5a for a quick review, the 8086/88 generates its 20-bit physical address by adding the 16-bit segment value (with zeroes appended to the least-significant

PAD VIEW

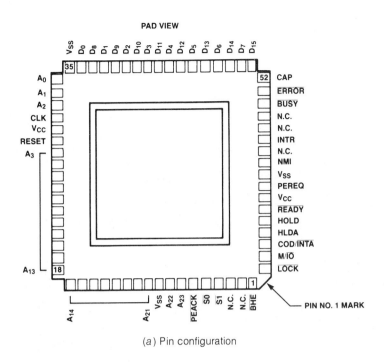

(a) Pin configuration

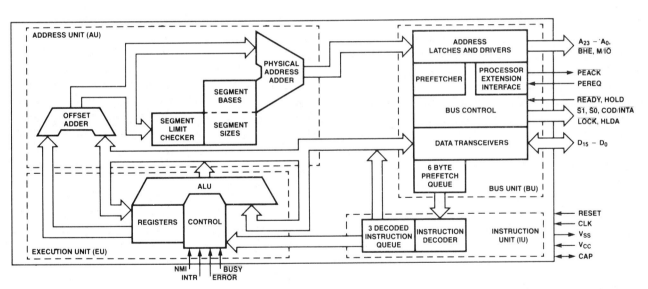

(b) Internal block diagram

Figure 26.3 The 80286 CPU. (*Courtesy Intel Corporation*)

4 bit positions) to the 16-bit offset. It is convenient to think of the segment value as pointing to the bottom of the 64K segment (the segment base) and the offset specifying a value from the base.

The 80286/88, on the other hand, generates its 30-bit virtual space by specifying 16K segments of 64K locations each (16K × 64K = 1 Gbyte). Figure 26.5*b* shows us how it is done. Instead of a segment register, we have a *segment selector* which uses 14 of its 16 bits to point to one of 16K *segment descriptors* located in physical memory. Each seg-

ment descriptor represents one 64K segment of virtual memory. To map the one Gbyte of virtual memory to the 16 Mbytes of physical memory, the segment descriptor sends a 24-bit segment base address to the CPU. The offset then specifies a value within this 64K segment.

When we enlarge the segment-descriptor/segment-base portion of the diagram to reveal more detail (Figure 26.6), we see that the segment base is part of a larger *task register* within the CPU. Also, the segment descriptor contains the segment size and access rights of the segment, in addition

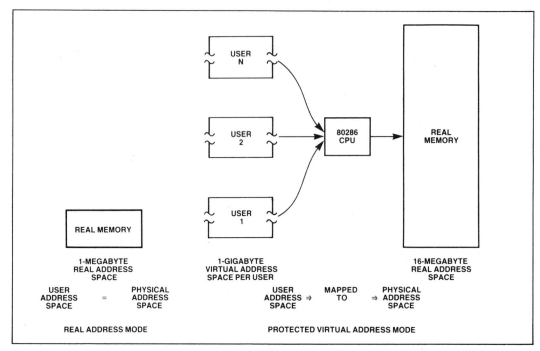

Figure 26.4   Comparing the address space of the *real* address mode vs the *protected virtual* address mode. (*Courtesy Intel Corporation*)

to the 24-bit base address. The net result is that the 16-bit segment selector has been expanded into a 48-bit *task register*. Once the CPU copies the descriptor information into the segment task register (also known as the *cache register*), it does not need to refer to a descriptor table again until the program requires access to another segment.

The system programmer locates the descriptor tables anywhere in memory by using the three descriptor table registers: a global descriptor table register (GDTR) for code and data common to all tasks, an interrupt descriptor table register (IDTR), and a local descriptor table register (LDTR) that defines the code and data private to each task (see Figure 26.6). *Switching from one task's memory space to another only requires changing the LDTR in the CPU.*

Memory Protection and Privilege

Consider a computer system that handles bank transactions. Clearly, the software that manipulates the data should be more highly *privileged* than the data. Furthermore, an application must be able to *use* the operating system (OS) services without taking control of the OS. Therefore, the following privilege rules must hold:

> A program may access data at only the same or a less-privileged level; it may call services at only the same or a more-privileged level.

The 80286/88 offers the programmer four levels of privilege (Figure 26.7). As shown, the operating system *kernel*

(the most basic part of the operating system) is given the highest level, while the applications are the least privileged.

Because each block of programs and data occupies its own variable-length segment, these segments constitute ideal units for privilege control. As shown in Figure 26.8a, each segment selector includes a *requested privilege level (RPL)*, and each segment descriptor (Figure 26.8b) includes a *descriptor privilege level (DPL)*. If the RPL and DPL do not match the rules for privilege, an *exception* (internally-generated interrupt) is issued.

In addition to privilege, memory *protection* is yet another technique used to improve security and help prevent the spread of software "bugs." For protection purposes, the iAPX 286 system provides four segments types:

- Execute-only.
- Execute and read.
- Read only.
- Read and write.

Referring to Figure 26.8b, the protection category for each segment is specified in the TYPE field of the segment descriptor. Any violation of the protection rules also generates an exception.

Virtual Memory

A major reason for adopting virtual memory is to support a system containing both primary and secondary memory. Primary memory (RAM) is required for high-speed operation,

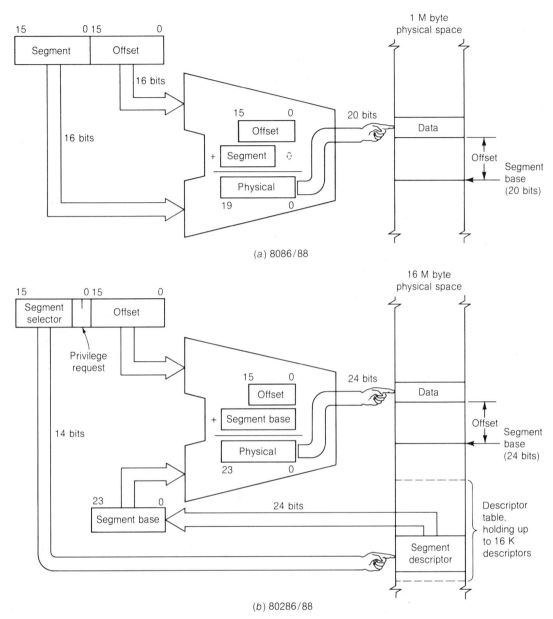

Figure 26.5   8086/88 vs 80286/88 address generation. (*Courtesy Intel Corporation*)

and secondary memory (usually a disk) is needed to hold large amounts of data at low cost. Any computer system that supports a virtual address space must effectively manage the swapping of programs and data between primary and secondary memory. As first explained in Chapter 4, program action tends to *cluster* about certain portions of memory. As time goes by, processing action gradually shifts to other memory regions. It is the job of the operating system to continuously monitor memory activity, and to place the more highly active (clustered) regions in primary memory, and the least-active regions in secondary memory.

To aid the virtual memory software, the segment descriptor contains the A field (see Figure 26.8b), which indicates

if the segment has been previously accessed (since the last time the A bit was reset).

In order for the operating system to determine which segments are in primary (real) memory and which are in secondary (virtual) memory, each segment descriptor contains a *Present (P)* field (Figure 26.8b). If P = 1, the segment is mapped into physical memory; if P = 0, it is mapped into secondary memory. Each time a segment is swapped between primary and secondary memory, the P field is changed. For example, if an instruction requests access to a segment that is not present in real memory, the P bit (0 for not-present) triggers a "segment not-present" exception, and the OS initiates a swap. (The S field indicates if the segment descriptor

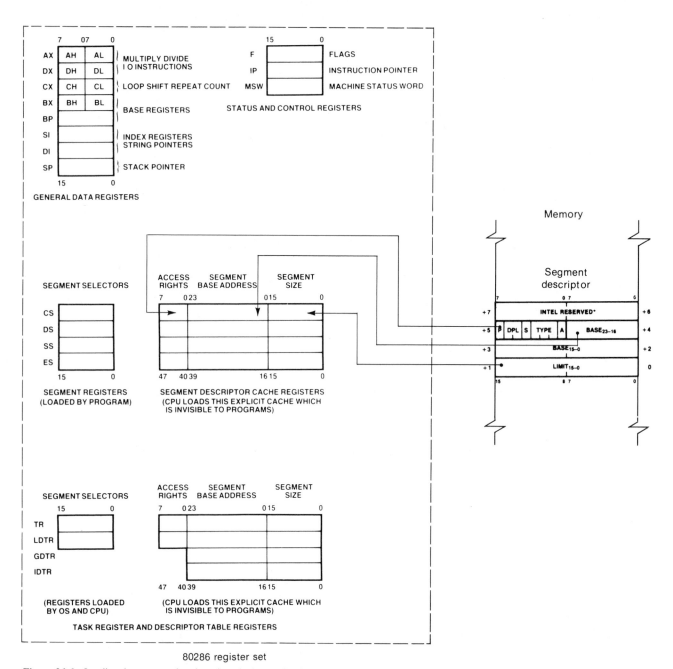

Figure 26.6 Loading the segment descriptor into the international cache register.

refers to a code or data segment, or to a nonsegment descriptor.)

Extended Capabilities

As stated earlier, we may wish to use the 80286/88 in the *real* mode simply for its many improvements, apart from memory protection and management. Let's wrap up our discussion of the 80286/88 by briefly reviewing several of these extended capabilities:

- The iAPX 286 can respond to an interrupt in less than 4 microseconds, and is therefore ideal for real-time control applications.

- A multiuser or multitasking system must switch from one task to another quickly. Due to special built-in dedicated, task-switching hardware, the 80288/86 can save the state of one task (all registers), load the state of another, and resume execution all in less than 17 microseconds.

- New instructions (not found on the 8088/86) are designed to speed the processing of code generated by a high-level

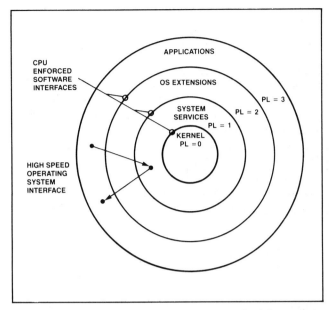

Figure 26.7 Hierarchical privilege levels. (Courtesy Intel Corporation)

language. In particular, these new instructions simplify and speed up the handling of stack operations, and of executing procedure entry and exit commands.

• Four independent processing units operate in parallel so that memory accesses, address calculations, protection checks, instruction decoding, and execution can overlap.

THE iAPX386 FAMILY

Continuing the logical progression, the iAPX386 carries the iAPX286 family into the 32-bit world. Those who have an investment in the 286 family will be pleased to learn that the upgrade into the 32-bit world can be made with existing operating software and support tools.

The heart of the iAPX386 family, the 80386 central processing unit, incorporates over 300,000 transistors on chip—over twice that of the 80286. As if to end the persistent shortage in memory space as systems and applications increase in size, the 80386 addresses 4 gigabytes of physical memory and 64 terabytes of virtual memory (1 terabyte = 10^{12} bytes). Continuing the trend started with the 286, the 386 offers on-chip memory management and protection.

As always, throughput and processing speed must improve in order to remain competitive. Overall, the 386 is two to three times faster than the 80286, offering special on-board hardware to speed up arithmetic calculations. A 32-by-32 bit integer multiply, for example, can be carried out in as little as .6 usec. To further enhance arithmetic calculations, the 386 family includes the 80387 floating-point coprocessor chip.

The 386 should find a ready home in the rapidly expanding technical workstation market, and then gradually expand into nearly every sector of microprocessor activity.

INTELLIGENT-MACHINE UPDATE

As so clearly demonstrated by the state of hypnosis, we all have some limited access to those innermost portions of our mind that control our most critical functions, such as breathing and heartbeat—*but we cannot change them*. To further protect this prime "kernel" of life-giving data, nature long ago endowed our automonic nervous system with an *execute only* level of protection.

Once again, as we have seen so often, several fundamental concepts of computer action—memory management and protection—occurred *in* the human mind before they occurred *to* the human mind.

QUESTIONS AND PROBLEMS

1. List the seven functional areas integrated within the 80186/88 chip.
2. What information is contained in the peripheral control block?
3. What is a type-8 vector, and how is it generated?
4. What is a *wait state*, and how is automatic wait-state generation included in the memory select process?
5. For each of the following, how is a segment base and physical address within the base determined?

    • iAPX 86/88 system
    • iAPX 286/88 system

6. How does a 14-bit segment selector address result in 1 Gbyte of virtual address space?
7. Within a segment descriptor, what information do each of the following fields hold?

    • BASE
    • LIMIT
    • TYPE
    • A
    • S
    • DPL
    • P

8. Each segment of an 80286/88 system is assigned a privilege level. How does the system determine if the requested segment obeys the privilege rules?
9. What basic rules does the operating system use to initiate swaps of information between primary and secondary memory?

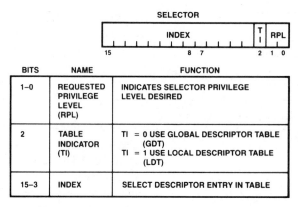

(a) Segment selector holds requested priviledge level

Segment Descriptor

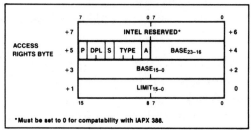

*Must be set to 0 for compatability with iAPX 386.

Access Rights Byte Definition

Bit Position	Name	Function		
7	Present (P)	P = 1	Segment is mapped into physical memory.	
		P = 0	No mapping to physical memory exists, base and limit are not used.	
6–5	Descriptor Privilege Level (DPL)		Segment privilege attribute used in privilege tests.	
4	Segment Descriptor (S)	S = 1 S = 0	Code or Data segment descriptor Non-segment descriptor	
3	Executable (E)	E = 0	Data segment descriptor type is:	**Data Segment**
2	Expansion Direction (ED)	ED = 0	Grow up segment, offsets must be ≤ limit.	
		ED = 1	Grow down segment, offsets must be > limit.	
1	Writeable (W)	W = 0 W = 1	Data segment may not be written into. Data segment may be written into.	
3	Executable (E)	E = 1	Code Segment Descriptor type is:	**Code Segment**
2	Conforming (C)	C = 0	Code segment may only be executed when CPL ≥ DPL.	
1	Readable (R)	R = 0	Code segment may not be read.	
		R = 1	Code segment may be read.	
0	Accessed (A)	A = 0 A = 1	Segment has not been accessed. Segment selector has been loaded into segment register or used by selector test instructions.	

Type Field Definition (spans the E/ED/W and E/C/R rows, bit positions 3–0)

(b) Segment descriptor holds present priviledge level

Figure 26.8 Segments and privilege levels in the 80286/88. (Courtesy Intel Corporation)

chapter 27

The 2920 Signal Processor

One advantage enjoyed by the human mind over a computer is the ability to process signals in both analog and digital. Now, with the advent of the signal (analog) processor, no longer are complex analog manipulations the sole property of the human mind.

THE 2920 SIGNAL PROCESSOR: AN OVERVIEW

The 2920 signal processor is a general-purpose analog system on a chip, bringing the power of programmability to analog designs. Working in the time domain, and processing signals by mathematical manipulation, it reduces a board full of analog components to a single device.

Basically, the 2920 consists of three blocks: an analog-to-digital front end, a digital processing section, and a digital-to-analog output section. All processing action is done in digital, but the inputs and outputs are purely analog.

There are many advantages to working in digital rather than analog. First of all, the production version of an analog design will act just as it was designed, with no complex component matching required. Also, a digital system is less expensive because the analog "parts" normally required are simulated mathematically and simply do not exist. Furthermore, digital circuits are easier to integrate than analog circuits. And finally, as with any programmable device, the design can be modified and improved simply by changing the software.

The 2920 is a sampled-data system. The input analog signal is sampled at regular intervals. Each sampled voltage is converted to digital, processed, reconverted back to analog, and output, producing a "squared off" output waveform.

In most cases, an *antialiasing filter* and *reconstruction filter* are added to the analog input and output. The function of the antialiasing filter is to eliminate or reduce the spectral noise caused when the analog signal is chopped into discrete voltages by sampling. The reconstruction filter smooths out the output waveform into a continuous analog signal. Figure 27.1 is a block diagram of a 2920-based sampled-data system.

Internal Architecture and Processing Action

A functional block diagram of the 2920 is shown in Figure 27.2. Once inside the analog/digital conversion blocks, it is a full-fledged, special-purpose microprocessor in its own right. An understanding of the 2920's internal architecture will come from following an analog signal through the device (refer to Figure 27.2).

An analog signal enters the device through one of four multiplexed (time-shared) inputs. Under program control, the input is selected and sampled. While held in a sample-and-hold capacitor, each analog signal is converted to a 9-bit digital word (a sign bit plus eight amplitude bits). During the analog-to-digital process, the digital bits accumulate in the Digital/Analog Register (DAR). The DAR is the interface between the analog and digital sections of the 2920. Following A/D conversion, the digital word is loaded into a 40-word, 25-bit scratch-pad RAM. The RAM is provided with two ports, allowing two words (A and B) to be read from the RAM simultaneously.

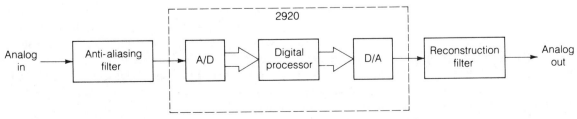

Figure 27.1   The 2920 signal processing system.

389

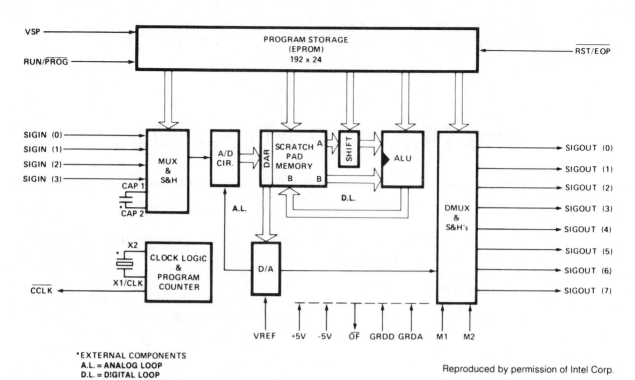

Reproduced by permission of Intel Corp.

*EXTERNAL COMPONENTS
A.L. = ANALOG LOOP
D.L. = DIGITAL LOOP

Figure 27.2   2920 functional block diagram.

Digital processing takes place in a loop. First, two data words are fetched simultaneously from the two RAM ports. The data from port A are passed through the binary shifter, which scales the A data word from 2^2 (2-position left shift) to 2^{-13} (13-position right shift). The scaled A value and the unscaled B value pass on to the ALU. After the two words are mathematically combined under program control, the result is returned to the same B RAM location (each B location therefore has properties of an accumulator).

When a data word is ready for output, it passes to the DAR, is converted to an analog voltage level, loaded into a sample-and-hold capacitor, and output on one of eight multiplexed lines.

All analog and digital processing is controlled by a stored program in the on-board 192 × 24 EPROM. Each pass through the stored program produces one digital-processing/analog-sampling loop. A full 192 instruction program, running at the maximum 10-MHz clock rate, results in a 13-KHz sample rate. (If the program requires only half of the 192 locations, the sampling rate is doubled.) To maintain a constant sampling rate, no conditional branching is allowed.

The Instruction Set

As detailed in Figure 27.3a, the instruction set of the 2920 contains 13 digital instructions and 8 analog instructions.

Figure 27.3b shows the format of each 24-bit instruction word stored in the EPROM. Digital and analog processing take place simultaneously; the first four fields control the

activities of the digital processing loop, and the last field commands the analog/digital conversion and input/output analog operations. Because of the complexity of each machine-language word, the conversion from assembly language to machine language is usually accomplished with a machine assembler.

A LOW-PASS FILTER

The best way to understand the capabilities and unique properties of the 2920 is through a specific example. In this section, we will program the 2920 to simulate the simple single-pole (one break frequency), low-pass filter of Figure 27.4.

We are well aware of the characterisitcs of a single-pole, low-pass filter in the frequency domain (Figure 27.4a), but the 2920 processes information in the time domain. For a simple step input, the response of a single-pole, low-pass filter is equally well known (Figure 27.4b).

The question is: can we simulate the RC curve of Figure 27.4b by using a repetitive loop equation that outputs a regular sequence of voltages, all lying along the RC curve? The answer is: we can, and it is done with a mathematical technique known as a *pseudo-moving average*. Here is how it works: *Add 63% of the 1-volt input signal to 37% of the current output value. The result becomes the new current value.*

The operation is graphed in time as shown in Figure 27.5.

Mnemonics		Operations		
Code	Condition			
Digital Instructions				
ADD		$(A \times 2^N) + B \longrightarrow B^{[1]}$		
SUB		$B - (A \times 2^N) \longrightarrow B$		
LDA[3]		$(A \times 2^N) + 0 \longrightarrow B$		
XOR[3]		$(A \times 2^N) \oplus B \longrightarrow B$		
AND		$(A \times 2^N) \cdot B \longrightarrow B$		
ABS[3]		$[(A \times 2^N)] \longrightarrow B$		
ABA		$[(A \times 2^N)] + B \longrightarrow B$		
LIM		$\text{Sign}(A) \rightarrow \pm \text{ F.S.} \rightarrow B^{[4]}$		
ADD	CND( )[2]	$(A \times 2^N) + B \longrightarrow B$		IFF DAR(K) = 1
		$B \longrightarrow B$		IFF DAR(K) = 0
SUB	CND( )[2][7]	$B - (A \times 2^N) \longrightarrow B$	$\& \text{ CY} \rightarrow \text{DAR(K)}$	IFF $CY_P = 1$
		$B + (A \times 2^N) \longrightarrow B$	$\& \text{ CY} \rightarrow \text{DAR(K)}$	IFF $CY_P = 0$ [5]
LDA	CND( )[2]	$(A \times 2^N) \longrightarrow B$		IFF DAR(K) = 1
		$B \longrightarrow B$		IFF DAR(K) = 0
ABA	CND( )[8]	$(A \times 2^N) + B \longrightarrow B$		
XOR	CND( )[8]	$(A \times 2^N) \oplus B \longrightarrow B$		
Analog Instructions				
IN(K)		Signal Sample from Input Channel K		
OUT(K)		D/A to Output Channel K		
CVTS		Determine Sign Bit		
CVT(K)		Perform A/D on Bit K		
EOP		Program Counter to Zero[6]		
NOP		No Operation		
CND(K)		Select Bit K for Conditional Instructions		
CNDS		Select Sign Bit for Conditional Instructions		

Notes:
1. Note that scaling of A always occurs before executing the digital operation.
2. CND( ) can be either CND(K) or CNDS testing amplitude bits or the sign bit of the DAR respectively.
3. Clarification of CY_{OUT} sense for certain operations. For LDA, XOR, AND, ABS: $CY_{OUT} \rightarrow 0$.
4. B is set to full scale (F.S.) amplitude with the same sign as the "A" port operand.
5. The previous carry bit (CY_P) is tested to determine the operation. The present carry bit (CY) is loaded into the Kth bit location of the DAR. "Present carry (CY) is generated independent of overflow. It will represent the carry (CY) of a calculated 28-bit result."
6. EOP will also enable overflow correction if it was disabled during a program pass. The EOP must occur in ROM location 188.
7. For SUB CNDS operation $\overline{CY} \rightarrow DAR(S)$.
8. Does not affect DAR. In this case, CND is used with XOR/ABA to enable/disable the ALU overflow saturation algorithm. Use of either instruction causes the ALU output to roll over rather than go to full scale with sign bit preserved. An EOP instruction will also enable the ALU overflow sturation algorithm.

Reproduced by permission
of Intel Corp.

(a) Assembly language instruction set

ALU instruction	B address (destination/source)	A address (source)	Shift code	Analog instruction
3 bits	6 bits	6 bits	4 bits	5 bits

(b) Instruction format

Figure 27.3 2920 software.

Note that G plus B is equal to 1 (necessary to produce the proper output amplitude).

Performing the loop operation, we obtain the following output sequence:

> 0.63
> 0.86
> 0.96
> 0.98
> 0.99

This sequence does indeed lie along the RC curve. (If the pseudo-moving average gives the correct value for a step input, we assume it gives the correct low-pass filter response for *all* inputs.) Therefore, the following loop equation (written in FORTRAN) will generate the RC curve, point by point:

$$Y0 = (G*X) + (B*Y1)$$

or, in our specific case:

$$Y0 = (0.63*X) + (0.37*Y1)$$

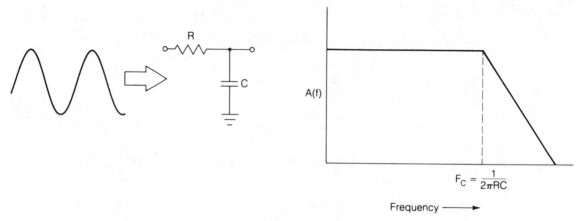

(a) Frequency-domain characteristics

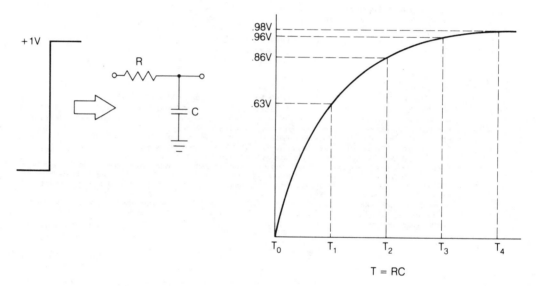

(b) Time-domain characteristics

Figure 27.4 Single-pole low-pass filter.

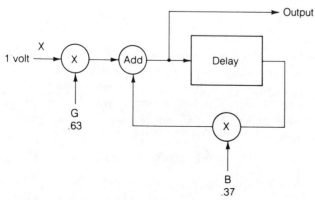

Figure 27.5 Graph of "moving average" technique.

Unfortunately, there are two problems with implementing this equation using the 2920 instruction set. First of all, we have assumed a sampling rate equal to the RC time constant of the low-pass filter. This seldom occurs; in fact the sampling period is usually much shorter than the RC time constant, since it is determined by the length of the program (each instruction processed requires 400 nsec at the 10-MHz clock rate). Second, each of the constants used in the loop equation (G and B) must ultimately be converted to binary. We will find that some values are easier to develop than others. To be specific, as shown in Figure 27.6, the easiest binary numbers to generate are those with a single 1 in the number (or 1 minus those numbers).

Binary number	n	2^{-n}	$1 - 2^{-n}$
0.1000000000	1	0.5	0.5
0.0100000000	2	0.25	0.75
0.0010000000	3	0.125	0.875
0.0001000000	4	0.0625	0.9375
0.0000100000	5	0.03125	0.96875
0.0000010000	6	0.015625	0.984375
0.0000001000	7	0.007812	0.992188
0.0000000100	8	0.00390625	0.99609375
0.0000000010	9	0.001953125	0.998046875
0.0000000001	10	0.0009765625	0.9990234375

Figure 27.6   Decimal number created by simple powers of 2.

Numbers not on this list can be generated by combinations of these "single 1" numbers. An example follows for the number 0.53125:

$$0.53125 = 0.5 + 0.03125$$
$$0.53125 = 2^{-1} + 2^{-5}$$

It clearly is an advantage to use numbers on the "single 1" list, for generating values by combinations of "single 1" numbers lengthens the program and reduces the sampling rate.

To see how both problems are handled, let us be very specific and design a low-pass filter with a cut-off frequency (3 dB down) of 50 Hz. Let us also assume (arbitrarily) that the sampling period (length of time between samples) is 96 μsec.

Somehow, from this specific information, we must calculate G and B. The two equations linking together the knowns (sample period and critical frequency) with the unknowns (G and B) are:

$$B = e^{-F_c \cdot T \cdot 2\pi} \text{ (where } T \text{ is the sample period)}$$
$$G + B = 1$$

The top relationship should look familiar, for it is very closely related to the equation of the output voltage rise in an RC filter circuit:

$$V_c = V_{in}(1 - e^{-t/RC})$$

Therefore, let us substitute our known values into the equations and come up with the G and B constants:

$$B = e^{-50 \cdot 96 \mu s \cdot 2\pi} \text{ (which equals 0.97029)}$$

Unfortunately, this number for B is not on our "single 1" list, but it is close to one (0.96875).

Therefore, to avoid combining "single 1" numbers to generate the required B value (at the expense of increased program length), why not fudge slightly on our break frequency? Surely it will not matter if it breaks slightly to one side of exactly 50 Hz. In fact, let us work backward and start with the "easy" number 0.96875. The operation is:

$$0.96875 = e^{-F_c \cdot 96 \mu sec \cdot 2\pi}$$

or: $$\ln 0.96875 = -F_c \cdot 96 \mu sec \cdot 2\pi$$

Solving for F_c, we obtain:

$$F_c = 52.6 \text{ Hz (close enough)}$$

Therefore, for a break frequency of 52.6 Hz, G and B are:

$$B = 0.96875$$
$$G = 0.03125$$

Substituting these values into our FORTRAN equation gives:

$$Y1 = Y0$$
$$Y0 = (0.03152*X) + (0.96875*Y1)$$

To ready the equation for assembly language, we convert the G and B constants into their "powers of 2" forms (or 1 minus powers of 2 forms):

$$Y1 = Y0$$
$$Y0 = 2**-5*X + (1 - 2**-5)*Y1$$

or, using conventional notation:

$$Y1 = Y0$$
$$Y0 = 2^{-5}X + Y1 - 2^{-5}Y1$$

The final equation involves only addition, subtraction, and shifting—all operations easily performed by the 2920. The high-level FORTRAN program is then conveted into an assembly-language program using instructions from the 2920 instruction set:

OP	DEST	SOURCE	SHIFT	COMMENTS
LDA	Y1	Y0	R00	$Y1 = Y0$
SUB	Y0	Y1	R05	$Y0 = Y1 - 2^{-5}Y1$
ADD	Y0	X	R05	$Y0 = 2^{-5}X + (Y1 - 2^{-5}Y1)$

When these three assembly-language instructions are processed at the rate of 10.4 KHz ($\frac{1}{96}$ μsec), the analog output will simulate a low-pass, single-pole filter with a break frequency of approximately 50 Hz.

When analog instructions are added to carry out the input, output, A/D, and D/A operations, the program will be complete and ready for assembly. A final version, using abbreviated analog instructions, is:

```
IN 0     Select input 0 and charge up input sample-and-hold capacitor
CVTS ⎤ Convert analog voltage to 9-bit digital word using
CVTO ⎦ successive-approximation sequence
LDA, X,DAR,R00  } Send DAR contents to memory location X
LDA Y1,Y0,R00 ⎤
SUB Y0,Y1,R05 ⎬ Generation of new value
ADD Y0,X,R05  ⎦
LDA DAR, Y0,R00   Begin D/A process
OUT0 ⎤ Output analog voltage to output line 0
EOP  ⎦ End of program—jump back to beginning
```

Remember, for the preceding program, we made the *assumption* that the program would cycle in 96 μsec. Should less time be required, our G and B values would have to be modified. (All trade-offs between cycle time, G and B are handled automatically by the 2920 machine assembler.)

Besides filters, the 2920 can implement virtually any analog system in the dc to 10-kHz range. Additional applications are shown in Figure 27.7.

INTELLIGENT-MACHINE UPDATE: A FINAL WORD

Bionics, the science of designing systems modeled after living organisms, has borne fruit many times since its inception 20 years ago. To increase the speed of oceangoing vessels, we study the flexible skin of the porpoise; to develop antifreeze solutions of great durability, we study the blood of the penguin; and to increase our knowledge of navigation, we study the amazing feats of migratory birds. To build better computers, then, perhaps we should study the human brain—the most complex entity in the known universe.

Consider the ordinary honey bee. Endowed with only 900 neurons, it can communicate with other members of the hive; navigate by polarized sunlight; simulate the guidance and flight-control system required for powered flight; sense the smallest changes in its light, sound, smell, magnetic, and electric environment; produce and care for its young; build structures of great geometric design and strength; and

meanwhile maintain its required bodily functions. Can *we* do as well with 900 logic gates and other components? Indeed, can we do as well with 900 LSI circuits? From honey bee to human being, what secrets of computing power lie hidden within the animals that share our planet?

Considering the accomplishments of the honey bee, with a brain no bigger than a grain of salt, is it any wonder that the power of the human brain—with its 10 billion neurons—far surpasses that of the computer? Yet, what is significant is not that the human brain far outclasses the computer of today, but that the computer is evolving much faster. Nearly every advance in computer technology introduced in this book—from RAM and ROM to cybernetics and distributed processing—has its counterpart in the human brain. Already the circuits from which we fashion our computers are as small as those of the brain—and they are much faster. But the computer is constrained to the step-by-step processing of logical and mathematical processes. The brain, on the other hand, is global in nature (holographic), processing and synthesizing information in a complex, interdependent network of both an analog and digital nature. However, this is also the direction we are now taking with the distributed parallel-processing capability of the 8086 and the analog nature of the 2920. It appears that once again the computer is traveling in the same evolutionary direction as the human mind. Would it not be far faster and more efficient to unlock the secrets of the human brain and apply the knowledge to the evolving computer?

This is a subject for the twenty-first century.

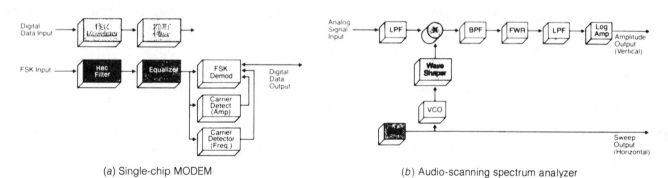

(a) Single-chip MODEM

Reproduced by permission of Intel Corp.

(b) Audio-scanning spectrum analyzer

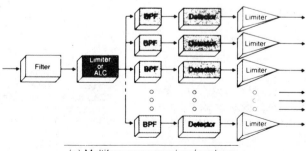

(c) Multifrequency receiver/analyzer

Figure 27.7   Additional applications of the 2920.

QUESTIONS AND PROBLEMS

1. What three basic blocks make up the 2920 system?
2. Name several advantages of processing analog signals in digital.
3. What are the functions of the *antialiasing* and *reconstruction* filters?
4. What is a two-port RAM?
5. How does the 2920 multiply and divide?
6. What is the mathematical technique for generating a *pseudo-moving average*?
7. Why is it easy to multiply by 0.0625 on a 2920 processor?
8. Does the 2920 work in the *frequency domain* or the *time domain*?
9. How is the port B location similar to the 8080/8085 accumulator?
10. How are numbers not on the "single 1" list generated?
11. What determines the sampling rate of the 2920?
12. Why are analog and digital processes performed simultaneously on the 2920?

Glossary

access time the time span from the start of the read cycle to when valid data are available at the output pins.

accumulator the primary data register within the CPU—holds the initial and final results of a number of processor operations.

active low the initiation of an action when a signal—normally high—goes low.

address a block of data specifying a memory or port location.

addressing mode a particular way of specifying the operand of an instruction.

algorithm a precisely defined set of steps for solving a problem.

aliasing noise distortion due to the sampling process.

analog a continuum of levels representing magnitudes.

archival storage long-term storage in a permanent storage medium.

arithmetic/logic unit (ALU) the portion of computer hardware that performs arithmetic and logic operations.

artificial intelligence (AI) the study of computer techniques to simulate the intellectual capabilities of humans.

ASCII (American Standard Code for Information Interchange) a 7-bit code widely used for information interchange.

assembler a computer program used to translate symbolic language into machine language.

assembly-language program a program written using mnemonics and listed in four fields: code, operand, label, and comment.

asynchronous the events or operations are not controlled by a common master clock.

backup memory high-capacity, high-reliability, but slow memory system; backup memory is usually sequential in nature.

bank switching the use of output-port lines as additional high-level address lines, thereby creating memory banks.

baud the number of code elements transmitted per second (often equal to 1 bit/second).

benchmark program a routine used to evaluate the relative performance of computers.

bidirectional information flow taking place in both directions.

binary coded decimal (BCD) a number system in which each nibble represents a coded decimal character.

BISYNC (Binary Synchronous Communication) an IBM communication protocol for half-duplex operations.

bit manipulation the software setting or resetting of individual selected bits within the total word.

bit slice the building block (usually 4 bits) used to construct custom-designed microcomputers of any word size.

branch a departure from normal sequential program flow.

breakpoint a point in the program at which processing is interrupted in order to allow analysis of the system state.

buffer a device that offers a high-input impedance and low-output impedance to isolate a circuit while providing driving power; also a register used to hold temporary information.

bus a set of conducting elements forming a common connection between many circuit elements.

bus contention two circuits transmitting onto a common bus at the same time.

Butterworth filter a filter having a flat response up to the breakpoint.

byte 8 bits.

bytewide memory memory units in which each addressable location stores a byte.

CAD/CAM (computer-aided design/computer-aided manufacturing) using a computer to aid in the design and manufacturing of mechanical and electronic systems.

central processing unit (CPU) an LSI circuit (such as a general-purpose microprocessor) that combines the ALU, control unit, and internal data registers.

character generator a preprogrammed ROM used to generate symbols in a dot-matrix video display.

charge-coupled device (CCD) a serial array of MOS gates, forming a high-speed, serial-shift register.

clock cycle an internal cycle used by Intel microprocessors for synchronizing all events.

closed loop a "circular" system whereby the output is continuously fed back to the input.

COBOL (Common Business-Oriented Language) a high-level language specifically designed for the data-processing industry.

codec (coder/decoder) used in PCM systems to perform digital-to-analog and analog-to-digital conversions.

communication protocol   a set of rules and conventions governing information flow.

compiler   a programming system that accepts high-level programs and converts them to machine-language programs.

controller   a unit that operates automatically to regulate a system.

coprocessor   a processor that must operate in conjunction with an independent processor, relying on the independent processor for instruction fetching.

current loop   the transmission of serial data by changes in current along a closed path linking receiver and transmitter.

cybernetics   the science of communication and control.

cycle stealing   a DMA process where information is transferred at least once each instruction cycle when the data bus is unused.

cyclic-redundancy-check character (CRCC)   the remainder term when a data polynomial is divided by a generator polynomial; the CRCC is transmitted along with the data and used for error checking.

DAC   digital-to-analog converter.

daisy chain   an interrupt technique whereby the interrupt acknowledge is hardware-propagated through the peripherals, looking for the highest-priority interrupt request.

damping   the reduction of oscillatory tendencies.

data acquisition   a system used to collect data, usually involving multiplexing of multiple analog inputs and conversion to digital.

data transfer   a process that moves information between CPU and external device by use of a where/when operation.

debouncing   the process of producing a single output for each activation of a mechanical switch.

decision   choosing one path among many.

decoded addressing   an address technique that makes use of decoders to allow all possible combinations of the high-level lines.

deposit   to place the program into memory.

development system   a computer system designed to aid the development of microprocessor-based systems; it allows the user to write and edit programs, test them in real time, and make modifications to the system.

direct memory access   a process whereby the processor is halted; its address, data, and control lines are floated; and external circuitry transfers data between peripherals at high speed.

disk controller   the interface electronics between floppy or Winchester disk and CPU.

disk operating system (DOS)   an operating system whose system files are usually stored on floppy or Winchester disk.

diskette   the Mylar-based recording system of a floppy-disk system.

displacement   the amount by which the data location differs from a reference location.

distributed processing   the use of intelligent peripherals to scatter the processing load among satellite stations.

duplex   two-way communication (full duplex is simultaneous two-way communication).

dynamic memory   a memory that stores information capacitively and requires regular recharging of capacitor states.

ECC   error checking and correcting.

ECL   emitter-coupled logic.

editor   an interactive program that allows users to write programs and make changes and corrections.

EE-PROM   a PROM erasable by electrical methods.

emulation   the ability of one system to imitate the actions of another, while allowing analysis of the system.

EPROM   a PROM erasable by ultraviolet light.

ergonomics   the science that seeks to adapt work or working conditions to suit the worker.

examine   determine the contents of a memory or register location.

execution   the part in the processing of an instruction in which a command is carried out.

feedback   the return of part of the output of a system back to the input.

FILO (first in/last out)   the sequence of data flow to the stack; the last data byte in is the first out.

firmware   a cross between hardware and software—programs stored in ROM.

flag   flip-flop used to signal the occurrence of a specific condition.

floating point   a number convention appropriate for large numbers in which the data bits are separated into fraction and exponent.

flowchart   a graphical representation of a program, using block symbols to represent functions.

FORTRAN (formula translation)   an early high-level language used for scientific applications.

foldback memory   when a page of memory is addressed by more than one high-level address; linear addressing results in foldback memory.

formatting   a predetermined arrangement of words used to allow for synchronization, identification, and error checking.

frequency-shift-keyed (FSK) modulation   a form of frequency modulation in which a logic 0 is represented by one frequency and a logic 1 by another.

gate array (master slice)   a semicustom MSI to VLSI array of basic logic elements, offering a wide variety of circuit elements and interconnections.

GCR (group-coded recording)   a coding scheme that eliminates the timing pulse by coding each nibble into a 5-bit word prior to floppy or Winchester storage.

generator polynomial   a specifically chosen polynomial designed to generate the CRCC when divided into the data polynomial.

GPIB (general-purpose interface bus)   a parallel communication standard used to interconnect instruments and devices.

graphics   the technique of placing nontextual images on a CRT screen by computer processing action.

handshaking   a request/acknowledge set of back-and-forth signals used to coordinate data flow in asynchronous systems.

hard-sectored   the correct sector of a floppy diskette is located by the use of 32 sector holes arranged about the diskette.

hardware the physical components of a computer system.

high-level address lines those lines that interface the memory module's CE inputs and select the desired module from the others in the system.

high-level flowchart a flowchart in which each block stands for a large number of instructions.

high-level language a computer language that generally uses English-like statements for each instruction; each instruction corresponds to a number of machine-code instructions.

hysteresis the difference between the turn-on threshold and the turn-off threshold, after turn-on.

ICE in-circuit emulation.

independent processor a processor that executes its program independently of other processors.

index register a register holding a memory address and used by certain instructions as a reference to locate a specific memory location.

input/output (I/O) hardware devices allowing data to flow between the computer system and the outside world.

instruction a computer command that can be decoded and used to direct a process.

instruction cycle the time required to fetch and execute one instruction.

instruction fetch to bring the operation code and operand into the CPU.

instruction lookahead (prefetching) future instructions fetched during execution of present instructions.

instruction register the register that holds the fetched op code.

instruction set the list of instruction types recognized by a given microprocessor.

integration a concept of calculus similar to multiplication, but used when the multiplicand is a variable rather than a constant.

interrupt an unscheduled request for special CPU action.

interrupt I/O the input or output of data under interrupt control.

interrupt-service routine the program used to service the needs of the interrupting device.

interrupt vector an interrupt whereby the processor automatically calls a specific memory location.

invisible subtraction a subtraction in which the answer is inhibited from going to the accumulator (the compare instruction subtracts invisibly).

ISO International Standards Organization.

isolated I/O a computer system in which memory is distinguished from I/O ports.

Kansas City standard the frequency-shift-keyed (FSK) encoding technique for cassette recorders.

LAN local area network.

label used in programming as a representation of an address.

large-scale integration (LSI) more than 1,000 transistor equivalents integrated on a single chip of silicon.

linear addressing an addressing technique that assigns each memory module to its own unique high-level address line.

logic analyzer a device used to test and troubleshoot microprocessor-based equipment; the acquisition of data is controlled by a number of user-selectable parameters, and the display of data can be in state, timing, or other modes.

logic array a semicustom array of logic elements fabricated on a single MSI base and usually exhibiting a sum-of-products format.

loop a repeating sequence of instructions.

low-level address lines those lines that feed the memory's address pins and are used to select a particular memory location within the selected memory module.

low-level flowchart a flowchart in which each flowchart block represents a very small number of instructions.

lunar landing vehicle (LLV) a spacecraft module designed to land on the moon.

machine cycle an internal cycle used by Intel microprocessors for data transfer and any required internal CPU operations.

machine language the lowest-level computer language, written in binary or hexadecimal.

magnetic bubbles small areas of reverse magnetism that can store logic data and can be propagated through the magnetic medium by external magnetic fields.

masking a form of bit manipulation in which the bits—when properly set or reset—inhibit an action.

memory-address register (MAR) the register used to hold the address of a data word (in the 8080/8085, the MAR is known as the WZ register pair).

memory cell that unit of memory holding a single bit of data.

memory hierarchy ranked categories of memory, from primary to secondary to backup.

memory map a listing of all memory programs showing address assignments.

memory-mapped I/O a computer system in which I/O ports are treated as memory locations.

memory segmentation the subdividing of the total memory space into smaller areas.

microcomputer a small-scale computer system, consisting of CPU, memory, and I/O, often dedicated to a specific purpose and usually using LSI blocks.

microprocessor an LSI component usually integrating the CPU and ALU on a single chip; single-chip microprocessors place all components on one chip.

microprogram the sequential list of subinstructions (microcode) stored within the CPU and used to carry out each main-program command.

minicomputer a small, general-purpose computer, between the microcomputer and mainframe (large-scale) computer in scale; minicomputers usually employ a high-level language.

mnemonic   a shorthand English-like symbol for an instruction type.

mode control   selecting the overall configuration of a system (often by writing a mode-control word to an internal register).

modem (modulator/demodulator)   an interface device that performs the modulation and demodulation functions in a communication link.

monitor program   a program in ROM used to perform a variety of functions, such as deposit, examine, and error checking; the monitor program gives the computer its initial "intelligence" upon startup.

multilevel interrupt structure   more than one vectored interrupt input.

multiple precision   numbers requiring two or more bytes for storage.

multiprocessing   use of more than one independent processor in order to process programs concurrently.

multitasking   allowing more than one user or program to share a computer system, often by time-sharing.

negative feedback   the returned output signal opposes the input (the returned signal is out of phase with the input).

nesting   a loop or subroutine placed within another loop or subroutine.

network   an interconnecting system of terminals and computer components.

nibble   4 bits (2 nibbles make a byte).

nonmaskable interrupt   an interrupt input that cannot be disabled.

object program   a program written in binary or hexadecimal machine language.

operand   the quantity on which the operation is performed.

operating system   a group of programs that manages the resources of the system and frees the user to concentrate on other tasks.

operation code (op code)   the part of the instruction that initiates specific actions when decoded.

page   a 256 × 8 block of memory.

PAL   programmable array logic.

parallel   information processed and moved about in multibit units.

parallel processing   the processing of more than one program at a time by more than one processor.

parameter   a variable required by a given subroutine; also a constant changed by the programmer to control a program.

phoneme   an elemental unit of speech.

PLA   programmable logic array.

polling   the periodic sampling of a control line (for example, to determine if a peripheral requires servicing); polling is used in programmed I/O operations.

POP   the process of removing register or flag data from the stack.

port   the interface between the computer system and the outside world.

positive feedback   the returned output signal reinforces the input (the returned signal is in phase with the input).

primary memory   memory fast enough to keep up with the speed of the microprocessor; primary memory achieves its speed through the property of random access.

priority   ranking the interrupt input lines according to the highest need for interrupt processing.

program counter   a sequencing 16-bit register, holding the consecutive addresses of the stored program.

programmable peripheral chip   a multifunctional IC whose characteristics are programmed under software control.

programmable read-only memory (PROM)   a user-programmable ROM.

programmed I/O   the input or output of data under software control.

programming   placing a sequential list of instructions into the computer's memory.

pseudo-instruction   an instruction that gives information for proper program development, but is not itself executed.

pulse-code modulation (PCM)   a modulation scheme in which the analog signal is sampled periodically and each level converted to digital and transmitted.

push   the process of adding register or flag data to the stack.

quasi-static RAM   a dynamic RAM with all refreshing circuitry on chip.

random access   each memory location can be accessed in the same amount of time.

read   to transfer information *to* the CPU.

reenterable   describing a routine that can be shared by several other routines.

relative addressing   an addressing mode in which the location of the data is known relative to the location of the instruction.

relocatable program   a program that may be stored and executed from many areas in memory.

robotics   adding artificial intelligence to computer-controlled machines in order to simulate human activities.

ROM   read only memory, usually nonvolatile DIP.

sampled-data system   making measurements of a function at periodic intervals.

scratchpad memory   an internal, easily accessible array of registers for holding intermediate data and addresses.

secondary memory   medium-capacity, medium-speed memory, usually quasi-sequential in structure.

sequential (serial) access   single-file storage and transmission of data.

signature analysis the conversion of serial data streams to hexadecimal characters (signatures); comparing the actual signature to the expected signature provides a means of troubleshooting the system.

signed numbers a convention that uses the most significant bit (sign bit) to specify positive or negative numbers (1 for negative, 0 for positive); the remaining bits are used to determine the magnitude.

sign magnitude a number convention using the sign bit for a positive or negative number, but always storing the magnitude in true (not 2's complement) form.

simplex transmission one-way communication.

single-chip microcontroller a single-chip microprocessor, including I/O and RAM, and specifically configured for control applications.

single-step to process a program by hand, one step at a time.

soft-sectored the correct sector of a floppy disk is identified by software reading of timing and address information included with every sector.

software computer programs.

source listing the original program written in assembly or high-level language.

stack a block of successive memory locations used to store return addresses and register and flag information during subroutine processing.

stack pointer a register used to point to the most recent data stored in the stack or the next piece of data to be removed.

state equal to one clock cycle, the smallest unit of time in the 8080/8085 system.

state (data domain) display display of data in binary, octal, or hex format.

static memory a memory device requiring only dc voltages to power its operation.

status register a register used to hold information relative to the present state of the system.

stepper motor a motor in which rotation takes place in discrete steps under control of pulses.

stored program the concept of storing the instructions along with the data.

streaming data flow continuous data flow onto a tape system, eliminating the starts and stops.

strobed-output mode an output technique using double buffering to speed data flow.

structured programming the technique of writing programs in blocks, with each block independent and jumps not allowed back and forth between blocks.

subroutine a routine that is part of another routine, but placed at a different memory location.

super-large-scale integration (SLSI) approximately 100,000 transistor equivalents integrated on a single chip of silicon.

synchronous the events or operations take place in step with a common master clock.

throughput the total amount of information processed in a specified time.

time multiplexing the time-sharing of a circuit or system.

timing display display of data in waveform format.

top-down programming program development by moving from the general to the specific—from the high-level conceptual to the low-level instructional stage.

transducer a device that converts analog states (temperature, pressure, etc.) to electrical signals.

tristate circuit a circuit especially designed to transmit information onto a bus; it can transmit the standard logic 1 or 0 states, or it can be floated to allow another circuit to transmit onto the bus.

tunneling quantum-mechanical penetration of an otherwise unsurmountable energy barrier.

two's (2's) complement a number format used in signed-number operations, and equal to the 1's complement + 1 (1's complement is equal to an inversion of all bits).

UART (universal asynchronous receiver/transmitter) a device used to interface a parallel CPU or data terminal to a serial asynchronous communication network.

USART (universal synchronous/asynchronous receiver/transmitter) a device used to interface a parallel CPU or data terminal to a serial synchronous or asynchronous communication network.

very-large-scale integration (VLSI) more than 50,000 transistor equivalents integrated on a single chip of silicon.

virtual memory the automatic page swapping of memory between primary and secondary memories.

volatile memory that loses data when power is removed (nonvolatile memory retains data when power is removed).

Winchester disk a medium-to-high capacity, high-reliability, hard-disk system that features a sealed-disk environment to allow the read/write head to "fly" very close to the surface of the recording medium.

word a 16-bit piece of data, as distinguished from the 8-bit byte.

write to transfer information *from* the CPU.

appendix I

8080/8085 Instruction Set

4.6 INSTRUCTION SET ENCYCLOPEDIA

In the ensuing dozen pages, the complete 8085A instruction set is described, grouped in order under five different functional headings, as follows:

1. **Data Transfer Group** — Moves data between registers or between memory locations and registers. Includes moves, loads, stores, and exchanges. (See below.)
2. **Arithmetic Group** — Adds, subtracts, increments, or decrements data in registers or memory. (See page 4-13.)
3. **Logic Group** — ANDs, ORs, XORs, compares, rotates, or complements data in registers or between memory and a register. (See page 4-16.)
4. **Branch Group** — Initiates conditional or unconditional jumps, calls, returns, and restarts. (See page 4-20.)
5. **Stack, I/O, and Machine Control Group** — Includes instructions for maintaining the stack, reading from input ports, writing to output ports, setting and reading interrupt masks, and setting and clearing flags. (See page 4-22.)

The formats described in the encyclopedia reflect the assembly language processed by Intel-supplied assembler, used with the Intellec® development systems.

4.6.1 Data Transfer Group

This group of instructions transfers data to and from registers and memory. **Condition flags are not affected by any instruction in this group.**

MOV r1, r2 (Move Register)
(r1) ← (r2)
The content of register r2 is moved to register r1.

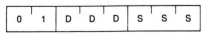

Cycles: 1
States: 4
Addressing: register
Flags: none

MOV r, M (Move from memory)
(r) ← ((H) (L))
The content of the memory location, whose address is in registers H and L, is moved to register r.

| 0 | 1 | D | D | D | 1 | 1 | 0 |

Cycles: 2
States: 7
Addressing: reg. indirect
Flags: none

MOV M, r (Move to memory)
((H) (L)) ← (r)
The content of register r is moved to the memory location whose address is in registers H and L.

| 0 | 1 | 1 | 0 | S | S | S |

Cycles: 2
States: 7
Addressing: reg. indirect
Flags: none

MVI r, data (Move Immediate)
(r) ← (byte 2)
The content of byte 2 of the instruction is moved to register r.

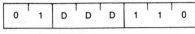

Cycles: 2
States: 7
Addressing: immediate
Flags: none

MVI M, data (Move to memory immediate)
((H) (L)) ← (byte 2)
The content of byte 2 of the instruction is moved to the memory location whose address is in registers H and L.

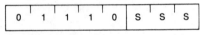

Cycles: 3
States: 10
Addressing: immed./reg. indirect
Flags: none

LXI rp, data 16 (Load register pair immediate)
(rh) ← (byte 3),
(rl) ← (byte 2)
Byte 3 of the instruction is moved into the high-order register (rh) of the register pair rp. Byte 2 of the instruction is moved into the low-order register (rl) of the register pair rp.

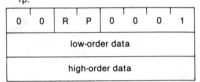

Cycles: 3
States: 10
Addressing: immediate
Flags: none

LDA addr (Load Accumulator direct)
(A) ← ((byte 3)(byte 2))
The content of the memory location, whose address is specified in byte 2 and byte 3 of the instruction, is moved to register A.

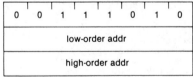

Cycles: 4
States: 13
Addressing: direct
Flags: none

STA addr (Store Accumulator direct)
((byte 3)(byte 2)) ← (A)
The content of the accumulator is moved to the memory location whose address is specified in byte 2 and byte 3 of the instruction.

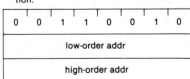

Cycles: 4
States: 13
Addressing: direct
Flags: none

LHLD addr   (Load H and L direct)
(L)←((byte 3)(byte 2))
(H)←((byte 3)(byte 2)+1)
The content of the memory location, whose address is specified in byte 2 and byte 3 of the instruction, is moved to register L. The content of the memory location at the succeeding address is moved to register H.

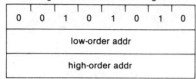

0	0	1	0	1	0	1	0
low-order addr								
high-order addr								

Cycles: 5
States: 16
Addressing: direct
Flags: none

SHLD addr   (Store H and L direct)
((byte 3)(byte 2))←(L)
((byte 3)(byte 2)+1)←(H)
The content of register L is moved to the memory location whose address is specified in byte 2 and byte 3. The content of register H is moved to the succeeding memory location.

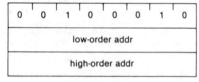

0	0	1	0	0	0	1	0
low-order addr								
high-order addr								

Cycles: 5
States: 16
Addressing: direct
Flags: none

LDAX rp   (Load accumulator indirect)
(A)←((rp))
The content of the memory location, whose address is in the register pair rp, is moved to register A. Note: only register pairs rp=B (registers B and C) or rp=D (registers D and E) may be specified.

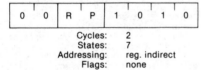

0	0	R	P	1	0	1	0

Cycles: 2
States: 7
Addressing: reg. indirect
Flags: none

STAX rp   (Store accumulator indirect)
((rp))←(A)
The content of register A is moved to the memory location whose address is in the register pair rp. Note: only register pairs rp=B (registers B and C) or rp=D (registers D and E) may be specified.

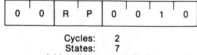

0	0	R	P	0	0	1	0

Cycles: 2
States: 7
Addressing: reg. indirect
Flags: none

XCHG   (Exchange H and L with D and E)
(H) ↔ (D)
(L) ↔ (E)
The contents of registers H and L are exchanged with the contents of registers D and E.

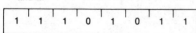

1	1	1	0	1	0	1	1

Cycles: 1
States: 4
Addressing: register
Flags: none

4.6.2 Arithmetic Group

This group of instructions performs arithmetic operations on data in registers and memory.

Unless indicated otherwise, all instructions in this group affect the Zero, Sign, Parity, Carry, and Auxiliary Carry flags according to the standard rules.

All subtraction operations are performed via two's complement arithmetic and set the carry flag to one to indicate a borrow and clear it to indicate no borrow.

ADD r   (Add Register)
(A) ← (A) + (r)
The content of register r is added to the content of the accumulator. The result is placed in the accumulator.

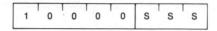

1	0	0	0	0	S	S	S

Cycles: 1
States: 4
Addressing: register
Flags: Z,S,P,CY,AC

ADD M   (Add memory)
(A) ← (A) + ((H) (L))
The content of the memory location whose address is contained in the H and L registers is added to the content of the accumulator. The result is placed in the accumulator.

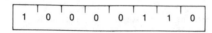

1	0	0	0	0	1	1	0

Cycles: 2
States: 7
Addressing: reg. indirect
Flags: Z,S,P,CY,AC

ADI data   (Add immediate)
(A) ← (A) + (byte 2)
The content of the second byte of the instruction is added to the content of the accumulator. The result is placed in the accumulator.

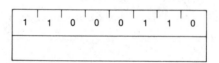

1	1	0	0	0	1	1	0
data								

Cycles: 2
States: 7
Addressing: immediate
Flags: Z,S,P,CY,AC

ADC r   (Add Register with carry)
(A) ← (A) + (r) + (CY)
The content of register r and the content of the carry bit are added to the content of the accumulator. The result is placed in the accumulator.

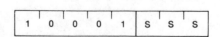

1	0	0	0	1	S	S	S

Cycles: 1
States: 4
Addressing: register
Flags: Z,S,P,CY,AC

ADC M   (Add memory with carry)
(A) ← (A) + ((H) (L)) + (CY)
The content of the memory location whose address is contained in the H and L registers and the content of the CY flag are added to the accumulator. The result is placed in the accumulator.

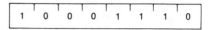

1	0	0	0	1	1	1	0

Cycles: 2
States: 7
Addressing: reg. indirect
Flags: Z,S,P,CY,AC

ACI data   (Add immediate with carry)
(A) ← (A) + (byte 2) + (CY)
The content of the second byte of the instruction and the content of the CY flag are added to the contents of the accumulator. The result is placed in the accumulator.

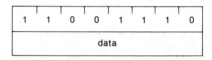

1	1	0	0	1	1	1	0
data								

Cycles: 2
States: 7
Addressing: immediate
Flags: Z,S,P,CY,AC

SUB r   (Subtract Register)
(A) ← (A) − (r)
The content of register r is subtracted from the content of the accumulator. The result is placed in the accumulator.

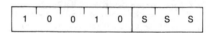

1	0	0	1	0	S	S	S

Cycles: 1
States: 4
Addressing: register
Flags: Z,S,P,CY,AC

SUB M   (Subtract memory)
(A) ← (A) − ((H) (L))
The content of the memory location whose address is contained in the H and L registers is subtracted from the content of the accumulator. The result is placed in the accumulator.

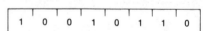

1	0	0	1	0	1	1	0

Cycles: 2
States: 7
Addressing: reg. indirect
Flags: Z,S,P,CY,AC

SUI data   (Subtract immediate)
(A) ← (A) − (byte 2)
The content of the second byte of the instruction is subtracted from the content of the accumulator. The result is placed in the accumulator.

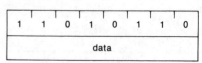

1	1	0	1	0	1	1	0
data								

Cycles: 2
States: 7
Addressing: immediate
Flags: Z,S,P,CY,AC

SBB r (Subtract Register with borrow)

(A) ← (A) − (r) − (CY)

The content of register r and the content of the CY flag are both subtracted from the accumulator. The result is placed in the accumulator.

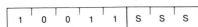

1	0	0	1	1	S	S	S

Cycles:	1
States:	4
Addressing:	register
Flags:	Z,S,P,CY,AC

SBB M (Subtract memory with borrow)

(A) ← (A) − ((H) (L)) − (CY)

The content of the memory location whose address is contained in the H and L registers and the content of the CY flag are both subtracted from the accumulator. The result is placed in the accumulator.

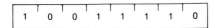

1	0	0	1	1	1	1	0

Cycles:	2
States:	7
Addressing:	reg. indirect
Flags:	Z,S,P,CY,AC

SBI data (Subtract immediate with borrow)

(A) ← (A) − (byte 2) − (CY)

The contents of the second byte of the instruction and the contents of the CY flag are both subtracted from the accumulator. The result is placed in the accumulator.

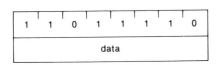

1	1	0	1	1	1	1	0

data

Cycles:	2
States:	7
Addressing:	immediate
Flags:	Z,S,P,CY,AC

INR r (Increment Register)

(r) ← (r) + 1

The content of register r is incremented by one. Note: All condition flags **except CY** are affected.

0	0	D	D	D	1	0	0

Cycles:	1
States:	4
Addressing:	register
Flags:	Z,S,P,AC

INR M (Increment memory)

((H) (L)) ← ((H) (L)) + 1

The content of the memory location whose address is contained in the H and L registers is incremented by one. Note: All condition flags **except CY** are affected.

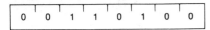

0	0	1	1	0	1	0	0

Cycles:	3
States:	10
Addressing:	reg. indirect
Flags:	Z,S,P,AC

DCR r (Decrement Register)

(r) ← (r) − 1

The content of register r is decremented by one. Note: All condition flags **except CY** are affected.

0	0	D	D	D	1	0	1

Cycles:	1
States:	4
Addressing:	register
Flags:	Z,S,P,AC

DCR M (Decrement memory)

((H) (L)) ← ((H) (L)) − 1

The content of the memory location whose address is contained in the H and L registers is decremented by one. Note: All condition flags **except CY** are affected.

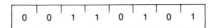

0	0	1	1	0	1	0	1

Cycles:	3
States:	10
Addressing:	reg. indirect
Flags:	Z,S,P,AC

INX rp (Increment register pair)

(rh) (rl) ← (rh) (rl) + 1

The content of the register pair rp is incremented by one. Note: **No condition flags are affected.**

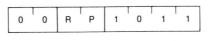

0	0	R	P	1	0	1	1

Cycles:	1
States:	6
Addressing:	register
Flags:	none

DCX rp (Decrement register pair)

(rh) (rl) ← (rh) (rl) − 1

The content of the register pair rp is decremented by one. Note: **No condition flags are affected.**

0	0	R	P	1	0	1	1

Cycles:	1
States:	6
Addressing:	register
Flags:	none

DAD rp (Add register pair to H and L)

(H) (L) ← (H) (L) + (rh) (rl)

The content of the register pair rp is added to the content of the register pair H and L. The result is placed in the register pair H and L. Note: **Only the CY flag is affected.** It is set if there is a carry out of the double precision add; otherwise it is reset.

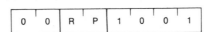

0	0	R	P	1	0	0	1

Cycles:	3
States:	10
Addressing:	register
Flags:	CY

DAA (Decimal Adjust Accumulator)

The eight-bit number in the accumulator is adjusted to form two four-bit Binary-Coded-Decimal digits by the following process:

1. If the value of the lease significant 4 bits of the accumulator is greater than 9 **or** if the AC flag is set, 6 is added to the accumulator.

2. If the value of the most significant 4 bits of the accumulator is now greater than 9, **or** if the CY flag is set, 6 is added to the most significant 4 bits of the accumulator.

NOTE: All flags are affected.

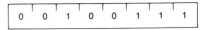

0	0	1	0	0	1	1	1

Cycles:	1
States:	4
Flags:	Z,S,P,CY,AC

4.6.3 Logic Group

This group of instructions performs logical (Boolean) operations on data in registers and memory and on condition flags.

Unless indicated otherwise, all instructions in this group affect the Zero, Sign, Parity, Auxiliary Carry, and Carry flags according to the standard rules.

ANA r (AND Register)

(A) ← (A) ∧ (r)

The content of register r is logically ANDed with the content of the accumulator. The result is placed in the accumulator. **The CY flag is cleared and AC is set.**

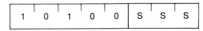

1	0	1	0	0	S	S	S

Cycles:	1
States:	4
Addressing:	register
Flags:	Z,S,P,CY,AC

ANA M (AND memory)

(A) ← (A) ∧ ((H) (L))

The contents of the memory location whose address is contained in the H and L registers is logically ANDed with the content of the accumulator. The result is placed in the accumulator. **The CY flag is cleared and AC is set.**

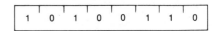

1	0	1	0	0	1	1	0

Cycles:	2
States:	7
Addressing:	reg. indirect
Flags:	Z,S,P,CY,AC

ANI data (AND immediate)

(A) ← (A) ∧ (byte 2)

The content of the second byte of the instruction is logically ANDed with the contents of the accumulator. The result is placed in the accumulator. **The CY flag is cleared and AC is set.**

1	1	1	0	0	1	1	0

data

Cycles:	2
States:	7
Addressing:	immediate
Flags:	Z,S,P,CY,AC

XRA r (Exclusive OR Register)

(A) ← (A) ⊻ (r)

The content of register r is exclusive-OR'd with the content of the accumulator. The result is placed in the accumulator. **The CY and AC flags are cleared.**

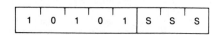

| 1 | 0 | 1 | 0 | 1 | S | S | S |

Cycles: 1
States: 4
Addressing: register
Flags: Z,S,P,CY,AC

XRA M (Exclusive OR Memory)

(A) ← (A) ⊻ ((H) (L))

The content of the memory location whose address is contained in the H and L registers is exclusive-OR'd with the content of the accumulator. The result is placed in the accumulator. **The CY and AC flags are cleared.**

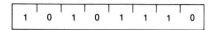

| 1 | 0 | 1 | 0 | 1 | 1 | 1 | 0 |

Cycles: 2
States: 7
Addressing: reg. indirect
Flags: Z,S,P,CY,AC

XRI data (Exclusive OR immediate)

(A) ← (A) ⊻ (byte 2)

The content of the second byte of the instruction is exclusive-OR'd with the content of the accumulator. The result is placed in the accumulator. **The CY and AC flags are cleared.**

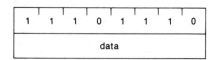

| 1 | 1 | 1 | 0 | 1 | 1 | 1 | 0 |
| data |

Cycles: 2
States: 7
Addressing: immediate
Flags: Z,S,P,CY,AC

ORA r (OR Register)

(A) ← (A) V (r)

The content of register r is inclusive-OR'd with the content of the accumulator. The result is placed in the accumulator. **The CY and AC flags are cleared.**

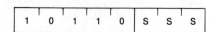

| 1 | 0 | 1 | 1 | 0 | S | S | S |

Cycles: 1
States: 4
Addressing: register
Flags: Z,S,P,CY,AC

ORA M (OR memory)

(A) ← (A) V ((H) (L))

The content of the memory location whose address is contained in the H and L registers is inclusive-OR'd with the content of the accumulator. The result is placed in the accumulator. **The CY and AC flags are cleared.**

| 1 | 0 | 1 | 1 | 0 | 1 | 1 | 0 |

Cycles: 2
States: 7
Addressing: reg. indirect
Flags: Z,S,P,CY,AC

ORI data (OR Immediate)

(A) ← (A) V (byte 2)

The content of the second byte of the instruction is inclusive-OR'd with the content of the accumulator. The result is placed in the accumulator. **The CY and AC flags are cleared..**

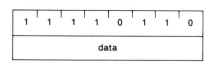

| 1 | 1 | 1 | 1 | 0 | 1 | 1 | 0 |
| data |

Cycles: 2
States: 7
Addressing: immediate
Flags: Z,S,P,CY,AC

CMP r (Compare Register)

(A) − (r)

The content of register r is subtracted from the accumulator. The accumulator remains unchanged. The condition flags are set as a result of the subtraction. **The Z flag is set to 1 if (A) = (r). The CY flag is set to 1 if (A) < (r).**

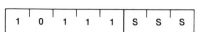

| 1 | 0 | 1 | 1 | 1 | S | S | S |

Cycles: 1
States: 4
Addressing: register
Flags: Z,S,P,CY,AC

CMP M (Compare memory)

(A) − ((H) (L))

The content of the memory location whose address is contained in the H and L registers is subtracted from the accumulator. The accumulator remains unchanged. The condition flags are set as a result of the subtraction. **The Z flag is set to 1 if (A) = ((H) (L)). The CY flag is set to 1 if (A) < ((H) (L)).**

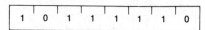

| 1 | 0 | 1 | 1 | 1 | 1 | 1 | 0 |

Cycles: 2
States: 7
Addressing: reg. indirect
Flags: Z,S,P,CY,AC

CPI data (Compare immediate)

(A) − (byte 2)

The content of the second byte of the instruction is subtracted from the accumulator. The condition flags are set by the result of the subtraction. **The Z flag is set to 1 if (A) = (byte 2). The CY flag is set to 1 if (A) < (byte 2).**

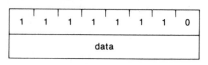

| 1 | 1 | 1 | 1 | 1 | 1 | 1 | 0 |
| data |

Cycles: 2
States: 7
Addressing: immediate
Flags: Z,S,P,CY,AC

RLC (Rotate left)

$(A_{n+1}) ← (A_n) ; (A_0) ← (A_7)$
$(CY) ← (A_7)$

The content of the accumulator is rotated left one position. The low order bit and the CY flag are both set to the value shifted out of the high order bit position. **Only the CY flag is affected.**

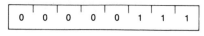

| 0 | 0 | 0 | 0 | 0 | 1 | 1 | 1 |

Cycles: 1
States: 4
Flags: CY

RRC (Rotate right)

$(A_n) ← (A_{n+1}); (A_7) ← (A_0)$
$(CY) ← (A_0)$

The content of the accumulator is rotated right one position. The high order bit and the CY flag are both set to the value shifted out of the low order bit position. **Only the CY flag is affected.**

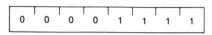

| 0 | 0 | 0 | 0 | 1 | 1 | 1 | 1 |

Cycles: 1
States: 4
Flags: CY

RAL (Rotate left through carry)

$(A_{n+1}) ← (A_n); (CY) ← (A_7)$
$(A_0) ← (CY)$

The content of the accumulator is rotated left one position through the CY flag. The low order bit is set equal to the CY flag and the CY flag is set to the value shifted out of the high order bit. **Only the CY flag is affected.**

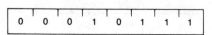

| 0 | 0 | 0 | 1 | 0 | 1 | 1 | 1 |

Cycles: 1
States: 4
Flags: CY

RAR   (Rotate right through carry)

$(A_n) \leftarrow (A_{n+1}); (CY) \leftarrow (A_0)$
$(A_7) \leftarrow (CY)$

The content of the accumulator is rotated right one position through the CY flag. The high order bit is set to the CY flag and the CY flag is set to the value shifted out of the low order bit. **Only the CY flag is affected.**

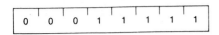

| 0 | 0 | 0 | 1 | 1 | 1 | 1 | 1 |

Cycles: 1
States: 4
Flags: CY

CMA   (Complement accumulator)

$(A) \leftarrow (\overline{A})$

The contents of the accumulator are complemented (zero bits become 1, one bits become 0). **No flags are affected.**

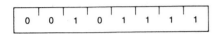

| 0 | 0 | 1 | 0 | 1 | 1 | 1 | 1 |

Cycles: 1
States: 4
Flags: none

CMC   (Complement carry)

$(CY) \leftarrow (\overline{CY})$

The CY flag is complemented. **No other flags are affected.**

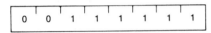

| 0 | 0 | 1 | 1 | 1 | 1 | 1 | 1 |

Cycles: 1
States: 4
Flags: CY

STC   (Set carry)

$(CY) \leftarrow 1$

The CY flag is set to 1. **No other flags are affected.**

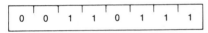

| 0 | 0 | 1 | 1 | 0 | 1 | 1 | 1 |

Cycles: 1
States: 4
Flags: CY

4.6.4 Branch Group

This group of instructions alter normal sequential program flow.

Condition flags are not affected by any instruction in this group.

The two types of branch instructions are unconditional and conditional. Unconditional transfers simply perform the specified operation on register PC (the program counter). Conditional transfers examine the status of one of the four processor flags to determine if the specified branch is to be executed. The conditions that may be specified are as follows:

CONDITION	CCC
NZ — not zero (Z = 0)	000
Z — zero (Z = 1)	001
NC — no carry (CY = 0)	010
C — carry (CY = 1)	011
PO — parity odd (P = 0)	100
PE — parity even (P = 1)	101
P — plus (S = 0)	110
M — minus (S = 1)	111

JMP addr   (Jump)

$(PC) \leftarrow (byte\ 3)(byte\ 2)$

Control is transferred to the instruction whose address is specified in byte 3 and byte 2 of the current instruction.

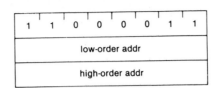

1	1	0	0	0	0	1	1
low-order addr							
high-order addr							

Cycles: 3
States: 10
Addressing: immediate
Flags: none

Jcondition addr (Conditional jump)

If (CCC),
$(PC) \leftarrow (byte\ 3)(byte\ 2)$

If the specified condition is true, control is transferred to the instruction whose address is specified in byte 3 and byte 2 of the current instruciton; otherwise, control continues sequentially.

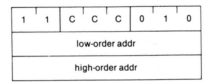

1	1	C	C	C	0	1	0
low-order addr							
high-order addr							

Cycles: 2/3
States: 7/10
Addressing: immediate
Flags: none

CALL addr   (Call)

$((SP) - 1) \leftarrow (PCH)$
$((SP) - 2) \leftarrow (PCL)$
$(SP) \leftarrow (SP) - 2$
$(PC) \leftarrow (byte\ 3)(byte\ 2)$

The high-order eight bits of the next instruction address are moved to the memory location whose address is one less than the content of register SP. The low-order eight bits of the next instruction address are moved to the memory location whose address is two less than the content of register SP. The content of register SP is decremented by 2. Control is transferred to the instruction whose address is specified in byte 3 and byte 2 of the current instruction.

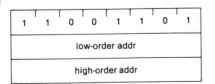

1	1	0	0	1	1	0	1
low-order addr							
high-order addr							

Cycles: 5
States: 18
Addressing: immediate/ reg. indirect
Flags: none

Ccondition addr (Condition call)

If (CCC),
$((SP) - 1) \leftarrow (PCH)$
$((SP) - 2) \leftarrow (PCL)$
$(SP) \leftarrow (SP) - 2$
$(PC) \leftarrow (byte\ 3)(byte\ 2)$

If the specified condition is true, the actions specified in the CALL instruction (see above) are performed; otherwise, control continues sequentially.

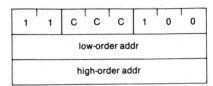

1	1	C	C	C	1	0	0
low-order addr							
high-order addr							

Cycles: 2/5
States: 9/18
Addressing: immediate/ reg. indirect
Flags: none

RET   (Return)

$(PCL) \leftarrow ((SP));$
$(PCH) \leftarrow ((SP) + 1);$
$(SP) \leftarrow (SP) + 2;$

The content of the memory location whose address is specified in register SP is moved to the low-order eight bits of register PC. The content of the memory location whose address is one more than the content of register SP is moved to the high-order eight bits of register PC. The content of register SP is incremented by 2.

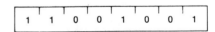

| 1 | 1 | 0 | 0 | 1 | 0 | 0 | 1 |

Cycles: 3
States: 10
Addressing: reg. indirect
Flags: none

Rcondition   (Conditional return)

If (CCC),
$(PCL) \leftarrow ((SP))$
$(PCH) \leftarrow ((SP) + 1)$
$(SP) \leftarrow (SP) + 2$

If the specified condition is true, the actions specified in the RET instruction (see above) are performed; otherwise, control continues sequentially.

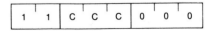

| 1 | 1 | C | C | C | 0 | 0 | 0 |

Cycles: 1/3
States: 6/12
Addressing: reg. indirect
Flags: none

RST n (Restart)

((SP) − 1) ← (PCH)
((SP) − 2) ← (PCL)
(SP) ← (SP) − 2
(PC) ← 8 * (NNN)

The high-order eight bits of the next instruction address are moved to the memory location whose address is one less than the content of register SP. The low-order eight bits of the next instruction address are moved to the memory location whose address is two less than the content of register SP. The content of register SP is decremented by two. Control is transferred to the instruction whose address is eight times the content of NNN.

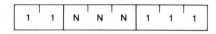

Cycles: 3
States: 12
Addressing: reg. indirect
Flags: none

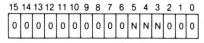

Program Counter After Restart

PCHL (Jump H and L indirect — move H and L to PC)

(PCH) ← (H)
(PCL) ← (L)

The content of register H is moved to the high-order eight bits of register PC. The content of register L is moved to the low-order eight bits of register PC.

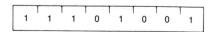

Cycles: 1
States: 6
Addressing: register
Flags: none

4.6.5 Stack, I/O, and Machine Control Group

This group of instructions performs I/O, manipulates the Stack, and alters internal control flags.

Unless otherwise specified, **condition flags are not affected by any instructions in this group.**

PUSH rp (Push)

((SP) − 1) ← (rh)
((SP) − 2) ← (rl)
(SP) ← (SP) − 2

The content of the high-order register of register pair rp is moved to the memory location whose address is one less than the content of register SP. The content of the low-order register of register pair rp is moved to the memory location whose address is two less than the content of register SP. The content of register SP is decremented by 2. **Note: Register pair rp = SP may not be specified.**

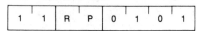

Cycles: 3
States: 12
Addressing: reg. indirect
Flags: none

PUSH PSW (Push processor status word)

((SP) − 1) ← (A)
((SP) − 2)$_0$ ← (CY) , ((SP) − 2)$_1$ ← X
((SP) − 2)$_2$ ← (P) , ((SP) − 2)$_3$ ← X
((SP) − 2)$_4$ ← (AC), ((SP) − 2)$_5$ ← X
((SP) − 2)$_6$ ← (Z) , ((SP) − 2)$_7$ ← (S)
(SP) ← (SP) − 2   X: Undefined.

The content of register A is moved to the memory location whose address is one less than register SP. The contents of the condition flags are assembled into a processor status word and the word is moved to the memory location whose address is two less than the content of register SP. The content of register SP is decremented by two.

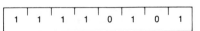

Cycles: 3
States: 12
Addressing: reg. indirect
Flags: none

FLAG WORD

D$_7$	D$_6$	D$_5$	D$_4$	D$_3$	D$_2$	D$_1$	D$_0$
S	Z	X	AC	X	P	X	CY

X: undefined

POP rp (POP)

(rl) ← ((SP))
(rh) ← ((SP) + 1)
(SP) ← (SP) + 2

The content of the memory location, whose address is specified by the content of register SP, is moved to the low-order register of register pair rp. The content of the memory location, whose address is one more than the content of register SP, is moved to the high-order register of register rp. The content of register SP is incremented by 2. **Note: Register pair rp = SP may not be specified.**

Cycles: 3
States: 10
Addressing: reg.indirect
Flags: none

POP PSW (Pop processor status word)

(CY) ← ((SP))$_0$
(P) ← ((SP))$_2$
(AC) ← ((SP))$_4$
(Z) ← ((SP))$_6$
(S) ← ((SP))$_7$
(A) ← ((SP) + 1)
(SP) ← (SP) + 2

The content of the memory location whose address is specified by the content of register SP is used to restore the condition flags. The content of the memory location whose address is one more than the content of register SP is moved to register A. The content of register SP is incremented by 2.

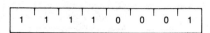

Cycles: 3
States: 10
Addressing: reg. indirect
Flags: Z,S,P,CY,AC

XTHL (Exchange stack top with H and L)

(L) ← ((SP))
(H) ← ((SP) + 1)

The content of the L register is exchanged with the content of the memory location whose address is specified by the content of register SP. The content of the H register is exchanged with the content of the memory location whose address is one more than the content of register SP.

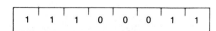

Cycles: 5
States: 16
Addressing: reg. indirect
Flags: none

SPHL (Move HL to SP)

(SP) ← (H) (L)

The contents of registers H and L (16 bits) are moved to register SP.

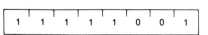

Cycles: 1
States: 6
Addressing: register
Flags: none

IN port (Input)

(A) ← (data)

The data placed on the eight bit bi-directional data bus by the specified port is moved to register A.

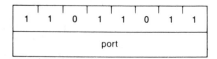

port

Cycles: 3
States: 10
Addressing: direct
Flags: none

OUT port (Output)

(data) ← (A)

The content of register A is placed on the eight bit bi-directional data bus for transmission to the specified port.

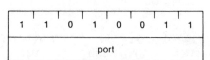

port

Cycles: 3
States: 10
Addressing: direct
Flags: none

EI (Enable interrupts)

The interrupt system is enabled **following the execution of the next instruction.**

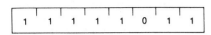

| 1 | 1 | 1 | 1 | 1 | 0 | 1 | 1 |

Cycles: 1
States: 4
Flags: none

NOTE: Interrupts are not recognized during the EI instruction. Placing an EI instruction on the bus in response to INTA during an INA cycle is prohibited.

DI (Disable interrupts)

The interrupt system is disabled **immediately following the execution of the DI instruction.**

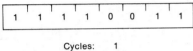

| 1 | 1 | 1 | 1 | 0 | 0 | 1 | 1 |

Cycles: 1
States: 4
Flags: none

NOTE: Interrupts are not recognized during the DI instruction. Placing a DI instruction on the bus in response to INTA during an INA cycle is prohibited.

HLT (Halt)

The processor is stopped. The registers and flags are unaffected. A second ALE is generated during the execution of HLT to strobe out the Halt cycle status information.

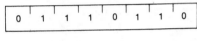

| 0 | 1 | 1 | 1 | 0 | 1 | 1 | 0 |

Cycles: 1+
States: 5
Flags: none

NOP (No op)

No operation is performed. The registers and flags are unaffected.

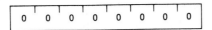

| 0 | 0 | 0 | 0 | 0 | 0 | 0 | 0 |

Cycles: 1
States: 4
Flags: none

RIM (Read Interrupt Masks)

The RIM instruction loads data into the accumulator relating to interrupts and the serial input. This data contains the following information:

- Current interrupt mask status for the RST 5.5, 6.5, and 7.5 hardware interrupts (1 = mask disabled)
- Current interrupt enable flag status (1 = interrupts enabled) except immediately following a TRAP interrupt. (See below.)
- Hardware interrupts pending (i.e., signal received but not yet serviced), on the RST 5.5, 6.5, and 7.5 lines.
- Serial input data.

Immediately following a TRAP interrupt, the RIM instruction must be executed as a part of the service routine if you need to retrieve current interrupt status later. Bit 3 of the accumulator is (in this special case only) loaded with the interrupt enable (IE) flag status that existed prior to the TRAP interrupt. Following an RST 5.5, 6.5, 7.5, or INTR interrupt, the interrupt flag flip-flop reflects the current interrupt enable status. Bit 6 of the accumulator (I7.5) is loaded with the status of the RST 7.5 flip-flop, which is always set (edge-triggered) by an input on the RST 7.5 input line, even when that interrupt has been previously masked. (See SIM Instruction.)

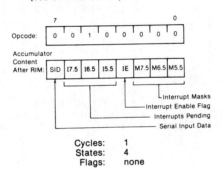

Cycles: 1
States: 4
Flags: none

SIM (Set Interrupt Masks)

The execution of the SIM instruction uses the contents of the accumulator (which must be previously loaded) to perform the following functions:

- Program the interrupt mask for the RST 5.5, 6.5, and 7.5 hardware interrupts.
- Reset the edge-triggered RST 7.5 input latch.
- Load the SOD output latch.

To program the interrupt masks, first set accumulator bit 3 to 1 and set to 1 any bits 0, 1, and 2, which disable interrupts RST 5.5, 6.5, and 7.5, respectively. Then do a SIM instruction. If accumulator bit 3 is 0 when the SIM instruction is executed, the interrupt mask register will not change. If accumulator bit 4 is 1 when the SIM instruction is executed, the RST 7.5 latch is then reset. RST 7.5 is distinguished by the fact that its latch is always set by a rising edge on the RST 7.5 input pin, even if the jump to service routine is inhibited by masking. This latch remains high until cleared by a RESET IN, by a SIM Instruction with accumulator bit 4 high, or by an internal processor acknowledge to an RST 7.5 interrupt subsequent to the removal of the mask (by a SIM instruction). The RESET IN signal always sets all three RST mask bits.

If accumulator bit 6 is at the 1 level when the SIM instruction is executed, the state of accumulator bit 7 is loaded into the SOD latch and thus becomes available for interface to an external device. The SOD latch is unaffected by the SIM instruction if bit 6 is 0. SOD is always reset by the RESET IN signal.

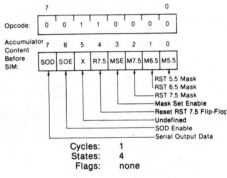

Cycles: 1
States: 4
Flags: none

8085A CPU INSTRUCTIONS IN OPERATION CODE SEQUENCE
Table 4-2

OP CODE	MNEMONIC	OP CODE	MNEMONIC	OP CODE	MNEMONIC	OP CODE	MNEMONIC	OP CODE	MNEMONIC	OP CODE	MNEMONIC	OP CODE	MNEMONIC
00	NOP	2B	DCX H	56	MOV D,M	81	ADD C	AC	XRA H	D7	RST 2		
01	LXI B,D16	2C	INR L	57	MOV D,A	82	ADD D	AD	XRA L	D8	RC		
02	STAX B	2D	DCR L	58	MOV E,B	83	ADD E	AE	XRA M	D9	–		
03	INX B	2E	MVI L,D8	59	MOV E,C	84	ADD H	AF	XRA A	DA	JC Adr		
04	INR B	2F	CMA	5A	MOV E,D	85	ADD L	B0	ORA B	DB	IN D8		
05	DCR B	30	SIM	5B	MOV E,E	86	ADD M	B1	ORA C	DC	CC Adr		
06	MVI B,D8	31	LXI SP,D16	5C	MOV E,H	87	ADD A	B2	ORA D	DD	–		
07	RLC	32	STA Adr	5D	MOV E,L	88	ADC B	B3	ORA E	DE	SBI D8		
08	–	33	INX SP	5E	MOV E,M	89	ADC C	B4	ORA H	DF	RST 3		
09	DAD B	34	INR M	5F	MOV E,A	8A	ADC D	B5	ORA L	E0	RPO		
0A	LDAX B	35	DCR M	60	MOV H,B	8B	ADC E	B6	ORA M	E1	POP H		
0B	DCX B	36	MVI M,D8	61	MOV H,C	8C	ADC H	B7	ORA A	E2	JPO Adr		
0C	INR C	37	STC	62	MOV H,D	8D	ADC L	B8	CMP B	E3	XTHL		
0D	DCR C	38	–	63	MOV H,E	8E	ADC M	B9	CMP C	E4	CPO Adr		
0E	MVI C,D8	39	DAD SP	64	MOV H,H	8F	ADC A	BA	CMP D	E5	PUSH H		
0F	RRC	3A	LDA Adr	65	MOV H,L	90	SUB B	BB	CMP E	E6	ANI D8		
10	–	3B	DCX SP	66	MOV H,M	91	SUB C	BC	CMP H	E7	RST 4		
11	LXI D,D16	3C	INR A	67	MOV H,A	92	SUB D	BD	CMP L	E8	RPE		
12	STAX D	3D	DCR A	68	MOV L,B	93	SUB E	BE	CMP M	E9	PCHL		
13	INX D	3E	MVI A,D8	69	MOV L,C	94	SUB H	BF	CMP A	EA	JPE Adr		
14	INR D	3F	CMC	6A	MOV L,D	95	SUB L	C0	RNZ	EB	XCHG		
15	DCR D	40	MOV B,B	6B	MOV L,E	96	SUB M	C1	POP B	EC	CPE Adr		
16	MVI D,D8	41	MOV B,C	6C	MOV L,H	97	SUB A	C2	JNZ Adr	ED	–		
17	RAL	42	MOV B,D	6D	MOV L,L	98	SBB B	C3	JMP Adr	EE	XRI D8		
18	–	43	MOV B,E	6E	MOV L,M	99	SBB C	C4	CNZ Adr	EF	RST 5		
19	DAD D	44	MOV B,H	6F	MOV L,A	9A	SBB D	C5	PUSH B	F0	RP		
1A	LDAX D	45	MOV B,L	70	MOV M,B	9B	SBB E	C6	ADI D8	F1	POP PSW		
1B	DCX D	46	MOV B,M	71	MOV M,C	9C	SBB H	C7	RST 0	F2	JP Adr		
1C	INR E	47	MOV B,A	72	MOV M,D	9D	SBB L	C8	RZ	F3	DI		
1D	DCR E	48	MOV C,B	73	MOV M,E	9E	SBB M	C9	RET Adr	F4	CP Adr		
1E	MVI E,D8	49	MOV C,C	74	MOV M,H	9F	SBB A	CA	JZ	F5	PUSH PSW		
1F	RAR	4A	MOV C,D	75	MOV M,L	A0	ANA B	CB	–	F6	ORI D8		
20	RIM	4B	MOV C,E	76	HLT	A1	ANA C	CC	CZ Adr	F7	RST 6		
21	LXI H,D16	4C	MOV C,H	77	MOV M,A	A2	ANA D	CD	CALL Adr	F8	RM		
22	SHLD Adr	4D	MOV C,L	78	MOV A,B	A3	ANA E	CE	ACI D8	F9	SPHL		
23	INX H	4E	MOV C,M	79	MOV A,C	A4	ANA H	CF	RST 1	FA	JM Adr		
24	INR H	4F	MOV C,A	7A	MOV A,D	A5	ANA L	D0	RNC	FB	EI		
25	DCR H	50	MOV D,B	7B	MOV A,E	A6	ANA M	D1	POP D	FC	CM Adr		
26	MVI H,D8	51	MOV D,C	7C	MOV A,H	A7	ANA A	D2	JNC Adr	FD	–		
27	DAA	52	MOV D,D	7D	MOV A,L	A8	XRA B	D3	OUT D8	FE	CPI D8		
28	–	53	MOV D,E	7E	MOV A,M	A9	XRA C	D4	CNC Adr	FF	RST 7		
29	DAD H	54	MOV D,H	7F	MOV A,A	AA	XRA D	D5	PUSH D				
2A	LHLD Adr	55	MOV D,L	80	ADD B	AB	XRA E	D6	SUI D8				

D8 = constant, or logical/arithmetic expression that evaluates to an 8 bit data quantity.

Adr = 16-bit address.

D16 = constant, or logical/arithmetic expression that evaluates to a 16 bit data quantity.

appendix II

SDK-85 Operation

In general, consult the *SDK-85 System Design Kit User's Manual* for proper operation of the SDK-85 single-board computer. However, to get the reader "up and running" quickly and to handle several idiosyncrasies of the SDK-85, we provide the following information.

USING THE SDK-85's BUILT-IN PORTS

There are five ports available on the SDK-85: three from the 8155A RAM/IO/Timer chip and two from the 8355 ROM/IO chip. Most of the programs in Part III (Chapters 10 through 16) can be testing using the three ports of the 8155A in the following configuration:

- Port A (8-bits)—Input
- Port B (8-bits)—Output
- Port C (6-bits)—Output

To set up the 8155A to match this configuration, we must program the chip by placing the following instructions at the beginning of a program:

```
MVI   A,0EH    (Place 0EH in the accumulator)
OUT   20H      (Write to port 20H)
```

RERUNNING A PROGRAM

When a program is executed, it will either enter the halt (HLT) state or remain in a continuous loop. The most natural way to exit either of these two states is to press RESET. However, activating RESET *may* destroy register and RAM information (RESET often can be used without problems). Should problems arise, the solution lies with the "warm start" capability of the SDK-85.

1. In programs which enter the HLT state, the solution is to replace the HLT instruction with the RST 1 (warm start) instruction. RST 1 (CFH) will direct the system to re-enter the monitor with no loss of information.

2. For programs in a loop, we must exit the system via an interrupt, which in turn causes an RST 1 warm start. Since the VECT INTR front panel key is the most convenient interrupt available, we enable the process by placing the following instructions at the beginning of every loop program (care must be exercised in those programs that themselves use interrupts):

```
MVI   A,0BH   (Load interrupt mask data)   3EH,0BH
SIM           (Enable RST 7.5 interrupt)   30H
EI            (Enable interrupt system)    FBH
```

To complete the process, we place CFH (warm start) at interrupt vector location 20CEH in RAM.

ADDITIONAL NOTES

- Don't forget to set the stack pointer to 20C2H via the front keypad.
- To single-step through programs that use the 8155A's ports, place the configuration data (0EH in most cases) in memory location 20FFH. (The reason is that the single-step process uses the command register within the 8155A to program the timer for each single-step—which destroys the command register information. To replace the destroyed information, the monitor automatically places the data at memory location 20FFH into the command register after each single-step operation.)

8080/8085 Instruction-Set Machine-Cycle Analysis

NOTES:

1. The first memory cycle (M1) is always an instruction fetch; the first (or only) byte, containing the op code, is fetched during this cycle.

2. If the READY input from memory is not high during T2 of each memory cycle, the processor will enter a wait state (TW) until READY is sampled as high.

3. States T4 and T5 are present, as required, for operations which are completely internal to the CPU. The contents of the internal bus during T4 and T5 are available at the data bus; this is designed for testing purposes only. An "X" denotes that the state is present, but is only used for such internal operations as instruction decoding.

4. Only register pairs rp = B (registers B and C) or rp = D (registers D and E) may be specified.

5. These states are skipped.

6. Memory read sub-cycles; an instruction or data word will be read.

7. Memory write sub-cycle.

8. The READY signal is not required during the second and third sub-cycles (M2 and M3). The HOLD signal is accepted during M2 and M3. The SYNC signal is not generated during M2 and M3. During the execution of DAD, M2 and M3 are required for an internal register-pair add; memory is not referenced.

9. The results of these arithmetic, logical or rotate instructions are not moved into the accumulator (A) until state T2 of the next instruction cycle. That is, A is loaded while the next instruction is being fetched; this overlapping of operations allows for faster processing.

10. If the value of the least significant 4-bits of the accumulator is greater than 9 or if the auxiliary carry bit is set, 6 is added to the accumulator. If the value of the most significant 4-bits of the accumulator is now greater than 9, or if the carry bit is set, 6 is added to the most significant 4-bits of the accumulator.

11. This represents the first sub-cycle (the instruction fetch) of the next instruction cycle.

12. If the condition was met, the contents of the register pair WZ are output on the address lines (A_{0-15}) instead of the contents of the program counter (PC).

13. If the condition was not met, sub-cycles M4 and M5 are skipped; the processor instead proceeds immediately to the instruction fetch (M1) of the next instruction cycle.

14. If the condition was not met, sub-cycles M2 and M3 are skipped; the processor instead proceeds immediately to the instruction fetch (M1) of the next instruction cycle.

15. Stack read sub-cycle.

16. Stack write sub-cycle.

17.
CONDITION		CCC
NZ	— not zero (Z = 0)	000
Z	— zero (Z = 1)	001
NC	— no carry (CY = 0)	010
C	— carry (CY = 1)	011
PO	— parity odd (P = 0)	100
PE	— parity even (P = 1)	101
P	— plus (S = 0)	110
M	— minus (S = 1)	111

18. I/O sub-cycle: the I/O port's 8-bit select code is duplicated on address lines 0-7 (A_{0-7}) and 8-15 (A_{8-15}).

19. Output sub-cycle.

20. The processor will remain idle in the halt state until an interrupt, a reset or a hold is accepted. When a hold request is accepted, the CPU enters the hold mode; after the hold mode is terminated, the processor returns to the halt state. After a reset is accepted, the processor begins execution at memory location zero. After an interrupt is accepted, the processor executes the instruction forced onto the data bus (usually a restart instruction).

SSS or DDD	Value	rp	Value
A	111	B	00
B	000	D	01
C	001	H	10
D	010	SP	11
E	011		
H	100		
L	101		

MNEMONIC	OP CODE		M1[1]					M2		
	$D_7 D_6 D_5 D_4$	$D_3 D_2 D_1 D_0$	T1	T2[2]	T3	T4	T5	T1	T2[2]	T3
MOV r1,r2	0 1 D D	D S S S	PC OUT STATUS	PC = PC +1	INST→TMP/IR	(SSS)→TMP	(TMP)→DDD			
MOV r, M	0 1 D D	D 1 1 0				x[3]		HL OUT STATUS[6]	DATA→DDD	
MOV M, r	0 1 1 1	0 S S S				(SSS)→TMP		HL OUT STATUS[7]	(TMP)→DATA BUS	
SPHL	1 1 1 1	1 0 0 1				(HL) ——→SP				
MVI r, data	0 0 D D	D 1 1 0				x		PC OUT STATUS[6]	B2→DDDD	
MVI M, data	0 0 1 1	0 1 1 0				x			B2→TMP	
LXI rp, data	0 0 R P	0 0 0 1				x			PC = PC + 1	B2→r1
LDA addr	0 0 1 1	1 0 1 0				x			PC = PC + 1	B2→Z
STA addr	0 0 1 1	0 0 1 0				x			PC = PC + 1	B2→Z
LHLD addr	0 0 1 0	1 0 1 0				x			PC = PC + 1	B2→Z
SHLD addr	0 0 1 0	0 0 1 0				x		PC OUT STATUS[6]	PC = PC + 1	B2→Z
LDAX rp[4]	0 0 R P	1 0 1 0				x		rp OUT STATUS[6]	DATA→A	
STAX rp[4]	0 0 R P	0 0 1 0				x		rp OUT STATUS[7]	(A)→DATA BUS	
XCHG	1 1 1 0	1 0 1 1				(HL)↔(DE)				
ADD r	1 0 0 0	0 S S S				(SSS)→TMP (A)→ACT		[9]	(ACT)+(TMP)→A	
ADD M	1 0 0 0	0 1 1 0				(A)→ACT		HL OUT STATUS[6]	DATA→TMP	
ADI data	1 1 0 0	0 1 1 0				(A)→ACT		PC OUT STATUS[6]	PC = PC + 1	B2→TMP
ADC r	1 0 0 0	1 S S S				(SSS)→TMP (A)→ACT		[9]	(ACT)+(TMP)+CY→A	
ADC M	1 0 0 0	1 1 1 0				(A)→ACT		HL OUT STATUS[6]	DATA→TMP	
ACI data	1 1 0 0	1 1 1 0				(A)→ACT		PC OUT STATUS[6]	PC = PC + 1	B2→TMP
SUB r	1 0 0 1	0 S S S				(SSS)→TMP (A)→ACT		[9]	(ACT)-(TMP)→A	
SUB M	1 0 0 1	0 1 1 0				(A)→ACT		HL OUT STATUS[6]	DATA→TMP	
SUI data	1 1 0 1	0 1 1 0				(A)→ACT		PC OUT STATUS[6]	PC = PC + 1	B2→TMP
SBB r	1 0 0 1	1 S S S				(SSS)→TMP (A)→ACT		[9]	(ACT)-(TMP)-CY→A	
SBB M	1 0 0 1	1 1 1 0				(A)→ACT		HL OUT STATUS[6]	DATA→TMP	
SBI data	1 1 0 1	1 1 1 0				(A)→ACT		PC OUT STATUS[6]	PC = PC + 1	B2→TMP
INR r	0 0 D D	D 1 0 0				(DDD)→TMP (TMP) + 1→ALU	ALU→DDD			
INR M	0 0 1 1	0 1 0 0				x		HL OUT STATUS[6]	DATA→TMP (TMP)+1→ALU	
DCR r	0 0 D D	D 1 0 1				(DDD)→TMP (TMP)+1→ALU	ALU→DDD			
DCR M	0 0 1 1	0 1 0 1				x		HL OUT STATUS[6]	DATA→TMP (TMP)-1→ALU	
INX rp	0 0 R P	0 0 1 1				(RP) + 1 ——→RP				
DCX rp	0 0 R P	1 0 1 1				(RP) - 1 ——→RP				
DAD rp[8]	0 0 R P	1 0 0 1				x		(ri)→ACT	(L)→TMP, (ACT)+(TMP)→ALU	ALU→L, CY
DAA	0 0 1 0	0 1 1 1				DAA→A, FLAGS[10]				
ANA r	1 0 1 0	0 S S S				(SSS)→TMP (A)→ACT		[9]	(ACT)+(TMP)→A	
ANA M	1 0 1 0	0 1 1 0	PC OUT STATUS	PC = PC + 1	INST→TMP/IR	(A)→ACT		HL OUT STATUS[6]	DATA→TMP	

	M3			M4			M5				
T1	T2[2]	T3	T1	T2[2]	T3	T1	T2[2]	T3	T4	T5	
HL OUT STATUS[7]	(TMP) ──► DATA BUS										
PC OUT STATUS[6]	PC = PC + 1	B3 ──► rh									
	PC = PC + 1	B3 ──► W	WZ OUT STATUS[6]	DATA ──────► A							
	PC = PC + 1	B3 ──► W	WZ OUT STATUS[7]	(A) ──────► DATA BUS							
	PC = PC + 1	B3 ──► W	WZ OUT STATUS[6]	DATA ──► L, WZ = WZ + 1		WZ OUT STATUS[6]	DATA ──► H				
PC OUT STATUS[6]	PC = PC + 1	B3 ──► W	WZ OUT STATUS[7]	(L) ──────► DATA BUS, WZ = WZ + 1		WZ OUT STATUS[7]	(H) ──────► DATA BUS				

[9]	(ACT)+(TMP)→A	
[9]	(ACT)+(TMP)→A	

[9]	(ACT)+(TMP)+CY→A	
[9]	(ACT)+(TMP)+CY→A	

[9]	(ACT)-(TMP)→A	
[9]	(ACT)-(TMP)→A	

[9]	(ACT)-(TMP)-CY→A	
[9]	(ACT)-(TMP)-CY→A	

HL OUT STATUS[7]	ALU ──► DATA BUS	

HL OUT STATUS[7]	ALU ──► DATA BUS	

(rh)→ACT	(H)→TMP (ACT)+(TMP)+CY→ALU	ALU→H, CY

[9]	(ACT)+(TMP)→A	

MNEMONIC	OP CODE		M1[1]					M2		
	$D_7 D_6 D_5 D_4$	$D_3 D_2 D_1 D_0$	T1	T2[2]	T3	T4	T5	T1	T2[2]	T3
ANI data	1 1 1 0	0 1 1 0	PC OUT STATUS	PC = PC + 1	INST→TMP/IR	(A)→ACT		PC OUT STATUS[6]	PC = PC + 1 B2	→TMP
XRA r	1 0 1 0	1 S S S				(A)→ACT (SSS)→TMP		[9]	(ACT)+(TPM)→A	
XRA M	1 0 1 0	1 1 1 0				(A)→ACT		HL OUT STATUS[6]	DATA	→TMP
XRI data	1 1 1 0	1 1 1 0				(A)→ACT		PC OUT STATUS[6]	PC = PC + 1 B2	→TMP
ORA r	1 0 1 1	0 S S S				(A)→ACT (SSS)→TMP		[9]	(ACT)+(TMP)→A	
ORA M	1 0 1 1	0 1 1 0				(A)→ACT		HL OUT STATUS[6]	DATA	→TMP
ORI data	1 1 1 1	0 1 1 0				(A)→ACT		PC OUT STATUS[6]	PC = PC + 1 B2	→TMP
CMP r	1 0 1 1	1 S S S				(A)→ACT (SSS)→TMP		[9]	(ACT)-(TMP), FLAGS	
CMP M	1 0 1 1	1 1 1 0				(A)→ACT		HL OUT STATUS[6]	DATA	→TMP
CPI data	1 1 1 1	1 1 1 0				(A)→ACT		PC OUT STATUS[6]	PC = PC + 1 B2	→TMP
RLC	0 0 0 0	0 1 1 1				(A)→ALU ROTATE		[9]	ALU→A, CY	
RRC	0 0 0 0	1 1 1 1				(A)→ALU ROTATE		[9]	ALU→A, CY	
RAL	0 0 0 1	0 1 1 1				(A), CY→ALU ROTATE		[9]	ALU→A, CY	
RAR	0 0 0 1	1 1 1 1				(A), CY→ALU ROTATE		[9]	ALU→A, CY	
CMA	0 0 1 0	1 1 1 1				(Ā)→A				
CMC	0 0 1 1	1 1 1 1				$\overline{CY}$→CY				
STC	0 0 1 1	0 1 1 1				1→CY				
JMP addr	1 1 0 0	0 0 1 1				X		PC OUT STATUS[6]	PC = PC + 1 B2	→Z
J cond addr[17]	1 1 C C	C 0 1 0				JUDGE CONDITION		PC OUT STATUS[6]	PC = PC + 1 B2	→Z
CALL addr	1 1 0 0	1 1 0 1				SP = SP - 1		PC OUT STATUS[6]	PC = PC + 1 B2	→Z
C cond addr[17]	1 1 C C	C 1 0 0				JUDGE CONDITION IF TRUE, SP = SP - 1		PC OUT STATUS[6]	PC = PC + 1 B2	→Z
RET	1 1 0 0	1 0 0 1				X		SP OUT STATUS[15]	SP = SP + 1 DATA	→Z
R cond addr[17]	1 1 C C	C 0 0 0			INST→TMP/IR	JUDGE CONDITION[14]		SP OUT STATUS[15]	SP = SP + 1 DATA	→Z
RST n	1 1 N N	N 1 1 1			φ→W INST→TMP/IR	SP = SP - 1		SP OUT STATUS[16]	SP = SP - 1 (PCH)	→DATA BUS
PCHL	1 1 1 0	1 0 0 1			INST→TMP/IR	(HL)──────→ PC				
PUSH rp	1 1 R P	0 1 0 1				SP = SP - 1		SP OUT STATUS[16]	SP = SP - 1 (rh)	→DATA BUS
PUSH PSW	1 1 1 1	0 1 0 1				SP = SP - 1		SP OUT STATUS[16]	SP = SP - 1 (A)	→DATA BUS
POP rp	1 1 R P	0 0 0 1				X		SP OUT STATUS[15]	SP = SP + 1 DATA	→r1
POP PSW	1 1 1 1	0 0 0 1				X		SP OUT STATUS[15]	SP = SP + 1 DATA	→FLAGS
XTHL	1 1 1 0	0 0 1 1				X		SP OUT STATUS[15]	SP = SP + 1 DATA	→Z
IN port	1 1 0 1	1 0 1 1				X		PC OUT STATUS[6]	PC = PC + 1 B2	→Z, W
OUT port	1 1 0 1	0 0 1 1				X		PC OUT STATUS[6]	PC = PC + 1 B2	→Z, W
EI	1 1 1 1	1 0 1 1				SET INTE F/F				
DI	1 1 1 1	0 0 1 1				RESET INTE F/F				
HLT	0 1 1 1	0 1 1 0				X		PC OUT STATUS	HALT MODE[20]	
NOP	0 0 0 0	0 0 0 0	PC OUT STATUS	PC = PC + 1	INST→TMP/IR	X				

| M3 | | | M4 | | | M5 | | | | |
T1	T2[2]	T3	T1	T2[2]	T3	T1	T2[2]	T3	T4	T5
[9]	(ACT)+(TMP)→A									
[9]	(ACT)+(TMP)→A									
[9]	(ACT)+(TMP)→A									
[9]	(ACT)+(TMP)→A									
[9]	(ACT)+(TMP)→A									
[9]	(ACT)−(TMP); FLAGS									
[9]	(ACT)−(TMP); FLAGS									
PC OUT STATUS[6]	PC = PC + 1 B3 →W								WZ OUT STATUS[11]	(WZ) + 1 → PC
PC OUT STATUS[6]	PC = PC + 1 B3 →W								WZ OUT STATUS[11,12]	(WZ) + 1 → PC
PC OUT STATUS[6]	PC = PC + 1 B3 →W		SP OUT STATUS[16]	(PCH)——→DATA BUS SP = SP − 1		SP OUT STATUS[16]	(PCL)—→DATA BUS		WZ OUT STATUS[11]	(WZ) + 1 → PC
PC OUT STATUS[6]	PC = PC + 1 B3 →W[13]		SP OUT STATUS[16]	(PCH)——→DATA BUS SP = SP − 1		SP OUT STATUS[16]	(PCL)—→DATA BUS SP-2		WZ OUT STATUS[11,12]	(WZ) + 1 → PC
SP OUT STATUS[15]	SP = SP + 1 DATA →W								WZ OUT STATUS[11]	(WZ) + 1 → PC
SP OUT STATUS[15]	SP = SP + 1 DATA →W								WZ OUT STATUS[11,12]	(WZ) + 1 → PC
SP OUT STATUS[16]	(TMP = 00NNN000)——→Z (PCL)——→DATA BUS								WZ OUT STATUS[11]	(WZ) + 1 → PC
SP OUT STATUS[16]	(rl)—→DATA BUS									
SP OUT STATUS[16]	FLAGS—→DATA BUS									
SP OUT STATUS[15]	SP = SP + 1 DATA—→rh									
SP OUT STATUS[15]	SP = SP + 1 DATA—→A									
SP OUT STATUS[15]	DATA—→W		SP OUT STATUS[16]	(H)———→DATA BUS		SP OUT STATUS[16]	(L)—→DATA BUS	(WZ)—→HL		
WZ OUT STATUS[18]	DATA—→A									
WZ OUT STATUS[18]	(A)—→DATA BUS									

PUSH PSW →

appendix IV

The Ten Secret Op Codes

Op codes	Mnemonics	Function
08	DSUB B	Subtract (B,C) from (H,L)
10	RHR	Rotate (H,L) right through carry
18	RDL	Rotate (D,E) left through carry
28xx	DMOV D,H	(H,L) plus immediate byte xx into (D,E)
38xx	DMOV D,SP	(SP) plus immediate byte xx into (D,E)
CB	RSTV	Restart at 0040 if V flag = 1
D9	SHLX	Store (H,L) at memory location (D,E)
DDyyxx	JND	Jump to location xxyy if D flag = 0
ED	LHLX	Load (H,L) from memory location (D,E)
FDyyxx	JD	Jump to location xxyy if D flag = 1

appendix V

8080/8085 Assembly-Language Reference Card

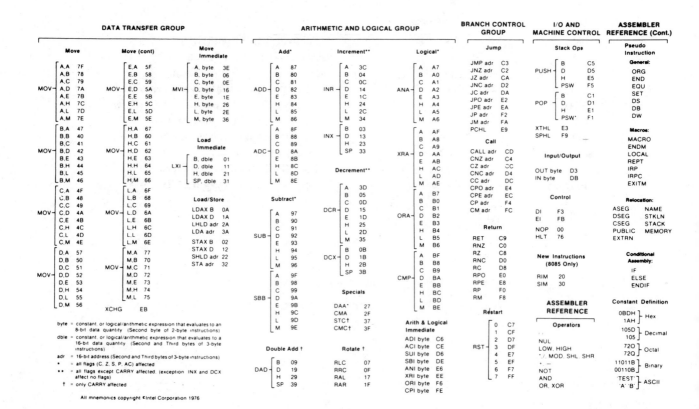

DATA TRANSFER GROUP

Move

MOV	A,A	7F
	A,B	78
	A,C	79
	A,D	7A
	A,E	7B
	A,H	7C
	A,L	7D
	A,M	7E
MOV	B,A	47
	B,B	40
	B,C	41
	B,D	42
	B,E	43
	B,H	44
	B,L	45
	B,M	46
MOV	C,A	4F
	C,B	48
	C,C	49
	C,D	4A
	C,E	4B
	C,H	4C
	C,L	4D
	C,M	4E
MOV	D,A	57
	D,B	50
	D,C	51
	D,D	52
	D,E	53
	D,H	54
	D,L	55
	D,M	56

Move (cont)

MOV	E,A	5F
	E,B	58
	E,C	59
	E,D	5A
	E,E	5B
	E,H	5C
	E,L	5D
	E,M	5E
MOV	H,A	67
	H,B	60
	H,C	61
	H,D	62
	H,E	63
	H,H	64
	H,L	65
	H,M	66
MOV	L,A	6F
	L,B	68
	L,C	69
	L,D	6A
	L,E	6B
	L,H	6C
	L,L	6D
	L,M	6E
MOV	M,A	77
	M,B	70
	M,C	71
	M,D	72
	M,E	73
	M,H	74
	M,L	75
XCHG		EB

Move Immediate

MVI	A, byte	3E
	B, byte	06
	C, byte	0E
	D, byte	16
	E, byte	1E
	H, byte	26
	L, byte	2E
	M, byte	36

Load Immediate

LXI	B, dble	01
	D, dble	11
	H, dble	21
	SP, dble	31

Load/Store

LDAX B	0A
LDAX D	1A
LHLD adr	2A
LDA adr	3A
STAX B	02
STAX D	12
SHLD adr	22
STA adr	32

byte = constant. or logical/arithmetic expression that evaluates to an 8-bit data quantity (Second byte of 2-byte instructions)
dble = constant. or logical/arithmetic expression that evaluates to a 16-bit data quantity (Second and Third bytes of 3-byte instructions)
adr = 16-bit address (Second and Third bytes of 3-byte instructions)
* = all flags (C, Z, S, P, AC) affected
** = all flags except CARRY affected. (exception INX and DCX affect no flags)
† = only CARRY affected

All mnemonics copyright ©Intel Corporation 1976

ARITHMETIC AND LOGICAL GROUP

Add*

ADD	A	87
	B	80
	C	81
	D	82
	E	83
	H	84
	L	85
	M	86
ADC	A	8F
	B	88
	C	89
	D	8A
	E	8B
	H	8C
	L	8D
	M	8E

Subtract*

SUB	A	97
	B	90
	C	91
	D	92
	E	93
	H	94
	L	95
	M	96
SBB	A	9F
	B	98
	C	99
	D	9A
	E	9B
	H	9C
	L	9D
	M	9E

Double Add †

DAD	B	09
	D	19
	H	29
	SP	39

Increment**

INR	A	3C
	B	04
	C	0C
	D	14
	E	1C
	H	24
	L	2C
	M	34
INX	B	03
	D	13
	H	23
	SP	33

Decrement**

DCR	A	3D
	B	05
	C	0D
	D	15
	E	1D
	H	25
	L	2D
	M	35
DCX	B	0B
	D	1B
	H	23
	SP	3B

Specials

DAA*	27
CMA	2F
STC†	37
CMC†	3F

Rotate †

RLC	07
RRC	0F
RAL	17
RAR	1F

Logical*

ANA	A	A7
	B	A0
	C	A1
	D	A2
	E	A3
	H	A4
	L	A5
	M	A6
XRA	A	AF
	B	A8
	C	A9
	D	AA
	E	AB
	H	AC
	L	AD
	M	AE
ORA	A	B7
	B	B0
	C	B1
	D	B2
	E	B3
	H	B4
	L	B5
	M	B6
CMP	A	BF
	B	B8
	C	B9
	D	BA
	E	BB
	H	BC
	L	BD
	M	BE

Arith & Logical Immediate

ADI byte	C6
ACI byte	CE
SUI byte	D6
SBI byte	DE
ANI byte	E6
XRI byte	EE
ORI byte	F6
CPI byte	FE

BRANCH CONTROL GROUP

Jump

JMP adr	C3
JNZ adr	C2
JZ adr	CA
JNC adr	D2
JC adr	DA
JPO adr	E2
JPE adr	EA
JP adr	F2
JM adr	FA
PCHL	E9

Call

CALL adr	CD
CNZ adr	C4
CZ adr	CC
CNC adr	D4
CC adr	DC
CPO adr	E4
CPE adr	EC
CP adr	F4
CM adr	FC

Return

RET	C9
RNZ	C0
RZ	C8
RNC	D0
RC	D8
RPO	E0
RPE	E8
RP	F0
RM	F8

Restart

RST	0	C7
	1	CF
	2	D7
	3	DF
	4	E7
	5	EF
	6	F7
	7	FF

I/O AND MACHINE CONTROL

Stack Ops

PUSH	B	C5
	D	D5
	H	E5
	PSW	F5
POP	B	C1
	D	D1
	H	E1
	PSW*	F1
XTHL		E3
SPHL		F9

Input/Output

| OUT byte | D3 |
| IN byte | DB |

Control

DI	F3
EI	FB
NOP	00
HLT	76

New Instructions (8085 Only)

| RIM | 20 |
| SIM | 30 |

ASSEMBLER REFERENCE

Operators

NUL
LOW, HIGH
*, /, MOD, SHL, SHR
NOT
AND
OR, XOR

ASSEMBLER REFERENCE (Cont.)

Pseudo Instruction

General:
ORG
END
EQU
SET
DS
DB
DW

Macros:
MACRO
ENDM
LOCAL
REPT
IRP
IRPC
EXITM

Relocation:

ASEG	NAME
DSEG	STKLN
CSEG	STACK
PUBLIC	MEMORY
EXTRN	

Conditional Assembly:
IF
ELSE
ENDIF

Constant Definition

0BDH	} Hex
1AH	
105D	} Decimal
105	
72Q	} Octal
72O	
11011B	} Binary
00110B	
'TEST'	} ASCII
'A' 'B'	

416

8048 Instruction Set

8048/8049
INSTRUCTION SET SUMMARY

Mnemonic	Description	Bytes	Cycle
Accumulator			
ADD A, R	Add register to A	1	1
ADD A, @R	Add data memory to A	1	1
ADD A, #data	Add immediate to A	2	2
ADDC A, R	Add register with carry	1	1
ADDC A, @R	Add data memory with carry	1	1
ADDC A, #data	Add immediate with carry	2	2
ANL A, R	And register to A	1	1
ANL A, @R	And data memory to A	1	1
ANL A, #data	And immediate to A	2	2
ORL A, R	Or register to A	1	1
ORL A, @R	Or data memory to A	1	1
ORL A, #data	Or immediate to A	2	2
XRL A, R	Exclusive Or register to A	1	1
XRL A, @R	Exclusive or data memory to A	1	1
XRL A, #data	Exclusive or immediate to A	2	2
INC A	Increment A	1	1
DEC A	Decrement A	1	1
CLR A	Clear A	1	1
CPL A	Complement A	1	1
DA A	Decimal Adjust A	1	1
SWAP A	Swap nibbles of A	1	1
RL A	Rotate A left	1	1
RLC A	Rotate A left through carry	1	1
RR A	Rotate A right	1	1
RRC A	Rotate A right through carry	1	1
Input/Output			
IN A, P	Input port to A	1	2
OUTL P, A	Output A to port	1	2
ANL P, #data	And immediate to port	2	2
ORL P, #data	Or immediate to port	2	2
INS A, BUS	Input BUS to A	1	2
OUTL BUS, A	Output A to BUS	1	2
ANL BUS, #data	And immediate to BUS	2	2
ORL BUS, #data	Or immediate to BUS	2	2
MOVD A, P	Input Expander port to A	1	2
MOVD P, A	Output A to Expander port	1	2
ANLD P, A	And A to Expander port	1	2
ORLD P, A	Or A to Expander port	1	2
Branch			
JMP addr	Jump unconditional	2	2
JMPP @A	Jump indirect	1	2
DJNZ R, addr	Decrement register and skip	2	2
JC addr	Jump on Carry = 1	2	2
JNC addr	Jump on Carry = 0	2	2
J Z addr	Jump on A Zero	2	2
JNZ addr	Jump on A not Zero	2	2
JT0 addr	Jump on T0 = 1	2	2
JNT0 addr	Jump on T0 = 0	2	2
JT1 addr	Jump on T1 = 1	2	2
JNT1 addr	Jump on T1 = 0	2	2
JF0 addr	Jump on F0 = 1	2	2
JF1 addr	Jump on F1 = 1	2	2
JTF addr	Jump on timer flag	2	2
JNI addr	Jump on $\overline{INT}$ = 0	2	2
JBb addr	Jump on Accumulator Bit	2	2

Mnemonic	Description	Bytes	Cycles
Registers			
INC R	Increment register	1	1
INC @R	Increment data memory	1	1
DEC R	Decrement register	1	1
Subroutine			
CALL	Jump to subroutine	2	2
RET	Return	1	2
RETR	Return and restore status	1	2
Flags			
CLR C	Clear Carry	1	1
CPL C	Complement Carry	1	1
CLR F0	Clear Flag 0	1	1
CPL F0	Complement Flag 0	1	1
CLR F1	Clear Flag 1	1	1
CPL F1	Complement Flag 1	1	1
Data Moves			
MOV A, R	Move register to A	1	1
MOV A, @R	Move data memory to A	1	1
MOV A, #data	Move immediate to A	2	2
MOV R, A	Move A to register	1	1
MOV @R, A	Move A to data memory	1	1
MOV R, #data	Move immediate to register	2	2
MOV @R, #data	Move immediate to data memory	2	2
MOV A, PSW	Move PSW to A	1	1
MOV PSW, A	Move A to PSW	1	1
XCH A, R	Exchange A and register	1	1
XCH A, @R	Exchange A and data memory	1	1
XCHD A, @R	Exchange nibble of A and register	1	1
MOVX A, @R	Move external data memory to A	1	2
MOVX @R, A	Move A to external data memory	1	2
MOVP A, @A	Move to A from current page	1	2
MOVP3 A, @A	Move to A from Page 3	1	2
Timer/Counter			
MOV A, T	Read Timer/Counter	1	1
MOV T, A	Load Timer/Counter	1	1
STRT T	Start Timer	1	1
STRT CNT	Start Counter	1	1
STOP TCNT	Stop Timer/Counter	1	1
EN TCNTI	Enable Timer/Counter Interrupt	1	1
DIS TCNTI	Disable Timer/Counter Interrupt	1	1
Control			
EN I	Enable external interrupt	1	1
DIS I	Disable external interrupt	1	1
SEL RB0	Select register bank 0	1	1
SEL RB1	Select register bank 1	1	1
SEL MB0	Select memory bank 0	1	1
SEL MB1	Select memory bank 1	1	1
ENT0 CLK	Enable Clock output on T0	1	1
NOP	No Operation	1	1

index